THE DISCOVERY OF AUSTRALIA

Illustrated

GEORGE COLLINGRIDGE

Copyright © 2015 George Collingridge
All rights reserved.
ISBN: 1517516269
ISBN-13: 978-1517516260

THE DISCOVERY OF AUSTRALIA

A Critical, Documentary and Historic Investigation Concerning the Priority of Discovery in Australasia by Europeans before the arrival of Lieutenant James Cook, in the Endeavour, in the year 1770.

With Illustrations, Charts, Maps, Diagrams, etc. Copious Notes, References, Geographical Index and Index to Names.

BY
GEORGE COLLINGRIDGE,

MEMBER OF THE COUNCIL OF THE ROYAL
GEOGRAPHICAL SOCIETY OF AUSTRALASIA, SYDNEY,
NEW SOUTH WALES.
HONORARY CORRESPONDING MEMBER OF THE
ROYAL GEOGRAPHICAL SOCIETY OF AUSTRALASIA,
MELBOURNE, VICTORIA.
HONORARY CORRESPONDING MEMBER OF THE
NEUCHATELOISE GEOGRAPHICAL SOCIETY,
NEUCHATEL, SWITZERLAND.
HONORARY CORRESPONDING MEMBER OF THE
PORTUGUESE GEOGRAPHICAL SOCIETY, LISBON.
HONORARY CORRESPONDING MEMBER OF THE
SPANISH GEOGRAPHICAL SOCIETY, MADRID, ETC.,
ETC.
FOUNDER AND FIRST VICE-PRESIDENT OF THE ART
SOCIETY OF NEW SOUTH WALES, SYDNEY.

SYDNEY:

HAYES BROTHERS, 55 & 57 ELIZABETH STREET.

1895.

TO
THE HONOURABLE
MR. JUSTICE SIR WILLIAM CHARLES WINDEYER, M.A.,
LL.D., KNT.,
CHANCELLOR OF THE UNIVERSITY OF SYDNEY,
AND
SENIOR PUISNE JUDGE OF THE SUPREME COURT,
DEPUTY JUDGE OF THE
VICE-ADMIRALTY COURT, AND JUDGE OF THE
DIVORCE AND MATRIMONIAL CAUSES COURT,
OF NEW SOUTH WALES,
EMINENT
NO LESS FOR HIS HIGH LEGAL AND SCHOLASTIC
ATTAINMENTS,
AND HIS WIDE AND ACTIVE LITERARY, SOCIAL, AND
INTELLECTUAL SYMPATHIES,
THAN FOR HIS DISTINGUISHED PUBLIC SERVICES,
THIS WORK,
DEVOTED TO AN ENQUIRY INTO THE FIRST
DISCOVERY OF THE COUNTRY WHICH
HAS BEEN THE SCENE OF HIS LIFE AND LABOURS,

THE DISCOVERY OF AUSTRALIA

PREFACE.

Of the many books which have been published on subjects relating to Australia and Australian History, I am not aware of any, since my late friend Mr. R.H. Major's introduction to his valuable work, Early Voyages to Terra Australis, which has attempted a systematic investigation into the earliest discoveries of the great Southern Island-Continent, and the first faint indications of knowledge that such a land existed. Mr. Major's work was published in 1859, at a time when the materials for such an enquiry were much smaller than at present. The means of reproducing and distributing copies of the many ancient maps which are scattered among the various libraries of Europe were then very imperfect, and the science of Comparative Cartography, of which the importance is now well recognised, was in its infancy. For these reasons, his discussion, useful though it still is, cannot be regarded as abreast of modern opportunities. It is indeed, after the lapse of more than a third of a century, somewhat out of date. Having therefore been led to give close attention during several years to the whole subject, I have thought the time ripe for the present work.

The distance from the great centres and stores of knowledge at which I have been compelled to labour will excuse to the candid critic the errors which will no doubt be discovered, yet I feel some confidence that these will prove to be omissions rather than positive mistakes. No pains have been spared in investigating the full body of documents now available. Though unable to examine personally some manuscripts of interest and value, I believe I can truly say that I have read every book, and examined every map, of real importance to the question, which has been produced in English, French, Spanish, Portuguese, Italian and Dutch. I have corresponded also largely, during the past four years, with many of the most eminent members of the Geographical Societies of London, Paris, Madrid, Lisbon, Rome, Amsterdam and Neuchatel. To these gentlemen I am deeply indebted for searches which they have made for me in the libraries and museums within their reach, for much information readily and kindly afforded, and for the interest and sympathy which they have at all times manifested in my labours. My thanks are due also to the gentlemen in charge of the Sydney Free Public Library, who kindly enriched their collection with many rare and very useful volumes of permanent importance which I was unable to procure myself, and who aided my researches by every means in their power. I cannot hope that in a subject so vast and interesting I shall be found to have said the last word, yet I trust that my book may prove to be of value, both in itself and as directing the attention of others to a field which should be mainly explored by residents in Australia. Such as it is, I now send it forth, with the natural solicitude of a parent, and commend it to the indulgence of the reader, and the kindly justice of the critic.

GEORGE COLLINGRIDGE.

Jave-la-Grande,
Hornsby Junction,
July, 1895.

CONTENTS.

PREFACE.

CHAPTER 1.
Introduction.

CHAPTER 2.
The Dawn of Geographical Knowledge, especially with Reference to the Southern Hemisphere.

CHAPTER 3.
An Inquiry concerning the Position of North and South in Ancient

Geography.
The Equatorial Regions Distorted.
Taprobana and Ceylon.

CHAPTER 4. A.D. 1 TO 150..
St. Thomas.
Strabo.
Ptolemy.
Galvano's Opinion on Ptolemy's Geography.

CHAPTER 5.
Early Manuscript Maps of the First Period of the Middle Ages.

CHAPTER 6. A.D. 1295.
Marco Polo.
Java Minor and Java Major.
Five types of Maps with Marco Polo's Nomenclature.
Mandeville.
Odoric de Pordenone.

CHAPTER 7.
Prince Henry the Navigator.

CHAPTER 8. A.D. 1444.
Nicolo de' Conti.

CHAPTER 9. A.D. 1457 TO 1459.
Fra Mauro Mappamundi.

CHAPTER 10. A.D. 1471 TO 1478.
The Equator crossed.
Revival of Ancient ideas concerning the sphericity of the Earth.
Toscanelli.
Columbus.

CHAPTER 11. A.D. 1479 TO 1484.
Toscanelli and Columbus.

CHAPTER 12. A.D. 1484 TO 1487.

The Cape of Good Hope Reached.

CHAPTER 13. A.D. 1487 TO 1489.
Bartholomew Columbus' Lost Map of the World.

CHAPTER 14. A.D. 1487 TO 1489.
British Museum Mappamundi.
A possible Copy from Bartholomew Columbus' Map of the World.

CHAPTER 15. A.D. 1492.
Martin Behaim's Globe.

CHAPTER 16. A.D. 1492.
The Australasian Regions on Martin Behaim's Globe.

CHAPTER 17. A.D. 1499.
Terra Australis.
Said to be Discovered.

CHAPTER 18. A.D. 1500.
Juan de la Cosa's Map.
Cantino's Map.
Australia the Baptismal Font of Brazil.

CHAPTER 19. A.D. 1503 TO 1508.
De Gonneville's Alleged Voyage to Australia.
Ludovico Barthema.

CHAPTER 20. A.D. 1506 TO 1511.
Hunt-Lenox Globe.
Ruysch's Mappamundi of 1507 to 1508.

CHAPTER 21. A.D. 1511.
Conquest of Malacca.
D'Abreu's Expedition to the Spice Islands.

CHAPTER 22. A.D. 1512 TO 1521.
Magalhaens and Serrano.
Francisco Rodriguez Portolanos.

CHAPTER 23. A.D. 1515 TO 1517.
The Frankfort-Schonerean Globe of 1515.
The Sunda and Molucca Islands as traced in Pedro Reinel's Chart.

CHAPTER 24. A.D. 1516 TO 1519.
Line of Demarcation of Magalhaens and Pope Alexander VI.

CHAPTER 25. A.D. 1520 TO 1522.
Vastness of the Pacific Ocean gradually Realised.
Petrus Apianus' Mappamundi of 1520.
Mappemonde La Salle, circa 1522.
Juan Vespuccius' Mappamundi of 1522/1523.
The First Circumnavigators.

CHAPTER 26. A.D. 1523.
Maximilianus Transylvanus' Letter.

CHAPTER 27. A.D. 1522 TO 1523.
Alleged Globe of Schoner of 1523.

CHAPTER 28. A.D. 1525 TO 1529.
Loaysa's Expedition to the Spice Islands.
Don Jorge de Menezes.
The Franciscus Monachus Mappamundi of 1526.
Alvaro de Saavedra Discovers nearly the whole of the North Coast of New Guinea.

CHAPTER 29. A.D. 1527 TO 1536.
Spanish Official Maps.
The Anonymous Weimar Mappamundi of 1527.
The Diego Ribeiro Mappamundi of 1529.
The Dauphin Chart, 1530 to 1536.

CHAPTER 30. A.D. 1530 TO 1550.
The Dauphin Chart of the Assigned Date of 1530 to 1536, and other Maps of the same School.

CHAPTER 31. 1531 TO 1542.

The Mappemonde of Orontius Finaeus of 1531.
Schoner's Weimar Globe of 1533.
G. Mercator's Double Cordiform Mappamundi of 1538.
Hernando de Grijalva's Expedition to the Spice Islands.
Two Maps of Australia by John Rotz (Jean Roze), 1542.

CHAPTER 32. A.D. 1540 TO 1545.
Villalobos' Expedition.
New Guinea named by Inigo Ortiz de Retez and Gaspar Rico.
Juan Gaetan's Account of the Homeward Voyage of the San Juan along the North Coast of New Guinea.

CHAPTER 33. A.D. 1544 TO 1569.
The Sebastian Cabot Mappamundi of 1544.
The Henri II (so called) Mappamundi of 1546.
Pierre Desceliers' Mappamundi of 1550. Mendana's Expedition of 1567.

CHAPTER 34. A.D. 1569 TO 1580.
Gerard Mercator's Mappamundi of 1569.
Ortelius' Mappamundi of 1570.
The Rise of England's Maritime Power.
Drake amongst the Islands to the North of Australia.

CHAPTER 35. A.D. 1537 TO 1588.
Cavendish amongst the Islands to the North of Australia.

CHAPTER 36. A.D. 1592 TO 1595.
The Rise of Holland's Maritime Power.
H. Linschoten.
Houtman.
Cornelius Claesz.
Peter Plancius.
The First Voyage of the Dutch to Australasia.

CHAPTER 37. A.D. 1595 TO 1605.
Mendana's Expedition in Search of the Great Southern Continent.
New Guinea, the Solomon Islands, and the Australian Continent on De Bry's and Wytfliet's Maps.

De Quiros and Torres.
Arrival of the Dutch in the East Indian Archipelago.

CHAPTER 38.
Extract from a Memorial addressed to His Catholic Majesty Phillip III of Spain, by Dr. Juan Luis Arias, respecting the Exploration, Colonisation, and Conversion of the Southern Land.

CHAPTER 39. A.D. 1605 TO 1606.
Relation of Luis Vaez de Torres, concerning the Discoveries of Quiros, as his Almirante, dated Manila, July 12 1607.

CHAPTER 40. A.D. 1605 TO 1607.
The First Claim of Dutch Discovery in Australia.
The Voyage of the Little Dove to the South Coast of New Guinea and the Gulf of Carpentaria.

CHAPTER 41. A.D. 1606 TO 1613.
Don Diego de Prado's Original Maps, made in 1606, showing the Discoveries made by the Spaniards that same year in the New Hebrides and New Guinea.
Two letters of Don Diego de Prado to the King of Spain, referring to de Quiros' Discoveries.

CHAPTER 42. A.D. 1616.
Dirck Hartog's Alleged Discovery on the western coast of Australia.

CHAPTER 43. A.D. 1617 TO 1623.
Other Dutch Discoveries on the western coast of Australia and south coast of New Guinea.
Abraham Goos' Globe of 1621.
The Discovery of the Land of the Leeuwin.
The Voyage of the Pera and Arnhem to the Gulf of Carpentaria.

CHAPTER 44. A.D. 1624 TO 1629.
An English Petition to King James the First for the right to Colonize the Terra Australis.
Discovery of the south coast of Australia, 1627.

The Vianen on the north-west coast in 1628.
The Wreck of the Batavia in 1629.

CHAPTER 45. A.D. 1630 TO 1640.
A Pre-Tasmanian Map of Australia.
Discoveries in the Gulf of Carpentaria.
Hoeius' Map, circa 1640.

CHAPTER 46. A.D. 1642 TO 1658.
Tasman's First Voyage round about Australia.
Tasman's Second Voyage along the northern and north-western coasts of Australia.
Wreck of the Golden Dragon.

CHAPTER 47. A.D. 1660 TO 1669.
P. Goos' Maps of Hollandia Nova, circa 1660 to 1669.

CHAPTER 48. A.D. 1688 TO 1700.
The Dawn of the English Period.
W. Dampier's First Voyage to New Holland.
W. de Vlamingh's Voyage.
W. Dampier's Second Voyage.

CHAPTER 49. A.D. 1700 TO 1717.
Voyage of the Nova Hollandia, the Wajer, and Vossenbosch to Melville Island and the Coburg Peninsula in 1705.
Dampier and Welbe.

CHAPTER 50. A.D. 1717 TO 1770.
John Purry's Propositions.
Roggeween's Expedition.
The Loss of the Zeewyck.
Conclusion.

Appendix.

Georgraphical Index.

Index of Names.

LIST OF MAPS AND ILLUSTRATIONS.

No. 1. ABRAHAM GOOS' GLOBE.
No. 2. ADAPTATION OF PORTION OF DAUPHIN CHART, SHOWING THE PROCESS OF DISTORTION RESORTED TO.
No. 3. AZTEC CALENDAR OR WATER-STONE.
No. 4. AUSTRALASIAN REGIONS ON M. BEHAIM'S GLOBE AND HUNT-LENOX GLOBE COMPARED.
No. 5. AUSTRALASIAN REGIONS ON G. MERCATOR'S [1569] MAPPAMUNDI.
No. 6. BAY OF ST. PETER OF ARLANZA.
No. 7. BOWREY'S MAP (CAPTAIN T.) SHOWING TASMAN'S TRACKS IN HIS FIRST AND SECOND VOYAGES.
No. 8. BRITISH MUSEUM MAPPAMUNDI.
No. 9. CANNIBALISM.
No. 10. CARTA MARINA O DA NAVIGARE.
No. 11. CAVENDISH.
No. 12. CAVENDISH'S TRACK AS IT WOULD APPEAR ON THE DAUPHIN CHART.
No. 13. CHALDEAN CONCEPTION OF THE SHAPE OF THE EARTH.
No. 14. CIRCULAR BOAT OF THE TIGRIS AND EUPHRATES FROM NINEVEH SCULPTURES.
No. 15. COPENHAGEN MAPPAMUNDI.
No. 16. DAMPIER.
No. 17. DAMPIER'S MAP OF SHARK'S BAY.
No. 18. DAMPIER'S ROSEMARY.
No. 19. DAUPHIN CHART OF AUSTRALIA.
No. 20. DAUPHIN CHART OF AUSTRALIA REDUCED.
No. 21. DIEGO DO COUTO'S HOG (JAVA)
No. 22. DIEGO RIBEIRO MAPPAMUNDI (1529).
No. 23. DRAKE.
No. 24. DRAKE'S AND CAVENDISH'S TRACKS AS SHOWN ON JODOCUS HONDIUS' MAP.
No. 25. DRAKE'S CHAIR.

No. 26. EGTIS SILLA ON BEHAIM'S GLOBE AND HAME DE SYLLA ON DAUPHIN CHART COMPARED.
No. 27. ELEPHANT OF CEYLON.
No. 28. EL ISTAHKRI MAPPAMUNDI.
No. 29. ESPIRITU SANTO (MODERN MAP).
No. 30. FRA MAURO MAPPAMUNDI.
No. 31. FRANCISCO RODRIGUEZ'S PORTOLANOS.
No. 32. FRANCISCUS MONACHUS MAPPAMUNDI.
No. 33. GERARD MERCATOR'S DOUBLE CORDIFORM MAPPAMUNDI.
No. 34. PETER GOOS'S MAP OF HOLLANDIA NOVA.
No. 35. GREAT BAY OF ST. PHILIP AND ST. JAMES.
No. 36. GREAT BAY OF ST. LAWRENCE AND PORT OF MONTEREY.
No. 37. GREEK CONCEPTION OF THE SHAPE OF THE EARTH.
No. 38. HENRY II MAPPAMUNDI.
No. 39. HOEIUS' MAP.
No. 40. HUNT-LENOX GLOBE AND RUYSCH'S MAPPAMUNDI COMPARED.
No. 41. IDOLATRY.
No. 42. ISLANDS OF GOMEZ DE SEQUEIRA.
No. 43. JAVA (LINSCHOTEN'S).
No. 44. JEAN ROZE'S MAP OF AUSTRALIA, NUMBER 1.
No. 45. JEAN ROZE'S MAP OF AUSTRALIA, NUMBER 2.
No. 46. JEAN ROZE'S MAP OF AUSTRALIA, NUMBER 2, ORIGINAL PROJECTION.
No. 47. JUAN VESPUCCIUS' MAPPAMUNDI.
No. 48. LA SALLE MAPPEMONDE.
No. 49. LINSCHOTEN.
No. 50. MAGALHAENS.
No. 51. MAGELLAN'S SHIP.
No. 52. MAP OF THE WORLD PUBLISHED WITH THE ACCOUNT OF FROBISHER'S VOYAGES.
No. 53. MAP SHOWING CENTRE OF MENDANA'S DISCOVERIES.
No. 54. MAR DI INDIA MAP.
No. 55. MARTIN BEHAIM, FROM THE PORTRAIT ON HIS GLOBE.

No. 56. NICOLAI GORES.3
No. 57. OANNES AND EA, THE GREEK AND CHALDEAN FISH-GODS.
No. 58. ORANGERIE BAY (MODERN MAP).
No. 59. ORONCE FINE'S MAPPAMUNDI ON OUR PROJECTION.
No. 60. ORONCE FINE'S TERRA AUSTRALIS.
No. 61. PARIS WOODEN GLOBE (CIRCA 1535).
No. 62. PENTAM, ETC., ON BEHAIM'S GLOBE, COMPARED WITH MODERN EASTERN COASTS OF AUSTRALIA AND TASMANIA.
No. 63. PETRUS APIANUS' MAPPAMUNDI.
No. 64. PIERRES DESCELIERS' MAP OF AUSTRALIA.
No. 65. PORTION OF DAUPHIN CHART.
No. 66. PORTS AND BAYS OF THE LAND OF ST. BONAVENTURE, AND MODERN MAP.
No. 67. PORTUGUESE CARAVEL.
No. 68. PRINCE HENRY THE NAVIGATOR.
No. 69. PTOLEMY'S INDIAN OCEAN, AND COMPARATIVE POSITION OF THE AUSTRALASIAN REGIONS.
No. 70. RUYSCH'S MAPPAMUNDI AND SCHONEREAN GORES COMPARED.
No. 71. SCHONER'S ALLEGED GLOBE.
No. 72. SCHONER'S WEIMAR GLOBE.
No. 73. SEBASTIAN CABOT MAPPAMUNDI.
No. 74. SOLOMON ISLANDS, SANTA CRUZ AND NEW HEBRIDES.
No. 75. ST. SEVER MAPPAMUNDI.
No. 76. ST. THOMAS CATECHISING THE NATIVES OF ZANZIBAR ISLAND, FROM BEHAIM'S GLOBE.
No. 77. SUNDA AND MOLUCCA ISLANDS AS TRACED ON PEDRO REINEL'S CHART.
No. 78. TORRES' TRACK FROM THE NEW HEBRIDES TO TORRES STRAITS.
No. 79. TRACK OF THE DUYFKEN.
No. 80. TRITON BAY (MODERN MAP).
No. 81. TURIN MAPPAMUNDI.
No. 82. VAUGONDY'S MAP OF NEW HOLLAND.
No. 83. VIEW OF TABLE MOUNTAIN, CAPE OF GOOD HOPE.

No. 84. WEST COAST OF BOGUS SUMATRA IN RUYSCH'S MAPPAMUNDI COMPARED WITH MODERN WEST COAST OF AUSTRALIA.
No. 85. WORLD AS APPREHENDED BY THE PORTUGUESE AND ITALIANS.
No. 86. WORLD OF PTOLEMY.
No. 87. WYTFLIET'S MAP OF THE CONTINENT OF AUSTRALIA.

THE DISCOVERY OF AUSTRALIA.

CHAPTER 1.
INTRODUCTION.

"Lifted up on the vast wave, he quickly beheld afar." HOMER.

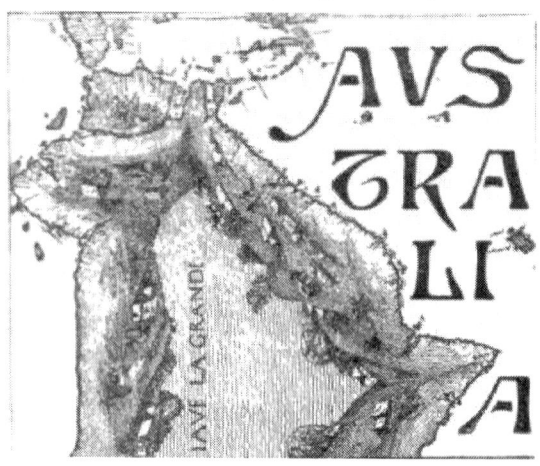

Australia may some day, perhaps in 1899, hold an International Exhibition, even as America held one in Chicago to commemorate the four-hundredth anniversary of her discovery.

(*Footnote. The initial sketch-map [left] is a very much reduced adaptation of the Dauphin Chart of Australia which accompanies Chapter 30.)

Looking broadly at the question of American discovery, C. Columbus may be said to have discovered America in 1492; but the controversy on the question, for the critic who likes to enquire into details, is not settled yet.

Concerning the discovery of Australia, we are further off still from a solution than our cousins of the New World. This is owing partly to the fact that the matter has not yet received with us the same amount of attention.

Lately there has been found a wooden globe, now in Paris,* on which an inscription occurs to the effect that the *Terra Australis* was discovered in 1499. The assertion needs confirmation, of course, like all other assertions, without exception, relating to discoveries.

(*Footnote. This curious globe is preserved in the geographical department of the Paris National Library (Number 386). For further particulars concerning this globe we refer our readers to the admirable work by Henry Harrisse, The Discovery of North America, where it is described, page 613. H. Harrisse ascribes to it the date of circa 1535.)

The whole question of early Australasian maritime discovery is so thoroughly enveloped in mystery that it will require not only the greatest care to fathom it, but also the greatest impartiality and circumspection to decide to whom the honor of priority of discovery is due.

As an instance, if we suppose that Captain Cook (Lieutenant at the time) discovered the eastern sea-board, which, by the way, is the generally accepted belief, we are met at the outset by the rebuffing testimony of old charts presenting every portion of that coast line clearly set down more than two hundred years before his arrival in these seas.

Then, if, taking a step backward, we consider the claims of the next candidate for the honor, we are confronted by Tasman. What discoveries did HE make? The old charts we have referred to preclude the possibility of a discovery by him of the western and eastern shores. As to the northern and southern coasts, which are not given on the said charts, there is much incertitude. Who shall say who discovered them?

Again, while, as we shall show, the Portuguese and Spaniards were as a nation the first Europeans to navigate in Australian waters and must have discovered Australia, we find no narrative of their discoveries as far as the continent of Australia is concerned. Furthermore, when we consult the maps, the prototypes of which were made by them, and on which the Australian continent, although evidently distorted for a purpose, is set down with a fair amount of accuracy, we find these very documents borrowing certain features and a certain nomenclature from older representations on globes and maps. We are thus thrown back to a period that antedates the arrival of their fleets in the southern hemisphere.

These older globes and maps connect us with the Ptolemaic period, which, being one of retrogression in a certain measure, makes it imperative for us to begin our inquiries with the very dawn of geographical knowledge.

CHAPTER 2.
THE DAWN OF GEOGRAPHICAL KNOWLEDGE, ESPECIALLY WITH REFERENCE TO THE SOUTHERN HEMISPHERE.

We have said that the Ptolemaic period was one of retrogression in a certain measure. This is apparent when we take into consideration the fact that the earlier ideas concerning the sphericity of the earth were generally discredited by Europeans during the prevalence of the Ptolemaic system, which lasted thirteen centuries. Ptolemy however is not altogether, if at all, responsible for this; as many errors got abroad during the prevalence of manuscript copying, and even after the introduction of printing, that were afterwards attributed to him and other classical authors. It is therefore a difficult task to separate the true teachings of early philosophers from the errors introduced subsequently and which became crystallized in the first printed editions of their works, appearing early in the sixteenth century. But it is a task that is being performed by comparing the traditions and records of western and eastern civilizations. During what has been termed the dark ages in Europe, Oriental writers preserved in many instances more faithful traditions, and were more versed in the sciences than the most eminent men of their time in Europe. Such men as Albert-le-Grand, Bacon, Pierre d'Abano, Dante, etc. began the work of revision; it is owing to their knowledge of Oriental languages that they became pre-eminent among their contemporaries, and they often refer to Oriental authors in matters connected with geography, cosmography, astronomy and kindred sciences.

(*Footnote. With the initial W are represented Oannes and Ea, the Greek and Chaldean Fish-Gods.)

However, in order to fully appreciate the changes that took place with regard to this matter, we must begin at the beginning, for, owing to the connection and continuity that exist in all geographical representations, we might overlook or fail to understand many cartographic particularities if we did not get a clear conception of their origin. We must bear in mind the theories of early cosmology and the motives that obtained later on, whereby many features of archaic cosmography may have been altered; as, for instance, the placing of islands in the northern hemisphere, which, in reality, belonged to the southern one.

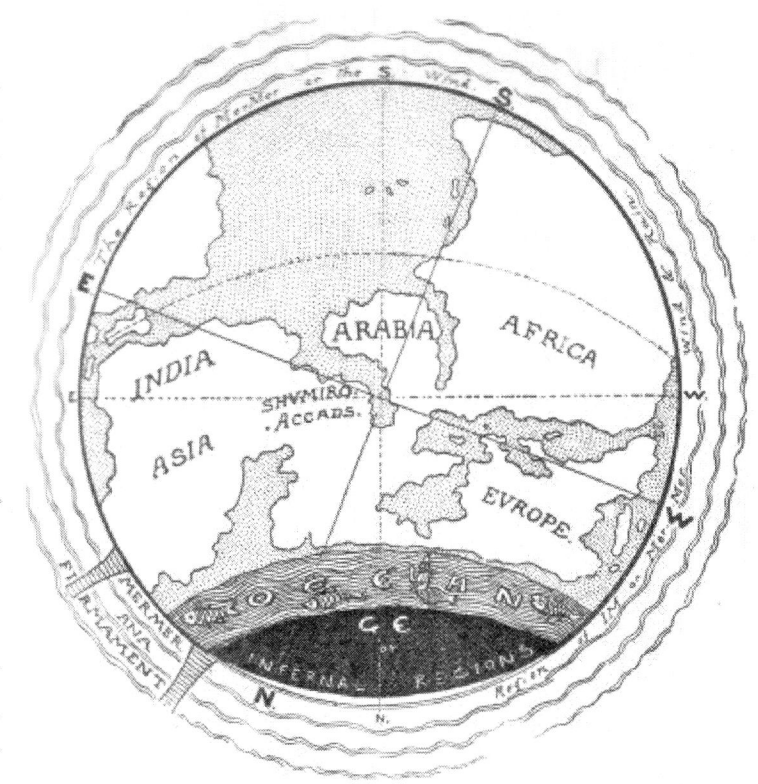

Chaldean conception of the shape of the earth.

CHALDEAN CONCEPTION OF THE SHAPE OF THE EARTH.

It has now been ascertained and demonstrated beyond doubt that the earliest ideas concerning the laws of the universe and the shape of the earth were, in many respects, more correct and clearer than those of a subsequent period.*

(*Footnote. Mr. Hyde Clarke has more than once pointed out: The legend of the Atlantis of Plato, Royal Historical Society 1886, etc., that Australia must have been known in the most remote antiquity of the early history of civilisation, at a time when the intercourse with America was still maintained. It is certainly remarkable, as we learn from classic authors, that the school of Pergamos taught that the earth was divided into four worlds or regions. These were the Great World or Northern Continent (Asia, Europe. and Africa), the Austral or Southern World (Australia), the Northern World, opposite this continent--speaking from Europe--(North America), and the Southern World, to balance the Austral World (South America). All these were stated to be inhabited. Navis, Australia and the Ancients, Notes and Queries volume 5 page 356 May 5 1888.)

Let us see what they were. The author of Chaldea* says:

"According to Mr. Francois Lenormant,* the Shumiro-Accads had formed a very elaborate and clever idea of what they supposed the world to be like; they imagined it to have the shape of an inverted* round boat or bowl, the thickness of which would represent the mixture of land and water (ki-a) which we call the crust of the earth, while the hollow beneath this inhabitable crust was fancied as a bottomless pit or abyss (ge), in which dwelt many powers.

(*Footnote. Chaldea from the Earliest Times to the Rise of Assyria, etc. by Zenalde A. Ragozin, London 1889 page 133.)

(*Footnote. Lenormant, in the English translation of his La magie chez les Chaldeens, which is a revised and enlarged edition of that French work which appeared in the autumn of 1874, says, page 151: "Let us imagine then a boat turned over, not such an one as we are in the habit of seeing, but a round skiff like those which are still used, under the name of Kufa, on the shores of the lower Tigris and Euphrates, and of which there are many representations in the historical sculptures of the Assyrian palaces, the sides of this round skiff bend upwards from the point of the greatest width, so that they are shaped like a hollow sphere deprived of two-thirds (sic, for one-third, as the context shows. G.C.) of its height, and showing a circular opening at the point of division. Such was the form of the earth according to the authors of the Accadian magical formulae and the Chaldean astrologers of after years. We should express the same idea in the present day by comparing it to an orange of which the top had been cut off, leaving the orange upright upon the flat surface thus produced.")

(Footnote. See sketch.)

Above the convex surface of the earth (ki-a) spread the sky (ana), itself divided into two regions--the highest heaven or firmament, which, with the fixed stars immovably attached to it, revolved, as round an axis or pivot, around an immensely high mountain, which joined it to the earth as a pillar, and was situated somewhere in the far North-East--some say North--and the lower heaven, where the planets--a sort of resplendent animals, seven in number, of beneficent nature--wandered forever on their appointed path. To these were opposed seven evil demons, sometimes called *The Seven Fiery Phantoms*. But above all these, higher in rank and greater in power, is the Spirit (*Zi*) of heaven (*ana*), ZI-ANA, or, as often, simply ANA--*Heaven*. Between the lower heaven and the surface of the earth is the atmospheric region, the realm of IM or MERMER, the Wind, where he drives the clouds, rouses the storms, and whence he pours down the rain, which is stored in the great reservoir of *Ana*, in the heavenly Ocean. As to the earthly Ocean, it is fancied as a broad river, or watery rim, flowing all round the edge of the imaginary inverted bowl; in its waters dwells EA,* or THE EXALTED FISH, or on a magnificent ship, with which he travels round the earth, guarding and protecting it." See accompanying sketch (Illustration 57) of an inverted Chaldean boat transformed into a terrestrial globe, which will give an idea of the possible appearance of early globes.

(Footnote. Berosus, the priestly historian of Babylon, in reporting the legend concerning the arrival of EA from the East, seems to have given the God's name EA-han (EA the Fish) under the corrupted Greek form of OANNES.)

Now, it is remarkable that the Greeks, adopting the earlier Chaldean ideas concerning the sphericity of the earth, believed also in the circumfluent ocean; but they appear to have removed its position from latitudes encircling the *Arctic regions* to a latitude in close proximity to the equator.

Notwithstanding this encroachment of the external ocean--*encroachment which may have obliterated indications of a certain northern portion of Australia, and which certainly filled those regions with the great earth--surrounding river*

Okeanos--the traditions relating to the existence of an island, of immense extent, beyond the known world, were kept up, for they pervade the writings of many of the authors of antiquity.

One of the most striking of the traditions we refer to is quoted by R.H. Major* in the following terms:

(Footnote. R.H. Major, Early Voyages to Australia, page ii line 27.)

"In a fragment of the works of Theopompus, preserved by Aelian, is the account of a conversation between Silenus and Midas, King of Phrygia, in which the former says that Europe, Asia, and Africa were lands surrounded by the sea; but that beyond this known world was another island, of immense extent, of which he gives a description. The account of this conversation, which is too lengthy here to give in full, was written three centuries and a half before the Christian era. Not to trouble the reader with Greek, we give an extract from the English version by Abraham Fleming, printed in 1576, in the amusingly quaint but vivid language of the time:

"*The Thirde Booke of Aelianus.* Page 37.

"Of the familiaritie of Midas, the Phrigian, and Selenus, and of certaine circumstances which he incredibly reported.

"Theopompus declareth that Midas, the Phrygian, and Selenus were knit in familiaritie and acquaintance. This Selenus was the sonne of a nymphe inferiour to the gods in condition and degree, but superiour to men concerning mortalytie and death. These twaine mingled communication of sundrye thynges. At length, in processe of talke, Selenus tolde Midas of certaine ilandes, named Europia, Asia, and Libia, which the ocean sea circumscribeth and compasseth round about; and that without this worlde there is a continent or percell of dry lande, which in greatnesse (as hee reported) was infinite and unmeasurable; that it nourished and maintained, by the benefite of the greene medowes and pasture plots, sundrye bigge and mighty beastes; that the men which inhabite the same climats exceede the stature of us twise, and yet the length of their life is not equall to ours; that there be many and divers great cities, manyfold orders and trades of living; that their lawes, statutes, and ordinaunces are different, or rather clean contrary to ours. Such and lyke thinges dyd he rehearce." Major adds: "The remainder of this curious conversation, however apparently fabulous, deserves attention from the thoughtful reader."

The peculiar Chaldean opinion relating to the boat-shaped form of the earth is commented upon by Mr. Gladstone in his Homeric Synchronysms. Speaking of F. Lenormant's description, Gladstone says: "He (Lenormant) observes that the meaning of *scaphoeides* is the form of a boat reversed, and that the boats of the rivers Tigris and Euphrates were circular. They are so represented on the Nineveh sculptures (Rawlinson, note on Herodotus, i. 194); and they may still be seen on these rivers in the like form."

"But he (Lenormant) does not notice," says Gladstone, "what we learn from Colonel Chesney (Expedition to the Euphrates and Tigris; volume i. page 57; volume ii. page 640; and Rawlinson as before cited) namely, that the side of the boat curves inwards, so that when reversed the figure of it would be like an orange with a slice taken off the top, and then set on its flat side. The Chaldean conception, thus rudely described, shows a yet nearer approximation (to say the least) to the true doctrine concerning the form of the globe, when we bear in mind that this actually is in shape a flattened sphere, with the vertical diameter (so to speak) the shorter one."

Comparing these early notions, as to the shape and extent of the habitable world, with the later ideas which limited the habitable portion of the globe to the equatorial regions, we may surmise how it came to pass that islands--to say nothing of continents which could not be represented for want of space*--belonging to the southern hemisphere were set down as belonging to the northern hemisphere.

(*Footnote. A curious example of the difficulties that early cartographers of the circumfluent ocean period had to contend with, and of the sans facon method of dealing with them, occurs in the celebrated Fra Mauro Mappamundi, which is one of the last in which the external ocean is still retained. On this map of the world the islands of the Malay Archipelago follow the shores of Asia from Malacca to Japan. Borneo, Scelebes and the Philippines are left out, and the cartographer, conscious of his omissions, excuses himself naively in these terms: "In questo Mar Oriental sono molte isole grande e famose che non ho posto per non aver luogo: In this Oriental sea there are great many large and well-known islands, that I have not set down, because I had no room." After this admission there was room for improvement.)

We have no positive proof of this having been done at a very early period, as the earlier globes and maps have all disappeared; but we may safely conjecture as much, judging from copies which have been handed down. Globes especially--as being more explicit, because not presenting the difficulties of planispheric projection--would have been useful, for they would have shown us exactly what early geographical knowledge must have been in this respect; unfortunately, whereas the earliest recorded *mention* of an earth globe is of the one made by Crates (200 B.C.), ten feet in diameter and described by Strabo, Geographica; Book ii. cap. v. paragraph 10--the earliest one extant dates no further back than the year 1492. This is the well-known globe of Martin Behaim, of Nuremberg.

Early maps of the world, as distinguished from globes, take us back to a somewhat remoter period; they all bear most of the disproportions of the Ptolemaic geography, for none belonging to the pre-Ptolemaic period are known to exist. The influence of the Ptolemaic astronomical and geographical system was very great, and lasted for over thirteen hundred years. Even the Arabs, who, after the fall of the Roman Empire, developed the geographical knowledge of the world during the first period of the middle ages, adopted many of its errors. With reference to the earliest opinions concerning a knowledge of an Australian Continent, R.H. Major says*: "Among the very early writers, the most striking quotation that the editor has lighted upon in connection with the southern continent, is that which occurs in the *astronomicon* of Manilius, lib. i. lin. 234, *et seq.*, where, after a lengthy dissertation, he says:

(*Footnote. R.H. Major, Early Voyages to Australia, Introduction, page xii. line 14th.)

Ex quo colligitur terrarum forma rotunda;

Hanc circum variae gentes hominum atque ferarum,

Aeriaeque colunt volucres. Pars ejus ad arctos

Eminet, *Austrinis pars est habitabilis oris,*

Sub pedibusque jacet nostris.

The latter clause of this sentence, so strikingly applying to the lands in question, has been quoted as a motto for the title page of this volume--Early Voyages to Australia. The date at which Manilius wrote, though not exactly ascertained, is supposed, upon the best conclusions to be drawn from the internal evidence supplied by his poem, to be of the time of Tiberius.

"Aristotle also, in his Meteorologica, lib. ii. cap. 5, has a passage which, though by no means so distinct as the preceding, speaks of two segments of the *habitable* globe, one towards the north, the other towards the south pole, and which have the form of a drum. Aratus, Strabo, and Geminus have also handed down a similar opinion, that the torrid zone was occupied throughout its length by the ocean, and that the band of sea divided our continent from another, situated, as they suppose, in the southern hemisphere. (See Aratus, Phoenom., 537; Strabo, i. 7, page 130, and i. 17; Crates apud Geminum, Elementa Astronomica, c. lxiii. in the Uranologia, page 31)."

In the 9th century Al-Mamoun had Ptolemy's geography translated, which became the Almageste, or Great Book of the Arabs. In the course of time, through practical experience acquired in their extensive voyages to the east and south-east, the Arabs wrought many improvements in their maps. An important one was introduced in their maps of the Indian Ocean, and that is: after having been set down as a Mediterranean, or enclosed sea, by their predecessors, they represented it as an open sea again, as in the days of Homer and in the geography of Erathosthenes.

Ptolemy's fantastic islands of the Indian Ocean--fantastic inasmuch as they had been shifted from the southern to the northern hemisphere--reappear during the later Arabian period in the southern hemisphere; but, strangely enough, with others, which in their turn become fantastic--so to speak--inasmuch as they are set down in the southern while belonging to the regions north of the equator; the latter mistake being traceable, principally, to an erroneous interpretation of the writings of the two great Venetian travellers Marco Polo and Nicolo de' Conti.

Thus we have a threefold source of information--a Greek, an Arabian, and an Italian--and we shall find this threefold character in the nomenclature of the islands we refer to.

CHAPTER 3.

AN INQUIRY CONCERNING THE POSITION OF NORTH AND SOUTH IN ANCIENT GEOGRAPHY. THE EQUATORIAL REGIONS DISTORTED. TAPROBANA AND CEYLON.

Io mi volsi a man destra, e posi mente

All' altro polo; e vidi quattro stelle

Non viste mai, fuor ch' alla prima gente

Goder pareva 'l ciel di lor fiammelle.

O settentrional vedovo sito,

Poiche privato se' di mirar quelle!

Dante, Purgatorio, Canto I.

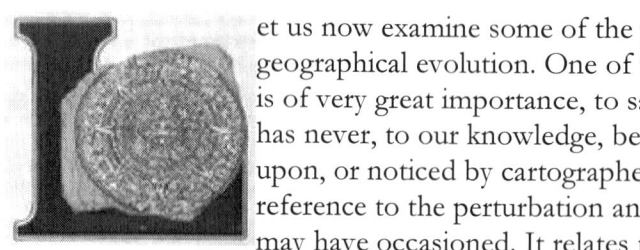et us now examine some of the peculiarities of geographical evolution. One of these peculiarities is of very great importance, to say the least, and has never, to our knowledge, been commented upon, or noticed by cartographers or others with reference to the perturbation and errors that it may have occasioned. It relates to the position of north and south.

(*Footnote. With the initial L of this Chapter is represented an Aztec Calendar or Water-Stone. drawn in facsimile and reduced from the illustration in Mr. Thomas Crawford Johnston's paper, Did the Phoenicians discover America? which appeared in a special bulletin of the Geographical Society of California; dated San Francisco, September 15 1892.

Speaking of this stone Mr. Johnston says: "And perhaps more curious still, we find among the remains of this people in the ancient and capital city of Mexico what has been called a calendar stone, which anyone may see at a glance is a national monument of a seafaring people in the form of a mariner's compass, and to which they probably attributed the fact that they had discovered the new world." Pages 12 and 13.)

We have seen that according to the earliest geographical notions the habitable world was represented as having the shape of an *inverted* round boat, with a broad river or ocean flowing all round its rim, beyond which opened out the *Abyss* or *bottomless pit*, which was beneath the habitable crust.

The description is sufficiently clear, and there is no mistaking its general sense, the only point that needs elucidation being that which refers to the position of the earth or globe as viewed by the spectator.

Our modern notions and our way of looking at a terrestrial globe or map with the north at the top, would lead us' to conclude that the *abyss* or *bottomless pit* of the inverted Chaldean boat, the Hades and Tartaros of the Greek conception, should be situated to the south, somewhere in the Antarctic regions.

There are reasons to believe however, apart from the evidence we gather in the Poems,* that these abyssal regions were supposed or believed to be situated around the North Pole.

(*Footnote. The internal evidence of the Poems points to a northern as well as a southern location for the entrance to the infernal regions. Mr. Gladstone seems to incline to this opinion when he says (Homer page 60 paragraph 4. The Outward Geography Eastwards): "The outer geography eastwards, or wonderland, has for its exterior boundary the great river Okeanos, a noble conception, in everlasting flux and reflux, roundabout the territory given to living man. On its farther bank lies the entrance to the Underworld; and the passage, which connects the sea (*Thalassa*, or *Pontos*) with Okeanos, lies in the east: 'where are the abodes of the morning goddess, and the risings of the sun' (Od. 12:3). Here however he makes his hero confess that he is wholly out of his bearings, and cannot well say where the sun is to set or to rise (Od. 10:139). This bewildered state of mind may be reasonably explained. The whole northern region, of sea as he supposed it, from west to east, was known to him only by Phoenician reports. One of these told him of a Kimmerian land deprived perpetually of sun or daylight. Another of a land, also in the north, where a man, who could dispense with sleep, might earn double wages, as there was hardly any night. He probably had the first account from some sailor who had visited the northern latitudes in summer; and the second from one who had done the like in winter. They were at once true, and for him irreconcilable. So he assigned the one tale to a northern country (Kimmerie) on the ocean-mouth eastwards, near the island of Kirke, and the other to the land of the Laistrugonas westwards but also northern, and lying at some days' distance from Aiolie; but was compelled, by the ostensible contradiction, to throw his latitudes into something like purposed confusion."

The author suggests the following as another probable source of information: The Phoinikes of Homer are the same Phoenicians who as pilots of King Solomon's fleets *brought gold and silver, ivory, apes and peacocks* from Asia beyond the Ganges and the East Indian islands. The Phoenician reports referred to by Mr. Gladstone came most likely therefore, not so much from the north, as from these regions which, tradition tells us (See Fra Mauro's Mappamundi), were situated *propinqua ale tenebre*. Volcanoes were supposed to be the entrances to the infernal regions, and towards the south-east the whole region beyond the river Okeanos of Homer, from Java to Sumbawa and the sea of Banda, was sufficiently studded with mighty peaks to warrant the idea they may have originated. Then in a north-easterly direction Homer's great river Okeanos would flow along the shores of the Sandwich group, where the volcanic peak of Mt. Kilauea towers three miles above the ocean. Indeed, wherever we look round the margin of the circumfluent ocean for an appropriate entrance to *Hades* and *Tartaros*, we find it, whether in Japan, Iceland, the Azores, or Cape Verde Islands.)

European mariners and geographers of the Homeric period considered the bearing of land and sea only in connection with the rising and setting of the sun and with the four winds Boreas, Euros, Notos, and Sephuros. These winds covered the arcs intervening between our four cardinal points of the compass, which points were not located exactly as with us; but the north leaning to the east, the east to the south, the south to the west and the west to the north (see Turin Map).

These mariners and geographers adopted the plan--an arbitrary one--of considering the earth as having the north above and the south below, and, after globes or maps had been constructed with the north at the top, and this method had been handed down to us, we took for granted that it had obtained universally and in all times.

Such has not been the case, for the earliest navigators, the Phoenicians, the Arabs, the Chinese, and perhaps all Asiatic nations, considered the south to be above and the north below.

The reason for this is plausible, for whereas the northern seaman regulated his navigation by the north star, the Asiatic sailor turned to southern constellations for his guidance. Many cartographers of the renascence, whose charts indeed we cannot read unless we reverse them, must have followed Asiatic cartographical methods, and this perhaps through copying local charts obtained in the countries visited by them.

It is strange that Mr. Gladstone, in pointing out so cleverly that the Chaldean conception was more in accordance with the true doctrine concerning the form of the globe than had been suspected, fails, at the same time, to notice that Homer in his brain-map reversed the Chaldean terrestrial globe and placed the north at the top. This is all the more strange when we take into consideration that, in the light of his context, the fact is apparent and of great importance as coinciding with other European views concerning the location of the north on terrestrial globes and maps. These are Mr. Gladstone's words:

"The surface of the vessel represented is the world which we inhabit. The mouth lies downward. In the hollow of the solid dwell the Earth-genii of Tartaros and the Spirits of the dead. Over it extends the compacted mass of Heaven, with its astral bodies. All this seems to have been adopted by Homer. But, moreover, the Chaldean Heaven rested upon columns, about which it revolved; these columns were not at the zenith of the heaven, which was immediately over Accad, but at the Mountain of the East.* And even so Homer sets his heaven upon columns, *but places them with his Atlas in the south.*"

(*Footnote. "North-east, some say north," according to Ragozin. Note of author.)

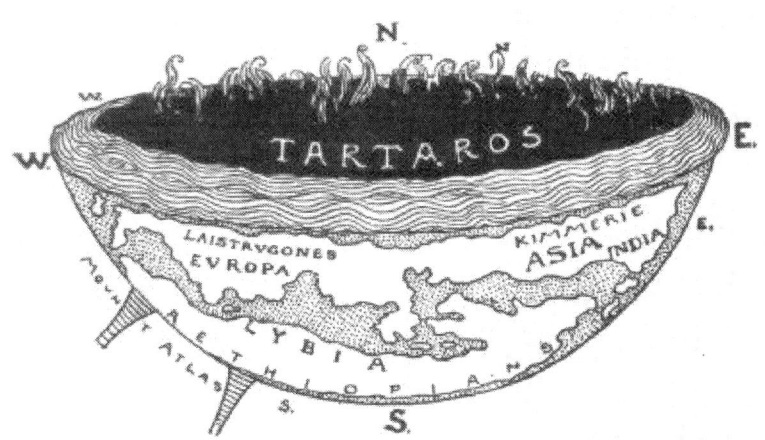

Greek conception of the shape of the earth.

GREEK CONCEPTION OF THE SHAPE OF THE EARTH.

To resume briefly: The Chaldeans placed their north below; Homer placed his north above. See Illustration 37. The Chaldeans placed their heaven in the east or north-east; Homer placed his heaven in the south or south-west.

During the middle ages, we shall see a reversion take place, and the terrestrial paradise and heavenly paradise placed according to the earlier Chaldean notions; and on maps of this epoch, encircling the known world from the North Pole to the equator, flows the antic Ocean, which in days of yore encircled the infernal regions. In this ocean we find also EA the *Exalted Fish*, but, deprived of his ancient grandeur and divinity, he is no doubt considered nothing more than a merman at the period when acquaintance is renewed with him on the Frankfort gores of Asiatic origin bearing date 1515. See Mappamundi bearing that date.

At a later period, during which planispheric maps, showing one hemisphere of the world, may have been constructed, the circumfluent ocean must have encircled the world as represented by the geographical exponents of the time being; albeit in a totally different way than expressed in the Shumiro-Accadian records. The divergence was probably owing in a great measure to the *inability of representing graphically the perspective appearance of the globe on a plane*; but may be also traceable to an erroneous interpretation of the original idea, caused by the reversion of the cardinal points of the compass.

Afterwards came the geographical period, 500 B.C., when Thales drew the equator across the globe; but the original design of this line of demarcation became confused also, and so misapplied that it was made to follow the southern rim of the ocean that girt the world. This extraordinary manner of distorting the equatorial regions was repeated in mediaeval charts, and one of its last representations is nowhere more remarkable than in Fra Mauro's celebrated Mappamundi of 1457/1459, a very much reduced facsimile of which is given elsewhere.

The zone or climate division of the world was propounded about the same time. According to this division other continents south of the equator were supposed to exist and habited, some said, but not to be approached by those inhabiting the northern hemisphere on account of the presumed impossibility of traversing the equatorial regions, the heat of which was believed to be too intense.

It follows from all this that, as mariners *did* actually traverse those regions and penetrate south of the equator, the islands they visited most, such as Java, its eastern prolongation of islands, Sumbawa, etc., were believed to be in the northern hemisphere, and were consequently placed there by geographers, as the earliest maps of the various editions of Ptolemy's Geography bear witness.

To these first sources of confusion may be added another that originated with the misleading accounts in which Ceylon and Sumatra were indiscriminately described under the Greek name of Taprobana,* and this confusion of one island with the other led to various forms of distortion; sometimes Ceylon was placed in the longitude and latitude of Sumatra; at other times Sumatra was placed where Ceylon stands; but, as Sumatra was known by some to be cut in two by the equator, Ceylon had to be enlarged so as to extend sufficiently south to allow for it being bisected by the equator as mentioned. Then again islands lying south of the equator came to be taken for Ceylon--Ceram, for instance.

(*Footnote. Taprobana was the Greek corruption of the Tamravarna of Arabian, or even perhaps Phoenician, nomenclature; our modern Sumatra. See Alberuni's India volume 1 page 296.)

These mistakes were the result doubtless of an erroneous interpretation of information received; and the most likely period during which cognizance of these islands was obtained was when Alexandria was the centre of the Eastern and Western commerce of the world. About this time Erathosthenes was the chief or great Librarian at Alexandria (230 to 220 B.C.). Geographical science was on the eve of reaching its apogee with the Greeks, ere it was doomed to retrograde with the decline of the Roman Empire. The views of the three great Greek astronomers and cartographers--Dicearchus, Erathosthenes and Hipparchus (300 to 125 B.C.)--comprising the origin of degrees of longitude and latitude, the inauguration of the principle of stereographic projection and the division of the circle into 360 degrees, give us an idea of the progress made at the time. Although these views were continued and developed to a certain extent by their successors, Strabo and Ptolemy, through the Roman period, and more or less entertained during the Middle Ages, they became obscured as time rolled on. The earliest known maps of the mediaeval epoch present the appearance of rough delineations of land and water, a corrupted nomenclature, and no reference whatsoever to degrees of longitude or latitude. No geographical progress, in fact, was made by Europeans until Marco Polo, Odoric of Pordenone, and Nicolo de' Conti, the three great Italian travellers, revealing afresh the vast extent and wonders of the eastern and southern hemisphere, created the interest that brought about the rediscovery of new worlds.

But to return to the earlier Pre-Ptolemaic period which we have left, and to form an idea of the chances of information which the traffic carried on in the Indian Ocean may have offered to the Greeks and Romans, let us listen to what Galvano* says, quoting Strabo and Pliny (Strabo, lib. 17; Plinius, lib. 12, cap. 18). The quaint phraseology of his translator runs thus: "For the trafficke grew so exceeding great that they sent every yeere into India a hundred and twenty ships laden with wares, which began to set saile from Myos-Hormos about the middle of July, and returned backe againe within one yeere. The marchandise which they did carrie amounted unto one million two hundred thousand crownes; and there was made in returne of every crown an hundred. In so much that, by reason of this increase of wealth the matrones, or noblewomen, of that time and place (Rome) spent infinitely in decking themselves with precious stones, purple, pearles, gum benzoin, frankincense, musk, amber, sandalwood, aloes, and other perfumes, and trinkets, and the like; whereof the writers and historians of that age speake very greatly."

(*Footnote. The discoveries of the world from their first original unto the year of our Lord 1555, by Antonio Galvano, Governor of Ternate. Corrected, quoted, and published in England by Richard Hakluyt 1601 page 47.)

Now as the above articles of commerce, mentioned by Strabo and Pliny, after leaving their original ports in Asia and Austral-Asia, were conveyed from one island to another, any information--when sought for--concerning the location of the islands from which the spices came, must necessarily have been of a very unreliable character, for the different islands at which any stay was made were invariably confounded with those from which the spices originally came.* We shall see, when dealing with Ptolemy's map of the world, some of the results of this confusion.

(*Footnote. Such misnomers as *Turkey-cock* and *Turkey rhubarb* remind one of the same peculiar way of confusing names.)

CHAPTER 4. A.D. 1 TO 150.

ST. THOMAS. STRABO. PTOLEMY. GALVANO'S OPINION ON PTOLEMY'S GEOGRAPHY.

During the first years of the first century of our epoch there lived two personages of a somewhat different character, but having both a claim on our attention as connected more or less with our subject. These two personages are: St. Thomas the Apostle, and Strabo the Greek geographer.

(*Footnote. With the initial D of this Chapter is represented St. Thomas catechising the inhabitants of Zanzibar island as represented on Martin Behaim's globe of 1492.)

According to the Lives of the Saints St. Thomas, after the dispersion of the Apostles, preached the Gospel to the Parthians and Persians; then went to India, where he gave up his life for Jesus Christ. John III, King of Portugal, ordered his remains to be sought for in a little ruined chapel that was over his tomb, outside Meliapur or Maliapor. The earth was dug in 1523, and a vault was discovered shaped like a chapel. The bones of the holy apostle were found, with some relics which were placed in a rich vase. The Portuguese built near this place a new town which they called St. Thomas or San-Thome. We shall have to refer to this town, when the name first appears in chronological sequence.

In Strabo's Geography* there are these four points of importance with reference to our subject:

1. That he corroborates Homer's views as to the sphericity of the earth by describing Crates' terrestrial globe (Geographica; Book ii. cap. v. section 10).

2. That he accentuates Homer's views concerning the black races which lived some in the west (the African race) others in the east (the Australian race).

3. That he shows the four cardinal points of the compass to have been situated somewhat differently than with us, for he says (Book 1, c. iv. section 6): "...*So that if the extent of the Atlantic Ocean were not an obstacle, we might easily pass from Iberia to India, still keeping in the same parallel, etc.*" This is the idea that C. Columbus endeavoured to put into practice; but had he followed the parallel mentioned, instead of reaching the islands now called the West Indies, he would have reached the latitude where New York now stands. Again, if we consider the Atlantic and North Pacific Oceans as devoid of the American Continent, and the Atlantic Ocean as stretching to the shores of Asia, as Strabo did, the parallel of Iberia (Spain) would have taken Columbus' ships to the north of Japan--i.e. much further north than the India of Strabo.

4. That he appears to be perpetuating an ancient tradition when he supposes the existence of a vast continent or *antichthonos* in the southern hemisphere to counterbalance the weight of the northern continents.

(*Footnote. Bohn's Classical Library.)

From these facts, and many others, such as the positions given to the Mountain of the East or North-East of the Shumiro-Accads, the Mountain of the South, or South-West, of Homer, and the Infernal Regions, we may conclude that the North Pole of the Ancients was situated somewhere in the neighbourhood of the Sea of Okhotsk. The relativeness of these positions appears to have been maintained on some mediaeval maps. See the Turin Mappamundi and Fra Mauro's.

PTOLEMY'S MAP OF THE WORLD.
A.D. 150.

If we consult the scanty evidence distributed here and there during the middle ages in old manuscripts, cosmographies, maps, etc. we shall see by the data they furnish how slowly the geographical evolution proceeded. Hundreds of years elapsed without any apparent progress. Yet progress of a practical kind was being made all the time. Whilst, as Galvano's Translator* quaintly puts it: "All the world was in a hurly burly"; the Arabs were extending their navigations and trade to Malacca and China.

(*Footnote. Our initial I has a representation of an elephant of Ceylon taken from an old edition of Ptolemy's geography.)

(*Footnote. Galvano page 51.)

Then the great period of general renascence brought about a revival in geography as in other studies, and conjecture gave way to truth, as navigators gradually penetrated to the furthermost regions of the earth.

But even then the first flush of revival brought back Ptolemy to the front, and it was some time before the errors and disproportions of his system were rejected. Witness the pertinacity with which C. Columbus maintained and always believed to the last, that he had reached India-- the India of Marco Polo, Nicolo de' Conti, Pierre d' Ailly, and Toscanelli--aye, the India of the Ancients--when amongst the islands of the West Indies and on the north coast of South America.

The early editions of Ptolemy contain a map of the world, which is,-- for aught we know to the contrary--in design and information contemporaneous with Ptolemy himself. The sketch given here shows the Indian Ocean of a map of the world in an edition of La Geografia di Claudio Tolomeo Alexandrino, published in Venice in 1574, the configuration of which map dates probably as far back as A.D. 150, which is about the period at which Ptolemy compiled his great work.

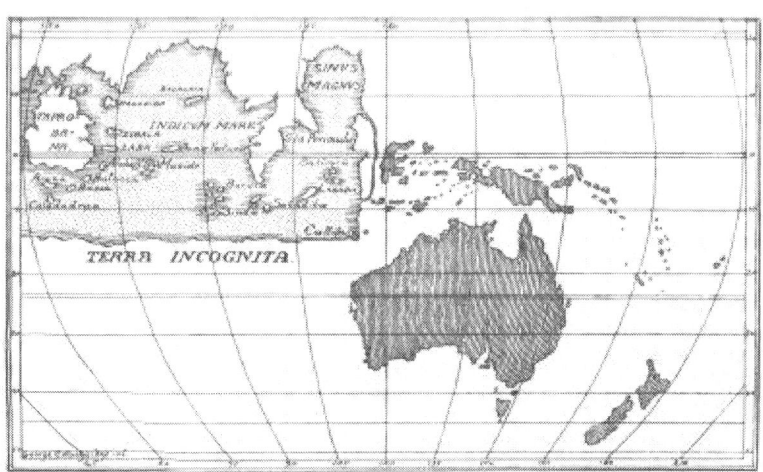

PTOLEMY'S INDIAN OCEAN, AND COMPARATIVE POSITION OF THE AUSTRALASIAN REGIONS.

In the entire map the degrees of longitude extend from the Canary Islands on the west coast of Africa to the longitude of Hong Kong, or thereabouts on the east coast of China. Towards the south the limits of the known world do not extend beyond the 16th degree of latitude.

In the portion of the southern hemisphere comprised within these limits--that is, to the south of the China Sea, we should find the greater or southern half of Sumatra, the island of Java, and a south-western portion of Borneo.

What do we really find depicted? The northern rim of a continent called *Terra incognita*, which might comprise a portion of the coast of Australia, but connected east and west by a continuous line of coast. On this coast the continuous line runs north, passes the equator, and, still running north, connects with the east coast of China.

On the west the continuous line of coast follows the 16th parallel until it reaches the east coast of Africa, a little below the island Menuthias, the modern Zanzibar.

By the above description we notice that the Indian Ocean becomes a Mediterranean or enclosed sea. The islands set down to the north of Australia are: Ceylon, which bears the Greek name *Taprobana*, and is traversed in its southern parts by the equatorial line, thus actually confounded with and in certain respects representing Sumatra; Java, called *Zaba*; Sumbawa, named *Zibala*; and the various Spice Islands in the Banda Sea, which appear to be represented under the names of *Maniole, Barusae, Sindae, Sabadibae* and *Labadii*; whereas *Satiroru* may refer to the north-western parts of New Guinea. It will be noticed that in this map, Sumatra, being confounded with Ceylon, is removed, together with the adjoining Eastern Islands, from its position near the Malay Peninsula.

We conclude from the position of most of these islands that all these places, although evidently visited, either by Phoenician, Malay or Arabian sailors, were set down by guess on Ptolemy's map of the world, from accounts more or less trustworthy received at second hand.

Otherwise, why should we find Java and Sumatra placed in the northern hemisphere and in the longitude of Ceylon; New Guinea, or its north-western extremity, where the south-west coast of Borneo should be? The Spice Islands are correctly placed, as far as latitude is concerned, but they are set down too far to the west.

A few more words on Ptolemy's map of the world before we dismiss this relic of a bygone age.

It is strange how its configuration, in that portion of it which occupies us just now, follows the outlines of lands represented in the latest surveys as having been above the sea level during a period when man was in existence, and who shall say to what extent those archaic representations may not have been correct at one time? It is only fair therefore to point out that excuses--not to say reasons--were not wanting to account for Ptolemy's discrepancies. As an instance of the firm belief in the soundness of his views and in the correctness of his geographical representations, the following few remarks from a man of rare talent--Galvano, the founder of historical geography--may be quoted. Writing towards the end of the first half of the 16th century, Galvano says*:

(*Footnote. Galvano's Discoveries of the World, printed for the Hakluyt Society, page 26 et seq.)

"In India also, and in the land of Malabar, although now there be great store of people, yet many writers affirme that it was once a maine sea into the foot of the mountaines; and that the Cape of Comarim and the Island of Zeilan were all one thing. As also that the Island of Samatra did ioine with the land of Malacca by the flats of Caypassia; and not far fro thence there stands now a little island, which feu yeeres past was part of the firme land that is ouer against it.

"Furthermore, it is to be seene how Ptolemy in his tables doth set the land of Malacca to the south of the line in three or fower degrees of latitude, whereas now it is at the point thereof, being called Jentana, in one degree on the north side, as appeereth in the Straight of Cincapura, where daily they doe passe through unto the coast of Sian and China, where the Island of Aynan standeth, which also they say did ioine hard to the land of China: and Ptolemy placeth it on the north side far from the line, standing now aboue 20 degrees from it towards the north, as Asia and Europe now stand.

"Well it may be that in time past the land of Malacca and China did end beyond the line on the south side, as Ptolemy doth set them foorth: because it might ioine with the point of the land called Jentana, with the Islands of Bintan, Banca, and Salitres being many that waies, and the land might be all slime and oaze; and so ye point of China might ioine with the Islands of Lucones, Borneos, Lequeos, Mindanaos, and others which stand in this parallele; they also as yet hauing in opinion that the Island of Samatra did ioine with Java by the channel of Sunda, and the Islands of Bali, Anjane, Sambana, Solor, Hogaleas, Maulua, Vintara, Rosalaguin, and others that be in this parallele and altitude, did all ioine with Jaua (and form one land); and so they seeme outwardly to those that descrie them. For at this day the islands stand so neere the one to the other, that they seeme all but one firme land; and whosoever passeth betweene some of them may touch with the hand the boughs of the trees on the one and on the other side also. And to come neerer to the matter, it is not long since that in the east the Islands of Banda were diuers of them overflowen and drowned by the sea.* And so likewise in China about nine score miles of firme ground is now become a lake, as it is reported. Which is not to be thought maruellous; considering that which Ptolemy and others haue written in such cases, which here I omit, to return to my purpose."

(*Footnote. The connection of these islands was well illustrated the other day when the volcanic disturbances in Sanghir were found to affect the volcanos of Borneo and Scelebes.)

CHAPTER 5. A.D. 1 TO 150.
EARLY MANUSCRIPT MAPS OF THE FIRST PERIOD OF THE MIDDLE AGES.

There are no maps of the world extant of the first centuries of our era, so says Santarem.* Those of the first period of the middle ages are exceedingly scarce. We shall give a few of these, because there may be, in some of them, preserved by tradition, or copied from earlier prototypes, certain features and nomenclature that, with the help of fresh data, will form, at the least, the disjecta membra of a chain of evidence that may throw additional light on ancient geography generally, and on the geography of Australasian regions in particular.

(*Footnote. The initial T of this Chapter is adapted from Ptolemy's geography.)

(*Footnote. Essai sur l'Histoire de la Cosmographie et de la Cartographie du Moyen-Age 1849.)

COPENHAGEN MAPPAMUNDI.

Number 1 is a Mappamundi given in Jomard's collection from the library of Copenhagen. It bears no date. The south is placed at the top as indicated by the lettering. In the northern hemisphere, which is placed below, we notice *Asia, Europa* and *Affrica*. Africa is set down according to the Homeric and Strabonean geography which limits its extent to the northern hemisphere. The Australian regions bear the name *Synti bygd*, which we are unable to explain. The circumfluent ocean surrounds the hemisphere represented, which is cut in two by the torrid zone, the two habitable temperate zones being bounded north and south by their respective glacial zones. A band cutting the equinoctial at the correct angle answers to the plane of the celestial ecliptic. It is a pity that the information it affords is so limited, but, such as it is, it is worth noting.

TURIN MAPPAMUNDI.

Number 2 is a Mappamundi given in Santarem's and Jomard's collections; it is from the Royal Library of Turin, where it is to be seen in a manuscript of the Apocalypse written in the 8th century. In it the east is at the top, where Adam and Eve form a conspicuous feature in the Asiatic landscape there represented by various mountains and rivers. Asia, Europe and Africa are represented as separated from each other by expanses of sea drawn at right angles; except where a connection between Asia and Africa is left at the head waters of the Blue Nile and the south-eastern extremity of the Red Sea. To the north-west of this isthmus--our modern isthmus of Suez--the White and Blue Nile, in a strangely overlapping way which reminds one of a flying pennant, flow into the Mediterranean opposite an island without name, intended no doubt for Crete or Cyprus.

The narrow isthmus of Suez, instead of being laved on the north side by the Mediterranean, is confined on that side by a spur of the mountains of the moon and the source of the Blue Nile indicated by a lake, which must be meant for Lake Tzana, otherwise called Dembea. On the side of the Red Sea the waters represented are those of the Gulf of Aden at the south entrance to the Red Sea; Mushkah Bay and the promontory that juts out to the north of the islands of that name being clearly set down close to the words *Mare rubrum* on the map. Away to the west another lake--either the Albert Nyanza or the Victoria Nyanza--indicate the source of the White Nile. The Persian Gulf and Indian Ocean are indicated, but bear no names. Of the two islands in the extreme east, i.e. at the top of the map, one bears the name of Crisa and is either meant for the Golden Chersonesus or Sumatra; the other island may be intended for Java.

We come now to a part of the map that has a distinct and decided interest for Australians. To the south of Africa *and Asia*, and separated by the Indian Ocean, a fourth part of the world is represented beyond the Equator. This fourth part of the world bears the following Latin legend written right across it: *Extra tres aut partes orbis quarta pars trans oceanum interior est qui solis ardore incognita nobis est cuius finibus Antipodes fabalatore inhabitare pduneur*. Besides these three parts of the world there is a fourth part beyond the interior ocean (Indian Ocean, supposed by some to be a Mediterranean ocean, hence the term *interior ocean*), which on account of the heat of the sun is unknown to us, and where may live the fabulous antipodeans.

This then is the origin of the *terra Australis incognita*; at least it is so far the first representation we have of it on a map. Nor can we argue that because it is roughly set down, it was not known, because Asia, Europe, and Africa are set down in the same way. The geometrical arrangement of the Mappamundi points to an archaic origin, preserved in later, and especially Arabian, maps.

Other features of this venerable specimen of cartography can be traced to an early period; we have seen, for instance, reference made to a southern continent* 350 years before our era. The immediate origin however of the Latin legend quoted above may be attributed to Isidore of Seville. Speaking of *Mela* and *Isidore de Seville* with reference to the *Alter orbis* and *Antichthone*, Santarem says (T.I., page 22) of Isidore de Seville, who lived in the 8th century, i.e., just before the Mappamundi we refer to was drawn: "Il admet aussi l'Antichthone, en soutenant qu'il y a une quatrieme partie du monde, au-dela de l'ocean interieur, c'est-a-dire au midi, qui en raison de l'ardeur du soleil, est inconnue, et dans l'extremite de laquelle on pretend que les Antipodes fabuleux font leur demeure."

(*Footnote. Above, Silenus.)

As another proof of the antiquity of the origin of this Mappamundi we cannot do better than call the critic's attention to those quaint figures dispensing wind and rain from sea shells and inflated skins in the atmospheric regions which correspond with the realm of IM or MERMER of the Shumiro-Accadian records. These figures represent *Boreas, Euros, Notos* and *Zephuros* of the early Greek period, as far as their respective positions are concerned. We shall see the idea perpetuated in later documents, the rain however being left out.

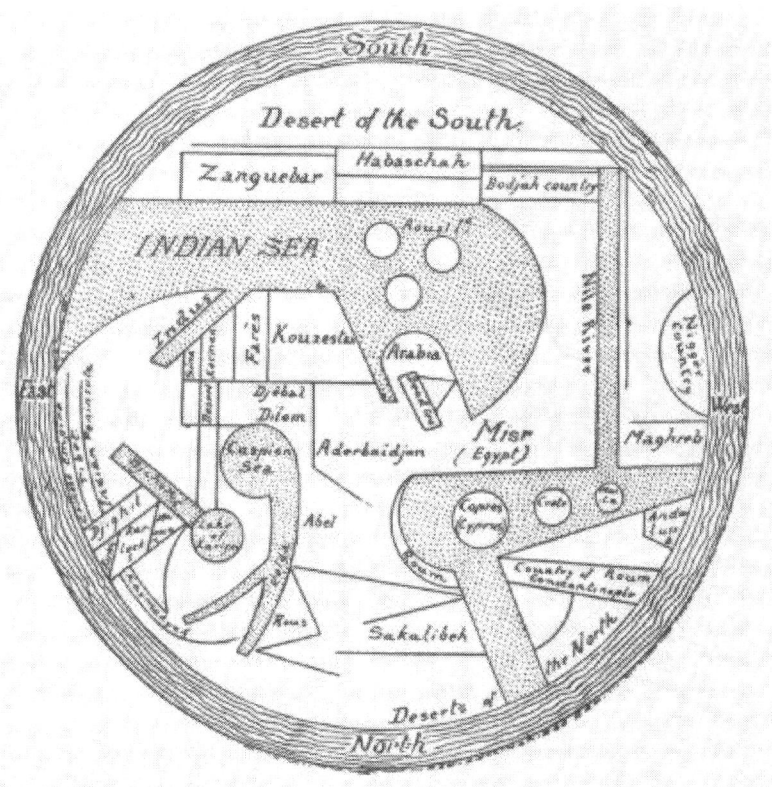

EL ISTAHKRI MAPPAMUNDI.

Number 3 is a Mappamundi of the 9th century from *El Istahkri*, the Arabian geographer. In it the circumfluent ocean is represented, and it is in communication with the Indian Sea. The coastal lines are drawn with rule and compass, a method which may be termed a decorative one, and often used by the Arabs. The south is at the top. At this period the geographical knowledge of the Arabs must have been far superior to what this miserable specimen of cartography would lead us to believe, for they had, at the time, passed the Straits of Malacca, and traded regularly between Omaun, on the Persian Gulf, and China. All the trade of China and India was in their hands, whilst the nation that possesses most of it nowadays was defending her coasts and ports against Danish pirates, and King Alfred, in consequence, was commanding boats and long ships to be built throughout the kingdom.

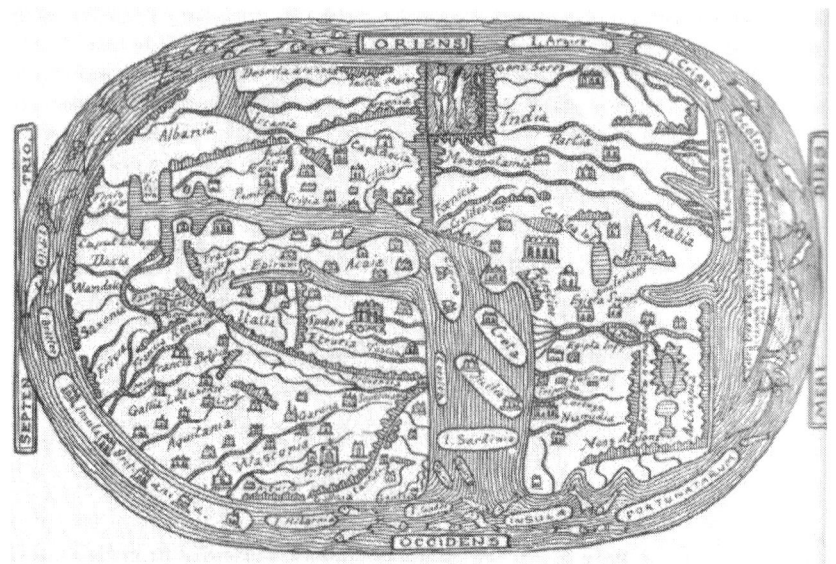

ST. SEVER MAPPAMUNDI.

Number 4 is a Mappamundi, the original of which covers two pages of the Latin manuscript Number 8878 in the French National Library, Paris. The manuscript was executed towards the middle of the 11th century in the Monastery of St. Sever in Gascony, under the guidance of *L'abbe Gregoire*, who administered the establishment from 1028 to 1072. The accompanying sketch is a facsimile of an abridged and reduced copy of the original taken from the Bulletin de la Societe de Geographie Commerciale de Bordeaux, Number 19, October 3 1892.

As in the Mappamundi Number 2, the east is placed at the top, where Adam and Eve, here also, hold a conspicuous position. To the south of India we notice a large island, *I. Tapaprone, Indie*--the Taprobana of the ancients. Whether it represents Ceylon or Sumatra is difficult to say. There are three other islands in the same ocean, *Scolera, Crise*, and *Argire*. According to the internal evidence of later maps, but as far only as nomenclature is concerned, *Scolera* (the Scoyra of the Frankfort gores) is meant for Socotra, and *Crise* for the Malay Peninsula. According however to the position of these two islands and of *Argire*, two of them, at least, may have been intended originally, i.e., in the prototype, for Sumatra and Java; whereas *Crise* represented probably the Malay Peninsula. In the original document, near the island *Argire*, there is a legend that has been omitted on the Mappamundi of the Bordeaux Bulletin. This legend however has been given by the author of the description; we translate it as follows: "This country is near India and the island Taprobane; it is also near the islands *Argire* and *Crise*, where quantities of gold and silver are collected. There are in these parts elephants and dragons, spices and aromatics, precious stones. Monsters prevent men from approaching." It is well to note this legend and fix its origin thus far, as we shall find it handed down and often repeated with slight variation on maps and in descriptions of a later period.

To the south of Africa and Asia, the fourth part of the world is set down with a little less importance than in Mappamundi Number 2. The Latin legend, also, is abridged, but this may not be so on the original, for the author of the French description, which accompanies the reduced copy of the map from which we have taken ours, wisely acknowledges the unwise act of leaving out a part of the nomenclature; in his words "pour eviter la confusion du dessin, nous ne donnons que quelques-uns des noms inscrits sur la carte, nos lecteurs pouvant se reporter a l'original pour les details qui les interesseraient plus particulierement, page 505, lin. 20."

The circumfluent ocean surrounds the elliptical form of the hemisphere represented.

CHAPTER 6. A.D. 1295.

MARCO POLO. JAVA MINOR AND JAVA MAJOR. FIVE TYPES OF MAPS WITH MARCO POLO'S NOMENCLATURE. MANDEVILLE. ODORIC DE PORDENONE.

In 1295, after an absence of many years, Marco Polo, the great Venetian traveller, returned to Venice. He had travelled more extensively in the East and had penetrated further than any other European. Since the days of Alexander the Great, no traveller had brought back from Asia such a store of information of every kind. On his way back, and in the vicinity of the straits of Malacca, the fleet that Marco Polo was with was compelled to wait for the favourable monsoon. Previous to this stay he had sojourned for some time on the coast of Cochin-China. Meanwhile, he gathered information concerning the islands that lay toward the south.

His chief informers, the Arabs, or Moors, as they were called, used to give the generic term iaoas to all the islands in those regions. The terms *Java Major* and *Java Minor* occur frequently in Marco Polo's descriptions, and, judging from the confusion which reigns supreme in subsequent descriptions and maps wherever these names appear, it would seem that Marco Polo's ideas on the subject were of a very mixed nature. Such was not the case.

At a later period Nicolo de' Conti was also in the same localities, and in describing them *he also* mentions Java Major and Java Minor; his Java Minor however does not apply to the same island as Marco Polo's.

The confusion we have referred to was brought about through the insufficiency of knowledge of subsequent writers, some having read Marco Polo's descriptions and not Nicolo de' Conti's, whilst other writers had done the reverse.

Mistakes of the kind will arise also when persons consider a subject from their point of view, instead of considering it from the point of view of the person who introduces the subject.

Marco Polo considered our modern *Java and Australia as one*--the south coast of Java being unknown--and called it Java Major. He also gave this generic name of Java to Sumatra; and to distinguish it from the larger one, he called it Java Minor.

We must bear this fact in mind, because many errors have occurred through mistaking Polo's Java Minor (*Sumatra*) for Java Major (*Australia and Java*).

For superficial inquirers the mistake was an easy one to make, as Java Minor seems to be the more suitable term for the lesser island; but then, as we have said, Marco Polo connected, in his mind, Java with Australia, describing it as *the largest island in the world*.

Although some time elapsed after the return of Marco Polo before the various manuscript editions of his travels appeared, the news of his voyages spread wide and far. He was interviewed by the learned men of the day, and the field of geographical knowledge was widened in consequence. We do not know whether Marco Polo brought back from the East any maps of the countries he visited; but, as an example of Marco Polo's descriptions, we give the following, which not only refers to our subject but is of the greatest importance in connection with it, as illustrating what enormous mistakes were possible when no degrees of latitude or longitude were given.

Owing to the word *Java* being used instead of *Chiampa*,* as a point of departure, a whole set of maps were constructed, in which the islands Marco Polo describes were set down in erroneous positions. Marco Polo's description, which caused these mistakes, runs thus: "When you leave Java and steer a course between south and south-west seven hundred miles, you fall in with two islands, the larger of which is named Sondur and the other Kondur. Both being uninhabited, it is unnecessary to say more respecting them. Having run the distance of fifty miles from these islands in a south-easterly direction, you reach an extensive and rich province that forms a part of the mainland, and is named Lochac. Its inhabitants are idolators. They have a language peculiar to themselves, and are governed by their own king, who pays no tribute to any other, the situation of the country being such as to protect it from any hostile attack. Were it assailable, the Grand Khan would not have delayed to bring it under his dominion.

(*Footnote. R.H. Major, in his biography of Prince Henry the Navigator, page 307, says: "Now, although all the manuscripts and texts of Marco Polo read 'when you leave Java,' Marsden has shown that the point of departure should really be Chiampa, a name in old times applied by Western Asiatics to a kingdom which embraced the whole coast between Tongking and Cambodia, including all that is now called Cochin China.")

"In this country sappan or brazil-wood is produced in large quantities. Gold is abundant to a degree scarcely credible; elephants are found there; and the objects of the chase, either with dogs or birds, are in plenty. From hence are exported all those porcelain shells which, being carried to other countries, are there circulated for money, as has been already noticed. Here they cultivate a species of fruit called berchi, in size about that of a lemon, and having a delicious flavour. Besides these circumstances there is nothing further that requires mention, unless it be that the country is wild and mountainous, and is little frequented by strangers, whose visits the king discourages, in order that his treasure and other secret matters of his realm may be as little known to the rest of the world as possible.

"Departing from Lochac and keeping a southerly course for five hundred miles, you reach an island named Pentam, the coast of which is wild and uncultivated, but the woods abound with sweet scented trees. Between the province of Lochac and this island of Pentam, the sea, for the space of sixty miles, is not more than four fathoms in depth, which obliges those who navigate it to lift the rudders of their ships, in order that they may not touch the bottom. After sailing these sixty miles in a south-easterly direction, and then proceeding thirty miles further, you arrive at an island, in itself a kingdom, named Malaiur, which is likewise the name of its city. The people are governed by a king, and have their own peculiar language. The town is large and well built. A considerable trade is there carried on in spices and drugs, with which the place abounds. Nothing else that requires notice presents itself. Proceeding onwards from thence, we shall now speak of Java Minor."

With Marsden's rectification--see note immediately above--it is easy to follow Marco Polo's route on the map; it extends from the coast of Cochin China to the Pulo Condore islands, thence to the coast of

Cambodia.* From the coast of Cambodia the next place mentioned is the island of Pentam, which has been identified, by good authority, as Bintang, near Singapore; then the island, *in itself a kingdom*, of the name of Malaiur, can be no other country than the Malay Peninsula. Following the itinerary, he afterwards describes Sumatra under the name of Java Minor.

(*Footnote. Marsden shows from the circumstances that it is highly probable that Lochac is intended for some part of the country of Cambodia, the capital of which was named Loech, according to the authority of Gaspar de Cruz, who visited it during the reign of Sebastian, King of Portugal. See Purchas, volume iii. page 169. The country of Cambodia, moreover, produces the gold, the spices, and the elephants which Marco Polo attributes to Lochac.)

The maps that began to appear after Marco Polo's and Nicolo de' Conti's return, and which bear their nomenclature, are of five different types.

If we consider them in chronological order, there is:

1st. Shortly after M. Polo's return, but prior to Nicolo de' Conti's, the primitive type; in it the circumfluent ocean is set down, and the southern portion of Africa, from the equator to the Cape of Good Hope, is bent round, so as to almost join the Malay Peninsula, like in the Arabian maps. There is no mention of the islands *Java Major, Java Minor, Pentan, Condur, etc.*, which form such a conspicuous feature in later maps. This class of map is best represented by the Mappamundi of Marino Sanuto, 1321.

In the 2nd type, of which only one specimen exists--the famous Fra-Mauro Mappamundi--the circumfluent ocean is still retained, and, in consequence, the islands of the Indian and Chinese seas lack space. Nevertheless, *Java Major, Java Minor, Pentan, etc.*, are represented. The date, 1457/1459, allows for the introduction of information derived from Nicolo de' Conti's writings.

In the 3rd type a decided progress is apparent. The circumfluent ocean is rejected. Africa and Asia stretch beyond the equator, the Southern Sea is studded with islands named after Marco Polo's descriptions, such as: *Java Major, Java Minor, Condur, Sondur, Pentan, Neucuram, Angania, etc.* This type, on which no Australian continent appears, is represented by what may be termed the Behaimean and Schonerean maps--1477 to 1535, and even to 1570.

The 4th type is of a mysterious kind; it shows signs of an early beginning, yet contains some of the latest features, features, indeed, that are still present on our modern maps and belong to the Australian regions. It appears to be more independent and less connected with the other three types than those types are relatively to each other. On maps of this type the Australian continent is called Java Major, according to the correct interpretation of Marco Polo's writings. This type of map is represented by the *Dauphin chart*, circa 1530.

The 5th type is a fantastic one, we were going to say altogether fantastic; it has however some features of actuality about it. It bears the nomenclature of Marco Polo, but the term Java Major no longer refers to Australia, which is called *Terra Australis*. The real Java is termed Java Major. Java Minor, Pentan, and other misplaced islands are thrown here and there at random. The Austral regions called *Terra Australis* envelope the South Pole and extend in the correct longitude sufficiently North to warrant the supposition of a knowledge of the Australian continent. A strait between New Guinea and the Terra Australis is another feature of this type. It is represented by the fine specimens of cartography of Ortelius (1570) and Mercator (1569 to 1587).

It will be seen that the influence of Marco Polo's writings was very great, and that their effect on the cartography of the Australasian regions lasted for nearly three hundred years; but during this period other travellers brought their quota of information to bear on the improvements and consequent modifications that were wrought in the maps we have alluded to.

There was Odoric of Pordenone and Mandeville, the mendacious Mandeville, as he has been called. Concerning him, we notice in B. Quaritch's catalogue, 1891, Number iii. page 39, the following: "The latest theory developed from a study of Sir John Mandeville's travels, and supported by Sir Henry Yule, Mr. E.B. Nicholson, and others, is destructive of the interesting personality of the Knight of St. Albans. Just as Raspe compiled the adventures of Munchhausen, so a certain Canon of Bruges is considered to have concocted these wonderful travels and invented the traveller. It is however at least probable that he met a real Englishman whose career suggested the work."

Whoever the traveller may have been, he is quoted as an authority under the name of *Johan de Mandevilla* on Martin Behaim's Globe, 1492.

Colonel H. Yule's verdict was that Mandeville's account of his voyages was mostly inspired, not to say plagiarised, from Odoric de Pordenone's descriptions. In those parts which concern our subject the plagiary is evident.

ODORIC OF PORDENONE.

After Marco Polo, Odoric of Pordenone was certainly one of the most renowned travellers in his days; he also, like the great Venetian traveller, visited far Cathay, following somewhat the itinerary of his predecessor, reaching however nearer to Australia than Marco Polo ever did, for, whereas the latter described the Australasian regions only from hearsay, the Franciscan Monk Odoric actually visited Java and some of the islands of the eastern Archipelago.

He started on his wanderings some time between 1316 and 1318, and returned to Italy in the beginning of the year 1330, where he died the following year from the hardships he had met with during his ten or twelve years' travels.

Numerous manuscripts of the blessed Odoric's narrative spread rapidly abroad during the fourteenth century, and his geographical descriptions had some influence on the cartography of the period. These manuscripts were derived from a copy dictated by the dying man, and written by a friar of less literary attainments than Odoric; hence no doubt the obscurity of many passages. Besides these obscure passages, there appears to have crept into the text of some of these manuscripts several interpolations, especially in those parts of the narrative that relate to the Australasian regions.

Yule says..."The real difficulties of Odoric's story are the accounts of the Islands of Nicoverra and Dondin"...etc.

We shall see with the help of comparative cartography whether these difficulties may be overcome, or explained to a certain extent.

Odoric's course of peregrinations may be rapidly sketched thus: Constantinople, Trebizond, Erzerum, Tabriz, Soltania, Kashan, Yezd, Persepolis, Shiraz, Bagdad, Persian Gulf, Hormuz, where he embarks for Tana in Salsette, Malabar, Pandarani, Cranganor, Kulam, Ceylon; the shrine of St. Thomas at Mailapoor, Sumatra, Java, and some other islands thereabouts, probably southern or eastern Borneo, Champa, and Canton. He returns overland to Venice.

We give here Odoric's account of the regions south of the equator from Yule's excellent and now scarce work, Cathay and the way Thither, published by the Hakluyt Society.--Volume. i., page 87.

"21. THE FRIAR SPEAKETH OF THE EXCELLENT ISLAND CALLED JAVA.

"In the neighbourhood of that realm is a great island, *Java* by name, which hath a compass of a good three thousand miles. And the king of it hath subject to himself seven crowned kings. Now this island is populous exceedingly, and is the second best of all islands that exist. For in it grow camphor, cubebs, cardamons, nutmegs, and many other precious spices. It hath also very great stores of all victuals save wine.

"The king of this island hath a palace which is truly marvellous. For it is very great, and hath very great staircases, broad and lofty, and the steps thereof are of gold and silver alternately. Likewise the pavement of the palace hath one tile of gold and the other of silver, and the wall of the same is on the inside plated all over with plate of gold, on which are sculptured knights all of gold, which have great golden circles round their heads, such as we give in these parts to the figures of saints. And these circles are all beset with precious stones. Moreover, the ceiling is all of pure gold, and to speak briefly, this palace is richer and finer than any existing at this day in the world.

"Now the Great Khan of Cathay many a time engaged in war with this king; but this king always vanquished and got the better of him. And many other things there be which I write not.

"22. OF THE LAND CALLED THALAMASIN, AND OF THE TREES THAT GIVE FLOUR, AND OTHER MARVELS.

"Near to this country is another which is called PANTEN, but others call it THALAMASYN, the king whereof hath many islands under him. Here be found trees that produce flour, and some that produce honey, others that produce wine, and others a poison the most deadly that existeth in the world. For there is no antidote to it known except one; and that is that if anyone hath imbibed that poison he shall take of *stercus humanum* and dilute it with water, and of this potion shall he drink, and so shall he be absolutely quit of the poison. [And the men of this country being nearly all rovers, when they go to battle they carry every man a cane in the hand about a fathom in length, and put into one end of it an iron bodkin poisoned with this poison; and when they blow into the cane, the bodkin flieth and striketh whom they list, and those who are thus stricken incontinently die.]*

(*Footnote. From Pal. This is a remarkable passage from the Palatine manuscript, and is, I suppose, the earliest mention of the Sumpit or blowpipe of the aborigines of the Archipelago. The length stated is a *braccio*, which I have rendered fathom, as nearest the truth, a meaning which the word seems to have in sea phraseology.)

"But, as for the trees that produce flour, 'tis after this fashion. These are thick, but not of any great height; they are cut into with an axe round about the foot of the stem, so that a certain liquor flows from them resembling size. Now this is put into bags made of leaves, and put for fifteen days in the sun; and after that space of time a flour is found to have formed from the liquor. This they steep for two days in seawater, and then wash it with fresh water. And the result is the best paste in the world, from which they make whatever they choose, cakes of sorts and excellent bread, of which I, Friar Odoric, have eaten; for all these things have I seen with mine own eyes. And this kind of bread is white outside, but inside it is somewhat blackish.

"By the coast of this country towards the south is the sea called the Dead Sea, the water whereof runneth ever towards the south, and if anyone falleth into that water he is never found more. And if the shipmen go but a little way from the shore they are carried rapidly downwards and never return again. And no one knoweth whither they are carried, and many have thus passed away, and it hath never been known what became of them.*

(*Footnote. From Pal. De Barros says that the natives believed that whoever should proceed beyond the Straits of Bali to the South would be hurried away by strong currents, so as never to return.)

"In this country, also, there be canes or reeds like great trees, and full sixty paces in length. There be also canes of another kind which are called *Cassan*, and these always grow along the ground like what we call dog's grass, and at each of their knots they send out roots, and in such wise extend themselves for a good mile in length. And in these canes are found certain stones which be such that if any man wear one of them upon his person he can never be hurt or wounded by iron in any shape, and so for the most part the men of that country do wear such stones upon them. And when their boys are still young they take them and make a little cut in the arm and insert one of these stones, to be a safeguard against any wound by steel. And the little wound thus made in the boy's arm is speedily healed by applying to it the powder of a certain fish.

"And thus, through the great virtue of those stones, the men who wear them become potent in battle and great corsairs at sea. But those who from being shipmen on that sea have suffered at their hands, have found out a remedy for the mischief. For they carry as weapons of offence sharp stakes of very hard wood, and arrows likewise that have no iron on the points; and as those corsairs are but poorly harnessed, the shipmen are able to wound and pierce them through with these wooden weapons, and by this device they succeed in defending themselves most manfully.

"Of these canes called *Cassan* they make sails for their ships, dishes, houses, and a vast number of other things of the greatest utility to them. And many other matters there be in that country which it would cause great astonishment to read or hear tell of; wherefore I am not careful to write them at present."

After the above description concerning the bamboo and rattan there follows a description of three islands which has puzzled many a critic, principally because it does not appear to refer to any islands in the vicinity of Java. These three islands bear the names of *Nicoverra or Nicoveran, Sillan,* and *Dondin.*

We are inclined to believe that the reference made to these islands has been interpolated from Marco Polo's work. Marco Polo describes *Nicoveran* (Nicobar Island) and *Sillan* (Ceylon). *Dondin* or *Dondyn* may refer to Candin or Candyn. If we turn to Martin Behaim's globe, 1492, or to any of the globes or maps which bear Marco Polo's nomenclature, we shall find all the islands in question set down in the vicinity of Java, which appears to solve the mystery.

CHAPTER 7.
PRINCE HENRY THE NAVIGATOR.

But the influence that these and other travellers brought to bear, after all, was but of slight importance as regards the discovery of the Australasian regions. Of quite another value was the influence of the great figure we must now introduce in pursuance of the chronological order of our scheme, an order which we have endeavoured to follow as closely as the subject would allow. This great figure--*Prince Henry the Navigator*--we cannot do better than introduce in the very words of the late R.H. Major, his able biographer. In the first chapter of Prince Henry the Navigator Major says:

(*Footnote. With the initial B of this Chapter is given a statue of Prince Henry the Navigator over the side gate of the monastery at Belem, from R.H. Major's Life of Prince Henry the Navigator.)

"The mystery which since creation had hung over the Atlantic, and hidden from man's knowledge one half of the surface of the globe, had reserved a field of noble enterprise for Prince Henry the Navigator. Until his day the pathways of the human race had been the mountain, the river, and the plain, the strait, the lake, and inland sea; but he it was who first conceived the thought of opening a road through the unexplored ocean, a road replete with danger but abundant in promise."

And again, page ix. preface:

"The glory of Prince Henry consists in the conception and persistent prosecution of a great idea, and in what followed therefrom...That glory is not a matter of fancy or bombast, but a mighty and momentous reality, a reality to which the Anglo-Saxon race, at least, have no excuse for indifference.

"*The coasts of Africa visited; the Cape of Good Hope rounded; the new world disclosed; the seaway to india, the Moluccas, and China laid open; the globe circumnavigated, and Australia discovered; within one century of continuous and connected exploration.* Such...were the stupendous results of a great thought, and of indomitable perseverance in spite of twelve years of costly failure and disheartening ridicule...To be duly appreciated, this comprehensive thought must be viewed in relation to the period in which it was conceived. 'The last of the dark ages,' the fifteenth century has been rightly named, but the light which displaced its obscurity had not yet begun to dawn when Prince Henry, with prophetic instinct, traced mentally a pathway to India by an anticipated Cape of Good Hope. No printing-press as yet gave forth to the world the accumulated wisdom and experience of the past. The compass, though known and in use, had not yet emboldened men to leave the shore and put out with confidence into the open sea; no sea-chart existed to guide the mariner along those perilous African coasts; no lighthouse reared its friendly head to warn or welcome him on his homeward track. The scientific and practical appliances which were to render possible the discovery of half a world had yet to be developed. But, with such objects in view, the Prince collected the information supplied by ancient geographers, unweariedly devoted himself to the study of mathematics, navigation, and cartography, and freely invited, with princely liberality of reward, the co-operation of the boldest and most skilful navigators of every country."

Not only did Prince Henry collect the information supplied by ancient geographers, but also all the most recent information obtainable in his days, for we cannot inquire into the geography of his times without finding him always the first and best informed in matters connected with the latest discoveries made, or else using all his efforts to obtain such information.

In 1428 Prince Henry's brother, Dom Pedro, after many years of travel, returned to Portugal. On his journey home the Prince went to Venice,* and there received from the Republic, in compliment to him as a traveller and a learned royal Prince, the priceless gift of a copy of the travels of Marco Polo, which had been preserved by the Venetians in their treasury as a work of great value, together with a map which had been supposed to have been either an original or the copy of one by the hand of the same illustrious explorer...On his return Dom Pedro devoted himself like his brother Prince Henry to scientific studies, among which the art of cartography took a leading place, and there is little doubt that to the genius and attainments of his elder brother Dom Pedro Prince Henry owed much of encouragement and enlightenment in his pursuit of geographical investigation. The Marco Polo Manuscript and the map brought from Venice would doubtless act as a potent stimulus to these investigations.

(*Footnote. R.H. Major, Prince Henry the Navigator page 51.)

Galvano* refers to the Venetian map in these terms: "In the yeere 1428 it is written that Don Peter (Dom Pedro), the King of Portugal's eldest sonne, was a great traveller. He went into England, France, Almaine, and from thence into the Holy Land, and to other places, and came home by Italie, taking Rome and Venice in his way: from whence he brought a map of the world, which had all the parts of the world and earth described.

(*Footnote. Galvano, Discoveries of the World page 66.)

The Streight of Magelan was called in it The Dragon's taile: The Cape of Bona Speranca, the forefront of Afrike (and so foorth of other places), by which map Don Henry, the King's third sonne,* was much helped and furthered in his discoueries."

(*Footnote. Don Henry was King Joao's 5th son; his two first sons, Branca and Alfonso, died in infancy. See Prince Henry the Navigator page 20.)

And Galvano adds, page 67: "It was tolde me by Francis de Sosa Tauares that in the yeere 1528 Don Fernando, the King's sonne and heire, did shew him a map, which was found in the studie of Alcobaza, which had been made 120 yeeres before, which map did set foorth all the nauigation of the East Indies with the Cape of Bona Speranca, according as our later maps have described it. Whereby it appeereth that in ancient time there was as much or more discouered than now there is. Notwithstanding all the trauaile, paines, and expences in this action of Don Henry, yet he was neuer wearie of his purposed discoueries."

It is no doubt the one and same map which is referred to as having been brought back in 1428 by Dom Pedro, and seen in 1528 by Francisco de Souza Tavarez, for Tavarez says it was made 120 years before, which would allow for its being 20 years old when presented to Dom Pedro by the Venetians. It was therefore apparently a copy from an Italian prototype. Unfortunately this map has disappeared.

Major remarks that "it is a notable fact, and one that greatly redounds to the honour of Italy, that the three Powers, which at this day possess almost all America, owe their first discoveries to the Italians: Spain to Columbus, a Genoese; England, the Cabots, Venetians; and France, to Verazzano, a Florentine; a circumstance which sufficiently proves that in those times no nation was equal to the Italians in point of maritime knowledge and extensive experience in navigation."

The same may be said as regards the earliest information in connection with the east and the Australasian regions--information that was only to be obtained from such writers as Marco Polo, the Venetian, Odoric of Pordenone, Nicolo de' Conti, the Venetian, Ludovico Barthema, the Bolognese, Giovanni da Empoli, the Florentine, Andrea Corsali, the Florentine, Hieronimo da San Stephano, the Genoese, etc, etc.

CHAPTER 8. A.D. 1444.
NICOLO DE' CONTI.

In 1444 Nicolo de' Conti, the emulator of Marco Polo, returned to Italy after an absence of 25 years. During his peregrinations *per tutte l' Indie orientali*, he had, in order to save his life, to renounce his faith, and Ramusio* tells us: *Bisogno ch'egli andasse al sommo Pontefice per farsi assoluere, che allhora era in Firenze & si chiamaua Papa Eugenio IIII, che fu dell' anno 1444, il qual dopo, la benedittione, gli dette per penitenza, che con ogni verita douesse narrar tutta la sua peregrinatione ad un valent huomo suo segretario detto Messer Poggio Fiorentino, il quale la scrisse con diligenza in lingua latino.*

(*Footnote. Ramusio, Navigationi at viaggi, fol. 338 C.)

Copies of the narrative of his voyages--narrative that Pope Eugene IV ordered him, as a penance, to dictate to his secretary, *Messer Poggio*--became very scarce about a hundred years later, for Ramusio could not find a single copy, *non solamente nella Citta di Venetia, ma in molte altre d' Italia.*

The patriotic Ramusio, wishing to make known to the world the exploits of his worthy fellow citizen, was compelled, not finding a single copy of his voyages in any town of Italy, to have recourse to a

Portuguese translation, printed in Lisbon, which he was fortunate enough to hear of.

Thus, the Portuguese were in possession of an account of the voyages of the Venetian traveller, the memory of which voyages was all that was left in the minds of Italians of a generation or two later; and Ramusio informs us how this came to pass in these terms:

Questa scrittura dopo molti anni (the manuscript account) peruenne a notitia del Serenissimo Don Emanuel primo di questo nome Re di Portogallo, & fu del 1500, in questo modo: che sapendosi da ogniuno che sua Maesta non pensaua mai ad altro, se non come potesse far penetrare le sue carauelle per tutte l' Indie Orientali, le fu fatto intendere, che questo Viaggio di Nicolo di Conti daria gran luce, & cognitione a i suoi Capitani & Pilotti, & pero di suo ordine fu tradotto di lingua latina nella Portoguese, per un Valentino Fernandes, il quale nel suo proemio dedicato a sua Maesta, tra i altre parole dice queste. Io mi son mosso a tradur questo Viaggio di Nicolo Venetiano, accio che si legga appresso di quello di Marco Polo, cognoscendo 'l grandissimo seruitio che ne resultera a Vostra Maesta, ammonendo, & auisando 1i Sudditi suoi delle cose dell' Indie, cioe quelle Citta, & popoli, che sieno de Mori, et quali degli Idolatri, & delle grandi utilita & ricchezze di spetierie, gioie, oro, & argento, che se ne traggona, & sopra tutto per consolar la travagliata menta di Vostra Maesta, la quale manda le sue carauelle in cosi lungo & pericoloso Viaggio, conciosia cosa che in questo Viaggio di Nicolo si parta particolarmente d' altre citta dell 'Indie, oltra Calicut, & Cochin, che gia al presente habbiamo Scoperte; & appresso per aggiugnere un testimonio al Libro di Marco Polo, il qual ando al tempo di Papa Gregorio X, nelle parti orientali fra 'lvento greco, & levante, & questo Nicolo dipoi al tempo di Pafa Eugenio IIII. per la parte di mezzodi penetro a quella volta, & trouo le medesime Terre descritte dal detto Marco Polo. & questa e stata la principal cagione d' havermi fatto pigliar la fatica di questa tradutione per ordine suo.

In the above we see that Dom Manoel, King of Portugal, in the year 1500, obtained a copy of Nicolo de' Conti's voyages, which he entrusted to Valentino Fernandes to translate into Portuguese, as the account of these voyages would be of great service to his captains and pilots. We see also that Valentino Fernandes, in his dedicatory proem, refers to the additional testimony that Nicolo de' Conti's account will give to Marco Polo's book.

In the preceding chapter we stated that Dom Pedro in 1428 brought back from Venice a manuscript of Marco Polo's travels. R.H. Major* says that *a Portuguese translation of this work* (Marco Polo's work) was made and edited at Lisbon in 1502 by a learned German printer named Valentim Fernandez, who had established himself in Lisbon at that time.

(*Footnote. R.H. Major, Prince Henry the Navigator page 51 note 3.)

This Valentim Fernandez is no doubt the author of the translation of Nicolo de' Conti's Voyages, mentioned by Ramusio under the Italian form of Valentino Fernandes. Unfortunately, this learned German printer does not appear--in the eyes of Ramusio--to have been a very *learned* Italian scholar, whatever his qualifications may have been in other branches of knowledge, for Ramusio says of his translation: "*l' ho ritrouato grandemente guasto & scorreto*," and he adds that he was on the point of abandoning the idea of publishing it. So that, with Ramusio, we must content ourselves with what information may be culled from the much translated translation*:--The first of any importance refers to the city of Malepur,* *situata pur alla costa del mare nell' altro colfo Verso' l' fiume Gange, doue il corpo di San Thommaso honoreuolmente e sepolto iu vna chiesa assai grande, & bella, gli habitatori della quale son christiani detti Nestorini, i quali sono sparsi per tutta l' India, come fra noi sono li giudei, & tutta questa prouincia si dimanda Malabar.*

(*Footnote. We make use of the Portuguese edition translated into Italian by Ramusio, because it contains the text that caused, in our opinion, the distortion of the Behaimean and Schonerean charts. The original Latin edition that Ramusio could not find turned up afterwards, vide note below.)

(*Footnote. Ramusio, Navigationi, F. 339, B.)

The above passage furnishes an item of information which connects it with and suggests that it may have served to form the prototype from which many important, highly interesting, and equally puzzling charts were made.

Nicolo de' Conti, referring to Malepur, *where the body of St. Thomas is buried*, calls that part of the Coromandel coast Malabar; but, as a little further on he refers to the real coast of Malabar, calling it also Malabar,* we may presume that he did not confound the one with the other.

(*Footnote. The original Latin description of Nicolo de' Conti's travels, which Ramusio could not find, appeared afterwards in the fourth book of Poggio's treatise *De Varietate Fortunae libri quatuor*, edited by the Abbe Oliva, Paris 1723 4to., and from that edition R.H. Major edited in 1857 the first English translation for the Hakluyt Society's volume India in the 15th Century. In this edition Malabar is written Melibaria. See page 7.)

The mistake resulted no doubt from the similarity of the contemporaneous names given to these two *provinces* (as they were called), namely: *Provincia di Malabar*, on the coast of Malabar. *Provincia di Ma'bar* or *Mobar*, on the Coromandel coast,* where the city of Malepur was situated and where afterwards the city of *San Thome* was built.

(*Footnote. See map in Yule's Cathay Volume i.)

But, to come to the item of information which may account, in a certain measure, for the distortions of Behaimean and Schonerean maps. It is this: Conti, after describing several towns visited by him on the Coromandel coast and referring to the location of Malepur, says: *situata pur alla costa del mare nell' altro colfo verso 'l' fiume Gange*: situated also on the sea coast in the other gulf towards the river Ganges.

Now, this passage is ambiguous. Conti spoke as though he were on the shores of the Arabian Sea, meaning by the *other gulf* the Bay of Bengal. Those who had to make out his descriptions and locate on charts the various places he described did not interpret him that way. By the *other gulf* they of course understood the Gulf of Martaban, and placed in consequence the *projected* San Thome on the Tenasserim coast opposite.

In this translatory operation--we must ask the question--what charts did they work on? They had no choice. There were no others but those of Ptolemy, *in which the indian peninsula was suppressed*. On the Ptolemy map the two important gulfs were: the *Sinus Gangeticus*, our modern Bay of Bengal, and the *Sinus Magnus*, the Chinese Sea represented as a gulf (see Ptolemy's map Illustration 69). San Thome was therefore placed in this *other gulf*, as may be seen in the 1489 British Museum map.

One fault begot another. Having duplicated in this way the Malay Peninsula--duplication, let it be said, already suggested in Ptolemy's map--the speculative cartographers proceeded without more ado to duplicate on their charts the missing Sumatra, which had been dragged out of place and stood for Ceylon in the Ptolemy maps, where its enormous size had no doubt prevented the proper charting of the Indian Peninsula. The missing Sumatra set down to the south of the duplicate Malay Peninsula received the name of Cayln, afterwards converted to Seillan, Seillan insulae pars, etc.; but, as we shall explain, when we come to the detailed description of these important documents, the west coast and, probably, north-west coast of this bogus Sumatra were in reality the west and north-west coasts of Australia.

In Ramusio's description of Nicolo de' Conti's travels we are brought by a sudden transition from *Zaiton* (China) to *Giava minore & maggiore*; the reason of this suddenness is explained in the text by the notice: *Qui mancan righe*; here lines are missing. The description runs thus: *Nell' India interiore vi sono due isole verso l' estremo confine del mondo, & ambe due sono sono dette le Giave, una delle quali ha di circuito tremila miglia, & l' altra due, poste verso 'l levante, & per il nome di maggiore & minore sono differenti l' una dal l' altra, ad arrivar allequal vi stette un mese continuo di navigatione nel suo ritorno. Da un' isola all' altra vi sono cento miglia di distantia, dove e la parte piu vicina. Quivi si fermo per spatio di nove mesi con la moglie, & con i figliuoli, & con la sua compagnia.*

It is strange that after a sojourn of nine months in the Javas, Nicolo de' Conti's description should be so imperfect. For *interiore*, we propose to read *inferiore*. The two islands in inferior or Austral-India, *Giava minore* and *Giava maggiore*, situated on the confines of the world, must be Java and Sumbawa, yet from his account we do not know in which he stayed. *Giava minore* cannot be Marco Polo's Java Minor, i.e., Sumatra, for Nicolo de' Conti describes that island under the name of *Sumatra anticamente detta Taprobana*, fol. 340 B. Moreover, he says of the two islands: *Da un' isola all' altra vi sono cento miglia di distantia*: from one island to the other the distance is one hundred miles. Again, his context, where he speaks of cock-fighting, the practice of running *amuck*, and the vicinity of the Spice Islands, the produce of which he describes, points to Bali, Lomboc or Sumbawa, but more probably to the latter as the island called by him Java Minor. He describes *Bandan* (Banda) and *Sandai*. Banda is one of the Spice Islands; Sandai may be one of them also, but is more difficult to make out, which may explain how it came to be identified with *Sunda* in the Fra Mauro Mappamundi.

The south coasts of the islands of the Indian Archipelago, such as Java, Bali, Lomboc, Sumbawa, etc., were little known, on account of the strong currents and consequent dangerous nature of the navigation through the straits that separate these islands. Nevertheless, the more westerly coasts of Australia *were known*, and the supposed connection that some of the above-mentioned islands had with the southern continent gave rise to the idea of great extent they were supposed to have, especially the *Java Major*.

CHAPTER 9. A.D. 1457 TO 1459.
FRA MAURO MAPPAMUNDI.

We have seen that in the year 1428 Prince Henry the Navigator and his brother, Dom Pedro, had become possessed of a manuscript of Marco Polo and of a map of the world. Twenty-nine years after, King Affonso V of Portugal sent some documents to Italy to help in the compilation of the famous mappamundi that forms the subject of this chapter. We shall find in this mappamundi many traces, not only of the above-mentioned documents, but also of Nicolo de' Conti's descriptions, showing that although Ramusio could not find towards 1563 one single copy of Conti's narrative of travels, the Portuguese Princes had either obtained a copy long before the year 1500, the year in which, according to Ramusio, D. Manoel obtained a copy, or copies were obtainable in Italy in 1457/1459, the date of the compilation of the Fra Mauro Monument of Geography.

Prince Henry, although 63 years of age at the time, does not seem to have lost sight of the task he had set himself in early life. Indeed Major says:

Prince Henry the Navigator. **Page 187.**

"During the long period in which Prince Henry was continuing his maritime explorations, he did not cease to cultivate the science of cartography. In this he was warmly seconded by his nephew, King Affonso V. We have unfortunately nothing to show as the result of the cartographical labours of the geographer Mestre Jayme, whom the

Prince had procured from Majorca, to superintend his school of navigation and astronomy at Sagres, whither he had also brought together the most able Arab and Jewish mathematicians that he could obtain from Morocco or the Peninsula; but at his instance the King caused to be made in Venice the finest specimen of mediaeval map-making that the world has ever produced, and which exists at the present day. The discovery that beyond Cape Verde the coast trended eastwards inspired the King with new energy, for he assumed therefrom that it would soon lead to India. He thought it possible that in that direction the meridian of Tunis, and perhaps even that of Alexandria, had been already passed. He gave names to rivers, gulfs, capes, and harbours in the new discovery, and sent to Venice draughts of maps on which these were laid down, with a commission for the construction of a mappemonde on which they should be portrayed.

It was to the Venetian Fra Mauro, of the Camaldolese Convent of San Miguel de Murano, that this commission was entrusted. King Affonso V spared no expense, and Fra Mauro paid the draughtsmen from twelve to fifteen sous a day, while from 1457 to 1459 he himself gave all possible pains to perfecting his task. The practiced draughtsman, Andrea Bianco, was called to take a part in its execution. At length this magnificent specimen of mediaeval cartography was completed, and by desire of the King despatched to Portugal, in charge of the noble Venetian Stefano Trevigiano on the 24th of April 1459. In the same year, on the 20th of October, the drawings and writings and a copy of the mappemonde were enclosed in a chest and sent to the Abbot of the convent, from which it would seem that Fra Mauro was then dead. It is to be presumed that while elaborating the mappemonde for King Affonso he made at the same time a copy which he intended to leave to the convent. In the convent library still exists the register of receipts and expenditure of the convent, written by the Abbot, afterwards Cardinal, Maffei Gerard, in which is a note of the current cost of the map.*

(*Footnote. Note in Prince Henry the Navigator, page 189. A photograph copy of this planisphere, of the size of the original, and the finest existing, having been made by Signor Naya, of Venice, under the express supervision of my friend, Mr. Rawdon Brown, is now in the Department of Maps and Charts in the British Museum.)

On this map, which preceded by forty years the rounding of the Cape of Good Hope by Vasco da Gama, we see clearly laid down the southern extremity of Africa, under the name of Cavo di Diab. Northeast of Cavo di Diab are inscribed the names of Soffala and Xengibar. The southern extremity is separated from the Continent by a narrow strait. An inscription on Cape Diab states that in 1420 an Indian junk from the east doubled the Cape in search of the islands of men and women (separately inhabited by each), and after a sail of two thousand miles in forty days, during which they saw nothing but sea and sky, they turned back, and in seventy days' sailing reached Cavo di Diab, where the sailors found on the shore an egg as big as a barrel, which they recognised as that of the bird Crocho, doubtless the roc or rukh of Marco Polo, a native bird of Madagascar."

There are other inscriptions and names on this wonderful chart, which have not been noticed by Major or any other critic that we are aware of, and which are of importance as connecting it with the later maps of the world of the Behaimean and Schonerean type. But, before we proceed to notice these, it may be well to consider, with the help of the accompanying sketch map, the general features of this last of the planispheric maps of the archaic type in which the circumfluent ocean is retained.

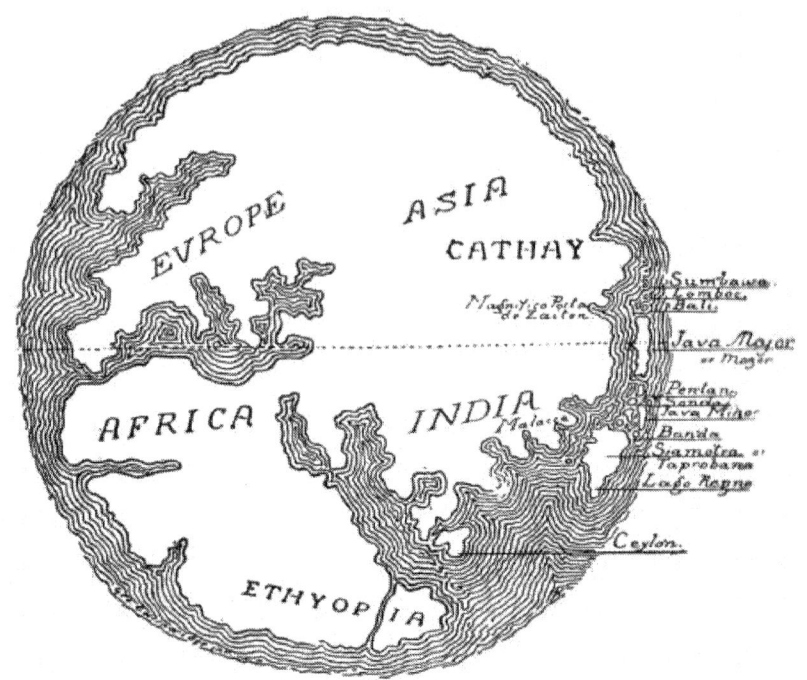

The above skeleton-map is a much reduced outline facsimile of Fra Mauro's celebrated Mappamundi.

Owing to the inability of representing graphically the hemisphere, or, strictly speaking, semi-hemisphere, intended, the longitudinal projection is confounded with the latitudinal. In this state of things it will be noticed that it is necessary to place the west at the top in order to recognise the Australasian regions; for what appears to be the equator with reference to Java and its eastern prolongation of islands is nothing else but the outward limit of the circumfluent ocean. We have here, on the extreme confines of the world, as the cartographer expresses it, Sumatra, Banda, Java, Bali, Lomboc, Sumbawa, etc. In the large original map, placed amongst the various islands there are represented rolls of paper on which the explanatory text shows that the map-maker evidently held views concerning the shape of the earth somewhat similar to those of the early Greek period; for the islands referred to are *propinqua ale tenebre*: near the exterior darkness.

Yet all kinds of spices are said to be produced in these beautiful islands, and notice is also taken of the various bright plumaged birds: *Item li se trova papaga tutti rossi salvo i piedi et el becco che son zali*; wherein we recognise Nicolo de' Conti's description. We must take note of this mention about parrots, because we shall find it revived later on, and the whole Australian Continent termed *Psittacorum regio*: the land of parrots.

We have remarked elsewhere concerning the omission of the islands of the Chinese Sea, such as Borneo, Scelebes, etc. There was clearly no room for them, and who knows but that the Australian Continent, or a part of it, at least, was omitted for the same reason, *per non aver luogo.*

The inexorable laws of *routine* and conservatism had not yet, in the year of grace 1459, sanctioned the breaking of the pagan shackles that prevented the expansion of the old world. It was reserved for Diaz, Columbus and Vasco da Gama to do this.

Taking the nomenclature in the order given in the accompanying sketch, that is, from the true east, westwards, it may be noticed that Sumbawa, Lomboc, Bali and Java are remarkably well charted, and that an open sea, albeit the old river Ocean, is shown to the south of these islands. It will be well to note this fact at this date, 1459, because we shall find this sea blocked, not without reason, at a subsequent date. Sumatra is charted nearly as well as Java and its eastern prolongation of islands, and much better than in many later maps. It is much split up in its southern extension, but this must not surprise us, as the southern parts of Sumatra were believed to be formed of several islands as late as the year 1784--vide map in Marsden's Sumatra. Amongst those islands we notice *Java Minor* and *Pentan* (Bintang), which tallies, in a certain measure, with Marco Polo's description--*Sondai* (written Sandai in Ramusio's account) and *Banda* are also there, corresponding to Nicolo de' Conti's text. The cartographer says: *Sondai insola propinqua a banda*, and describes the nutmegs, spices, parrots, and white cockatoos found there; this also corresponds with Nicolo's description. But Nicolo de' Conti describes the Spice Islands from hearsay, and no doubt confounds some of them with some port of call on the coast of Sumatra where the spices were conveyed to, which may explain how *Banda* came to be placed in propinquity to *Sondai* (Sunda). The larger portion of Sumatra bears the name first given to it by Nicolo de' Conti, *Isola Siamotra* over Taprobana*--and in large type TAPROBANA. Another name for Sumatra is referred to in an inscription in the centre of the island: Questa isola antichissamente era nominata *Si modi* (sic for Sismondi). So that there is no mistaking Sumatra.

(*Footnote. In Ramusio's translation from the Portuguese, this island is named Sumatra; but in the original Latin of Poggio Bracciolini the name is Sciamuthera.)

The most interesting inscription however, and one that gave rise to many strange complications, is set down to the north of some lofty hills on the north coast, where a couple of lakes are portrayed. *Lago* and *Lago regno* is the inscription. We shall refer to this lake district in due course.

We may conclude by drawing attention to the fact--an important one-- that the straits of Malacca are shown. Malacca is also set down in its proper place; but Milapur, Conti's Malepur, is set down on a duplicate Indian peninsula, for we see towards the west *Saylam*, i.e. Ceylon, and the true Indian Peninsula clearly marked.

CHAPTER 10. A.D. 1471 TO 1478.

THE EQUATOR CROSSED. REVIVAL OF ANCIENT IDEAS CONCERNING THE SPHERICITY OF THE EARTH. TOSCANELLI. COLUMBUS.

The example set by Prince Henry the Navigator was followed by his nephew, King Affonso V of Portugal, and the voyages towards the south along the west coast of Africa were continued; nor were these voyages, strictly speaking, made along the coasts only, as expressed in a paper which has recently appeared in the Century Magazine,* where the writer says: "The Portuguese merely felt their way along the coast in all these voyages;...the coast-line served for a leading-string, holding to which they felt themselves safe;...they only dared to leave the land in regions with which they had long been acquainted."

(*Footnote. Columbus, by Professor Dr. S. Ruge, Harper's Monthly Magazine page 682 line 9 October 1893.)

For Major, on the contrary, says: "It will have been noticed that in previous voyages, when islands at a distance from the mainland, as for example Porto Santo and the Cape Verde Islands, had been discovered, it had been through the vessels being driven on them by storms; but in the present case we have islands, one, S. Thome, more than fifty, the other, Annoban, more than eighty leagues distant from the mainland, discovered without the interference of any storm whatever of which we are informed. The reasonable inference seems to be that the navigators used their newly improved nautical instruments to good purpose, *and were able to leave the coast with impunity*, which their predecessors were not in the position to do, for want of being able to take the altitude. In this same year 1471, *for the first time within the memory or even the knowledge of man the equinoctial line was crossed from North to South.* As Cape Lopo

Gonsalvez, now Cape Lopez, was the first locality, south of the equator, to have a geographical name attached to it, it may fairly be inferred that this was the name of the navigator who first crossed the line."*

(*Footnote. R.H. Major, Prince Henry the Navigator pages 199 to 200.)

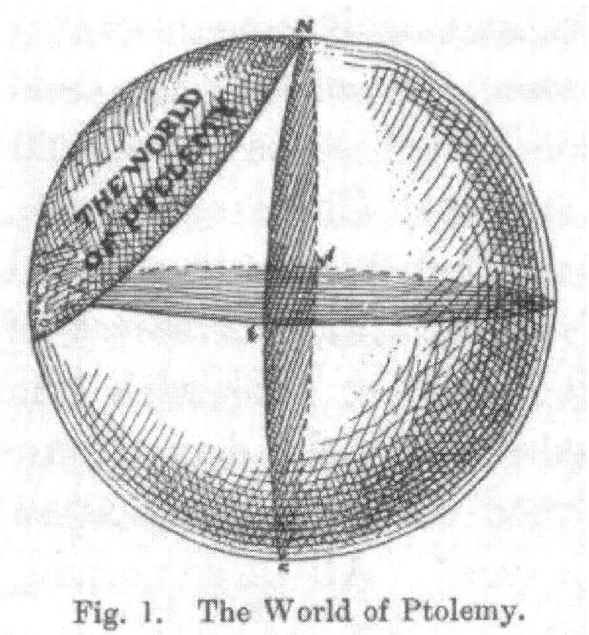

Fig. 1. The World of Ptolemy.

Figure 1. The World of Ptolemy.

The crossing of the line was the first act in the upsetting of the old world theories concerning the inaccessibility of the regions lying beyond the circumfluent ocean, and the equatorial regions also inaccessible on account of the intense heat. Once the equator crossed, the gates of the ocean were opened and all parts of the world brought into communication. No objection could henceforth be raised against the habitableness of the southern hemisphere, and in future maps we shall see the Australasian regions invaded by the hitherto cramped islands and other features that the former cartographer could not set down *per non aver luogo*. The world which had been represented *within a circle* was in reality only a *quarter of the sphere*. See Figure 1.

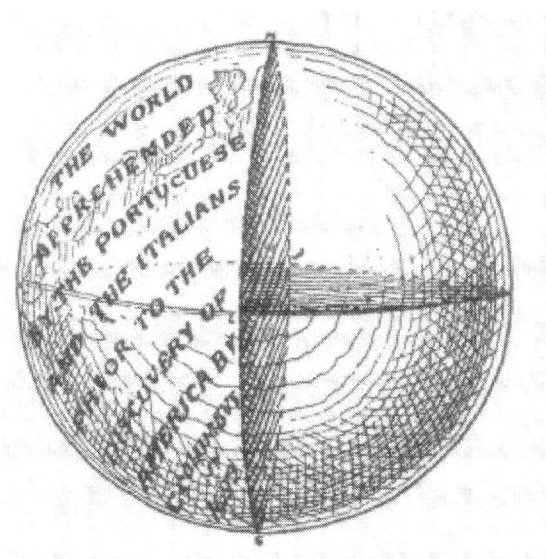

Fig. 2. The world as apprehended by the Portuguese and Italians.

Figure 2. The world as apprehended by the Portuguese and Italians..

After the bursting of the Archaic ocean, half the sphere was apprehended (see Figure 2, the natural result of the widening of the sphere being the enlargement of various configurations of land and water which had been, with or without reason, supposed to have been dwarfed.

The next task for thinking minds of the day, cartographers and others, was, once the sphericity of the earth practically demonstrated, to ascertain what remained to be discovered. Cartographers set to work to construct maps and globes in order to clearly ascertain the proportions of the undiscovered surface of the globe. Since the days of Crates, who is mentioned by Strabo as having constructed a terrestrial globe, that is since 200 years before Christ, little could have been done in the way of constructing earth-globes, for none have been handed down to us from that period to the one we are now dealing with. We shall now find--to use an expressive modern term--a boom in map and globe making. In the construction of these the older documents were used until fresh data could be obtained; but, as the world was now enlarged, geographers naturally thought fit to enlarge the dimensions of the various configurations of land and water, and in this process the less well known regions, that is, those most distant, suffered most.

The amount of progress achieved latitudinally had also been made longitudinally by the Portuguese. In this respect they had also anticipated the discoveries made under the Spanish flag. As Mr Harrisse remarks, speaking of C. Columbus:* "It cannot be denied that notwithstanding his extensive display of Scriptural and scientific authorities, the great Genoese was also influenced by the attempts of the Portuguese; from which, in point of history, his theories and achievements cannot be separated, although they were not precisely of the same character. The bold seafaring men of Portugal sought to reach insular regions supposed to be cast far away into the ocean, whilst Columbus endeavoured to arrive at China and Japan. Still, those islands were so much believed to be on the route that Toscanelli referred to them as landing places, when Affonso V should send an expedition in search of the east coast of Asia. What is more, the map which Columbus took with him when he started from Spain on his first voyage contained oceanic isles depicted by himself. Those were necessarily borrowed from charts then current: '*donde segun parece tenia pintadas el Almirante ciertas islas por aquella mar.*' All those notions therefore were not only co-eval but also closely connected.

(*Footnote. H. Harrisse, The Discovery of North America page 651 2nd paragraph.)

"It is unquestionable that Roger Bacon, Pierre d'Ailly, Toscanelli, Munzmeister, and a host of thinkers, derived their ideas concerning the existence of transatlantic lands from the hypothesis of Aristotle, more or less directly; the mariners of the first half of the fifteenth century however were actuated by different inferences. They firmly believed that the islands which stud the western seas in all maps and globes of that period, so far from being imaginary, existed really, and could be reached. Hence repeated efforts on the part of adventurers, chiefly Lusitanian, or from the Azores, whose habits of thought precluded them from entertaining learned or theoretical opinions on the subject, and who were impelled only by practical ideas.

"We possess abundant proofs that such was actually the case. Where did Prince Henry send Gonzalo Velho Cabral? In search of the islands marked on the map which Dom Pedro had brought from Italy in 1428.

Where did Diogo de Teive direct his ship? To the south-west of Fayal to find the Antilia. What was the island which Affonso V conceded to Fernam Tellez, and which Joao II afterwards granted to Fernam d' Ulmo? The Island of the Seven Cities. What isle did the captain in the employ of the Infant Henry pretend to have discovered? Again, the Antilia. What was the object of the voyage of Thomas Lloyd? To find the island of Brazil. What captainship was given to Joao Vogado? That of the Ovo and Capraria islands, known then chiefly from being marked on charts: 'As quaaes segumdo a carta de marear.' Did not the Bristol people during seven years previous to 1498 equip every year two, three, or four caravels to go in search of the islands of Brazil and of the Seven Cities? None of these fantastic islands are mentioned in the *Opus Majus* or in the *Imago Mundi*; but they figure in almost every mappamundi and atlas of the fifteenth century. Nay, do we not see Martin Alonso Pinzon claiming to have been shown in the Pope's library at Rome, in 1491, a map setting forth the transatlantic lands which, in company with Columbus, he was destined to discover a year afterwards?"

Toscanelli appears to have been the first in the field to put these ideas into shape, by giving the relative distances as considered in connection with the projection of the earth. The wonderful piece of mediaeval cartography known as Fra Mauro's Mappamundi served him as a ground plan to work on; it had no degrees of longitude or latitude; he undertook to indicate by what he called spaces the missing degrees. On the 25th of June 1474 he sent to Portugal a copy of a map he had constructed; this was addressed to Fernam Martins, King Affonso's chaplain, and a letter accompanied it, in which he says*: "I send to His Majesty a map which I have designed with my own hands, and on which I have marked the coasts and islands which may serve to you as a starting point when you undertake that navigation, in steering always westward."

(*Footnote. H. Harrisse, Discovery of North America page 378.)

On this subject, and with reference to Nicolo de' Conti, Professor Ruge says*: "After his return (Nicolo de' Conti's return to Italy from the East) he made a report of his journey to the Pope, and Toscanelli also gained information from him by word of mouth. Toscanelli possessed energy and genius. His experience of life was wide. He lived to be a hundred years old, and he had considerable geographical knowledge. It was natural enough that such a man should conceive the idea of representing in visible form on a globe the distribution of land and water. The coast line of Europe from Scotland southwards, and the western coast of Africa as far as Guinea, had been correctly depicted by the skilled cartographers of Italy and Spain. Now it was necessary, from the information given by Polo in writing and by Conti in conversation, to construct a picture of the position and size of the countries of Asia, a picture which might claim to give a true, or, at all events, a probable, presentation of the facts. A sketch made it quite clear to the Italian cosmographer that the western ocean was very small. The conviction gradually grew stronger, and he came to think that a man in the neighbourhood of Mexico, for example--if I may borrow the geographical language of our own time--would be on the east coast of Japan. He knew how the Portuguese were exerting themselves to find a way to India round Africa. From the Italian agents at Lisbon he constantly heard of new attempts. His sketch map showed him that this route must be decidedly longer, even without taking into account the fact that no one had the least idea how far Africa extended to the south. He wished to put the Portuguese on the right track, and with this object he made an indirect application to the King of Portugal."

(*Footnote. Columbus, by Professor Dr. S. Ruge, Harper's Monthly Magazine page 687 line 4 2nd column.)

Manuscript copies of Marco Polo's travels were no doubt very difficult to obtain; but, when the *Editio Princeps* (Fricz Creuszner zu Nurmberg Nach eristi gepurdt Tausent vierhundert un im siben un sibenczigte iar) (1477) of his travels, published in any language, appeared, geographers and cartographers, especially in Germany, were enabled to make use of his descriptions of countries in the East in the construction of their new maps of the world. It is no doubt from this date that the various types of maps that we have mentioned as belonging to the 3rd type began to make their appearance. The first edition of the Ptolemy Atlas, with the first set of maps ever produced by copper engraving, which appeared the following year, 1478, shows the interest that was taken at the time in connection with geography and cartography.

CHAPTER 11. A.D. 1479 TO 1484.

TOSCANELLI AND COLUMBUS.

The following year, 1479, C. Columbus may have received* from Toscanelli a letter and map in answer to inquiries made by him concerning the *Land of Spice*. This letter and map appear to have been duplicates of those sent in 1474 to Affonso V, King of Portugal. Concerning this map and letter Mr. Harrisse says: "This map was crossed with longitudinal lines indicating the distances from east to west, and with horizontal ones showing the distances from north to south. The intervals between those lines was called a space, and each space measured from east to west 250 Italian miles. *The Italian mile was equal to 1481 meters. The early Spanish navigators considered the nautical league as equal to four miles: 'Volunt leguam Hispani millia passuum quatuor continere mari prasertim; terra vero tria.'* Anghiera Decad. ii., cap. x., page 174.

(*Footnote. The date fixed by Mr. Harrisse is between 1479 and 1484. See Discovery of North America pages 379, 380.)

"From Lisbon to the city of Quinsay there were 26 such spaces, which 26 spaces represented, in the opinion of Toscanelli, about one-third of the surface of the entire globe. *Las Casas* says: 'Tenia en circuito 2,400 millas, que son 600 leguas.' Historia General, lib. i. cap. i. volume i. page 360.

"On that map were marked, adjoining the coast of Portugal, islands which we assume to have been the Azores, and, west of the same, that is, on the opposite shores of the Atlantic Ocean, the province of Mango, near Cathay, and the Empire of the Great Khan, the extremity of which bore the name of Zaitam.

"Nearly in the middle of the Atlantic was the imaginary Antilla Island, 10 spaces distant from the island of Cipango.

"Finally, the map stated 'how much it was necessary to deviate from the pole and from the equinoctial line.'

"This primitive and original chart was in the possession of Las Casas when he wrote his History of the Indies, and apparently until the time of his death, which occurred in 1566. It doubtless belonged originally to the library of Fernando Columbus, and we are of opinion that it was given to Las Casas by the Dominican friars, who were yet in charge of that library as residuary legatees, when he was ordained bishop in their monastery of San Pablo, at Seville, in 1544.

"There is a minute description of the map in Book I., chapter L., of Las Casas' *Historia General de las Indias*, to which we refer the reader.

"But if the map itself is irretrievably lost, we still have the letter which Toscanelli sent to Columbus at the same time. It is to be found among the manuscript annotations added by the Great Genoese to the few books which he possessed, and are now preserved in the Colombina Library, where they have been an object of curiosity for three centuries, without anyone suspecting until May 8 1871 that they contain the original Latin text of Toscanelli's important epistle, theretofore supposed to have been originally written in Italian.*

(*Footnote. It is owing to Mr. H. Harrisse's indefatigable and intelligent researches that the Latin text of Toscanelli's letter has become known to the world. We may therefore be allowed to join the Chief Librarian of the Colombiana Library who thanks him for having caused the fact to be known that the text referred to was the original one. George Collingridge.)

"That letter is so inseparable from the geographical data which led to the discovery of the New World; it has played so great a part in the evolution of American cartography in its incipient stage, and it serves in such a high degree to comprehend the lost map of Toscanelli, that we feel constrained to reproduce it in connection with the present chapter."

The above paragraph applies with equal if not greater force to Australia; for was it not to the *Land of Spice*--that is to the AUSTRALASIAN REGIONS--that C. Columbus directed his course?*

(*Footnote. See also The Early Cartography of Japan, By George Collingridge, in the Proceedings of the Royal Geographical Society, London, May 1894. In that paper the author shows that the famous island of Cipango that Ch. Columbus was in search of was not Japan but Java.)

We shall also therefore reproduce Toscanelli's letter, contenting ourselves with the vernacular which accompanies in Mr. H. Harrisse's work the Latin text of Toscanelli.

We continue the quotation as follows: "As the reader is aware, Columbus wrote a letter to Toscanelli, which is lost. We know however that it was a request for information concerning the *Land of Spice*, which he thought possible to reach direct from Europe by sea. Judging from the Florentine's reply, Columbus desired more particularly to ascertain what route he should take, the distance to sail over, the stations on the way, landfalls, and landing places.

"Toscanelli replied by sending him the above-mentioned map, together with a copy of a letter which he had formerly addressed to Fernam Martins, the chaplain of the King of Portugal, in answer to just such a request.

"The letter written to Martins was dated from Florence, June 25 1474, but Columbus only received communication of it years afterwards. In the note accompanying the package, Toscanelli says that the original letter had been written: Antes de las guerras de Castilla--before the wars in Castille. Consequently the copy was sent after September 24 1479, when the treaty of peace between Spain and Portugal was signed.

"That letter was translated into Spanish probably by Fernando Columbus when engaged writing the life of his father. That translation has been inserted by Las Casas in his *Historia General de las Indias*, but it is far from being literal. Certain geographical descriptions, borrowed apparently from Toscanelli's map, explanations which are regular commentaries, and personal details, of which we do not know the source, have been intercalated. Several passages are also inserted not in their proper place. It follows that the critic can no longer remain satisfied with the Italian version first published in the *Historia* in 1571, and which was the only one known, until the Spanish translation from which it had been taken was printed with Las Casas' work in 1875. Nor is the latter version any more satisfactory, as it contains the same defects.

"The original Latin text of that letter is as follows: Copia misa christofaro, etc. The English translation being: Copy sent to Christopher Colombo by Paul the physician, with a nautical chart.

"To Ferdinand Martins, a canon in Lisbon, Paul the physician, greeting: I have learnt with pleasure that your health is good, and that you are on terms of intimacy with your very generous and very magnificent sovereign. On a previous occasion I have spoken to you of a sea route to the land of spice shorter than the one which you (i.e. the Portuguese) take by the way of Guinea. That is the reason why the Most Serene King (Affonso V, surnamed The African, (cross symbol) 1481) asks of me today information on the subject, or rather an explanation sufficiently clear to enable men, even but little learned, to understand the existence of such a route. Although I know that it is a consequence of the spherical form of the earth, I have decided, nevertheless, so as to be better understood and to facilitate the enterprise, to demonstrate in constructing a nautical chart that the said route is proved to exist. I therefore send to His Majesty a map which has been drawn with my own hands, and on which are marked your coasts and the islands which may be taken as a starting point, when you undertake the voyage, by steering constantly towards the west. (Las Casas here--volume 1 page 93--makes the following interpolation: En la cual esta pintado todo el fin del Poniente, tornando desde Irlanda al Austro hasta el fin de Guinea...con las islas. These details may be added to his description of the map.) You will also find thereon the indication of the countries which you must fall in with; how much you will have to deviate from the pole, and from the equinoctial line; and finally, the space--that is to say, the number of leagues--you have to sail over to reach the country, which is so rich in spice and precious stones of all sorts. Do not be surprised if I call the country of spices a *western* country, whilst it is the custom to call it *eastern*. The reason is that in making the voyage by sea, in the hemisphere which is opposite our own, that country will always be found on the west side. If, on the contrary, the land route is adopted, in crossing the higher hemisphere it will always be found in the east. The longitudinal lines traced on the map show the distance from east to west; the horizontal ones show the distance from south to north. I have also marked, for the use of navigators, several countries where you may touch in case contrary winds or some accident should drive mariners to some other coast than the one intended. I wanted to enable them to show the aborigines that we were not without possessing some knowledge of their country, which must please them. Only merchants, as we are informed, settle in those islands; for there is such a great concourse of navigators with goods that the port of Zaiton alone, which is famous, contains a greater number of them than all the rest of the world together. It is asserted that every year one hundred large vessels, loaded with pepper, arrive in that port; without speaking of the other ships which bring different kinds of spice. That country is very much peopled, and very rich. It is composed of a multitude of provinces, kingdoms, and innumerable cities, all of which are under the sway of a single prince, called The Grand Khan. That title means, in Latin, The King of Kings. His residence is mostly in the province of Cathay. His ancestors being desirous to have intercourse with the Christians, sent, two hundred years ago, an embassy to the Pope to obtain doctors in theology to teach them the Catholic religion; but the envoys were prevented from continuing their route, and returned home. In the time of Eugene,* one of them visited the Pope, and assured him that his countrymen entertained very good feelings towards Christians. I have conversed with him a great deal on all topics. He spoke to me of the large size of the royal palaces; of the prodigious extent of rivers in breadth and length; of the multitude of cities built on their banks (nearly two hundred towns were on the banks of a single river); finally, of marble bridges very wide and very long, adorned with a double row of columns. That country deserves to be sought after by the Latins, not only because enormous wealth can be acquired there, in gold, in silver, in precious stones of all kinds, and in certain sorts of spice which never reach our country, but on account of the scholars, philosophers, and learned astrologers (from India), who may teach us by what means a province so powerful and so magnificent is governed, and their manner of waging war.

(*Footnote. See the relation of N. Conti in Poggii Bracciolini Florent. Historiae de Varietate Fortunae; Paris 1723 4to lib. iv. Also Yule, Cathay and the way thither; London 1866 page cxxxviii.; and Cordier, Bibliotheca Sinica volume i.)

"Let these short details suffice to satisfy, in a measure, the king who asked for information. My occupations, which absorb my entire time, do not allow me to speak more at length. But, later on, I shall be disposed to comply with the desires of His Royal Majesty as extensively as he may wish.

"Given at Florence on the 25th of June 1474.

"From the city of Lisbon, towards the west, in a direct line, there are twenty-six spaces (of 250 miles each) marked on the map as far as the famous and very large city of Quinsay. The circumference of that city is 100 miles. It possesses ten bridges, and its name means The city of the Heavens. They relate marvellous things relative to the multitude of objects (of art ?) found there, and the amount of its revenue. That space is about one-third of the entire globe.* The city is in the province of Mango, near that of Cathay, in which is the royal residence. From the Antilia Island, which you know, to the famous island of Cipango there are ten spaces. That island yields quantities of gold, pearls, and precious stones. The temples and palaces of the king are inlaid with plates of gold. It will not be necessary therefore to cross very extensive spaces over the sea on an unknown route. Perhaps I should have given more minute details on many things, but a careful observer can, of himself, supply much of what may be wanting. Goodbye, dearest."

(*Footnote. Conti here says: Piu oltre de questa provincia di Mangi, se ne troua un' altra che e la miglior di tutte l' altre del mondo nominata il Cataio...et la principal citta, et la piu nobil si chiama Cambalu nella quale e posto il palazzo del Re. Viaggio di Nicolo di Conti, scritto por Messer Poggio; in Ramusio.)

Mr. Harrisse adds: "That important letter must not be considered simply as a familiar communication of which Toscanelli had kept a copy for ten years or more. It was evidently based upon some scientific paper, which embodied notions shared by a certain class of thinkers in quarters where the problems of cosmography were frequently mooted, and whose writings have not all come down to us. We are even justified in supposing that the idea of the existence of transatlantic lands which could be easily reached by steering westward, had been the subject of conversations in the Italian cities. This is shown by the fact that the Duke of Ferrara viewed the discovery accomplished by Columbus as a confirmation of the ideas advanced by Toscanelli, and in 1494 requested his ambassador at Florence to institute researches among the papers of the Florentine astronomer, then in the possession of his nephew Ludovico, and to secure any note or writing on the subject."*

(*Footnote. See H. Harrisse, Discovery of North America pages 2 and 3.)

CHAPTER 12. A.D. 1484 TO 1487.

THE CAPE OF GOOD HOPE REACHED.

In 1481 King Affonso V of Portugal died, and his son and successor Joao II, The Perfect, entered with zeal into the views of his predecessors. R.H. Major tells us*: "Hitherto the Portuguese in making their explorations had contented themselves by setting up crosses by way of taking formal possession of any country; but these crosses soon disappeared, and the object in setting them up was frustrated. They would also carve on trees the motto of Prince Henry, Talent de bien faire, together with the name which they gave to the newly discovered land. In the reign of King Joao however they began to erect stone pillars surmounted by a cross. These pillars, which were designed by the king, were fourteen or fifteen hands high, with the royal arms sculptured in front, and on the sides were inscribed the names of the king and of the discoverer, as well as the date of the discovery, in Latin and Portuguese. These pillars were called Padraos.

(*Footnote. "Prince Henry the Navigator" page 203.)

"In 1484, Diogo Cam, a knight of the king's household, carried out with him one of these stone pillars and, passing Cape St. Catherine, the last point discovered in the reign of King Affonso, reached the mouth of a mighty river, on the south side of which he set up the pillar, and accordingly called the river the Rio do Padrao. The natives called it Zaire. It was afterwards named the Congo, from the country through which it flowed. Diogo Cam ascended the river to a little distance, and fell in with a great number of natives, who were very peacefully inclined, but although he had interpreters of several of the African languages, none of them could make themselves understood. He accordingly determined to take some of the natives back with him to Portugal, that they might learn the Portuguese language and act as interpreters for the future. This was easily managed, and without any violence, by sending Portuguese hostages to the King of Congo, with a promise that in fifteen months the negroes should be restored to their country. He took with him four of the natives, and on the voyage they learned enough Portuguese to enable them to give a fair account of their own country and of those which lay to the south of it. King Joao was greatly gratified, and treated the negroes with much kindness and even munificence, and when Diogo Cam took them back the following year, the king charged them with many presents for their own sovereign, accompanied by the earnest desire that he and his people would embrace the Christian religion. Up to the year 1485 Joao II used the title of King of Portugal and the Algarves on this side the sea and beyond the sea in Africa, but in this year he added thereto that of Lord of Guinea.

View of Table Mountain, Cape of Good Hope.

"In this remarkable voyage Diogo Cam was accompanied by the celebrated Martin Behaim, the inventor of the application of the astrolabe to navigation."

A curious parallel might be drawn, in many ways, between Martin Behaim and Alexander Dalrymple on one side and C. Columbus and Captain Cook on the other, the principal features being that M. Behaim and Alex Dalrymple were both sailors and *savants*, and came, both of them, very near being sent out on the two expeditions which resulted in the rediscovery of New Worlds. C. Columbus and Cook were better sailors than *savants*, but were both pre-eminently practical men, and both of them must be considered as the principal agents in the practical rediscovery of America and Australia respectively.

To return to the voyage of the Portuguese that led to the opening of the sea-way to India and Australasia we must here introduce a personage that greatly exercised the minds of the period. Prester John was the name given to him. He was supposed, in his twofold character of priest and king, to rule over vast tracts of country, and, if we judge from the tales that were told concerning him, and from the localities marked on maps, over which he was said to rule, he would have been a mighty prince indeed; for he is represented as having under his sway all the eastern parts of Africa and the larger part of Asia.

King Joao II, believing that such a monarch might be of the greatest service to him, determined to reach his country both by land and sea. Major tells us*:

(*Footnote. Prince Henry the Navigator page 212 et seq.)

"The first persons whom he sent out with this object were Father Antonio de Lisboa and one Pedro de Montarryo; but when they reached Jerusalem they found that without knowing Arabic it would be useless to continue their voyage, and therefore they returned.

"On the 7th of May 1487 however the king despatched two men who were not wanting in that respect, namely Pedro de Covilham and Affonso de Payva. They went by Naples and Rhodes to Alexandria and Cairo, and so to Aden, where they separated with an agreement to meet at a certain time at Cairo. They left Lisbon for Naples, where their bills of exchange were paid by the son of Cosmo de Medicis; and from Naples they sailed to the island of Rhodes. Then, crossing over to Alexandria, they travelled to Cairo as merchants, and proceeding with the caravan to Tor on the Red Sea, at the foot of Mount Sinai, gained some information relative to the trade with Calicut. Thence they sailed to Aden, where they parted; Covilham directed his course towards India, and Payva towards Suakem in Abyssinia, appointing Cairo as the future place of their rendezvous.

"At Aden Covilham embarked in a Moorish ship for Cananor, on the Malabar coast, and after some stay in that city went to Calicut and Goa, being the first of his countrymen who had sailed on the Indian Ocean.

He then passed over to Sofala, on the eastern coast of Africa, and examined its gold-mines, where he procured some intelligence of the island of St. Lawrence, called by the Moors the Island of the Moon, now known as Madagascar.

"Covilham had now heard of cloves and cinnamon, and seen pepper and ginger; he therefore resolved to venture no further until the valuable information he possessed was conveyed to Portugal. With this idea he returned to Egypt; but found on his arrival at Cairo, where he met with messengers from King Joao, that Payva had died a short time before. The names of these messengers were Rabbi Abraham of Beja, and Joseph of Lamego; the latter immediately returned with letters from Covilham, containing, among other curious facts, the following remarkable report:

"That the ships which sailed down the coast of Guinea might be sure of reaching the termination of the continent, by persisting in a course to the south, and that when they should arrive in the eastern ocean, their best direction must be to inquire for Sofala, and the Island of the Moon..."*

(*Footnote. The Arabs called Madagascar AL-CAMAR, the Island of the Moon; but this name got to be corrupted on charts and maps to such an extent that the island was believed by some to be a fictitious one. The following are some of the corrupted forms of Al-Camar: Camar, Comor, Comr, Comar, Comari, Comair, Camrou, Camroun, Comara, etc. For further particulars on this subject, we refer our readers to J. Codine's Memoire Geographique sur le mer des Indes. Paris, 1868. George Collingridge.)

"From his letter to King Joao it will be seen that to Covilham is to be assigned the honour of the theoretical discovery of the Cape of Good Hope, as that of the practical discovery will presently be shown to belong to Bartholomeu Dias...

"By sea Joao sent, in August 1486, two vessels of fifty tons respectively, under the command of Bartholomeu Dias and Joao Infante. A smaller craft which carried the provisions was commanded by Pedro Dias, Bartholomeu's brother...It was fitting that a Dias should be the first to accomplish the great task which it had been the ruling desire of the life of Prince Henry to see effected. It was a family of daring navigators. Joao Dias had been one of the first who had doubled Cape Bajador, and Lorenzo Dias was the first to reach the Bay of Arguin, while Diniz Dias was the first to reach the land of the Blacks and even Cape Verde, to which he gave its name. The expedition of Bartholomeu started about the end of August, and made directly for the south. Passing the Manga das Areas where Diogo Cam had placed his furthest pillar, they reached a bay to which they gave the name of Angra dos Ilheos. Here Dias erected a pillar, which was broken some eighty years ago. The point is now called Dias Point or Pedestal Point. From seaward is seen what looks like two conical shaped islands, on the highest of which stood the cross. These hillocks stand out dark from the surrounding land, and probably gave rise from their tint to the name of Serra Parda, or the Dark Hills, in which Barros places this monument. Proceeding southward, Dias reached another point, where he was delayed five days in struggling against the weather, and the frequent tacks that he had to make induced him to call it Angra das Voltas, or Cape of the Turns and Tacks. It is called Cape Voltas, and forms the south point of Orange River. From this they were driven before the wind for thirteen days, due south, with half-reefed sails, and of course out of sight of land, when suddenly they were surprised to find a striking change in the temperature, the cold increasing greatly as they advanced. When the wind abated, Dias, not doubting that the coast still ran north and south, as it had done hitherto, steered in an easterly direction with the view of striking it, but, finding that no land made its appearance, he altered his course for the north, and came upon a bay where were a number of cowherds tending their kine, who were greatly alarmed at the sight of the Portuguese and drove their cattle inland. Dias gave the bay the name of Angra dos Vaqueiros, or the Bay of Cowherds. It is the present Flesh Bay, near Gauritz River. He had rounded the Cape without knowing it.

"It is a fact specially worthy of notice that in this voyage an entirely different system was adopted with respect to the natives than had prevailed hitherto. Instead of capturing the negroes that they chanced to find on the coast, they had orders to leave on the shore at intervals negroes and negresses well dressed and well affected towards Portugal, to gather information respecting Prester John, to speak in praise of the Portuguese from experience of kindnesses received, and to infuse a desire to contract alliances with them. In accordance with those instructions, two negroes had been restored at Angra do Salto (the Bay of the Capture), so called from Diogo Cam having captured them at this place. They had left also a negress at Angra dos Ilheos (Angra Pequena), and another at Angra das Voltas. An unfortunate event however occurred which neutralized the effect of this well intended plan. In proceeding eastward from Flesh Bay, Dias reached another bay, to which he gave the name of San Bras, where he put in to take water. In doing this he met with determined opposition from the natives, who threw stones at his men. They were thus compelled to resort to their own weapons in self-defence, and an unfortunate shot from an arblast struck one of the Caffres dead, and thus the favourable impressions which had been looked for from a pacific system of procedure were nullified by an act of violence which they would gladly have avoided. Continuing east, Dias reached a small island in Algoa Bay, on which he set up another pillar with its cross, and the name of Santa Cruz which he gave to the rock still survives; and as they found two springs in it, many called it the Penedo das Fontes. This was the first land beyond the Cape which was trodden by European feet, and here they set on shore another negress.

"The crews now began to complain, for they were worn out with fatigue, and alarmed at the heavy seas through which they were passing. With one voice they protested against proceeding farther. Dias however was most anxious to prosecute the voyage. By way of compromise he proposed that they should sail on in the same direction for two or three days, and if they then found no reason for proceeding farther, he promised they should return. This was acceded to. At the end of that time they reached a river some twenty-five leagues beyond the island of Santa Cruz, and as Joao Infante, the captain of the second ship, the *S. Pantaleon*, was the first to land, they called the river the Rio do Infante. It was the river now known as the Great Fish River.

"Here the remonstrances and complaints of the crews compelled Dias to turn back. When he reached the little island of Santa Cruz, and bade farewell to the cross which he had there erected, it was with grief as intense as if he were leaving his child in the wilderness with no hope of ever seeing him again. The recollection of all the dangers that he and his men had gone through in that long voyage, and the reflection that they were to terminate thus fruitlessly, caused him the keenest sorrow. He was, in fact, unconscious of what he had accomplished. But his eyes were soon to be opened. As he sailed onwards to the west of Santa Cruz he at length came in sight of that remarkable cape which had been hidden from the eyes of man for so many centuries. In remembrance of the perils they had encountered in passing that tempestuous point, he gave to it the name of Cabo Tormentoso, or Stormy Cape, but when he reached Portugal, and made his report to

Joao, the King, foreseeing the realization of the long coveted passage to India, gave it the enduring name of Cape of Good Hope.

"The one grand discovery which had been the object of Prince Henry's unceasing desire was now effected. The joy of the homeward voyage was however marred by a most painful incident. Dias had, by way of precaution, left behind him, off the coast of Guinea, the small vessel containing the supplies of provisions. He now went in search of it, it being nine months since they had parted company. When they reached it, they found three men only surviving out of the nine that had been left, and one of these, named Fernando Colaco, a scrivener from Lumiar, near Lisbon, was so weakened by illness that he died of joy when he saw his companions. The cause of the loss had been that, while the Portuguese were holding friendly communication with the negroes, the latter were seized with a covetous desire to possess some of the articles which were being bartered, and, as a short means of obtaining them, killed the owners. Not to return empty handed, Dias put in at St. George da Mina, and received from the commander, Joao Fogaza, the gold which he had taken in barter. He then proceeded to Lisbon, which he reached in December 1487, after an absence of sixteen months and seventeen days.

"In that voyage he had discovered three hundred and fifty leagues of coast, which was almost as much as Diogo Cam had discovered in his two voyages. This great and memorable discovery was the last that was made in the reign of King Joao II."

CHAPTER 13. A.D. 1487 TO 1489.

BARTHOLOMEW COLUMBUS' LOST MAP OF THE WORLD.

nce the Cape of Good Hope and the southern extremity of Africa rounded, the sea-way to India and Australasia lay open to the adventurous sailor of the day. But now, Portugal and Spain being at war with one another, no further expeditions were sent out by the Portuguese until Vasco da Gama--ten years after the successful voyage of Dias--made his way to Calicut with the first European fleet that ever entered the waters of the Indian Ocean. Prior to this, Columbus had made a proposition to the King of Portugal to reach the Land of Spice by the west. Joao however preferred to carry out the designs inaugurated by Prince Henry. Columbus then went to Spain, where after many weary years of solicitation his projects were at last listened to.

The race to the Spice Islands now fairly began, but, like in the fable of the hare and the tortoise, he who started first won the race. Columbus' expedition nevertheless resulted in something better than the discovery of the Land of Spice. The vast continent extending from the north to the south pole, and now known to us as America, was revealed to the world. That continent, which was to assume such an immense importance, was unknown to Columbus, for he believed to the very last that he had reached India and the Spice Islands.

Let us now examine the maps and charts of the period we have just briefly considered. Fra Mauro's Mappamundi served pre-eminently as a model for all cartographers who were then pointing out the regions to be discovered. Toscanelli used that prototype freely, although he altered its features considerably. Behaim and others copied him more or less. Christopher Columbus made a globe which he sent to Toscanelli together with a letter asking for information. Bartholomew, Christopher Columbus' younger brother, one of the most efficient cartographers of the day, demonstrated to Christopher, according to Antonio Gallo, "that by starting from the south coast of Ethiopia, and steering westward on the right in the open sea, a continent would certainly be reached;" which is as strange as it is true. According to the notions of the time however it was not South America that would have been reached, but a continental land which occupied in the maps of the world, as then delineated, the Australasian regions.

According to Mr. H. Harrisse Bartholomew Columbus made a map of the world in London for Henry VI. This map, which is now lost, contained some indifferent verses, which have been preserved in two different Latin versions: Las Casas' and the *Historie*.

We give here Mr. Harrisse's translation of the *Historie* version*: "Whomsoever you may be, who desires to know the earth and the seas, this picture will give you the detail thereof in full; which has already been related by Strabo, Ptolemy, Pliny, and Isidor (of Seville). Yet their information differs. Here is represented the torrid zone recently navigated by the Spanish (*sic*)* vessels, until then unknown, and now well known.

(*Footnote. Mr. Harrisse's note: "This is evidently an allusion to the discovery of the Cape of Good Hope which Bartholomew Diaz had recently accomplished (August 1486 to December 1487) after crossing the torrid zone, then supposed to extend throughout the ocean (Santarem, Hist. de la Cosmographie au moyen age, volume iii. page 212). But Diaz sailed under the Portuguese flag, and the Spaniards had nothing whatever to do with this or any other similar expedition during the fifteenth century.)

(*Footnote. Discovery of North America, page 387.)

"As to the author or painter, Genoa is his native country, his name is Bartholomew Columbus, of Terra Rubra; he has executed this work at London, in the year of our Lord 1480, and, besides, the year 8, and the tenth day, with the 3rd of the month of February."

Mr. Harrisse here remarks: "That is, for those who are compelled to distort words in order to construct poor verse: "On the 13th day of the month of February 1488." And again:..."the wording of the *Historie* differs somewhat from that of Las Casas, which should not be the case if both had copied the original document, but Las Casas assigns the date of February 10th: decimaque die mensis Februarii, instead of

February 13th, decimaque die cum tertia mensis Februarii. Nor are we certain that their 1488 is not 1489, new style.

"Neither Las Casas nor the *Historie* give any description of the map, and the above is all that we know concerning it. What is said on the subject, or relative to the presence of Bartholomew Columbus in London, by Hakluyt, Bacon, Purchas, and Herrara, was entirely borrowed from the *Historie*."

Now, there is a map--and we don't know why Mr. Harrisse does not mention it--that answers sufficiently to the above description to make it, at least, interesting. But, for Australians, the map we refer to has an intrinsic value and interest as being *the earliest specimen on which the possible outline of the western coasts of our continent are delineated.*

CHAPTER 14. A.D. 1487 TO 1489.

BRITISH MUSEUM MAPPAMUNDI. A POSSIBLE COPY FROM BARTHOLOMEW COLUMBUS' MAP OF THE WORLD.

The map referred to at the close of the preceding chapter is to be found in the British Museum. It bears no date that we are aware of. A copy of this map is given in Santarem's collection, and the date 1489 is assigned to it. We think that date is about correct, for the map shows information up to 1487; yet is much more primitive than M. Behaim's globe of 1492. The name of the cartographer who designed it does not transpire; but there are in it several features that point to its being a copy of Bartholomew Columbus' lost map. The date assigned to it being one of these features, this date is corroborated, to a certain extent, by an inscription in a scroll near the Cape of Good Hope, which inscription reads thus: *Huc usque ad ilha de fonti pe vnit ultima navigatio portugalensium anno domini 1489*. The date in that inscription is no doubt a bad reading for 1487; for it was, as we have seen, in the year 1487 that Bartholomew Dias doubled the Cape of Good Hope and reached the Rio do Infante, whence he turned back and arrived at Lisbon in December 1487.

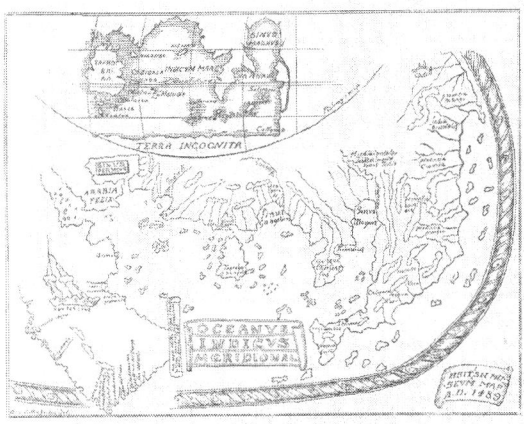

British Museum Mappamundi.

This mappamundi bears the appearance of being connected with the earliest class of maps belonging to the new departure in map-making. The departure was made from Fra Mauro's map of the world, in which, as we have seen, the ancient ocean surrounded the world at the equator in its southerly limits; and legends spread here and there on the confines of that world indicated that in the mind of the cartographer transilience was out of the question. The Portuguese by their navigations towards the south had broken that spell. This fact would seem to be graphically represented in this map, where the southern extremity of the African continent bursts through the marginal *postes*--a compromise for the circumfluent ocean of mediaeval and older maps. The fear of openly discarding the traditions of the past is also amusingly apparent in this early attempt at geographical reform.

This will be at once noticeable if one compares this map with Ptolemy's. Ptolemy connected the southern extremity of Africa with a fictitious prolongation of the coast of China. In this map the fictitious coastline is left out. The cartographer was sufficiently well informed to know that it did not exist, but he appears to have made a kind of concession by filling the gap with those two scrolls of paper, the upper line of the larger scroll actually running over and parallel with Ptolemy's fictitious coastline.

The whole of the coastline of the Indian Ocean above that large scroll on which OCEANUS INDICUS MERIDIONAL is inscribed belongs to Ptolemy's geography. Marco Polo is responsible for the extreme eastern sea-board dotted with islands which in this map bear no names; but the short line of coast running almost parallel to the right hand side of the large paper scroll does not belong to his description.

Unfortunately we cannot treat this map with the importance that it might have acquired had it been a more faithful representation of its prototype. It has no degrees of longitude or latitude, although we have seen that in 1474 Toscanelli had made use of these divisions.

Nevertheless, taking into consideration its general features, we notice that the portion of coastline referred to above is situated to the south of the *Aureus Chersonesus* (the Malay Peninsula) and in the latitude of the southern parts of Africa. This coastline therefore cannot be any other but the west coast of Australia.

Here we might ask the question: Who informed this Portuguese, Spanish, or Italian map-maker that this portion of coast did not run out towards the west as far as the east coast of Africa, as in Ptolemy's map?

The only navigators in these seas who constructed maps and charts and who could therefore have charted these coasts with anything like their approximate correctness, were the Chinese and the Arabs. Of these two nations the Arabs may be considered the more likely draughtsmen, for they had long before the period we are dealing with set down on their maps Madagascar and other islands lying eastward of Madagascar in the latitudes and neighbourhood of the Australian continent.

On the fictitious peninsula, the westernmost extremity of which is bounded from north to south by the western coast of Australia, are set down the following place-names: *S. Thome, regnum lac and regnum Cayln.*

Those names are of importance because they form the clue that will lead us to understand how the distortion of these parts was set about. We shall refer to them by and by.

We must first endeavour to follow the evolution that always obtains in cartographical representations, and with that object in view we must compare this map with its predesigned prototype, the Fra Mauro Mappamundi.

When constructing the Fra Mauro Mappamundi, the cartographer, not being constrained by Ptolemy's equatorial line, brought the Indian Peninsula down in something more like its actual position with regard to Ceylon; but nevertheless, instead of correcting or obliterating Ptolemy's duplicate Indian Peninsula which figures to the east of Ceylon, he made it more prominent and endorsed the mistake by setting down on its western and eastern shores respectively the double nomenclature originating from Nicolo de' Conti's descriptions: *Questa region dita Mahabar, and Milapur, Pudipeten, etc.*

The author of the new prototype, the various copies of which we shall now have to consider, may have been Toscanelli, B. Columbus or M. Behaim; but whosoever he be, he formed his new prototype with the aid of the map of Ptolemy, Fra Mauro's, and other data, in this way:

1. He used Ptolemy's configuration of coasts from *Catigara*, away north to the Sinus Magnus, thence in a westerly direction to the *Sinus Persicus*, then in a southerly direction to the extreme limits of Ptolemy's south, i.e. 16 degrees south of the equator, where the coastline is cut off by the smaller paper scroll relating to the Portuguese discoveries in 1487.

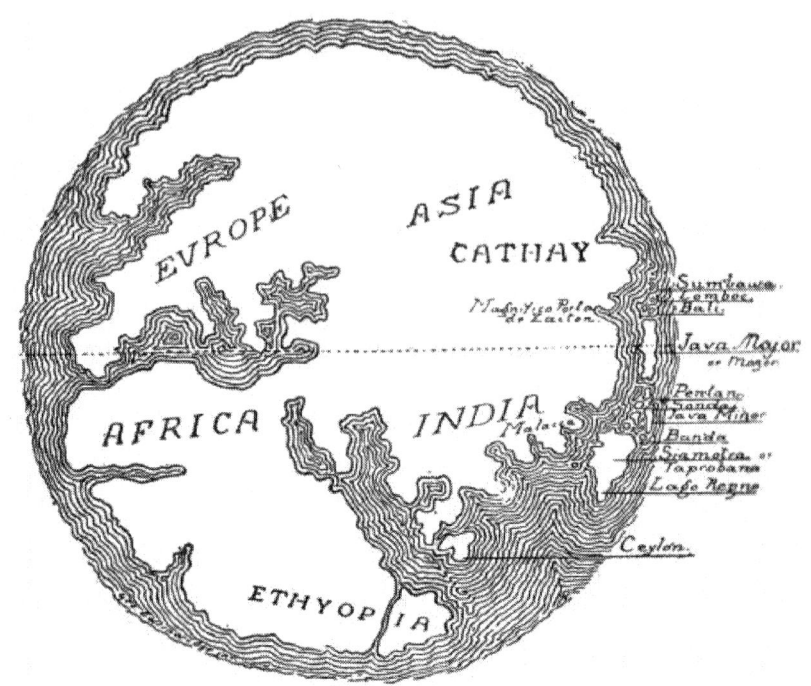

The above skeleton-map is a much reduced outline facsimile of Fra Mauro's celebrated Mappamundi.

2. He borrowed from Fra Mauro's map by using his Siamotra (Sumatra) in the following extraordinary manner: he connected it with Ptolemy's fictitious coastline at *Catigara*.

On the northern coast of Fra Mauro's Sumatra there is a region called *lago regno*, where a couple of lakes are set down; this region, in the map we are now dealing with, is called *regnum lac*, and a lake separates it from *regnum Cayln*.

What does *regnum Cayln* mean? Two hypotheses present themselves. It may be meant for *Ceylon*, or it may be meant for *Coilum*, the modern *Quilon* on the coast of Travancore, Indian Peninsula.

Whatever it was meant for however it became subsequently in most maps of the Behaimean and Schonerean types, *a bogus Sumatra*, as the *regnum lac* above it became the extremity of a bogus Malay Peninsula, that, from that time till the present day, puzzled many cartographers.

Even in the present map we may notice the initiation of the evolution, for it will be noticed that *regnum Cayln* is actually separated from *regnum lac* by the two rivers that flow from the lake situated between these two regions--*regnum Cayln* is therefore an island, strictly speaking. We shall find this particularity emphasized in subsequent maps in which these rivers become arms of the sea, or straits. *Regnum Cayln* also suffers some modification in nomenclature; it becomes *Caylur* and *Seylan insulae* in Martin Behaim's globe 1492--*Provincia Seilan* in the Lenox Globe 1506 to 1511--*Seilan Insulae pars*, in Ruysch's Mappamundi 1508--*Coilu regnu* and *Seyla*, in the Schonerean Frankfort gores of 1515, etc.

The little town of *S. Thome** set down on the western shores of the bogus Malay Peninsula confirmed subsequent geographers and cartographers in the belief that this was indeed the real Malay Peninsula; and the representation of its eastern shores bearing Marco Polo's nomenclature gave strength to their belief.

(*Footnote. In Yule's Cathay, volume ii. page 374 note 4 we find the following reference to San Thome: "Mirapolis is a Grecized form of Mailapur, Meliapur, or, as the Catalan map has it, Mirapor, the place since called San Thome, near the modern Madras. *Mailapuram* means or may mean Peacock Town. A suburb still retains the name of Mailapur. It is near the shore, about three miles and a half south of Fort St. George, at the mouth of the Sydrapetta River.")

The evolution of Fra Mauro's *lago regno* with its lakes and surrounding hills of a more or less lofty and inaccessible character is equally interesting, and extends subsequently to the continental regions surrounding the south pole. The representation of this region on various maps, now lost no doubt, led to a curious description which has not, to our knowledge, been attributed, as it ought, to these cartographical representations. This is the description*: "Thirty leagues from Java the Less is Gatigara, nineteen degrees the other side of the equinoctial towards the south. Of the lands beyond this point nothing is known, for navigation has not been extended further, and it is impossible to proceed by land on account of the *numerous lakes and lofty mountains in those parts*. It is even said that there is the site of the Terrestrial Paradise."

(*Footnote. R.H. Major, Early Voyages to Australia, pages lxiv and lxv. Extract from a work entitled El libro de las costumbres de todas las gentes del mundo y de las Indias, translated and compiled by the Bachelor Francisco Themara. Antwerp 1556.)

We cannot agree with R.H. Major, who before giving the above quotation says: "A notion may be found of the knowledge possessed by the Spaniards in the middle of the sixteenth century, on the part of the world (Australia) on which we treat, from the following extract"...and "Although this was not originally written in Spanish, but was translated from Johannes Bohemus, it would scarce have been given forth to the Spaniards had better information on such a subject existed among that people." We cannot agree with R.H. Major, for we might as well quote any of the hundred and one ignorant remarks made daily at our antipodes concerning Australia, as a notion to be formed of the knowledge possessed by Europeans concerning things Australian. The title of the work marks its level.

Which suggested to the Revd. F.T. Woods the following judicious and witty remarks*: "I am sure no one even suspected the information which I now give from Francisco Themara's *El Libro de las Costumbres de todas las Gentes del Mundo y de las Indias*--a book on the Customs of all Nations of the World and of the Indies. It was published at Antwerp in 1556. The title is quaint, nay, even droll. All the nations of the world, the Indies besides, reminds one of the book about everything, and a few other things, with a catalogue of subjects not otherwise mentioned.

(*Footnote. The Australian Monthly Magazine volume 3 1866, Australian Bibliography page 278 line 2.)

But about Australia. Themara did not profess to speak of Australian manners and customs, though they might as easily have been described with the brevity of the Yankee, who said, "manners, none; customs, nasty." He only spoke of a land of whose inhabitants he knew nothing, for he says: *Thirty leagues from Java the Less is GATIGARA, nineteen degrees on the other side of the equinoctial, towards the south. Of the lands beyond this point nothing is known, for navigation has not been extended further, and it is impossible to proceed by land, in consequence of the large lakes and lofty mountains in those parts. It is even said that there is the site of the Terrestrial Paradise.*

"I think we are in a position to give a most complete denial to the last supposition. I dare say even a good many people smile at the first, but it is worth a moment's thought. A land, nineteen degrees from the equator, where people could not travel because of the mountains and lakes. Was this prophecy? Were not the early colonists stopped by the Blue Mountains, and when they got over them, were not the early explorers stopped by the lakes. At any rate, here is material for a theory."

When Fra Mauro set down those lakes and mountains on the north coast of Sumatra he little thought that they would give rise to such complications.

CHAPTER 15. A.D. 1492.
MARTIN BEHAIM'S GLOBE.

We have now arrived at the important period of reliable geographical data as embodied in the oldest known globe extant, that of Martin Behaim of Nuremberg, the celebrated cosmographer of the close of the fifteenth century.

We cannot do better than reproduce here what Mr. H. Harrisse says concerning Behaim's globe in his admirable work on The Discovery of North America, from which we have freely quoted, because it is the most reliable work of its kind we have yet come across. After which we shall examine the Australasian regions on this old globe and show how its nomenclature in those parts was handed down, modified, yet was still traceable on the maps of New Holland at a time when Flinders, P.P. King and others surveyed the western shores of our continent.

Mr. H. Harrisse says*: "Its diameter measures 530mm. The globe is pasted over with vellum, and the configurations exhibit flags, figures of kings, and inscriptions in gold and colours. It is mounted on an iron stand, with brass meridian and horizon, on the edge of which is inscribed the date *Anno Domini 1510 die 5 Novembris*, which refers to these two metallic additions.

(*Footnote. The Discovery of North America page 391.)

"There are numerous legends, in old German language, which have been reproduced by De Murr, at a time when they were yet perfectly legible; although the vellum had already turned nearly black. Parts of these are omitted or imperfectly rendered in Ghillany's facsimile of the western hemisphere.

"The globe was repaired in 1825, and it is after having been thus put in order that Jomard obtained in 1847 from Baron Frederic Carl von Behaim senior familiae, that it should be temporarily removed from that gentleman's mansion to the School of Arts of Nuremberg, to be facsimiled entirely at the expense of the French Government, for the Geographical Department of the Paris National Library. That facsimile is now on exhibition in the latter place, but very difficult to decipher, on account of the fading away of the colouring. As to the original globe, it is still preserved in the archives of the Behaim family, in Nuremberg, Egydienplatz, Number 15.

"The following legend, which is inscribed in German on the globe, gives the history of that important geographical monument:

'At the request of the wise and venerable magistrates of the noble imperial city of Nuremberg, who govern it at present, namely, Gabriel Nutzel, P. Volkhamer, and Nicholas Groland, this globe was devised and executed according to the discoveries and indications of the Knight Martin Behaim, who is well versed in the art of cosmography, and has navigated around one-third of the earth. The whole was borrowed with great care from the works of Ptolemy, Pliny, Strabo, and Marco Polo, and brought together, both lands and seas, according to their configuration and position, in conformity with the order given by the aforesaid magistrates to George Holzschuer, who participated in the making of this globe, in 1492. It was left by the said gentleman, Martin Behaim, to the city of Nuremberg, as a recollection and homage on his part, before returning to meet his wife (Johanna de Macedo, daughter of Job de Huerter, whom he married in 1486) who lives in an island (at Fayal) seven hundred leagues from this place, and where he has his home, and intends to end his days.'

"Our interpretation of the above quotation is that Martin Behaim furnished the geographical data and legends, but that the globe was constructed, painted, and inscribed by a gentleman* of the name of George Holzschuer.

(*Footnote. Author's note: The *Holzschuers* were Nuremberg patricians; one of that family, Wolf, lived in Portugal and, having rendered services to King Manoel, received from that monarch, February 2 1503, an additional escutcheon. The arms of the Holzschuer family are also painted on Behaim's globe.)

"For a complete geographical description of the globe, we refer the reader to the following works:

"De Murr, *Diplomatische Geschichte des Portug, beruhmten Ritters Martin Behaims, Nurnberg*, 1779, 8vo.; and in French by Jansen, Paris and Strasburg, 1802, 8vo.

Humboldt, *Examen Critique de l'Histoire de la Geographie du Nouveau Continent* et des progres de l'astronomie nautique dans les XVe et XVIe siecles, volume 1 pages 257 to 274.

"Breusing, *Zur Geschichte der Geographie, Regiomontanus, Martin Behaim und der Jacobstab, Zeitsch, der Gesellsch. F. Erdk, zu Berlin* 1869 8vo.

"Ghillany, *Geschichte des Seefahrers* Ritter Martin Behaim; Nurenberg 1853 4to.

"Lelewel, *Epilogue de la Geographie du Moyen Age, Bruxelles* 1857 pages 184 a 191; and

"Kohl, *Documentary History of the State of Maine*, pages 147 to 150.

"There is a good (but not a facsimile) reduced copy of the configurations and legends in Doppelmayr, *Historische Nachricht von den Nurnbergischen Mathematicis und Kunstlern*; Nurnberg 1730 fol.

"Johan Muller, the artist who reproduced the globe for the French Government in 1847, also made a lithographed facsimile for Ghillany in 1853. In Jomard's *Monuments de la Geographie* it is incomplete and otherwise imperfect.

"Our chief reason for inserting Behaim's globe in our list, is that it exhibits the geographical notions which would have guided him if Joao II had listened to the Emperor Maximilian's advice to go in search of Cathay by a maritime route westward, and to Dr. Jerome Munzmeister's suggestion to secure the services of Martin Behaim for that bold and great undertaking.

"This fact, which is not generally known, is proved by the following extremely curious letter, namely:

'*A letter which Hieronymus Monetarius (MUNZER or MUNZMEISTER), a German doctor from the city of Nuremberg in Germany, sent to the Most Serene King Dom Joao II of Portugal, concerning the discovery in the Oceanic Sea and province of the Great Khan of Cathay. Translated from Latin in (the Portuguese) language by Master Alvaro da Torre, a Master of Theology, of the order of Dominicans, Preacher to our lord the said King.*

'To the Most Serene and Invincible King of Portugal, of the Algarves and of Mauritania, (who is) the first discoverer of the Fortunate Islands, Canaries, Madeira, and Azores, Hieronymus Monetarius, a learned German, most humbly recommends himself.

'As you have laudably imitated the Most Serene Infant Dom Henry, your uncle,* in sparing neither efforts nor expense to demonstrate the sphericity of the earth, and succeeded in bringing under your sway the people of the coast of Ethiopia and of the sea of Guinea as far as the tropic of Capricorn, with the products thereof, namely, gold, grains of Paradise,* you have won praises, immortality, and glory, together with very great profits.

(*Footnote. Great uncle. George Collingridge.)

(*Footnote. Amomum Melegueta, also called Guinea Grains and Malaguetta pepper.)

'It cannot be doubted that within a short time the Ethiopians, who are animals almost, but with the appearance of men, and entirely ignorant of Divine worship, will, through your efforts, lose their bestiality, and embrace the Catholic religion.

'Maximilian, the Most Invincible King of the Romans, noticing all those things, has requested your Majesty to search for the very rich coast of Cathay, because Aristotle states at the end of Book ii., *De Caelo et Mundo*, and also Seneca, Book v. of *Naturalium Quaestionum*, and Cardinal Peter de Alyaco,* a great savant in his day, and many illustrious persons think that the inhabitable extreme East is very near the West, as is shown by the numerous elephants found in both, and by the bamboo stalks which are driven by storms to the shores of the Azore islands.

(*Footnote. Pierre D'Ailly, the "Eagle of the doctors of France," who died in 1420.)

'Numberless arguments, so to speak, prove that after sailing but a few days the east coast of Cathay could be reached. No notice must be taken of Alfragano and other inexperienced individuals who affirm that only one-fourth of the earth is above the sea, and that the other three-fourths are under water; as in such matters we should believe experience and trustworthy accounts rather than fantastical suppositions.

'You know, doubtless, that several astronomers of great repute have denied the possibility of living under the tropics and in the equinoctial regions, yet you have effectually proved* that those were erroneous and groundless affirmations. No attention should be paid to (the statement) that the greatest part of the earth is submerged, because, on the contrary, it is the sea which is smaller than the earth. Moreover, there is the fact that the earth is round.

(*Footnote. By the discoveries accomplished in Africa.)

'You possess ample wealth and very able mariners who are eager to acquire immortality and fame. How glorious it would be for you to disclose the East to your West! How trade (with those new regions) would prove profitable! You should also bear in mind that the eastern islands will become your tributaries, and that the majority of kings, carried away by their admiration, will readily place themselves under your protection.

'Already the Germans, Italians, and Rhutenians, and Apollonians of Scythia, who dwell under the dry star of the Arctic Pole, all sing your praises, together with those of the Grand Duke of Moscovia,* who, only a few years since, has found under that star the great island of Greenland, three hundred leagues long, which, with a numerous population, is (now) under the sway of the said Duke.

(*Iwan III, who died in 1505, celebrated for his great territorial accessions as far as Siberia and Laponia, but who never discovered or conquered Greenland.)

'If you succeed in that undertaking, you will be praised as a god or as another Hercules. At your bidding you may secure, to accompany the expedition, the envoy of our King Maximilian (namely:) His Lordship Martin of Bohemia, who is so well fitted for carrying out the undertaking, and also several other expert mariners, who will cross the broad sea, starting from the Azores, and who by their skill and by means of the quadrant, cylinder, astrolabe, and other instruments, and fearing neither the cold nor the heat, will sail to the East, with a favourable wind and smooth sea.

'All those arguments should convince your Majesty. But why spur on the running courser? And this so much the less as you are yourself able to fathom all things! To expatiate on the subject is to impede the runner in his course. Let the Almighty preserve you in this design; and when the crossing shall have been effected, may your knights (sic) confer on you immortality. Farewell. From Nuremberg, a city of upper-Germany; July 14 A.D. 1493."

"Maximilian I was the son of Leonora of Portugal, and therefore the cousin of Joao II. He was Emperor of the Romans from February 16th 1486 until August 17 following, when he became Emperor of Germany. He waged war in person against France from 1492 until May 23 1493. It is consequently prior to the spring of 1492, or between the end of May and the second week in July 1493, that Maximilian wrote on the subject to Joao II.

"On the other hand, Martin Behaim was at Nuremberg from 1491 until 1493, and as it was an imperial residence, whilst his birth and position allowed him to frequent the Court, we may infer that he met Maximilian in that city; and, after suggesting a transatlantic voyage of discovery, requested the Emperor to write to his cousin the King of Portugal on the subject, apparently in 1491 or 1492. This seems to imply unsuccessful efforts in that respect on the part of Behaim when he was at Lisbon, previous to 1491.

"Another curious coincidence is the fact that the arguments used by Munzmeister to convince Joao II are precisely those which were advanced by Toscanelli, and adduced by Columbus to convince Ferdinand and Isabella, namely:

"1. 'Aristotle states at the end of Book ii., *De Caelo et Mundo*...that the east is very near the west,' alleged Munzmeister.

"Columbus said: 'It is possible to sail from the western coast of Africa and Spain westward to the easternmost part of India, because there is no wide sea between the two; as Aristotle states at the end of Book ii. of The Heaven and Earth.'

"2. 'It is not true that the greatest part of the earth is submerged. On the contrary it is the sea which is smaller than the earth,' pretended Munzmeister.

"Columbus said: 'Six parts of the world are dry land; only the seventh is submerged.'

"3. 'After sailing but a few days the coast of Cathay can be reached,' affirmed Munzmeister.

"Columbus said: 'If the intervening space is sea, then it will be easy to cross it in a few days.'

"4. 'There is also the fact that the earth is round,' remarked Munzmeister.

"Columbus said: 'As all the seas and lands of the world form a sphere, and the earth consequently is round, it is possible to go from east to west.'

"5. 'Bamboo stalks are driven by storms to the shores of the Azore Islands,' wrote Munzmeister.

"Columbus, referring to a statement of his brother-in-law, said: 'Pedro Correa told him (i.e. Columbus) that in the island of Porto Santo he had seen another piece of wood driven by the same (west) wind, and in the same manner thick canes.'

"Finally, both the Nuremberg doctor and Columbus quote in support of their assertions the same authorities, namely, Aristotle, Seneca, and the then celebrated Cardinal Pierre D'Ailly.

"As to the writer of that curious letter, his name was Jerome Munzer or Munzmeister, in Latin Hieronymus Monetarius, a Nuremberg savant, who is evidently the Doctor Ieronimus mentioned by Martin Behaim* in the postscript of his letter of March 11 1494, and consequently one of his personal friends. He is called Philosophus et medecinae doctor, and is the author of a work on the discoveries of the Portuguese in Africa. He also wrote an account of his travels during the years 1494 to 1495 in Germany, France, Spain, and Portugal. The first of those works has been published by Kunstmann, who gave only an analysis of the second, and an excellent introduction."

(*Footnote. In Ghillany, Geschichte des seefahrers Ritter Martin Behaim, Urkunde xi. page 107.)

CHAPTER 16. A.D. 1492.
THE AUSTRALASIAN REGIONS ON MARTIN BEHAIM'S GLOBE.

Martin Behaim's globe is the first document that introduces to us the *revived* use of the early earth divisions of the ancients now so well-known by their names of longitude and latitude. We have seen that Toscanelli, the Florentine doctor, made use of these divisions on a map which he sent to C. Columbus, describing them to him, in a letter, in the following terms: "The longitudinal lines traced on the map show the distance from east to west; the horizontal ones show the distance from south to north." (See Toscanelli's letter above).

When--owing to the construction of terrestrial globes--the relative proportions of land and water began to be seriously discussed, we can well imagine the various theories and arguments that arose amongst the learned men of the day. One line of argument was that *one-fourth only of the earth was above the sea*, whereas Toscanelli, Columbus and others argued that it was the other way about, and that *the sea was smaller than the earth*. They contended that from Lisbon to Quinsay in Cathay (China) *one-third* only of the entire globe remained to be explored. These opposite views are easily accounted for, if we take into consideration their various sources.

The Arabs, who had from the beginning of the eighth century traded with China, knew more about those parts than those who followed a theoretical line of argument based on Ptolemy's views and configurations. The Arabs maintained that the earth presented more water than land surface. Toscanelli, Munzmeister, Columbus and others maintained the reverse, and in support of their arguments pointed to the distorted maps on which the bogus and duplicate Malay Peninsula invaded the southern hemisphere in the latitude and longitude of Australia; whereas the eastern shores of this duplicate peninsula and the shores of China--the Mangi and Cathay of Marco

Polo fame--swelled out to such a phenomenal size as to reach the longitude of the Sandwich Islands, to the east of which the islands of Cipango and Antilia (of marvellous wealth) acted as stepping-stones to invite the timorous navigator to launch out in search of those wonderful regions.

There is a particularity about Toscanelli's description which has not been generally noticed, and which is of some value as showing that Behaim's globe was no doubt copied from Toscanelli's map. Toscanelli's map is lost, but we have his letter in which he says: "From the city of Lisbon, towards the west, in a direct line, there are twenty-six spaces (of 250 miles each) marked on the map as far as the famous and very large city of Quinsay...That space is about one-third of the entire globe...From the Antilia island...to the famous island of Cipango there are ten spaces." (See remarks on Toscanelli's letter, Chapter 11.)

Now these distances only give us a vague notion of Toscanelli's measurements. We have the whole distance between Lisbon and China, 26 spaces; and the distance between Antilia and Cipango, 10 spaces; but, where were those two islands situated with reference to Lisbon, or, with reference to China? Toscanelli's letter gives no clue. If however we refer to Behaim's globe we shall find Cipango and Antilia on one side, and Quinsay and Lisbon on the other, placed respectively at distances corresponding to Toscanelli's description, showing that Behaim's globe was either a copy or had been compiled from Toscanelli's data.

By the above we have established the continuity of the geographical evolution and brought back the origin of those features of this globe to the year 1474--the date of Toscanelli's map. We may presume furthermore that the Florentine doctor compiled his map from Fra Mauro's, for there was no better model to go by that we are aware of. In doing so he introduced the features that formed the prototype of the class of maps we shall have now to deal with.

At that time there must have existed a portolano or sea-chart on which the western coasts of Australia were set down from the vicinity of Dampier's Archipelago to Cape Leeuwin, for we find in Behaim's globe the features of this coastline, roughly charted it is true, but nevertheless unmistakably intended for the said coasts; and the longitudes and latitudes correspond approximately. When dealing with Ruysch's mappamundi of Arabian origin (1507/8) we shall find these coasts set down at the tropic of Capricorn, in the exact longitude of the western coast of Australia as shown in Illustration 84; and Cape Leeuwin is not far out from its proper position, being placed in 39 degrees of south latitude instead of 35 degrees.

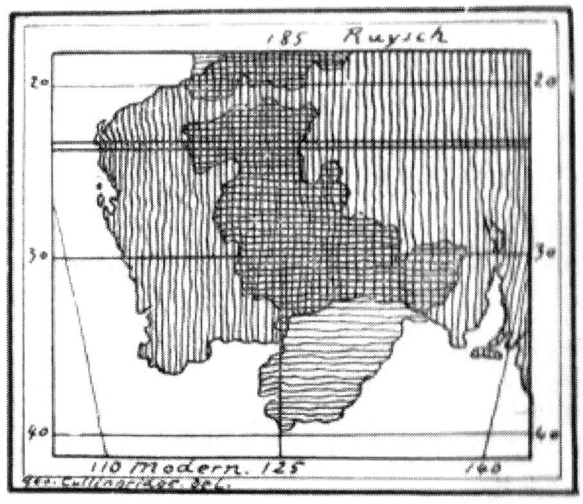

Portion of the west coast of the bogus Sumatra in Ruysch's Mappamundi compared with modern west coast of Australia. Australia is lined perpendicularly--Ruysch's map is lined horizontally.

Before proceeding any further in the description of this map and of others belonging to the same class, we must here state, with reference to measurements of longitude, that we have not fixed our point of departure at our antipodes. Our reason for not doing so will be obvious when the fact is considered that in the maps we are dealing with all measurements were made from west to east only. The further the cartographers of the period proceeded eastward with their measurements the more they exaggerated the proportions of the less known land configurations, lying in that direction, in order to fill up the vacant space on the globe. It was only after the return in 1522 of the *Vittoria* with the remnant of the first circumnavigators that the real size of the vast Pacific Ocean was realised and that the regions of Asia and Australasia shrank back to more correct dimensions.

The only correct way therefore of considering the relative proportions of the Australasian regions was to make them the centre, as we have done, of the eastern and western configurations.

With this object in view we have placed our zero, so to speak, at the extreme limit of Ptolemy's world, the point of departure for the representation of Marco Polo's descriptions. This central point between Ptolemy's and Marco Polo's geography was situated at 180 degrees from the *Insulae Fortunatae* (Canary Islands) of the ancients. It corresponds with our modern 120 degrees east of Greenwich. The modern degrees of longitude will be found at the bottom of each map, and the original degrees (when expressed) at the top. Having thus given our reasons for adopting this point of departure for comparing the relative proportions of these old maps and globes, we may add that, in order to facilitate their comprehension, we have drawn them to a uniform scale and translated them to the same projection. This, it will be understood, was necessary for comparative purposes.

We may now ask, How did it come to pass that indications of our western coasts came to be confounded with the western shores of Sumatra?

Our explanation is this: When Toscanelli, or the author of the first map of the type we are considering, compiled his map of the world from Fra Mauro's, he was no longer compelled to restrict its limits to the northern hemisphere.

On the contrary, once the regions south of the equator were revealed by the Portuguese navigations to the Cape of Good Hope, he must have been impressed with the belief that Fra Mauro's manner of displaying his various configurations of land and water was an erroneous one. Furthermore, he had Fra Mauro's authority--so to speak--to outstep his boundaries. Had not Fra Mauro placed on record that *in that Oriental sea there were many islands large and famous that he had not set down because he had no room for them*? His very words were: *In questo mar Oriental sono molte isole grande e famose che non ho posto per non aver luogo.* Toscanelli must have been actuated by the inclination to fill those regions of the southern hemisphere which had been ignored and cramped.

He therefore--we argue--placed Fra Mauro's Sumatra to the south of the equator, thinking no doubt that the tropic of Capricorn, not the equator, divided Sumatra in two. In confirmation of this belief he may have observed on some Arabian portulano the outlines of the western coasts of Australia thus cut in two by the tropic of Capricorn. Availing himself of these configurations, he must have united them to the eastern shores of Fra Mauro's Sumatra, and connected both with the coasts of China as in Ptolemy's map--the straits of Malacca being obliterated at the point where we find the name *Mallaqua* set down on the Schonerean Frankfort gores of 1515, and where the word Lack may be noticed in the map we are considering.

If we examine carefully Fra Mauro's Mappamundi we shall find that there is little doubt but that this was the method employed by Toscanelli of reconstructing Fra Mauro's data, for we find in most of the maps of this type Fra Mauro's eastern prolongation of islands, together with his nomenclature, to which have been added the islands that he did not set down *per non aver luogo*.

Toscanelli was a man of superior intellect in his day, and little influenced by popular prejudice or error. He was evidently an innovator, and to him we owe doubtless the representation on maps of those more or less fantastic islands that were set down according to the interpretation of Marco Polo's writings. There appears however to have been several of these interpretations.

Let us compare some of them with the interpretation given on Behaim's globe.

Unfortunately we have not been able to procure as yet any better copy of this important document than the one given here from Jomard's *Monuments de la Geographie*, and we have been to some trouble in procuring this. It is incomplete, as Mr. H. Harrisse remarks (see above); other charts however may help to fill the lacunae.

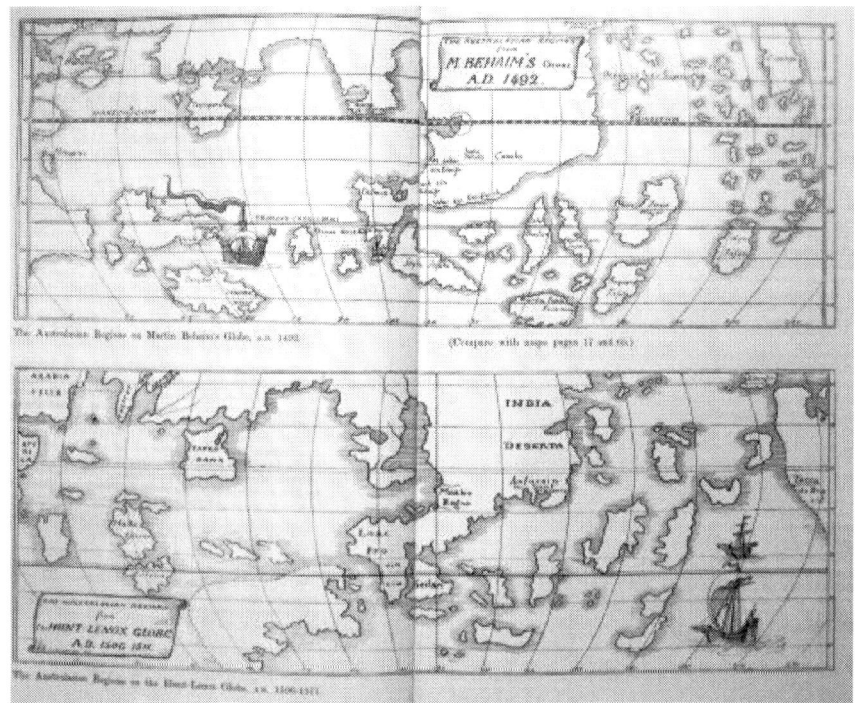

AUSTRALASIAN REGIONS ON M. BEHAIM'S GLOBE AND HUNT-LENOX COMPARED.

Marco Polo says*: "Upon leaving Champa, and steering a course between south and south-west* seven hundred miles, you fall in with two islands, the larger of which is named Sondur, and the other *Kondur*."

(*Footnote. Marsden's Marco Polo.)

(*Footnote. Allowing for the projection this course will be found to be correct.)

Now, west of 165 degrees of east longitude, 20 degrees north latitude, the reader will notice *Ciampo porto*, which is probably a little to the south and a good deal to the west of the point of departure mentioned by Polo; and to the south, south-west of this point of departure, two islands may be noticed in 10 degrees of latitude north, which, we may presume, are meant for *Sondur* and *Kondur*, for in map Number 3 *Sodur* is placed on the equator and *Candur* below it. Map Number 4 places *Sandio* and *Candur* in about 11 degrees south of the equator.

Then Marco Polo's description introduces us to *Lochac* on the mainland, the name of which province, we may notice, has been corrupted, and appears in 135 degrees east, 10 degrees south, as *Coachs*, *Lo* and *Loach ac*, in map Number 3; *Loach provin*, in map Number 4.

Marco Polo's description then continues thus: "Departing from Lochac and keeping a southerly course for five hundred miles, you reach an island named *Pentam*, the coast of which is wild and uncultivated, but the woods abound with sweet scented trees."

This island of *Pentam* will be noticed in 150 degrees east longitude, cut in two by the tropic of Capricorn. In map Number 3 it is placed just above *Java Minor*. In map Number 4 it has the same position as on Behaim's globe.

Marco Polo's description then takes us to *Malaiur* on the mainland and to *Java Minor*, where that portion of his description ends.

Malaiur, although spoken of as an island--which is often the case with eastern descriptions in which the whole extent of a country is not well known--has been identified by Marsden, Major, and others as the Malay Peninsula, and we believe this interpretation to be the correct one. But the identification certainly presented some little difficulty, which may account for the fact that the name does not appear on Martin Behaim's globe; or, at least, on Jomard's copy of it, nor in any of the maps we are now dealing with. Later on, and in a class of maps in which Marco Polo's descriptions have been less faithfully interpreted, we shall find it set down as an island, and also as a province pertaining to a fantastic representation of Australia.

Java Minor is set down to the south-east of Australia and between the 150th and 165th degree of east longitude, thus, strangely enough, occupying the position of Tasmania. This is all the more strange when coupled with the fact that, on our modern maps, to the south of Tasmania, appear the *unaccounted for* Spanish or Portuguese words *Piedra Blanca* or *Pedra branca*. In map Number 3 *Java Minor* is placed in the same longitude as on the Behaim globe, but to the north of the tropic of Capricorn, whereas in map Number 4 it resumes the same position as on the Behaim globe. Unfortunately we have not been able to procure

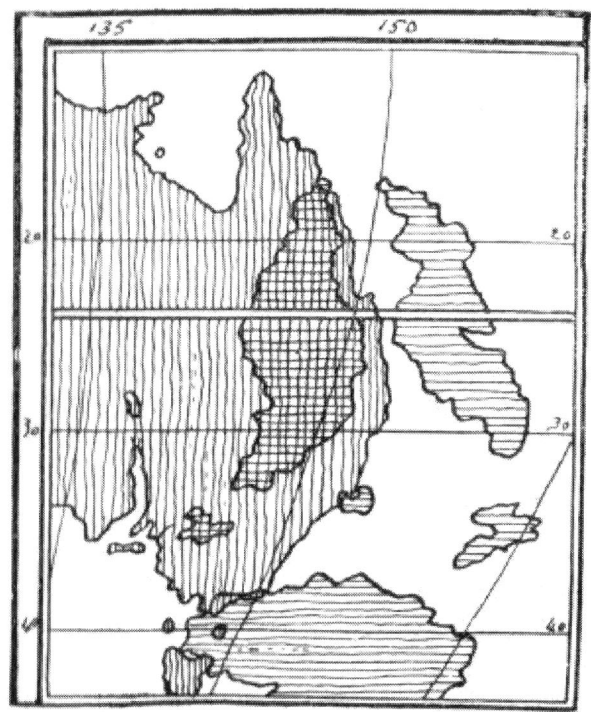

Pentam, etc., in Behaim's globe, compared with modern eastern coasts of Australia and Tasmania. The modern charting is shaded perpendicularly--the old features are shaded horizontally.

**Pentam, etc. in Behaim's globe, compared with modern eastern coasts of Australia and Tasmania.
The modern charting is shaded perpendicularly--the old features are shaded horizontally.**

The other islands of the Australasian regions on Behaim's globe are: *Java Major, Candyn, Anguana, Neucuram, Seylan, Zanzibar,* and *Madagascar*. There are other islands besides, but they bear no names. *Candyn* is altogether outside the Australasian sphere; it is described under the name Dondin by Odoric of Pordenone. *Java Major* is a distorted representation of Fra Mauro's *Siamotra*. *Anguana* occupies the site of New Zealand, and might be derived from a representation of those islands; it will become the Ysles de Magna of the Dauphin Chart 1530/36. Its name however is simply a corruption of the Angaman of Marco Polo, who described the Andaman Islands under that name. *Neucuram* and *Pentam* also belong to his nomenclature. Under the first name he describes the Nicobar Islands, and *Pentam* has been identified as Bintang, near Singapore; but the eastern coast lines of both these islands--*Neucuram* and *Pentam*--have a remarkable resemblance to the eastern coasts of Australia, both as to shape and position; *Pentam* especially, the eastern coast of which actually follows the greater part of our eastern coastlines, as may be seen in Illustration 62. The southern coast of *Seylan* falls in also, to a certain extent, with our southern shores.

Madagascar and *Zanzibar* deserve notice. Madagascar, it will be observed, runs east and west, thus fulfilling the function of a certain portion of Ptolemy's *bogus* continent in those parts. *Zanzibar* is placed away from its proper position on the coast of Africa owing to a particularity in Marco Polo's account that might naturally lead the cartographer to place it where he did.

We shall find the position of Zanzibar maintained in many maps of later date until the Portuguese reached these parts and made more accurate surveys.

With reference to the Dauphin and similar charts wherein the Australian coasts are so remarkably well delineated, we have now to mention in connection with the present globe some of its most curious and extraordinary features--features which will show that the Dauphin and similar charts were not entirely due to Portuguese and Spanish surveys. On the portion of coast in 105 degrees west longitude and above the tropic of Capricorn appears the word *Calmia*. *Calmia* bears no resemblance to lago regno, which occupies the same position in Fra Mauro's Mappamundi, nor to *regnum lac* of the British Museum map of 1489, nor to any other more or less similar name on maps of this class. But it corresponds with *quabe se quiesce* of the Dauphin chart, which has been read erroneously *quabesegmesce*, and which appears as *ap quieta* on Descelier's map of 1550. We should not be so sure about it though, if another word did not occur, which shows that the nomenclature of this globe, or better, of its prototype, served in the following instance, at least, in the Dauphin chart nomenclature.

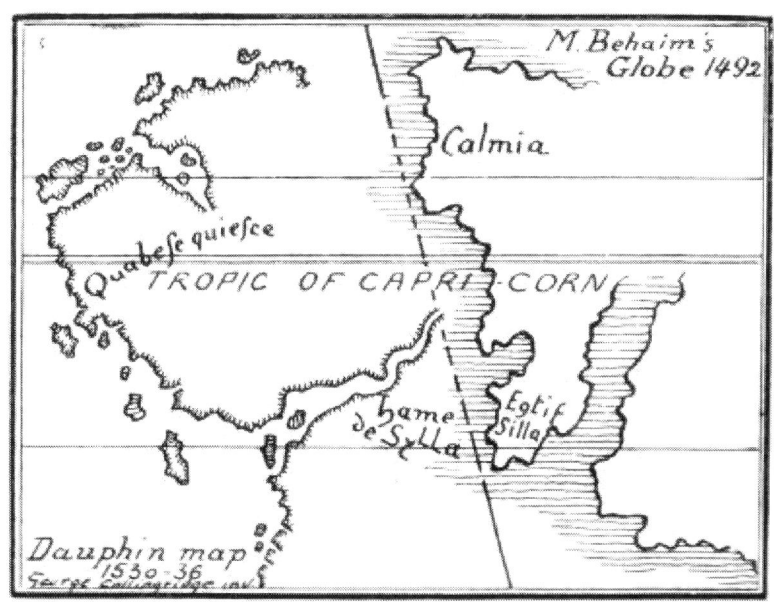

Egtis Silla in Behaim's globe and ***Hame de Sylla*** in Dauphin chart compared.

To the south of the tropic of Capricorn and in the same regions *Egtis-Silla* occurs. *Egtis-Silla* belongs to the following inscription, which, on our reduced copy, we have not given in full: *das land margenannt Egtis-Silla*. Whatever primitive form it may have been corrupted from, it certainly *is* the origin of *Hame de Sylla* which on the Dauphin chart occurs in the same locality, as may be seen in Illustration 26.

CHAPTER 17. A.D. 1499.
TERRA AUSTRALIS.--SAID TO BE DISCOVERED IN 1499.

Rapid strides were being made now in the work of discovery, westwardly and eastwardly.

In 1497 Vasco da Gama sailed round the Cape of Good Hope and arrived at Calicut with Paolo da Gama, Nicolas Coelho, Pedro Nunez, Pero de Alemquer, Joao de Coimbra, and Pero Escobar.

The same year John and Sebastian Cabot left Bristol on the 2nd of May, sighted the continent of America June 24th, and returned to Bristol on August the 9th.

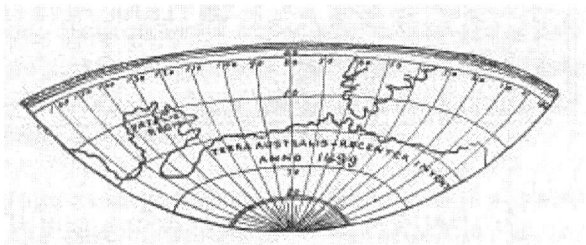

Portion of Paris wooden globe circa 1535, showing inscription on Austral land and *Patalis Regio*, indicating a discovery made in 1499.

**Portion of Paris wooden globe circa 1535, showing inscription on Austral land
and Patalis Regio, indicating a discovery made in 1499.**

There occurs about this time, which was a most active period, a claim of Australasian discovery to which we have alluded in the introductory chapter of this work. We must now inquire into this claim, for although as yet the evidence in support of it appears to be scanty there is no telling what further research may reveal. The claim is in the form of an inscription on a wooden globe, as represented in Illustration 61.

Concerning this claim Mr. H. Harrisse, from whose work* we have borrowed our sketch, says: "The Austral lands bear an inscription somewhat surprising: The simply cordiform map of Finaeus inscribes there: Terra Australis nuper inventa, sed nondum plene examinata. The Austral land, recently discovered, but not yet entirely explored. The wooden globe modifies the legend as follows: Terra Australis recenter inventa anno 1499 (*sic*), sed nondum plene cognita. That is, it gives the date of 1499 for the discovery of the Austral region. We are inclined to think that it is a reference to the voyage of Magellan, coupled with an erroneous rendering of the date in the account of Maximilianus Transylvanus: Soluit itaque Magellanus die decimo Augusti, Anno, M.D. XIX."

(*Footnote. The Discovery of North America page 613 4th paragraph.)

We cannot say that we are of Mr. Harrisse's opinion, because there is no possibility of mistaking that date M.D. XIX for 1499, which would have been rendered thus: MCCCCIC.; and because the data of this wooden globe does not appear to be based on Maximilianus Transylvanus' account.

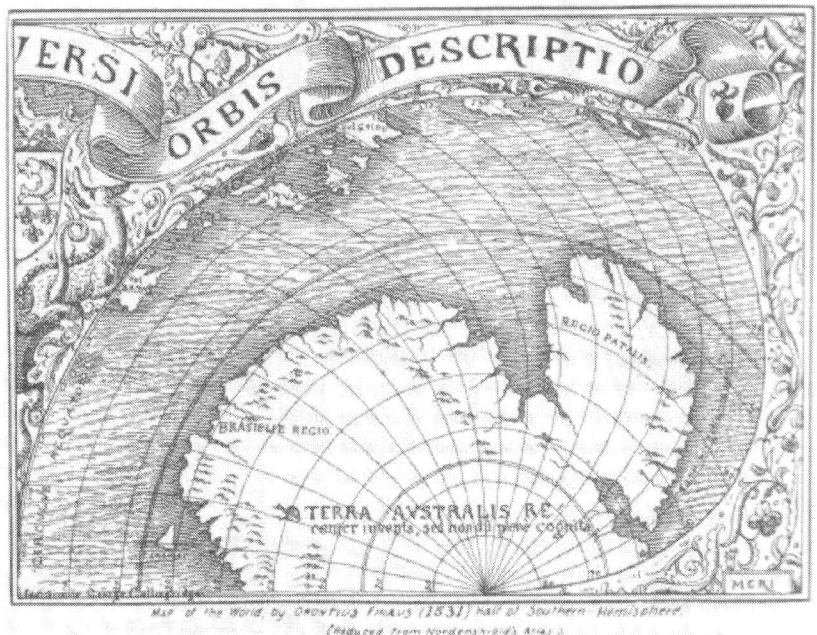

**Map of the World by Orontius Finaeus (1531) Half of Southern Hemisphere.
(Reduced from Nordenskiold's Atlas.)**

Mr. Harrisse refers to a cordiform map of Finaeus* later than the one, a portion of which we reproduce here, and ours bears a somewhat different legend, as will be observed. Our reason for giving it here however is to show that, owing to the connection that exists between it and the wooden globe, the term *Terra Australis* may have applied originally to *Australia* as well as to those regions now known to us as *Terra del Fuego*.

(*Footnote. Mr. Harrisse, alluding to Finaeus' map of 1531, which is the one we reproduce here, remarks, same work, page 618: "In regard to the Austral land, if we sketch its configuration (as given in the mappamundi of 1531) so as to give it the form which would be imparted by the projection of the present, it will be found to exhibit precisely the same elements. The names Regio Patalis and Brasilie regio, together with the main legend, are to be found in both. The only difference is that in 1531 Finaeus writes: Terra Australis recenter inventa, sed nondum plene cognita,' while in 1536. he adopts the phrase: "Terra Australis recenter inventa, sed nondum plene examinata.")

Patalis regio in the wooden globe answers to New Zealand, and the prolongation of the coastline westwardly indicated no doubt the east coast of Australia. We have not the eastern hemisphere of this wooden globe to judge how this coastline runs in its more northerly bearings, but, judging from globes and maps similar to Finaeus', we may safely conclude that the above-mentioned coastline was intended for the east coast of Australia.

Who were the discoverers? It would be difficult to say. Mr. Harrisse, referring to westerly *expeditions carried out by virtue of regular licenses*, says: "That, between 1493 and 1500, a number of vessels were, besides, unlawfully equipped in the ports of Spain, Portugal, and France, for the purpose of exploiting the New World, and sailed secretly or without being provided with any license whatever, does not admit of a doubt. The glowing accounts which Columbus gave of the newly discovered regions; the hope to find gold in quantity; the Indians kidnapped and sold as slaves in Andalusia; the cargoes of dyewood, spun cotton, and novel objects brought from America, were surely of such a character as to induce the bold mariners of the Peninsula to engage in the venture.

"So far as Portugal is concerned we see, from the start in 1493, a caravel sail from Madeira to find the countries which Columbus had just discovered, and King Manoel immediately send three vessels after the alleged truant ship, apparently to arrest her, but in reality to join in the expedition: y podria ser que esto se fuiese con otros respetos, o' que los mismos que fueron en las carabelas, una y otras, querran descubrir algo en lo que pertenece a' Nos, Navarette, doc. lxxi. Volume ii. page 109. The fact is that the Azores were the hot-bed, so to speak, of transatlantic expeditions. And the Portuguese notarial archives, as well as those of the Torre do Tombo, may yet yield information of that character, and of a date prior to the letters patent granted in October 1499 to Joam Fernandez of Terceira, authorising a voyage to the New World, before any such privilege had yet been conceded to Gaspar Corte-Real, or before anything was known of the latter's maritime attempts.

"As to such secret and illegal Portuguese expeditions, we can know only of those which were the object of protests on the part of the Spanish Government; as for instance the incursion of four Lusitanian ships which early in the year 1503 went to the country discovered by Rodrigo de Bastidas, and returned to Lisbon loaded with dyewood and Indian slaves. Weare loth to believe that this was a solitary case; and if Portuguese shipowners sent vessels in the track of Bastidas, we may rest assured that they acted in the same manner, on a venture, when informed of the quantities of pearls brought by Cristobal Guerra, if not before.

"The French, who in the beginning of the sixteenth century exhibited such a great maritime activity, at least in their western seaports, showed just as little scruple. We have authentic documents on that point. In the affidavit subscribed at Rouen by Binot Paulmier de Gonneville, June 19 1505, mention is made of *Dieppe and St. Malo mariners, as well as other Normands and Britons, who for years past go to the West Indies in search of dyewood, cotton, monkeys, parrots, and other articles.* As this information must have been possessed by Gonneville before June 24 1503 (when he sailed from Honfleur) we have in his deposition evidence that for years prior to 1503: *d' empuis aucunes annees en ca les Dieppois et les Malouins et autres Normands et Bretons vont querir aux Indes occidentalles du bois a teindre en rouge, cotons, guenons, et perroquets, et autres denrees.* But who can tell how far those seafaring men (who rank among the boldest that *ever existed, and were sometimes accompanied by Portuguese mariners*) went and what countries they may have explored?

"As regards Spain, the Crown rendered lawful enterprises to the newly discovered regions extremely difficult. Licenses were granted only to the subjects of Queen Isabella, that is, inhabitants of Castile, Leon, Asturias, Galicia, Estramadura, Murcia, and Andalusia; while not only foreigners, but even her husband's own subjects (Aragonese, Catalans, and Valencians) were strictly excluded. Nay, Isabella attached so much importance to such an exclusive right that if in her testament she speaks only once of the Indies it is to affirm her absolute and personal prerogative on the subject.

"The royalty to be paid to the Crown, exclusively of Columbus' 10 percent on the tonnage of every vessel, the obligation to have constantly on board State officials to watch proceedings and record minutely the receipts, together with a strict requirement to equip all ships in the only port of Seville, where the law compelled them also to return and unload, were likewise impediments which could but result in the fitting out of numerous clandestine expeditions to the New World, both for the purpose of barter and maritime discovery.

"The damage occasioned to the Crown from that cause compelled their Catholic Majesties several times to issue stringent orders to repress such illegal enterprises. The warning issued September 3 1501 recalls similar defences already published, and enacts very severe penalties against all those who should dare in the future to undertake unauthorised voyages in the Atlantic Ocean.

"It must not be supposed, nevertheless, that those prohibitions ever prevented adventurers from running the gauntlet. As far back as 1497 we see two of Columbus' own officers, one of whom, Alonso Medel, had been the master of the *Nina* during the second voyage of discovery, elope with two armed vessels equipped by the Crown, and of which they were in command. Disregarding the orders of Columbus, and surreptitiously, this Medel, with Bartolome Colin, set sail for unknown regions. When they returned to Cadiz Columbus asked their Majesties to instigate legal proceedings, on the plea that the bold adventurers had been guilty, to use Navarette's expressions, of *Viages arbitrarios*. We do not know where those truant mariners went, but they certainly avoided the transatlantic ports and coasts visited by licensed Spanish ships and officials.

"Later, February 4 1500, we see another instance of the kind, when Ferdinand and Isabella charter three vessels for the purpose of overtaking in the open sea two ships which had sailed unlawfully from Seville to the New World. It is worthy of notice that they belonged to a Genoese, Francesco de Rivarolla, the friend and banker of Christopher Columbus.

"It is plain that under the circumstances unlicensed adventurers eschewed, as much as possible, the localities where they ran the risk of meeting with caravels sailing under the royal flag, or the points of the coast already exploited by duly authorised traders and seafaring men. This would lead them to unknown parts, the secret of which they kept to themselves, or marked on maps intended exclusively for the information of their employers." Mr. Harrisse then remarks, with reference to the north-east coast of America, that "we can well realise how geographical information gathered during such secret and dangerous voyages may have remained unknown to the pilots and cosmographers of the Spanish Crown, and, as a matter of course, failed to figure on the official charts of the Sevillan Hydrography," and adds, "Those facts will certainly be viewed by just critics as indicating several of the various sources whence may have been derived the cartographical data which appear on the Lusitano-Germanic maps."

Yes, and Mr. Harrisse's remarks are quite true, but they may and ought to apply likewise to voyages south of the equator--to voyages in search of a southern passage to the Spice Islands as well as to voyages in search of a northern passage. A passage leading to the Spice Islands was one of the foremost desiderata of mariners of the day, for few believed, as Columbus appears to have believed, that the eastern regions beyond the Golden Chersonesus were attained.

There are reasons to believe that this glittering Eldorado was sought for and reached years before the recorded expeditions to it that we know of. What we know positively is that Antonio de Abreu in 1511 eastwardly, and Magellan in 1521 westwardly, attained these regions. We have however representations on maps of the pathways traversed by Abreu and Magellan, combined with other data, which go far to show that, since these regions were charted before the arrival of those hitherto accepted pioneers, they must have been known.

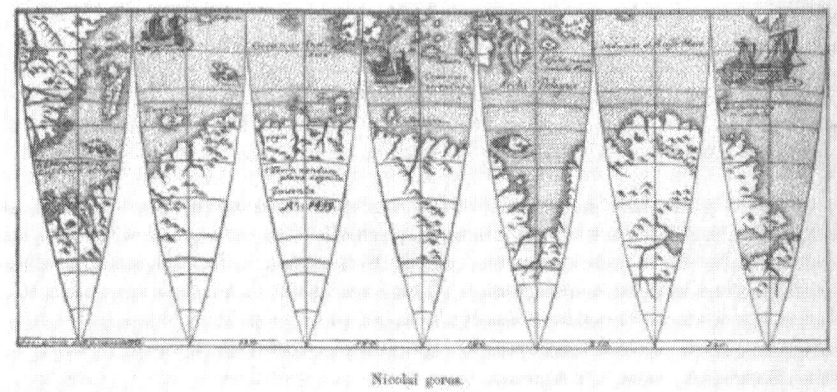

Nicolai gores.

Since writing the above another mappamundi has come to our notice, in which the statement with reference to the discovery of the *Terra Australis* is repeated.

It is a mappamundi in gores of the date 1603, published at Lyons in France by Guiliemus Nicolai Belga. We give here a reduced facsimile of the Australasian regions on this interesting map. The legend--*Terra nondum plene cognita, Inventa Anno 1499*--is set down in a more correct position than on the Paris wooden globe of 1535, and to the west of it, on the margin of the Australian Continent, may be noticed the inscription *Brasilia regio* and *Psitacorum terra*.

CHAPTER 18. A.D. 1500.
JUAN DE LA COSA'S MAP. CANTINO'S MAP. AUSTRALIA THE BAPTISMAL FONT OF BRAZIL.

It is strange that, precisely the year following the one in which the *Terra Australis* was said to have been discovered, we should find, as it were, a contrary statement made, by the non-appearance of that recorded discovery on the first important document on which it should have appeared--the famous planisphere of Juan de la Cosa, constructed towards the end of the year 1500, and on which Cabral's discovery of Brazil, the year preceding, is recorded.

Was the omission intentional? We cannot say; but from that date a special class of maps was issued, on which the example set by the celebrated Basque cartographer was followed, although not implicitly, for whereas de la Cosa's map does not extend eastwardly beyond the *Sinus Gangeticus*, or Bay of Bengal, omitting therefore the Malay Peninsula and the regions to the east of it as far as America, the special class of maps we refer to give the full extent of the earth's circumference, but omit, in the Australasian regions heretofore crowded with islands, even the merest suspicion or indication of land, if we except the real Sumatra, Java, and its eastern prolongation of islands as far as Gilolo.

CANTINO'S MAP 1501 TO 1502.

The document next in order is the Cantino map of 1501/2. Cantino was Hercules d'Este's ambassador at the Court of Portugal, and the map that bears his name was sent by him to his Lordship Hercules d'Este, Duke of Ferrara.

This planisphere sets forth, as Juan de la Cosa's did, Cabral's discovery on the coast of Brazil. It must be remembered here that the name given originally to that part of the southern continent of America was not Brazil, but *Terra de Santa Cruz*; and if we notice a *Rio de brasil* on this map it is there merely on account of the frequent use to which the name was put at the time, without in any way applying to the mainland, and in this way we see it applied also to a small island off the coast of Venezuela in de la Cosa's map.

It would be curious however to find that the term was applied to some large island or continental land in the Australasian regions before it came to be adopted as the name of the large South American region to which it now belongs. We suggest that it may have thus been given by some learned cosmographer, as it was afterwards by Schoner, with the belief that the Australasian regions were connected with and formed the western coasts of the South American Continent, for it was only after the return of the survivors of Magellan's fleet that the vastness of the Pacific Ocean was realised.

In the map now before us there is a small island with the following inscription: *Ilha timoua en este ilha ha brasil carata seda*; it lies in about 14 degrees south of the equator, and in not quite the same number of degrees east of Malacca, which in this map extends towards the tropic of Capricorn. Judging from the position of this island with reference to the southern extremity of the Malay Peninsula on the same map, we might take it for one of the Anamba islands; otherwise it lies sufficiently south to be some island off the west coast of Australia. We think it is intended for *Timor*, as Timor is so situated in Schoner's globe of 1533. As far as we have been able to ascertain it is the first cartographical appearance of the term Brasil in the Australasian regions.

Let us see now what reasons we may find in other documents in support of our suggestion that the term may have been given to some large island or continental land, south of Asia, before it came to be applied in South America.

We have first Marco Polo's account of LOCACH: "*In this country* (Locach, corrupted afterwards to Beach) *the brazil which we make use of grows in great plenty.*"*

(*Footnote. Marco Polo, 3rd book 7th chapter.)

In Martin Behaim's globe, 1492, *Locach*, corrupted to *Coachs*, is situated in the southern hemisphere, occupying a position midway between New Guinea and Australia. The prototype from which Behaim,

Toscanelli, and others constructed those early globes and maps of the Behaimean and Schonerean type was no doubt of Arabian origin, and may have been similar to the lost map referred to by Albuquerque. This lost map was used by Francisco Rodriguez, the Portuguese pilot, in making that extract or copy that was sent to the King of Portugal, before Rodriguez set out with Abreu in 1511 on his expedition to the Moluccas. Albuquerque's allusion to the lost map is made in a letter dated April 1st 1512, and which has been recently published.*

(*Footnote. Cartas de Affonso de Albuquerque seguitas de Documentos que as elucidam, etc. t. 1 page 64 to 65. Lisboa, Typ. da Acad. Real das sciencias, 1884, in 4to. The following is Albuquerque's text: Tambem vos vay hum pedaco de padram que se tirou dua gramde carta dum piloto de jaoa, aquall tinha ho cabo de booa esperamca, portugall e a terra de brasyll, ho mar rroxo e ho mar da persia, as ilhas de crauo, a navegacam dos chins e gores, com suas lynhas e caminhos dercytos por omde as naos hiam, e ho sertam. quaees reynos comfynauam huns cos outros; parece me, senhor, que foy a milhor cousa que eu nunca vy, e voss alteza ounera de folgar muyto de ha ver; tinha os nomes por letra jaoa, e eu trazio jao que sabia ler e espreuer; mamdou esse pedaco a voss alteza, *que francisco rrodriquez em pramtou sobre a outra*, domde vos alteza podera ver verdadeiramente os chins domde ven e os gores, e as vossas naos ho caminho que am de fazer pera as ilhas de crauo e as minas do ouro omde sam, e a ilha de jaoa e de bamdam, de nos nozcada e macas e a terra del rrey de Syam e asy o cabo da terra de nauegacam dos chins, e asy para omde volve e como daly a diamte nam nauegam: A CARTA PRIMCIPALL SE PERDEO EM FROLL DE LA MAR; co piloto e com pero dalpoem pratiquey ho symtir desta carta, pera la saberem, dar rezam a voss alteza; temde este pedaco de padram por cousa muyto certa e muyto sabida, porque he a mesma nauegcam por omde eles vam o vem mingua lhe o arcepedego das ilhas que se chamam *celate*, que jazem amtre jaoa e malaca.)

Commenting on this letter in his L'Oeuvre geographique des Reinel et la decouverte des Moluques, Dr. E.T. Hamy says:

Il parait resulter de cette lettre d'Albuquerque que Rodriguez avait fait une sorte d'adaptation d'une grande carte javanaise, on plutot arabe, detruite depuis lors, et sur laquelle on ne s'explique pas aisement, il faut bien le reconnaitre, les indications relatives au Portugal et surtout au Bresil. Il est assez probable que, suivant les habitudes des cartographes de son temps, Rodriguez avait introduit dans un cadre de sa fabrication les dessins fournis par la composition indigene et que c'est a l'ensemble ainsi obtenu que s'adressent les eloges d'Albuquerque.

The Javanese map (or Arabian, as Dr. E.T. Hamy suggests) referred to by Albuquerque represented then the land of Brazil. Now, what land could this be? The Arabs, at the time, could hardly have any knowledge of the continent of America, and it is still less probable that they knew anything about Cabral's discovery. Their navigations were confined to the Indian Ocean, and we must look within their sphere for an explanation. Albuquerque's letter, which has puzzled learned critics, if viewed in the light of the term Brazil being applied to Australia, is easily understood. Then again another perplexing subject of controversy will be solved if we consider Brazil to apply to Australia. It relates to the Straits of Magellan, Brazil, and the alleged proximity of Brazil to Malacca.

On Schoner's globe of 1515, that is five years before Magellan passed through the straits that bear his name, a passage from the South Atlantic ocean to the South Pacific Ocean is marked. The charting of this strait is certainly mysterious, and led to the following remarks in F.H.H. Guillemard's Life of Ferdinand Magellan*:

(*Footnote. Ferdinand Magellan, F.H.H. Guillemard, page 192 third paragraph.)

"What had Schoner in his mind when he gave this strait a place upon his globes? What were his sources of information? Was it fact or conjecture that guided his pencil? These are the questions we have to answer. Some light is thrown upon them by a work of the cosmographer which was published at the same time as his early globe, and intended to be in great measure illustrative of it.*

(*Footnote. Luculentissima quaeda terrae totius descriptio, Schoner, Nuremberg 1515 4to.)

"In it he speaks of his Brasilae regio--that the country was not far from the Cape of Good Hope; that the Portuguese had explored it, and had discovered a strait going from east to west; that this strait resembled the Strait of Gibraltar; and that Mallaqua was not far distant therefrom.* All this information was, nevertheless, not gathered at first hand by Schoner. Shortly before he wrote--but how long we do not know, for the title-page bears no date--was published a certain pamphlet in bad German, anonymous and apparently a confused translation of a Portuguese original--the *Copia der Newen, Zeytung aus Presillg Landt*. From this he apparently took his description almost word for word, and the question thus shifts itself a point further back into the examination of the provenance and authorities of the *Copia*."

(*Footnote. Schoner op. cit. Tract ii. cap. ii. fol. 60v. A capite bonae spei (quod Itali Capo de bona speranza vocitant) parum distat. Circumnavigaverunt itaque Portugalienses eam regionem, et comperierunt illum transitum fere conformem nostrae Europae (quam nos incolimus) et lateraliter infra orientum et occidentum situm. Ex altero insuper latera etiam terra visa est, et penes caput hujus regionis circa miliaria 60, eo videlicet modo; ac si quis navigaret orientum versus et transitum sive strictum Gibel terrae aut Sibiliae navigaret, et Barbarium, hoc est Mauretaniam in Aphrica intueretur; ut ostendet Globus noster versus Polum antarcticum. Insuper modica est distantia ab hoc Brasiliae regione ad Mallaquam.)

Now the *Copia* speaks of the strait as being in 40 degrees south, but Schoner's globe shows two straits, one to the south of America in 45 degrees and one between the Australian regions and an antarctic continent which bears the name of *Brasilie Regio*. This strait runs from east to west and is in 40 degrees south as the *Copia* states; moreover, as it is nearer Malacca than the former strait, it is only fair to presume that the *Land of Brazil* alluded to in the Copia was not the land in South America, especially when we take into consideration the fact that the South American region which now bears the name of Brazil had not, in Schoner's map, been christened otherwise than with its first name *Sacte Crucis*, which is the name given to the cape forming the Brazilian elbow.

Andrea Corsali,* speaking of a continental land to the south-east of the Spice Islands, that is, in the vicinity of New Guinea, says:

Et nauigado verso le parti d' Oriente, dicono esserui terra de piccinacoli, & e di molti openione che questa terra vada a tenere, & congiungersi per la Banda di Leuante & mezogiorno, con la costa del Brezil o' Verzino perche per la grandezza di detta terra del Verzino, non si e per anchora da tutta le parti discoperta. And navigating towards the east, they say there lies the land of *Piccinacoli*,* and many believe that this land is connected towards the east in the south with the coast of *Bresil* or *Verzino*,* because, on account of the size of this land of *Verzino*, it is not as yet on all sides discovered.

(*Footnote. Ramusio, Lettera di Andrea Corsali Fiorentino allo illustrissimo Signor Duca Giuliano de Medici, Lettera scritta in Cochinterra del' India nell l' anno MDXV alli VI di Gennaio, Fol. 280 (sic for 180) C.)

(*Footnote. Piccinacoli is the name given to New Guinea in G. Mercator's map of 1569.)

(*Footnote. Verzino is the Italian for Brazil-wood.)

As New Guinea was supposed to be connected with Australia, it follows that we have in the above statement of Andrea Corsali the reason, at least, for the presence on subsequent maps of the Shonerean term Brasielie Regio, as applied to the Austral Continent.

CHAPTER 19. A.D. 1503 TO 1508.

DE GONNEVILLE'S ALLEGED VOYAGE TO AUSTRALIA. LUDOVICO BARTHEMA.

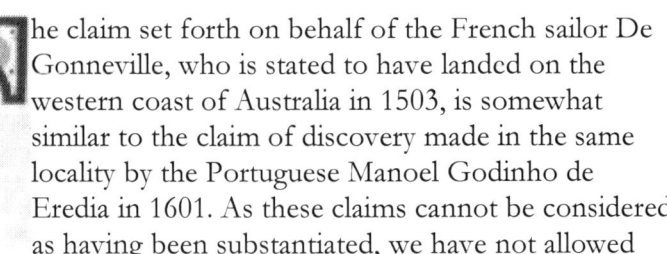

The claim set forth on behalf of the French sailor De Gonneville, who is stated to have landed on the western coast of Australia in 1503, is somewhat similar to the claim of discovery made in the same locality by the Portuguese Manoel Godinho de Eredia in 1601. As these claims cannot be considered as having been substantiated, we have not allowed them to interfere with the chronological sequence of historical facts and documents. But, as both these claims of discovery present sufficient interest to the Australasian student, and are indirectly connected with our subject, we have not dismissed them entirely. They will be found discussed in the appendix at the end of this volume.

LUDOVICO BARTHEMA.

We must now give an account of a traveller whose descriptions have had some influence on Australian geography.

About this time also, 1502/1503, the influence of Marco Polo and Nicolo de' Conti on the cartography of the Eastern regions was at its apogy, for their voyages had just been published in the Portuguese language at Lisbon.*

(*Footnote. See above, Chapter 8.)

Ludovico Barthema's account of his travels ranges over a period of five years, from 1503 to 1508.

He visited those regions that were soon to fall under the sway of the Portuguese, and on his way back to Europe met the latter at Calicut, and stayed for some time there imparting to them knowledge of the countries he had visited.

Barthema visited Java, and from this furthest point south he retraced his steps back to India and Europe.

We give here *verbatim* the portions of his voyages that describe the regions visited by him south of the equator and in proximity to Australia.

Dr. E.T. Hamy and other critics believe that Barthema never visited the Spice Islands, but described them in the same manner that Java was described by Marco Polo, from the accounts of his fellow travellers.

Ludovico Barthema's account of his travels appears to have been very little known, even by his own countrymen. George Percy Badger, in the introduction to The Travels of Ludovico di Varthema, etc.,* says: "One would have thought that Ramusio might have picked up some information respecting the early life and subsequent career of our author; but his *Discorso Breve* to Varthema's book is briefer than many of the notices prefixed to other far less important voyages and travels contained in his valuable collection.

(*Footnote. Hakluyt Society Edition.)

"Moreover, it is clear that the first authorised edition of the Itinerary, printed at Rome in 1510, was either unknown to him or beyond his reach; since he tells us that his revised exemplar was prepared from a Spanish version made from the Latin translation--a third-hand process, which accounts for the many variations existing between his copy and the original Italian edition. The following is all that he says: 'This *Itinerary* of Lodovico Barthema, a Bolognese, wherein the things concerning India and the Spice Islands are so fully and so correctly narrated as to transcend all that has been written either by ancient or modern authors, has hitherto been read replete with errors and inaccuracies, and might have been so read in future, had not God caused to be put into our hands the book of Christofero di Arco, a clerk of Seville, who, being in possession of the Latin exemplar of that voyage, made from the original itself, and dedicated to the Most Reverend Monsignor Bernardino, Cardinal Carvaial of the Santa Croce, translated it with great care into the Spanish language, by the aid of which we have been enabled to correct in many places the present book, which was originally written by the author himself in our own vulgar tongue and dedicated to the Most Illustrious Madonna Agnesina, one of the pre-eminent and excellent women of Italy at that period. She was the daughter of the Most Illustrious Signor Federico, Duke of Urbino, and sister of the Most Excellent Guidobaldo, wife of the Most Illustrious Signor Fabricio Colonna, and mother of the Most Excellent Signor Ascanio Colonna and of the Lady Vittoria Marchioness Dal Guasto, the ornament and light of the present age. And the aforesaid Lodovico divided this volume into seven Books, in the First of which he narrates his journey to Egypt, Syria, and Arabia Deserta. In the Second, he treats of Arabia Felix. In the Third, of Persia. In the Fourth, Fifth, and Sixth, he comprises all India and the Molucca Islands, where the spices grow. In the Seventh and last, he recounts his return to Portugal, passing along the coast of Ethiopia, the Cape of Good Hope and several islands of the western ocean."

In the course of his travels, having arrived at Shiraz, "accident threw him in the way of a Persian merchant called Cazazionor, by whom he was recognised as a fellow pilgrim at Meccah, and whose friendly overtures on the occasion were destined to exert a powerful influence in shaping his subsequent course."*

(*Footnote. The Travels of Ludovico di Varthema, etc. page iii. Translated by J. Winter Jones, Esquire, F.S.A., and edited, with Notes and an Introduction, by the Rev. George Percy Badger 1863.)

He then, in company with the Persian merchant, started for Samarcand; owing however to some warfaring then going on in the locality, they were unable to reach their destination and returned to Shiraz. "The Persian merchant became so much attached to our traveller during the abortive attempt to reach Samarcand that, on their return to Shiraz, he intimated to the latter his intention of giving him the hand of his niece, who was called Samis, that is, the Sun, and so far transgressed Musulman etiquette in his favour as to present him personally to the damsel, with whom Varthema 'pretended to be much pleased, although his mind was intent on other things.' He tells us however that his destined bride was 'extremely beautiful, and had a name which suited her;' and lest the designation should be considered a misnomer, it must be remembered that the sun takes the feminine gender in most of the Oriental languages."*

(*Footnote. Ludovico di Varthema, Hakluyt Edition page lvii.)

Starting afresh from Shiraz, the two travellers reached Hormuz, where they embarked for India. Having reached India, at Cannanore, Barthema or Varthema avoided coming into contact with the Portuguese, fearing that his assumed profession of Islam might be detected by his companion traveller, for he could not have been friendly with the Portuguese without revealing to them his true character, and, had he done so, his future travelling prospects with his friend, the Persian merchant, would have been frustrated. Pursuing therefore their peregrinations they reached *Benghalla*, where they met two Nestorian Christians who had come there from a place called *Sarnau* in China. These two Christians from Sarnau, noticing some branches of coral which Cazazionor or Cogiazanor, the Persian merchant, had for sale, advised him and his friend to accompany them to Pegu, where they were going, and where he would find, they said, a ready market for such kind of wares. They travelled together and reached Pegu, where, after a short stay, they set off again for *Pider* in Sumatra. "A desire on the part of Cogiazanor to see the place where the nutmegs and cloves were produced induced him and Varthema to put themselves under the guidance of these two Christian companions, who were now anxious to return to their own country, but who eventually consented to accompany them, on hearing that Varthema had been a Christian and had seen Jerusalem, where he had been purchased as a slave, and brought up as a Musulman. This fabricated story so delighted the simple Sarnau couple that they endeavoured to persuade Varthema to go with them to China, promising that he should be made very rich there, and be allowed the free exercise of his adopted faith. Cogiazanor objected to the latter arrangement, informing them that his companion was the destined husband of his bright-eyed niece Samis, which finally settled the matter. Smaller boats being required for the projected trip, wherein there were no dangers to be apprehended from pirates, though the Christians would not promise them immunity from the chances of the sea, two Sampans, ready manned, were bought by the Persian for 400 *pardai* (about 280 pounds) and, after taking on board a stock of provisions, including the best fruits which Varthema had ever tasted, the party sailed from the island of Sumatra."*

(*Footnote. Ludovico di Varthema, Hakluyt Edition page xc.)

As we arrive now at the part of Ludovico Barthema's travels which affects more particularly our subject, and as certain learned critics* are of opinion, after a careful study of the question, that Barthema never visited the Spice Islands, we shall give verbatim the account of the part of his travels which refers to Australasia as found in Ramusio, with the English of the Hakluyt Society's edition, in order that our readers may judge for themselves. We know of many Australians whose practical knowledge of the Spice Islands will lead them to believe, like Tiele, Schefer, and Hamy, that Barthema never did visit the islands in question.

(*Footnote. In his L'oeuvre geographique des Reinel et la decouverte des MOLUQUES Dr. E.T. Hamy says: L'etude du recit de Varthema m'a conduit a admettre avec Tiele (*De Europeers in der Maleischen Archipel Bijdragen tot de Taal--Land--en Volken-Kunde van Nederlandsch Indie*, IV v. 1 D page 322 1878) et avec M. Schefer, que jamais le Voyageur n'avait reellement fait le voyage aux iles des Epices, qu'il a raconte a la suite de celui de Sumatra et de la cite de Pedir," page 20 N 1.)

Be this however as it may, the fact remains, and it is an interesting one for us, that at the early period of Barthema's travels, Chinese merchants were accustomed to visit and trade with the Spice islanders.

DELL' ISOLA DI BANDAN DOUE NASCONO LE NOCI MOSCATE & MACIS--CAP. XXIIII.*

(*Footnote. Primo Volume, et Terza editione Delle Navigationi et Viaggi raccolta gia da M. Gio. Battista Ramusio, etc., In Venetia nella stamperia de Giunti, 1563 folio 168 E.)

Infra il detto cammino trouammo cerca venti isole parte habitate & parte no, & in spatio di quindici giorni arriuammo alla detta isola, laqual e molta bruta & trista, e di circuito cerca cento miglia, & e terra molto bassa & piana, qui non v'e, ne Re, ne gouernatore, ma vi sono alcuni villani quasi come bestie senza alcuno ingegno, le case di questa isola sono di legname molto triste & basse, l' habito di costoro e che vanno in camicia, scalzi, senza alcuna cosa in testa, portano li capelli lunghi, il viso loro e largo & tondo, il suo colore e bianco, & sono picoli di statura, la sua fede e getile, ma sono di questa sorte che sono li piu triste di Calicut, chiamati *Poliar* & *Hirava*, sono molto debili d' ingegno & di forza, non hanno alcuna virtu, ma viuono come bestie, qui non nasce altre cose che noci moscate, il piede della noce moscata, e fatto a modo di vno arboro persico & fa la foglia in quel modo, ma sono piu strette, & avanti che la noce e matura, il macis l' abbracia, & cosi la colgono del mese di settembre, perche in questa isola va la stagione come a noi, & ciascun huomo raccoglie piu che puo, pche tutte sono comuni et a detti arbori: non si dura fatica alcuna, ma lasciano fare alla natura, queste noci si vendono a misura, laqual pesa ventisei libbre, per prezzo di mezzo carlino, la moneta corre qui ad vsanza di Calicut, qui no bisogna far ragione, per che la gente e tanto grossa, che volendo, non saperiano far male, & in termine di duoi giorni disse il mio compagno alli christiani, li garofani doue nascono? risposero che nasceuano lontano da qui sei giornate in vna isola chiamata Maluch, & che le genti di quella sono piu bestiali, et piu vili & dappoche, che no sono queste de Bandan, alla fine deliberammo di andar a quell' isola fussero le genti come si volessero, & cosi facemo vela, & in dodici giorni arriuammo alla detta isola.

THE CHAPTER CONCERNING THE ISLAND OF BANDAN, WHERE NUTMEGS AND MACE GROW.*

(*Footnote. Ludovico di Varthema, Hakluyt Society's Edition page 243.)

In the course of the said journey we found about twenty islands, part inhabited and part not, and in the space of fifteen days we arrived at the said island, which is very ugly and gloomy, and is about one hundred miles in circumference, and is a very low and flat country. There is no king here, nor even a governor, but there are some peasants, like beasts, without understanding. The houses of this island are of timber, very gloomy, and low. Their dress consists of a shirt; they go barefooted, with nothing on their heads; their hair long, the face broad and round, their colour is white, and they are small of stature. Their faith is Pagan, but they are of that most gloomy class of Calicut called *Poliar* and *Hirava*; they are very weak of understanding, and in strength they have no vigour, but live like beasts. Nothing grows here but nutmegs and some fruits. The trunk of the nutmeg is formed like a peach-tree, and produces its leaves in like manner; but the branches are more close, and before the nut arrives at perfection the mace stands round it like an open rose, and when the nut is ripe the mace clasps it, and so they gather it in the month of September; for in this island the seasons go as with us, and every man gathers as much as he can, for all are common, and no labour is bestowed upon the said trees, but nature is left to do her own work. These knots are sold by a measure, which weighs twenty-six pounds, for the price of half a *carlino*. Money circulates here as in Calicut. It is not necessary to administer justice here, for the people are so stupid that if they wished to do evil they would not know how to accomplish it. At the end of two days my companion said to the Christians: "Where do the cloves grow?" They answered: "That they grew six days' journey hence, in an island called Monoch, and that the people of that island are beastly, and more vile and worthless than those of Bandan." At last we determined to go to that island be the people what they might, and so we set sail, and in twelve days arrived at the said island.

DELL' ISOLA DI MALUCH DOUE NASCONO LI GAROFANI-- CAP. XXV.

Smontammo in questa isola di Maluch, laqual e molto piu piccola di Bandan, ma la gente e peggiore, & viuono pur a quel modo, & sono piu bianchi, & l' aere e vn poco piu freddo, qui nascono li garofani & in molte altre isole circouicine, ma sono piccole & dishabitate, l' arboro delli garofani e proprio come l' arboro del busso, cioe cosi folto, & la sua foglia e quasi come quella della canella, ma vn poco piu tonda, & e di quel colore come gia vi dissi in Zeilan laqual e quasi come la foglia del lauro. Quado sono maturi, li detti huomini sbattono li garofani con le canne, & mettono sotto al detto arbore alcune stuore p raccoglierli, la terra doue sono questi arbori e come arena, cioe di quel medesimo colore, no pero che sia arena, il paese e volto verso mezzodi, & di qui non si vede la stella tramontana. Veduto che hauemmo questa isola, & questa gente, dimandammo alli christiani, se altro v' era da vedere, ci risposero, vediamo vn poco in che modo vendono questi garofani, trouammo che si vendeuano il doppio piu che le noci moscate, pure a misura, perche quelle persone non intendono pesi.

THE CHAPTER CONCERNING THE ISLAND OF MONOCH, WHERE THE CLOVES GROW.

We disembarked in this island of Monoch, which is much smaller than Bandan; but the people are worse than those of Bandan, but live in the same manner, and are a little more white, and the air is a little more cold. Here the cloves grow, and in many other neighbouring islands, but they are small and uninhabited. The tree of the clove is exactly like the box tree--that is, thick, and the leaf is like that of the cinnamon, but it is a little more round, and is of that colour which I have already mentioned to you in Zeilan (Ceylon), which is almost like the leaf of the laurel. When these cloves are ripe, the said men beat them down with canes, and place some mats under the said tree to catch them. The place where these trees are is like sand--that is, it is of the same colour, not that it is sand. The country is very low* (meaning perhaps as to latitude), and the north star is not seen from it. When we had seen this island and these people, we asked the Christians if there was anything else to see. They replied: "Let us see a little how they sell these cloves." We found that they were sold for twice as much as the nutmegs, but by measure, because these people do not understand weights.

(*Footnote. Those critics who think that Barthema never visited the Spice Islands have no doubt given good reasons for believing so. We do not know their reasons; but, if the passage which has been translated--*The country is very low*--has in any way given strength to their arguments, it ought not to have done so, for it is not to be found with that meaning in the Italian text. It is in fact, we believe, a wrong translation, *Volto verso* having been read *Molto basso*.)

Our travellers then agree to visit Java, "the largest island in the world." They proceed by way of Borneo, in order to "take a large ship, for the sea is more rough."

IN CHE MODO LI MARINARI SI GOUERNANO NAUIGANDO VERSO L' ISOLA GIAUA--CAP. XXVII.

Fornita che fu la noleggiata naue di vettouaglia, pigliammo il nostro cammino verso la bella isola chiamata Giaua, allaquale arriuammo in cinque giorni, nauigando pure verso mezzo giorno, il padrone di detta naue portaua la bussola con la calamita ad vsanza nostra, & haueua vna charta, laquel era tutta rigata per lungo & per trauerso: dimando il mio compagno alli christiani, poi che noi abbiamo perso la tramontana, come si gouerna costui, euui altra stella tramotana che questa, con laqual noi nauighiamo? li christiani ricercorono il padron della naue questa medesima cosa, & egli ci mostro quattro o cinque stelle bellissime, infra lequalli ve n' era vna, qual disse ch' era all' incontro della nostra tramontana; ch' egli nauigando seguiva quella, pche la calamita era acconcia & tiraua alla tramontana nostra, ci disse anchora che dell' altra banda di detta isola verso mezzo giorno vi sono alcune genti, lequali nauigano con le dette quattro o cinque stelle che sono per mezza la nostra tramontana, & piu ci disse, che di la dalla detta isola si nauiga tanto che trouano che il giorno non dura piu che quattro hore, & che iui era maggior freddo, che in luogo del mondo. Vdendo questo noi restammo molto contenti & satisfatti.

THE CHAPTER SHOWING HOW THE MARINERS MANAGE THE NAVIGATION TOWARDS THE ISLAND OF GIAVA.

When the chartered vessel was supplied with provisions we took our way towards the beautiful island called Giava, at which we arrived in five days, sailing towards the south. The captain of the said ship carried the compass with the magnet after our manner, and had a chart which was all marked with lines, perpendicular and across. My companion asked the Christians: "Now that we have lost the north star, how does he steer us? Is there any other north star than this by which we steer?" The Christians asked the captain of the ship the same thing, and he showed us four or five stars, among which there was one which he said was *contrario della* (opposite to) our north star, and that he sailed by the north because the magnet was adjusted and subjected to our north. He also told us that on the other side of the said island, towards the south, there are some other races, who navigate by the said four or five stars opposite to ours; and moreover they gave us to understand that beyond the said island the day does not last more than four hours, and that there it was colder than in any other part of the world. Hearing this we were much pleased and satisfied.

The information furnished above is valuable and interesting; it requires however careful examination and a more accurate translation if we are to judge of its true meaning.

The last short chapter suggests four leading questions, as follows:

1. Was the padron of the ship they had chartered a Moorish or a Malay captain?

2. What sort of compass did he use?

3. What kind of chart did he use?

4. What country to the south of Java did he refer to?

In answer to the first question, we may notice that the Persian merchant seeking information from the captain asks the Christians to address him. Now the Christians had been acting as guides to the Persian and his friend Barthema, they had been in these regions before, and could no doubt speak the Malay language. We may conclude therefore that the padron was a Malay, for had he been an Arab or Moor the Persian merchant could have asked the captain himself.

In answer to the second question, we should say that the compass with the magnet after *our* manner was one of European workmanship, a compass in which the magnet or needle pointed to the north. We have seen* that in Asiatic compasses generally, the needle pointed to the south; the mention therefore of the fact that the captain's compass was ad usanza *nostra*--i.e. with the needle pointing to the north, as in European compasses--shows plainly that the case was an extraordinary one. Moreover this is corroborated by the captain's answer, in which he refers to the star which is (*all' incontro della nostra tramontana*) opposite to *our* north star. This south star was the one he navigated by, because the magnet of his compass pointed to *our* north: *perche la calamita era acconcia & tirava alla tramontana nostra.*

(*Footnote. Chapter 3.)

This sentence has been translated wrong in the Hakluyt Society's edition. The Italian text does not say that he sailed by the north; on the contrary it clearly says, & ch' egli navigando seguiva quella: and that he navigating followed it, i.e. that particular star of the Southern Cross.

The third question suggested refers to the charts used. It was no doubt an Arabian chart, unless the Javanese and Malays had charts of their own, which is a difficult point to settle, and which involves also the possibility of Chinese charts having been used.

One thing however is almost certain, and that is that the chart used had the south at the top. It may have resembled therefore the 1542 chart of the *Sea of Orient*. It was also like this chart and other charts of the period in being all marked with lines perpendicular and across.*

(*Footnote. Shakespeare in *Twelfth Night* alludes to a chart of this description when he makes Maria say to Malvolio--"He does smile his face into more lines than are in the new map with the augmentation of the Indies.")

The fourth question: "What country to the south of Java did the Javanese captain allude to?" is easily answered, since no country except

Australia could be meant. The notes given in the Hakluyt Society's edition of Barthema's travels concerning this particular question are of great interest; we shall therefore give them here in full. These notes were the result of a communication of G.P. Badger to Markham and Major for information.

Says C.R. Markham, the Honorary Secretary of the Hakluyt Society:

"This sentence is very important if it should point to latitudes on a line with or south of Australia. The point where the shortest day would only last four hours would be 15 degrees south of the southern point of Van Diemen's Land. It is most improbable that the Malay skipper should have been so far south; yet his statements indicate a knowledge of countries as far south at least as Australia."

R.H. Major's answer to the editor's query is as follows:

"Vague as this sentence is, it either means nothing, or it contains information of very great importance. It is difficult to suppose that the Malay skipper should have been so far south as the Great Southern Continent; yet it is more difficult to believe him capable of describing a phenomenon natural to these high latitudes, except from his own observation, or that of other navigators of that early period. But even should we feel disposed to withhold our belief in the probability of an event so astonishing as this would be, there yet remains the almost unavoidable conclusion that Australians are alluded to in the description of people to the south of Java who navigate by the four or five stars, doubtless the constellation of the Southern Cross. This reference to Australia is the more remarkable that it precedes in time even those early indications of the discovery of that country which I have shown to exist on manuscript maps of the first half of the sixteenth century, although the discoverers' names, most probably Portuguese, and the date of the discovery as yet remain a mystery." 1863.

DELLA ISOLA GIAUA, DELLA FEDE, ETC.

Seguendo adunque il camin nostro, in cinque giorni arriuammo a questa isola Giaua, nella quale sono molti reami, li Re delli quali sono gentili, la fede loro e questa, alcuni adorano gl' idoli come fanno in Calicut, & alcuni sono che adorano il Sole, altri la Luna, molti adorano il Bue, gran parte la prima cosa che scontrano la mattina, & altri adorano il Diauolo al modo che gia vi dissi, questa isola produce grandissima quantita di seta, parte al modo nostro, & parte ne i boschi sopra gli arbori saluatichi, qui si truouano li migliori & piu fini smeraldi del mondo, et oro & rame in gran quantita grano assaissimo al modo nostro, & frutti bonissimi, ad vsanza di Calicut, si truouano in questa paese carni di tutte le sorti ad vsanza nostra, credo che questi habitanti siano i piu fedeli huomini del mondo, sono bianchi, & di altezza come noi, ma hanno il viso assai piu largo di noi, gli occhi grandi & verdi, il naso molto ammaccato, & li capelli lunghi, qui sono vccelli in grandissima moltitudine, & tutti differenti dalli nostri, & eccetto li pauoni, tortore & cornacchie negre, le quali tre sorti sono come le nostre. Fra queste genti si fa grandissima giustitia, & vanno vestiti all' apostolica, di panni di seta, ciambellotto, & di bombagio, & non vsano troppe armatura, perche non combattono, saluo quelli che vanno por mare, iquali portano alcuni archi, & la maggior pte freccie di canna, accostumano anchora alcune cerbottane, cole quali tirano freccie attossiccate, & le tirano con la bocca, & ogni poco che faccino di sangue, muore la persona, qui non vi usa artiglieria di sorte alcuna, & manco le sanno fare, questi mangiano pane di grano, alcuni altri anchora mangiano came di castrati, o di ceruo, o vera di porco salnaticho, & altri mangiana pesci & frutti.

THE CHAPTER CONCERNING THE ISLAND OF GIAVA OF ITS FAITH, ETC.

Following then our route, in five days we arrived at this island of Giava, in which there are many kingdoms, the kings of which are Pagans, Their faith is this: some adore idols as they do in Calicut, and there are some who worship the sun, others the moon; many worship the ox; a great many the first thing they meet in the morning; and others worship the devil in the manner I have already told you. The island produces an immense quantity of silk, part in our manner and part wild, and the best emeralds in the world are found here, and gold and copper in great quantity; very much grain like ours, and excellent fruits like those of Calicut. Animal food of all kinds like ours is found in this country. I believe that these inhabitants are the most trustworthy men in the world; they are white and of about our stature, but they have the face much broader than ours, their eyes large and green, the nose much depressed, and the hair long. The birds here are in great multitudes, and all different from ours, excepting the peacocks, turtle-doves, and black crows, which three kinds are like ours. The strictest justice is administered among these people, and they go clothed *all' apostolica* in stuffs of silk, camelot, and cotton, and they do not use many arms, because those only fight who go to sea. These carry bows, and the greater part darts of cane. Some also use *zarabottane* (blow pipes), with which they throw poisoned darts; and they throw them with the mouth, and however little they draw blood the (wounded) person dies. No artillery of any kind is used here, nor do they know at all how to make it. These people eat bread made of corn, some also eat the flesh of sheep, or of stags, or indeed of wild hogs, and some others eat fish and fruits.

COME IN QUESTA ISOLA LI UECCHI SI UENDONO DA FIGLIUOLI OUERO DA PARENTI, ET POI SE LI MANGIANO--CAP. XXIX.

Vi sono huomini in questa isola che mangiano carne humana, hanno questa costume, che essendo il padre vecchio, di modo che non possi far piu essercitio alcuno, li figliuoli, ouer li parenti, lo mettono in piazza a vendere, & quelli che lo comprano, l' ammazzano, & poi se lo mangia no cotto, et se alcun giouane venisse in gran de infirmita, che paresse alli suoi che 'l fusse per morire di quella, il padre ouero fratello del infermo, l' amazzano, & no aspettano che 'l muora, & poi che l' hanno morto, lo vendono ad altre persone per mangiare, stupefatti noi di simil cose, ci fu detto da alcuni mercatanti del paese. O poueri Persiani, perche tanto bella carne lasciate mangiar alli vermi? inteso questo subito il mio compagno disse, presto presto andiamo alla nostra naue, che costoro piu non mi giungeranno in terra.

THE CHAPTER SHOWING HOW IN THIS ISLAND THE OLD PEOPLE ARE SOLD BY THEIR CHILDREN OR THEIR RELATIONS, AND AFTERWARDS ARE EATEN.

The people in this island who eat flesh, when their fathers become so old that they can no longer do any work, their children or relations set them up in the marketplace for sale, and those who purchase them kill them and eat them, cooked. And if any young man should be attacked by any great sickness, and that it should appear to the skilful that he might die of it, the father or the brother of the sick man kills him, and they do not wait for him to die. And when they have killed him they sell him to others to be eaten. We being astonished at such a thing some merchants of the country said to us: "O you poor Persians, why do you leave such charming flesh to be eaten by the worms?" My companion hearing this immediately exclaimed: "Quick, quick, let us go to our ship, for these people shall never more come near me on land!"

Before leaving Java, where our travellers evidently landed at some out-of-the-way and comparatively uncivilized place, the Christians, who accompanied them, said to Barthema: "O, my friend, take this news (the news of the cruelty of the people) to your country, and take this other also which we will show you. Look there, now that it is midday, turn your eyes towards where the sun sets." To which Barthema remarks for himself and his companion (the Persian merchant): "And raising our eyes we saw that the sun cast a shadow to the left more than a *palmo*. And by this we understood that we were far distant from our country, at which we remained exceedingly astonished. And, according to what my companion said, I think that this was the month of June; for I had lost our months, and sometimes the name of the day...Having remained in this Island of Giava altogether fourteen days, we determined to return back, because, partly through the fear of their cruelty in eating men, partly also through the extreme cold, we did not dare to proceed further, and also because there was hardly any other place known to them (the Christians).

"Wherefore we chartered a large vessel, that is, a giunco, and took our way outside the islands towards the east, because on this side there is no archipelago, and the navigation is more safe..."

They arrived at *Malacha*, and Barthema proceeding homeward after leaving Calicut, met at Cannanore Don Lorenzo, the son of Don Francisco de Almeyda, the Portuguese Viceroy, who questioned him on the state of affairs at Calicut. Barthema was then escorted to the Viceroy, then in Cochin...On the 12th of March 1506 the Indian fleet, of 209 sails, set out from Pannani, Calicut, Capogat, Pandarani and Tormapatan to meet the Portuguese. Barthema says: "When we saw this fleet, which was on the 16th of the month above mentioned (March), truly, seeing so many ships together, it appeared as though one saw a very large wood. We Christians always hoped that God would aid us to confound the Pagan faith. And the most valiant knight, the captain of the (Portuguese) fleet, son of Don Francisco dal Meda, Viceroy of India, was here with eleven ships, amongst which there were two galleys and one brigantine."...They fought, and the Moors were defeated with great slaughter. Barthema afterwards, for a period of eighteen months, acted as factor to the Portuguese at Cochin, and then returned to Europe by the Cape of Good Hope and Portugal, arriving in Rome after an absence from his country of about five years.

CHAPTER 20. A.D. 1506 TO 1511.
HUNT-LENOX GLOBE. RUYSCH'S MAPPAMUNDI OF 1507 TO 1508.

We shall now describe, as being the next in chronological order, the Lenox globe, recently found. Mr. C.H. Coote, of the British Museum, in his historical introduction to Henry Stevens' *Johann Schoner*,* (page xii. line 8) remarks: "As there are several misleading narratives of this globe, we will here insert Mr. Stevens' own account of it. He writes as follows:

(*Footnote. Johann Schoner, Professor of Mathematics at Nuremberg etc. London 1888.)

"In 1870, while residing at the Clarendon in New York, I dined one evening with Mr. R.M. Hunt, the architect of the Lenox Library, a son of my father's old friend, Jonathan Hunt, who represented the State of Vermont in Congress from 1827 to 1832. While talking on library conveniences and plans I chanced to notice a small copper globe, a child's plaything, rolling about the floor. On inquiry I was told that he picked it up in some town in France for a song, and now, as it opened at the equator and was hollow, the children had appropriated it for their amusement. I saw at once by its outlines that it was probably older than any other globe known, except Martin Behaim's at Nuremberg, and perhaps the Laon globe, and told Mr. Hunt my opinion of its geography, requesting him to take great care of it, for it would some day make a noise in the geographical world. Subsequently I borrowed it for two or three months, studied it, took it to

Washington, exhibited it to Dr. Hilgard and others at the Coast Survey Office, and employed one of the draughtsmen there to project it in a two-hemisphere map, with a diameter of the original, about four and a half inches, at a cost to me of 20 dollars. On returning to New York I delivered it into the hands of Mr. Hunt, telling him that it was unquestionably as early as 1510, and perhaps 1505; and was, in historical and geographical interest, second to hardly any other globe, small as it was, and concluded by recommending him, when he and his children had done playing with it, to present it to the Lenox Library, the plans of which he was then engaged upon. I also told Mr. Lenox of it and its value, and recommended him to keep his eye upon it, and secure it if possible for preservation in his library. My pains and powder were not thrown away. Not long after Mr. Hunt presented it to the library, and from that time, it has been known and styled as the Hunt-Lenox Globe. On my return to London I showed my drawing of it to my friend Mr. C.H. Coote of the map department of the British Museum, and lent it to him for the reduced facsimile in his article on GLOBES in the new edition of the *Encyclopaedia Britannica*. Thus the Hunt-Lenox Globe won its (first) geographical niche in literature."*

(*Footnote. Recollections of Mr. James Lenox of New York, 1886 pages 140 to 143.)

Mr. Henry Stevens assigns the date 1506/1507 to this globe,* whereas Mr. Harrisse brings it under the date of *about* 1511.

(*Footnote. See Johann Schoner etc. by Henry Stevens; edited with an introduction and bibliography by C.H. Coote, page xii.)

It certainly bears signs of an early date in that portion of it that claims more especially our attention. The protuberant part of the south-east coast of Africa which in the earlier Behaim globe extends in such an extraordinary way eastward is, in this globe, cut off, and forms an island which may have been intended for Madagascar. In the engraving of this part of the east coast of Africa due notice had evidently been taken of the Portuguese navigations through the Mozambique channel, and along the eastern coasts of Africa to Calicut.*

(*Footnote. This coast was already set down correctly in Juan de la Cosa's map of 1500.)

Madagascar, discovered in 1506, if known to have been discovered at the time the globe was engraved, and intended to be represented by this severed portion of Behaim's Africa, bears no name. This nameless island nevertheless, lying as it does in a more northerly situation than Behaim's protuberant part of Africa, would lead one to believe that it was meant for Madagascar. To the east, in the same longitude as in Behaim's globe, we find Marco Polo's Madagascar; but its length, contrary to the direction that it assumes in Behaim's representation, runs north and south, as it should. Between Madagascar and the western coast of Australia, which bears the name of *Loac Provincia*, there is a curious continental land that has been taken by some critics as a representation of Australia. It lies too far to the west to warrant this conclusion, unless we consider the dotted line as an erroneous addition; but even then, if we suppose the eastern coastline of the nameless continental land to have been intended for the western coastline of Australia, the position of this coastline would be too far to the south. The western coasts of Australia bear an inscription which appears for the first time in the southern hemisphere. *Loac Provincia* is the inscription we refer to. What is the origin of this name as applied to these regions? Is it a corruption of Fra Mauro's *Lago Regnum*, or is it derived from Marco Polo's *Loach?* It is evidently intended for one of the two; but it is difficult to say which the cartographer intended it for. It gave rise, we believe, to the use of the term *Lucach* and *Beach* (a corruption of Lucach) as applied by G. Mercator and his school to the Australian continent, for we shall find it set down on G. Mercator's epochal mappamundi of 1569, and copied by many subsequent cartographers until the Dutch altered the name of the Australian continent to *New Holland*. Seilan is represented to the east of Loac Provincia, corresponding with Behaim's *Seylan Insula*. In the three nameless islands, above the 20th degree of latitude and between *Madagascar* and *Loac Provincia*, we see an embodiment of those three islands which have been called the *three Arabian Islands*,* and which, on maps that allow a more detailed nomenclature, bear the names of *Dina Morare*, or Moraze; *Dimo baz*, or Margabim; and *Dina Aroby*, or Arobi--corruptions of the Arabian names *Diva Moraze*, *Diva Margabim*, and *Diva Arobi*; and which, in our opinion, correspond with Bourbon, Mauritius and Rodriguez.

(*Footnote. Memoire Geographique sur la Mer des Indes, par J. Codine; Paris 1868 chap. v. In a lengthy and remarkably clever dissertation on the origin of the charting and naming of these islands Mr. J. Codine comes to the conclusion (see page 155) that *Dina Morare* corresponds with the *Banc de*

Nazareth, Dimo baz with *Bourbon*, and *Dina Aroby* with *Mauritius*.)

The small size of this copper globe, only 127 mm. diameter, is the reason for the scarcity of names on it. It will be observed, nevertheless, by comparing it with Behaim's configurations, that many of the names may be restored. The two nameless large islands, *par exemple*, in 165 and 180 longitude, correspond with Behaim's *Java Major*. In about twenty or thirty degrees east of these two islands, and therefore at a distance answering approximately to New Guinea, and on the parallel of New Guinea, appears the legend *Terra de Brazil*. This *Terra de Brazil* is however set down on a fictitious westerly prolongation of the South American continent, whereas the real Brazil occurs more than eighty degrees away to the east, bearing its early name of *Terra Sanctae Crucis*.* The probabilities are in favour of this *Land of Brazil* being intended for New Guinea.

(*Footnote. See chap. 18. Andrea Corsali's Description of Terra de Piccinacoli.)

RUYSCH'S MAPPAMUNDI, A.D. 1507/1508.

There has been various opinions expressed as to the origin of Ruysch's Mappamundi. C.H. Coote of the British Museum says: "The Ruysch map of Rome, 1507/1508, is of the *Spanish* school."*

("Footnote. Johann Schoner, by H. Stevens, page xxi. l. 11.)

Harrisse on the contrary says*: "The basis of *the entire map* was a purely Lusitanian planisphere," and further adds however, "Now, was the model followed by Ruysch a purely Lusitanian chart, or one made in Germany with Portuguese elements? Our opinion is that Ruysch has copied merely a Lusitano-Germanic map. Our reasons are based upon the fact that Ruysch inscribed an erroneous name, which was certainly taken from the Latin account of the *cosmographiae introductio*, first printed at St. Diey, in Lorraine, in May 1507, namely: Omnium Sanctorum abbatiam. As we have frequently proved, none of the Lusitanian charts known commit that extraordinary mistake, which may be considered as the touchstone of Lusitano-Germanic maps. The Portuguese charts all inscribe A BAIA *de todos sanctos*, and even A BAIA *de tutti santi*, or

BAIE *de tutti li santi*, when copied by an Italian cartographer. That is, the Bay and not the *Abbey* of All Saints."

(*Footnote. The Discovery of North America by Henry Harrisse, page 449 paragraph 6 and page 452 line 2.)

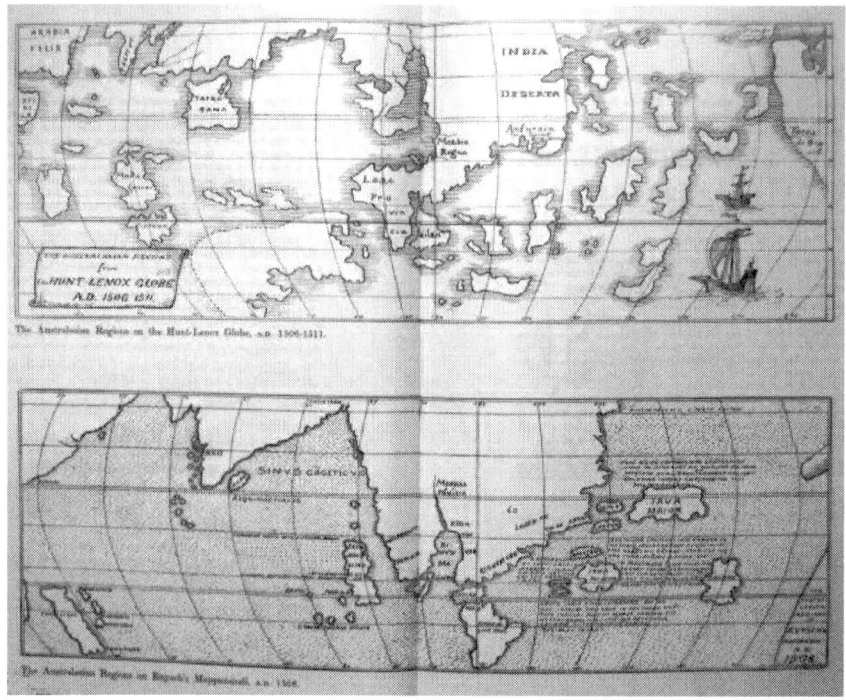

HUNT-LENOX GLOBE AND RUYSCH'S MAPPAMUNDI COMPARED.

Ruysch's Mappamundi is unique in many respects. It presents many improvements on the maps of an earlier date, although certain distortions are very remarkable for their magnitude. In the regions which are connected with our inquiries, for instance, the *Sinus Magnus* is brought down below the equator. This extraordinary misplacement of the China Sea can be accounted for in the following way. The cartographer, recognising no doubt the error of previous charts on which *two malay peninsulas* were represented (see preceding maps), rejected one of these representations; but in doing so he preserved the wrong one, extending to the tropic of Capricorn, the logical sequence being to represent the *Sinus Magnus* to the east of it.

Sumatra, which had been grafted on the West Australian coasts and connected with the duplicate Malay Peninsula on earlier charts, is now separated from the continental bogus prolongation and assumes a greater likeness to the real Sumatra, although retaining its erroneous position, its southern parts being traversed by the tropic of Capricorn.*

(*Footnote. Galvano informs us (Discoveries of the World, page 106 line 3) that in the year 1506, "Tristan de Acuna and Alfonso de Albuquerque went vnto Mossambique, and Aluaro Telez ran so far that he came to the Island of Sumatra, and so back againe vnto the Cape of Guardafu; hauing discouered many islands, sea, and land neuer seene before that time of any Portugall." This discovery of Sumatra is recorded in a legend set down to the west of Sumatra, and the date of 1507 is given as the date of the discovery. Was it the western coast of Australia on which Alvaro Telez was driven?)

It bears the name of *Taprobana alias Zoilon*, thus suggesting *Ceylon* as another name for *Taprobana*, whereas the true Ceylon under the name of *Ceilam* is set down in its correct position and size to the south-east of the Indian Peninsula.

The *Seylan Insula* of Behaim and *Seilan* of the Hunt-Lenox globe still retains its position corresponding to the western parts of Australia; it is called *Seylan insule pars* twice, and that part of the Indian Ocean that laves its western shores is set down as the *Seylan Oceanus*.

The South Pacific Ocean of modern charts is studded with Marco Polo's islands, *Iava maior, Iava minor, Sodur, Candur, pevtan, Nevca, agama*, and *Candyn*.

On the continent of Asia eastwardly we notice LO* and LOACH AC, already placed in the southern hemisphere in the Hunt-Lenox globe, and which, in later maps, will appear on a southern continent altered to *Lucach* and *Beach*.

(*Footnote. With reference to LO and LOACH AC, R.H. Major in his Prince Henry the Navigator, page 307 line 26, makes the following remark: "Colonel Yule has shown that the country meant by *Locach* was *Lo-kok*, or the kingdom of *Lo*, which, previous to the middle of the fourteenth century, formed the lower part of what is now Siam.")

An important feature of this map--which we believe to be of Portuguese, not Spanish origin--is that it shows signs of having been compiled, in parts, of Moorish or Arabian charts or descriptions.

This is observable in the names given to various islands to the west of Australia; Madagascar, for instance, is called *Camaeocada*, an evident corruption from *Camar diva*, Island of the Moon; *Dinanorca, Dinarobin* and *Maroabyn* are corruptions of *Diva Moraze, Diva Arobi,* and *Diva Margabym.*

On the subject of these and other islands of the Indian Ocean visited by the Malays and charted by the Arabs, Mr. J. Codine, in his valuable Memoire Geographique sur la Mer des Indes, page 153, 2nd paragraph, says:

L'existence, au milieu de la Mer des Indes, d'iles connues des Maures, est tout a coup revelee par leur figuration sur des mappemondes du commencement du seizieme siecle, les indications ont ete recueillies des recits oraux de quelques marins marchands de la Mer des Indes, et surtout des cartes de ces marins, trouvees dans les navires Maures dont s'emparerent les Portugais qui furent maitres de cette mer aussitot qu'ils y parurent. The existence, in the middle of the Indian Ocean, of islands known to the Moors, is suddenly revealed by their appearance on maps of the world of the beginning of the sixteenth century. Those indications have been gathered from the verbal recitals of some trading seamen of the Indian Ocean, and especially from the charts of those seamen, found in Moorish vessels seized by the Portuguese, who were masters of these seas as soon as they appeared upon them.

CHAPTER 21. A.D. 1511.
CONQUEST OF MALACCA. D'ABREU'S EXPEDITION TO THE SPICE ISLANDS.

From 1505 to 1507 the Court of Spain was earnestly engaged in the project of finding a direct route to the Spice Islands by the west, and according to Navarrette, on the 29th of June 1508, Vicente Yanez Pinzon and Juan Diaz de Solis sailed from San Lucar and explored the coasts of South America from C. St. Augustine to the 40th degree of south latitude.

The Portuguese, on their side, were making rapid progress eastwardly, and Diogo Lopez de Sequeira was commissioned in 1508 to discover Malacca. R.H. Major says*: "On the 11th of September 1509 Sequeira anchored at Malacca, the great emporium of the east, to which were brought cloves from the Moluccas, nutmegs from Banda, sandalwood from Timor, camphor from Borneo, gold from Sumatra and Loo Choo, and gums, spices and other precious commodities from China, Japan, Siam, Pegu, etc. There he established a factory. Fernam de Magalhaens was in this expedition."

(*Footnote. Prince Henry the Navigator page 267.)

After this expedition, which opened the gates to the extreme east, and before the conquest of Malacca in 1511, the Portuguese appear to have penetrated as far as the Spice Islands, but to have kept the matter secret.*

(*Footnote. Pinkerton page 292.)

In 1511 Albuquerque lost no time in sending out an expedition to Sumatra, Java and the Spice Islands. The journals of this important voyage have not been preserved, but Antonio Galvano, the conqueror and apostle of the Moluccas, has left us a detailed description, which we give here:

ANTONIO GALVANO'S DESCRIPTION OF THE FIRST PORTUGUESE EXPEDITION TO THE SPICE ISLANDS.

*

(*Footnote. The Discoveries of the World by Antonio Galvano, Hakluyt Society's Edition page 115.)

In the end of this yeere 1511, Alfonso de Albuquerque sent three ships to the Islands of Banda and Maluco. And there went as generall of them one Antonio de Breu, and with him also went one Francis Serrano; and in these ships there were 120 persons.* [Not more vessels nor men went to discouer New Spain with C. Columbus, nor with Vasco de Gama to India; nor in comparison with these is Maluco less wealthy, nor ought it to be held in less esteem.]

(*Footnote. Dr. E.T. Hamy in his L'Oeuvre Geographique des Reinel et la Decouverte des Molugues says (page 21 note 1): Il y avait, en outre, huit esclaves sur chaque bord pour le service des pompes. For further particulars concerning this important expedition we refer the critic to Dr. Hamy's interesting paper.)

They passed through the Streight of Saban, and along the Island of Samatra, and [in sight of] many others, leauing them on the left hand, towards the east; and they called them the Salites. They went also to the Islands of Palimbam* and Lusuparam, from whence they sailed by the noble Island of Iaua, and they ran their course east, sailing betweene it and the Island of Madura. The people of this island are very warlike and strong, and doe little regard their liues [as any known in the world]. The women also are there hired for the warres; and they fall out often together, and kill one another, as the Mocos doe (and they contrive that cocks should fight with spurs, as their principal diversion is blood-shedding), delighting onely in shedding of blood.

(*Footnote. The district of Palembang and other southern parts of Sumatra were long believed to be separate islands. We find the southern parts of Sumatra split up into islands in Fra Mauro's Mappamundi 1547 (see Chapter 9), and as late as 1784, in Marsden's Sumatra, "the district of Palembang is still believed to form an island. In Pedro Reinel's chart of 1517, a southern section of Sumatra bears the name *Ilha de Jaavaa*, and Dr. E.T. Hamy, describing Reinel's chart, and recognising that cartographer's error, says: C'est pour nous, sans le moindre doute, le pays de Palembang avec le district des Lampongs, considere par le geographe Portugais, comme une terre distincte du reste de Sumatra, erreur qui s'explique aisement par la nature meme des atterrages formes de vastes plaines, basses et marecageuses, s'etendant au de la du large estuaire de Banjou Assin.)

Beyond the Island of Iaua they sailed along by another called Bali; and then came also vnto others called Aujaue,* Cambaba, Solor, Galav or Guliam, Mallua, Vitara, Rosalanquin, and Arus, from whence are brought delicate birds, which are of great estimation because of their feathers.

(*Footnote. The island called here *Aujaue* is named Anjano in the Portuguese text of Galvano. It corresponds with Lomboc. Dr. E.T. Hamy suggests Rindjani (L'Oeuvre Geographique des Reinel et la Decouverte des Moluques, page 23 note 2), the name of the volcanic peak in Lomboc, as the origin of *Aujaue* or *Anjano*. We fear the similarity of names in this instance is only coincidental. It is probable that Galvano in his invaluable work--*Tratado que compos o nobre & notauel capitao Antonio Galuao, dos diuersos & desuayrados caminhos, por onde nos tempos passados a pimenta & especearia veyo da India as nossas partes, & assi de todos os descobrimentos antigos & modernos, que sao feitos ate a era de mil & quinhentos & cincoenta, com os nomes particulares das pessoas que os fizeram: & em que tempos & as suas alturas, obra certo muy notauel & copiosa*--which was finished towards 1553, consulted contemporaneous charts for his nomenclature. On some of the earliest charts the original nomenclature of the islands visited by D'Abreu and Serrano had already suffered mutilation and corruption, due no doubt to bad reading. On a chart of the early assigned date of 1517, only six years therefore after the event we write of, the district of Palembang, mistaken for an island, as in Galvano's description, bears the name of Ilha de Jaavaa, whereas Java proper receives the name of Simbabau. On later maps bearing dates that would still show that they may have been consulted by Galvano, we find the Island of Lomboc bearing the name of Autane (Pierres Desceliers' map of 1550); Aintama (Henry II's map of 1546); an tane (Jean Roze's map of 1542). On these maps the Island of Bali, situated to the west of Lomboc, bears a name that is difficult to reconcile with Bali; in the 1550 and 1546 maps it is bamcha; in the 1542 map it is bacha. This word in the three instances is written with a small b. Now, there is an earlier map called the Dauphin Chart drawn by Pierres Desceliers, and of the assigned date of 1530/1536, which has been copied from a prototype now lost, and on which the apparent names of the two islands in question is *Anda ne Barcha*. That nautical phrase--no boats go here--has no other reference to the Islands of Bali and Lomboc than that which its meaning implies, i.e., that the navigation in those parts was either dangerous or impossible. The difficult nature of the navigation between Bali and Lomboc is a known fact. A few days ago Captain Carpenter, of the Costa Rica Packet, who is now in Sydney, referring to the navigation in those parts, in the presence of Mr. J. Mann, honorary secretary to our Royal Geographical Society, said that many a time he had been compelled to take another and roundabout route owing to the extraordinary rapidity of the tide that flows between Bali and Lomboc. We might give many other proofs on this point were it necessary. At the present stage however, although it is in our opinion almost certain that Galvano's Anjano is a bad reading for Anda ne, we are not so certain about the original location of this phrase Anda ne barcha. Owing to the peculiar distortion of all the maps we have mentioned it may apply to the Gulf of Carpentaria, which offers a different impediment to navigation, that of shallowness. This peculiarity of distortion we allude to may be observed in all the maps in which the Cape York of Australia is connected with the southern shores of Sumbawa, the next island in an easterly direction after leaving Bali and Lomboc. For further information on this subject see our concluding chapter.)

They came also to other islands lying in the same parallel on the south side in 7 or 8 degrees of latitude.*

(*Footnote. Probably the Timor Laut group of Islands.)

And they be so nere the one to the other that they seeme at the first to be one entire and maine land. The course by these islands is above fiue hundred leagues. The ancient cosmographers call all these islands by the name Iauos; but late experience hath found their names to be very diuers, as you see. Beyonde these (it is said) there are other islands, which are inhabited with whiter people going arraied in shirts, doublets and slops, like vnto the Portugals, hauing also money of silver. The gouernours among them doe carrie in their hands red staues, whereby they seeme to have some affinitie with the people of China; and not only these, but there are other islands and people about this place which are redde*; and it is reported that they are of the people of China.*

(*Footnote. *Gentes pintadas*, says the Portuguese text--i.e. painted people-- tattooed.)

(*Footnote. This part of Galvano's description referring to a whiter and more civilized race of people, and also to a tattooed race, is evidently a digression borrowed from the accounts of travellers that visited the Spice Islands shortly after his arrival there as governor. Saavedra in 1528, on his way back to America from the Spice Islands, sailed along the north-east coasts of Papuasia or New Guinea, and again in 1529 he followed the same route. Herrera, in his *Decada* iv. lib. 111 cap. vi., thus describes the portion of their two voyages that refer to our subject: Anduvieron 250 leguas hasta la isla del Oro, grande y de gente negra, con los cabellos crespos...Corrieron 250 leguas hasta dar en otras islas, en altura de 7 [degrees] pobladas de gente blanca, barbuda, que salieron a la nao, amenazando de tirar piedras con las hondas; y fue cosa maravillosa ver en tan poca distancia hombres tan diferentes de color. Hallaron, otras islas pequenes...pobladas de gente morena, con barbas, desnudos...estan en 7 [degrees], mil leguas de Tidore y otras tantas de Nueva Espana. Corrieron al NE, anduvieron 80 leguas, hallaron otras islas bajas y en una de ellas surgieron...Esta gente es blanca, pintados los brazos y cuerpos; las mujeros parecian hermosas, con cabellos negros y largos...Estan estas islas en 8 [degrees] de la banda del N de la linea."

Antonio de Breu and those that went with him tooke their course toward the north, where is a small island called Gumnape* (or Ternate), from the highest place whereof there fall continually into the sea flakes or streams like vnto fire, which is a wonderfull thing to behold.

(*Footnote. *Gumnape* is meant for *Gunong Api*, the native name for volcano or mountain of fire. There are several in these seas. The one referred to is not the one near Ternate, but in the Banda Sea.)

From thence they went to the Islands of Burro and Amboino (and coasted along what is called Muar d' Amboina), and came to an anker in an hauen of it called Guliguli, where they went on land and tooke a village standing by the river, where they found dead men hanging in the houses; for the people there are eaters of man's flesh. Here the Portugals burnt the ship wherein Francis Serrano was, for she was old and rotten. They went to a place on the other side standing in 8 degrees* towards the south, where they laded cloues, nutmegs, and mace, in a junco or barke, which Francis Serrano bought here.

(*Footnote. The Banda Islands are situated in 4 and 5 degrees latitude south. The Portuguese text reads: *banda q'estaa em oito graos da parte do Sul*. Dr. Hamy supposes that in composing Galvano's text, 5 may have been taken for 8, and that the composer substituted the word *oito* for the mistaken cipher.)

They say that not far from the Islands of Banda there is an island where there breedeth nothing else but snakes, and the most are in one caue in the middest of the land (some great and others small go always rolled together). This is a thing not much to be wondered at; for as much as in the Levant Sea, hard by the Isles of Maiorca and Minorca, there is another island of old named Ophinsa, and now Formentera, wherein there is great abundance of these vermine; and in the rest of the islands lying by it there are none.

In the yeere 1512 they departed from Banda toward Malacca, and on the baxos or flats of Lucapinho Francis Serrano perished (was wrecked with his junk) in his junke or barke, from whence escaped (had returned) vnto the Isle of Mindanao (with) nine or ten Portugals which were (went) with him, and the Kings of Maluco sent for them.*

(*Footnote. This sentence has not been understood by Galvano's translator, owing no doubt to the wrong construction given to se perdeo Francisco Serram co o seu junco. The Portuguese text runs thus: No ano de 1512 partiram de Banda pera Malaca, & nos baixos de Lusupino, se perdeo Francisco Serram co o seu junco, donde se tornou ailha de Midanao co 9 ou 10 portugueses q' co ele hia, & os reis d' Maluco madara por eles. We correct the phrase, which should read thus: In the year 1512 they departed from Banda toward Malacca, and on the baxos or flats of Lucapinho Francis Serrano was wrecked with his junk, from whence he escaped unto the Isle of Amboina with nine or ten Portugals which were with him, and the Kings of Maluco sent for them.)

These were the first Portugals that came to the Islands of Cloues, which stand from the equinoctiall line towards the north in one degree, where they lived seuen or eight yeeres. (A. Dabreu made his way to Malacca having discovered all the sea and land above named.)

CHAPTER 22. A.D. 1512 TO 1521.

MAGALHAENS AND SERRANO. FRANCISCO RODRIGUEZ PORTOLANOS.

There is much mystery concerning Magalhaens' and Serrano's doings in the Molucca regions.

With regard to Magalhaens, it has often been asked: Did he or did he not command one of the ships in D' Abreu's expedition to the Moluccas in 1511?

It is said there were three ships in that expedition--D' Abreu's, Serrano's, and, according to De Goes and Correa, the third ship was commanded by Simao Afonso Bisagudo. (Chronica de D. Manoel, 3 3a parte, cap. xxv. fol. 51.)

Neither De Barros, Castanheda, Correa, De Goes nor Galvano mention Magalhaens as having sailed with D' Abreu; but Argensola says that Magalhaens went as captain of the third ship.

D' Abreu, *capitao mor*, commanded the *Santa Caterina*; Francisco Serrao, his second captain, commanded a ship, the name of which is not mentioned; Simao Afonso Bisagudo commanded a lateen caravel, constructed specially for the voyage. The pilots were: Goncalo d'Oliveira, *piloto mor*, Luys Botim, Francisco Rodriguez. A rich merchant of Malacca was allowed to send a junk loaded with merchandise, and an agent to teach the Portuguese the spice trade accompanied the expedition.

The confusion that arose as to the third ship, commanded by Magalhaens, was no doubt due to the fact that the lateen caravel was, by some authors, counted as the third ship, while others either reckoned it as a fourth, or failed to count it at all, setting it down merely as a convoy.

Whatever may have been the origin of the confusion, Magalhaens evidently commanded a ship, and sailed either with the expedition or shortly after, entrusted with some special and secret mission for Albuquerque.

As to his starting Argensola is very explicit, and his evidence is corroborated by other writers. Argensola says:

En este mismo tepo (at this same time), aviendo Magalhaens passado seys cientas leguas adelante hazia Malaca, se hallaua en vnas Islas, desde donde se correspondia co Serrano. El qual, como le auia sucedido ta bien en Ternate co Boleyse, escriuio a su amigo los fauores y riquezas, que del anio recibido, y que per se boluiesse a su compania. Magallanes dexando persuadir, propuso la yda al Maluco: pero en caso que en Portugal no premiassen sus servidos como pretedia, desde donde luego tomaria la derrota de Ternate, co cuyo Reye en nueue anos enriquecio Serrano tanto.*

(*Footnote. Argensola, conquista de las islas Malucas, page 15.

According to the above, Magalhaens may have sailed about the same time (en este mismo tepo) as D' Abreu, and indeed he could not have retarded much, nor spent much time in the vicinity of the Spice Islands, since he was back in Lisbon in 1512, where we find him signing a receipt for a monthly pension on the 12th of June of that year.*

(*Footnote. Book vi. of Moradias da Casa Real, fol. 47 v.)

What were the islands 600 leagues to the east of Malacca, and from which he held communication with Serrano? Six hundred leagues from Malacca would bring him in close proximity to the Spice Islands, and, if allowance is made for strong currents and other matters rendering the computation of distances difficult, Magalhaens may have reached even more distant lands.

There are reasons to believe that, about this time, the Portuguese were in hopes of falling in with the western shores of the *Terra Sanctae Crucis* (South America), for as we have seen it was represented on the charts of the period as lying at no great distance from the Spice Islands, and known since 1503 from Giovanni da Empoli's account as the *Terra Della Vera Croce, ouer del Bresil cosi nominata...nellaqual si fa buona soma di Cassia, & di Verzino.**

(*Footnote. Ramusio, fol. 145 C. Compare with Andrea Corsali's letter concerning the location of the *Costa del Brezil, o Verzino*. See above.)

Dr. Hamy thinks that the islands mentioned as having been reached by Magalhaens may correspond with some point of the north coast of New Guinea, the discovery of which island was attributed, many years later, to Magalhaens by Texeira.*

(*Footnote. On ignore quelles sont ces iles; il pourrait bien se faire qu'elles correspondent a quelque point de la cote nord de la Nouvelle Guinee, dont Texeira, beaucoup plus tard, attribuait a Magellan la decouverte. *L'Oeuvre des Reinel et la decouverte des Moluques*, page 27.)

Serrano's long sojourn of nine years in the Moluccas enabled him to make many voyages and discoveries. At the present time it would be difficult to ascertain what he may or may not have accomplished in this way, for the data to hand are meagre, and the secrecy observed at the time by the Lusitano-Indian Government renders the chances of information turning up very small.*

(*Footnote. With reference to the secrecy observed and enforced Ramusio says in his prefatory *Discorso sopra il libro di Odoardo Barbosa, etc.:...fu sforzato di leuarne via tutta quella parte che nel fine dell' opera trattana delle isole Molucche*. Ramusio, folio 287 F.)

We have copies of passages from letters written by Magalhaens to Serrano, and by the latter to Magalhaens, that throw a little light on the question.

Referring to Serrano's letters, F.H.H. Guillemard, in his *Life of Magellan* (page 71), says:

"From Ternate he (Serrano) wrote many letters to his friends, and especially to Magellan, 'giving him to understand that he had discovered yet another new world, larger and richer than that found by Vasco da Gama.' These letters," says Guillemard, "joined possibly with a personal knowledge of those regions, formed, it may safely be conjectured, no slight inducement to the undertaking of the voyage which ended our hero's life and made his name immortal...The letters written by Magellan to Serrao were found among the papers left at the latter's death. In them he promises 'that he will be with him soon, if not by way of Portugal, by way of Spain,' for to that issue his affairs seemed to be leading." (*Navarette*, volume iv. note v. page lxxiv.; *Barros*, Dec. iii. lib. v. cap. viii.)

Alas! a few years later, Magalhaens, the first of mortals who made the circuit of the world, reaching by the west the regions wherein he had left his friend Serrano, died without meeting him; and Serrano, it is said, perished in the same manner, at the hands of Indians, the very same day as Magalhaens--21st April 1521.*

(*Footnote. Argensola, page 17.)

FRANCISCO RODRIGUEZ' PORTOLANOS.

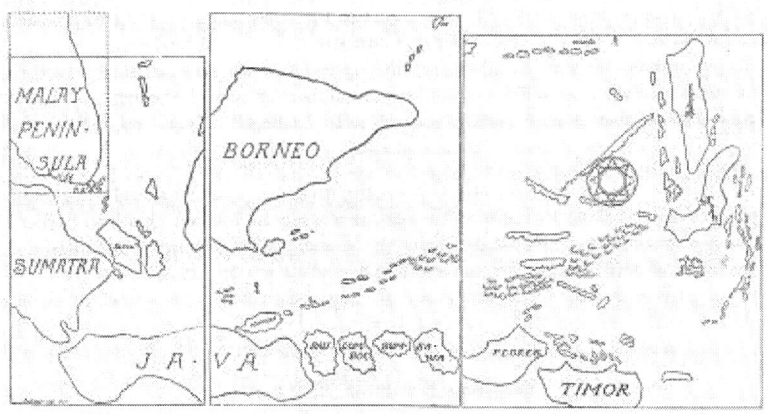

F. Rodriguez' portolanos of East Indian Archipelago.

We have seen that Francisco Rodriguez was one of the pilots of D'Abreu's expedition. He is the author of a set of sailing charts, drafted no doubt during that memorable voyage. These portolanos or sailing charts are of great interest to the Australasian student, not only because they depict for the first time the Molucca Islands, but also because Java, Bali, Lomboc and Sumbawa are set down on them as distinct and separate islands, whereas on a class of maps a little later in date, on which the Australian Continent is represented, some of those islands are indicated as forming part of the northern shores of Australia.

This at first may seem of little importance; it is of great importance however for it shows that, as an accurate knowledge had been obtained of the south coasts of the above-named islands, it was owing to deliberate distortion that they were made to form part and parcel of the southern continent; nor can it be argued that the later charts were not purposely distorted, or that Rodriguez' charting was not known at the time, since, as we can prove, the portolanos in question served as models in the compilation of a prototype from which all the distorted charts of Australia, to which we refer, were copied.

When dealing with the distorted charts, we hope to be able to show satisfactorily, with all the data we have collected on the subject, how and why those old maps were altered.

But let us first examine some of F. Rodriguez' portolanos. There are six in the atlas preserved at Lisbon; they have been reproduced in *outline* in Santarem's collection, and our facsimiles of four of them are taken from that valuable work, a copy of which may be seen in the Sydney Free Public Library. The collection of six sailing charts bears the title Portulan dresse entre les annees 1524 a 1530 par Francisco Rodriguez, pilote portugais qui a fait le voyage aux Moluques. The dates assigned to this atlas, remarks our friend Dr. E.T. Hamy,* were given by Santarem, who ignored that Rodriguez was already at Malacca in 1511.

(*Footnote. L'Oeuvre Geographique des Reinel et la Decouverte des Moluques page 32 note 3.)

Our belief is that Rodriguez' charts of the Moluccas, the earliest ever made by Europeans, are the result of D' Abreu's surveys during his expedition in 1511, or of Joam Lopez Alvrin's voyage in 1513, and that they are, on this account, quite independent from Pedro Reinel's charts, to which the date of 1517 has been assigned.*

(*Footnote. We appear to agree in this respect with Dr. E.T. Hamy, who says in his memoire already quoted: *Rodriguez connait aussi, bien mieux que ses devanciers, les cotes de la Chine et l'une de ses cartes remonte jusqu'a Pekin, dont elle dresse le plan et enseigne la route.* Ou peut se demander dans quelle mesure les contours relativement precis des cartes de Rodriguez n'ont pas ete empruntes par ce pilote a une piece indigene dont Albuquerque lui avait fait faire un extrait pour le roi de Portugal avant son depart avec Abreu.--L'Oeuvre Geographique des Reinel et la Decouverte des Moluques, page 33 note 4. It will be noticed that in the first sentence, which we have [caps], Dr. Barny seems to admit that Rodriguez' charts were not the earliest, since he speaks of his *devanciers*. In the next sentence however he expresses a somewhat different opinion, which we endorse. G.C.)

There are three maps, in the set of six, which are of special interest as connected with our subject. A map of Java, with part of Sumatra; a map of part of Java, with Bali, Lomboc, Sumbawa, etc.; a map of the Spice Islands and Papoia.

The map of Java, with part of Sumatra, bears an inscription* in 7 degrees of latitude south, and in the longitude approximately of Cheribon in modern maps, thus:

Agoada Joham Lopez D'ollunn elle descobrio d'aqui afi Japara.

Which we have rendered:

Watering-place of John Lopez Alvrin, from which place you can discover (see) as far as Japara.

(*Footnote. We had not sufficient space to set down this inscription in our much reduced copy.)

On a clear day the magnificent coast scenery from Cheribon to Japara is one of the well-known sights of Java, so that it is not astonishing to find this hydrographical note on the portolano that we are considering.

Who was this Joham Lopez or Lopiz? We do not know; there is no mention of any such name among the officers of D' Abreu's expedition. Was he a pioneer sent out to these regions to prepare the way for D' Abreu? Was he a pilot on Magalhaens' ship? Who shall say?

Sir Thomas Stamford Raffles, F.R.S., formerly Lieutenant-Governor of Java and its dependencies, and President of the Society of Arts and Sciences at Batavia, in the introduction of his valuable History of Java (page xiv.), gives us, from Barros' Decadas, I expect, the following information, in which Joam Lopez Alvrin's name occurs: "*Nakoda Ismael* returning from the Moluccas with a cargo of nutmegs, his vessel was wrecked on the coast of Java, near Tuban. The cargo of the *Nakoda's* vessel having been saved, JOAM LOPEZ ALVRIN was sent (A.D. 1513) by the Governor of Malacca with four vessels to receive it. Alvrin was well received in all the ports of Java where he touched, but particularly at *Sidayu* belonging to PATEH UNRUG, a Prince, who had been defeated by Fernan Peres at Malacca."

We have noticed particularly the above inscription--in itself not very clear, it must be allowed--because we shall find it repeated on later charts of a distorted type, on which the Australian continent is set down, whereby their connection with Francisco Rodriguez' chart is proved.

The map with part of Java, Bali, Lomboc, Sumbawa, etc. bears the following nomenclature: *Ilha de Madura* (Madura Island); *Agaci* (Gresic); *Ssurabaia* (Surabaia); and the inscription, *A fin da Ilha de Jaoa* (end of the

Island of Java). In later maps this inscription is altered thus: Dauphin Chart, *Fin de Iaoa*; Jean Roze's Chart, *Fin de Iana*. Curiously enough, in later maps, this hydrographical notice is corrupted to *Fideoia*; and on G. Mercator's celebrated large map of the world of 1569 a castellated township is depicted on this eastern extremity of Java, with the name *Fideida*. Bali is called *Ballaram*, Lomboc *Lomboquo*, and Sumbawa is represented as two islands--*Ssimbana* and *Aramaram*. The deep gulf which almost cuts Sumbawa in two, is accountable for this segregation.

The map of the Spice Islands offers this striking feature--that a northwestern portion of New Guinea, or perhaps Gilolo, is marked on it under the name of *Papoia*, which might lead one to conclude that this map is of a much later date, or that--which is much more probable--New Guinea was discovered by D'Abreu and his party.

The hitherto accepted version is that New Guinea was first discovered by Don Jorge de Menezes, who gave it the name of Papua. The account of his voyage, which is to be found in Couto,* is not very precise, the date is given as being either 1528 or 1533; Major fixes the date as 1526.*

(*Footnote. Asia of de Barros, continued by do Couto, 3rd book 3rd chapter 4th decada.)

(*Footnote. Early Voyages to Australia page lxiv.)

CHAPTER 23. A.D. 1515 TO 1517.

THE FRANKFORT-SCHONEREAN GLOBE OF 1515. THE SUNDA AND MOLUCCA ISLANDS AS TRACED IN PEDRO REINEL'S CHART.

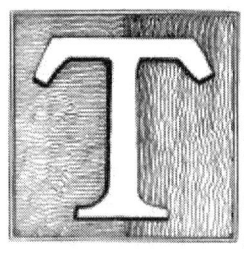

The Spanish still continued their attempts to reach the Spice Islands by the west; and on the 8th of October 1515* Juan Diaz de Solis sailed with that intention. He reached the Rio de la Plata, where "he was killed and eaten up by the natives of the Charruas tribe, before September 1516, when the expedition returned to Spain under the command of Francisco de Torres, his brother-in-law."*

(*Footnote. Herrera, Decada II. ii.)

(*Footnote. Harrisse, The Discovery of North America page 738.)

THE FRANKFORT GLOBE OF 1515.

We arrive now at one of the important geographical monuments of the beginning of the 16th century--The Frankfort-on-the-Main Schonerean globe of 1515. This globe is believed by Dr. Wieser* to be the work of Schoner, hence its name. Our sketch is taken from the reproduction in form of gores in Jomard's collection.* Schoner is the first cartographer to give a more decided form and a different name to the Austral continent already represented in 1506/1511 on the Hunt-Lenox globe, but without a name.

(*Footnote. Wieser, Magalhaes-Strasse page 22.)

(*Footnote. E.F. Jomard, *Les Monuments de la Geographie*; Paris 1854 fol. plates xv. and xvi., entitled: *Globe terrestre de la premiere moitie du seizieme siecle*.)

The Austral continent, supposed by *Andrea Corsali* and others to extend from the region of New Guinea (*Terra de Piccinnacoli*) to the land of *Sanctae Crucis*, then known as the coast of *Bresil* or *Verzino*,* was also known as the *Papagalli terra*--i.e., land of parrots. The origin of this denomination has been supposed to have been given first to Brazil, because either Gaspar de Lemos in 1500, or Pedralvarez Cabral in 1501,* it is not known which, or when, brought some parrots to Europe from Brazil.

(*Footnote. Ramusio, fol. 280 (sic. for 180) c. *Andrea Corsali having described the Spice Islands says*: Et nauigado verso le parti d' Oriente, dicono esserui terra de Piccinnacoli, & e di molti openione che questa terra vada a tenere, & congiungersi per la banda di leuante & mezo giorno, con la costa del Bresil, o verzino, perche per la grandezza di detta terra del verzino, non si e per anchora da tutte la parti discoperta.)

(*Footnote. See Harrisse, The Discovery of North America, page 491.)

On the other hand, Nicolo de' Conti may also have brought back to Europe in 1444 parrots from Australasia, for he describes them in his narrative*; and in those regions, on the famous Fra Mauro Mappamundi of 1457, we find the following legend*: *Item li se trova papaga tutti rossi salvo i piedi et el becco che son zali*: also, you find there parrots all red except their feet and beak, which are yellow.

(*Footnote. See above.)

(*Footnote. See chap. ix. page 44, and chap. 18, Australia the Baptismal Font of Brazil.)

The denomination *Papagalli terra* may have been applied therefore to Australia, and the term *Patalis Regio*, which is found on later maps in connection with *Brasilie Regio*, and, later still, *Psittacorum regio*, may be a corruption of (Pa)Pagalli Regio, the first syllable being dropped, or as we have suggested elsewhere, its origin may be traced to the nomenclature that obtained after Magalhaens' voyage, when *Patalis Regio*, the Latin for *Tierra Patagonia*, may have been given, not only to *Patagonia*, but also to *Tierra del Fuego* and its supposed circumpolar prolongation; unless indeed Schoner borrowed the term from Behaim's globe, on which we find, to the north of the equator it is true, *Patalis regio* or *Potutis regio*.

On the Frankfort map, which we shall now describe, the western coasts of Australia are set down in much the same way as in the preceding maps of this type, the nomenclature being *Lac regnum* and *Coilu regnu*.

The island to the east of Coilu regnu bears the following Latin legend: *Seyla idolatre sut ambulant nude nullum habent bladum Rixo excepto*. Eastward may be noticed Marco Polo's islands. *Java minor in ea sunt octo regna et sunt idolatre, Pentan idolatre sut, Necuram idolatre bestialiter vivunt, Iavva maior variaz Spetierum dives sunt idolatre*, with the addition of nutmegs and pepper *nuces muscata pipe*. The other islands are *Candin*, and the two Pulo Condor Islands, *Sandio* & *Candur*.

On the Asiatic continent may be observed *Loach provin*, just below the equator and between the 135 and 150 degrees of longitude. *Mallaqua* is set down where it is suggested by its termination *Lack* on Behaim's globe. Above Mallaqua may be seen *Egrisillani*, which is a curious corruption of *Christiani*, and refers to Nicolo de' Conti's description of the Nestorian Christians, as does the inscription below the Island of Socotra, *Scoyra Christiana babet*! (habet) *Archiepiscopu*. We find also another curious bad reading referring to San Thome, *ibionidisu S. Thomas*. To the east of this legend will be noticed *Varre regio*, undoubtedly corrupted from *barr in M' barr*, the b and v being interchangeable. In Behaim's globe may be seen *War ein Konigreich* in the same locality, and *Varr Varr regnum* in the British Museum map of 1489.

To the west of the Australasian regions there are fourteen islands, five of which bear no names. The first of those that are named is *Callezuan*, which will be found nameless in earlier maps, and which in later maps is altered to *Callenzuaz*, etc. We have not yet found a meaning for this name, although we suspect it is a variation of Ptolemy's *Caladadrua*. The next island bears the legend: *Tona ibi bombex & porcellana*, and is apparently nameless, unless *Tona* be the remnant of some prototypic name.

The insufficiency of data renders the task of hunting down the origin of names like these not only difficult but risky, as owing to an apparent parity one is liable sometimes to make mistakes. Noticing however the number of words which have suffered mutilation on this otherwise exceedingly instructive globe, we have been led to suspect that this word *Tona* is nothing else but the corruption of the first word that occurs in a legend in this locality on M. Behaim's globe, the word being *Thomas*. To the west of the large island just described we notice the three Arabian islands, which in Ruysch's map, 1507/1508, occur in closer proximity to Madagascar; they are called here: *Dinamora, Dino baz* and *Dina Aroby*. Marco Polo's Madagascar bears the legend: *Madagascar insula no hz rege sunt Sarraceni & Mahumenste*. An eastern prolongation bears the inscription *Sandalos silve*. To the south-west of Madagascar there is an island named *Circobena*; it is nameless on Behaim's globe, and corresponds with *Cirtena* on the Hunt-Lenox globe. It is probably a corruption of *Comor diva*, an alternative Arabian name for Madagascar.

The real Madagascar, discovered by the Portuguese the 10th of August 1506 is set down to the west of Marco Polo's Madagascar, and bears the name of *Dauxety*.

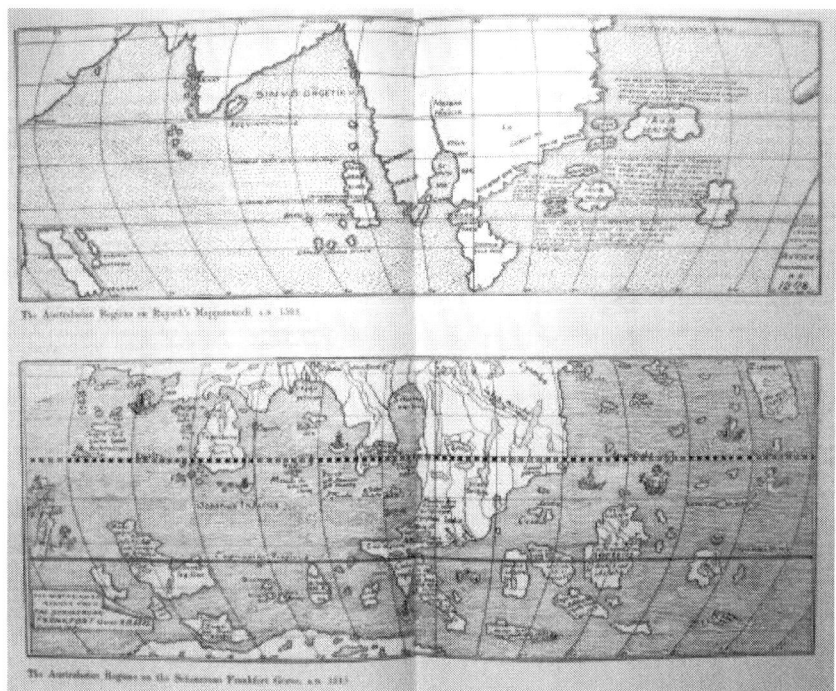

RUYSCH'S MAPPAMUNDI AND SCHONEREAN GORES COMPARED

In connection with this globe and the name Dauxety a strange mistake was made some years ago by a very clever French geographer, who, commenting on its origin and on the various names of Madagascar, said* that the general information that this globe presented was derived from two sources, neither of them Portuguese, since no Portuguese name was to be found on this globe. In the next sentence he said: At some distance from Africa is situated a Dauxety Island, etc. Now, had he known the origin of Dauxety, he would not have said that there was no Portuguese name on this globe, for Dauxety is a corruption of Laurentij, the Latin for San Lourenco, the name given by the Portuguese to Madagascar, discovered by them in the year 1506 on the 10th of August, the feast of St. Laurence.

(*Footnote. Ce globe n'est pas, dans l'ordre chronologique, le premier document utile a consulter, mais il presente un ensemble de renseignements tires de deux sources, toutes deux etrangeres aux Portugais, car aucun nom Portugais n'y figure. A quelque distance de l'Afrique est placee une ile Dauxety dont la forme allongee, les dimensions propres et relatives, et la distance du continent Africain, conviennent parfaitement a Madagascar; c'est bien reellement Madagascar, puisque au nord-ouest de cette ile Dauxety, et dans, la position qui leur convient, sont representees les iles que nous nommons aujourd'hui Comores et qui ont nom: *Comoro*.)

To the south of the regions we have described lies the Polar Continent, which in outline corresponds in a most striking manner with what we know of those regions. It extends north however in several places, to the 40th degree of latitude.

On the portion of this continent that lies to the south of America occurs the legend Brasiliae Regio, and on the same continent, to the south of Australia, a vast lake is depicted surrounded by mountains, with the inscription *Laco int Montaras*, which seems to be a repetition of the *Lac regnum*, situated under the tropic of Capricorn in the Australian regions.

THE SUNDA AND MOLUCCA ISLANDS AS TRACED IN PEDRO REINEL'S CHART.

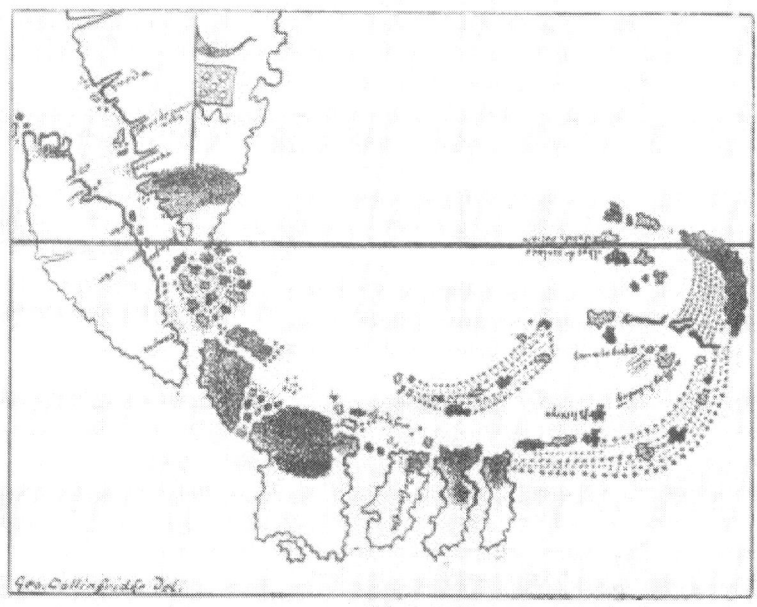

The Sunda and Molucca Islands as traced in Pedro Reinel's chart of the assigned date 1517.

the Sunda and Molucca islands as traced in Pedro Reinel's chart of the assigned date 1517.

Dr. E.T. Hamy, in his interesting memoire L'Oeuvre Geographique des Reinel, read at the Academie des Inscriptions et Belles-Lettres on the 26th of June 1891, describes exhaustively the geographical work of the two Reinels, father and son, with reference especially to the discovery of the Moluccas or Spice Islands. We have borrowed freely in the preceding chapter from that careful and clever memoire, and now we give here a sketch of the map which accompanies it, together with a few remarks on that precious document.

Reinel's map shows to perfection how that constant feature of cartography which we have called the *geographical evolution* obtained.

Referring to the special deformation of certain islands on this map, Dr. Hamy says* that it is remarkable that Java, Sumbawa, Flores and another island of the eastern prolongation extend considerably, all four, in a southerly direction, *thus supplying the first model of those peculiar distortions that will be found reproduced and magnified* in so many Portuguese and French maps.

(*Footnote. Il est remarquable que Java (Simbabau), Sumbawa (Frroresta),

Flores et une autre ile encore de la chaine se prolongent considerablement, toutes quatres, dans la direction du sud, fournissant, ainsi le premier modele de ces deformations speciales que reproduirent en les amplifiant taut de cartes Portugaises et Francaises.)

Strictly speaking, Dr. Hamy is quite right; but we think he will agree with us when we say that it is not exactly the *first model* supplied. In our opinion the FIRST MODEL of those peculiar distortions is to be found on Martin Behaim's globe of 1492.

When Behaim, or Toscanelli, corrected the direction of Fra Mauro's pseudo-equatorial line, or regions, which ran parallel with the Archaic Ocean, and neglecting to perform the same office for Java and its neighbouring isles--left them as they were on the Venetian Mappamundi, instead of giving them the new position that the alteration of the equatorial line required--then was the first model supplied. Thus, subsequently, Java and the other islands assume in most maps a longitudinal, instead of a latitudinal, position. This was a natural consequence of the slow evolutional process. Another reason for the maintenance and amplification of the deformation was the account of the large size of Java given by Marco Polo.

Fra Mauro's *Giava mazor* however seems to have been set down from actual knowledge of its coastlines, so superior are its proportions and the delineation of its shores to the general design of the Javas of later maps, which were merely rough representations jotted down, *errant a l'aventure*, in an ocean unknown to Europeans, and placed according to Marco Polo's descriptions.

Albeit certain outlines of shores, roughly drafted by Arabian, or even perhaps Phoenician, pilots, may have served as a *maquette* for the construction of some of those islands.

Dr. Hamy assigns the date of 1517 to Reinel's map--*puisqu'elle renferme dans ses portions orientales des traces inconnus des cartographes avant le retour d' Abreu de son voyage des Moluques (1512), et la vulgarisation tres imparfaite de ses decouvertes dans les Indes, puis en Europe (1516)* [page 14]--but if D' Abreu was back in 1512, he brought back his maps with him, and may they not have been copied there and then by Reinel? That this one was copied is evident; no sea captain, pilot, or cartographer who had seen the localities charted on this map would make the mistake that Reinel makes in misnaming nearly all the islands represented.

In naming that peculiarly deformed quartette of islands situated midway between Papua and Sumatra, how did he proceed? Was it from east to west, or *vice-versa*? The largest is Java. Then, to the east, we notice two small islands--they are Bali and Lomboc, and have escaped the distortion that their neighbours have suffered. The next island is Sumbawa, then comes Flores. The last of the group of four is made up no doubt of Solor, Adenara and Lomblen.

Now, evidently--and here we agree with Dr. Hamy--our cartographer began too far to the west and set down the name of *Jaavaa* (Java) on that detached section of Sumatra, the Palembang and Lampong territory, and continued his error in an easterly direction by giving to Java the name belonging to Sumbawa, and to Sumbawa that which belonged to Flores, leaving the two last islands nameless. Timor is not represented. The whole representation seems to correspond so exclusively with Galvano's description of D' Abreu's expedition that we are inclined to believe that it is a copy either of D' Abreu's or some of his officers' portolanos.

CHAPTER 24. A.D. 1516 TO 1519.
LINE OF DEMARCATION OF MAGALHAENS AND POPE ALEXANDER VI.

After seven* years' service in India, Magalhaens returned to Europe, where, having distinguished himself on the battlefield, he applied to the King for promotion. His application however was not favourably considered. Events of little importance have sometimes great consequences.

(*Footnote. Gomara gives the length of his Indian service as seven years: Gomara, Histoire General de las Indias cap. xci.)

Faria y Souza remarks* that the refusal of one King to raise the pay of an old and faithful servant thirteen shillings per annum led to endless disagreements with another, to a great loss of profit to the first power of Europe, and to a still greater loss of glory.

(*Footnote. Asia Portugueza, volume I. part iii. chap. v.)

This referred to a refusal on the part of Dom Manoel of Portugal to recognise Magalhaens' long services in the east. In his Life of Magellan F.H.H. Guillemard says*: "It was the custom in those days that all who belonged to the King's household--the criacao de El Rey--should receive a stipend which, though merely nominal in value, corresponded to their rank.*

("Footnote. Life of Magellan, page 72 line 9; and page 77 bottom of page.)

(*Footnote. Osorio, *De Rebus Emmanuelis*, lib. xi. page 327 (Ed. Col. Agrip MDLXXVI.), tells us the origin of this stipend: Olim erat apud Lusitanos in more positum, ut in Regia, qui Regi serviebant ipsius Regis sumptibus alerentur. Cum vero multitudo domesticorum tanta fuisset, difficillimum videbatur cibos tantae multitudini praeparare. Quocirca fuit a Portugallix Regibus statutum, ut sumptum, quem quilibet erat in

Regia facturus, ipse sibi ex regia pecunia faceret. Sic autem factum est, ut cuilibet certa pecuniae summa, singulis mensibus assignaretur.)

MAGALHAENS.

"This stipend was known as the *moradia*. Magellan, borne on the books as moco hidalgo, received a monthly pension of a milreis, and an *alqueire* of barley daily. The *milreis* or dollar, although at that period of considerably greater value, is now worth about 4 shillings 5 pence of our English money. The *alqueire* is as nearly as possible 28 pounds..." And further on: "Doubtless he looked forward with certainty to the coveted rise in the *moradia*--that minute increase which, paltry though it was in actual value, meant so much to those who were of the King's household. Foremost in his mind however must have been the hope of a command--of a return to India. He was doomed to disappointment: Sempre lhe El Rey teve hum entejo--the King always loathed him, Barros tells us (Decadas, Dec. iii. liv. v. cap. viii.) His reception was not more gracious than it had been on the occasion of their last meeting. Dom Manoel turned a deaf ear to his entreaties, and Magellan, cruelly hurt at the ingratitude shown him after his years of honourable service, was left to realise that, so far as his King and country were concerned, his career was over." It is not astonishing therefore to find him a few years later denaturalising himself and making his way to the Court of Spain, for shortly after his interview with the King of Portugal he wrote to Serrano in the Moluccas to tell him that he would be with him soon--"if not by Portugal, then by way of Spain"; which meant if not by the east then by the west. As we have said, events of little importance have sometimes great consequences. After Magalhaens' arrival in Spain in 1517 we find that country disputing with Portugal the possession of the Moluccas. R.H. Major on this subject says*:

(*Footnote. Early Voyages to Australia, page xxxvii.)

"Now, after 1516 or 1517, Spain began to dispute with Portugal the possession of the Moluccas, as being situated within the hemisphere which had been allotted to them by the bull of Pope Alexander VI, dated the 4th of July 1493. This Pope, in consequence of the disputes which had arisen between the Courts of Lisbon and Toledo, had arranged that all the discoveries which might be made on the globe to the east of a meridian one hundred leagues west of the Azores and Cape Verde Islands (which he seemed to think lay under the same meridian), for the space of a hundred and eighty degrees of longitude, should belong to the Portuguese; and that those to the westward of the same meridian, for the same space, should belong to the Spaniards. This division has been since called the line of demarcation of Pope Alexander VI. Don John II however, who was then King of Portugal, being dissatisfied with this bull, which seemed to deprive him of considerable possessions in the west, made another arrangement in the following year with Isabella and Ferdinand of Spain, by which this line was pushed further west, and definitely fixed at three hundred and seventy leagues to the westward of the Cape Verde Islands. This agreement was signed the 4th of June 1494; and it was arranged that in the space of ten months persons should be sent out who were well informed in geography to fix exactly the places through which this line should pass. This engagement once entered upon, no more consideration was given to the sending out competent persons to the places indicated, and the two governments continued their discoveries, each on its own behalf. Under the guidance of Cabral the Portuguese, on the 9th of March 1500, discovered Brazil, which lay in their own hemisphere. Under the guidance of Vincent Yanez Pinzon the Spaniards had in this same or preceding year sailed along the whole of this coast as far as the embouchure of the Oronoco. After this time the line, without further examination, was reckoned to pass by the mouth of the Maranon, or river of the Amazons, which had been already explored, and it is in this part that it is found traced on the Spanish maps of Herrera. The Portuguese, while they took possession of Brazil, continued their discoveries towards the east, and reached the Moluccas, where they established themselves, as we have said, in 1512. The proprietorship of the Spices, which the possession of these islands gave them, produced such considerable profits that it soon excited the jealousy of the Spaniards. The latter pretended that the Moluccas were in the hemisphere which had been allotted to them. This idea was particularly suggested to them by Magellan, who, being discontented with the treatment of King Emanuel, in having refused him an increase of allowance, took refuge about the year 1516 in Spain, and offered his services to the Government of Charles V. Not only did he assert that the hemisphere belonging to the Spaniards comprised the Moluccas, but also the Islands of Java and Sumatra, and a part of the Malay Peninsula. In fact, from the difficulty which then existed in determining longitudes, the discoveries of the Portuguese appeared to appropriate more than one hundred and eighty degrees in this direction, so great was the amount of space given to them in their maps; nevertheless, if we examine modern maps we shall see that, measuring from the mouth of the Maranon, the Moluccas still came within the hemisphere of the Portuguese.

"Cardinal Ximenes, who at that time governed Spain in the absence of Charles V, at the outset received Magellan very well, and Charles V himself afterwards entrusted him with the command of a squadron of five vessels, which, as we know, sailed from San Lucar on the 20th of September 1519, on a western passage in search of the Spice Islands or Moluccas."

CHAPTER 25. A.D. 1520 TO 1522.

VASTNESS OF THE PACIFIC OCEAN GRADUALLY REALISED. PETRUS APIANUS' MAPPAMUNDI OF 1520. MAPPEMONDE LA SALLE, CIRCA 1522. JUAN VESPUCCIUS' MAPPAMUNDI OF 1522/1523. THE FIRST CIRCUMNAVIGATORS.

For all those who cared to investigate the subject, the extent of the South Sea, afterwards to be called the Pacific Ocean, dawned gradually. Vasco Nunez de Balboa, who had been placed in command of a small colony on the Gulf of Darien, had sighted this *Mar del Sur* in 1513 from the heights of the Sierra de Quarequa, and, having reached its shores, not without difficulty, had taken formal possession "for Castille and for Leon" by entering knee-deep into the water, with his uplifted sword in one hand and the standard of Castille in the other.

Meanwhile, Rafael Perestello and Andrade, after their return from China,* had shown that an extensive sea, probably not the Atlantic Ocean,* laved the shores visited by them.

(*Footnote. According to Dr. Hamy, Perestello was in China in 1514, and was followed a few years after by Andrade and Pires; L'Oeuvre Geog. des Reinel, etc. pages 29 and 32. According to R.H. Major, Fernam Peres de Andrade sailed to China in 1517 and returned to India in 1519. Thome Pires was cast into prison in China, and died there after a captivity of many years--- Prince Henry the Navigator, page 268.)

(*Footnote. Certain maps of the period represent North America split up into comparatively small islands, and with therefore an uninterrupted Atlantic Ocean extending to the shores of China. See the Boulengier Gores of 1514/1517.)

The vastness however of that sea was not yet fully realised; it required the practical experience of the first circumnavigators to bring forth such exclamations as uttered by Maximilian in his letter*--the first document which made known Magalhaens' great achievement. Maximilian writes*: "A sea so vast that the human mind can scarcely grasp it."

(*Footnote. Printed at Cologne in January 1523. See below.)

(*Footnote. Our quotation is from F.H.H. Guillemard's Life of Magellan page 223.)

PETRUS APIANUS' MAPPAMUNDI OF 1520.

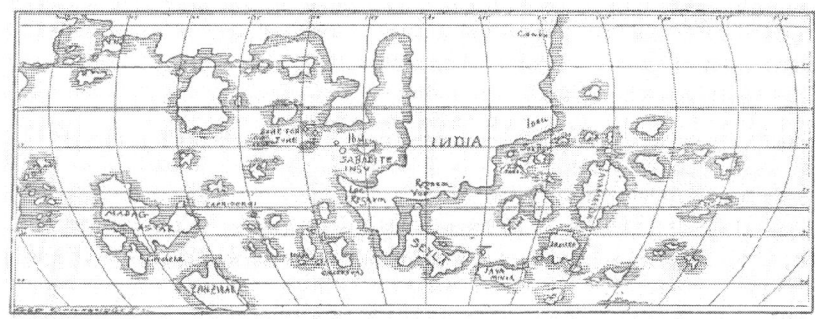

Petrus Apianus' Mappamundi of 1520.

Our sketch of Apianus' map is taken from the one given in Nordenskiold's collection. The original is a cordiform mappamundi engraved on wood, and first published in 1520 at Vienna by Camers to accompany his Solinus' *Polyhistor*. It was also inserted in the *Pomponius Mela*, printed at Basles in 1522. It is rather rough in execution, but nevertheless, its geographical configurations are carefully depicted, and closely resemble the 1515 Frankfort gores of Schonerean origin. The artist who designed it on the woodblock was evidently a novice in his profession, as may be observed by the N's in *Bone fortune, Iona, Callensuaz*, and *India*, which he failed to reverse as is the custom when drawing on the block for the wood engraver.

The western coast of Australia is represented as in the previous maps, the bogus Sumatra or continental promontory on which this coast is grafted bearing the usual legend *Lac regnum*; a large island to the southeast bears the inscription in large letters--SEYLA. To the east we notice Marco Polo's Islands *Java maior, Java minor, Angiana, Penta*. Penta, half demolished by the slips of the engraver's burin, reads PLVIA; the E, the N, and the T have been half cut away. The other islands bearing names are *Sondur* and *Canduz*. On the Asiatic continent, *Ioach** answers to *Loach*, and *Ciambo* to *Ciamba*. *Ma'Bar* is indicated by *Regnum Var*. Eastward we notice *Callensuaz, Iona*, which we have suggested may be altered from *Tona* in the 1515 map. *Zanzibar, Madagastar* and *Circobena* resemble those islands on the 1515 Frankfort map. The three Arabian Islands (Maurice, Bourbon and Rodriguez) are also represented, but without any nomenclature.

(*Footnote. Rendered *Ioca* by mistake on our map.)

In the latitudes in which the Antarctic continent is represented on the Schonerean globe of 1515 there is no such representation here.

With reference to Zanzibar, it will be well to note here that about this time--i.e. in 1521--Zanzibar (Marco Polo's Zanzibar) was said to be inhabited by giants, hence no doubt the appellation on the Dauphin and other charts: *Zanzibar iles des Geants*.*

(*Footnote. See Memoire Geographique sur la mer des Indes by J. Codine, Paris 1868 page 154: Cette double representation de Madagascar peut etre remarquee aussi dans la mappemonde de Bernardi Sylvani de 1511, sous les noms *Comortina* et *Madax*. Elle existe aussi sur la mappemonde de Benedetto Bordone de 1521; dans l'Isolario de ce geographe, Madagascar est reconnaissable a sa forme allongee placee parallelement a la cote d'Afrique; elle n'y a pas de nom; elle s'etend jusqu'a une latitude plus meridionale que le cap de Bonne-Esperance; a l'est sont trois iles dont la latitude correspond a celle du cap de Bonne-Esperance; elles ne portent pas de noms; en pleine mer des Indes (voir au verso de la page lxx.) sont deux grandes iles; l'une nommee *Maidegascar*; au nord ouest de Maidegascar est l'ile *Zanzibar* dont les habitants, dit l'auteur tant hommes que femmes, *sont des geants*; opinion qui se transforme dans la Cosmographie de Sebastien Munster disant seulement que si les naturels etaient grands en proportion de leur grosseur ce seraient des geants; opinion egalement reprouvee par Thevet, qui certifie que les naturels sont de petite taille.)

MAPPEMONDE LA SALLE, CIRCA 1522.

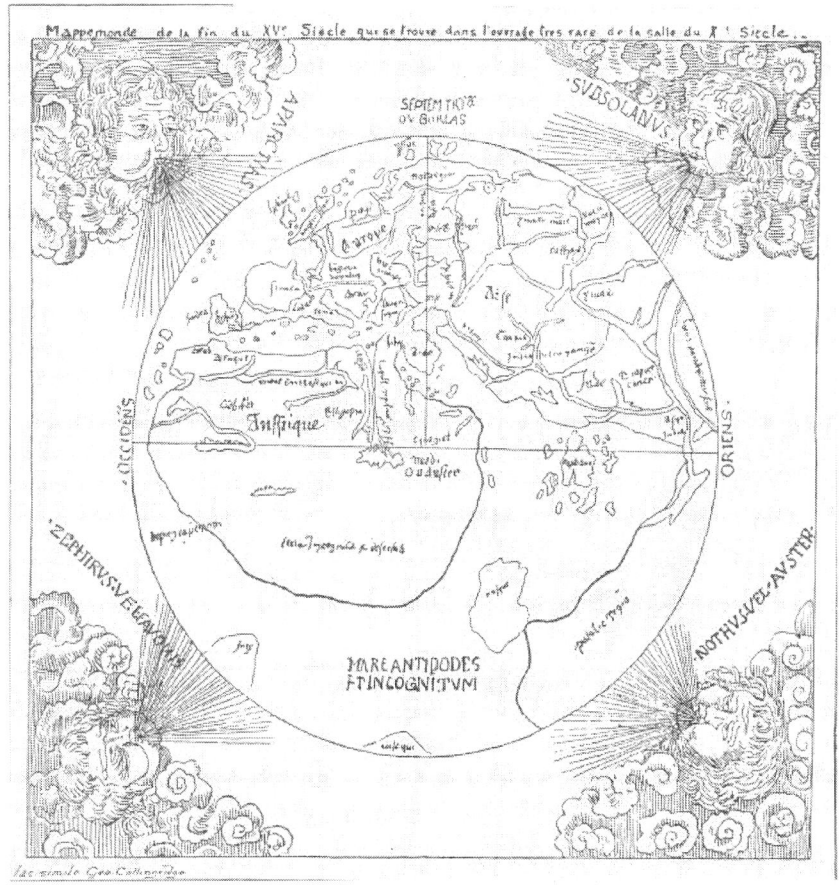

Mappemonde La Salle, circa 1522.

The reproduction we give here of the La Salle map, which was published with a work on geography by La Salle, is taken from the copy given in Santarem's Atlas. Mr. Delmar Morgan says: "There are two versions of the La Salle map, the one reproduced in the Vicomte de Santarem's Atlas, and that in the Royal Library, Stockholm, facsimiled in the English edition of Baron Nordenskiold's Atlas." Mr. D. Morgan further remarks* that this map "as originally drawn, probably dated from the 15th century, the Australian part being added subsequently. The name given to this roughly delineated Terra Australis is Patalie Regio, meaning, according to the Vicomte de Santarem, who derives it from the Sanskrit, the nether region, i.e. hell. Wieser derives Patalis from the Latin Pateo, meaning that it was the open region masking the hidden interior of the continent. Mr.

Petherick, a well-known writer on Australian discovery, has suggested that Patalis should be Pratalis, a name given by the Spaniards to a part of South America--the Rio de la Plata; the letters l and r being interchangeable. His argument is based on the occurrence of another American name, Brazil, on the Austral continent."

(*Footnote. Remarks on the Early Discovery of Australia by E. Delmar Morgan, F.R.G.S., London 1891 page 7.)

We have suggested elsewhere that Patalie Regio or Patalis Regio may be a corruption of (Pa)pagali regio, The Land of Parrots, or Psittacorum Regio of later charts. (See above.)

JUAN VESPUCCIUS' MAPPAMUNDI OF 1522/1523.

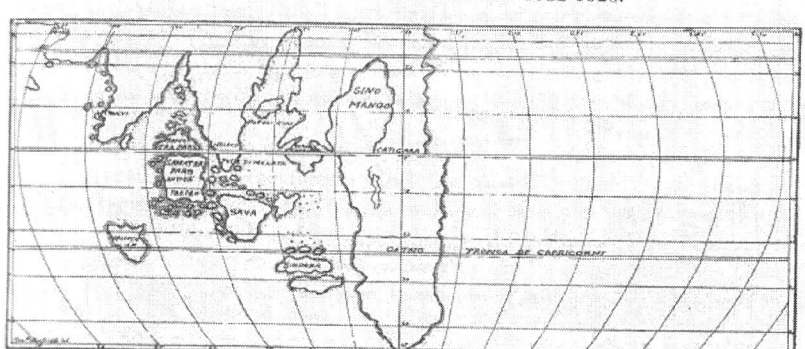

Juan Vespuccius' Mappamundi of 1522/1523.

We must now say a few words about Juan Vespuccius' Mappamundi, an important geographical document which closes the data of the pre-Magellanic period. It shows for the Australasian regions totally different configurations. Juan Vespuccius' Mappamundi is on an equidistant polar projection, which renders the original design rather difficult to understand. A glance at the translation we give here will show that the cartographer himself must have been somewhat puzzled by his own scheme, for, as may be observed, the continental land to the south of the equator bearing the name *Gataio* fails, when translated to our more reasonable projection, to join the continent of Asia at *Catigara* as it ought to do. The same disconnection may be noticed with regard to Sumatra; but, notwithstanding the disjunction at the equator to which this mappamundi is subjected in the original, the southern extremity of the Malay Peninsula, *Puta di Metala*, falls in its position with remarkable accuracy as shown in our sketch. To the south of *Puta di Melata* Point of Malacca, a large island bearing the name *Sava* answers to Java, and a smaller one to the east of it is intended no doubt for Sumbawa, although that island is duplicated to the south-east under the name of *Sindoba*. To the south-west of Sumatra an island called *Calensuan*, bisected by the tropic of Capricorn, is the last remnant of the Behaimean and Schonerean bogus Sumatra which had been grafted on the western coast of Australia, and it may prove of some interest to note that this original survey is maintained on this map in conjunction with and notwithstanding the presence of the real Sumatra above it.

By far the most interesting feature however on this extremely curious mappamundi is the representation of the huge continental land in the southern hemisphere. It bears a name which at first sight appears ridiculous, for *Gataio* is meant for Cataio, China. China is certainly a strange name for Australia, but in a cartographical sense not altogether impossible at the period we are dealing with, for we must remember that this mappamundi was constructed before the return of the first circumnavigators, when the Pacific Ocean to the east of the Spice Islands was not yet known.

If we imagine a flying survey with the Solomon Islands for point of departure, and Tasmania for the goal, we might expect to find that survey charted somewhat after the style of Juan Vespuccius' southern continent, and that continent might reasonably be supposed to form part of China. We have said with Tasmania for the goal because, strangely enough, the southern extremity of this continental Cathay reaches in longitude and latitude the exact position of an old Spanish survey to the south of Tasmania that bears to the present day a name which proves its Spanish Origin; we refer to *Piedra blanca*.'*

(*Footnote. *Piedra blanca*, or Pedra Branca, are words of Portuguese or Spanish origin, but it is only probable that they refer to an old Spanish or Portuguese survey made in the southern parts of Tasmania. George Collingridge.)

THE FIRST CIRCUMNAVIGATORS.

Reverting to the first circumnavigators, Magalhaens' squadron of five vessels was now sorely reduced. Major thus describes the return of this glorious but disastrous expedition and its results*:

(*Footnote. R.H. Major, Early Voyages to Terra Australis page xxxix. et sequit.)

"Two of the vessels of this fleet arrived on the 8th of November 1521, at the Island of Tidore, after having passed through the straits, since called the Straits of Magellan. That navigator was now no more; he had been killed in one of the islands of the Archipelago of St. Lazaro, since called the Philippines, and, nearly all his squadron having been destroyed, one vessel only, named the *Victoria*, returned to Europe with eighteen persons, all very sick, under the guidance of Sebastian del Cano, who landed on the 6th of September 1522, at the same port of San Lucar de Barrameda from which the fleet had set sail three years before.

"Whether it was from policy, or because the currents which exist in the Great Pacific Ocean had carried Magellan's fleet rapidly down to the Philippines and Moluccas, those who returned from this expedition always maintained that these latter islands were in the hemisphere of the Spaniards, who consequently laid claim to traffic there. They were even on the point of sending out a new expedition thither, when King John III begged Charles V to have the question examined by competent persons, and promised to acquiesce in their decision. The two governments appointed twenty-four, or even a greater number, both Spaniards and Portuguese, well skilled in geography and navigation, who from the commencement of March 1524 met alternately in the two cities of Badajos and Elvas, on the frontiers of the two States. Three months were allowed them to decide definitely to whom these islands belonged.

"These commissioners, among whom was Sebastian del Cano, who had brought back the *Victoria*, consumed at the outset a considerable time in consulting globes and charts, and in comparing the journals of pilots. They examined the distance between the Moluccas and the line of demarcation. They disputed much, and came to no conclusion. More than two months passed away in this manner; and they reached the latter part of May, which had been fixed as the term of the conferences.

"The Spanish commissioners then settled the line of demarcation at three hundred and seventy leagues west of the Cape Verde Islands, as it had been fixed in 1494; and, as on the basis of the charts which they had then before them, they made the opposite line, which was to be at the distance of a hundred and eighty degrees, pass through the Malay Peninsula, they included in their own hemisphere not only the Moluccas, but also the Islands of Java and Borneo, part of Sumatra, the coast of China, and part of the Malay Peninsula itself. The Portuguese did not agree to this limitation, which was too disadvantageous for themselves; on the contrary they went away very discontented, storming, and threatening war, which gave occasion to the jocose observation of Peter Martyr of Anghiera, a talented man, at that time the historiographer of the Court of Spain, that the commissioners, after having well syllogized, concluded by being unable to decide the question except by cannonballs.

"In spite of the unsuccessful issue of this negotiation, the two Courts did not come to a quarrel; they were on the point of forming alliances. The question of the marriage of the Infanta Catherine, the Emperor's sister, with King John, which was celebrated in 1525, was being then entertained. In the following year, 1526, the Emperor espoused, with great pomp, Isabella, King John's sister. Charles V however, believing himself in the right, continued to permit his subjects to carry on commerce with the Spice Islands; and he himself fitted out fleets to dispute the possession of them with the Portuguese. Some of these vessels landed at the Moluccas in 1527 and 1528; but, as these expeditions were generally unsuccessful, and as moreover he was in need of money for his coronation in Italy, he listened to the proposals of King John to purchase his right to these islands. He parted with them by a secret treaty, which was signed at Saragossa the 22nd of April 1529 for the sum, it is said, of 350,000 golden ducats, against the express wish of his subjects, who often but in vain besought him to retract it. By his refusal it was thought that he had received much more. Thenceforth the Spaniards were not permitted to traffic with the Moluccas.

"This termination of the quarrel on the part of Portugal was a justification of the claims of the Spaniards, and an acknowledgment in some sort that the Moluccas were in their hemisphere. After such an arrangement the Portuguese could not show any discoveries made to the eastward, or even under the meridian of these islands. The greatest part of New Holland is more to the east than the Moluccas; hence it is to be believed that for this reason the Portuguese have kept silence respecting their discovery of it."

There is in Galvano's account of the return of the *Victoria* a curious reference to the discovery of "certain islands" which could not have been far distant from the west coast of Australia. As the mention of this discovery is not found elsewhere, we give here Galvano's description of it, as follows:

"In the yeere 1521 there went from Maluco one of Magellan's ships with cloues (Captain and pilot--John Sebastian del Cano); they victualled themselves in the Island of Burro (which is in 24 degrees* south latitude, and passed between Vitara and Malua,* which are in 8 degrees), and from thence went to Timor, which standeth in 11 degrees of southerly latitude. Beyond this island one hundred leagues they discouered certain islands under the tropic of Capricorn [and further on others. All are peopled thenceforward; nor did they see land (without inhabitants) except it might be some islet, up to the Cape of Good Hope, where it is said they took in wood and water] (one named Ende finding the places from thenceforward peopled. Afterward passing without Samatra they met with no land till they fell with the Cape of Bona Speranca, where they tooke in fresh water and wood). So they came by the Islands of Cape Verde, and from thence to Siuill, where they were notably receiued as well for the cloues that they brought as that they had compassed about the world: No anno de 1521 partio de Maluco hua das naos pera Castella, em q' o Magalhaes fora carregada de crauo, capita & piloto della Joam Sebastiam del cano. Foram tomar mantimento aa ilha de Burro q' estaa em vinte quatro graos daltura da parte do Sul, passaram por antre Vitara & Malua, que estam em oyto graos: & dahi foram a Thimor q' estaa em onze, ate delle cem legoas, descobriram huas ylhas diante outras debaxo do tropico de Capricornio. Todas sam pouoadas daqui por diate; nam sey terra que vissem ate o Cabo de boa esperanca senam algua ylheta sem gente: onde diz que tomaram agoa & lenha, E ao logo daquella costa vieram aas ylhas do Cabo verde, & dahi aa cidade de Seuilha, onde foram com grande aluoroco recebidos, assi pello crauo que traziam, como por darem hua volta ao mundo."

(*Footnote. Burro or Booro is in 4 degrees. 24 is no doubt a misprint, as the context shows.)

(*Footnote. Wetter and Ombai, modern.)

CHAPTER 26. A.D. 1523.
MAXIMILIANUS TRANSYLVANUS' LETTER.

After the return of the survivors of Magalhaens' expedition the whole crew and officers went up to Valladolid to report to the Emperor and show themselves. C.H. Coote in his Introduction to Stevens' Johann Schoner, page xxi., says: "A young man (Maximilianus Transylvanus), the natural son of Matthaes Lang, Archbishop of Saltzburg, was at Court, under the care of Peter Martyr, as one of his pupils, and sometimes acting with the young superior of his own age, as private secretary. Peter sent him these returned men, and gave him the task of writing out an account of the expedition to his father, then in Germany, as good practice in writing Latin. Maximilian having (with Ferdinand Columbus) accompanied the Emperor in his recent swing round Germany and Flanders, and having only recently returned to Spain with the travelling Court, very naturally sent his *Latin Exercise* to Cologne to be printed, where the *first Edition* appeared in a very neat sm. 8vo. in January 1523 (at Cologne the new year began 1st January, so that this was not really January 1524, as has been claimed, and therefore a reprint of the Rome edition of November 1523)."

The translation of Maximilianus Transylvanus' letter given here is from H. Stevens' Johann Schoner.*

(*Footnote. Johann Schoner by Henry Stevens of Vermont; London, H. Stevens & Son 1888.)

TRANSLATION OF THE LETTER OF MAXIMILIANUS TRANSYLVANUS TO THE CARDINAL OF SALTZBURG.

Prima ego velivolis ambivi cursibus orbem
Magellane novo te duce ducta freto
Ambivi, meritoq vocor Victoria: sunt mi
Vela alae, precium gloria; pugna, mare.

I was the first with flying sails
To course the world around;
Under thy guidance, Magellan,
Have we the new strait found:
Victoria is my rightful name,
Sails are my wings, my guerdon fame,
The sea my battlefield I claim.

Magellan's Ship, The Victoria.

A letter from Maximilianus Transylvanus to the Most Reverend Cardinal of Saltzburg, very delightful to read, concerning the Molucca Islands, and also many other wonders which the latest voyage of the Spaniards has just discovered, made under the auspices of the Most Serene Emperor Charles V:

MOST REVEREND AND ILLUSTRIOUS LORD: My only Lord, to you I most humbly commend myself. Not long ago one of those five ships returned which the Emperor, while he was at Saragossa some years ago, had sent into a strange and hitherto unknown part of the world, to search for the islands in which Spices grow. For although the Portuguese bring us a great quantity of them from the Golden Chersonesus, which we now call Malacca, nevertheless their own Indian possessions produce none but pepper. For it is well-known that the other spices, as cinnamon, cloves, and the nutmeg, which we call muscat, and its covering (mace), which we call muscat-flower, are brought to their Indian possessions from distant islands, hitherto only known by name, in ships held together not by iron fastenings, but merely by palm-leaves, and having round sails also woven out of palm-fibres. Ships of this sort they call junks, and they are impelled by the wind only when it blows directly fore or aft.

Nor is it wonderful that these islands have not been known to any mortal almost up to our time. For whatever statements of ancient authors we have hitherto read with respect to the native soil of these spices, are partly entirely fabulous, and partly so far from truth that the very regions in which they asserted that these spices were produced are scarcely less distant from the countries in which it is now ascertained that they grow than we are ourselves.

For, not to mention others, Herodotus, in other respects a very good authority, states that cinnamon was found in bird's nests, into which the birds had brought it from very distant regions, among which birds he mentions especially the Phoenix--and I know not who has ever seen the nest of a Phoenix. But Pliny, who might have been thought to have had better means of knowing the facts, since long before his time many discoveries had been made by the fleets of Alexander the Great, and by other expeditions, states the cinnamon was produced in Ethiopia, on the borders of the land of the Troglodytes. Whereas we know now that cinnamon is produced at a very great distance from any part of Ethiopia, and especially from the country of the Troglodytes--i.e. dwellers in subterraneous caves.

Now it was necessary for our sailors, who have recently returned, who knew more about Ethiopia than about other countries, to sail round the whole world, and that in a very wide circuit, before they discovered these islands and returned to Europe; and, since this voyage was a very remarkable one, and neither in our own time nor in any former age has such a voyage been accomplished, or even attempted, I have determined to send your Lordship a full and accurate account of the expedition.

I have taken much care in obtaining an account of the facts from the commanding officer of the squadron,* and from the individual sailors who have returned with him. They also made a statement to the Emperor, and to several other persons, with such good faith and sincerity that they appeared in their narrative not merely to have abstained from fabulous statements, but also to contradict and refute the fabulous statements made by ancient authors.

(*Footnote. Juan Sebastian del Cano.)

For who ever believed that the Monosceli, or Sciapodes (one-legged men), the Scirites, the Spithamaei (persons a span--7 1/2 inches--high), the Pigmies (height 13 1/2 inches), and such like were rather monsters than men? Yet, although the Castilians in their voyages westwards, and the Portuguese sailing eastwards, have sought out, discovered and surveyed so many places even beyond the tropic of Capricorn, and now these countrymen of ours have sailed completely round the world, none of them have found any trustworthy evidence in favour of the existence of such monsters, and therefore all such accounts ought to be regarded as fabulous and as old wives' tales, handed down from one writer to another without any basis of truth; but, as I have to make a voyage round the world, I will not extend my prefatory remarks but will come at once to the point.

Some thirty years ago, when the Castilians in the West, and the Portuguese in the East, had begun to search after new and unknown lands, in order to avoid any interference of one with the other the kings of these countries divided the whole world between them, by the authority probably of Pope Alexander VI, on this plan, that a line should be drawn from the North to the South Pole through a point three hundred and sixty leagues west of the Hesperides, which they now call Cape Verde Islands, which would divide the earth's surface into two equal portions. All unknown lands hereafter discovered to the east of this line were assigned to the Portuguese, all on the west to the Castilians. Hence it came to pass that the Castilians always sailed south-west, and there discovered a very extensive continent, besides numerous large islands, abounding in gold, pearls and other valuable commodities; and have quite recently discovered a large inland city named Tenoxtica (Mexico), situated in a lake like Venice. Peter Martyr, an author who is more careful as to the accuracy of his statements than of the elegance of his style, has given a full but truthful description of this city. But the Portuguese, sailing southward past the Hesperides (Cape Verde Islands), and the Fish-eating Ethiopians (West Coast of Africa), crossed the Equator and the tropic of Capricorn, and sailing eastward discovered several very large islands heretofore unknown, and also the sources of the Nile and the Troglodytes. Thence, by way of the Arabian and Persian Gulfs, they arrived at the shores of India, within the Ganges, where now there is the very great trading station and the Kingdom of Calicut. Hence they sailed to Taprobane, which is now called Zamatara (Sumatra). For where Ptolemy, Pliny, and other geographers placed Taprobane, there is now no island which can possibly be identified with it. Thence they came to the Golden Chersonesus, where now stands the well-peopled city of Malacca, the principal place of business of the East. After this they penetrated into a great gulf, as far as the nation of the Sinae, who are now called Schinae (Chinese), where they found a fair-complexioned and tolerably-civilised people, like our folks in Germany. They believe that the Seres and Asiatic Scythians extend as far as these parts.

And although there was a somewhat doubtful rumour afloat that the Portuguese had advanced so far to the east that they had come to the end of their own limits, and had passed over into the territory appointed for the Castilians, and that Malacca and the Great Gulf were within our limits, all this was more said than believed, until four years ago Ferdinand Magellan, a distinguished Portuguese, who had for many years sailed about the Eastern Seas as admiral of the Portuguese fleet, having quarrelled with his king, who, he considered, had acted ungratefully towards him, and Christopher Haro, brother of my father-in-law, of Lisbon, who had, through his agents, for many years carried on trade with those Eastern countries, and more recently with the Chinese, so that he was well acquainted with these matters (he also having been ill-used by the King of Portugal, had returned to his native country, Castille), pointed out to the Emperor that it was not yet clearly ascertained whether Malacca was within the boundaries of the Portuguese or of the Castilians, because hitherto its longitude had not been definitely known; but that it was an undoubted fact that the Great Gulf and the Chinese nations were within the Castilian limits. They asserted also that it was absolutely certain that the islands called the Moluccas, in which all sorts of spices grow, and from which they were brought to Malacca, were contained in the Western or Castilian division, and that it would be possible to sail to them, and to bring the spices at less trouble and expense from their native soil to Castille.

The plan of the voyage was to sail to the west, and then coasting the Southern hemisphere round the south of America to the east. Yet it appeared to be a difficult undertaking, and one of which the practicability was doubtful. Not that it was impossible, *prima facie*, to sail from the west round the Southern hemisphere to the east; but that it was uncertain, whether ingenious Nature, all whose works are wisely conceived, had so arranged the sea and the land that it might be possible to arrive by this course at the Eastern Seas. For it had not been ascertained whether that extensive region, which is called Terra Firma, separated the Western Ocean (the Atlantic) from the eastern (the Pacific); but it was plain that that continent extended in a southerly direction, and afterwards inclined to the west. Moreover two regions had been discovered in the north, one called Baccalearum, from a new kind of fish, the other called Florida; and if these were connected with Terra Firma it would not be possible to pass from the Western Ocean to the Eastern; since although much trouble had been taken to discover any strait which might exist connecting the two oceans, none had yet been found. At the same time it was considered that to attempt to sail through the Portuguese concessions and the Eastern seas would be a hazardous enterprise, and dangerous in the highest degree.

The Emperor and his council considered that the plan proposed by Magellan and Haro, though holding out considerable advantages, was one of very considerable difficulty as to execution. After some delay Magellan offered to go out himself, but Haro undertook to fit out a squadron at the expense of himself and his friends, provided that they were allowed to sail under the authority and patronage of his Majesty. As each resolutely upheld his own scheme, the Emperor himself fitted out a squadron of five ships, and appointed Magellan to the command. It was ordered that they should sail southwards by the coast of Terra Firma until they found either the end of that country or some strait by which they might arrive at the spice-bearing Moluccas.

Accordingly on the 10th of August 1519 Ferdinand Magellan, with his five ships, sailed from Seville. In a few days they arrived at the

Fortunate Islands, now called the Canaries. Thence they sailed to the islands of the Hesperides (Cape Verde); and thence sailed in a south-westerly direction towards that continent which I have already mentioned (Terra Firma or South America), and after a favourable voyage of a few days discovered a promontory, which they called St. Mary's. Here Admiral John Ruy Dias Solis, while exploring the shores of this continent by command of King Ferdinand the Catholic, was, with some of his companions, eaten by the Anthropophagi, whom the Indians call cannibals. Hence they coasted along this continent, which extends far on southwards, and which I now think should be called the Southern Polar Land, then gradually slopes off in a westerly direction, and so sailed several degrees south of the tropic of Capricorn. But it was not so easy for them to do it as for me to relate it. For not till the end of March in the following year (1520) did they arrive at a bay, which they called St. Julian's Bay. Here the Antarctic Pole Star was 49 1/3 degrees above the horizon, this result being deduced from the sun's declination and altitude, and this star is principally used by our navigators for observations. They stated that the longitude was 56 degrees west of the Canaries. For since the ancient geographers, and especially Ptolemy, reckoned the distance easterly from the Fortunate Islands (Canaries) as far as Cattigara to be 180 degrees, and our sailors have sailed as far as possible in a westerly direction, they reckoned the distance from the Canaries westward to Cattigara to be also 180 degrees. Yet even though our sailors in so long a voyage, and in one so distant from the land, lay down and mark out certain signs and limits of their longitude, they appear to me rather to have made some error in their method of reckoning of the longitude than to have attained any trustworthy result.

Meanwhile, however this may be, until more certain results are arrived at I do not think that their statements should be absolutely rejected, but merely accepted provisionally. This bay appeared to be of great extent, and had rather the appearance of a strait. Therefore Admiral Magellan directed two ships to survey the bay; and remained with the rest at anchor. After two days they returned, and reported that the bay was shallow, and did not extend far inland. Our men on their return saw some Indians gathering shell-fish on the sea-shore, for the natives of all unknown countries are commonly called Indians. These Indians were very tall, ten spans high (7 feet 6 inches), clad in skins of wild beasts, darker-complexioned than would have been expected in that part of the world; and when some of our men went on shore and showed them bells and pictures, they began to dance round our men with a hoarse noise and unintelligible chant, and to excite our admiration they took arrows, a cubit and a half long, and put them down their own throats to the bottom of their stomachs without seeming any the worse for it. Then they drew them up again, and seemed much pleased at having shown their bravery. At length three men came up as a deputation, and by means of signs requested our men to come with them further inland, as though they would receive them hospitably. Magellan sent with them seven men well equipped, to find out as much as possible about the country and its inhabitants. These seven went with the Indians some seven miles up the country, and came to a desolate and pathless wood. Here was a very low-built cottage, roofed with skins of beasts. In it were two rooms, in one of which dwelt the women and children, and in the other the men. The women and children were thirteen in number, and the men five. These received their guests with a barbarous entertainment, but which they considered to be quite a royal one. For they slaughtered an animal much resembling a wild ass, and set before our men half-roasted steaks of it, but no other food or drink. Our men had to cover themselves at night with skins, on account of the severity of the wind and snow.

Before they went to sleep they arranged for a watch to be kept; the Indians did the same, and lay near our men by the fire, snoring horribly. When day dawned our men requested them to return with them, accompanied by their families, to our ships. When the Indians persisted in refusing to do so, and our men had also persisted somewhat imperiously in their demands, the men went into the women's room. The Spaniards supposed that they had gone to consult their wives about this expedition. But they came out again as if to battle, wrapt up from head to foot in hideous skins, with their faces painted in various colours, and with bows and arrows, all ready for fighting, and appearing taller than ever. The Spaniards, thinking a skirmish was likely to take place, fired a gun. Although nobody was hit yet these enormous giants, who just before seemed as though they were ready to fight and conquer Jove himself, were so alarmed at the sound that they began to sue for peace. It was arranged that three men, leaving the rest behind, should return with our men to the ships; and so they started. But as our men not only could not run as fast as the giants, but could not even run as fast as the giants could walk, two of the three, seeing a wild ass grazing on a mountain at some distance, as they were going along, ran off after it, and so escaped. The third was brought to the ships, but in a few days he died, having starved himself after the Indian fashion through homesickness. And although the Admiral returned to that cottage, in order to make another of the giants prisoner and bring him to the Emperor as a novelty, no one was found there, as all of them had removed elsewhere and the cottage had disappeared. Hence it is plain that this nation is a nomad race, and although our men remained some time in that bay, as we shall presently mention, they never again saw an Indian on that coast; nor did they think that there was anything in that country that would make it worth while to explore the inland districts any further. And though Magellen was convinced that a longer stay there would be of no use, yet, since for some days the sea was very rough and the weather tempestuous, and the land extended still further southward, so that the further they advanced the colder they would find the country, their departure was unavoidably put off from day to day till the month of May arrived, at which time the winter sets in with great severity in those parts, so much so that, though it was our summertime, they had to make preparations for wintering there. Magellan, perceiving that the voyage would be a long one, in order that the provisions might last longer ordered the rations to be diminished. The Spaniards endured this with patience for some days, but, alarmed at the length of the winter and the barrenness of the land, at last petitioned their Admiral, Magellan, saying that it was evident that this continent extended an indefinite distance southwards, and that there was no hope of discovering the end of it, or of discovering a strait; that a hard winter was setting in, and that several men had already died through scanty food and the hardships of the voyage; that they would not long be able to endure that restriction of provisions which he had enacted; that the emperor never intended that they should obstinately persevere in attempting to do what the natural circumstances of the case rendered it impossible to accomplish; that the toils they had already endured would be acknowledged and approved, since they had already advanced further than the boldest and most adventurous navigators had dared to do; that, if a south wind should spring up in a few days, they might easily sail to the north, and arrive at a milder climate. In reply Magellan, who had already made up his mind either to carry out his design or to die in the attempt, said that the Emperor had ordered him to sail according to a certain plan, from which he could not and would not depart on any consideration whatever; and that therefore he should continue this voyage till he found either the end of this continent or a strait; that, though he could not do this at present, as the winter prevented him, yet it would be easy enough in the summer of this region; that if they would only sail along the coast to the south the summer would be all one perpetual day; that they had means of providing against want of food and the inclemency of the weather, inasmuch as there was a great quantity of wood, that the sea produced shell-fish and numerous sorts of excellent fish; that there were springs of good water, and they could also help their stores by hunting and by shooting wild fowl; that bread and wine had not yet run short, and would not run short in future, provided that they used them for necessity and for the preservation of health, and not for pleasure and luxury; that nothing had yet been done worthy of much admiration, nor such as could give them reasonable grounds for returning; that the Portuguese, not only yearly, but almost daily, in their voyages to the east, made no difficulty about sailing twelve degrees south of the tropic of Capricorn. What had they then to boast of when they had only advanced some four degrees south of it? that he for his part had made up his mind to suffer anything that might happen rather than return to Spain with disgrace; that he believed that his companions, or at any rate those in whom the generous spirit of Spaniards was not totally extinct, were of the same way of thinking; that he had only to exhort them fearlessly to face the remainder of winter; that the greater their dangers and hardships were the richer their reward would be for having opened up for the Emperor a new world rich in spices and gold.

Magellan thought that by this address he had soothed and encouraged the minds of his men, but within a few days he was troubled by a wicked and disgraceful mutiny. For the sailors began to talk to one another of the long-standing ill-feeling existing between the Portuguese and the Castillians, and of Magellan being a Portuguese; that there was nothing that he could do more to the credit of his own country than to lose this fleet with so many men on board; that it was not to be believed that he wished to find the Moluccas, even if he could, but that he would think it enough if he could delude the Emperor for some years by holding out vain hopes, and that in the meanwhile something new would turn up whereby the Castillians might be completely put out of the way of looking for spices; nor indeed was the direction of the voyage really towards the fertile Molucca Islands, but towards snow and ice and everlasting bad weather. Magellan was exceedingly irritated by these conversations, and punished some of the men, but with somewhat more severity than was becoming to a foreigner, especially to one holding command in a distant part of the world. So they mutinied, and took possession of one of the ships, and began to make preparations to return to Spain; but Magellan, with the rest of his men who had remained faithful to him, boarded that ship and executed the ringleader* and other leading mutineers, even some who could not legally be so treated, for they were royal officials, who were only liable to capital punishment by the Emperor and his council. However under the circumstances no one ventured to resist. Yet there were some who whispered to one another that Magellan would go on exercising the same severity amongst the Castillians as long as one was left, until having got rid of every one of them he could sail home to his own country again with the few Portuguese he had with him. The Castillians therefore remained still more hostile to the Admiral. As soon as Magellan observed that the weather was less stormy and that winter began to break up he sailed out of St Julian's Bay on 24th August 1520, as before.

(*Footnote. Gaspar de Quesada.)

For some days he coasted along to the southward and at last sighted a cape, which they called Cape Santa Cruz. Here a storm from the east caught them and one of the five ships was driven on shore and wrecked, but the crew and all goods on board were saved, except an African slave, who was drowned. After this the coast seemed to stretch a little south-eastwards, and as they continued to explore it, on the 26th November (1520), an opening was observed having the appearance of a strait; Magellan at once sailed in with his whole fleet, and, seeing several bays in various directions, directed three of the ships to cruise about to ascertain whether there was any way through, undertaking to wait for them five days at the entrance of the strait, so that they might report what success they had. One of these ships* was commanded by Alvaro de Mezquita, son of Magellan's brother, and this by the windings of the channel came out again into the ocean whence it had set out. When the Spaniards* saw that they were at a considerable distance from the other ships they plotted among themselves to return home, and, having put Alvaro, their captain, in irons, they sailed northwards, and at last reached the coast of Africa, and there took in provisions, and eight months after leaving the other ships they arrived in Spain, where they brought Alvaro to trial on the charge that it had chiefly been through his advice and persuasion that his uncle Magellan had adopted such severe measures against the Castillians.

(*Footnote. The San Antonio.)

(*Footnote. Among them was Esteven Gomez.)

Magellan waited some days over the appointed time for this ship, and meanwhile one ship had returned and reported that they had found nothing but a shallow bay, and the shores stoney, and with high cliffs; but the other reported that the greatest bay had the appearance of a strait, as they had sailed on for three days and had found no way out, but that the further they went the narrower the passage became, and it was so deep that in many places they sounded without finding the bottom; they also noticed from the tide of the sea that the flow was somewhat stronger than the ebb, and thence they concluded that there was a passage that way into some other sea. On hearing this Magellan determined to sail along this channel. This strait, though not then known to be such, was of the breadth in some places of three, in others of two, in others of five or ten Italian miles, and inclined slightly to the west. The latitude south was found to be 52 degrees, the longitude they estimated as the same as that of St. Julian's Bay. It being now hard upon the month of November, the length of the night was not much more than five hours; they saw no one on the shore. One night however a great number of fires were seen, especially on the left side, whence they conjectured that they had been seen by the inhabitants of those regions. But Magellan, seeing that the land was craggy, and bleak with perpetual winter, did not think it worth while to spend his time in exploring it, and so with his three ships continued his voyage along the channel, until on the twenty-second day after he had set sail, he came out into another vast and open sea; the length of the strait they reckoned at about one hundred Spanish miles. The land which they had to the right was no doubt the continent we have before mentioned (South America). On the left hand they thought that there was no continent, but only islands, as they occasionally heard on that side the reverberation and roar of the sea at a more distant part of the coast. Magellan saw that the mainland extended due north, and therefore gave orders to turn away from that great continent, leaving it on the right hand, and to sail over that vast and extensive ocean, which had probably never been traversed by our ships or by those of any other nation, in a north-westerly direction, so that they might arrive at last at the Eastern Ocean, coming at it from the west, and again enter the torrid zone, for he was satisfied that the Moluccas were in the extreme east, and could not be far off the equator. They continued in this course, never deviating from it, except when compelled to do so now and then by the force of the wind; and when they had sailed on this course for forty days across the ocean with a strong wind, mostly favourable, and had seen nothing all around them but sea, and had now almost reached again the tropic of Capricorn, they came in sight of two islands, small and barren, and on directing their course to them found that they were uninhabited; but they stayed there two days for repose and refreshment, as plenty of fish was to be caught there. However they unanimously agreed to call these islands the Unfortunate Islands. Then they set sail again, and continued on the same course as before. After sailing for three months and twenty days with good fortune over this ocean, and having traversed a distance almost too long to estimate, having had a strong wind aft almost the whole of the time, and having again crossed the equator, they saw an island, which they afterwards learnt from the neighbouring people was called Inuagana. When they came nearer to it they found the latitude to be 11 degrees north; the longitude they reckoned to be 158 degrees west of Cadiz. From this point they saw more and more islands, so that they found themselves in an extensive archipelago, but on arriving at Inuagana they found that it was uninhabited. Then they sailed towards another small island, where they saw two Indian canoes, for such is the Indian name of these strange boats; these canoes are scooped out of the single trunk of a tree, and hold one or at most two persons; and they are used to talk with each other by signs, like dumb people. They asked the Indians what the names of the islands were, and whence provisions could be procured, of which they were very deficient; they were given to understand that the first island they had seen was called Inuagana; that near which they then were Acacan, but that both were uninhabited; but that there was another island almost in sight, in the direction of which they pointed, called Selani, and that abundance of provisions of all sorts was to be had there. Our men took in water at Acacan, and then sailed towards Selani. But a storm caught them so that they could not land there, but they were driven to another island called Massana, where the king of three islands resides. From this island they sailed to Subuth, a very large island and well supplied, where, having come to a friendly arrangement with the chief, they immediately landed to celebrate divine worship according to Christian usage--for the festival for the Resurrection of Him who has saved us was at hand. Accordingly, with some of the sails of the ships and branches of trees they erected a chapel, and in it constructed an altar in the Christian fashion, and divine service was duly performed. The chief and a large crowd of Indians came up, and seemed much pleased with these religious rites. They brought the Admiral and some of the officers into the chief's cabin, and set before them what food they had. The bread was made of sago, which is obtained from the trunk of a tree not much unlike the palm. This is chopped up small, and fried in oil, and used as bread, a specimen of which I send to your lordship. Their drink was a liquor which flows from the branches of palm-trees when cut. Some birds also were served up at this meal, and also some of the fruit of the country. Magellan, having noticed in the chief's house a sick person in a very wasted condition, asked who he was and from what disease he was suffering. He was told that it was the chief's grandson, and that he had been suffering for two years from a violent fever. Magellan exhorted him to be of good courage, that if he would devote himself to Christ he would immediately recover his former health and strength. The Indian consented, and adored the Cross, and received baptism, and the next day declared that he was well again, rose from his bed and walked about, and took his meals like the others. What visions he may have told to his friends I cannot say; but the chief and over 2,200 Indians were baptized and professed the name and faith of Christ. Magellan, seeing that this island was rich in gold and ginger, and that it was so conveniently situated with respect to the neighbouring islands that it would be easy, making this his headquarters, to explore their resources and natural productions. He therefore went to the chief of Subuth and suggested to him that since he had turned away from the foolish and impious worship of false gods to the Christian religion it would be proper that the chiefs of the neighbouring islands should obey his rule; that he had determined to send envoys for this purpose, and, if any of the chiefs should refuse to obey this summons, to compel them to do so by force of arms. The proposal pleased the savage, and the envoys were sent; the chiefs came in one by one and did homage to the chief of Subuth in the manner adopted in those countries. But the nearest island to Subuth is called

Mauthan, and its king was superior in military force to the other chiefs; and he declined to do homage to one whom he had been accustomed to command for so long. Magellan, anxious to carry out his plan, ordered forty of his men, whom he could rely on for valour and military skill, to arm themselves, and passed over to the island Mauthan in boats, for it was very near. The chief of Subuth furnished him with some of his own people to guide him as to the topography of the island and the character of the country, and if it should be necessary to help him in the battle. The King of Mauthan, seeing the arrival of our men, led into the field some 3,000 of his people. Magellan drew up his own men and what artillery he had, though his force was somewhat small, on the shore, and, although he saw that his own force was much inferior in numbers, and that his opponents were a warlike race and were equipped with lances and other weapons, nevertheless thought it more advisable to face the enemy with them than to retreat or to avail himself of the aid of the Subuth islanders. Accordingly he exhorted his men to take courage and not to be alarmed at the superior force of the enemy; since it had often been the case, as had recently happened in the island [peninsula] of Yucatan, that two hundred Spaniards had routed two or even three hundred thousand Indians. He said to the Subuth islanders that he had not brought them with him to fight, but to see the valour and military prowess of his men. Then he attacked the Mauthan islanders, and both sides fought boldly; but as the enemy surpassed our men in number and used longer lances, to the great damage of our men, at last Magellan himself was thrust through and slain. Although the survivors did not consider themselves fairly beaten, yet, as they had lost their leader, they retreated; but as they retreated in good order the enemy did not venture to pursue them. The Spaniards then, having lost their Admiral (Magellan) and seven of their comrades, returned to Subuth, where they chose as their new admiral John Serrano, a man of no contemptible ability. He renewed the alliance with the chief of Subuth by making him additional presents, and undertook to conquer the King of Mauthan. Magellan had been the owner of a slave, a native of the Moluccas, whom he had formerly bought in Malacca; and by means of this slave, who was able to speak Spanish fluently, and of an interpreter of Subuth, who could speak the Moluccan language, our men carried on their negotiations. This slave had taken part in the fight with the Mauthan islanders, and had been slightly wounded, for which reason he lay by all day intending to nurse himself. Serrano, who could do no business without his help, rated him soundly, and told him that though his master (Magellan) was dead, he was still a slave, and that he would find that such was the case, and would get a good flogging into the bargain, if he did not exert himself and do what was required of him more zealously. This speech much incensed the slave against our people; but he concealed his anger, and in a few days he went to the chief of Subuth and told him that the avarice of the Spaniards was insatiable; that they had determined, as soon as they should have defeated the king of Mauthan, to turn round upon him and take him away as a prisoner; and that the only course for him (the chief of Subuth) to adopt was to anticipate treachery by treachery. The savage believed this, and secretly came to an understanding with the king of Mauthan, and made arrangements with him for common action against our people. Admiral Serrano and twenty-seven of the principal officers and men were invited to a solemn banquet. These, quite unsuspectingly, for the natives had carefully dissembled their intentions, went on shore without any precautions to take their dinner with the chief. While they were at table some armed men, who had been concealed close by, ran in and slew them. A great outcry was made. It was reported in our ships that our men were killed, and that the whole island was hostile to us. Our men saw, from on board the ships, that the handsome cross, which they had set up in a tree, was torn down by the natives and cut up into fragments. When the Spaniards, who had remained on board, heard of the slaughter of our men they feared further treachery; so they weighed anchor and began to set sail without delay. Soon afterward Serrano was brought to the coast a prisoner; he entreated them to deliver him from so miserable a captivity, saying that he had got leave to be ransomed if his men would agree to it. Although our men thought it was disgraceful to leave their commander behind in this way, their fear of the treachery of the islanders was so great that they put out to sea, leaving Serrano on the shore in vain lamenting and beseeching his comrades to rescue him. The Spaniards, having lost their commander and several of their comrades, sailed on sad and anxious, not merely on account of the loss they had suffered, but also because their numbers had been so diminished that it was no longer possible to work the three remaining ships.

On this question they consulted together and unanimously came to the conclusion that the best plan would be to burn one of the ships, and to sail home in the two remaining. They therefore sailed to a neighbouring island, called Cohol,* and, having put the rigging and stores of one of the ships on board the two others, set it on fire. Hence they proceeded to the island of Gibeth. Although they found that this island was well supplied with gold and ginger and many other things, they did not think it desirable to stay there any length of time, as they could not establish friendly relations with the natives; and they were too few in number to venture to use force. From Gibeth they proceeded to the island of Porne.*

(*Footnote. A misprint for Bohol.)

(*Footnote. Borneo.)

In this archipelago there are two large islands, one of which is called Siloli, whose king has six hundred children. Siloli is larger than Porne, for Siloli can hardly be circumnavigated in six months, but Porne in three months. Although Siloli is larger than Porne, yet the latter is more fertile, and distinguished as containing a large city of the same name as the island. And since Porne must be considered to be more important than the other islands which they had hitherto visited, and it was from it that the other islanders had learnt the arts of civilised life, I have determined to describe briefly the manners and customs of these nations. All these islanders are Caphrae or Kafirs, i.e. heathens, they worship the sun and moon as gods; they assign the government of the day to the sun, and that of the night to the moon; the sun they consider to be male, and the moon female, and that they are the parents of the other stars, all of which they consider to be gods, though little ones. They salute rather than adore the rising sun with certain hymns. Also they salute the bright moon at night, from whom they ask for children, for the increase of their flocks and herds, for an abundant supply of the fruits of the earth, and for other things of that sort. But they practise piety and justice; and especially love peace and quiet, and have great aversion to war. As long as their king maintains peace they show him divine honours; but if he is anxious for war they never rest till he is slain by the enemy in battle. When the king has determined on war, which very seldom happens, his men set him in the first rank, where he has to stand the whole brunt of the combat: and they do not exert themselves vigorously against the enemy till they know that the king has fallen; then they begin to fight for liberty and for their new king; nor has any king of theirs entered on a war without being slain in battle. For this reason they seldom engage in war, and they think it unjust to extend their frontiers. Their chief care is to avoid giving offence to the neighbouring nations or to strangers. But if at any time they are attacked they retaliate; and yet, lest further ill should arise, they at once endeavour to come to terms. They think that party acts most creditably which is the first to propose terms of peace; that it is disgraceful to be anticipated in so doing, and that it is scandalous and detestable to refuse peace to those who ask for it, even though the latter should have been the aggressors. All the neighbouring people unite in destroying such refusers of peace as impious and abominable. Hence they mostly pass their lives in peace and leisure. Robberies and murders are quite unknown among them. No one may speak to the king but his wives and children, except at a distance by hollow canes, which they apply to his ear, and through which they whisper what they have to say. They think that at death men have no perception as they had none before they were born. Their houses are small, built of wood and earth, covered partly with rubble and partly with palm leaves. It is ascertained that there are 20,000 houses in the city of Porne. They marry as many wives as they can afford to keep; they eat birds and fish, make bread of rice, and drink a liquor drawn from the palm-tree--of which we have spoken before. Some carry on trade with the neighbouring islands, to which they sail in junks, some are employed in hunting and shooting, some in fishing, some in agriculture. Their clothes are made of cotton. Their animals are nearly the same as ours, excepting sheep, oxen, and asses; their horses are very slight and small. They have a great supply of camphor, ginger, and cinnamon. On leaving this island our men, having paid their respects to the king and propitiated him by presents, sailed to the Moluccas, their way to which had been pointed out to them by the king. Then they came to the coast of the island of Solo, where they heard that pearls were to be found as large as doves' eggs, or even hen's eggs, but that they were only to be had in very deep water. Our men did not bring home any single large pearl, as they were not there at the season of the year for pearl-fishing. They said however that they found an oyster there the flesh of which weighed 47 pounds. Hence I should be disposed to believe that pearls of the size mentioned would be found there; for it is certain that large pearls are found in oysters. And, not to forget it, I will add that our men reported that the islanders of Porne asserted that the king wore two pearls in his crown as large as goose eggs. After this they came to the island of Gilona, where they saw some men with such long ears that they reached down to their shoulders; and when they expressed their astonishment the natives told them that, in an island not far off, there were men who had such long and wide ears that one ear could, when they liked, cover the whole of their heads. But as our men were not in search of monsters but of spices they did not trouble themselves about such rubbish, but sailed direct for the Moluccas, where they arrived in the eighth month after their Admiral (Magellan) had been slain in the island of Mauthan. The islands are five in number, and are called Tarante, Muthil, Thedori, Mare, and Matthien*, situated partly to the north, partly to the south, and partly on the equator; the productions are cloves, nutmegs, and cinnamon. They are all close together, but of small extent.

(* Ternate, Moter, Tidore, Maru, Mutjan.)

A few years ago the kings (of) Marmin began to believe that the soul is immortal. They were induced to believe this solely from the following reason, that they observed that a certain very beautiful small bird never settled on the earth, or on anything that was on the earth; but that these birds sometimes fell dead from the sky to the earth. And when the Mohammedans, who visited them for trading purposes, declared that these birds came from Paradise, the place of abode of departed souls, these princes adopted the Mohammedan faith, which makes wonderful promises respecting this same Paradise. They call this bird Mamuco Diata, and they venerate it so highly that the kings think themselves safe to battle under their protection, even when, according to their custom, they are placed in the front line of the army in battle. The common people are Kafirs, and have much the same manners and customs as the islanders of Porne, already spoken of. They are much in need of supplies from abroad, inasmuch as their country only produces spices, which they willingly exchange for the poisonous articles, arsenic and sublimated mercury, and for the linen which they generally wear, but what use they make of these poisons has not yet been ascertained. They live on sago-bread, fish, and sometimes parrots. They live in very low-built cabins; in short, all they esteem and value is peace, leisure and spices. The former, the greatest of blessings, the wickedness of mankind seems to have banished from our part of the world to theirs; but our avarice and insatiable desire of the luxuries of the table has urged us to seek for spices even in those distant lands. To such a degree has the perversity of human nature persisted in driving away as far as possible that which is conducive to happiness, and in seeking for articles of luxury in the remotest parts of the world. Our men, having carefully examined the position of the Moluccas, and of each separate island, and also into the character of the chiefs, sailed to Thedori, because they understood that this island produced a greater abundance of cloves than the others, and also that the king excelled the other kings in prudence and humanity. Providing themselves with presents they went on shore, and paid their respects to the king, and handed him the presents as the gift of the Emperor. He accepted the presents graciously, and looking up to heaven said: "It is now two years since I learnt from observation of the stars that you were sent by the great King of Kings to seek for these lands. Wherefore your arrival is the more agreeable to me inasmuch as it has already been foreseen from the signification of the stars. And since I know that nothing happens to men which has not long since been ordained by the decree of Fate and of the stars, I will not be the man to resist the determination of Fate and the stars, but will spontaneously abdicate my royal power, and consider myself for the future as carrying on the government of this island as your king's viceroy. So bring your ships into the harbour, and order the rest of your companions to land in safety, so that now, after so much tossing about on the sea and so many dangers, you may securely enjoy the comforts of life on shore, and recruit your strength, and consider yourselves to be coming into your own king's dominions."

Having thus spoken, the king laid aside his diadem, and embraced each of our men, and directed such refreshments as the country produced to be set on table. Our men, delighted at this, returned to their companions and told them what had taken place. They were much delighted by the graciousness and benevolence of the king, and took up their quarters in the island. When they had been entertained for some days by the king's munificence they sent envoys thence to the other kings to investigate the resources of the islands and to secure the goodwill of the chiefs. Tarante was the nearest; it is a very small island, its circumference being a little over six Italian miles. The next is Matthien, and that also is small. These three produce a great quantity of cloves, but every fourth year the crop is far larger than at other times. These trees only grow on precipitous rocks, and they grow so close together as to form groves. The tree resembles the laurel as regards its leaves, its closeness of growth, and its height; the clove, so called from its resemblance to a nail (Latin *clavus*) grows at the very tip of each twig. First a bud appears, and then a blossom much like that of the orange; the point of the clove first shows itself at the end of the twig, until it attains its full growth; at first it is reddish, but the heat of the sun soon turns it black. The natives share groves of this tree among themselves, just as we do vineyards. They keep the cloves in pits till the merchants fetch them away. The fourth island, Muthil, is no larger than the rest. This island produces cinnamon; the tree is full of shoots, and in other respects fruitless; it thrives best in a dry soil, and is very much like the pomegranate tree. When the bark cracks through the heat of the sun it is pulled off the tree, and being dried in the sun a short time becomes cinnamon. Near Muthil is another island, called Bada, more extensive than the Moluccas; in it the nutmeg grows. The tree is tall and wide-spreading, a good deal like a walnut-tree. The fruit too is produced just in the same way as a walnut, being protected by a double covering, first a soft envelope, and under this a thin reticulated membrane which encloses the nut. This membrane we call muskatbluthe, the Spaniards call it mace; it is an excellent and wholesome spice. Within this is a hard shell, like that of a filbert, inside which is the nutmeg, properly so called. Ginger also is produced in all the islands of this archipelago; some is sown, some grows spontaneously; but the sown ginger is the best. The plant is like the saffron-plant, and its root, which resembles the root of saffron, is what we call ginger. Our men were kindly received by the various chiefs who all, after the example of the king of Thedori, spontaneously submitted themselves to the Imperial Government. But the Spaniards, having now only two ships, determined to bring with them specimens of all sorts of spices, but to load the ship mainly with cloves because there had been a very abundant crop of it this season, and the ships could contain a great quantity of this kind of spice. Having laden their ships with cloves, and received letters and presents from the chiefs to the Emperor, they prepared to sail away. The letters were filled with assurances of fidelity and respect; the gifts were Indian swords, etc. The most remarkable curiosities were some of the birds called Mamuco Diata--that is the Bird of God with which they think themselves safe and invincible in battle. Five of these were sent, one of which I procured from the captain of the ship, and now send it to your lordship--not that you will think it a defence against treachery and violence, but because you will be pleased with its rarity and beauty. I also send some cinnamon, nutmegs, and cloves, that you may see that our spices are not only not inferior to those imported by the Venetians and Portuguese, but of superior quality because they are fresher. Soon after our men had sailed from Thedori the larger of the two ships sprang a leak, which let in so much water that they were obliged to return to Thedori. The Spaniards, seeing that this defect could not be put right except with much labour and loss of time, agreed that the other ship should sail to the Cape of Cattigara, thence across the ocean as far as possible from the Indian coast, lest they should be seen by the Portuguese, until they came in sight of the southern point of Africa, beyond the tropic of Capricorn, which the Portuguese call the Cape of Good Hope, for thence the voyage to Spain would be easy. It was also arranged that when the repairs of the other ship were completed it should sail back through the archipelago and the vast (Pacific) Ocean to the coast of the continent which we have already mentioned (South America), until they came to the Isthmus of Darien, where only a narrow neck of land divides the South Sea from the Western Sea, in which are the islands belonging to Spain. The smaller ship accordingly set sail again from Thedori, and though they went as far as 12 degrees south they did not find Cattigara, which Ptolemy considered to lie considerably south of the equator; however after a long voyage they arrived in sight of the Cape of Good Hope, and thence sailed to the Cape Verde Islands. Here this ship also, after having been so long at sea, began to be leaky, and the men, who had lost several of their companions through hardships in the course of their adventures, were unable to keep the water pumped out, They therefore landed at one of the islands, called Santiago, to buy slaves. As our men, sailor-like, had no money, they offered cloves in exchange for slaves. When the Portuguese officials heard of this they committed thirteen of our men to prison. The rest, eighteen in number, being alarmed at the position in which they found themselves, left their companions behind, and sailed direct to Spain. Sixteen months after they had sailed from Thedori, on the 6th September 1522, they arrived safe and sound at a port near Seville. These sailors are certainly more worthy of perpetual fame than the Argonauts who sailed with Jason to Colchis; and the ship itself deserves to be placed among the constellations more than the ship *Argo*. For the *Argo* only sailed from Greece through the Black Sea, but our ship setting out from Seville sailed first southwards, then through the whole of the West, into the Eastern Seas, then back again into the Western.

I humbly commend myself to your Most Reverend Lordship.

Written at Valladolid, 24th October 1522.

Your Most Reverend and Most Illustrious Lordship's most humble and perpetual servant,

MAXIMILIANUS TRANSYLVANUS.

Cologne--(printed) at the house of Eucharius Cervicornus, A.D. 1523, in the month of January.

CHAPTER 27. A.D. 1522 TO 1523.

ALLEGED GLOBE OF SCHONER OF 1523.

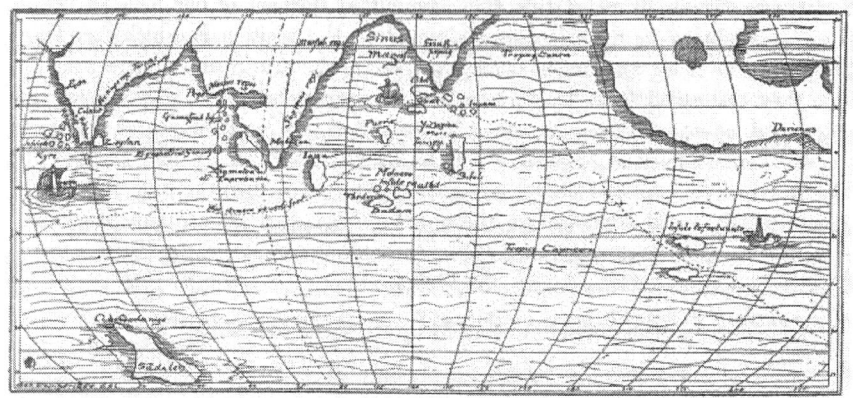

ALLEGED GLOBE OF SCHONER OF 1523.

he voyage of the *Vittoria* had a marked influence on the geography of Australasia at the period immediately following the return of the first circumnavigators. Its influence on cartography is of a strange character, and this period might be termed the *no Australia period*, its strangeness consisting in the transitory total disappearance of the Australian continent; for although the Great South Land appears again in a new form and under a new name with the Desceliers Lusitano-Spanish type of map, ranging between 1530 and 1556, yet its effacement is maintained in such an important document as the Sebastian Cabot mappamundi of 1544. Whether the leaving out of the Australian continent was a matter of political purpose, or whether the inclusion on the maps of the period of a continent which had not been sufficiently surveyed, was not deemed advisable, are questions which remain to be considered. It must be conceded however that the previous periods were periods of geographical incunabula as far as

Australia is concerned, for the indications of a Great South Land on maps previous to 1530/1536 were of a very rough nature. Those indications showed a mere knowledge of the existence of certain portions of the coastlines which geographers had taken upon themselves to join together in a more or less arbitrary manner. The voyage of the first circumnavigators demolished in a great measure certain theories and vagaries, and relegated towards the South Pole the unknown continent. On the other hand the absence on the charts of the *terra incognita* may have been a provisory measure adopted until better information was available.

ALLEGED GLOBE OF SCHONER OF 1523.

The late Henry Stevens considered the globe which we are going to deal with--and which with Mr. Henry Harrisse and for want of a better name we shall describe as the Alleged Globe of Schoner of 1523*--as "one of the immediate results of the publication of the celebrated first edition of the Letter of Maximilianus of Transylvanus, printed at Cologne in January of that year, and not 1524, as has been generally held.

(*Footnote. The Munich gores is another name given by Mr. H. Harrisse to the Alleged Globe of Schoner of 1523.)

He also credits Schoner with laying down the precise routes of Magellan's fleet, with the latitudes and longitudes given, projected and worked over 360 degrees of the world in a far more correct and intelligible manner than ever had been done before";* and, in support of his belief that the globe we are considering was constructed by Schoner, Mr. H. Stevens refers his readers to Schoner's description of his 1523 globe, *De Nuper*, etc. But we do not possess that globe, as Mr. Harrisse has proved most conclusively.*

(*Footnote. Johann Schoner etc. by Henry Stevens of Vermont, page xxiv. line 17. C.H. Coote of the British Museum in voce.)

(*Footnote. The Discovery of North America by Henry Harrisse, page 519 et sequit Number 147.)

Schoner's lost globe of 1523 was copied from his globe of 1520, which, as far as the Australasian regions are concerned, is identical with his globe of 1515. Now, this Alleged Globe of Schoner of 1523 is totally different, as may be observed, from the Schonerean gores of 1515, and cannot therefore be accepted as the work of Schoner.

A passage occurs in Schoner's description of his 1523 lost globe which is sufficient proof to that effect, for he says: "I do not however wish to set aside the globe I constructed some time ago, as it fully showed all that had, at that time, been discovered; so that the former, as far as it goes, agrees with the latter."

Our sketch of the Alleged Schoner's Globe of 1523 is taken from the reproduction of the original gores formerly in the possession of the late Mr. Henry Stevens. Concerning these reprinted gores Mr. H. Harrisse remarks* "that the original woodcut, from which the reprint was made recently (1885), does not bear the date of 1523 or the name of Schoner. On the contrary, it is entirely anonymous and dateless."

(*Footnote. The Discovery of North America, page 520 line 15.)

Moreover, as regards at least the Australasian regions and its fantastic islands, the leading feature inaugurated in this important wood block is a marked departure from the Behaimean and Schonerean configurations, one strange phase of this new departure being the total disappearance of the Austral-Asian continental protuberance which occupied in previous charts the site of Australia. In this map Magalhaens' course is set down. After leaving the straits that bear his name* Magalhaens' track runs through a group of islands where the word Crete may be noticed; reaching the tropic of Capricorn it passes between two islands which bear the name *Insule Infortunate*, then, following the same course, the equator is crossed and the first land reached is the island *Iuuana*, the Inuagana of Maximilian's letter.

(*Footnote. The entrance to this strait on the South Atlantic side bears the name *Sinus Juliana*, Bay of St. Julian, and is placed too far north.)

In proximity to Iuuana may be noticed five islands without names. Had there been sufficient space for naming them we might expect to find Maximilian's nomenclature, i.e. Acacan, Selani, Massana, Subuth, and Mauthan. *Cohol*, left to the north, has preserved its original orthography, and *Gibith* to the south stands for Gibeth; the track then passes by *Porne*, leaving in an easterly direction *Yciagina?--a* name not to be found in Maximilian's letter; whereas of the nine islands mentioned under the names Siloli, Solo, Gilona, Tarante, Muthil, Thedori, Mare,

Matthien, and Bada* six only are named on this map, namely *Mare, Taraze* (Tarante?), *Siloli, Muthil, Thedori,* and *Badam*.

(*Footnote. An error occurs in Stevens' Johann Schoner, page 142 note 2, where *Bada*, the nutmeg producing Banda, is mistaken for Badjan or Batchian.)

Upon leaving the Spice Islands the course of the remaining ship of Magalhaens' fleet is set down to the south of *Iaua*, that island being placed longitudinally according to the erroneous interpretation initiated after the altering of Fra Mauro's mappamundi.

To the south of the track of the *Vittoria* and halfway between Java and the Cape of Good Hope we notice a large island, bearing the name *Sadales*, which recalls the *Sandalos silve* of the Frankfort gores of 1515. This island is a remnant of the bogus Madagascar of Marco Polo, but *Cabo Godanige*, the name of the north cape of this island, is here introduced for the first time as far as we are aware.

In conclusion, we may say, with reference to this map and to the voyage of the first circumnavigators, that the nomenclature in the Spice Island region is certainly derived from Maximilian's letter; and, although the track of Magalhaens' vessels is very carelessly indicated and does not always agree with the above-mentioned letter, it nevertheless bears signs of being derived from the same source as the nomenclature.

CHAPTER 28. A.D. 1525 TO 1529.

LOAYSA'S EXPEDITION TO THE SPICE ISLANDS. DON JORGE DE MENEZES. THE FRANCISCUS MONACHUS MAPPAMUNDI OF 1526. ALVARO DE SAAVEDRA DISCOVERS NEARLY THE WHOLE OF THE NORTH COAST OF NEW GUINEA.

After the return of the *Vittoria* the old dispute between the Portuguese and Spanish about the line of demarcation was resumed and referred to the Badajos convocation of learned cosmographers and pilots. No decision however was arrived at, and another expedition to the Spice Islands was fitted out by Spain.

This was entrusted to Garcia Jofre de Loaysa with Sebastian del Cano as pilot-major and other survivors of Magalhaens' expedition.

They sailed from Coruna in July 1525 with an armament consisting of seven ships.*

(*Footnote. Nombrose por Capitan general de esta armada y capitan de la primera nave llamada *Santa Maria de la Victoria* a Garcia Jofre de Loaisa, Caballero del Avito de San Juan, natural de Ciudad-Real, con 450 castellanos; a Juan Sebastian del Cano, por capitan de la segundo nave, dicha *Sancti Spiritus*; a Pedro de Vera, continuo de la Casa Real, por capitan de la tercera, i de la 40a, dicha *San Gabriel*, a D. Rodrigo de Acuna; y de la 5a llamada *Santa Maria del Parral*, a D. Jorge Manrique de Naxera; y de la 6a que llamaban *San Lesmes*, a Francisco de Hoces, y de un patage a Santiago de Guevara. Herrera. Decada III lib vii. cap. v.)

The expedition proved a most disastrous one. Sebastian del Cano's vessel was wrecked at the entrance to Magalhaens' strait and the captain-general was separated from the fleet. Francisco de Hoces, who commandad the *San Lesmes*, is reported to have been driven by the storm to 55 degrees of south latitude, where he sighted land, which, if we consider the evidence of the *De orbi situ* of Franciscus Monacus,* must have been either the South Georgia or South Sandwich Islands. Francisco de Hoces believed it to belong to an Austral continent and to be connected with the *Tierra del Fuego*.

(*Footnote. See below The Franciscus Monacus Mappamundi.)

It was April before they entered Magalhaens' strait, and the passage was tedious and dismal, several of the sailors dying from the extreme cold. At last, on the 25th of May 1526, they entered the Pacific Ocean, where they were met by another violent storm which dispersed them right and left. One of the small vessels, a rowboat called a patache, in command of Joam de Resaga, ran along the coast of Peru and reached New Spain, where they gave an account to the celebrated Cortez, telling him that Loaysa was on his way to the islands of cloves; the others steered a north-westerly course.

By this time they had met with many hardships, several seamen had died, and Loaysa and Sebastian del Cano were very sick. At last the commander of the expedition died, July 30 1526, and Sebastian del Cano soon followed his commander, expiring a few days later. Alonso de Salazar was now appointed to the command of the fleet; he steered for the Ladrones.

When they reached this group of islands they had lost thirty-eight seamen. From the Ladrones they sailed to the Philippines, and on their journey lost their third commander, Alonso de Salazar. They then made their way to the Spice Islands.

Galvano informs us that only one vessel of Loaysa's fleet reached the Moluccas or Spice Islands. The fourth commander, Martin Iniquez de Carquicano, died, poisoned, it is said, and the command of the remnant of the expedition was entrusted to Hernando della Torre. Disputes immediately arose between the Portuguese and the Spaniards, eventuating in a warfare that lasted several years.

Meanwhile in the year 1526* Don Jorge de Menezes, in his passage from Malacca to the Spice Islands, was carried by currents, and through his want of information respecting the route to the north coast of Papua, probably to Waigiu, which appears to be the island known at the time under the name of *Versija*.*

(*Footnote. 1526, 1527, 1528, according to various authors.)

(*Footnote. See above.)

Having spent some time in a good port at this island of Versija, he continued his journey towards the east and made other discoveries along the north-west coast of New Guinea. It is in these regions that we find on old charts *Os Papuas* and the legend *Hic hibernavit Georgius de Menezes*.*

(*Footnote. See G. de Barros, Asia, Decad. iv. lib. i. c. xvi., and Lavanha, Voyage of Menezes page 53. Madrid 1615.

THE FRANCISCUS MONACHUS MAPPAMUNDI OF 1526 OR 1527.

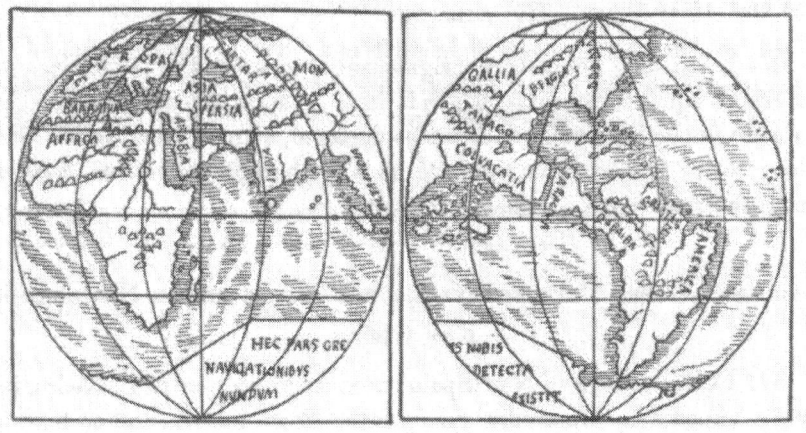

The two spheres of Franciscus Monachus, which we borrow from Harrisse's valuable work,* form an important geographical document. They are of the year 1526 or 1527, and belong to a work *De orbis situ*, which contains the following remarkable passage: "*Praterea inventa anno abhinc millesimo quingentesimo vigesimo sexto, terra longitudine 0. meridionali latitudine, 52. partium cultoribus vacua. Reliqua Australis ora etianum in obscuro latent*: Moreover in the year 1526 a land has been discovered by 0 degrees longitude and 52 degrees south latitude, which is not inhabited. The other parts of that Austral country are yet in the dark." Mr. Harrisse asks: "What is that Austral country beginning on a line with the initial meridian, and in such extreme southern latitude, which Franciscus Monacus says was discovered in 1526? The latter date can only be a *lapsus pennae*, as no such discovery was accomplished in that year. As to the country itself we have only to compare its delineation and position in Franciscus' woodcuts with the antarctic land in the various globes of Schoner to see at a glance that it can only be the region on which the Nuremberg mathematician has inscribed, in 1533, the legend: Terra Australis recenter inventa, sed nondum plene cognita. The difference is that Franciscus makes another *lapsus* in inserting in his map the following statement: Hec pars ore* (*sic pro* orb) is nobis navigationibus detecta nondum existit: This part of the world has not yet been discovered [*sic*] in our navigations."

(*Footnote. Harrisse, The Discovery of North America.)

(*Footnote. The E of ORE is only due to a slip of the wood engraver's burin. G. Collingridge.)

Mr. Harrisse adds, and we agree with him, that "Franciscus evidently meant that the country had not been entirely explored or made known, since he says so explicitly in his text, adding even a latitude and a longitude, and configurates the region in his map." Now, why should there be any *lapsus* at all? This land in 0 degrees longitude 52 degrees south latitude can be no other than South Georgia or the South Sandwich Islands, which we have seen* was discovered by Francisco de Hoces in the San Lesmes in 1526; and if we ask how did the news of such discovery reach Europe we have the answer in the fact that Joam de Resaga ran along the west coast of South America until he reached New Spain, where he rendered an account to Cortez concerning, the proceedings of Loaysa's fleet.

(*Footnote. Above.)

If the remarkable passage in the *De orbis situ*, confirmed by the Franciscus Monachus mappamundi and other documents, such as the Paris Gilt Globe, establishes another claim in favour of Spanish priority of discovery, the Monachus mappamundi seems to settle another in favour of the Portuguese. We refer to the further discovery of New Guinea, the north-westernmost parts of which had already been seen in 1511/1512.

On this small and apparently insignificant mappamundi New Guinea is represented in size as equal to Sumatra, which in itself is approximately correct; but, and which is more important, its periplus is also depicted, showing that Torres' Strait was known long before that navigator wended his way through its waters. Nevertheless in this map the Australian continent is left out.

ALVARO DE SAAVEDRA DISCOVERS NEARLY THE WHOLE OF THE NORTH COAST OF NEW GUINEA.

In 1527 Cortez sent from New Spain his kinsman, Alvaro de Saavedra, in search of Loaysa's expedition. Saavedra reached the Spice Islands, and on his way back, in endeavouring to reach America, in June 1528, he fell in with land 250 leagues east of the Spice Islands, which land has been identified as lying to the north of New Guinea and was named by him the *Isla del Oro*, the Island of Gold: *Anduvieron 250 leguas hasta la isla del Oro, grande y de gente negra, con los cabellos crespos...Corrieron 250 leguas hasta dar en otras islas, en altura de 7 degrees* pobladas de gente blanca, barbuda, que salieron a la nao, amenazando de tirar piedras con las hondas; y fue cosa maravillosa ver en tan poco distancia hombres tan diferentes de color. (Herrera, Decada iv. lib. iii. cap. vi.) If we accept Herrera's description concerning the variety of races met with by the Spaniards--variety which is known to exist nearer the equator--it is not difficult to reconcile it even with modern experience, but we must take for erroneous the latitude of 7 degrees mentioned in the Spanish text.

In November 1528 Saavedra returned to the Spice Islands, arriving at Tidor on the 19th. He had been unable, owing to calms and headwinds, to make his way back to America; nor was he more successful in a second attempt made the following year, when, after having followed his previous course, and having vainly attempted to sail eastward, he met with his death soon after leaving the Good Gardens Islands. The ship's company was compelled once more to seek the refuge of the Spice Islands where they remained for seven years, when a favourable opportunity enabled them to return to Spain by way of Lisbon, in the year 1536.

According to Galvano, Saavedra's discoveries in 1529 were more extensive than in 1528. He says:* "In the yeere 1529, in May, Saavedra returned back againe towards New Spaine, and he had sight of a land towards the south in two degrees, and he ran east along by it aboue fiue hundred leagues till the end of August [according to their account].

The coast was cleane and of good ankerage, but the people blacke and of curled haire; from the girdle downward they did weare* a certaine thing plaited to couer their lower parts. The people of Maluco call them Papuas, because they be blacke and friseled in their haire; and so also do the Portugals call them. [Alvaro] Saavedra hauing sailed four or five degrees to the south of the line, returned unto it, and passed the equinoctiall towards the north..."

(*Footnote. Galvano, page 176.)

(*Footnote. Skirts of feathers, well made, of various colours.)

CHAPTER 29. A.D. 1527 TO 1536.

SPANISH OFFICIAL MAPS. THE ANONYMOUS WEIMAR MAPPAMUNDI OF 1527. THE DIEGO RIBEIRO MAPPAMUNDI OF 1529. THE DAUPHIN CHART, 1530 TO 1536.

A few years after the discovery of the New World the Spanish Government found it necessary, in order to regulate her navigations and ascertain what new discoveries were being made, to order the creation of an official map of the world, in the composition of which the skill and knowledge of all her pilots and captains were sought.

This official map, from which copies were made, was called the *Padron Real* and afterwards the Padron general. The Diego Ribeiro mappamundi of 1529, a portion of which is reproduced here, belongs to the Padron general category of maps. In this class of Spanish maps the Australian continent has been left out. With reference to our subject this mappamundi is nevertheless of importance, because it shows graphically that such documents were prepared and used in Spain by the highest authorities in cartographical matters, for this mappamundi is a duplicate or replica of an earlier map by the same author as the anonymous Weimar mappamundi of 1527, which, according to Mr. Harrisse, is "the earliest complete specimen which we possess of a chart made with data collected in the *Casa de contratacion*, and on that account of great importance."

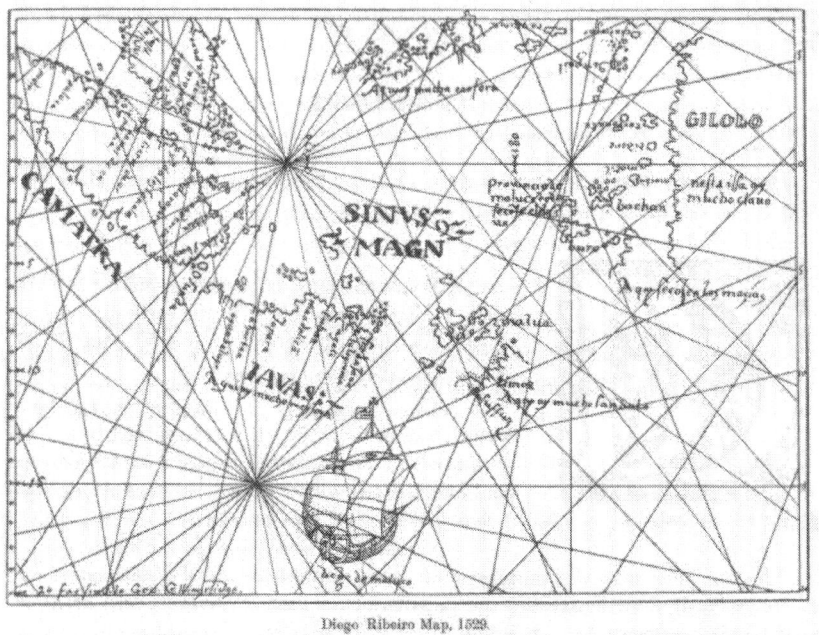

Diego Ribeiro Map, 1529.

The importance that it has with us is that it shows what were the claims of the Spanish Crown in connection with the famous line of demarcation.

According to the King of Spain's cosmographer, and as shown in this map, the Spice Islands fell within Spanish territory, so that with regard to Australia Portugal could only have claimed Western Australia; whereas the remainder of the continent, the lion's share, would have fallen to Spain. In the Propaganda Diego Ribeiro map of same date the same division may be observed, and the flags of Spain and Portugal float over the space which the Australian continent ought to occupy.

In the maps which we shall consider next, maps which, although showing Spanish influence, are essentially more Portuguese in their origin, the reverse occurs, and the line of demarcation is placed so as to include the Spice Islands in Portuguese territory.

Before we dismiss Diego Ribeiro's map, it may be well to notice that to the south of Java and below the pretty ship that announces that she comes from Maluco, the Spice Islands, *Vego de Maluco*, there is an open sea, called in the Propaganda copy *Occeanus Oriemtalis*. We draw attention to this fact because in the Dauphin chart, which we shall presently consider, we shall find that this ocean or sea is blocked by the Australian continent.

CHAPTER 30. A.D. 1530 TO 1550.

THE DAUPHIN MAP* OF THE ASSIGNED DATE OF 1530 TO 1536, AND OTHER MAPS OF THE SAME SCHOOL.

(*Footnote. This map has been called the Harleyan map, having belonged to Edward Harley, Earl of Oxford. See also The Early Discovery of Australia by George Collingridge. Journal and Proceedings of the Royal Geographical Society of Australasia, Sydney 1891/1892 Volume V.)

We now arrive at the most important document hitherto come to light connected with the early discovery of Australia--the map or chart which the late R.H. Major has called the Dauphin Map.

It belongs to a type of manuscript Lusitano-French planispheres, which is represented by several specimens, all of which are copies from a prototype which has either been destroyed or has not yet been found.

As we infer that the prototype of these planispheres is of a date anterior to 1530* we shall, notwithstanding the apparent later date of those we shall speak of, consider them collectively. According to Mr. Harrisse this planisphere, or at least its American portion, dates from after 1536.*

(*Footnote. Mr. Harrisse says: Le redacteur du catalogue du British Museum, ou cette carte est conservee (Add. Manuscripts 5, 413), en infere qu'elle est anterieur a l'annee 1536. Nous n'oserions l'affirmer. Jean et Sebastien Cabot, page 198.)

(*Footnote. Jean et Sebastien Cabot, page 200.)

One thing certain is that it has not been copied from the other maps of its class considered in this chapter, for it bears a legend in Portuguese, to which we shall refer, that has been corrupted in the other maps. Referring to these Lusitano-French maps in general, and describing this one in particular, the late R.H. Major says:* "The earliest in all probability, and the most fully detailed of these maps, is the one from which we give the annexed reduction of that portion immediately under consideration. It is a large chart of the world, on a plane scale, on vellum, 8 feet 2 inches by 3 feet 10 inches, highly ornamented, with figures, etc., and with the names in French. At the upper corner, on the left hand, is a shield of the arms of France, with the collar of St. Michael; and on the right, another shield of France and Dauphiny, quarterly. It was probably executed in the time of Francis I of France, for his son, the Dauphin, afterwards Henry II. This chart formerly belonged to Edward Harley, Earl of Oxford, after whose death it was taken away by one of his servants. It was subsequently purchased by Sir Joseph Banks, Bart., and presented by him to the British Museum in 1790."

(*Footnote. Early Voyages to Australia, Introduction. Page xxvii. A reduced copy of the Dauphin map is given, facing same page.)

It may not be out of place to state here that Edward Harley was one of the principal Lords of the Admiralty, and that he was instrumental in sending Dampier out to Australia.*

(*Footnote. See W. Dampier by W. Clark Russell. London, Macmillan & Co. 1889.)

The strongest evidence of discovery as yet brought to light is shown in the drafting of these old charts of Australia. Unfortunately, as we have said, they are all mere copies, more or less altered in outline and corrupted in nomenclature, from a prototype which has not yet been found.

But, if the internal evidence of these old charts clearly shows the original or originals to have been Portuguese and Spanish, one point of the question will be settled, and the Portuguese and Spanish will undoubtedly be entitled to the claim and honour of having discovered Australia.

As to the question of date, that is of less importance, and can be fixed approximately, for the discovery must have taken place at some period between the arrival of the Portuguese and Spaniards in these seas and the drafting of the earliest known chart, that is between 1511 and 1542.*

(*Footnote. See below. John Rotz' charts 1542.)

But after all, until the very date of the expedition which resulted in the first discovery can be ascertained, the question of the nationality of the first discoverers is a much more interesting one. Having no other documentary evidence except these old charts, the first conclusion drawn was, that as they are all written in French, the French, although no claim was made by them, were the discoverers.

The late R.H. Major, having thoroughly considered the possibility of a French claim, came to the conclusion that such a claim is untenable. Being somewhat shaken however in his first belief of a Portuguese discovery, he was led to adopt a Provencal theory to explain certain words on these old Gallicized charts which were neither Portuguese nor French. The whole question was in this state of incertitude when, a few years ago, having occasion to examine minutely these old documents, we discovered on this particular one a phrase in Portuguese, which curiously enough had escaped the notice of all those who had made a study of this early specimen of cartography. This phrase, *anda ne barcha* (no boats go here), situated as it is in the Gulf of Carpentaria, had in our mind a very great significance, since it not only proves the Portuguese origin of the chart but also the genuineness of the discovery made in that locality, as it showed that the discoverers were fully aware of the shallowness of the water off this part of the coast of Australia.

It must be admitted however that on the original chart the phrase anda ne barcha may refer to the difficulty of navigating the strait between Java and Bali or Lomboc.

When we say that this legend proves the Portuguese origin of the chart we do not mean to convey the idea that we accepted it there and then as a proof of Portuguese origin, but we took it as a clue, for the meaning of these words had evidently not been understood by the copyist, since he had left them in their original form instead of translating them into French, and had mistaken them for the names of two islands. This clue led us to make a special study of every word on the chart that had proved so interesting, the result being that we came to the conclusion that the western coasts of Australia had been charted by the Portuguese, whereas the eastern coasts, which fell within the sphere allotted to the Spaniards, had been discovered and charted by them.

If we take for granted that these charts are unquestionably of Portuguese and Spanish origin the next point of importance that calls for our attention relates to the peculiar configuration, or, to be more precise, the strange distortion which all these charts have undergone. This distortion is so great that one might fail to recognise Australia within the coastline set down were it not for the general fitness of the terms used as descriptive of this coastline, terms which have been handed down to us, and some of which are recorded in the very maps we use every day. Further we have the equally important fact that within the latitude and longitude charted Australia does actually hold its place in the vast ocean around.

We must make great allowance for the measurement of longitude as computed in the days when Magalhaens was called upon to determine whether the Moluccas fell within the Spanish or Portuguese territory, for after the return of the remnant of his glorious but disastrous expedition the matter was as unsettled as ever. Albeit the errors of these charts are far more suggestive of deliberate distortion than of inaccurate charting.

A contemporaneous Spanish pilot, Juan Gaetan, who navigated the seas to the north of Australia, reports that the Portuguese purposely distorted and otherwise altered their charts: Che cautelosamente le portano false.*

(*Footnote. The passage is worth giving in full. It will be found in Ramusio, Venetia 1563. Delle Navigationi et Viaggi, Primo Volume Fol. 377 B. Da malaccha nauigammo a Caniai con li lor nauilij, nelliquali ne codussero, et essendo io Pilotto stato in tutte le nauigationi che si fecero dipoi che vscimmo da Malaccho, conobbi tutte le lor carte, che cautelosamente le portano false, & fuori delle altezze & parizzi veri, & nauigano per certi derotteri, cioe pariggi, & libri che portano senza tener posta alcuna longitudine in quelli, di maniera che si ristringe & ritira la terra di Maluccho al capo di Buona speranza, al mio giudicio, piu di cinquecento 50 leghe, secondo quello che io nauigai & considerat in questa nauigatione; perche ordinariamente ogni giorno io pigliano la mia altezza, et derotta, et ne tengo fatta vna carta, la quale, come dico, e differente & discorde da quello che essi pongono la quatita sopradetta, & quiui lascio molte altre particolarita che mi passorno in questa andata, perche questo mi pare che solo faccia al capo principale, et e cosa certa che li Portoghesi vedendo ch'io intendeua le cose della lor nauigatione, procurono che io restassi con loro & mi offersero molti partiti, liquali io non volsi accettare per venir a servire la Maesta Cesarea.)

The Portuguese, who were the first to make discoveries in these seas, must have been perfectly aware that the coasts they had charted lay more to the east than shown in these maps, and if they placed them more to the west it was in order to secure to themselves the lion's share, for their line of demarcation, as fixed by Pope Alexander VI, did not extend much beyond the east coast of Timor. They could not have believed that Timor was situated to the east of the peninsula now known as York Peninsula, and clearly shown in these charts, nor that there was not an open sea to the south of Java, although the south coast of that island was not known at the time.

When that memorable council was convened on the shores of the Guadiana, a few years before these charts were made, to settle the dispute between the Spanish and Portuguese, after the return of Magalhaens' expedition, there may or may not have been collusion between both parties in connection with a distortion of the original charts used in the council, but both nations had something to gain by showing the sea-way blocked as it is in these maps.

In confirmation of this theory a very significant passage occurs in the Portuguese Asia of Barros (continued by Diego do Couto) relative to the blocking of the sea-way which we allude to. Diego do Couto, writing about 1570, having described the fort in the Canal de Sunda, and referring to the advisability of blocking the Straits of Malacca, says:

"And it was the opinion of our forefathers that if the king (king of Portugal) possessed three fortresses, one in this situation (Strait of Sunda), one on Acheen Head, and one on the coast of Pegu, the navigation of the East could in a manner be *locked by those keys*, and the king would be lord of all its riches; and they gave many reasons in support of their opinions which we *forbear to repeat*."

Now these fortresses in the Straits of Sunda and Malacca would have been ineffectual unless some means were also adopted of blocking the passage to the south of Java. Fortresses and cannon were of no avail here, the passage was too wide, but, by connecting the south coast of Java with Australia, and the surveyed coastline of Australia with an imaginary continent extending to and around the South Pole, the question was solved, the respective possessions of Portugal and Spain defined, and further discoveries by other nations discouraged.

To effect this connection of the surveyed coasts with the imaginary continent certain fictitious coastlines were laid down, and a portion of the north-west coast was left out, from Dampier's Archipelago to King Sound, in order to compensate in a certain measure for the extreme westing given to the western and north-western part of *Jave la Grande*, which had been placed under Java.

That the Portuguese and Spanish knew of an open sea to the south of Java is certain, since Sebastian del Cano, returning to Spain from Timor with the last ship of Magalhaens' fleet, sailed through it. But the secret was so well kept that seventy-eight years after Magalhaens' voyage Java and Australia were still believed to be one and the same continent by certain well-informed navigators, as will be seen from Linschoten's Discours of Voyages into ye East and West Indies, London 1598, in which the following description of Java Major occurs: "South, south-east, right over against the last point or corner of the Isle of Sumatra, on the south side of the equinoctial line, lyeth the island called Jaua Maior, or Great Java, where there is a strait or narrow passage, called the Strait of Sunda, of a place so called, lying not far from thence within the Isle of Java. This island beginneth under 7 degrees on the south side, and runneth east and by south 150 miles long; but touching the breadth it is not found, because as yet it is not discovered, nor by the inhabitants themselves well known. Some think it to be firme land and parcel of the countrie called *terra incognita*, which being so should reach from that place to the Cape de Bona Sperace; but as yet it is not certainly known, and therefore it is accounted an island."

With regard to the distortion of the eastern coast of Australia we confess to have been somewhat startled by the discovery that we made--startled not so much at the proof of distortion we found, but because this proof of distortion bore witness to a more accurate survey of the eastern coast than could have been expected or even dreamt of.

It occurred to us that, in order to duly appreciate the displacement occasioned by Cape York having been placed under the island of Sumbawa, it would be well to establish a comparison by scaling the map we are describing and setting down the continent of Australia in its true position.

Having marked the degrees of longitude and latitude in the modern style, we were just going to begin drafting the eastern coast from Cape York when we found the place already occupied by an island that bears the name *ye de Tnbanos?* Strange to say, this island gave us the correct outline of the portion of Cape York Peninsula that extends from Cairncross Island to Cape Grenville, and thence to Cape Direction. Then, continuing our coastline in a south-easterly direction, we came across another island in the latitude of the tropic of Capricorn and extending thence to the 26th degree of south latitude.

These islands also formed part, and occupied the exact site of, that portion of the coast of Queensland that extends from Curtis Island to the southern extremity of Great Sandy Island.

But these were not the only landmarks that had been left in their true position. C. de Fremose, which seems to jut out in such an extraordinary way on this chart, occupied the position of Cape St. George (Jervis Bay), and the line of coast we were drafting had to follow the one on the Dauphin chart from C. *de Fremose to Gouffre* (gulf), where we found Corner Inlet and Wilson's Promontory set down for us.

Then, turning north again, we found another group of islands occupying the position of Cape Arnheim in the northern territory. These were set down as *ye de Alioter*, or *Aliofer*.

Portugese Caravel

Now, could it be through mere coincidence that these fictitious islands and stretches of coast were set down and actually occupied such portions of our coast, with such extraordinary accuracy, not only as to configuration, but also as to longitude and latitude? It does not seem likely.

The illuminations form a conspicuous feature in these old maps, and lend a great charm to such productions of a bygone age; it would be a useless task however to seek in these quaint devices a strict pourtrayal of the scenes appertaining to the countries they are supposed to illustrate; to do so would be to forget their chief purpose--the decorative. But, allowing for the liberty usually granted to the artist and often exacted by him, the scenes depicted are not borrowed from the realms of Idealism to the extent that has been supposed by certain commentators. The kangaroo is not represented; no, nor the gum-tree either, perhaps? But that clump of bamboos on the top of the hill is not a volcano in full eruption, as a learned critic ventured to assert. We see on these charts fairly correct presentments of that animal seen for the first time by the Spaniards in the straits to which Magalhaens gave his name, and thus described by Pigafetta, who accompanied the first circumnavigators: "This animal has the head and ears of a mule, the body of a camel, the legs of a stag, and the tail of a horse, and like this animal it neighs."*

(*Footnote. The same author describes the Patagonians, an illustration of which is given in its proper place, in the 1550 chart, under the heading of *Geants trouve par les Espaignals*. Pigafetta says, speaking of one of these giants:

"This man likewise wore a sort of shoe, made of the same skin." The Patagonians covered their feet with the skin of the guanaco; it is on account of this shoe, which made their feet resemble somewhat those of an animal, that the Spaniards called these people *Patagones*, and their country was probably called *Regia Patalis*, and *Patagonia*, from Pata, an animal's foot.)

The animal thus described by Pigafetto is the Guanaco (camelus huanacus), and it is not astonishing to find it depicted on the continent of Australia, for we know that this continent was supposed to be connected with *Tierra del Fuego*. It is indeed described in certain old maps of the *post*-Magellanic period as *Regio Patalis*,* which Latin appellation may correspond to the Spanish *Tierra Patagonia*, as *Terra Australis* corresponds to *Tierra Australia*.

(*Footnote. See above.)

Now this brings us to the subject of the name given to Australia, on this and other early charts of this type. In the chart we are describing Australia is called *Jave la Grande*. La Grande Jave would have been the French construction, but this term--Jave la Grande--is merely the translation of Java Maior, the Portuguese for Marco Polo's Java Major.

The Dauphin Chart, A.D. 1530 to 1536.

Marco Polo described Java, from hearsay, as being the largest island in the world, and, the Portuguese finding this to be incorrect, as far as their knowledge of Java went, but finding nevertheless this "largest island in the world" to the south-east of Java, in fact, approximately in the longitude and latitude described by Marco Polo, the Portuguese, we say, did the best thing they could, both for Marco Polo's sake and their own, when they marked it on their charts where it was said to be, and with the name given to it by Polo, for he calls it Java Major to distinguish it from Sumatra, which island he calls Java Minor.

The channel marked between Java and Australia is evidently a concession due to the fact that a passage was known to exist. This channel, which is left white in the chart we are describing, is painted over in the 1550 specimen, as if it were blocked, and two men are represented with pick and shovel as if in the act of cutting it open. It is curious to notice how in both maps the upper silhouette of the landscape in this part defines the real south shore of Java. The Australian Alps, the range of hills on the western and north-western coast, and the great sandy interior of Australia, are also roughly sketched in.

NOMENCLATURE.

The names on the Dauphin map will be found compared in the following list with the nomenclature of other charts of the same class. Modern names are given in the last column.

NORTH COASTS OF SUMBAWA AND JAVA.

1530-1542. Dauphin.	1542-1546. De Rotz.	1546-1550 Henri II.	1550-1644. Desceliers.	1644-1894. Dutch to Modern period
G : Annape	Gunape	Guimape	Guanape	Gunong Api
	Cape	Cape	Cape	
Lima	bima	bouina	Bnuina	Bima
Arāāram	C : Vatraare	Arāāte	Aramaro	Kamara ?
Symbana	Sinbana	Sinbaua	Sinbaua	Sumbawa
	moro	maio	maro	
medan	modā	medam	medam	
...	Fiu de Jaua	...	...	(end of Java)
		panaruca		
...	lungrania	pularacā	pinaracā	...
Carabaia	Sieubina	Catabaia	Carnbaia	Surabaya
Agacim	Agizim	Agacim	Agadim	Gresic
Tumbam	Tnbā	Tabaur	Tabaur	
Mandalican	...	Mandalicā	Mandalicā	
		je tona		
...	...	...	Taroua	
Jappara	Japan	japara	Jaypara	Japara
Jana	Jane	Jana	Jaua	Java
Chnmbar	elibao	Carham	Carham	
		ye de cobras	y des cobras	
Agnada doilnu *	Guada doilim	Agnada dallom	agoada d'allom	
Simda	Sunda	Cumda	Cunda	Sunda
Canal de Sonda	Canal de Sonda	Canal de	Canal de	
Canal	...	Souda	Cunda	
P : des G⁰		Charbam	Charbam	
C : de	...	...	...	
Pallimbam	palinbaij	palimbam	pali mbam	
...	...	...	R.	
		Cap.	Cap.	

* As this work was going through the press, the following additional information concerning this corrupted legend to which we have already referred in connection with Francisco Rodriguez' Portolanos (see p. 114 et sequit.) was kindly forwarded by Mr. C. H. Coote, the worthy successor of the late R. H. Major of the British Museum. Mr. Coote's reading of the legend on the original portolano is as follows :—"Agoada da Joham lopiz dallvim elle desoobrio da que ate Japara." —"Watering place of Joao Lopez Dalvim, he discovered from this (place understood) as far as Japara." And Mr. Coote adds :—"If you will turn to my friend W. de Gray Birch's 'Commentaries of Alboquerque,' vol. 3, p. 166, you will find that Dalvim was captain of one of the vessels ordered by Alboquerque to remain at Malacca under the orders of Fernão Perez Andrade during the absence of Antonio D'Abreu's expedition to the Banda or Spice Islands, 1511-12. Rodriguez we know served under D'Abreu as pilot during this expedition. Upon his return he was probably transferred to Dalvim's ship upon a surveying expedition along the N. coast of Java; hence the legend on chart 16 of the portolano. The copyist on the Dauphin chart of 1536, unaware that dalvim was a proper name, and not a common term, makes nonsense of the whole thing.

Western Coasts of Jave-la-Grande.

....	....	G.	R.	
R.	....	R.	....	
....	....	R.	R.	
R des¹ p°	....	playne	plaine	
....	....	R de St pierre	R de St P	
Coste p°uro	....	....	Cap :	
R. Grande	Abaie de	Coste prune	Coste	
Baye bassa	Abaie a basse	R Grande	R : Grande	
C: de	....	R	Baye basse	
		C : de g°	Cap	
		....	R.	
Terre Ennegade	Terra en negade	Terre enneguade	C bo (cabo ?)	
Baye bresille	Abaie bresille	Baye Brasille	Terre onnega de	
Y⁸ des	illa da	ys de d°	Baye bresill	t'Landt de Eendracht ?
Baye basse	....	Baye basse	....	Pieter Goos' map c⁼ 1650 ?
B : de gao	....	R. de gao	R	
C : de grace	....	C : de grace	B : de.	
C : de St drao	....	C de Sᵗ A°	C : de grace	
Baye des y⁸	....	Cap	R	
Quabesegmence	....	Graibese qunesce	Roches	
C. des	....	R	ap quieta	Jacob Remmesens R ?
....	....	....	R	(J. Andrews' map)
....	....	....	Cap	1787
Coste blanche	....	Coste blanche	R	
yles	....	Ya	Coste br	
port de	....	R	....	
Lama de Sylla	....	Llame de Sille	P	I. des Filles ?
....	....	R de Silla	hama do Sille	Vaugondy's map 1756
Cap	....	Cap double	Cap	
coste bracq	....	....	....	
R de y°	....	R	Coste blanche	
R. de	....	Roches	....	
....	....	G⁰	R. de g°	
....	....	R	R.	
			R.	

Below 35° of south latitude the coastline is evidently fictitious, and the names in consequence cease on the Dauphin chart.

Eastern Coasts of Jave la Grande.

....	....	....	basses	
R	....	R Grande	R	
....	....	G°	Cap	
R	....	R	G°	
....	....	Cap	R.	
Coste dangereuse	Coste dägerose	R	....	In the locality of the Great Barrier Reef.
R		Coste perilleuse	Coste perilleuse	
R	....	....	....	
R	....	R	R	
Baye perdue	....	Baye perdue	R	
....	....	prayrye	Baye perdue	
R de beaucoup d'isles	....	R	Cap	
R	....	R	R.	
Rios	....	R : des basses	R. des 3 y⁸	
R	....	....	y de le	
....	....	....	R.	
....	....	....	R	
....	....	....	ansse	
Coste des herbaiges	....	Coste des herbaiges	Cap des herbaiges	
R.	....	R	....	
....	....	Cap p⁰	....	
R		R		
Y° de		R		
Coste de Graral		Coste de Gratal		
....		playne		
R		R		
R		R		
R		R		
Baye neusne		Baye neusne		
R		R		
R		R		
C : de Fremose		Cap de freinose		
R		R		
R		Gouffre		
....		R		
Gouffre		G°		
R		Bay Grande		
....		R		

Islands to the North of Jave-la-Grande and South of the Equator.

Abachachina		Abatochina	Abatochina		Gilolo
Les Papnas		Les Papuas	Papuas		Papua
Airrom		Arnim	Ariuz		Arroo islands
Conoir		Canoir	Canoie		
curam		Cutam	Curà		Goram ?
Seillan		dabeino ?	Seiloa		Ceram
Abillaro		Abillato	abillato		
Bacham		bacham	bacham		Batchian
....	....	Xulo			
bamda		banida	banida		Banda
....	....	barro			Booro
Adia					
bomraboir	botombor ?	bitibor			
Sollic	Sollic	Sollic	Sollic		Solor ?
Collorico	calorico	Lucapinho			
....	....	Lucalam			
Terre haute	Tierra alta		oorealta		High Land
Timoros	Tymor	Timor { Y° de Timor	Timor { T mor		Timor
Alanso	afaso	Tudor	ye de Timor		Allas ?
bamrera		Alanso	Tidor		
Lenr ree de Solor			clr ree de Solor		The Sea of Selor
C : de flonis	C : dos flores	C : fleurs	c des pol		C. Flores
Baenleao	bagnaiar	bacalico	balia		
C : de ferra	lizara gnefr	Lucarā	ucaro ate		
	C. de ferro	Gete	neecal		
....		Lucaraio	fer		
		C : Fer			
Anda ne	an tane	Amjana	an taue		No boats go here
barcha	bacha	bamcha	bamcha		Madura
Amadura	Amadura	Amadura	Amadura		
....	....	p : babia			
Crimacana	crimagane	quirima Jaoa	quirimojao		
bintam	bintan	bintam	bentam		Bintang
lingua	llinga	Lingua	ligua		Linga
		Veilato	velicitao		Billiton ?
....	....	Vanica	vanica		Banca
vamca	Banca	quirimata	....		Carimata
crimata	erimata				

Islands on the Western Coast of Jave-la-Grande.

Ye de Lame	Ysle de Llame	Ye de Laine	de Laine		
de neige	isle nege	Ye de Neige	de neige		
			arenes		Abrolhos

Islands on the Eastern Coasts of Jave-la-Grande.

Ye de Aliofer	....	Ye de Altofer	....	Tiburon
Ye de Tubaros	....	Ye des marsouyns	....	
Yslas de Magna	....	Ye de magas	....	
		Magna		
Ye de Saill	....	Ye de Saill	....	

CHAPTER 31. A.D. 1531 TO 1542.

THE MAPPEMONDE OF ORONTIUS FINAEUS OF 1531. SCHONER'S WEIMAR GLOBE OF 1533. G. MERCATOR'S DOUBLE CORDIFORM MAPPAMUNDI OF 1538. HERNANDO DE GRIJALVA'S EXPEDITION TO THE SPICE ISLANDS. TWO MAPS OF AUSTRALIA BY JOHN ROTZ (JEAN ROZE), 1542.

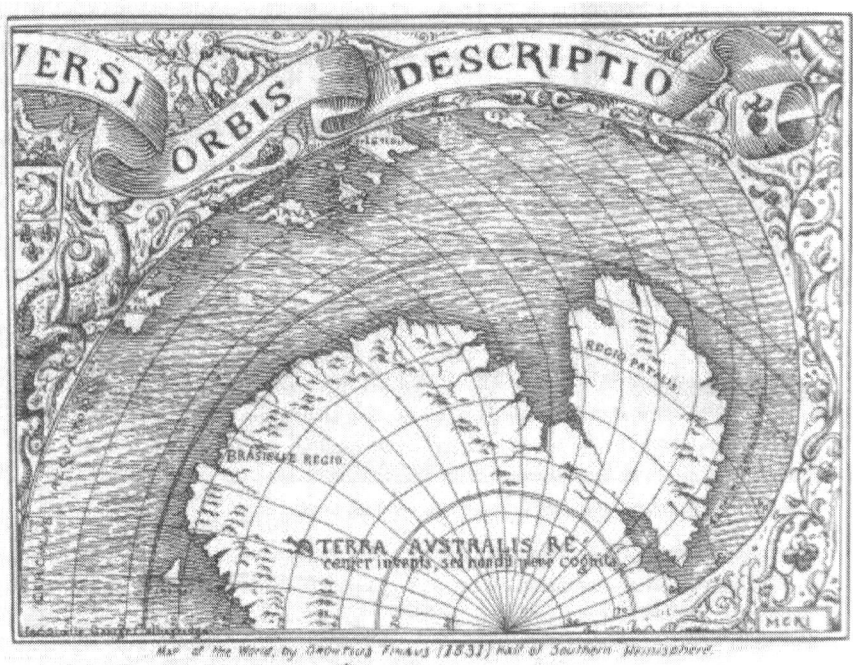

Map of the World by Orontius Finaeus (1531) Half of Southern Hemisphere.
(Reduced from Nordenskiold's Atlas.)

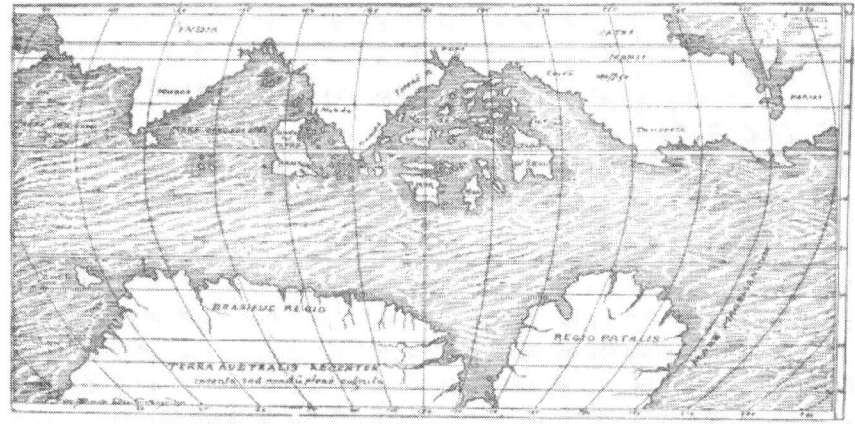

Mappemonde of Oronce Finé--1531--on our projection.

Mappemonde of Oronce Fine--1531--on our projection.

The first of the three maps that we shall examine briefly at the beginning of this chapter is a very rare engraved map of the world by the celebrated French astronomer and mathematician, Oronce Fine. The projection is a double cordiform one, of which we reproduce from Nordenskiold's atlas half of the hemisphere in which the TERRA AUSTRALIS occurs. In order to show the interesting features of the northern portions of many Australasian islands, and for the purposes of comparison with older and later maps, we give also a more comprehensive sketch map on our adopted projection.

Oronce Fine's information was borrowed from Lusitano-Spanish charts through the intermedium no doubt of Schoner's maps and globes, for we find on the *Terra Australis recenter inventa, sed nondum plene cognita*, his *Brasielie regio* and *Regio Patalis*.

The Malay peninsula is left out, or, at least, Cambodia and French Cochin-China is made to serve for it, as those regions are brought down south to the equator. Sumatra (*Samotra vel* TAPROBANA) lies too far to the west, Java (IAVA) is in its place. A kind of duplicate Java above it, without any name, may have been originally an indication of the south coast of Borneo, which appears above under the name of *burney*. To the east of Iava an island occupying the position approximately of Sumbawa or Timor bears the name Minor, which may have been intended for Java Minor, or is a bad reading for Timor. It appears however to have given rise to Sumbawa being called Java Minor, as we shall find it called in some later maps. Gilolo (*Gelolo vel Siloli**) is greatly exaggerated in size, and appears to include in its area the island of Ceram, other islands of the Banda Sea, and perhaps what was known of New Guinea.

(*Footnote. Mr. A.F. Calvert, in his book The Discovery of Australia (between pages 18 and 19) gives a reproduction of the Australian half of the southern hemisphere, in which *Siloli* appears under the name of Sylon. The mistake however is ours. This is how it happened; through the kindness of Mr. Delmar Morgan we received some time ago a photo-lithograpic copy of the portion we refer to. The Royal Geographical Society of Australasia wished to reproduce Mr. Delmar Morgan's reproduction. Everyone knows how blurred these repeated reproductions come out. In consequence we were asked to make a pen and ink facsimile of Mr. Delmar Morgan's photo-litho. At the time we had not seen the northern hemisphere of this map, the word read like Sylon, and as the island of Ceram in that locality has often been written Seillan, Seylan, and Sylon in old maps, we took it to be Sylon. When we saw the *whole map* shortly after we perceived our mistake at once, and also that the S of Siloli in the original was a bad reading for G. Had our signature been left on the reproduction of our map made by Mr. A.F. Calvert there would have been no need for this explanation. We have corrected the mistake in the present map.)

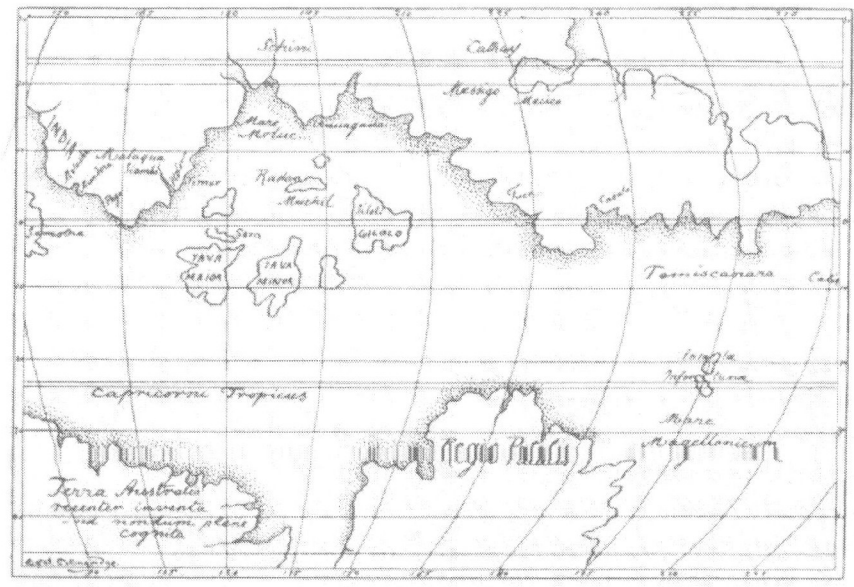

Schoner's Weimar Globe of 1533.

Schoner's Weimar Globe of 1533.

Schoner's Weimar Globe of 1533 is reproduced here on our projection from Mr. Harrisse's Discovery of North America. When compared with the preceding map it appears to have been copied from it. But we must remember that Schoner's lost globe of 1523, based on the knowledge of Magalhaens' voyage, contained, according to Schoner's own statements, features similar to those of this 1533 globe of his; and also that Schoner was the first geographer who joined America with Asia, and not Oronce Fine. There is a notable difference between this globe and Schoner's 1515 globe: In this one the islands, which in 1515 were placed on the Tropic of Capricorn, are placed on the equator. *Java Major* and *Java Minor* correspond to Java and Sumbawa, and bear the longitudinal deformation to which we have already referred.* Gilolo (*Siloli Gilolo*) is on the equator instead of above it. Magalhaens' *Insulae Infortunatae* are placed on the Tropic of Capricorn in the longitude of the Tonga islands. *Timor* is right out of its latitude to the north-west of Borneo, which bears no name.

(*Footnote. See above.)

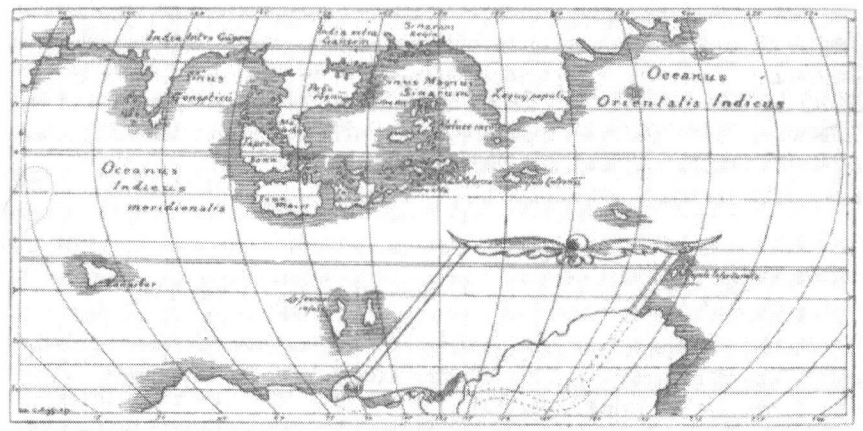

Gerard Mercator's double cordiform mappamundi of 1538.

Gerard Mercator's double cordiform mappamundi of 1538.

Gerard Mercator's double cordiform mappamundi of 1538 is translated here from the copperprint made by Lafreri and published in Rome in 1560. The fictitious Australian continent of Schonerean maps is less prominent here and bears no name. In this region appears for the first time, as far as we have been able to ascertain, two islands which in latitude and longitude correspond to some of the largest islands on the western coast of Australia. These islands are named *Los roccos insule.** Java is called *Jaua Maior*; it assumes the correct latitudinal position of its early cartography. Sumbawa, greatly exaggerated in size, is called *Jaua Minor*. We notice the *Terra alta* high land of the Ribeiro maps. The Spice Islands (*Insulae Molucce*) and the Ladrones of Magalhaens (*Insule Latronum*) are placed to the south of the equator instead of north. The *Insulae Infortunatae*, which in Schoner's globe of 1533 are placed in the longitude of the Tonga Islands, are here situated 15 degrees to the east of them, somewhere near Rarotonga.

(*Footnote. For further information with regard to these islands, we beg to refer our readers to the Journal and Proceedings of the Royal Geographical Society of Australia, Sydney, New South Wales 1891/1892, Volume V, Point Cloates (Western Australia), and the bird called Rock or Ruck, by Marco Polo. By George Collingridge, C.M.N.G.S.)

HERNANDO DE GRIJALVA'S EXPEDITION.

The year that witnessed the return from the Moluccas of the survivors of Saavedra's expedition, 1536, witnessed also the sailing of another expedition sent out from Acapulco by Cortes to discover in the same waters. It consisted of two ships commanded by Hernando de Grijalva and Fernando de Alvarado. The account of this voyage of discovery is very vague, and the various writers on the subject do not entirely agree. It appears certain however that many islands on the north coast of New Guinea were visited, and one in particular called *isla de los Crespos* at the entrance to Gcelvink Bay, near which a bloody tragedy was enacted and Grijalva murdered by his revolted crew. The expedition came to an end, a few of the survivors reaching the Spice Islands in 1539. It is supposed that the second in command, Fernando de Alvarado, returned to New Spain.

Most of the names given during the course of exploration are difficult to localise. Besides the various place names mentioned by Galvano, *Ostrich Point* is perhaps an interesting reminiscence of this untimely voyage. A casoar would of course be called an ostrich, and here we have for the first time a picturesque description of that Australasian bird. Galvano's translator says: "There is heere a bird as bigge as a crane; he flieth not, nor hath any wings wherewith to flee, he runneth on the ground like a deere: of their small feathers they do make haire for their idols."

TWO MAPS OF AUSTRALIA BY JOHN ROTZ (JEAN ROZE), 1542.

These two maps of Jean Roze, portions of which we give here, are described as Numbers 10 and 20 respectively in the following extract from the Catalogue of Maps and Drawings in the British Museum.

"John Rotz, his book of Hydrography, so called, being an account of the compass, elevation of the pole, latitude, sea coasts, etc., finely painted. Anno 1542."

This book is dedicated by the author to King Henry VIII, and the diagrams and maps have illuminated borders, and are otherwise ornamented in gold and colours.

It is mentioned by Malte-Brun in his Histoire de la Geographie, who on one point compares it with the additional Manuscript 5413, that is, the one containing the Dauphin chart, and adds the following, which we have translated:

"This curious and important manuscript is written in English, on vellum, but the dedication is French. The author was perhaps one of those Flamands who went over to England with Anne of Cleves in 1540. Besides a calendar and some instructions on navigation there are several charts executed with exactness and elegance, especially a planisphere, which ends the collection. New Holland is drawn almost like in the charts of the seventeenth century, before the voyage of Abel Tasman. It bears the name of Land of Java. In comparing this work with the map of the world spoken of above one is inclined to believe that the charts of Rotz are the original ones, for they contain many Portuguese names, which in the other are translated into French. In both the western coast of Borneo is placed where it should be, with the names of Porto de Borneo and Paseos de Borne. To the north of Borneo is to be seen Palaouan or Palawan; to the east are the Moluccas. These details render inadmissible the opinion of those who have pretended to see in the New Holland of these charts only an erroneous repetition of the island of Borneo, named Grand Java by Marco Polo. In the map of the world Borneo is in fact represented by an oblong much too small, but this error is common to all the charts of the same century. Mr. Coquebert-Montbret has seen a collection of charts that belonged to a certain Jean Valard, of Dieppe, and which bears date 1552, and the same information is found in them as in the two charts of the British Museum."

Before proceeding to further describe these two charts we shall correct some of the statements in the above description. We have received lately from our learned friend, Dr. E.T. Hamy, a monograph bearing for title Jean Roze, Hydrographe Dieppois du Milieu du seizieme siecle. This pamphlet clearly sets forth the following facts:

1. John Rotz was a Frenchman, a native of Dieppe, his correct name being Jean Roze or Rose.

2. He dedicated his atlas first to the King of France: *Parce que ja lons temps ayant le desir et affection de faire quelque oeuvre plaisante et agreable an Roy de France quy adonc estoyt mon souverain et naturel signeur Et apprez auoyr considre le monde estre assez Remply de cartes marines selon la maniere vulgaire ie maduisay por le mieux de luy faire et drecer vng liure contenant toutte lidrographie ou science marine Pour ce quil seroyt plus vtille et proffitable et de plus grand esprit*

et plus ayse et plus facile a manyer et regarder que ne seroyt vgne longue carte marine de quatre ou cinq verges de long Parquoy (Sire) apprez auoyr mis accord entre l'oppinion et le desir. Je commencay loeuure avec lentention deuant proposee mays comme ja elle estoit ou peu s'en falloit (accomplie) notre signeur quy de toutte choses veult disposer selon son plaisir la voullu adrecer vgne aultre part auec milleure fortune que moy mesme nesperoys comme jestime veu que telle en a este lordonnance divine...

3. Jean Roze went over to England in 1542, and,

4. his atlas was inspired from the Dieppese school of hydrography, the first and leading school in France.

So that Jean Rose or Roze was not a Fleming, nor did he go over to England with Anne of Cleves in 1540.

Moreover, his charts are not the original ones, for the legend ANDA NE BARCHA and other Portuguese legends and place-names render that inadmissible.

Malte-Brun is wrong also when he states that Marco Polo named Borneo Java Major*

(*Footnote. See above.)

CHART NUMBER 1.

CHART NUMBER 1. Jean Roze's Chart of Australia, A.D. 1542.

The first and largest of Jean Roze's maps given here, Number 20 of the catalogue of maps and drawings in the British Museum, is contained in a chart of the Indian Ocean from Cape Comorin on the west to Aimoey Bay, in China, on the east, and from 25 degrees north to 19 degrees south, including *Lytil Jaua*, and only a small portion of the Australian continent, which is cut off from east to west just below our modern Cape Grafton on the east, and our modern King Sound on the west. In this chart the south is placed at the top. We reproduce here all that is given of Australia, with Java and portion of Sumatra. Java is called *Lytil Jaua*, Australia bears no name, although in Roze's other map it is called The Londe, or Lande, of Java.*

(*Footnote. Referring to these maps in his excellent work on the Discovery of North America Mr. H. Harrisse says: "In the Lusitano-French maps of the world which originated in the year 1542 with Dieppe cosmographers such as Pierre Desceliers and his school, there is a continental configuration which of late has greatly exercised the historians of maritime discovery. South of the well-known island of Java, and separated by a strait, these mappamundi exhibit an extensive continent, stretching southward, and the north coast of which is dotted with numerous designations of dangerous coasts, capes, rivers, and landing places. That region, called therein Terre de Java la grande, or, as John Rotz (Jean Roze) names it so far back as 1542, the Londe of Java, in contradistinction to Lytil Java, stands, historically speaking, relative to the Sunda archipelago, precisely in the same position as the north-western continent in the Cantino chart stands as regards the West Indies. No historian, no documents of the sixteenth century mention the existence of such an Austral mainland. We also see it disappear from subsequent maps until long afterwards, when the region looms up again, but this time as an alleged discovery accomplished recently by Dutch navigators.

"That continental land, nevertheless, so far from being imaginary or an invention of cartographers, was nothing else than Australia, now justly considered by competent judges as having been discovered, visited, and named by unknown Portuguese mariners--whose maps furnished the cartographical data used in the Dieppe charts--sixty or seventy years before the Dutch first sighted the shores of that extensive country." The Discovery of North America, pages 96 to 97.

Mr. Harrisse adds the following note: Page 97 Note 4--The Sandwich Islands and the Falkland Islands present other instances of the kind. "That the Spaniards knew the Sandwich Islands a long time before COOK, that they had a name for them, that they probably visited them repeatedly, was proved by a map which Admiral ANSON found on board a Spanish vessel, and on which those islands were laid down in their true position." J.G. KOHL. *Substance of a lecture delivered at the Smithsonian Institution in General Appendix to the Report for 1856.* Washington D.C. 4to. page 111.)

It is contrary to all precedent for Java to be called Lytil Java. This name may have been suggested by a chart similar to the Dauphin chart, that is, a chart bearing the name Java Maior or Jave la Grande, on the Australian continent, for this name given to Australia would naturally suggest Java Minor, Jave la Petite, or Lytil Java for the smaller of the two islands. But such a name, as we have said, is without precedent in the historical nomenclature of this part of the world. In other words, it is an error.

Marco Polo, who was the first to use the terms Java Major and *Java Minor*, applied the term Java Minor to Sumatra to distinguish it from "the largest island in the world," which he called *Java Major*. A careful study of mediaeval geographical literature and cartography will show that whenever the term *Java Minor*, or *Menor*, is not applied to Sumatra, as it should be according to Marco Polo's meaning, it indicates, according to the various interpretations of divers historians and cartographers who have written about these islands, the island of Bali, Lomboc, Madura or Sumbawa--all islands smaller than Java, and having therefore an appearance of claim to the term. The nomenclature of the portions of coast shown north, east, and west, is as follows:

North coast--*Lytil Jaua*; and *Fin de Jaua*, end of Java. For other names on this island we beg leave to refer the reader to the map published in the Journal and Proceedings of the Royal Geographical Society of Australasia, Sydney, New South Wales; volume v. 1891/1892.

In the Gulf of Carpentaria, or perhaps to the east of Java, and if so, referring to the rapid tides between Java and Bali, Bali and Lomboc, we find the legend ANDA NE BARCHA (*no boats go here*) of the Dauphin chart corrupted to *Au fane bacha*. Erroneously it appears to refer to, and name, two islands situated between York Peninsula and the east end of Java. Those two nameless islands are probably charted for Bali and Lomboc, since Sumbawa is there also to the east of them. Sumbawa however is undistinguishable because forming the apex of York Peninsula, to which it has been joined. With reference to *Anda ne barcha*, the elision of the letter r in the word bacha indicated by the stroke above its position in the word, and the fact of the same word being spelt in full, barcha, on the Dauphin chart, proves beyond the slightest doubt two important points: first, that these charts are not the originals; and second, that they were copied from different originals, since the copyist in each case set down mechanically the two correct forms of spelling the word *boat* or *ship, bacha* and *barcha*, without knowing what it meant, as is evidenced by his incorrect spelling of the first portion of the phrase in this chart, and the incorrect spelling of most of the nomenclature in the Dauphin chart. The nomenclature of the island of Sumbawa, which we have omitted for want of space on our sketch, is as follows: From east to west, *gumape, cape bima, c: vatraar or ratraar, Sinbana, moro,* and *moda.*

Which we interpret as follows: *Gumape*--modern Gunong Api, a small island lying off the north-east coast of Sumbawa. It is important however because it contains a volcano which forms one of the most remarkable physical features of the Indian archipelago.

Cape bima--modern name, Bima--north-east coast of Sumbawa.

C: *Vatraar*, or *ratraar*--probably a bad reading for Aramaram in F. Rodriguez' Portolano 1511/1512; or it may be a corruption of Masaram or Massaram, another name for Bramble Cay, an island situated at the extreme north end of Cape York.

Sinbana--the name of the island, the modern Sumbawa. It is written Simbana in F. Rodriguez' Portolano, 1511/1512.

Moro, or *Maro*, may be intended for Maio, a small island at the entrance of Salee Gulf, Sumbawa.

Moda (?)--a name on the north-western coast of Sumbawa. We have not been able to identify it.

On the east coast, which is the coast of Queensland, one name only occurs, not far distant from the spot where Cook was nearly wrecked in the *Endeavour*. This name--*coste dangerose*--speaks for itself; it appears along a coast lined with reefs, clearly shown on this map.

On the west coast appear the following names:

Ille de llame (?) may be a corruption of *ilha llana*--Low island, or Level island.

Illa or *Ille da*, an unfinished appellation.

Isle Mege or *Nege* (?)

abaie bressille, Brazil Bay.

terra en negade, a corruption of *terra anegada*, submerged land.

Abaie a besse (?)

Abaie de, an unfinished appellation.

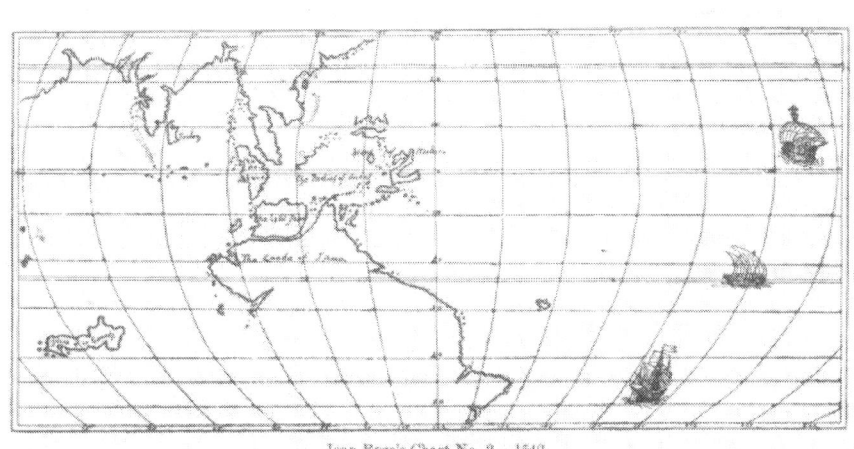

Jean Roze's Chart Number 2. 1542.

CHART NUMBER 2.

Chart Number 2 is a reduced copy of portion of Jean Roze's outline map of Southern Asia and Australia. As will appear from our sketch the information to be obtained from this document as regards nomenclature is meagre; one item however of great importance is that the west coast of the Londe of Java terminates precisely in the latitude of Cape Lioness, or Leeuwin of modern charts; this points to the discovery of Cape Leeuwin. We have suggested elsewhere that the peculiar shape of the Australian continent might have suggested the name *Lioness*. Since then we have received a photographic copy of another of these old charts of the Lusitano-Dieppese school, and we offer now another suggestion, *quantum valeat*. Tigers and lions have been supposed to inhabit Australia, but on the document we have lately received a lion, or lioness (we would not be quite certain as to the artist's intention), is represented as having taken up his or her abode in the latitude of Cape Leeuwin, where Jean Roze's chart comes to an end.

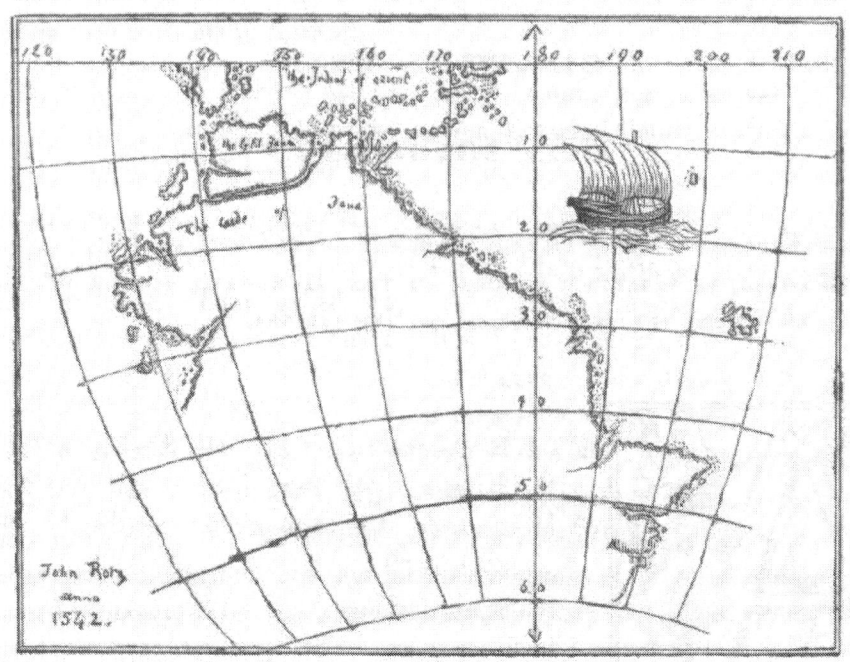

Chart Number 2. Original projection.

Java is called *The Lytil Jaua*, and Australia *The Londe*, or *Land of Jaua*. The outline of the Australian continent shows that it belongs to the same class of maps as the Dauphin chart, although in the latter the prolongation of coast from Cape Leeuwin to the South Pole constitutes a notable difference that may have some meaning. It is obvious that Jean Roze, in presenting this map to Henry VIII, had no intention or interest in showing the sea-way blocked as it is in all the other maps of this school.

CHAPTER 32. A.D. 1540 TO 1545.

VILLALOBOS' EXPEDITION. NEW GUINEA NAMED BY INIGO ORTIZ DE RETEZ AND GASPAR RICO. JUAN GAETAN'S ACCOUNT OF THE HOMEWARD VOYAGE OF THE SAN JUAN ALONG THE NORTH COAST OF NEW GUINEA.

After the treaties of Segovia, Seville, and Zaragoza the King of Spain renounced at last his claim to the Moluccas for the sum of 350,000 ducats. But this agreement did not interfere with other possessions of the Spanish Crown, nor did it prevent it from making fresh conquests. The Spanish Government continued therefore to send out their armadas to those quarters that were on the confines of the Portuguese settlements; for islands to which they lay claim, such as the Archipelago of St. Lazarus, discovered by Magalhaens, afterwards called the Philippines in honour of Philip II of Spain, invited their eager enterprise.

One of these maritime excursions belongs to our subject as it gave rise to a further survey of *Papua*, and to the naming of that island as it is now called New Guinea. We refer to the expedition of Ruiz Lopez de Villalobos, which set sail from the port of Juan Gallego in New Spain, on the 1st of November 1542, for the purpose of settling the colony now known as the *Philippines*. The armada was composed of six ships and four or five hundred soldiers, and as many Indians of the country, says Galvano. On their way from the west coast of North America to the islands discovered by Magalhaens they discovered many islands in the North Pacific Ocean, among others the group of islands afterwards named by Cook* the Sandwich Islands.

(*Footnote. See Chapter 31.)

In 1543 one of the ships belonging to the fleet, the *San Juan*, commanded by Bernardo de La Torre, with Gaspar Rico as pilot, made an unsuccessful attempt to return to New Spain.

The Spaniards in their numerous efforts to reach New Spain from the great Asiatic Archipelago had not yet found out the proper season nor latitude to sail in, and through their want of knowledge concerning the periodicity of the winds in those regions they met with many mishaps.

In Bernardo de La Torre's attempt many islands were discovered; but, after sailing seven hundred leagues in their estimation, the wind failing, they were compelled to return to the Philippine Islands.

The fleet had now reached the Moluccas, and in 1545 the *San Juan* was despatched again. She was now commanded by Inigo Ortiz de Retez, Gaspar Rico being still the pilot. They sailed from Tidor in the month of May, and made extensive discoveries on the north coast of OS PAPUAS, or Papua. One of the three great Papuan rivers, the river now called the AMBERNO, was discovered. It received the name of St. Augustin River.* Formal possession of the island was taken in the name of the King of Spain, and, says Galvano's translator, "*because the people there were black and had frisled hair, they named it NUEVA GUINEA*"..."*and because they knew not that Saavedra had been there before, they chalenged the honour and fame of that discouerie.*"..."*For the memorie of Saavedra as then was almost lost, as all things else do fall into oblivion, which are not recorded, and illustrated by writing.*"

(*Footnote. See Chapter 45, Hoeius' map 1640.)

Juan Gaetan, one of Villalobos' pilots, has written an account of this expedition which is given in Ramusio's collection. We give here the portion of it relating to New Guinea, because it corroborates Herrera's, Galvano's, and other descriptions, and mentions the return of the little ship *San Juan* to New Spain: Ramusio, fol. 377 F:...*essendo gia l'anno 1545, al principio di quello, & muto il parizzo, che noi altri per auanti haueuamo fatto, & volse che si andasse per la parte di mezzodi, il nauilio il qual seguitte la sua nauigatione, & secondo che dapoi da loro sapemmo, navigarono cento leghe per quella altezza al leuante, & trouarono la costa, & terra da mezzo grado, alla banda di mezzodi, & andarono costeggiando & nauigando 650, leghe senza perder vista di quella, quasi al leuante, & ponente, salvo che montarono sei in sette gradi della banda di mezzodi, la qual terra trouarono tutta habitata da negri, che vennero alla costa con freccie, & bastoni senza veleno a fargli la guerra, & sono negri molto agili, & con li capelli corti, & ritorti finalmente dopo molti trauagli, & fortune che hebbero, giunsero nella nuoua Spagna, & diedero nuoua al Vice Re, di quanto per noi era stato fatto, ma noi nola sapemmo se non dapoi.*

With reference to the description of New Guinea natives given in the passage above we may be allowed to correct a statement made lately by Mr. Petherick, and endorsed by Mr. Delmar Morgan, two eminent writers on Australasian maritime discovery. These writers appear to have taken Gaetan's description as referring to Australian natives, if both of these gentlemen did not indeed believe that the *San Juan* ran along the coast of Queensland. This points to the necessity of referring to original documents. Mr. Delmar Morgan says*: "The only allusion to one (a southern continent) is that given by Ramusio from the account of the pilot Gaetan, who heard that a small vessel, the *San Juan*, sailed 650 leagues (2,600 miles) without losing sight of land, running nearly east and west, and that this land was found to be inhabited by naked black people with short hair, who came to the coast carrying darts and clubs to make war, and that they were very active. This, observes Mr. Petherick in an article contributed to the *Melbourne Review*, is the earliest account we have of the natives of Australia, and may be taken as a true picture of the inhabitants of Queensland 250 years ago."

(*Footnote. Remarks on the Early Discovery of Australia by E. DELMAR MORGAN, F.R.G.S., with maps, for the Geographical Congress at Berne. London 1891 page 14.)

Had Mr. Petherick, and after him Mr. Delmar Morgan, only referred to Ramusio's text, they would have noticed that the *San Juan* was ordered to follow the equator--*Volse che si andasse per la parte di mezzodi*, which she did, sighting land in 1/2 a degree south of the equator---..." "*trouarono la costa, & terra da mezzo grado, alla banda di mezzodi*, and following this land until they stood in six or seven degrees of south latitude--"*salvo che montarono sei in sette gradi della banda di mezzodi*," In other words, they sighted New Guinea at its north-west extremity, or Cape of Good Hope, and never lost sight of land till they reached Cape King William or thereabouts, making the passage between New Britain and New Guinea. Nor is the distance correctly translated, for 650 leagues do not make 2,600 miles.

CHAPTER 33. A.D. 1544 TO 1569.

THE SEBASTIAN CABOT MAPPAMUNDI OF 1544.
THE HENRI II (SO CALLED) MAPPAMUNDI OF 1546.
PIERRE DESCELIERS' MAPPAMUNDI OF 1550.
MENDANA'S EXPEDITION OF 1567.

The Sebastian Cabot Mappamundi of 1544 is an engraved map drawn in one ellipsis on the Bordone projection. The Australasian portion of it, reproduced here from Jomard's Atlas, we have limited to 10 degrees south, as there is no Australian continent represented. The East Indian Archipelago follows the features of the Diego Ribeiro type of map, inasmuch as the southern shores of most of the islands composing that group are not defined; but the islands between Java and Flores, left out in the Diego Ribeiro map of 1529, are set down in this one.

Jaua Maior applies to Java, and *Jaua Minor* seems to apply to the East Indian Archipelago from Java to Flores. Sumbawa is indicated by the name *Simbana*.

The interest of the map for us lies in the representation of a portion of New Guinea, and an island bearing the name of *Camabam*.

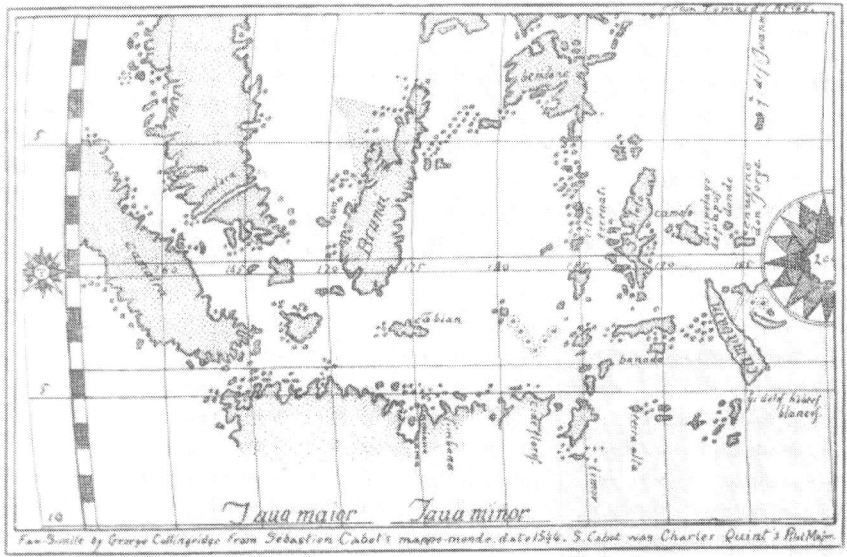

Camabam appears to represent that portion of the north-west coast of New Guinea situated below the McCluer Inlet, from Deri, Cape Peninsula, to Adi Island, and which to the present day figures on the latest Admiralty charts as a possible island.

Ysla de los hobres blancos, island of white men, in the same locality, reminds one of a similar appellation given by Saavedra to some islands on the north coast of New Guinea.

The *Los roccos* islands of G. Mercator's map of 1538 are set down on this map, but in a different longitude and latitude. They are in 120 degrees longitude, and between 15 and 20 degrees latitude, and do not appear therefore in our sketch. They bear the name *islas Rocos* with the marginal note *Enestas islas Rocos ay aues de tal grandeza [segum dizen] y fuerza que tomam un boy ylo traienuolando para comer, y mas dizen que tomam un batel por grande que sea ylo leuantan en grande altura, y despues lo dexan caer, y comense los hombres, y el Petrarcha semeiantemente lo dize en su libro de prospera y aduersa fortuna.* In these Roc Islands there are birds of such a size (as some say) and strength, that they can carry away an ox to eat it, and many say that they take a boat, no matter how big, lift it to a great height, and then let it fall and eat the men, and Petrarch says the same in his treatise on prosperity and adversity.

The fictitious Antarctic continent of earlier charts has been left out, but an inscription in those regions reads thus: *Terra vel mare incognitum.* Land or sea unknown, which is a very wise statement.

THE HENRI II MAPPAMUNDI (SO-CALLED). DATE, 1546.

This is a large manuscript planisphere by Pierre Desceliers, a priest of Arques, near Dieppe, who was a celebrated cosmographer and cartographer, and the author of several maps of this type.

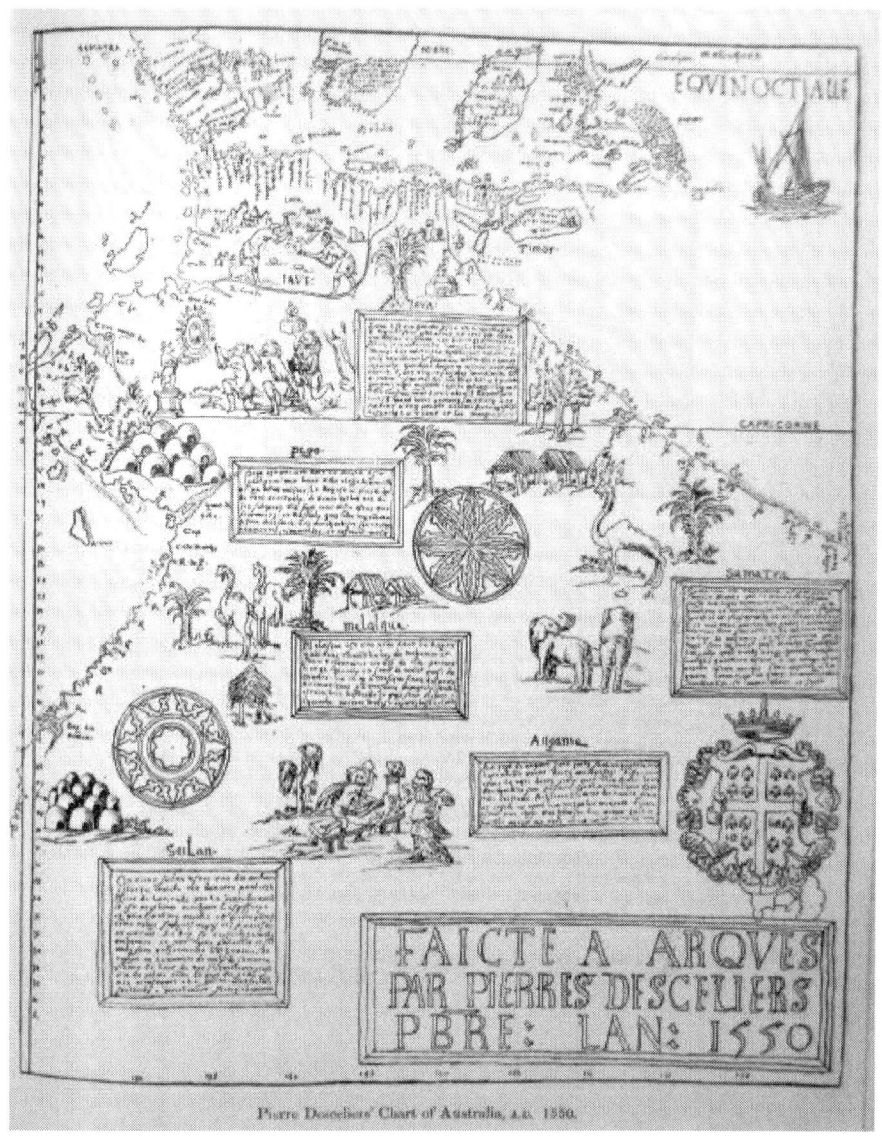

Pierre Desceliers' Chart of Australia, A.D. 1550.

It bears the inscription *Mappemonde peinte sur parchemin par ordre de Henri II roi de France*, and for this reason has sometimes been called the Henri II map. Java bears the name of *IAVA petite*. The Australian continent is called *IAVA LA GRANDE*. The west coast is prolonged further south than in the Dauphin and Roze charts; the other Australian coastal features of this map are almost similar to those described in maps of this class. The island of Timor is larger than in the Dauphin chart, and the island of Flores is placed latitudinally, as it ought to be, whereas in the Dauphin chart it is placed longitudinally. For the nomenclature we beg leave to refer the reader to the list given above Chapter 30.

PIERRE DESCELIERS' MAPPAMUNDI OF 1550.

This is another large manuscript planisphere, by the priest of Arques, and it bears in bold characters the inscription: FAICTE A ARQVES PAR PIERRES DESCELIERS PBRE: LAN: 1550. It is now in the British Museum. The general features of the Australian continent are the same as those of the maps of this class which we have already described. In the position of the Abrolhos group on the western coast of Australia there is an island on this map which bears the name *arenes*. This island is also set down on the Dauphin map, on the Jean Roze reduced map, and on the Henri II map, but on all of them it bears no name. Thus we have been unable to compare the word *arenes* and fix its meaning by corroborative evidence. We do not believe it to be a corruption of *arenas* sand, but rather of *abrolhos*, the name it has preserved to this day. Other similar charts might solve the mystery. The full nomenclature of this interesting document will be found above Chapter 30.

The Portuguese and Spanish origin of this chart is as apparent as in the others we have described belonging to this class, although many of the words that have not been translated into French have suffered greater mutilation. At first sight the most remarkable feature is the display of descriptive matter contained in cartouches spread here and there between the illuminations, and which have perhaps blocked out *Jave la Grande*, or some similar name, describing the vast locality occupied by these cartouches, and the quaint figures with which this map is profusely ornamented. However there may have been an intention in this, for all the descriptions are extracts taken from Marco Polo's and Barthema's writings, and Marco Polo's description of Java Major has been, no doubt purposely, left out also. With reference to the term *major* we must remember that the general belief of Marco Polo's informers, whether Chinese, Malays, or Arabs, was that the present Java and Australia were but one and the same large island, and Marco Polo called it Java Major, or the *largest island in the world*.

Cannibalism.

Idolatry.

We have had some difficulty in translating the nondescript old French contained in the cartouches we have referred to, and still greater difficulty in localising these descriptions, for the name of place above each frame is not in every instance the right name according to the description below it. The result of our researches is as follows: The descriptive matter under the respective headings of *Java* and *Sumatra* is taken from Marco Polo's description of Java Minor, i.e. Sumatra. *Pego* refers to Pegu, *Melasque* to Malacca, *Seilan* to Ceylon, and *Angania* to the Andaman Isles. As none of these descriptions refer to Australia we shall only point out that, as the figures representing cannibalism and idolatry are alluded to in the text contiguous to them, they have no connection with Australia; the same may be said of the two elephants, which evidently are meant to illustrate the text on the right hand side, namely under the heading of *Sumatra*. The only illustrations which might be supposed to appertain to Australia are those *not alluded to in the french text*, such as the representations of trees, rough* guniah-looking dwellings, guanacos, and those strange huts on the western coast which may have been inspired by some such freak of nature as was seen by Dampier on the same coast some hundred and thirty odd years after these charts were depicted. Dampier says: "There were several things like haycocks standing in the savannah, which at a distance we thought were houses, looking just like the Hottentots' houses at the Cape of Good Hope; but we found them to be so many rocks." Dampier and his companions may have mistaken some ant-hills for rocks. Peron describes some huge dome-shaped ant-hills seen on this coast, and Captain Pelsart, in 1629, also describes some ant-hills seen by him and his companions when in search for water on this same coast in latitude 22 degrees south. In 1818 Allan Cunningham, when on the west coast of Australia, at the Bay of Rest, took occasion to measure one of these gigantic ant-hills of that coast. He found it to be eight feet in height and twenty-six in girth. Pelsart's account runs thus: "On the 16th of June in the morning they returned on shore in hopes of getting more water, but were disappointed; and having no time to observe the country it gave them no great hopes of better success, even if they had travelled farther within land, which appeared a thirsty, barren plain, covered with *ant-hills, so high that they looked afar off like the huts of negroes*."

(*Footnote. Pigafetta, in describing the houses of the inhabitants of the Ladrone islands, was no doubt responsible for the delineation of these rough and ready sheds. He says: "Their houses are of wood, covered with planks, over which leaves of their fig-trees (banana-trees), four feet in length, are spread.")

Dampier in his second voyage to this coast in 1699, but more than one hundred miles further south, describes again some of these evidently very remarkable features of the western coast of Australia. He says: "Here are a great many rocks in the large savannah we were in, which are five or six feet high and round at top like a haycock, very remarkable; some red and some white." But Flinders when on this coast actually came across native huts similar to those depicted on P. Desceliers' chart of Australia.

As for the European buildings representing forts and castles, they are mostly situated where we know them to have been, excepting of course those two which are placed on York Peninsula.

The Portuguese legend *Anda ne barcha* has entirely lost its signification on this map; it is altered to *Autane bamcha*, the only clue to the transformation being that the second word still retains the initial small b of *barcha*. Although, as we have remarked, the continent of Australia bears no name (unless we reckon as such TERRE AUSTRALLE, which appears on the imaginary part, prolonged towards the South Pole), the island of Java bears a double name, JAVE, in large letters on the extreme border of the Southern coast, and *iaua* in small, marked on the northernmost part.

Now this small name, *iaua*, occupying the true centre of what should be, and probably was, the original shape given to Java, shows beyond doubt that the south coast of Java has been deliberately extended further south in order to block the passage between the south of Java and the north coast of Australia; otherwise, had this been the original shape given to Java, we might expect to see the name set down only once, in the centre of the island. The term *iaua* is also older than *Jave*, which indicates that the chart has been compiled from several sources.

Diego do Couto's hog

Diego do Couto's hog.

In Diego do Couto's description of Java appears the following, which tends to show that the Portuguese soon became aware of a more correct shape for *Java* than that under which it appears in this and the other charts of this class. Quoth Diego do Couto, writing about 1570: "The figure* of the island of Java resembles a hog couched on its fore legs, with its snout to the channel of Balabero, and its hind legs towards the mouth of the Straits of Sunda, which is much frequented by our ships...its length about 160 and its breadth about 70 leagues. The southern coast (hog's back), is not frequented by us, and its bays and ports are not known; but the northern coast (hog's belly) is much frequented, and has many good ports."

(*Footnote. Placing the south at the top was a common practice among cartographers at the time these charts were made.)

In the above description we have a more accurate idea of the proportion of Java, and an explanation for that unnatural sleek curve representing the south coast, because unexplored, and described by Couto as the *hog's back*.

MENDANA'S EXPEDITION OF 1567.

In pursuance of their object to attain the Spice Islands from America to the westward and make fresh discoveries the Spaniards continued to send out expeditions whenever an opportunity offered.

Most Spanish writers agree in ascribing the voyage in which Mendana discovered the Solomon Islands to the period in which Lopez Garcia de Castro governed Peru, and Dalrymple,* quoting Figueroa, says of this voyage: "They sailed from Callao the 10th January 1567, and reached the coast of Mexico 22nd of January 1568. They ran from Callao with contrary winds 1450 leagues, when they discovered a small island inhabited in 6 degrees 45 minutes south, which Mendana named Isla de Jesus. At 160 leagues from this island they fell in with a large ledge of rocks and small islands within them in 6 degrees 15 minutes south, which were named the Baxos de la Candaleria; they lay north-east and south-west, and might be 15 leagues in circuit altogether. They saw another land, which they named Santa Isabella, very populous; at 6 leagues to the south-east of a port in it they found two small islands in 8 degrees south." Dalrymple further says: "Figueroa then gives an account of the rest of the Solomon Islands; the farthest south he mentions, except St Christoval, which has a port in 11 degrees south, is a volcano named Segarga, 8 leagues in circuit in 9 degrees 45 minutes south, beyond which is Guadalcanal. Figueroa does not mention the latitude of Guadalcanal, nor does he give any longitude of these islands. He says they stood in north from Christoval into 3 degrees south, where they had signs of land, and thought it was New Guinea."

(*Footnote. An historical collection of the several voyages and discoveries in the South Pacific Ocean, 1770/1771.)

According to modern Spanish geographers* Mendana left Callao on the 20th November 1567; sighted an island fifty days after, which they called *la isla de Jesus*, and, continuing their course in a south and south-westerly direction, came to anchor in a port of the island of *Santa Isabel*, belonging to the Solomon Group.

(*Footnote. Descubrimiento de la Oceania por los Espanoles. D. Ricardo Beltran y Rozpide. Ateneo de Madrid 1892.)

This group was so called because the legends of the time reported that from those islands were derived the gold and other treasures that served for the decoration of King Solomon's temple.

At the island of Santa Isabel they built a brigantine, and Mendana sent Pedro Ortega and the chief pilot, Hernan Gallego, with 12 sailors and 18 soldiers to discover the whole group; some of the principal islands discovered and named being Buena Vista, Sesarga, Guadalcanar, San Jorge, San Nicolas, etc. In the month of August they returned to America, where they arrived in January 1569.

Other islands of the same archipelago were named as follows: Ramos o Malaita, Galera, Florida, San Dimas, San German, Guadalupe, Arrecifes, San Marcos, Treguada, Tres Marias, Santiago, San Urban, San Christobal o Pauro, Santa Catalina o Aguari y Santa Ana o Itapa.

We subjoin the following extract from C.M. Woodford's valuable book, A Naturalist Among the Head Hunters: A translation of portions of Gallego's Journal, a copy of which is in the British Museum, describing many of the events that took place during the voyage of the Spaniards, is given in Dr. Guppy's book, The Solomon Islands. The original manuscript of Catoira, a much fuller account of the voyages than that of Gallego, is in the possession of Mr. W. Amherst Tyssen Amherst, M.P., and has never been printed. During my last visit to the Solomons I was furnished with a translation of this journal which enabled me to identify the places visited by the Spaniards. I have taken photographs of some of the most interesting localities, and made copious notes upon the journal. It will, I hope, shortly be published."

The original manuscript in which Mendana's voyage in 1567 is narrated was found in the *Bibliotheque Nationale*, Paris, by Dr. E.T. Hamy, its title being: *Relacion breve de lo suscedido en el viaje que hizo Alvaro de Mendana en la demanda de la Nueva Guinea, laqual ya estava descubierta por Inigo Ortiz de Retez que fue con Villalobos de la tierra de Nueva Espana, en el ano de 1541.*

CHAPTER 34. A.D. 1569 TO 1580.

GERARD MERCATOR'S MAPPAMUNDI OF 1569. ORTELIUS' MAPPAMUNDI OF 1570. THE RISE OF ENGLAND'S MARITIME POWER. DRAKE AMONGST THE ISLANDS TO THE NORTH OF AUSTRALIA.

erard Mercator's map of the world disregards previous cartographical representations of Australia, and lays down a more or less fictitious continent instead, which does not appear to be based on any definite discovery or charting, but merely on a vague knowledge of the existence of the Australian continent.

The nomenclature is taken chiefly from Marco Polo's writings, to which however a false interpretation has been given, inasmuch as the islands in the northern hemisphere mentioned by him have been placed in the southern hemisphere on this mappamundi, and his Java Major is made to apply to Java.

On the southern continental land, which occupies the site of Australia, such names as *Lucach, Beach, Maletur*,* etc. may be seen, and a gulf which looks something like the Gulf of Carpentaria is occupied by a couple of islands named *Petan* and *Jaua Minor*.

(*Footnote. Maletur, through an oversight, has been omitted on our map; it should occur under Beach thus: Maletur regnum in quo maxima est copia aromatum.)

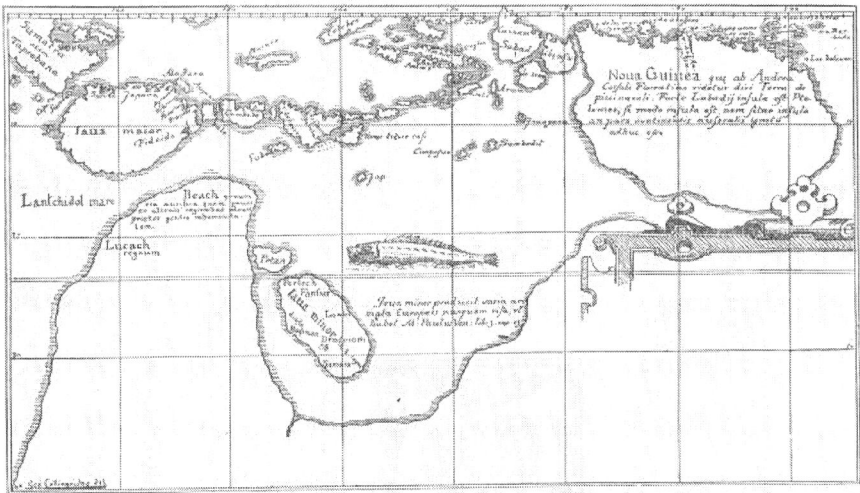

The Australian Regions in Mercator's Mappamundi of 1569.

Lucach and Maletur, in Polo's writings, belong to Asia. Beach* is a corruption of Lucach. Petan has been identified as Bintang, and Java Minor refers to Sumatra.

(*Footnote. With reference to Beach, Major says in Early Voyages to Australia, page xvii.: "We have already explained from Marsden's notes the reasonable rendering of the name of Lucach or Lochac. The name of Beach, or rather Boeach, is another form of the same name, which crept into the Basle edition of Marco Polo of 1532, and was blunderingly repeated by the cartographers; while for Maletur we have the suggestion of the Burgomaster Witsen, in his Noord en Oost Tartarye, fol. 169, that it is taken from Maleto, on the north side of the island of Timor, a suggestion rendered null by the fact, apparently unknown to Witsen, that Maletur, as already stated, was but a mis-spelling in the Basle edition for Malaiur. The sea in which, on these early maps, this remarkable land is made to lie, is called Mare Lantchidol, another perplexing piece of mis-spelling upon which all the cartographers have likewise stumbled, and which finds its explanation in the Malay words, Laut Kidol, or Chidol, *the South Sea*." For another interpretation of Laut Kidol see also *Verhandelingen Betrekkelijk Het Zeewezen*, volume 27 pages 165, 166.

In Prince Henry the Navigator, Appendix page 307, Major insists on the blunder committed by the printer of the Basle edition of Marco Polo thus: "In the Basle edition of Marco Polo in 1532 the printer unluckily altered the L into a B, and the first c into an e, so that the word Locach became Boeach. This was afterwards shortened into Beach, and the blunder was repeated in books and on maps with so much confidence that we find it even occurring on a semi-globe which adorns the monument of the learned Sir Henry Savile in Merton College Chapel, Oxford; and strangely enough it is the only geographical name thereon inscribed. As however some editions of Marco Polo retained the word Locach, and others Beach, both names came to be copied on to maps, and, the point of departure being Java, the mapmakers, following the course indicated in Marco Polo, laid these countries down as forming part of the great southern land which was supposed to occupy the entire south part of the globe."

We are not quite sure that the printer of the Basle edition of Marco Polo had no authority for altering the L of Lucach into a B, for the alteration had already been made before the year 1532. It may be noticed on the 1489 map of Bartholomew Columbus, where we read provintia bocaach. See Chapter 14.

On Martin Behaim's globe Lucach or Lochac is altered to Coachs.)

New Guinea forms an important feature in this famous mappamundi. It is separated from the Australian continent by a narrow strait, although the cartographer expresses his doubts as to its being thus separated....*si modo insula est, nam sitne insula an pars continentis Australis ignotu adhuc est.*

The inscription on New Guinea which contains the above remark reads thus: *Noua Guinea que ab Andrea Corsali Florentino videtur dici Terra de piccinacoli. Forte Labadij insula est Ptolomeo, si modo insula est, nam sitne insula an pars continentis australis ignoti adhuc est.*

The information contained in that inscription is very faulty. Andrea Corsali never saw New Guinea himself, but described it from hearsay. Writing from Cochin China to the Duke of Medici on the 6th of January 1515 he says: *Et nauigando verso le parti d' oriente, dicono esserui terra de piccinacoli, & e di molti openione che questa terra vada a tenere, & congiungersi per la Banda di Leuante & mezogiorno, con la costa del Brezil o' verzino, perche per la grandezza di detta terra del Verzino non si e per anchora da tutta le parti* *discoperta. And navigating towards the east, they say there lies the land of Piccinacoli, and many believe that this land is connected towards the east in the south with the coast of Bresil, or Verzino,* because, on account of the size of this land of Verzino, it is not as yet on all sides discovered.*

(*Footnote. See above. Australia and Brasielie regio.)

Mercator, in attempting to rectify the cartography of his time, made it worse in many respects, and certainly made great confusion of the Eastern and Australasian portion of it. In endeavouring to rename the islands in those regions he made use of Ptolemy's and Marco Polo's nomenclature, but failed generally to understand or locate their descriptions. He was the first cartographer, we believe, to alter Fra Mauro's Java to Japan, and the Java* of Ptolemy, which had been set down in a duplicate manner under the names Labadii* and Sabadibae he confounds with New Guinea, which he splits up into four islands, naming the three smaller ones to the west *Cainam Sabadibe insule tres*, and the large one to the east "is no doubt," he says, "Ptolemy's Labadij."

(*Footnote. There is a triplicate Java in Ptolemy's map bearing the name Zaba. See above.)

(*Footnote. Labadii and Sabadibae are corrupted forms of Java Dwipa or Jaoa diva of Sanscrit or Arabic origin.)

A strange thing happened, owing no doubt to Corsali's remarks, which cast a doubt on the insularity of New Guinea,* and this is what happened. Geographers, following Mercator's map, continued to represent New Guinea as an island, and, notwithstanding, placed thereon an inscription to the effect that it was not known whether it were an island or not.* Mendana's discoveries to the east of New Guinea are not charted.

(*Footnote. New Guinea had been nearly circumnavigated before Mercator's map was made. Coming from the north-west, Gomez de Sequeira (see Appendix) had no doubt navigated the straits of Torres in 1525, and Mendana in 1567 had reached the north-east end of New Guinea.)

(*Footnote. We think that Andrea Corsali's remarks give the clue to the uncertainty which prevailed from that date until Captain Cook set the matter at rest. On this subject, and referring to the chart in de Brosses' work, Mr. G.B. Barton in History of New South Wales from the Records, Volume 1 pages xxvii. and xxviii., says: "Looking at one of these charts, we observe that there is nothing to indicate the existence of the straits between the mainland and Van Diemen's Land; but the passage now known as Torres Straits is distinctly shown, although in the text the author repeatedly expresses a doubt whether the mainland touched New Guinea or not.

"Why this doubt should have been expressed by de Brosses when the position of the straits is shown so clearly in his charts is a question not easily answered. The discovery of the fact that Torres had sailed through the straits in 1606 is attributed to Dalrymple, who made it known to the world in his Account of the Discoveries in the South Pacific Ocean previous to 1764, published in 1767--a work which we may safely assume had its place in the *Endeavour's* library. Flinders states in his introduction that 'the existence of such a strait was generally unknown until 1770, when it was again discovered and passed by our great circumnavigator, Captain Cook.' In making this statement he seems to have repeated a remark made in the introduction (page xvi.) to Cook's Third Voyage, where the reader is told that 'though the great sagacity and extensive reading of Mr. Dalrymple had discovered some traces of such a passage having been found before, yet those traces were so obscure and so little known in the present age that,' among other things, 'the President de Brosses had not been able to satisfy himself about them.' But, unless he had satisfied himself on the subject, why did he construct his maps of New Holland and New Guinea in such a manner as to show the straits? This is one of the many little puzzles connected with Australian geography of the last century which deserves the attention of those who are interested in it. The only answer to the question seems to be that de Brosses looked upon New Holland as an island, probably considering that fact established; but not having seen the Relation, written by Torres of his passage through the straits, he thought that there was just room for a doubt on the subject. Nothing was known about Tasman's second voyage in his time.

"Dalrymple's Historical Collection of Voyages and Discoveries in the South Pacific Ocean was another work of great authority at the time it was published--1770. It contained a chart of the South Pacific, 'pointing out the discoveries made therein previous to 1764,' which showed Torres' track in 1606 through the straits. The work made its appearance too late to form part of the *Endeavour's* library..."

But although Dalrymple's Historical Collection of Voyages, etc., mentioned above, appeared too late to form part of the *Endeavour's* library, Captain Cook and Sir Joseph Banks were in possession of the information contained in that work when they passed through Torres Straits. This would appear from a letter written by Dalrymple to the editor of Cook's Voyages. We do not know whether this letter has been published in any English work, but it was published in 1774 in a translation of Dalrymple's work by Mr. de Freville, entitled Voyages dans le mer du Sud. From page 469 to 502 of that work there is a long letter from Dalrymple to Hawkesworth, in which Dalrymple states that he gave to Mr. Banks (since Sir Joseph Banks) a collection of the discoveries attempted in the Pacific Ocean with a map of those discoveries drawn by himself and which he published only after the return of Mr. de Bougainville. Dalrymple also states that he had marked Torres' track on his map from information contained in Arias' memorial, and that the track thus marked determined the course of the Endeavour between New Guinea and New Holland. Opinions, he says, were at first divided: Captain Cook. on the authority of Mr. Pingre, pretended that Torres had sailed to the north of New Guinea: Mr. Banks on the contrary maintained that he had left New Guinea on his right hand side. The route marked on my map, says Dalrymple, was at last unanimously adopted, etc., Il n'est pas moins vrai, que la route de Torrez que j'avois dessinee sur ma carte d'apres le memoire d' Arias, determina l'*Endeavour* a passer entre la Nouvelle Hollande and la Nouvelle Guinee. Les opinions avoient d' abord ete partagees; le Capitaine Cook, s'appuyant sur l'autorite de M. Pingre, pretendoit que Torres avoit fait voile au Nord de la Nouvelle Guinee; M. Banks soutenoit all contraire qu'il avoit laisse la Nouvelle Guinee a droite. La route dessinee sur ma carte reunit enfin les suffrages. And Dalrymple adds that his map was not compiled from conjectures, but from facts.)

The Australasian regions on Ortelius' mappamundi of the following year, 1570, are so similar to G. Mercator's in cartographical details and nomenclature that we have not thought it necessary to reproduce here that sample of cartography.

At the date we have now reached other European nations were on the eve of contending with Portugal and Spain for the right to trade with distant countries. The daring sea rovers of France and England first began the conflict, to be followed afterwards by resolute Dutch sea captains and merchants. "During the reign of Elizabeth," says an English historian,* "that spirit of commercial enterprise which had been awakened under Mary seemed to pervade and animate every description of men. For the extension of trade and the discovery of unknown lands associations were formed, companies were incorporated, expeditions were planned; and the prospect of immense profit, which, though always anticipated, was seldom realised, seduced many to sacrifice their whole fortunes, prevailed even on the ministers, the nobility, and the Queen herself, to risk considerable sums in these hazardous undertakings. The renowned Sir John Hawkins first acquired celebrity by opening the trade in slaves. He made three voyages to the coast of Africa; bartered articles of trifling value for numerous lots of negroes; crossed the Atlantic to Hispaniola and the Spanish settlement in America, and in exchange for his captives returned with large quantities of hides, sugar, ginger, and pearls. This trade was however illicit; and during his third voyage in the bay of St. Juan d' Ulloa Hawkins was surprised by the arrival of the Spanish viceroy with a fleet of twelve sail from Europe. The hostile squadrons viewed each other with jealousy and distrust; a doubtful truce was terminated by a general engagement; and in the end, though the Spaniards suffered severely, Hawkins lost his fleet, his treasure, and the majority of his followers. Out of six ships under his command two only escaped; and of these one foundered at sea, the other, called the *Judith*, a barque of fifty tons, commanded by Francis Drake, brought back the remnant of the adventurers to Europe."

(*Footnote. Lingard's History of England volume vi. chap. vii.)

The English and Dutch opportunity for discovery on the coasts of Australia began with the decline of Portuguese and Spanish supremacy. If we trace the growth of maritime preponderance in Europe we shall see that its results, so far as Australian maritime discovery is concerned, were due to the natural consequences which forced the English and the Dutch to invade the spheres of Portuguese and Spanish activity.

From Italy had come the first impulse which led to the re-discovery of the New World; the great movement of maritime exploration was continued by the Portuguese, the Spanish, and the French; and then began the struggle of commercial enterprise and ambition in which England and Holland had to join, owing to their geographical positions, or else forsake their very nationality.

It was a question of life or death; the contest for supremacy was a long one, and numerous were the naval combats between the rival Powers.

With Drake begins the rise of the naval fame of England; meanwhile the power of Portugal and Spain began to decline. After the battle of Alcacer Quibir in 1578, in which Don Sebastian was defeated and killed, and his army utterly destroyed, Portugal never recovered from the blow. For sixty years her throne became an appanage of Spain. Even when, in 1640, Portugal threw off the yoke, and the Government was compelled to leave Lisbon, and Portuguese India, and Brazil expelled the Spaniards, it was too late for either Portugal or Spain to set forth any claim to Australia, for the Dutch were by that time firmly planted in Java and Amboyna, and Tasman's first expedition was on the eve of being sent out. Before this time Spanish supremacy had also come to an end, and the very same gale that Cavendish experienced when nearing the coast of England, on his return from his voyage of circumnavigation, had already brought ominous disaster on the famous Armada, and after the defeat of that great Spanish fleet Spain gradually lost her hold on her zealously guarded possessions.

At this period the idea of colonization or even discovery did not forcibly suggest itself to the English mind.*

(*Footnote. The earliest English references to the colonization of the Great South Land appear in the shape of certain proposals made to the British Government in the sixteenth century. The manuscript containing these proposals, which is endorsed by Lord Burleigh, *A Discovery of Lands Beyond the Equinoctial*, 1573, has been printed in the Hakluyt Society's edition of Frobisher's Voyages, 1867 pages 4 to 8, and is entitled The discoverie, traffique and enjoyeuge for the Queen's Majesty and her subjects of all or anie landes, islands and countries southwards beyond the aequinoctial, or when the pole antartik hathe anie elevation above the horizon. and which lands, islandes and countries be not already possessed or subdued by or to the use of any Christian prince in Europe as by the charts and descriptions shall appere. Landsdowne Manuscript C. folio 142 to 6.

There is also in the same work (The Three Voyages of Sir Martin Frobisher) a very rough map and rather interesting description. The delineation of the Australian continent, which is joined to the Antarctic lands, is taken from the preceding Mercator type of map. The description of the *Terra Australis* is as follows:

Terra Australis seemeth to be a great firme land, lying under and about the South Pole, being in many places a fruitefull soyle, and is not yet thoroughly discovered, but onlye seene and touched on the north edge therof, by the travaile of the Portingals and Spaniards in their voyages to their East and West *Indies*.

It is included almost by a paralell, passing at 40 degrees in south latitude, yet in some places it reacheth into the sea with greate promontories, even into the tropicke Capricornus. Onely these partes are best knowen as over against *Capo d' buona Speranza* (where the Portingales see popingayes commonly of a wonderfull greatnesse), and againe it is knowen at the south side of the straight of Magellanus, and is called Terra del Fuego.

It is thoughte this south lande, aboute the pole Antartike, is farre bigger than the north land aboute the pole Artike, but whether it be so or not we have no certaine knowledge, for we have no particular description hereof, as we have of the lande under and aboute the north pole.

Referring to the map and above description Mr. G.B. Barton, in the first volume of the History of New South Wales, from the Records, says: "To understand exactly what the old geographers had in their minds when they wrote about Terra Australis we must go back at least three centuries, when the theory of its existence was in high favour among them. What they thought about it may be seen in the map of the world published with the account of Frobisher's voyages in the year 1578, and the description of the country given by the writer."

Mr. Barton's observations, we must bear in mind, may apply to the old [*English*] geographers; but certainly do not apply to more enlightened continental geographers and sailors of the period, if we are to Judge from the Carta Marina, o 'da Navigare, published some years before the one which accompanies Frobisher's narrative. The sailing chart we refer to was published with many of the numerous editions of Ptolemy, and may for aught we know have been published even before the year 1574. The facsimile we give here is taken from La Geografia di Clavdio Tolomeo Alexandrino, published in Venice in 1574. The editor states that it is a much reduced copy given only as a sample of the large charts used generally by sailors.

The following is his description of this chart:

QUESTA Carta e la Generale, che usano i marinari. Et e qui fatta come solamente per uno essempio, non perche in effeto cosi picciola ella fosse comoda o buona d'adoperare, se non a chi pero fosse molto pratico del mare in ciascuna sua parte & del modo d'adoperarla, che ogni picciola aiuto, o segno, gli fosse assai. I marinari l'usano quanto piu grandi lor sia possibile. Et hanno oltre alla generate o uniuersal, com 'e questa piu altre Carte particolari Della qual carta, & del modo di usarla, se n' e trattato distesamente nell' ultimo cap. dell' Espositioni uniuersali sopra tutto il Libro di Tolomeo.

The reader will notice that in the Carta da Navigare the Tierra Del Fuego is set down as an island, and is therefore unconnected with any South Polar continent. He will also notice that, following the example set in the year 1500, not only is the Australian continent purposely left out, but also New Guinea, which was charted in the earlier maps of the period we refer to.)

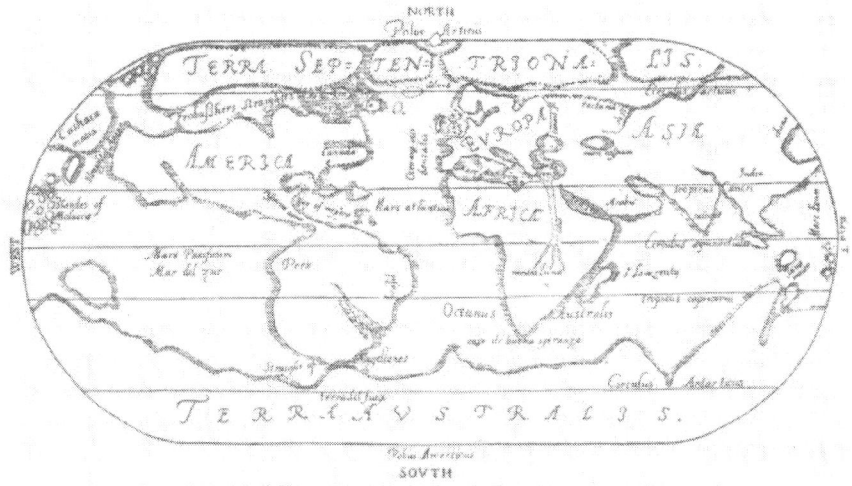

Map of the World, published with the account of Frobisher's Voyages, 1578.

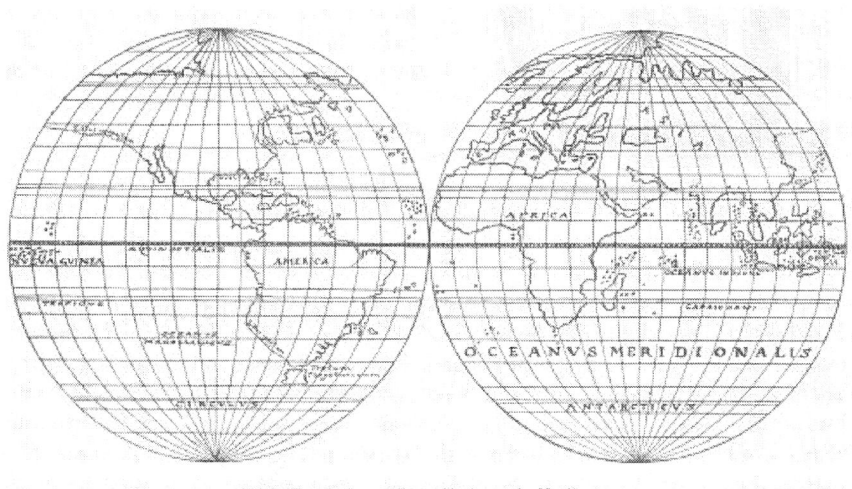

Orbis Descriptio. Carta Marina o da Navigare.

Drake's, Cavendish's, and many other voyages made by Englishmen during Queen Elizabeth's reign were mere piratical expeditions, undertaken with the more or less avowed object of plunder, and in pursuance of a well matured set of schemes for "singeing the king of Spain's beard." Otherwise both Drake and Cavendish stood as good a chance as the Dutch of coming in contact with the coasts of Australia, and that fifteen years before the arrival of the Dutch in Australasian waters. Drake, the first sea captain to complete the circumnavigation of the world, had sailed through the straits to the north-west of Australia on his way back to England, and Cavendish, eight years after, in 1588, had also sailed through the same straits, and anchored on the south coast of Java. Both these navigators, when among the Spice Islands, had many offers made them which, if accepted by England, would have made her sole mistress of all the islands in the Indian Ocean to the north of Australia; but England's hour had not come. There are in the narratives of Drake and Cavendish several passages which we shall quote, on account of their interest, as exemplifying the reception given to those early sea captains, and because the place-names therein mentioned bear witness to the genuineness of early Portuguese and Spanish discovery.

DRAKE AMONGST THE ISLANDS TO THE NORTH OF AUSTRALIA.

DRAKE, having sailed through the Straits of Magalhaens with safety and ease, and having discovered the falsehood of the traditional description, according to which the passage was long and intricate, the shores dreary and inhospitable, the weather always bleak and tempestuous, and the danger of shipwreck continual, reached the Molucca Islands, also without any great difficulty.

Then the narrative runs thus:

"Leaving this island the night after we fell in with it, on October 18 1579, we lighted upon divers others, some whereof made a great show of inhabitants. We continued our course by the islands of Tagulanda, Zelon, and Zewarra, being friends to the Portuguese, the first whereof hath growing in it great store of cinnamon. On November 14 we fell in with the islands of Molucca. Which day, at night (having directed our course to run with Tidore), in casting along the island of Mutyr, belonging to the king of Ternate, his deputy, or vice-king, seeing us at sea, came with his canoe to us without all fear, and came aboard, and after some conference with our General willed him in wise to run in with Ternate, and not with Tidore, assuring him that the king would be glad of his coming, and would be ready to do what he would require, for which purpose he himself would be that night with the king, and tell him the news, with whom if he once dealt we should find that as he was a king, so his word should stand; adding further that if he went to Tidore before he came to Ternate the king would have nothing to do with us, because he held the Portugals as his enemy. Whereupon our General resolved to run with Ternate, where the next morning early we came to anchor, at which time our General sent a messenger to the king, with a velvet cloak for a present and token of his coming to be in peace, and that he required nothing but traffic and exchange of merchandise, whereof he had good store in such things as he wanted.

"In the meantime the vice-king had been with the king according to his promise, signifying unto him what good things he might receive from us by traffic, whereby the king was moved with great liking towards us, and sent to our General with special message that he should have what things he needed and would require, with peace and friendship, and moreover that he would yield himself and the right of his island to be at the pleasure and commandment of so famous a prince as we served. In token whereof he sent to our General a signet, and within short time after came in his own person, with boats and canoes, to our ship, to bring her into a better and safer road than she was in at that present. In the meantime our General's messenger, being come to the court, was met by certain noble personages with great solemnity and brought to the king, at whose hands he was most friendly and graciously entertained.

Sir Francis Drake.

"The king, purposing to come to our ship, sent before four great and large canoes, in every one whereof were certain of his greatest statesmen that were about him, attired in white lawn of cloth of Calicut, having over their heads, from the one end of the canoe to the other, a covering of their perfumed mats, borne up with a frame made of reeds* for the same use, under which everyone did sit in his order according to his dignity, to keep him from the heat of the sun, divers of whom being of good age and gravity did make an ancient and fatherly show.

(*Footnote. Bamboos, evidently.)

"There were also divers young and comely men attired in white as were the others; the rest were soldiers, which stood in comely order round about on both sides, without whom sat the rowers, in certain galleries, which, being three on a side all along the canoes, did lie off from the side thereof three or four yards, one being orderly built lower than another, in every of which galleries were the number of fourscore rowers. These canoes were furnished with warlike munition, every man for the most part having his sword and target, with his dagger, besides other weapons, as lances, calivers, darts, bows and arrows; also every canoe had a small cast base mounted, at the least, one full yard upon a stock set upright. Thus coming near our ship, in order, they rowed about us one after another, and, passing by, did their homage with great solemnity, the great personages beginning with great gravity and fatherly countenance signifying that the king had sent them to conduct our ship into a better road. Soon after the king himself repaired, accompanied with six grave and ancient persons, who did their obeisance with marvellous humility. The king was a man of tall stature, and seemed to be much delighted with the sound of our music, to whom, as also to his nobility, our General gave presents, wherewith they were passing well contented...This island is the chief of all the islands of Molucca, and the king hereof is king of seventy islands besides. The king with his people are Moors in religion, observing certain new moons with fastings; during which fast they neither eat nor drink in the day, but in the night. After that our gentlemen were returned, and that we had here by the favour of the king received all necessary things that the place could yield us; our General considering the great distances, and how far he was yet off from his country, thought it not best here to linger the time any longer, but, weighing his anchor, set out of the island and sailed to a certain little island to the southward of Celebes, where we graved our ship and continued there in that and other business twenty-six days. This island is thoroughly grown with wood of a large and high growth, very straight and without boughs, save only in the head or top, whose leaves are not much differing from our broom in England. Amongst these trees night by night through the whole land did show themselves an infinite swarm of fiery worms flying in the air, whose bodies, being no bigger than our common English flies, make such a show and light as if every twig or tree had been a burning candle. In this place breedeth also wonderful store of bats, as big as large hens; of crayfishes also here wanted no plenty, and they of exceeding bigness, one whereof was sufficient for four hungry stomachs at a dinner, being also very good and restoring meat, whereof we had experience; and they dig themselves holes in the earth like coneys.

"When we had ended our business here we weighed and set sail to run for the Moluccas; but, having at that time a bad wind, and being amongst the islands, with much difficulty were covered to the northward of the island of Celebes, where, by reason of contrary winds, not being able to continue our course to run westwards, we were forced to alter the same to the southward again, finding that course also to be very hard and dangerous by reason of infinite shoals which lie off and among the islands, whereof we had too much trial to the hazard and danger of our ship and lives. For, of all other days, upon January 9 in the year 1580, we ran suddenly upon a rock where we stuck fast from eight o'clock at night till four o'clock in the afternoon the next day, being indeed out of all hope to escape the danger; but our General, as he had always hitherto showed himself courageous, and of a good confidence in the mercy and protection of God, so now he continued in the same; and lest he should seem to perish wilfully, both he and we did our best endeavour to save ourselves, which it pleased God so to bless that in the end we cleared ourselves most happily of the danger.

"We lightened our ship upon the rocks of three tons of cloves, eight pieces of ordnance, and certain meal and beans, and then the wind (as it were in a moment, by the special grace of God), changing from the starboard to the larboard of the ship, we hoisted our sails, and the happy gale drove our ship off the rock into the sea again, to the no little comfort of all our hearts, for which we gave God such praise and thanks as so great a benefit required.

"On February 8 following we fell in with the fruitful island of Barateue,* having in the meantime suffered many dangers by winds and shoals. The people of this island are comely in body and stature, and of civil behaviour, just in dealing, and courteous to strangers, whereof we had the experience sundry ways, they being most glad of our presence, and were ready to relieve our wants in those things which their country did yield.

(*Footnote. Bouton.)

"The men go naked, saving their head and privities, every man having something or other hanging at their ears. The women are covered from the middle down to the foot, wearing a great number of bracelets upon their arms, for some had eight upon each arm, being made, some of bone, some of horn, and some of brass, the lightest whereof by our estimation weighed two ounces apiece. With this people linen cloth is good merchandise and of good request, whereof they make rolls for their heads and girdles to wear about them. Their island is both rich and fruitful--rich in gold, silver, copper, and sulphur, wherein they seem skilful and expert, not only to try the same, but in working it also artificially into any form and fashion that pleaseth them.

"Their fruits be divers and plentiful, as nutmegs, ginger, long pepper, lemons, cucumbers, cocoas, figs, sago, with divers other sorts; and among all the rest we had one fruit, in bigness, form, and husk, like a bay berry, hard of substance, and pleasing of taste, which being sodden becometh soft, and is a most good and wholesome victual, whereof we took reasonable store, as we did also of the other fruits and spices; so that, to confess the truth, since the time that we first set out of our own country of England we happened upon no place (Ternate only excepted) wherein we found more comfort and better means of refreshing.

"At our departure from Barateue we set our course for Java Major, where arriving we found great courtesy and honourable entertainment. This island is governed by five kings, whom they call Rajas, as Raja Donan, and Raja Mang Bange, and Raja Cabuccapollo, which live as having one spirit and one mind. Of the five we had four a-shipboard at once, and two or three often. They are wonderfully delighted in coloured clothes, as red and green. The upper part of their bodies are naked, save their heads, whereupon they wear a Turkish roll, as do the Moluccians. From the middle downwards they wear a pintado of silk, trailing upon the ground, in colours as they best like..."

Here there follows a description of bread made with rice..."Not long before our departure they told us that not far off there were such great ships as ours, wishing us to beware. Upon this our captain would stay no longer. From Java Major we sailed for the Cape of Good Hope, which was the first land, until we came to Sierra Leone upon the coast of Guinea. Notwithstanding we ran hard aboard the Cape, finding the report of the Portuguese to be most false, who affirm that it is the most dangerous cape of the world, never without intolerable storms and present dangers to travellers which come near the same. This cape is a most stately thing and the fairest cape we saw in the whole circumference of the earth, and we passed by it on June 18 1580. From thence we continued our course to Sierra Leone, on the coast of Guinea, where we arrived on July 22, and found necessary provisions, great store of elephants, oysters upon trees of one kind, spawning and increasing infinitely, the oyster suffering no bud to grow. We departed thence on the 24th day. We arrived in England on November 3 1580, being the third year of our departure."

Drake's old ship, the *Pelican*, was named the *Golden Hind* after his voyage round the world. She was long an object of veneration to the seamen of Deptford. When she was broken up John Davis caused a chair to be made from her timbers (see initial letter of this chapter, Illustration 25), and presented it to the University of Oxford. This interesting relic is still preserved in the Bodleian library. Cowley's fine lines, written while sitting and drinking in it, are well known.

Great Relic! thou, too, in this port of ease,

Hast still one way of making voyages;

The breath of fame, like an auspicious gale

(The greater trade wind, which does never fail),

Shall drive thee round the world; and thou shalt run

As long around it as the sun.

The straits of time too narrow are for thee--

Launch forth into an undiscovered sea,

And steer the endless course of vast eternity.

Take for thy sail this verse, and for pilot me.

No sooner had Drake returned from his voyage of circumnavigation than another project* was formed for establishing a company to trade beyond the equinoctial line--Drake to be Governor for life. This project, in Secretary Walsingham's handwriting, still exists in the Record office. It eventually collapsed.

(*Footnote. An earlier project was prepared in 1573. See above footnote.)

CHAPTER 35. A.D. 1587 TO 1588.

CAVENDISH AMONGST THE ISLANDS TO THE NORTH OF AUSTRALIA.

The Australasian portion of Cavendish's narrative is as follows:

"On the 8th day of February, by eight of the clock in the morning, we espied an island near Gilolo, called Batochina, which standeth in one degree from the equinoctial line northward. On the 14th day of February we fell in with eleven or twelve very small islands, lying very low and flat, full of trees, and passed by some islands which be sunk and have the dry sands lying in the main sea. These islands, near the Moluccas, stand in three degrees and ten minutes to the southward of the line.

"On the 17th day one John Gameford, a cooper, died, which had been sick of an old disease a long time. On the 20th day we fell in with certain other islands, which had many small islands among them, standing four degrees to the southward of the line. On the 21st day of February, being Ash Wednesday, Captain Havers died of a most severe and pestilent ague, which held him furiously some seven or eight days, to the no small grief of our General and of all the rest of the company, who caused two falchions and one saker to be shot off, with all the small shot in the ship; who, after he was shrouded in a sheet and a prayer said, was heaved overboard, with great lamentation of us all. Moreover, presently after his death, myself, with divers others in the ship, fell marvellously sick, and so continued in very great pain for the space of three weeks or a month, by reason of the extreme heat and intemperateness of the climate.

"On the 1st of March, having passed through the Straits of Java Minor and Java Major, we came to an anchor under the south-west parts of Java Major, where we espied certain of the people which were fishing by the sea side, in a bay which was under the island. Then our General, taking into the ship's boat certain of his company, and a negro which could speak the Morisco tongue, which he had taken out of the Great St. Anna, made towards those fishers, which, having espied our boat, ran on shore into the wood for fear of our men; but our General caused his negro to call unto them, who no sooner heard him call but presently one of them came out to the shore side and made reply. Our General, by the negro, enquired of him for fresh water, which they found, and caused the fisher to go to the king and to certify him of a ship, that was come to have traffic for victuals, and for diamonds, pearls, or any other jewels that he had, for which he should have either gold or other merchandise in exchange. The fisherman answered that we should have all manner of victuals that we would request. Thus the boat came aboard again. Within a while after we went about to furnish our ship thoroughly with wood and water.

Cavendish's Portrait.

"About the 8th of March two or three canoes came from the town unto us with eggs, hens, fresh fish, oranges and limes; and brought word we should have had victuals more plentifully but that they were so far to be brought to us where we rode. Which, when our General heard, he weighed anchor and stood in nearer for the town, and as we were under sail we met with one of the king's canoes coming towards us, whereupon we shook the ship in the wind and stayed for the canoe until it came aboard of us, and stood into the bay which was hard by, and came to an anchor. In this canoe was the king's secretary, who had on his head a piece of dyed linen cloth, folded up like unto a Turk's turban; he was all naked saving about the waist; his breast was carved with the broad arrow upon it; he went barefooted; he had an interpreter with him, which was a Mestizo, that is, half an Indian and half a Portugal, who could speak very good Portuguese. This secretary signified unto our General that he had brought him an hog, hens, eggs, fresh fish, sugar canes and wine (which wine was as strong as any *aqua vitae* and as clear as any rock water); he told him further that he would bring victuals so sufficiently for him as he and his company would request, and that within the space of four days. Our General used him singularly well, banqueted him most royally with the choice of many and sundry conserves, wines, both sweet and other, and caused his musicians to make him music. This done, our General told him that he and his company were Englishmen, and that we had been at China, and had had traffic there with them, and that we were come thither to discover, and purposed to go to Molucca. The people of Java told our General that there were certain Portugals in the island which lay there as factors continually to traffic with them, to buy negroes, cloves, pepper, sugar, and many other commodities.

"This secretary of the king, with his interpreter, lay one night aboard our ship. The same night, because they lay aboard in the evening at the setting of the watch, our General commanded every man in the ship to provide his arquebuse and his shot, and so, with shooting off forty or fifty small shot and one saker, himself set the watch with them. This was no small marvel unto these heathen people, who had not commonly seen any ship so furnished with men and ordnance. The next morning we dismissed the secretary and his interpreter with all humanity.

"On the fourth day after, which was the 12th of March, according to their appointment, came the king's canoes; but the wind being somewhat scant they could not get aboard that night, but put into a bay under the island until the next day, and presently, after the break of day, there came to the number of nine or ten of the king's canoes so deeply laden with victuals as they could swim--with two great live oxen, half a score of wonderful great and fat hogs, a number of hens (which were alive), drakes, geese, eggs, plantains, sugar canes, sugar in plates, cocoa, sweet oranges and sour, limes, great store of wine and *aqua vitae*, salt to season victuals withal, and almost all manner of victuals else, with divers of the king's officers which were there. Among all the rest of the people, in one of these canoes came two Portugals, which were of middle stature, and men of marvellous proper personage. They were each of them in a loose jerkin and hose, which came down from the waist to the ancle, because of the use of the country, and partly because it was Lent, and a time for doing of their penance (for they account it as a thing of great dislike among these heathens to wear either hose or shoes on their feet). They had on each of them a very fair and a white lawn shirt, with falling bands on the same, very decently, only their bare legs excepted. These Portugals were no small joy unto our General and all the rest of our company, for we had not seen any Christian that was our friend of a year and a half before. Our General used and entreated them singularly well with banquets and music. They told us that they were no less glad to see us than we to see them, and enquired of the state of their country, and what was become of Don Antonio, their king, and whether he were living or no, for that they had not of long time been in Portugal, and that the Spaniards had always brought them word that he was dead. Then our General satisfied them in every demand, assuring them that their king was alive, and in England, and had honourable allowance of our Queen, and that there was war between Spain and England, and that we were come under the King of Portugal into the South Sea, and had warred upon the Spaniards there, and had fired, spoiled, and sunk all the ships along the coast that we could meet withal, to the number of eighteen or twenty sail. With this report they were sufficiently satisfied.

"On the other side they declared unto us the state of the island of Java. First, the plentifulness and great choice and store of victuals of all sorts, and of all manner of fruits as before is set down. Then they described the properties and nature of the people as followeth: The name of the king of that part of the island was Raja Bolamboam, who was a man had in great majesty and fear among them. The common people may not bargain, sell, or exchange anything with any other nation without special license from their king; and if any so do it is present death for him. The king himself is a man of great years, and hath a hundred wives; his son hath fifty. The custom of the country is that whensoever the king doeth die they take the body so dead and burn it, and preserve the ashes of him; and within five days next after, the wives of the said king so dead, according to the custom and use of the country, everyone of them go together to a place appointed, and the chief of the women, which was nearest unto him in account, hath a ball in her hand, and throweth it from her, and to the place where the ball resteth thither they go all, and turn their faces to the eastward, and everyone, with a dagger in her hand (which dagger they call a creese, and is as sharp as a razor), stab themselves to the heart, and with their hands all do bebathe themselves in their own blood, and falling grovelling on their faces so end their days. This thing is as true as it seemeth to any hearer to be strange...

"After we had fully contented these Portugals and the people of Java which brought us victuals in their canoes, they took their leave of us, with promise of all good entertainment at our returns, and our General gave them three great pieces of ordnance at their departure. Thus the next day, being the 16th of March (1588), we set sail towards the Cape of Good Hope, called by the Portuguese Cabo be Buena Esperanza, on the southernmost coast of Africa."

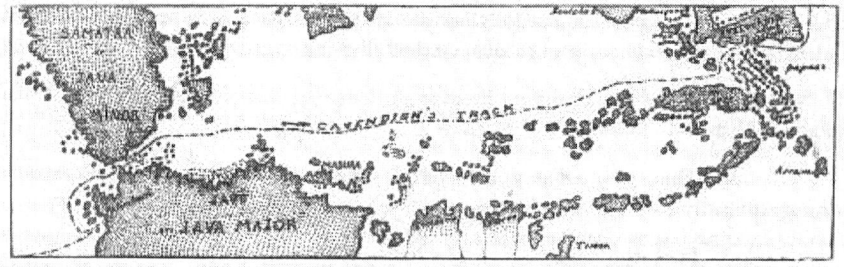

Cavendish's track, as it would appear on the Dauphin Chart.

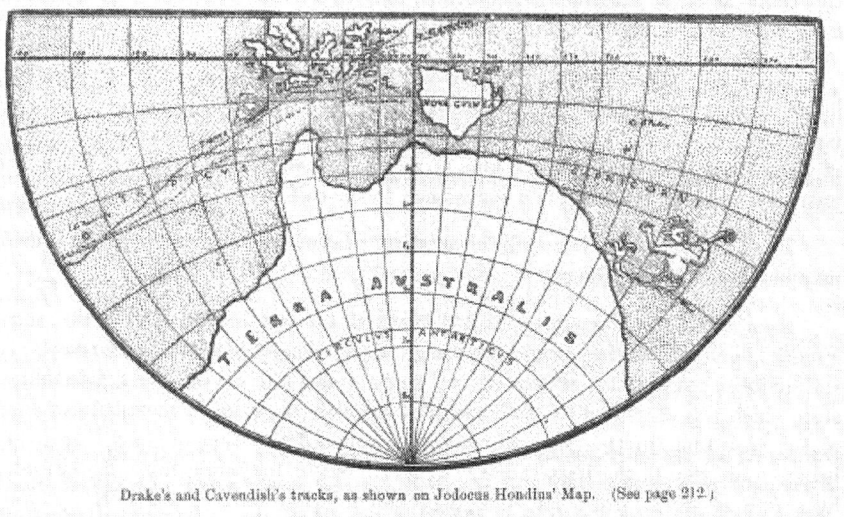

Drake's and Cavendish's tracks, as shown on Jodocus Hondius' Map. (See page 212.)

Cavendish's track as it would appear on the Dauphin Chart.

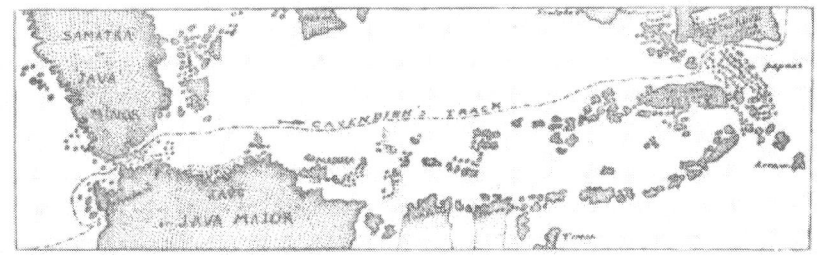

Cavendish's track, as it would appear on the Dauphin Chart.

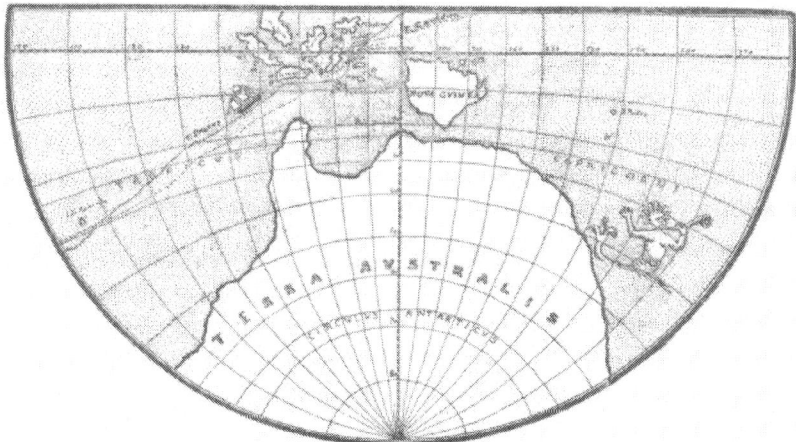

Drake's and Cavendish's tracks, as shown on Jodocus Hondius' Map.

Drake's and Cavendish's tracks, as shown on Jodocus Hondius' Map.

In the quaint narratives of Drake and Cavendish we see that the term Java Major is restricted to Java, whereas in the oldest Australasian charts it is extended to Australia. The island of Sumatra, which in old charts bears the various names of Camatra, Samatra, Ciamotra, and Siamotra, is called Java Minor, as in Marco Polo's descriptions; unless, which is quite possible, the term Java Minor in Drake's and Cavendish's narratives applies to some of the small islands to the east of Java. There are several examples of this term being so applied about this time, tending to show that it may have become customary. Then, according to both Drake's and Cavendish's tracks, as given in Hondius' map, which we give here,* these navigators appear to have passed either through the straits of Bali, Lomboc, or Allas; but it is questionable whether these tracks are correctly laid down, for

Cavendish's narrative says: "We came to an anchor under the south-west parts of Java Major, etc.," and in Hondius' map there is no indication of this course.

(*Footnote. Dauphin chart and Hondius' map, Illustrations 12 and 24.)

Moreover Linschoten, a contemporary, says distinctly, when describing the strait of Sunda: "Through this strait, or narrowe passage, Thomas Candish, an Inglish Captaine, passed with his ship, as he came out of the south parts (the Pacific Ocean) from Noua Spaigne."* Batochina in Cavendish's narrative is another name about which there appears to be some confusion, inasmuch as it originally described the island of Gilolo, and is so used in the Dauphin chart (1530/1536).

(*Footnote. English translation.)

At the time of Cavendish's voyage it seems to apply to an island on the east coast of Gilolo. Compare map with text. With reference to Cavendish's track the following interesting piece of information, written about ten years after, would go to prove that he landed on the south-east coast of Java, instead of the south-west: Le 22 (Janvier 1597) on alla mouiller sur la cote, environ, a une lieue nord-ouest quart a l'ouest de la place assiegee. La un Gentilhomme se rendit a bord, & fit le recit de l'etat du siege. Entr'autres choses il dit que le pere du Roi regnant vivoit encore, & que c'etoit un homme fort vieux, qui s'etoit retire assez avant dans l'Isle. Et comme ce pere avoit parle d'un vaisseau a peu pres de la meme fabrique que ceux des Hollandais, qui avoit ete sur ces memes cotes depuis dix ans, on presuma que ce vieux Roi pouvoit etre celui dont Sir Thomas Candish fait la description dans son voyage, & dont il dit qu'il avoit alors plus de cent cinquante ans.*

(*Footnote. Voyages de la Compagnie premier Voyage des Hollandais. Tome II page 106.)

The Dutch were then (January 1597) in sight of *Balambuam* on the south-east coast of Java, and Cavendish's *Raja Bolamboam* appears to be the father of the king who was reigning at the time of their first voyage.

Another passage in the same work--*Voyages de la Compagnie*, Tome II page 110--would show that Drake made a stay on the south-west coast of Bali in the bay of Padan. The passage runs thus: Cependant, le 9 du mois, le *Maurice* entra dans une grande baie nommee Padan, ou les habitants de la cote dirent a l'equipage, qu'il y avoit dix huit ans qu'il etoit aussi venu la d'autres gens faits comme eux, qui ayant coupe une corde en cinq ou six morceaux, l'avoient ensuite rejointe. On presuma que ce pouvoit etre Sir Francois Drake.

CHAPTER 36. A.D. 1592 TO 1595.

THE RISE OF HOLLAND'S MARITIME POWER. H. LINSCHOTEN. HOUTMAN. CORNELIUS CLAESZ. PETER PLANCIUS. THE FIRST VOYAGE OF THE DUTCH TO AUSTRALASIA.

Linschoten and Hootman, or Houtman, were the pioneers of Holland in the East; both had been for some considerable time in the service of Portugal. Linschoten, the son of a Frieslander, had lived for two years in Lisbon, and afterwards, as one of the servants of the Archbishop of Goa, he resided for thirteen years in India. During his sojourn in the East he patiently collected all the information he could get about the customs, trade, etc. of the countries in which he lived, and, from the Portuguese, all the details concerning the voyage to India and the Spice Islands. A book by him, published in Holland in 1595/1596, and subsequently in London in 1598 (Discours of Voyages into ye East and West Indies), bears all the appearance of being a translation from some Portuguese manuscript or work; perhaps Barros' Treatise on Geography.* The maps which accompany the text in Linschoten's work are of Portuguese origin, as the nomenclature and notes thereon show, for they are in the Portuguese language. Moreover the work concludes with a short history of Portugal, a rather strange addendum to a Dutch or English publication of the kind.

(*Footnote. Barros, the Portuguese historian, wrote a treatise on geography in which most of the countries discovered by the Portuguese were described; but it was never finished or published; it disappeared mysteriously at his death.)

On his return to his native land Linschoten was well received by his countrymen. We find him in 1594 accompanying Barentsz in that wild attempt to reach India by the Polar Seas in order to take the Portuguese and Spaniards in the rear. This route, tried also by Frobisher and other English navigators, was abandoned after several disastrous and ineffectual attempts.

"While they were in quest of this Northern Passage," says a Dutch historian, "one *Cornelius Hootman*, a *Hollander*, happen'd to be in *Portugal*, and there satisfied his curiosity by a diligent enquiry into the state of the *East Indies*, and the course that one must steer in order to come at it. He had frequent conferences upon this subject with the *Portuguese*, who gave notice of it to the Court.

"At that time all foreigners were strictly prohibited to make such enquiries, and upon that score *Hootman* was put in prison and ordered to lie there till he paid a severe fine. In order to raise such a considerable sum of money he addressed himself to the merchants of *Amsterdam*, and gave 'em to know that if they would pay his fine he would discover to them all that related to the *East Indies*, and the *Passage* thither. Accordingly they granted his request, and he perform'd his promise."*

(*Footnote. Voyages de la Compagnie. English translation of first volume. Introduction.)

Linschoten.

Prince Roland Bonaparte, an enthusiast in matters relating to Dutch discoveries, points out* that Linschoten's and Houtman's knowledge of the road to India was not alone conducive to the sending out of the first Dutch fleets by way of the Cape of Good Hope, but that the Dutch had premeditated their designs in the East.

(*Footnote. Les premiers Voyages des Neerlandais dans l'Insulinde, 1595 a 1602, Versailles 1884 page 4.)

Speaking of the former ideas according to which Linschoten, and especially Houtman, were supposed to be the only promoters of Dutch discovery in the East, Prince Roland Bonaparte says: "Documents published more recently enable us to demonstrate that it is not so, and that these voyages (the first voyages of the Dutch to Java) were the result of a long premeditated plan, followed with much perseverance. For the Dutch, preoccupied with those Indies, the products of which had been so often carried by their ships from Spanish ports to other ports in Europe, tried to collect all the documents that might guide them on the way to India. These researches were difficult and dangerous, for the Spaniards and Portuguese punished with death whomsoever would have sold maps to foreigners.

"Nevertheless on April 17 1592 the publisher, Cornelius Claesz, of Amsterdam, came and declared to the States-General that he had succeeded in procuring, at his expense, by the instrumentality of the learned Peter Plancius, twenty-five sea charts relative to India, China, and Africa. It was the cosmographer, Bartolomeo de Lasso, chief of the navigation in Spain, who had sent them to Plancius. The States-General gave orders to have them printed; they gave orders at the same time to construct a large chart of the world, that was to serve as a basis for future discoveries."

It is easy to see the importance of this communication, made six months before the return of Linschoten. It is at this time that the merchants of Amsterdam sent to Lisbon the two brothers Houtman to complete the documents of Plancius, and if necessary to verify them. Linschoten, who returned home in September 1595, added fresh information to that already obtained. This shows that Houtman, far from being the promoter of the expedition, was in reality only the agent of the merchants of Amsterdam. Besides it is known now that he was only the *commercial chief*, and that the fleet was commanded by the clever pilot Pieter Dircksz Keyser, who died in the straits of Sunda.

Houtman's sole merit therefore consists in having returned alive; and, as the dead are soon forgotten, it is he that history points out as having conducted the first Dutch fleet to the Indies.

The first expedition consisted of four ships, all small craft comparatively; these were, the *Mauritius* of 400 tons, carrying 6 large and 14 small guns, 4 large and 8 small bombards, and a crew of 84 men. The master was Jean Jansz Molenaar, and the supercargo Cornelius Houtman. The second ship was named the *Holland*, with the same tonnage and armament as the *Mauritius*. The master was Jean Dignumsz, the supercargo Gerard Van Beuningen. The third ship, *Amsterdam*, of 200 tons, was manned by 59 men, had 6 large and 10 small guns, 4 large and 6 small bombards. The master's name was Jean Jacobsz Schellinger, and the supercargo's Rene Van Hel. The fourth vessel was a small yacht named the *Little Dove*,* of 30 tons, carrying 20 men, and having 2 large and 6 small guns, with 2 bombards. The master was Simon Lambertsz Mau. The crews consisted therefore of a total of 247 men.

(*Footnote. The vessel named here the Little Dove, Duyfken in Dutch, but always erroneously spelt Duyfphen, or *Duyfhen*, by English writers, is the identical vessel that sailed eleven years later into the Gulf of Carpentaria and ran along the western shores of York Peninsula till a point was reached in 14 1/2 degrees, which retains to this day the name *Keer Weer* (Turnagain), given to it on early Dutch charts, which represent this part of the coast of Queensland as a prolongation of the south coast of New Guinea.)

On the 2nd of April 1595 those four ships left the Texel.

CHAPTER 37. A.D. 1595 TO 1605.

MENDANA'S EXPEDITION IN SEARCH OF THE GREAT SOUTHERN CONTINENT. NEW GUINEA, THE SOLOMON ISLANDS, AND THE AUSTRALIAN CONTINENT ON DE BRY'S AND WYTFLIET'S MAPS. DE QUIROS AND TORRES. ARRIVAL OF THE DUTCH IN THE EAST INDIAN ARCHIPELAGO.

hilst the Dutch were seeking to establish themselves in the East and were actually on their way to Java the Spaniards, who had still a lingering remembrance of the early explorations of their pioneers, sent out Mendana (1595), with the object of founding a colony at the island of San Christoval, one of the Solomon Group, previously discovered by him in 1567/1569; *and from thence attempting the discovery of the southern Terra Firma*, or continent, which formed such a conspicuous feature on the maps of the time.

Mendana's fleet was composed of four vessels. His captain and chief pilot was Pedro Fernandez de Quiros, the other officers were Lope de

Vega, who commanded the *Santa Isabel*, Felipe Corzo, who commanded the *San Felipe*, and Alonzo de Leyva, who commanded the frigate *Santa Catalina*; the name of Mendana's galleon was the *San Jeronimo*.

As it was intended to settle a colony on the Australian continent many took their wives with them, and amongst these were Dona Isabel de Barreto, Mendana's wife; and Dona Mariana de Castro, the wife of Lope de Vega.

Map of Solomon Islands, Santa Cruz and New Hebrides.

They set sail from Callao on the 9th of April 1595, and, after discovering the Marquesas and the group afterwards called by Carteret

Queen Charlotte's Islands, they sighted land on September 7th, which Mendana believed at first to be the Solomon Islands, of which he was in search. They soon found out their mistake, and named the island Santa Cruz. See chart of Solomon, Santa Cruz, and New Hebrides Islands, Illustration 74.

Here an attempt at colonization was made, but what with the hostility of the natives, sickness, and a mutinous spirit, the young colony did not progress favourably. To make matters worse Mendana himself fell ill and died; and the grand scheme which under favourable circumstances might have resulted in the foundation of a Spanish-Australian Empire was perforce abandoned for the while.

The remnant of this disastrous expedition, having repaired to the Philippine Islands, returned to New Spain in 1596.

De Quiros however never abandoned the project of discovery. His belief in the existence of a southern continent, a belief which, as he says, *had grown up with him from the cradle*, must have acquired considerable force, since it led him to persist in his determination to discover and settle that Australian continent, notwithstanding the almost unparalleled disasters of Mendana's last expedition and the opposition he subsequently met with from the court of Spain.

The earliest map on which Mendana's Solomon Islands were charted appears to be the one published at Francfort by De Bry in 1596, the very year in which the remnant of Mendana's expedition reached the Philippine Islands. It was published therefore without cognisance of the results of his second voyage to those islands. The Solomon Islands, according to De Bry's map, were confounded with the islands now known as New Britain and New Ireland.

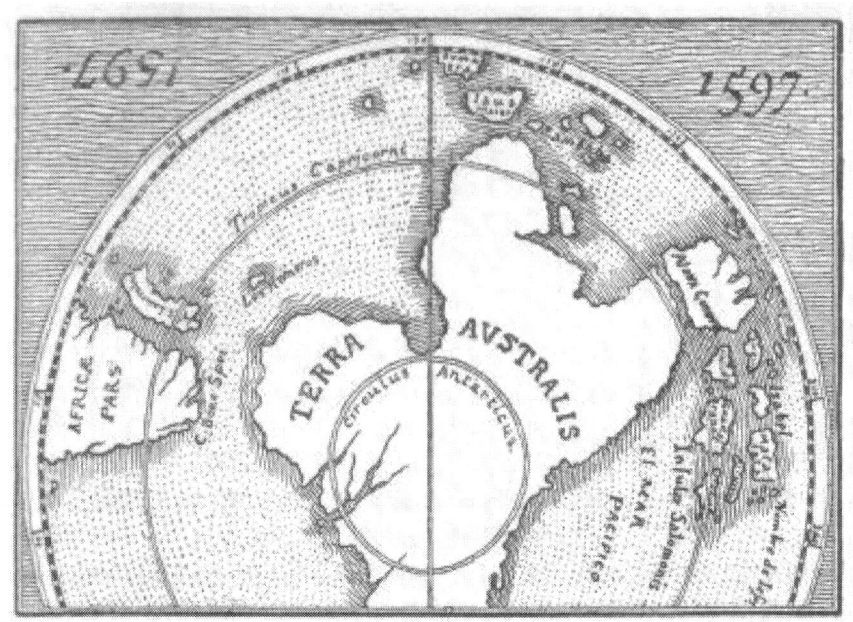

The Continent of Australia in Wytfliet's Map.

The Continent of Australia in Wytfliet's Map.

Wytfliet's map on the contrary, published one year later in 1597, places some of the Solomon Islands too far south, two out of the three largest islands of the group being placed on the tropic of Capricorn, which would lead one to believe that Mendana's Solomon group comprised New Caledonia and the New Hebrides as well as the group known to us as the Solomon Islands. The strait between *Nova Guinea* and *Terra Australis* is also placed in the longitude of the most southerly of the Solomon Islands; which is correct according to the actual position of those islands as determined by modern identification and survey.

Other islands of the group, such as *Nombre de Iesus, Isola Atreguada, Matalota, Isabel, Arracifes,* are in their true latitude. *I de los Crespos, I. d. los Martires, la Barbude, La Casimana, Los Volcanes,* and other names on the north coast of New Guinea belong to an earlier discovery.

The eastern and western coasts of Australia are roughly indicated, and also the Gulf of Carpentaria. All the names however, with the exception of TERRA AUSTRALIS, are fictitious. They are the same as those which occur on G. Mercator's map, i.e. Beach, Lucach, Maletur, etc., and have not been given on our copy through want of space. Java and Sumbawa bear respectively the names *Iaua Maior* and *Sambaba*. Wytfliet's work, *Descriptionis Ptolemaicae Augmentum*, containing 200 printed pages and 19 maps handsomely engraved on copper, reached seven editions between 1597 and 1611. An English edition was published at Louvain in 1597, and a passage occurs in it which is of very great importance because it bears witness to a discovery of the Australian continent made before the arrival of the Dutch in these seas. It is a known fact that the Dutch appropriated to themselves Portuguese and Spanish documents and charts which, when altered to serve their purpose, made them appear to be the actual discoverers, whereas in reality the countries described in such documents and charts had at the time never been visited by them. It is a curious fact that in all the works--and they are legion--in which the history of early Australian maritime discovery has been treated these frauds have never been noticed. Thus we find, without any enquiry as to its origin, the following often quoted passage we refer to:

"The Australis Terra is the most southern of all lands. It is separated from New Guinea by a narrow strait. Its shores are hitherto but little known since, after one voyage and another, that route has been deserted, and seldom is the country visited unless when sailors are driven there by storms. The Australis Terra begins at two or three degrees from the equator, and is maintained by some to be of so great an extent that, if it were thoroughly explored, it would be regarded as a fifth part of the world."

The above passage has always been supposed to refer to Dutch voyages; but, as in 1597 when it was published the Dutch had only sent out *one* expedition, which expedition did not return till August 14 1597, it cannot apply to Dutch voyages. What can be meant by "its shores are hitherto but little known since, *after one voyage and another* that route has been deserted?" It refers of course to some Portuguese or Spanish voyages, and the Dutch were not speaking for themselves but simply translating a Portuguese or Spanish text relating thereto. Linschoten's work contains a somewhat similar passage derived from Portuguese sources of information. It is as follows: "South-south-east, right over against the last point or corner of the Isle of Sumatra, on the south side of the equinoctial line, lyeth the island called Iaua Maior, or Great Java, where there is a strait, or narrow passage, called the Strait of Sunda, of a place so called lying not far from thence, within the isle of Java. This island beginneth under seven degrees on the south side, and runneth east and by south 150 miles long, but, touching the breadth, it is not found, because as yet it is not discovered, nor by the inhabitants themselves well known. Some think it to be firme land, and parcell of the countrie called *Terra incognita*, which being so should reach from that place to the *Cape de Bona Sperace*, but as yet it is not certainly known, and therefore it is accounted an island." Linschoten's Discours of Voyages into ye East and West Indies; London 1598. The same knowledge of the existence of a vast continent immediately below Java was expressed in Camoens' immortal poem long before the arrival of the Dutch in Java.

Olha a Sunda tao larga, que huma banda

Esconde para o sul difficultuoso.

Os. Lusiadas. Camoens.

Java behold, so large that one vast end

It covers towards the south tempestuous.

J.J. Aubertin's translation.

But Linschoten's information with reference to the *breadth* of Java was much out of date in 1598, and a map of Java of Portuguese origin, which he publishes in his book, contradicts his statement, for it shows an open sea to the south of Java called the *Laut Chidol* by the Javanese, or *South Sea*. On this map the term sea is repeated and Laut changed to Lant. Mare Lantchidol.

The work of Linschoten (London 1598) to which we have had access did not contain any map of the *Terra Australis* or Australia; possibly it had been torn out. Speaking of the indications of Australia on Mercator's and Ortelius' maps of the same period R.H. Major says: "In the map of Peter Plancius, given in the English edition of the Voyages of Linschoten 1598, similar indications of Australia occur, but leaving the question of the insular character of New Guinea doubtful."

(*Footnote. Early Voyages to Australia page lxvii.)

Linschoten's Map of Java.

There is a map said to be from Linschoten's work in A.E. Nordenskiold's splendid facsimile Atlas, Number 61 page 97, bearing the following title: Chart on Mercator's projection in: *Navigatio ac Itinerarum Iohannis Hugonis Linscotani.* Hagae-Comitis 1599, and on page 96 of the same work, under the date 1599: A map of Henricus Hondius in *Navigatio ac Itinerarum Johannis Linscotani*...Hagae-Comitis 1599. The map, given by Nordenskiold on page 97, is by H. Hondius as he says; but the date is wrong, and the information therefore wrong, because we find a legend on that map written across New Guinea as follows: *Terra dos Papous a Iacobo le Maire dicta Nova Guinea.*

We need not attach much importance to what that legend seems to imply, i.e. that Le Maire had discovered and named New Guinea, but we must bear in mind that his voyage along the northern coast of that island was performed in the year 1616, and therefore the map cannot belong to the Latin edition of Linschoten's work published in 1599. Moreover the T' LANDT VAN D'EENDRACHT said to have been discovered the same year (1616) on the west coast of Australia is also set down on this chart.

The Dutch of the first expedition to Australasia, having made a long stay at Madagascar, reached at last the south-west coast of Sumatra near the island of ENGANO on the 1st of June 1596. Afterwards they sailed along the north coast of Java, calling at various ports and reaching the island of BALI in 1597. They set sail from Bali and the south coast of Java on their homeward voyage by the Cape of Good Hope on the 26th of February, reaching the Texel in Holland on the 14th of August 1597.

According to de Constantin* the second, third, and fourth expeditions of the Dutch left Holland in 1598. The second expedition was composed of eight ships, and sailed to Java by the Cape of Good Hope. The third was composed of five vessels, or seven according to other accounts. They sailed from Holland with the intention of reaching the South Sea by way of Magalhaens' Strait; but this expedition, unlike Drake's and Cavendish's, met with a most disastrous fate; of the seven ships under command of Jacob Mahu, Simon de Cordes, and Sebald de Weerdt, only one, that of Sebaldt de Weerdt, ever returned to Holland.

(*Footnote. Recueil des Voyages qui ont servi a l'etablissement et aux progrez de la Compagnie des Indes Orientales formee dans les Provinces Unies des Pais-Bas. Rouen 1725.)

The fourth expedition, composed of four ships, had an English pilot with them who had been round the world with Cavendish. In 1599 Peter Both's fleet of eight ships set sail, arriving at Bantam on the 6th of August 1600; and Van den Hagen's expedition, consisting of three vessels, set sail also in 1599. In 1600 the English East Indian Company was formed, and in 1602 the Dutch East India Company. This year Captain Lancaster sailed from London, went to Achen, then to Bantam, where he settled a factory, which was the first possession of the English in the East Indies.

There appears to be much incertitude with reference to the dates of departure and to the number of ships which sailed from Holland to Australasia at this period. We give below a list from a good authority, Prince Roland Bonaparte.*

(*Footnote. Les premiers Voyages des Neerlandais dans l'Insulinde (1595 a 1602) Versailles 1884.)

SYNOPTIC TABLE OF THE FIRST VOYAGES OF THE DUTCH IN INSULINDIA.

	Commanders of Expeditions.	Companies that sent the Expeditions out.	Numb'r of ships	Date of Departure.	Date of Return.
1	Houtman	Cie van Verre, Amsterdam	4	2 April, 1595	14 April, 1597
2	Jakob Cornelisz Van Neck	Oude Compagnie, Amsterdam	8	1 May, 1598	19 July, 1599 / 19 May, 1600 / Sept., 1600
3	Houtman	Moucheron, Veere	2	15 March, 1598	29 July, 1600
4	Gerard Leroy and Laurens Bikker	Comp^ie de Middelbourg	3	1598.	1600
5	Jacques Mahu and Simon de Cordes	....	5	June, 1598	
6	Olivier de Noort	....	4	2 July, 1598	12 August, 1601
7	Steven van der Hagen	Oude Cie Amsterdam	3	26 April, 1599	July, 1601
8	Pieter Both van Amersfoort	Nieuwe Brabantsche, Cie Amsterdam	4	21 Dec., 1599	——— 1601
9	Jakob Wilkens	Oude Cie Amsterdam	4	21 Dec., 1599	1601
10	Van Neck	Oude Cie Amsterdam	6	28 June, 1600	15 July, 1602
11	Guljam Seneschal	Nieuwe Brabantsche, Cie Amsterdam	2	28 June, 1600	1601
12	Cornelis Bastiaansz	Cie de Middelbourg	4	28 January, 1601	6 July, 1602 / May, 1603
13	Jakob van Hoemakerck	Vereenigde Hollandsche, Cie Amsterdam	8	23 April, 1601	1602, 1604
14	Wolphert Harmensz	Vereenigde Hollandsche Cie Amsterdam	5	23 April, 1601	March, 1603
15	Joris van Spilbergh	Moucheron, Veere	3	5 May, 1601	1604
			65		

During the first four or five years of the 17th century several new Dutch companies were formed and fleet after fleet was sent out with marvellous rapidity.

England and Holland, after having combined in 1588 to defeat the famous Spanish Armada, began about this time those petty squabbles which resulted in a succession of naval combats that for many years left the claim of supremacy between them an undecided one.

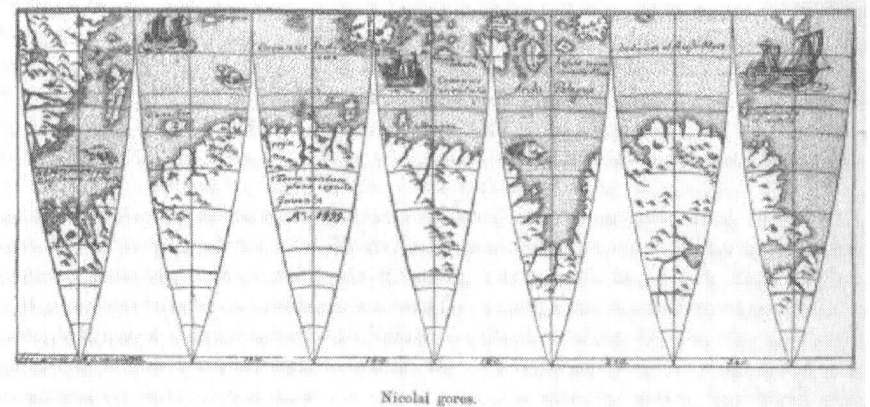

Nicolai Belga's Globe 1603.

We have reached the year 1605, in the month of December of which de Quiros, now the leader of another Spanish expedition, set sail from the coast of Peru with the object of renewing the attempt at settlement in the island of Santa Cruz, and from thence to search for the "deep and spacious, populous and fertile continent towards the south," the "often confirmed indications" of which had been given to him by the Indians of the island of Taumaco.

In connection with de Quiros' expedition of discovery there are two important items, to which we shall draw the attention of our readers because they are not generally known, namely first That de Quiros was only continuing the work of exploration begun by Mendana in 1567 to 1595; second That the strait between Australia and New Guinea was known to the Spanish, since it is marked on Wytfliet's map, dedicated in 1597 to the King of Spain. These two items of intelligence, which appear in the next chapter, have an important bearing on the often repeated statements that have been made to the effect: first That de Quiros is the first navigator who is known to have actually gone in search of a southern continent; and second That Torres, his lieutenant, passed through the strait that bears his name as by mere chance, not knowing beforehand that such a passage existed.

In 1762 Admiral Cornish and General Draper reduced the Philippines and bombarded and plundered Manila. A few years after that event, in 1764 or 1767, a copy of the memorial which forms the subject of the next chapter appears to have been communicated to Dalrymple, for, with the help of this memorial and other data mentioned by him,* he published in 1767 a chart of New Guinea, indicating roughly the southern coast running in a westerly direction from the Guadalcanal of the Solomon Islands, inscribing thereunder the name TORRES.

(*Footnote. *Hist. Coll.* Volume 1 page 163; and the *Biblioteca Oriental y Occidental* page 671. *Hist. Coll.* Volume 1 Introduction towards the end.)

CHAPTER 38.
EXTRACT FROM A MEMORIAL ADDRESSED TO HIS CATHOLIC MAJESTY PHILLIP III OF SPAIN, BY DR. JUAN LUIS ARIAS, RESPECTING THE EXPLORATION, COLONISATION, AND CONVERSION OF THE SOUTHERN LAND.

(*Footnote. For the translation in extenso of this interesting document (too lengthy to give here in full) we beg to refer our readers to Major's Early Voyages to Australia. Major gives no date to this memorial. In the collective volume in the British Museum which contains the original are several memorials to the same king from the Fray Juan de Silva, advocating the same cause on general religious and political grounds. Don Juan de Silva was governor in the Spice Islands before 1611, in which year he took from the Dutch the Fort of Sabongo in Gilolo. See Voyages de la Compagnie Tome vii. page 250. Whether he is the author of the memorials or not we however cannot say. George Collingridge.)

T must be observed that, although the arguments we have hitherto advanced refer to the entire southern, yet that which we now propose to have explored, discovered, and evangelically subdued is that part of the said hemisphere which lies in the Pacific Ocean, between the longitude of the coast of Peru, as far as the Baia de San Felipe y Santiago,* and the longitude

which remains up to Bachan and Ternate,* in which longitude the following most remarkable discoveries have already been made.

(*Footnote. New Hebrides.)

(*Footnote. In this passage it will be observed that the Spanish proposed to colonise that portion of Australia that fell within their sphere according to the Pope's grant, namely that portion lying between the Baia de San Felipe y Santiago (New Hebrides) and Bachan and Ternate in the Moluccas; in other words the territory now known as New South Wales, Queensland, Victoria, and South Australia, including the Northern Territory. George Collingridge.)

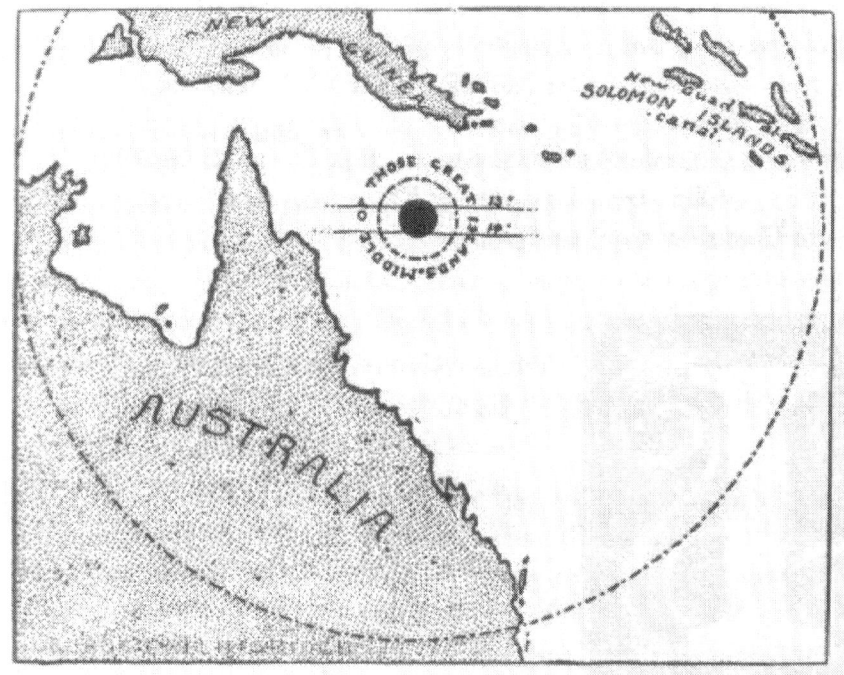

Map Shewing Centre of Mendana's Discoveries.

Map Shewing Centre of Mendana's Discoveries.

The adelantado Alvaro Mendana de Meyra first discovered New Guadalcanal, which is a very large island very near New Guinea; and some have imagined that what Mendana called New Guadalcanal was part of New Guinea; but this is of no consequence whatever. New Guinea belongs also to the southern hemisphere, and was discovered some time before; and almost all of it has been since discovered on the outside [northern side]. *It is a country encompassed with water,** and, according to the greater number of those who have seen it, it is seven hundred leagues in circuit; others make it much more.

(*Footnote. We have italicised this important remark, which shows that the Spanish had a knowledge of the insularity of New Guinea. George Collingridge.)

We do not give a close calculation here because what has been said is sufficient for the intention of this discourse. The rest will be said in its proper place. *The middle of those great islands are in from thirteen to fourteen degrees of south latitude.**

(*Footnote. We have italicised this passage which, if middle is to be taken in its true sense, would show the sphere of Mendana's discoveries to have extended as appears in the accompanying map. George Collingridge.)

The adelantado Mendana afterwards discovered the archipelago of islands, which he called the Islands of Solomon, whereof, great and small, he saw thirty-three of very fine appearance, the middle of which was, according to his account, in eleven degrees south latitude. After this he discovered, in the year 1565,* the island of San Christobal, not far from the said archipelago, the middle of which was in from seven to eight degrees of south latitude.

(*Footnote. 1567 in Figueroa's account. See Chapter 33.)

The island was one hundred and ten leagues in circuit. Subsequently, in the year '95, the said adelantado sailed for the last time from Peru, taking with him for his chief pilot the Pedro Fernandez de Quiros, with the purpose of colonising the island of San Christobal and from thence attempting the discovery of the southern terra firma. He shortly after discovered, to the east of the said island of San Christobal, the island of Santa Cruz, in ten degrees south latitude. The island was more than one hundred leagues in circuit, very fertile and populous, as indeed appeared all those islands which we have mentioned, and most of them of very beautiful aspect. In this island of Santa Cruz the adelantado had such great contentions with his soldiers that he had some of the chief of them killed, because he understood that they intended to mutiny, and in a few days after he died. Whereupon, as the admiral of the fleet had parted company a short time before they had reached the said island, the whole project was frustrated, and Pedro Fernandez de

Quiros took Dona Isabel Garreto, the wife of the adelantado, and the remainder of the fleet to Manila.

Some time afterwards Pedro Fernandez de Quiros, being at Valladolid, came to this court to petition for the same discovery, and was dispatched to the Viceroy of Peru, who was to supply him with all that was requisite. He sailed from Lima in January of the year 1605* with three vessels, the Capitana, the Almiranta, and one zabra, with Luis Vaez de Torres for his admiral, in order to colonise the island of Santa Cruz, and to follow out the intentions of the adelantado Mendana.

(*Footnote. 21st December 1605, according to Torres' account. George Collingridge.)

After discovering in this voyage many islands and islets he put in at the island of Taumaco, which is from eight to nine leagues in circuit, in ten degrees south latitude, and about one thousand seven hundred leagues distant from Lima, which is about eighty leagues to the eastward of the island of Santa Cruz. The cacique, or chief of Taumaco, informed him, as well as he could make himself understood, that if he sought the coast of the great Terra Firma he would light upon it sooner by going to the south than to the island of Santa Cruz; for in the south there were lands very fertile and populous, and running down to a great depth towards the said south. In consequence of which Pedro Fernandez de Quiros abandoned his idea of going to colonise the island of Santa Cruz, and sailed southward with a slight variation to the south-west, discovering many islands and islets, which were very populous and of pleasing appearance, until in fifteen degrees and twenty minutes south he discovered the land of the Baia de San Felipe y Santiago, which, on the side that he first came upon, ran from east to west. It appeared to be more than one hundred leagues long; the country was very populous, and although the people were dark they were very well favoured; there were also many plantations of trees, and the temperature was so mild that they seemed to be in Paradise; the air also was so healthy that in a few days after they arrived all the men who were sick recovered. The land produced most abundantly many kinds of very delicious fruits, as well as animals and birds in great variety. The bay also was no less abundant in fish of excellent flavour, and of all the kinds which are found on the coast of the sea in Spain. The Indians ate for bread certain roots like the batata, either roasted or boiled, which, when the Spaniards tasted, they found them better eating and more sustaining than biscuit.

For certain reasons (they ought to have been very weighty) which hitherto have not been ascertained with entire certainty, Pedro Fernandez de Quiros left the Almiranta and the zabra in the said bay and himself sailed with his ship, the Capitana, for Mexico, from whence he again came to this court to advocate anew the colonization of that land, and was again sent back to the viceroy of Peru, and died at Panama on his return voyage to Lima. The Admiral (Luis Vaez de Torres) being left in the bay, and most disconsolate for the loss of the Capitana, resolved, with the consent of his companions, to continue the discovery. Being prevented by stress of weather from making the circuit of the land of the Baia, to see whether it were an island or mainland as they had imagined, and finding himself in great straits in twenty-one degrees south, to which high latitude he had persevered in sailing in about a south-westerly direction from the fifteen or* twenty minutes south, in which lay the aforesaid Baia, he put back to the north-west and north-east up to fourteen degrees,* in which he sighted a very extensive coast, which he took for that of New Guadalcanal; *from thence he sailed westwards, having constantly on the right hand the coast of another very great land, which he continued coasting, according to his own reckoning, more than six hundred leagues, having it still to the right hand** (in which course may be understood to be comprehended New Guadalcanal and New Guinea). Along the same coast he discovered a great diversity of islands. The whole country was very fertile and populous; he continued his voyage on to Bachan and Ternate, and from thence to Manila, which was the end of this discovery...

(*Footnote. Or is evidently a misprint for 0 degrees. See above, 15 degrees 20 minutes south. George Collingridge.)

(*Footnote. Guadalcanal and St. Christoval of the Solomon group are respectively to the north and south of the 10th parallel; the context places the middle of the Islands of Solomon in the 11th parallel; so that we must take fourteen degrees as a misprint. According to Torres the latitude reached was 11 1/2 degrees south. George Collingridge.)

(*Footnote. It is from this sentence that Dalrymple observed the passage of Torres through these dangerous straits, and consequently gave to them the name of that navigator.)

CHAPTER 39. A.D. 1605 TO 1607.

RELATION OF LUIS VAEZ DE TORRES CONCERNING THE DISCOVERIES OF QUIROS, AS HIS ALMIRANTE. DATED MANILA, JULY 12TH 1607.

(*Footnote. A translation, nearly literal, by Alexander Dalrymple, from a Spanish manuscript copy in his possession.* First printed in Burney's *Discoveries in the South Sea*. Part 2 page 467 4to. London 1806.

(*Footnote. The original letter is in the archives of Simancas.)

Track of Duyfken.

eing in this city of Manila, at the end of a year and a half of navigation and making discovery of the lands and seas in the southern parts; and seeing that the Royal Audience of Manila have not hitherto thought proper to give me dispatches for completing the voyage as Your Majesty commanded, and as I was in hopes of being the first to give yourself a relation of the discovery, etc.; but being detained here, and not knowing if, in this city of Manila, I shall receive my dispatches, I have thought proper to send Your Majesty Fray Juan de Merlo, of the order of San Francisco, one of the three religious who were on board with me, who having been an eye-witness will give a full relation to Your Majesty. The account from me is the following:

We sailed from Callao, in Peru, on December 21st 1605, with two ships and a launch* under the command of Captain Pedro Fernandez de Quiros, and I for his almirante; and without losing company we stood west-south-west, and went on this course 800 leagues.

(*Footnote. According to Gonzalez de Leza, the pilot of the expedition, the name of Quiros' ship or galleon was the *San Pedro y San Pablo*. Torres' ship was named the *San Pedro*; the launch, zabra, or patache was named the *Tres-Reyes*, and was commanded by Pedro Bernal Cermeno. George Collingridge.)

In latitude 26 degrees south it appeared proper to our commander not to pass that latitude because of changes in the weather; on which account I gave a declaration under my hand that it was not a thing obvious that we ought to diminish our latitude, if the season would allow, till we got beyond 30 degrees. My opinion had no effect; for from the said 26 degrees south we decreased our latitude in a west-north-west course to 24 1/2 degrees south. In this situation we found a small low island, about two leagues long, uninhabited, and without anchoring ground.

From hence we sailed west by north to 24 degrees south. In this situation we found another island, uninhabited, and without anchorage. It was about ten leagues in circumference. We named it San Valerio.

From hence we sailed west by north one day, and then west-north-west to 21 1/3 degrees south, where we found another small low island without soundings, uninhabited, and divided into pIeces.

We passed on in the same course, and sailed twenty-five leagues. We found four islands in a triangle, five or six leagues each, low, uninhabited, and without soundings. We named them las Virgines (the Virgins). Here the variation was north-easterly.

From hence we sailed north-west to 19 degrees south. In this situation we saw a small island to the eastward, about three leagues distant. It appeared like those we had passed. We named it Santa Polonia.

Diminishing our latitude from hence half a degree, we saw a low island with a point to the south-east, full of palms; it is in 18 1/2 degrees south. We arrived at it. It had no anchorage. We saw people on the beach. The boats went to the shore, and when they reached it they could not land on account of the great surf and rocks. The Indians called to them from the land; two Spaniards swam ashore; these they received well, throwing their arms upon the ground, and embraced them, and kissed them in the face. On this friendship a chief among them came on board the *Capitana* to converse, and an old woman, who were clothed, and other presents were made to them; and they returned ashore presently, for they were in great fear. In return for these good offices they sent a heap or locks of hair, and some bad feathers, and some wrought pearl oyster shells--these were all their valuables. They were a savage people, mulattoes, and corpulent; the arms they use are lances, very long and thick. As we could not land nor get anchoring ground we passed on, steering west-north-west.

We went in this direction from that island, getting sight of land. We could not reach it from the first on account of the wind being contrary and strong with much rain. It was all of it very low, so as in parts to be overflowed.

From this place in 16 1/2 degrees south we stood north-west by north to 10 3/4 degrees south. In this situation we saw an island, which was supposed to be that of San Bernado because it was in pieces; but it was not San Bernado, from what we afterwards saw. We did not find anchoring ground at it, though the boats went on shore to search for water, which we were in want of, but could not find any; they only found some cocoa-nut trees, though small. Our commander, seeing we wanted water, agreed that we should go to the island Santa Cruz, where he had been with the adelantado Alvaro de Mendana, saying we might there supply ourselves with water and wood, and then he would determine what was most expedient for Your Majesty's service. The crew of the *Capitana* at this time were mutinous, designing to go directly to Manila. On this account he sent the chief pilot a prisoner on board my ship, without doing anything further to him or others, though I strongly importuned him to punish them, or give me leave to punish them. But he did not choose to do it, from whence succeeded what Your Majesty knows, since they made him turn from the course [voyage], as will be mentioned, and he has probably said at Your Majesty's court.

We sailed from the above island west by north and found nearly a point easterly variation. We continued this course till in full 10 degrees south latitude. In this situation we found a low island of five or six leagues, overflowed, and without soundings; it was inhabited, the people and arms like those we had left, but their vessels were different. They came close to the ship, talking to us, and taking what we gave them, begging more, and stealing what was hanging to the ship, throwing lances, thinking we could not do them any arm. Seeing we could not anchor, on account of the want we were in of water, our commander ordered me ashore with two boats and fifty men. As soon as we came to the shore they opposed my entrance, without any longer keeping peace, which obliged me to skirmish with them. When we had done them some mischief three of them came out to make peace with me, singing, with branches in their hands, and one with a lighted torch, and on his knees. We received them well, and embraced them, and then clothed them, for they were some of the chiefs; and asking them for water they did not choose to show it me, making signs as if they did not understand me. Keeping the three chiefs with me I ordered the sergeant with twelve men to search for water, and having fallen in with it the Indians came out on their flank and attacked them, wounding one Spaniard. Seeing their treachery they were attacked and defeated, without other harm whatever. The land being in my power, I went over the town without finding anything but dried oysters and fish, and many cocoanuts, with which the land was well provided. We found no birds nor animals except little dogs. They have many covered embarcations with which they are accustomed to navigate to other islands, with latine sails made curiously of mats; and of the same cloth their women are clothed with little shifts and petticoats, and the men only round their waists and hips. From hence we put off with the boats loaded with water, but by the great swell we were overset with much risk of our lives, and so we were obliged to go on without getting water at this island. We named it Matanza.

We sailed in this parallel thirty-two days. In all this route we had very strong currents, and many drifts of wood and snakes, and many birds, all of which were signs of land on both sides of us. We did not search for it that we might not leave the latitude of the island of Santa Cruz, for we always supposed ourselves near it; and with reason, if it had been where the first voyage when it was discovered had represented; but it was much further on, as by the account will be seen. So that about sixty leagues before reaching it, and 1,940 from the city of Lima, we found a small island of six leagues, very high, and all round it very good soundings; and other small islands near it, under shelter of which the ships anchored. I went with the two boats and fifty men to reconnoitre the people of this island; and at the distance of a musket shot separate from the island we found a town surrounded with a wall, with only one entrance, without a gate. Being near with the two boats with an intention of investing them, as they did not by signs choose peace, at length their chief came into the water up to his neck, with a staff in his hand, and without fear came directly to the boats; where he was very well received, and by signs which we very well understood he told me that his people were in great terror of the muskets, and therefore he entreated us not to land, and said that they would bring water and wood if we gave them vessels. I told him that it was necessary to remain five days on shore to refresh. Seeing he could not do more with me he quieted his people, who were very uneasy and turbulent, and so it happened that no hostility was committed on either side. We went into the fort very safely; and, having halted, I made them give up their arms, and made them bring from their houses their effects, which were not of any value, and go with them to the island to other towns. They thanked me very much; the chief always continued with me. They then told me the name of the country. All came to me to make peace, and the chiefs assisted me, making their people get water and wood and carry it on board the ships. In this we spent six days.

The people of this island are of an agreeable conversation, understanding us very well, desirous of learning our language and to teach us theirs. They are great cruizers; they have much beard; they are great archers and hurlers of darts; the vessels in which they sail are large, and can go a great way. They informed us of more than forty islands, great and small, all peopled, naming them by their names, and telling us that they were at war with many of them. They also gave us intelligence of the island Santa Cruz, and of what had happened when the adelantado was there.

The people of this island are of ordinary stature. They have amongst them people white and red, some in colour like those of the Indies, others woolly-headed blacks and mulattoes. Slavery is in use amongst them. Their food is yams, fish, cocoanuts, and they have hogs and fowls.

This island is named Taomaco, and the name of the chief is Tomai. We departed from thence with four Indians whom we took, at which they were not much pleased; and as we here got wood and water there was no necessity for us to go to the island Santa Cruz, which, as I have said, is in this parallel sixty leagues further on.

So we sailed from hence, steering south-south-east, to 12 1/2 south latitude, where we found an island like that of Taomaco, and with the same kind of people, named Chucupia.* There is only one small anchoring place; and, passing in the offing, a small canoe with only two men came to me to make peace, and presented me some bark of a tree, which appeared like a very fine handkerchief, four yards long and three palms wide; on this I parted from them.

(*Footnote. Tucopia, to the north-east of the New Hebrides. George Collingridge.)

From hence we steered south. We had a hard gale of wind from the north, which obliged us to lie to for two days; at the end of that time it was thought, as it was winter, that we could not exceed the latitude of 14 degrees south, in which we were, though my opinion was always directly contrary, thinking we should search for the islands named by the Indians of Taomaco. Wherefore, sailing from this place we steered west, and in one day's sail we discovered a volcano, very high and large, above three leagues in circuit, full of trees, and of black people with much beard.

To the westward, and in sight of this volcano, was an island, not very high, and pleasant in appearance. There are few anchoring places, and those very close to the shore; it was very full of black people. Here we caught two in some canoes, whom we cloathed and gave them presents, and the next day we put them ashore. In return for this they shot a flight of arrows at a Spaniard, though in truth it was not in the same port, but about a musket shot further on. They are however a people that never miss an opportunity of doing mischief.

In sight of this island and around it are many islands, very high and large, and to the southward one so large that we stood for it, naming the island where our man was wounded Santa Maria.

Sailing thence to the southward towards the large island we discovered a very large bay, well peopled, and very fertile in yams and fruits, hogs and fowls. They are all black people and naked. They fight with bows, darts, and clubs. They did not choose to have peace with us, though we frequently spoke to them and made presents; and they never, with their goodwill, let us set foot on shore.

This bay is very refreshing, and in it fall many and large rivers. It is in 15 2/3 degrees south latitude, and in circuit it is twenty-five leagues. We named it the bay de San Felipe y Santiago, and the land del Espiritu Santo.

There we remained fifty days; we took possession in the name of Your Majesty. From within this bay, and from the most sheltered part of it, the *Capitana* departed at one hour past midnight, without any notice given to us, and without making any signal. This happened the 11th of June. And although the next morning we went out to seek for them, and made all proper efforts, it was not possible for us to find them, for they did not sail on the proper course, nor with good intention. So I was obliged to return to the bay to see if by chance they had returned thither. And on the same account we remained in this bay fifteen days, at the end of which we took Your Majesty's orders and held a consultation with the officers of the frigate. It was determined that we should fulfil them, although contrary to the inclination of many, I may say of the greater part; but my condition was different from that of Captain Pedro Fernandez de Quiros.

At length we sailed from this bay, in conformity to the order, although with intention to sail round this island, but the season and the strong currents would not allow of this, although I ran along a great part of it. In what I saw there are very large mountains. It has many ports, though some of them are small. All of it is well watered with rivers. We had at this time nothing but bread and water. It was the height of winter, with sea, wind, and ill will [of his crew]. All this did not prevent me from reaching the mentioned latitude,* which I passed one degree, and would have gone farther if the weather had permitted, for the ship was good. It was proper to act in this manner, for these are not voyages performed every day, nor could Your Majesty otherwise be properly informed. Going into the said latitude on a south-west course we had no signs of land that way.

(*Footnote. The latitude which is here called the mentioned latitude, and which is again spoken of a little further on, in an equally mysterious way, as the said latitude, or, as the Spanish document has it, Todo esto no fue poderoso a estorvarme que no llegase a la altura, de la qual pase un grado...Entiendese yr haciendo esta derrota al altura, was no doubt purposely kept secret, and refers evidently to a certain degree of latitude which had been determined beforehand, and to which the expedition intended to proceed. In Dr. Juan Luis Arias' memorial Torres is said to have reached what is amusingly termed the "high latitude" of 21 degrees south. It is remarkable that this degree of latitude south corresponds with the most correctly charted portion of the Australian coast as given in the Dauphin chart (1530/1536), namely to that part in the vicinity of the Cumberland islands, Port Denison, Repulse Bay, and Broad Sound. Port Denison is one of the best ports on the eastern coast of Australia, and escaped the notice of Australians till said to have been discovered in 1859 by Captain Sinclair. Repulse Bay would correspond better with the degree of latitude, and Broad Sound, a little to the south, bears the name of Baia Perdita, Lost Bay, on the old chart mentioned above. If Torres was really in search of one of these "lost bays" or ports he was not far from reaching it, for his run in a south-west direction from the New Hebrides must have brought him to a point somewhere between New Caledonia and Broad Sound. See map showing Torres' track from the New Hebrides to Torres Strait, Illustration 78. In those days, when dead reckoning was the only means of ascertaining the degrees of longitude, navigators were at a loss to determine the distance they had run when they happened to fall in with currents, either favourable or adverse. George Collingridge.)

From hence I stood back to the north-west to 11 1/2 degrees south latitude; there we fell in with the beginning of New Guinea, the coast of which runs west by north and east by south. I could not weather the east point, so I coasted along to the westward on the south side.

All this land of New Guinea is peopled with Indians, not very white, and naked except their waists, which are covered with a cloth made of the bark of trees. and much painted. They fight with darts, targets, and some stone clubs, which are made fine with plumage. Along the coast are many islands and habitations. All the coast has many ports, very large, with very large rivers, and many plains. Without these islands there runs a reef of shoals, and between them [the shoals] and the mainland are the islands. There is a channel within. In these ports I took possession for Your Majesty.

We went along three hundred leagues of coast, as I have mentioned, and diminished the latitude 2 1/2 degrees, which brought us into 9 degrees. From hence we fell in with a bank of from three to nine fathoms, which extends along the coast above 180 leagues. We went over it along the coast to 7 1/2 degrees south latitude, and the end of it is in 5 degrees.*

(*Footnote. There is a mistake or miscalculation here, for the farthest northing they could make, in the gulf they were in (Gulf of Papua), would be in about 8 degrees north. George Collingridge.)

We could not go farther on for the many shoals and great currents, so we were obliged to sail out south-west in that depth to 11 degrees south latitude. There is all over it an archipelago of islands, without number, by which we passed, and at the end of the eleventh degree the bank became shoaler. Here were very large islands, and there appeared more to the southward.* They were inhabited by black people, very corpulent, and naked; their arms were lances, arrows, and clubs of stone ill-fashioned. We caught in all this land twenty persons of different nations, that with them we might be able to give a better account to Your Majesty. They give much notice of other people, although as yet they do not make themselves well understood.

(*Footnote. These are the large islands near Cape York. George Collingridge.)

We went upon this bank for two months, at the end of which time we found ourselves in twenty-five fathoms, and in 5 degrees south latitude, and ten leagues from the coast. And having gone 480 leagues, here the coast goes to the north-east.*

(*Footnote. The only portion of the coast trending north-east in anything like the latitude mentioned is from False Cape to Cape Kollf, along Frederick Henry Island; this portion of the coast line is however in 7 or 8 degrees latitude south instead of 5 degrees. There is reason to believe that this is nevertheless the portion of coast described as going north-east, because, as we have seen above, the head of the gulf they had previously visited (Gulf of Papua), the latitude of which corresponds to this same degree of latitude south, is also said to be in 5 degrees south, whereas it is in 8 degrees south. George Collingridge.)

I did not reach it for the bank became very shallow. So we stood to the north, and in twenty-five fathoms to 4 degrees latitude, where we fell in with a coast which likewise lay in a direction east and west. We did not see the eastern termination, but from what we understood of it it joins the other we had left on account of the bank, the sea being very smooth. This land is peopled by blacks, different from all the others; they are better adorned; they use arrows, darts, and large shields, and some sticks of bamboo filled with lime, with which, by throwing it out, they blind their enemies. Finally we stood to the west-north-west along the coast, always finding this people, for we landed in many places; also in it we took possession for Your Majesty. In this land also we found iron, china bells, and other things, by which we knew we were near the Malucas; and so we ran along this coast about 130 leagues, where it comes to a termination fifty leagues before you reach the Malucas. There is an infinity of islands to the southward, and very large, which for the want of provisions we did not approach; for I doubt if in ten years could be examined the coasts of all the islands we descried. We observed the variation in all this land of New Guinea to the Moluccas; and in all of it the variation agrees with the meridian of the Ladrone Islands and of the Philippine Islands.

At the termination of this land we found Mahometans, who were cloathed, and had firearms and swords. They sold us fowls, goats, fruit, and some pepper, and biscuit which they call sagoe, which will keep more than twenty years. The whole they sold us was but little, for they wanted cloth, and we had not any; for all the things that had been given us for traffic were carried away by the Capitana, even to tools and medicines, and many other things which I do not mention as there is no help for it; but without them God took care of us.

These Moors gave us news of the events at the Malucas,* and told us of Dutch ships, though none of them came here, although they said that in all this land there was much gold and other good things, such as pepper and nutmegs.

(*Footnote. According to the Moors the Dutch had not then (end of October 1606) sent out their expedition of 1606.

The events of the Moluccas were of a stirring nature at that time. Numerous Dutch and English vessels were establishing a trade with the natives notwithstanding the opposition met with from the Portuguese and Spanish. Captain Saris of Middleton's expedition was there taking notes which may serve to throw some light on the first Dutch voyage to Australia. (1606). The Little Sun, the Duyfken, and other yachts belonging to the Dutch were in very active service, and the question arises, did the Dutch learn of Torres' discoveries along the south coast of New Guinea, and did they in consequence send out at once their expedition of 1606 to that coast? See below.)

From hence to the Malucas it is all islands, and on the south side are many uniting with those of Banda and Amboyna, where the Dutch carry on a trade. We came to the islands of Bachian, which are the first

Malucas, where we found a *Theatine** with about 100 Christians in the country of a Mahometan king friendly to us, who begged me to subdue one of the Ternate islands inhabited by revolted Mahometans, to whom Don Pedro de Acunha had given pardon in Your Majesty's name, which I had maintained; and I sent advice to the M. de Campo, Juan de Esquivel, who governed the islands of Ternate, of my arrival, and demanded if it was expedient to give this assistance to the king of Bachian, to which he [Juan de Esquivel] answered that it would be of great service to Your Majesty if I brought force for that purpose. On this, with forty Spaniards and 400 Moors of the King of Bachian, I made war, and in only four days I defeated them and took the fort, and put the king of Bachian in possession of it in Your Majesty's name, to whom we administered the usual oaths, stipulating with him that he should never go to war against Christians, and that he should ever be a faithful vassal to Your Majesty. I did not find those people of so intrepid a spirit as those we had left.

(*Footnote. A regular order of clergy established at Rome in 1524. George Collingridge.)

It must be ascribed to the Almighty that in all these labours and victories we lost only one Spaniard. I do not make a relation of them to Your Majesty, for I hope to give it at large.

The king being put in possession, I departed for Ternate, which was twelve leagues from this island, where Juan de Esquivel was, by whom I was very well received; for he had great scarcity of people, and the nations of Ternate were in rebellion, and assistance to him was very unexpected in so roundabout a way.

In a few days afterwards arrived succour from Manila, which was much desired, for half of the people left by Don Pedro de Acunha were no more, and there was a scarcity of provisions, for, as I said, the nations of the island were in rebellion; but by the prudence of the M. de Campo, Juan de Esquivel, he went on putting the affairs of the island in good order, although he was in want of money.

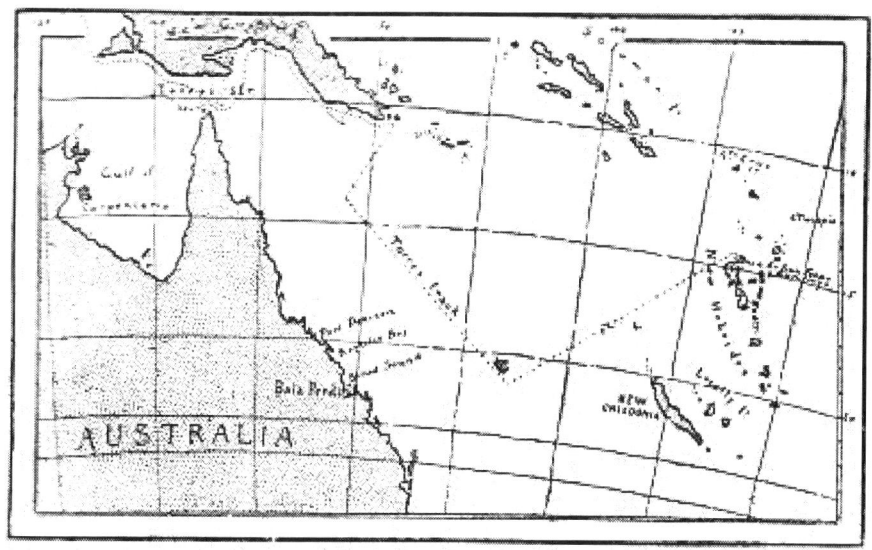

Map shewing Torres' Track from New Hebrides to Torres' Strait.

Map shewing Torres' Track from New Hebrides to Torres' Strait.

I left the *Patache* here and about twenty men, as it was expedient for the service of Your Majesty. From thence I departed for the city of Manila, where they gave me so bad a dispatch, as I have mentioned; and hitherto, which is now two months, they have not given provisions to the crew; and so I know not when I can sail from hence to give account to Your Majesty.

Whom may God preserve prosperous,

For Sovereign of the world,

Your Majesty's servant,

LUIS VAEZ DE TORRES.

Done at Manila, July 12th 1607.

De Quiros' and Torres' expedition closes the period of Spanish activity; it is true that De Quiros set sail again a few years later, still in search of the Great Australian Continent, but he died at Panama on his way out; and by the abandonment of the expedition the Dutch were allowed to remain the sole masters of the situation.

CHAPTER 40. A.D. 1605 TO 1607.

THE FIRST CLAIM OF DUTCH DISCOVERY IN AUSTRALIA.
THE VOYAGE OF THE LITTLE DOVE TO THE SOUTH COAST OF NEW GUINEA AND THE GULF OF CARPENTARIA.

We now enter upon the Dutch period of discovery, and in doing so we acknowledge that we feel very diffident and ill at ease. This feeling on our part is chiefly owing to our lack of knowledge of the Dutch language, but is also due to scarcity of reliable data and to the knowledge of the fact that Prince Roland Bonaparte, an authority on matters connected with geographical research and a Dutch scholar, has undertaken the task of preparing for the French press some important documents, said to have been recently found, bearing on Dutch discovery in Australia. We do not know whether the documents we refer to will throw any new light on the much disputed and rather obscure claims of Dutch discovery, and we may add that, to say the least, it is surprising to learn that, if the anticipated light can be produced, it has taken all these years to bring it forth:*

(*Footnote. It must be acknowledged however that those who should be the most interested in matters connected with the early history of Australia have shown hitherto but little interest in the subject. Over twelve months ago now we were offered Tasman's original manuscript map of Australia. We proposed the purchase of this valuable document at the time by the New South Wales Government, then by the Free Public Library; our proposition was not accepted, and subsequently Tasman's chart became the property of Prince Roland Bonaparte.)

Thirty-five years ago, in 1859, R.H. Major, writing on this subject, said*: "It is with pleasure that we indulge the hope that the veil which has thus hung over these valuable materials is likely before very long to be entirely removed. The archives of the Dutch East India Company, a yet unsifted mass of thousands of volumes and myriads of loose papers, have a short time since been handed over to the State Archives at the Hague, where the greatest liberality is shown in allowing access to the treasures they possess. Meanwhile the editor of the present volume need hardly plead any excuse for not having attempted what no foreigner, be his stay in Holland ever so long, could possibly accomplish; and he must leave to those who will take up this matter after him the satisfaction of availing themselves of materials the importance of which he knows, and the want of which he deeply deplores."

(*Footnote. Early Voyages to Australia. Introduction page lxxiii.)

And further on*: "Of the discoveries made by the Dutch on the coasts of Australia our ancestors of a hundred years ago, and even the Dutch themselves, knew but little. That which was known was preserved in the *Relations de divers voyages curieux* of Melchisedech Thevenot (Paris 1663 a 1672 fol.); in the *Noord en Oost Tartarye* of Nicolas Witsen (Amst. 1692 to 1705 fol.); in Valentyn's *Oud en Nieuw Oost Indien* (Amst. 1724 to 1726 fol.); and in the *Inleidning tot de algemeen Geographie* of Nicolas Struyk (Amst. 1740 4to). We have however since gained a variety of information through a document which fell into the possession of Sir Joseph Banks and was published by Alexander Dalrymple, at that time hydrographer to the Admiralty and the East India Company, in his collection concerning Papua. This curious and interesting document is a copy of the instructions to Commodore Abel Yansz Tasman for his second voyage of discovery. That distinguished commander had already, in 1642, discovered not only the island now named after him, Tasmania (but more generally known as Van Diemen's Land, in compliment to the then governor of the Dutch East India Company at Batavia), but New Zealand also; and, passing round the east side of Australia, but without seeing it, sailed on his return voyage along the northern shores of New Guinea. In January 1644 he was despatched on his second voyage; and his instructions, signed by the governor-general Antonio Van Diemen and the members of the council, are prefaced by a recital, in chronological order, of the previous discoveries of the Dutch. The document is reprinted in the present volume.

"From this recital, combined with a passage from Saris, given in Purchas, volume i. page 385, we learn that, 'On the 18th of November 1605 the Dutch yacht, the *Duyfhen* (the Dove), was despatched from Bantam to explore the islands of New Guinea, and that she sailed along what was thought to be the west side of that country, to 19 3/4 degrees* of south latitude.'

(*Footnote. The latitude given should read 13 3/4 degrees. George Collingridge.)

"This extensive country was found, for the greatest part, desert; but in some places inhabited by wild, cruel, black savages, by whom some of the crew were murdered; for which reason they could not learn anything of the land or waters, as had been desired of them; and from want of provisions and other necessaries they were obliged to leave the discovery unfinished. The furthest point of the land, in their maps, was called Cape Keer Weer, or Turn Again. As Flinders observes: 'The course of the *Duyfhen* from New Guinea was southward, along the islands of the west side of Torres' Strait, to that part of Terra Australis a little to the west and south of Cape York. But all these lands were thought to be connected, and to form the west coast of New Guinea.' Thus, without being conscious of it, the commander of the *Duyfhen* made the first *authenticated* discovery of any part of the great south land about the month of March 1606; for it appears that he had returned to Banda in or before the beginning of June of that year."

Track of the Duyfken.

Track of the Duyfken.

It appears then that the first Dutch craft sent out for purposes of exploration in the vicinity of Australia was the *Duyfhen*, or *Duyfken* (Little Dove*), as it should be written.

(*Footnote. The vessel named above *Little Dove*, *Duyfken* in Dutch, has always been written erroneously *Duyfhen* by English writers.)

Now a yacht of that name accompanied the first expedition leaving Holland for Java in 1595, and she was doubtless the same vessel. In the account of the first voyage she is said to be a yacht of 30 tons. In the expedition commanded by Steven Van der Hagen, equipped in 1603, a yacht of the same name but of 60 tons came out to the East Indies. Is the tonnage wrong, or is the *Little Dove* of Van der Hagen's expedition another vessel? It is difficult to say, but Van der Hagen's *Little Dove* is the yacht that was sent to New Guinea. She was commanded by Captain Guillaume Yansz, and did good service for many years.

The account of the voyage is very short, and was first given in Tasman's instructions for his second voyage. Father Tenison Woods says* that this document was doubtless found by Sir Joseph Banks when all the old archives were turned over at Batavia, on the occasion of Captain Cook's visit to that place after exploring the east coast of this continent. The document, in referring to the various voyages made by the Dutch before Tasman's time, describes the voyage of the *Duyfken* in the following terms: "First By order of the President, John Williamson Verschoor, who at that time directed the company's trade at Bantam, which was in the year 1606, with the yacht the *Duyfhen*, who in their passage sailed by the islands Key and Aroum, and discovered the south and the west coast of Nova Guinea, for about 220 miles (880) from 5 to 13 3/4 degrees south latitude, and found this extensive country for the greatest part desert, but in some places inhabited by wild, cruel, black savages, by whom some of the crew were murdered; for which reason they could not learn anything of the land or waters, as had been desired of them, and by want of provisions and other necessaries they were obliged to leave the discovery unfinished. The furthest point of the land was called in their map Cape Keer-Weer, situated in 13 3/4 degrees south."

(*Footnote. The Australian Monthly Magazine page 440 volume 3 1866.)

It will be noticed that in the above paragraph the names of the commanders of the expedition have been left out, hence the incomplete form of wording. "With the yacht the *Duyfhen*, who in their passage," etc. instead of "with the yacht, the Duyjhen, under command of so-and-so, and so-and-so, who in their passage," etc. But this omission may be only apparent and due to faulty translation. It is strange that R.H. Major, generally so careful, did not make use of the Dutch text instead of Dalrymple's faulty and incomplete translation, considering that the Dutch text was available at the time, having been published in 1844 in Jhr G.A. Tindal and Jacob Swart's Verhandelingen en Berigten betrekkelijk het Zeewezen en de zeevaartkunde.*

(*Footnote. Amsterdam 1844 G. Hulst Van Keulen.)

As an example of the faultiness and insufficiency of Dalrymple's version we draw the attention of our readers to the 6th paragraph referring to the voyages performed in 1616, 1618, 1619, and 1622. Dalrymple's paragraph, as given by Major, runs thus:

"But in the meantime, in the years 1616, 1618, 1619, and 1622, the west coast of this great unknown south land, from 35 to 22 degrees south latitude, was discovered by outward bound ships, and among them by the ship *Endraght*; for the nearer discovery of which the governor-general, Jan Pietersz Coen (of worthy memory) in September 1622 despatched the yachts *De Haring* and *Harewind*; but this voyage was rendered abortive by meeting the ship Mauritius and searching after the ship *Rotterdam*."

The Dutch account, given by Tindal and Swart, in the second half of the 5th paragraph, is as follows:...gelyck mede middelerwyle in den Yare 1616, 1618, 1619, en 1622, de west custe van het grote onbekende Zuytlaent van 35 tot 22 graden by de uit 't vaderland comende scepen d'Eendracht, Mauritius, Amsterdam, Dordrecht en de Leeuwin onvoordacht ondect geworden is, om welck gelegentheden nader te vernemen, den Gouverneur Generael Yan Pietersz Coch, losselycker gedachte in September, Anno 1622, de Yachten Harnigh en de Hasewindt, derwaerts hadde uytgeset, welcke reyse door 't bejegenen van 't schip Mauritius en 't Soecken van 't schip Rotterdam verhindert wiert, waerover op zyn Edisordre.

Now in the above paragraph the names of five ships are given as having made discoveries during the years 1616, 1618, 1619, and 1622, whereas in Major's paragraph only one ship, the *Eendracht*, is mentioned. These five ships were the *Eendracht*, the *Mauritius*, the *Amsterdam*, the *Dordrecht*, and the *Leeuwin*. It was a serious mistake to omit the names of these ships, especially the *Leeuwin*, because the omission cast a doubt on the authenticity of the discovery of that part of the south-west coast of Australia which now bears the name of Cape Leeuwin, a doubt which is now cleared up for the first time, as far as the English-speaking world is concerned, by our more complete translation of the paragraph in question.

But, to return to the voyage of the *Duyfken*, it is necessary to elucidate here the apparently contradictory versions of a passage from Saris given by R.H. Major and F.T. Woods, two good authorities on Australasian maritime discovery. Major says: "From this recital (the recital given in the instructions to Tasman), combined with a passage from Saris, given in Purchas, volume i. page 385, we learn that 'on the 18th of November 1605 the Dutch yacht the *Duyfhen* (the Dove), was despatched from Bantam to explore the islands of New Guinea,'" etc.; whereas F.T. Woods* from the same authority says: "We find this discovery mentioned in another work besides Tasman's letter of instructions. In the *Haklvytus Posthumus*; or *Purchas, his Pilgrimes*, *containing a history of the World in Sea Voyages and Land Trauells, by Englishmen and others*, by Samuel Purchas, B.D. (London 1625/1626 5 volumes) there is a passage from Saris (Purchas volume i. page 385) telling us of the *Duyfhen*'s voyage. But who was Saris? He was, my dear reader, an English captain, whose Christian name was John, and I would read you a useful example of the pursuit of knowledge under difficulties in relating what trouble I have been at to find out any more about him than is furnished by Purchas. He is one of the 'Pilgrimes,' and has handed himself down to posterity as the hero of the 'Eighth Voyage of the East India Society,' wherein were employed three ships, under the command of Captain John Saris. His course and acts to and in the Red Sea, Java, Moluccas, and Japan (by the inhabitants called Niffoon), where also he first began and settled an English trade factory with other remarkable varieties, from 1611 to 1614. Saris's expedition will be better understood if it be remembered that the English East India Company or Society was established in 1600, and was at first confined to sending out a small squadron for the purposes of trade. A settlement in India was not made until 1612; but Saris, from another work of his, got his Australian information during his residence at Bantam from 1605 to 1609. Among his 'observations of Occurrents which happened in the East Indies during his abode' was the sailing of the *Duyfhen* in November 1605, and her return in June 1606. This *Duyfhen* or *Dove* found no rest for the sole of her foot during her eight months' cruise among the islands and gulfs of Australia, and was not worthy of more than a mere mention.

(*Footnote. The Australian Monthly Magazine 1866 volume iii. page 439.)

"Through the kindness of a friend I am able to supplement my notice of Saris with the following extract from his Journal, as given in Purchas, 1606: A small vessel, called the *Little Sun*, being sent by the Dutch from the Molucca Islands for the discovery of New Guinea, which country they knew nothing of at that time, but where they imagined gold was to be found. In the following year I was told by a Chinese captain, just come from Bunda,* that the Dutch vessel had put in there on her return from New Guinea.

(*Footnote. Banda. George Collingridge.)

The crew gave an account that, having made a descent on the coast in order to learn something of the country, the natives received them with a shower of arrows which had killed nine Dutchmen. They represent these people as very barbarous, and even cannibals; and, very afraid to stay longer on these inhospitable shores, they returned without doing anything. Nothing is here said about Australia, and from the use of arrows it must have been at New Guinea that the Dutch were killed. The name of the vessel differs too, but this has been explained by supposing Saris to have mistaken the word *Duyfhen* for another similar."

Why do not authors, especially historians, consult original documents for themselves instead of trusting friends or relying on second-hand information? How could Saris have mistaken the word *Duyfhen* or *Duyfken* (Little Dove), for *Zonneken* or *Zonnetje* (Little Sun)?

If we consult Purchas we shall find that R.H. Major and F.T. Woods are both wrong, for neither the *Duyfken*, *Duyfhen*, nor the *Zonneken* (or Little Sun) are mentioned in that work as having been sent to New Guinea. This is Purchas' text:

"Bantam, the thirteenth (November 1605), heere arrived a small ship of the *Flemmings*, from the *Moluccas*, called the little *sunne*.

"The eighteenth, heere departed a small Pinnasse of the *Flemmings*, for the discovery of the Iland called Noua ginnea, which, as it is said, affordeth great store of gold.

"The fifteenth of June, heere arrived *Nockhoda Tingall*, a cling-man from Banda, in a Jaua Juncke, laden with Mace and Nutmegs, the which he sold heere to the *Guzerats* for an hundred and fiftie Rialls of eight the Bahar *Bantam*...He told me that the *Flemings* Pinnasse, which went vpon discouery for Noua Ginny, was returned to Banda hauing found the Iland; but in sending their men on shoare to intreate of Trade, there were nine of them killed by the Heathens, which are man-eaters, so they were constrained to returne, finding no good to be done there."

F.T. Woods' friend should have left out the paragraph in the "observations of Occurents" (our first paragraph) referring to the *little sunne*. We have quoted it to show that that small ship arrived at Bantam from the Moluccas five days before the departure from Bantam of the vessel that made the voyage to New Guinea. It will also be noticed that the passage from Purchas does not mention the name of that small vessel.

There is however another passage which has not been noticed by critics, and which confirms the recital given in the instructions to Tasman. It occurs in Commelyn's *Begin ende Voortganh*, the great Dutch collection of voyages published at Amsterdam in 1646. We have not seen the original work, and have been obliged to content ourselves with De Constantin's translation, published at Rouen in 1725. In the 5th volume of that work* page 212 Paul van Soldt, the author of the Journal that deals with Etienne Van der Hagen's second voyage, says:

"Le 4, nous mouillames l'ancre sous le Fort sur 7 brasses de profondeur n'aiant plus qu'une pipe & demie d'eau qui etoit corrompue. Nous y trouvames le yacht *Enchuise*, qui avoit sa charge de clou de gerofle, & *le Pigeonnau* qui etoit revenu de la Nouvelle Guinee."

(*Footnote. Voyages de la Compagnie.)

The context shows that the Fort where Paul van Soldt met the *Pigeonnau* (Little Dove), which had returned from New Guinea, was the Fort of Amboyna, and that the date was the 4th of March 1607. Nearly nine months therefore had elapsed since Captain Saris had heard of the return of the *Pinnasse* of the *Flemings*, and she was apparently still amongst the Spice Islands in company with the *Little Sun*, as is also shown in the course of Paul van Soldt's narrative.

We must now consider another phase of the question or controversy; for it has been questioned whether the *Duyfken* ever coasted along the shores of Carpentaria.

Ch. Ruelens, in the preface which he wrote to accompany the publication of the valuable manuscript of Godinho de Eredia,* argued that on the occasion of that memorable expedition the *Duyfken* never got further south than 8 degrees 15 minutes, and consequently never discovered any part of the shores of Australia. The chief points that led him to form such a conclusion are: first That the *Duyfken* could not have followed the coasts of New Guinea *and Australia* without noticing the opening at Torres' Straits; second That the extreme point said to have been visited in 13 3/4 degrees south, and to which the name Keer-Weer was said to have been given, does not bear that appellation on subsequent charts; whereas another point on the coast of New Guinea does.

(*Footnote. MALACA, L'Inde meridionale et le Cathay. Manuscript originale autographe de Godinho de Eredia, appartenant a la Bibliotheque Royale de

Bruxelles, reproduit en facsimile et traduit par M. Leon Janssen, membre de la Societe de Geographie de Bruxelles. Avec une preface de M. Ch. Ruelens conservateur a la Bibliotheque Royale, membre du comite de la Societe de Geographie de Bruxelles 1882.)

Ch. Ruelens maintains that the Keer-Weer on the coast of New Guinea is the extreme termination of the *Duyfken's* southern course, and in support of his argument states that all maps from F. De Wit's of the end of the seventeenth century down to the fine map which accompanied the memoire by MM. Bennet and Van Wyk (1825) show Cape Keer-Weer on the west coast of New Guinea, in the latitude of Frederick Henry Island, and north of *Valsche Kaep* (False Cape), which is, according to MM. Bennet and Van Wyk, in 8 degrees 15 minutes latitude, 138 degrees longitude.*

(*Footnote. Verhandeling over de Nederlandsche ontdekkingen in Amerika, Australie, enz, door R.G. Bennet en J. Van Wyk, Utrecht 1827, in 8o.)

Furthermore Ch. Ruelens says that Flinders, by using the narrative which had fallen into Dalrymple's hands, a narrative which guided Flinders in his attempts to trace the course of the Duyfken, is responsible for the confusion that was brought about.*

(*Footnote. It is a known fact that Flinders gave several Dutch names to the part of the coast of Australia alleged to have been visited by the Duyfken.)

The question remains now to be ascertained, did the voyage of the *Duyfken* extend to Australia or not? Did that yacht stop short at 8 degrees 15 minutes latitude south, or come on five or six degrees further south?

Since Ch. Ruelens arrived at the conclusion that she did not extend her voyage to Australia other documents have turned up which tend to prove that she did, and at the present stage the whole matter seems to resume itself into the examination of the *provenance* or authenticity of the said documents.

We have alluded to them in the beginning of this chapter. The principal document however is the alleged original manuscript map of the two voyages of Abel Yansz Tasman and Frans Yacobsz Visscher, the opper piloot-majoor and second in command of the expedition of 1644.

In a copy of the original manuscript now before us Cape Keer-Weer is set down in about 14 degrees 15 minutes south latitude, thus lending strength to the argument in favour of a discovery extending to that locality.

CHAPTER 41. A.D. 1606 TO 1613.

DON DIEGO DE PRADO'S ORIGINAL MAPS, MADE IN 1606, SHOWING THE DISCOVERIES MADE BY THE SPANIARDS THAT SAME YEAR IN THE NEW HEBRIDES AND NEW GUINEA.
TWO LETTERS OF DON DIEGO DE PRADO TO THE KING OF SPAIN, REFERRING TO DE QUIROS' DISCOVERIES.

When de Quiros appointed officers for the new colony in the Bay of St. Philip and St. James, Don Diego de Prado y Tovar was made *Depositario General*. He is the author of the four very remarkable and extremely interesting maps which are here presented for the first time to the English speaking world. Our copies are taken from those published in the Boletin de la Sociedad Geografica de Madrid, Tomo iv. January 1878. They have been reduced to three-eighths of the originals, and with each design we give a modern map of the same locality for comparison. The originals are now in the magnificent collections of the castle of Simancas, having been restored to their rightful owners, together with other documents appropriated by Napoleon the First.

MAP NUMBER 1. LAGRAN BAYA DE S. PHILIPPE Y S. SANTIAGO.
(The Great Bay of St. Philip and St. James.)

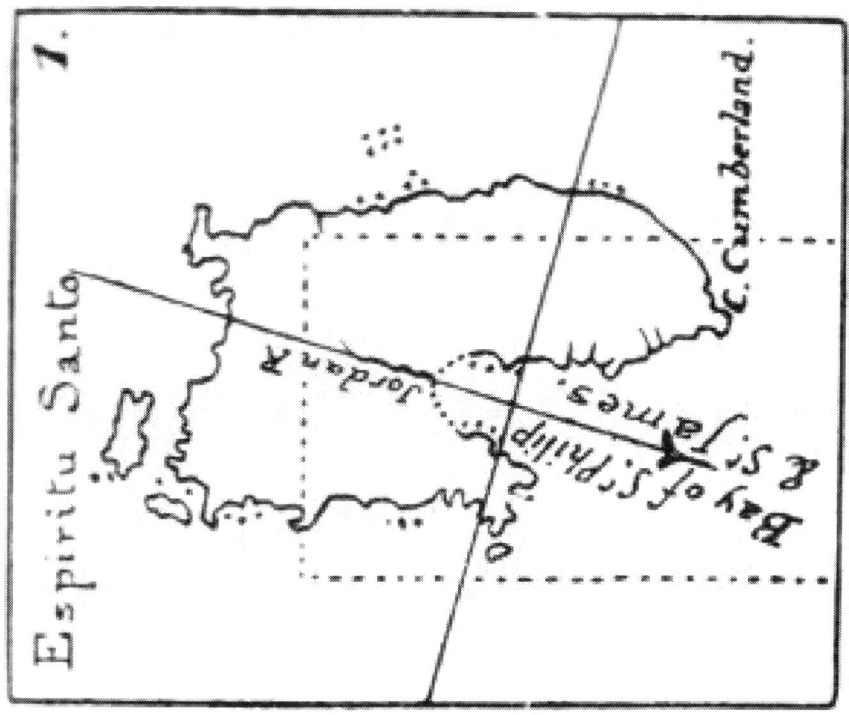

Modern Map of Espiritu Santo.

Towards the end of April 1606 Captain Pedro Fernandez de Quiros discovered in the New Hebrides group an island (Espiritu Santo), which he called *la Austrialia del spiritu Santo*. Coasting along this island, his two ships and the launch entered a bay on the feast of St. Philip and St. James (1st of May), and gave the names of those saints to it.

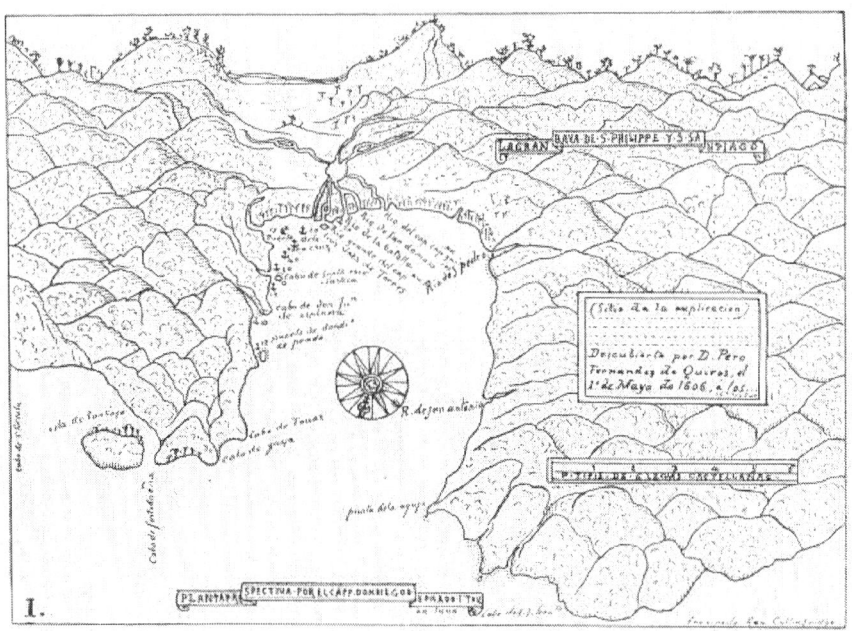

Map No. 1.—The Great Bay of St. Philip and St. James in the Island of Espiritu Santo (New Hebrides.)

MAP NUMBER 1. The Great Bay of St. Philip and St. James in the Island of Espiritu Santo (New Hebrides).

On the 3rd of May they anchored in the south-east corner of the bay, and named the port where they had decided to settle the young colony *el puerto de la vera cruz* (Port of the true cross). The town in the new colony was to be called the *New Jerusalem*, and one of the rivers that flowed into the bay was called the *Jordan*. These two names are mentioned in the narrative but not on the map. We shall now proceed to explain most of the names on this map. Those of de Quiros, of his lieutenant (Luis Vaez de Torres), and of D. Diego de Prado y Tovar, do not require any explanation; they have been given to one cape, one port, and several rivers in the Great Bay. The name of *don Jun de espinosa, gaya, fontiduena y Touar*, given to the eastern capes are names of officers belonging to the expedition, the last mentioned name being also the second name of Don Diego de Prado. The *Rio de la batalla* records no doubt the attacks made by the natives at that river. The *punta de la aguja* (Cape or Point of the Needle) may refer to some local peculiarity. The island of *Santiago* received its name through having been seen no doubt on the 1st of May, and in the same manner the *Rio de S. Pedro*, the *R. de San antonio*, and the *cabo de S. J. bauta* (Cape of St.

John the Baptist), referring as they do to feasts which occur in May and June, that is during the stay that the Spaniards made in the Bay, were named no doubt respectively on the days of the feasts of those saints. The name of *San damaso* given to a river and those of *santa escolastica* and *S. Ursula*, given to two capes, are not so easily explained, because the feasts of those saints do not occur at a time corresponding to the stay made at the place. They may however refer to some particular devotion, family record, or other circumstance.

As the term *Austrialia*, or *Australia*, given to these lands has been a matter for discussion, and some have thought that there was an error, and that *Austrialia* should be read *Australia*, we shall note briefly the reasons for one and the other opinion. In de Quiros' diary or journal, where he speaks of the taking possession of this land, which he believed to form part of a continent, he makes use of the term Australia. Formal possession of the country was taken on the day of the Pasch of the Holy Ghost, the 14th of May, and he says that he took possession of all the lands, those seen and those to be seen, of all that part of the south as far as the South Pole, that from that day was to be called *Australia del Espiritu Santo*. His words are:... *de todas las tierras que dejo vistas y estoy viendo, y de toda esta parte del Sur hasta su polo, que desde ahora se ha de llamar AUSTRALIA del Espiritu Santo*.

An alteration however appears to have been made in the manuscript in the Library of the *Ministerio de Marina*, which suggests that the word was originally written AUSTRIALIA.

Gonzalez de Leza gives an account of the ceremony of taking possession almost in the same words, but using the term *Austral* instead of *Australia*; he says:...*que desde agora se ha de llamar la parte AUSTRAL del Espiritu Santo*.

Owing to the want of space on our maps we reproduce in these pages the inscriptions contained in the originals. Those inscriptions fill, in the originals, the four cartouches which may be noticed in our copies. The first is as follows:

Ano de 1606, al postrero de abril descubrio el capan pero fernandez de quiros esta isla y la llamo la austrialia del spiritu Santo. y costeandola condos nauios y vn lancha entro en esta baya el capna luis vaes de Torres su almirante el dia de S. philippe y santiago y assi le pusieron este nombre el qual son dando la costa que esta norte sur. hallo el puerto y Rios en ella contenidos y por auer surgido el dia de santa cruz le pusieron por nonbre el puerto de la uera cruz. en las partes que estan senaladas las ancoras es el surgidero my bueno y linpio con las bracas numeradas. Lo demas es sinfondo ya cantilado--esta poblade de gente negra q traen los bestidos que sacaron del bientre de sus madres cubren sus berguencas con ojas de arboles. las armas con q pen son flechas laemacas macanas y dardos arrojadizos con puntas de guesos. su mantenimto es Raizes de names bafafas plantanos cocos y naranjas y algunos puercos. aqui senos desaparecio la nao capna a los ii. de Junio y no se hallo mas esta en altura de 15 grados 2/3 de la parte austral, etc.

In the above inscription the term used is unmistakably *Austrialia* and--which appears to settle the question--in one of de Quiros' memorials, the first no doubt sent to Philip III and printed probably in October 1607, de Quiros says:

Por felice memoria de V. M. y por el apellido de Austria, le di por nombre (a aquella tierra) la AUSTRIALIA *del Espiritu Santo*, porque es su mismo dia tome posesion de ella. For the happy memory of Your Majesty and for the sake of the name of *Austria*, I named it (the said land) la *Austrialia del espiritu Santo*, because in your day (the anniversary of your birth) I took possession of it.

MAP NUMBER 2. PUERTOS. I. BAYAS. DE TIERRA DE SANBVENAVENTVRA,
(Ports and Bays of the Land of St. Bonaventure.)

Our second map represents what is now known as Milne Bay, with the various ports, islands, and headlands adjacent thereto. That part of the extreme south-east coast of New Guinea, so admirably charted in 1606 by the Spaniards, and which Torres so accurately describes as the "*beginning Of New Guinea*," remained almost a *terra incognita* to Europeans up to quite a recent date, and was represented on maps in a very rough and incorrect manner prior to J. Moresby's visit and resurvey in 1873.

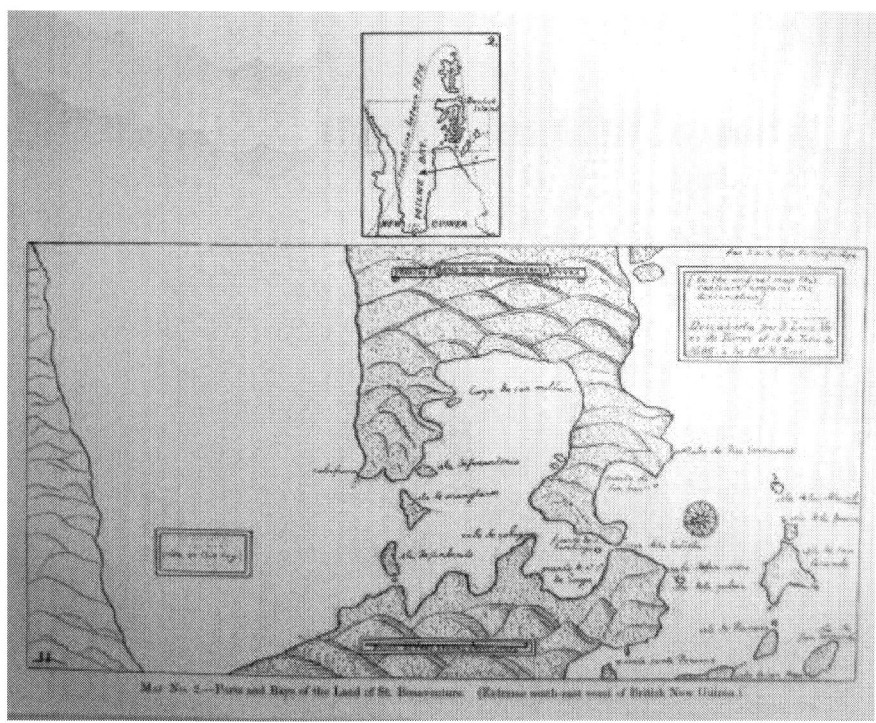

MAP NUMBER 2. Ports and Bays of the Land of St. Bonaventure. (Extreme south-east coast of British New Guinea.)

It is strange however that, before D. Diego de Prado's maps had been found, a Frenchman, of remarkable ability it must be said, was able to detect and point out, with the help of very inferior data, not only the priority of Spanish discoveries in the locality we are considering, but also the exact date of such discoveries. This was done by Dr. E.T. Hamy, the Frenchman we refer to, in 1877, a few months after the publication of Captain John Moresby's book.*

(*Footnote. New Guinea and Polynesia. Discoveries and Surveys in New Guinea and the d'Entrecasteaux Islands. A Cruise in Polynesia and Visits to the Pearl-shelling Stations in Torres Straits of H.M.S. Basilisk. By Captain John Moresby, R.N., London 1876.)

Dr. Hamy's views on the subject were published in a small pamphlet* which appeared in May 1877.

(*Footnote. Commentaires sur quelques cartes anciennes de la Nouvelle-Guinee, pour servir a l'histoire de la decouverte de ce pays par les navigateurs Espagnols (1528 a 1608) par Le Dr. E.T. Hamy. Paris Mai 1877.)

In that monograph, with the help of a map which forms part of an atlas published by Pierre Mortier,* at Amsterdam in 1700, and bearing the title *Suite du Neptune francois, ou Atlas nouveau des cartes marines*, etc., etc., he followed Torres' track from the extreme south-east end of New Guinea westward through Torres Straits and along the south coast to where that navigator left it on his way to the Spice Islands and Manila.

(*Footnote. Suite du Neptune Francois on Atlas nouveau des cartes marines levees par ordre expres des Roys de Portugal sous qui on a fait la decouverte de l'Afrique, etc., et donnees au public par les soins de feu M. d'Ablancourt, dans lequel on voit la description exacte de toutes les cotes du monde, du detroit de Gibraltar, de la mer Oceane meridionale ou Ethiopienne, de la des Indes orientales et occidentales, etc. Ou sont exactement marquees les routes qu'il faut tenir, les bancs de sable, rochers et brasses d'eau, et generalement tout ce qui concerne la navigation, le tout fait sur les observations et l'experience de plus habiles ingenieurs et pilotes. Amsterdam, Pierre Mortier 1700.)

We refer our readers to Dr. Hamy's *Commentaires* for a fuller description of Mortier's map, and we return to the description of Map Number 2.

The inscription in the cartouch of the original map is as follows:

Ano de 1606 a los 18 dias del mes de Julio descubrio esta tierra y puertos el capan ycano luis vaes de Torres y lepuso por nonbre la tierra desan buena uentura auiendola costeado cinco dias antes y por causa de los grandes arracifes muy peligrosos nosepudo tomar tierra astal dia dcho. es poblada de gente blanca ban desnudos y cubren las berguencas conpanillas de esteras de palma de cocos. sus mantentos son names cocos yalgunos puercos pescados y mariscos. sus armas son macanas de madera dardos pequenos arrojadizos y Rodelas esta en altura 10 gra. 2/3 por' la parte austral. puedese dar fondo en todas partes de las bayas y puertos quees linpio y sin mucaras ni Ratones solamte junto atierra tiene bajos de mucaras con forme esta senalado en las dchas partes: tiena agua en todas partes buena debeuer aunq no son Rios.--Por el capan don diego de prado y Touar.

Note in the Great Bay to the North (Milne Bay).

Esta baya tiene mas de 40 leguas de sircunferencia y llegando conel batel mas adelante de cauo fresco q es lo que sepudo salir conel batel porla parte del este no lebimos Remate sino algunos islotes porlo qual sejuzga tiene bocas grandes y porla del oest nole bimos boca sino toda tierra alta y cerrada y continuada al oest dejose de costear porno tener nauio de Remos suficiente para esto. In the year 1606, on the 18th day of July, Captain and Pilot Luis Vaes de Torres discovered this land and its ports, naming it the land of St. Bonaventure, having coasted it five days previously without being able to land before the said day on account of the large and very dangerous reefs. It is inhabited, etc., etc.

Of the four maps the one we are now considering is undoubtedly the most important because it proves that Torres discovered this part of the south-east coast of New Guinea which is mentioned in Moresby's preface in the following terms:

"It seems desirable to state, for the information of the general reader, that the line of New Guinea coast, first placed on the chart by H.M.S. *Basilisk*, had never been visited, and was actually unknown as to its conformation (as far as I have been able to discover any record), up to the period of her first visit in 1873, between the wide limits of Heath Island and Huon Gulf."

The bay, called Jenkins' Bay by Moresby, which is closed in on three sides by the island to which he gave the name of H.M.S. Basilisk, is easily recognised as the *bayo de san millan* of the Spanish map and Basilisk Island as the TIERA DESANBVENA VENTVRA. The great bay named Milne Bay (after the senior Naval Lord of the English Admiralty) was not thoroughly explored by Torres, otherwise, had he reached its north-eastern extremity (East Cape), he would have steered his course for the Philippine Islands by the north of New Guinea instead of proceeding by the south-west passage. He does not appear to have extended his surveys of Milne Bay in the north-east beyond *cabo fresco*, which corresponds to Challis Head, and in the north-west, beyond the mainland of New Guinea, in the vicinity of the Paples Island, which the Spanish chart names *isla de sanbenito*.

The passage called Rocky Pass, between Hayter and Basilisk islands, is set down as the *boca de la batalla* in the Spanish map, recording no doubt an encounter with the natives; and a little island in the middle of the pass, bearing no name in Moresby's map, had evidently suggested a suitable place for building a fort, for it is called the *fuerte de S. Santiago*. The bay within, not named in Moresby's chart, is called *puerto de na sa de Honga*.

China Strait, discovered by C. Moresby, is not marked on the Spanish map. It is evident that Mt. Haines masked its view to the Spanish and that they did not penetrate in that direction as far as Head or Brewer islands, for those islands are not marked on their chart.*

(*Footnote. Captain Moresby records his discovery of this channel in the following terms: "...We continued to track Jenkins Bay round, and watch for what it would develop; and the farther we went the more the formation of the land led us to suppose that even now we had not found the real terminating point of New Guinea. After pulling six or seven miles to the west we found our conjectures verified by the discovery of a clear broad blue channel two miles wide, leading fair from sea to sea, fit for a fleet to pass through under sail. Our hearts filled with delight and wonder as we looked. There and then I named it China Straits; the wish being father to the thought that I had found a new highway between Australia and China." Discoveries and Surveys in New Guinea, etc. page 201.)

Thus Hayter Island is marked as a peninsula on the Spanish map and the southern portion of China Strait is set down as a port, the *puerto santo Torinio (Toribio)*. Blanchard Island is called *isla de san facundo*. Didymus Island is the Spanish *isla de manglares*, and West Island *isla de san antonio*. The *cabo de casagun* or *cahagun* is marked in the English map, but bears no name. Bead Island is the *isla de la palma*.

Other islands, marked in both maps but bearing no names on the English one, have the following Spanish nomenclature: *isla de las altas palmas*, islands of the tall palm trees; *isla de la sauana*, Savanna Island; *isla de san bernardo*, Island of St. Bernard. St. Bernard's feast occurs on the 23rd of July, but this name may also be intended in commemoration of Juan Bernardo de Fuentiduena, an officer of the expedition, as also the *cabo de san diego* may commemorate the name of D. Diego Barrantes y Maldonad. *isla de Ranedo*, Island of Ranedo, or St. Ranedo. The *puerto de san franco* (Francisco) is no doubt the port where Torres first sighted land on the 14th of July. On the 14th of July the Spanish celebrate the feast of S. *Buenaventura* and also S. *Francisco Solano*.

MAP NUMBER 3. LA GRAN BAYA DE. S. LORENCO. I. PVERTO DE MONTEREY.
(The Great Bay of St. Lawrence and Port of Monterey.)

Our third map represents the site known in modern maps as Orangerie Bay. Bougainville, with the *Boudeuse* and *l'Etoile*, visited this easternmost bay of the south coast of New Guinea in June 1768, one hundred and sixty-two years after Torres and D. Diego de Prado. He called it the *Golphe de la Louisiade*, and of the country at the back of the inner portion of the bay, which he called the *cul de sac de l'Orangerie*, he says: J'ai peu vu de pays dont le coup d'oeil fut plus beau. I have seen few countries presenting a finer aspect.* His description throughout corresponds exactly with D. Diego de Prado's map.

(*Footnote. Voyage autour du monde par la fregate du Roi La Boudeuse et la flute L'Etoile, en 1766, 1767, 1768 et 1769. Paris 1772. Tom. II. page 167.)

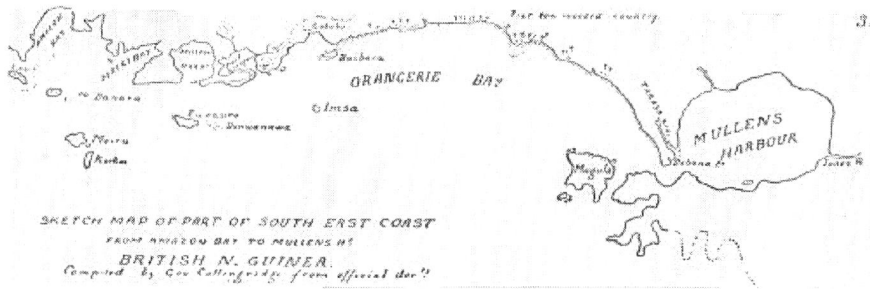

Modern Map of Orangerie Bay.

The Spanish description is as follows: Esta baya de sanct lorenco y puerto de monte Rey descubrio el capan y cauo luis vaes de Torres a 10 de agosto del ano de 1606 y porser el puerto tanbueno lepuso este nombre. dista del puerto de sanct franco beinte leguas mas. o. menos ala parte del oest. es muy hermosa y agradable y de lindo y linpio fondo pues sepuede seguramte surgir per todas partes la tierra delaparte del norte es de lindas llanuras y bien cultiuadas con mucha cantidad de aguas y palmeras de cocos. Raizes de names y camotes y mafafas plantanos y otras frutas no conocidas y much os y buenos puercos. los naturales son de color de mulatos. dispuestos de querpo y menbrudos y todos Retajados como Judios. cubren los hombres las berguencas con panpanillas y las mujeres las traen como ferdugadas asta las Rodillas. sus armas son dardos arrojadizos macanas y Rodelas largas. esta enaltura de 10 gra. 1/6 es la mejor tierra y mas fertil para poblar delas que sean descubierto.--por el cappan don diego de prado y Touar. The captain and pilot* Luis Vaes de Torres discovered this Bay of St. Lawrence and Port of Monterey on the 10th of August of the year 1606, and on account of the excellence of the port he gave it this name.* This port is distant from the port of San Francisco (Basilisk Island) 20 leagues, more or less, in a westerly direction. It is very beautiful and pleasant with good and clean anchorage. On all the north side, which is level country, there is good and secure landing. The country is well cultivated, plentifully watered and produces great quantities of cocoanut palms, etc., etc.

(*Footnote. *cauo cabo*, may mean also chief.)

(*Footnote. The Count de Monterey was the Viceroy of Peru, under whose auspices de Quiros' expedition was sent out the year before.)

Twenty leagues is exactly the distance which separates the two ports described in the Spanish narrative, and the configurations given on the old Spanish map are more complete than those given either by Bougainville in 1768, Dumont D'Urville in 1840, or Owen Stanley in 1848.

Whether the division of the land into allotments was suggested by actual features of the place at the time of Torres' stay in this bay, or whether it was the result of a special intention, is not shown in the documents we are now dealing with. Recent knowledge of the locality goes to show that the natives are rather apt to shift their dwellings and abandon their plantations without much ado.*

(*Footnote. 1892 Queensland. Annual Report on British New Guinea, from 1st July 1890 to 30th June 1891; with appendices. Page 60 paragraph 15.)

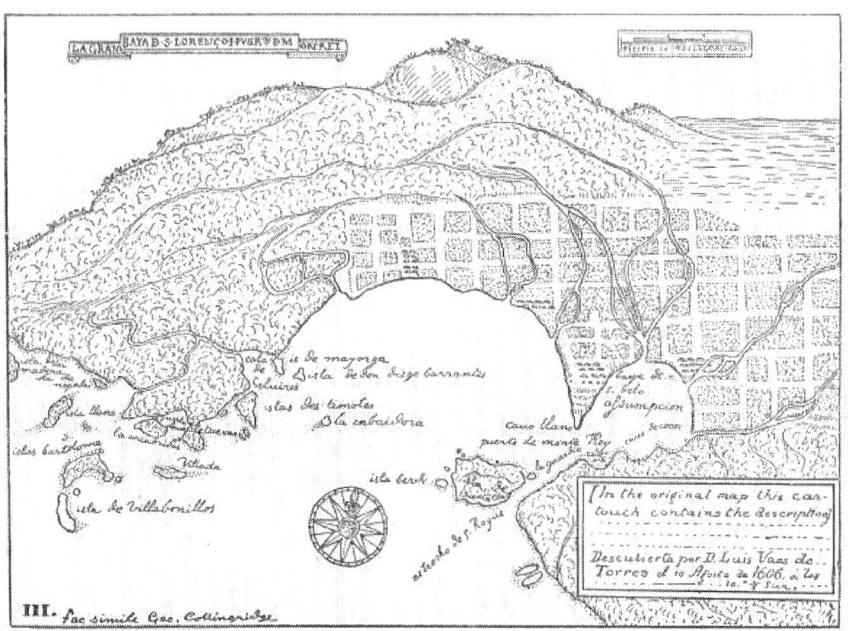

MAP NUMBER 3. The Great Bay of St. Lawrence and Port of Monterey. (Orangerie Bay, British New Guinea.)

We now come to the description of the nomenclature. The name of St. Lawrence Bay was given to Orangerie Bay because it was discovered on the 10th of August, feast of St. Lawrence.*

(*Footnote. Just one hundred years before the name of St. Lawrence was given to Madagascar by Joao Gomez d'Abreu, who discovered the west coast of that island on the 10th of August 1506.)

The name given to Dufaure or Mugula (native appellation) Island is *isla de santa clara*; the feast of St. Clair occurs on the 12th of August. The bay known under the name of Mullens' Harbour (uncharted in Moresby's map) is well laid down in the Spanish chart, and is called the baya *de n. s. dela assumpcion*, the Bay of Our Lady of the Assumption, corresponding to the 15th of August. Three rivers flow into this bay; they bear no names. The latest surveys give names to two of these rivers--the larger, to the north-west, is called the Tarasa river, and the smaller one, to the east, is named Jones River.

Sir William Macgregor, who explored some portion of the Tarasa river a few years ago, and described it in his despatch reporting his visit to this eastern part of New Guinea,* says that he found it to be a saltwater inlet running up into a great mangrove swamp. This level delta, with its mangrove islands, is well indicated in D. Diego de Prado's map. The channel between the mainland and Mugula Island (*Isla de Santa Clara*) is called the *estrecho de S. Roque*, Straits of St. Roch (16th August). This name at least should be retained by modern usurpers, as this channel does not bear any name that we are aware of to the present day.*

(*Footnote. Despatch from Samaria, 12th of June 1891.)

(*Footnote. The Admiralty chart, published June 9 1886 and corrected up to 1888, leaves this strait nameless, as also Sir William Macgregor's sketch map of this part of British New Guinea, published two years ago. Apart from the pre-emptive right which the Spanish have, without a doubt, the preservation of a few Spanish names would only be fair-- they would sound well and relieve the monotony of the Joneses, Mullenses, and Jenkinses.)

The *islas des timoteo*, Islands of St. Timothy (22nd August), include evidently the promontory which forms the eastern entrance to Port

Glasgow. This promontory is almost separated from the mainland by a creek, and was, with the two islands alongside it, set down as *islas des timotes (Islas de S. Timoteo)*.

The *islas bartolome*, Island of St. Bartholomew (24th August) which, with the previous nomenclature, indicates the progression of Torres' navigation towards the west, corresponds to Toulon Island (Mairu) of French nomenclature.

Other names, such as *isla berde*, Green Island; *cauo alto*, High Cape; *cauo de cocos*, Cocoanut Cape; *cauo llano*, Level Cape; *la enfaidora (embaidora)*, The Deceitful; *las encubridores*, The Hidden; *isla llana*, Level Island; and *isla de la Madera*, Wooded Island; indicate peculiarities borne out by the evidence of modern charts. For *isla berde* is the beautiful little green island situated at the eastern entrance to Orangerie Bay; *cauo alto* is the elevated land or high cape at the south entrance to Mullens' Harbour; *cauo de cocos* is the cape covered with cocoanut trees to this day; *cauo llano* is the low land which forms a cape at the northern entrance into Mullens' Harbour, i.e. Debana Point.

The island that stands alone at the western extremity of Orangerie Bay, and named *la enbaidora* in the Spanish map, is easily identified as Imsa of modern charts. The islets called *las encubridores* are the two small rocky islets at the eastern entrance to Millport Harbour. The coral reefs marked dry at low water between Mairy Bay and Amazon Bay correspond with the *isla llana*, Level or Low Island of the Spanish map, and the *isla de la madera*, or Wooded Island, with the wooded island of Ainioro. The very small island at the north-eastern extremity of Dufaure island marked on the Admiralty chart, but without a name, might, if thoroughly searched, reveal some traces, well worth looking for, of Spanish occupation. This island is called *la guardia* on Tovar's map, and was probably the camping ground of Torres' party, the garrisoned stronghold of the expedition during its stay in this bay.

Baibara and another island in its neighbourhood are marked on the Spanish map as *isla de don diego barrantes* and *islas de mayorga*. D. Diego de Barrantes was one of the principal officers of the expedition. The little bay where now stands the native village of Gobubu at the back of Baibara Island is named in the Spanish chart the *cala de helvires*, recording a name from Spain, as do also such names as *ualdetuexar* or Valdetuejar, *mayorga, villada, villabonillos*, and *nogales*.

The *puerto de ualdetuexar* is the port now known as Millport Harbour, the Losoa Don-Don of the natives. *villada* is an island marking the entrance of the above port. It is well charted with its eastern prolongation of reefs dry only at low water. The native name of *villada* is Eunauro or Euna, and the reef is called Bonuanawa. The native name for *isla de villabonillos*, the south-westernmost island of our map, is Koikoi, and the *isla de nogales* corresponds no doubt with the Boioro Peninsula. The harbour between the mainland and Mugula Island is called the *puerto de monte Rey*, Port of Monterey, after the Count of Monterey, Viceroy of Peru.

MAP NUMBER 4. BAYA. DE SANCT. PEDRO DE ARLANCA.
(The Bay of St. Peter of Arlanza.)

The locality represented in our fourth map and named the Bay of St. Peter of Arlanza is situated on the south-west coast of New Guinea in Dutch territory.

Torres left Orangerie Bay towards the end of August, passed between Australia and New Guinea, and, still continuing his course along the coasts of New Guinea, put in at this bay now known as Triton Bay, having received that name in 1828, when the Dutch ships *Triton* and *Iris* made a visit to it.

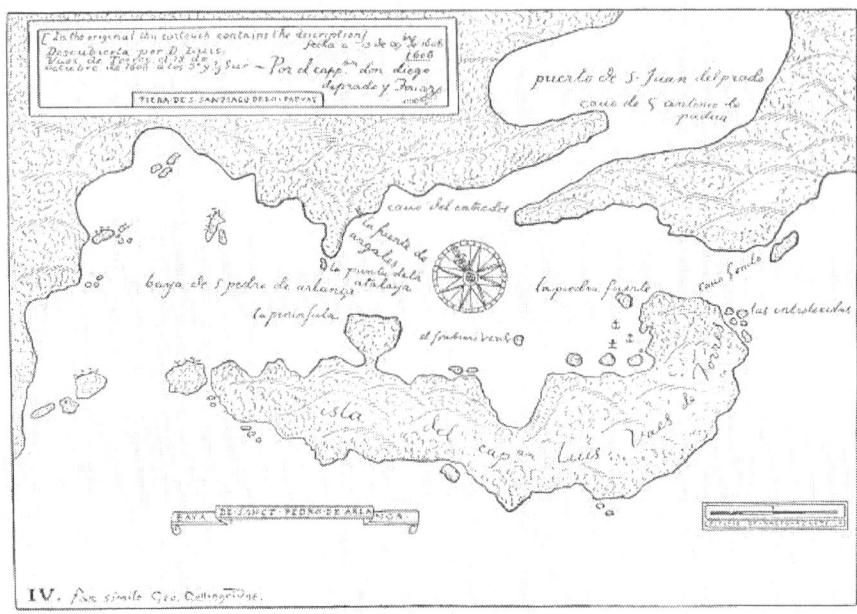

MAP NUMBER 4. The Bay of St. Peter of Arlanza. (Dutch New Guinea.)

The Spanish description of the place as contained in the cartouch on the map is as follows:

Esta baya de sanct pedro de arlanca y puerto de sanct lucas y el de sanct Juan del prado hallo el capan luis vaes de Torres a 18 dias de octubre de 1606 es tierra. de los papuas distante del puerto de s. franco 270 leguas Tiene mucho fondo portodas partes y sea de surgir junto atierra. la qual es muy montuosa y aspera con grandes arboledas y sin llanuras. la poblacion es de gente negra y muy poca por dcha aspereza y entrellos alguna parda y bien dispuesta y menbruda. la comida es muy poca porq no tienen sino pocos cocos y Raizes el mayor mantenimto es pescado y marisco sus armas son dardos arrojadizos y flechas con arcos de cana y puntas de guesos y paueses de madera largos siete palmos y anchos tres muy bien labrados de talla de medio Relieve traen panpanillas en las berguencas como los demas esta en altura de 3 grados y 2/3 aqui sehallo hierro labrado en anzuelos y fisgas y fuelles decanes con toueras de barro. conq labran cosillas de hierro--no se hallo agua en abundancia sino en la dcha fuente de argales q nace debajo de un cerro muy alto de penas.--fecha a 13 de xbre de 1606 1606--Por el cappan don Diego de prado y Touar. This bay of St. Peter of Arlanza (Alcantara), port of St. Luke, and that of St. John *del Prado*, were discovered by Captain Luis Vaez de Torres on the 18th day of October 1606. It is in the Land of the Papuas, distant 270* leagues. There is great depth all along this shore, and you have to get out close up to the land, which is very mountainous and rough, with big trees and no plains. The people are, etc., etc.

(*Footnote. Should read probably 370 leagues.)

Modern Map of Triton Bay.

By following the same method as that used with the other charts the nomenclature is as easily explained. The feast of St. Luke the Evangelist falls on the 18th of October, that of St. Peter of Arlanza on the 19th of the same month, and these are the names given to the two principal bays. The island of Aidoema was named *isla del capan luis vaes de Torres* after the commander of the expedition. The names of *puerto de s. Juan delprado* and *cauo de S. antonio de padua* were no doubt records of some particular devotion. The island named *la piedra fuerte* may refer to a place fortified during the stay made in these parts. *las tres hermanas*, the Three Brothers, are three islands not shown in the Dutch chart of 1876, nor in the map of Dutch New Guinea published with Prince Roland Bonaparte's Les derniers voyages des Neerlandais a la Nouvelle-Guinee, 1885, not because they do not exist but more probably because the Dutch survey at this particular point is far less accurate than the Spanish one. *el sonbrero* (sombrero) *verde*, the Green Hat, is the name given to a little round island, and records no doubt the circumstance of resemblance as the word suggests.

Other names refer in the same way either to local peculiarities or family records, such are: *la peninsula, la fuente de argales, cauo del entredos, la enpanada, islas de Sta leocadia, cauo de s. lucas, punta de fontiduena, las entretexidas* and *cauo hondo.*

DE PRADO'S LETTERS TO THE KING OF SPAIN.

The two following letters of D. Diego de Prado to the King of Spain (the first addressed to the king's secretary, and the second addressed to the king) respecting dc Quiros' expedition and Torres' discoveries in New Guinea do not appear to be generally known. In these letters New Guinea is referred to as the *Magna Margarita*, a name which does not appear on the four maps which we have considered in this chapter.

The name is easily explained, for Torres took formal possession on the 20th of July, i.e. on the day of the feast of St. Marguerite, one week after his arrival at the east end of New Guinea.

In his first letter Prado speaks of a map which must have been the principal document relating to the discoveries made during the expedition. This map has not yet been found although diligent research has been made and is still being made for it at Simancas and elsewhere.

Carta de Diego de Prado al Secretario Antonio de Arostegui, fecha en Goa a 24 de Diciembre de 1613: recibida en 12 de Octubre de 1614. Archivo de Simancas.

Secretaria de Estado. Leg. o 252.

Por bia del senor birrey de la India enbio a su magd el mapa del descubrimiento que acabo Luis Vaes de Torres, capitan de la nao Almiranta de Pero Fernandez de Quiros, guardando la horden que le dio el conde de Monterrey, que es la isla llamada por nos la *Magna Margarita*, que tiene 680 leguas de costa. Como vera v. m. por el dicho mapa lo que descubrio Pero Fernandez de Quiros el embustero, fueron aquellos escollos e islas pequenas, porque se le amotino la gente dentro de la baya de la isla del Spiritu Santo. Yo venia por capitan de la nao Capitana y fuy sabidor de lo que se iba hordenando en la nao; dile parte dello, y como hera el mayor sobre gueso que tenia, por decirle lo que conbenia al seruicio de su magd no me podia tragar y assi me desembarque en *Taumaco* y me fuy a la Almiranta, de que hubo mucha alegria en la nao. Para mejor efectuar su negocio, a los 11 de Junio de 1606 estando en la baya, que beniamos de una isla que estaba cerca, bino a las ocho de la noche el viento Sul algo fresco, conque los amotinados pusieron por hobra su mal intento, y siendo de noche, y lejos de nosotros alsaron en popa, sin berlo ese hablador por estar en su camara de popa. Por la manana no parecio la tierra de do hauian salido. no hoso hablar, antes le dixeron que se metiese en su camara y callase la boca, por lo qual le salbaron la uida y le desenbarcaron en Acapulco; sus proprias camaradas, dijeron al marques' de Montes claros quien hera, y como le podian atar por loco, el qual le trato como quien hera. Yo no se que rrespecto auian de tener los espanoles del Piru, a uno que ayer hera escribano de vna nao de mercaderes y portugueses; si lo conociesen como le conoce el capitan Alonzo Corco, acabarian de entender esos senores del Estado, que de tan baxos honbres y mentirosos no auian de hacer caso.

Yo partire para Ormuz a los 8 de Febrero del ano que biene, plaziendo a Dios, para hirme por tierra hasta el puerto de Leppe (Alepo) y de alli a Benencia, y no parar asta llegar a esa corte, a besar las manos de su magd y de v. m. Enbio vn indio de los de la tierra que se descubrio para testigo de abono, el qual lleba a su cargo el senor Rui Lorenco de Tabora, birrey que fue desta India, con horden de no entregarle a ninguno, si no fuere por horden de v. m. o. mia. La muerte del senor secretario Andres de Prada, me a dado mucha pena; pero como es camino que todos hemos de azer, encomendarle a Dios, el qual de a v. m. la salud que este su serbidor desea. De Goa 24 de xbre 1613.=D. Diego de Prado.

Letter of D. Diego de Prado to the secretary, Antonio de Arostegui, dated Goa, 24th December 1613; received 12th October 1614.*

(*Footnote. Our translation is from the Hakluyt Society's edition of De

Morga's Philippine Islands.)

I send to His Majesty, by means of the Viceroy of the Indies, the map of the discovery which was effected by Luis Vaez de Torres, captain of the *Almiranta*, of Pedro Fernandez de Quiros, who followed the instructions given by the Conde de Monterrey, which discovery was the island called by us La Magna Margarita, which has 680 leagues of coast, as your worship will see by the said map. That which was discovered by Pedro Fernandez de Quiros, the liar, were those rocks and small islands, because his crew mutinied at the bay of the island Espiritu Santo. I came as captain of the flag-ship, and had knowledge of what was being arranged in the ship. I informed him of it, and, as it was a most difficult and delicate matter to tell him of, and of what was best for His Majesty's service, he could not stand me. So I disembarked in Trumaco (*Taumaco*), and went on board the *Almiranta*, at which there was great joy on the flag-ship, as they could better carry out their design. On the 11th of June of 1606, being in the bay as we were coming from an island which was near, there came a rather fresh wind from the south at eight in the evening, upon which the mutineers carried out their evil designs; and as it was night and far from us they put the ship about, and the prattler did not see it as he was in his cabin in the stern; and in the morning the country from which they had come out did not appear. He did not venture to speak; on the contrary he was told to get into his cabin and hold his tongue, on which account they spared his life and landed him at Acapulco. His own companions told the Marquis of Montesclaros who he was, and how they might as well tie him up as mad, and he treated him as such a man as he was. I do not know what respect the Spaniards of Piru were to have for a man who yesterday was a clerk of a merchant ship and a Portuguese; if they knew him as Captain Alonzo Corzo knows him those gentlemen of the state would end by knowing that they ought not to take account of such low and lying men. I shall leave for Ormuz on the 8th of February of next year, if it please God, to go by land to the port of Leppe (Aleppo), and thence to Venice, and I shall not stop till I reach the court to kiss the hands of His Majesty; and, your worship, I send an Indian of the country which was discovered as a witness to certify it, who is taken at the charge of Senor Ruy Lorenzo de Tavora, the ex-Viceroy of India, with directions not to give him up to anyone unless by order of your worship or mine. The death of the secretary, Andres de Prada, has given me much sorrow, but as it is the journey we all have to take I recommend him to God. May He give to your worship the health which your servant desires for you. From Goa, 24th December 1613.

DON DIEGO DE PRADO.

DE PRADO'S SECOND LETTER.
Carta de Don Diego de Prado a S. M. (el rey don Felipe iii), fecha en Goa a 25 de Diciembre de 1613: y recibida en 12 de Octubre de 1614.

SENOR.--Enbio a V. magd el descubrimiento de la *Magna Margarita*, tierra austral, que hizo Luis Vaez de Torres, almirante de Pero Fernandez de Quiros, porque ya es tiempo que llegue a manos de V. magd; cuya tardanca, ha sido por causa del gobernador de Manila, don Juan de Silua, que mas mira su propio interez, que lo que conbiene al seruicio de V. magd, de que dare quenta a su tiempo. Por no tener con que enbarcarme en la nao en que ba el birrey Ruy Lorenco de Tauora, por auerlo perdido con la nao San Andres, he determinado hirme a Ormuz y de alli, por tierra, con la cafila de los mercaderes benecianos, y peregrinando poco a poco asta Alepo, y de alli a Benencia y otras partes, asta llegar a esa Corte y besar las manos a V. magd y darle quenta de todo muy en particular, y que entienda V. magd que todo lo que dice Pero Fernandez de Quiros, es mentira y falsedad, porque por su culpa no se descubrio lo que mas estimaua el conde de Monterrey, que es la coronilla del polo antartico, pues estubimos tan cerca della. Y no de V. magd credito a honbre, que sufris en su nao vn motin tal qual hicieron sus marineros, auiendo sido auisado; y assi, le trataron como quien es, que basta ser de la Ruanoua de Lisboa, in cujus hore, no ay sino enbuste, mentira y deslealtad. Y assi, abiso a V. magd que fie del como de vn escribano de nao de mercadez, y que fue este honbre causa que el adelantado Auendano se perdiese con su armada; esto dicho por el capitan Felipe Corso justicia mayor de la punta de Cabite de Manila.

Abiso esto a V. magd porque no gaste su hazienda con semejantes. Cuya persona Nuestro Senor guarde largos anos, como este su fiel criado desea.--De Goa, 25 de xbre de 1613.--DON DIEGO DE PRADO.

De Prado's first letter was dated from Goa, December 24. The one above was written apparently the next day, and dated from the same place, December 25. In it he repeats what he wrote in his first letter, saying: "I send to Your Majesty the discovery of the *Magna Margarita*, Southern Land, which discovery was made by Luis Vaez de Torres, de Quiros' *Almirante*, etc." He blames Don Juan de Silva, the Governor of Manila, for delaying his despatches, refers to the route he intends to take on his return to Spain, and reiterates his warnings concerning de Quiros, blaming him for not having discovered the southern continent, porque por su culpa no se descubrio lo que mas estimaua el conde de Monterrey, *que es fa coronilla del polo antartico pues estubimos tan cerca della*, because through his fault he did not discover that which the Count of Monterrey considered the most worthy of discovery, *that is the crown of the Antarctic Pole, to which we came so close.*

In these two letters de Prado shows a decided antagonism to de Quiros, yet he does not blame him for leaving Torres and returning *purposely* to New Spain. This he appears to have been accused of by Juan de Iturbe,* his accountant, who also blames him for having disobeyed instructions which were "*to go as far as 40 degrees south latitude.*"

(*Footnote. See De Morga's Philippine Islands. Notes by Lord Stanley of Alderley, page 406 et sequit.)

Had de Quiros obeyed the instructions referred to by Juan de Iturbe, Torres, and others he would certainly have discovered New Zealand and perhaps Australia. He discovered neither the one nor the other, but the report spread abroad nevertheless that he had discovered the southern continent, and this accounts for the strange manner in which his New Hebrides discoveries are joined to the eastern coast of Australia in many maps up to the date of Lieutenant James Cook's arrival and re-survey of the eastern coast of Australia.

The expedition of de Quiros and Torres closes the period of Spanish activity; it is true that de Quiros still urged the King of Spain to send him out again in order to continue his discoveries, but, owing to want of money, and no doubt to intrigues, his propositions were not entertained as in earlier days. Torres' discoveries, charted in such a remarkable way by de Prado, were however not to be abandoned so easily. The Spanish evidently intended to make some settlement in the localities surveyed by them in New Guinea. We have come across a passage in Constantin* which bears out this fact.

(*Footnote. Constantin, Voyages de la Compagnie, 1725. Rouen. Tome vii. pages 189, 190, 191, 192.)

It is there stated on the authority of two Dutchmen, five years after Torres' voyage, that the Spaniards intended to colonise that country and that they were constructing ships in New Spain to carry out the scheme, because there was every likelihood of great profits to be derived from the undertaking. It is further stated that several Spaniards had been left in New Guinea in order to explore the inland parts. These projects were nevertheless abandoned; besides, the Spanish were at the time losing their power and influence in Austral-Asia, although they retained it in the Philippine Islands. At the time Don Diego de Prado was writing home to the King of Spain the Dutch were rapidly gaining ground in the East Indian Archipelago. In 1610 Paul Van Caerden was proclaimed Governor of all the Spice Islands. The Dutch had at Ternate Fort Melaia or Malaie, and Fort Tacomma or Willemstadt. At Machian they had three forts, Tassaso, Noseckia or Fort Maurice and Tabilola. At Mortir or Motier they had Fort Nassau. At Bachian or Labova, which was comprised under Bachian, they had Fort Barneveldt.

CHAPTER 42. A.D. 1616.
DIRCK HARTOG'S ALLEGED DISCOVERY ON THE WESTERN COAST OF AUSTRALIA.

he second Dutch discovery was made, according to the *Instructions*, in the year 1616. The paragraph in the *Instructions* which refers to this claim is rather vague; it mentions the names of several ships without particularising the discoveries they made, giving the dates 1616, 1618, 1619, and 1622 as the years during which the western coasts were visited from 22 degrees [North-west Cape] to 35 degrees [Cape Leeuwin].

But in 1801 the French found a plate with an inscription on it recording a Dutch discovery made in 1616.

The document was picked up by one of a party of three men that had been sent ashore during the stay of the *Naturaliste* on that coast. After a copy of the inscription had been taken the plate was reverentially and carefully fixed on a new post occupying the position of the old one at the foot of which it had been found.

The inscription, that is faulty copies of it, are well known to writers on Australian maritime discovery, but few if any have taken the trouble to inquire about its origin and the actual existence of the plate.

A plate, tin, pewter, or lead, the versions vary, found on an island which bears the name of the alleged discoverer.

We have made particular enquiries about this plate, thinking that its proper place should be the Sydney Museum or Public Library. We were guided to a certain extent in our researches, because the locality where the plate was found by the French expedition that so carefully charted a great portion of our coasts in the early days of the mother colony is a well determined point, since named Cape *Inscription*. That locality was searched by a friend of ours, but without any result.

Meanwhile our attention was drawn to a passage in Mr. E. Favenc's History of Australian Exploration, page 436. Favenc says, speaking of this plate: "In 1819, M. L. de Freycinet, while on his voyage round the world, took it home with him, and placed it in the Museum of the Institute, Paris."

Mr. E. Favenc is a careful and scrupulous writer, and, although he could not inform us where he had obtained his information, nor could we procure in Australia at the time a copy of Freycinet's voyages* in order to verify it, we thought nevertheless that Mr. Favenc's information was worth acting upon.

(*Footnote. L. Claude de Freycinet. Voyage autour du monde. Uranie et Physicienne de 1817 a 1820 Paris 1823 14 volumes.)

We wrote to our friend, Dr. E.T. Hamy, himself a member of the French Institute in question, and one of the best informed scientists in matters relating to Australasian maritime discovery. Dr. Hamy's answer was: J'ai vainement cherche la relique rapportee par Freycinet; l'indication de son depot a l'Institut que j'avais prise dans Rienzi,* est malheureusement inexact. I have sought in vain for the relic brought back by Freycinet; the mention of its deposit at the Institute, that I had found in Rienzi, is unfortunately inexact. E.T. HAMY, Ministere de l'Instruction Publique et des Beaux-Arts, Palais du Trocadero, Musee d'Ethnographie, Paris, le 10 Mai 1892.

(*Footnote. Oceanie. Tome iii. page 477.)

This was perplexing, but we did not give up our search, and we found other inexactitudes in connection with Dirck Hartog's plate.

The French account of the finding of it is given in Peron's work,* volume 1 page 194. Peron, the author of the narrative, was on board the *Naturaliste* when the plate was brought back by the *chef de timonnerie*, who with two others had been sent ashore to signal the *Geographe* in case she appeared at the entry of the bay. In his description of the plate Peron does not give the Dutch but the French translation of the inscription only, as follows:

(*Footnote. Voyages de Decouvertes aux Terres Australes, execute par ordre de Sa Majeste l'Empereur et Roi, sur les corvettes le Geographe, le Naturaliste, et la Goelette le Casuarina, pendant les annees 1800, 1801, 1802, 1803, et 1804, etc. A Paris 1807.)

1616.

Le 25 octobre est arrive ici le navire l'Endraght, d'Amsterdam: premier marchand, GILLES MIEBAIS VAN-LUCK; capitaine DIRCK-HARTIGHS, d'Amsterdam; il remit sous voile le 27 du meme mois: BANTUM etoit sous-marchand; JANSTINS, premier pilote; PIETER ECOORES VAN-BU...Annee 1616.

The French translation as given above appears to be faulty. Major has pointed out that, owing to an error in punctuation, "a droll mistake is made," and "that Bantam, in Java, for which they set sail, is transformed into the under-merchant, and the person who really held that post is converted into chief pilot, while poor Pieter Dockes,* whose name, perhaps more feebly scratched at the close of the inscription, had become obliterated by more than a century's rough usage, is deprived of the honour of holding any post whatever."

(*Footnote. Ecoores in Peron's account. Doore, according to Rienzi, quoting Freycinet. George Collingridge.)

But Major's transcription is faulty also;* after *Gilles Mibais* he leaves out five words, which, in Rienzi, are given thus: "*Luick, schipper Dirck-Hatichs, van.*"

(*Footnote. See Introduction page lxxxi. Early Voyages to Terra Australis. R.H. Major.)

Why does Major say "more than a *century's* rough usage," when, in the preceding page, translating Peron's words, he says: "Captain Hamelin had a new post made, and sent back the plate to be refixed on the same spot from which it had been taken; he would have looked upon it as sacrilege to have kept on board this plate, which for *nearly two centuries* had been spared by nature and by those who might have observed it before him."

We do not believe it is a *lapsus* on Major's part because, as we shall see, he knew that the plate found by the French expedition was not the original one placed there by Dirck Hartog, but one containing a copy of Dirck Hartog's inscription and which had been placed at the spot whence Hartog's original plate had been taken away by Vlamingh on the 3rd of February 1697.

But then, why does he not say so? And another question might be asked also at this juncture: Where did Major get his Dutch text of the inscription? Not from Vlamingh's narrative, a copy of which Major tells us* he "deemed himself fortunate in procuring." The account of this voyage, which was printed in Amsterdam in 1701, 4to, is exceedingly scarce. We have however a copy of it in our Sydney Public Library, and it does not give the inscription. Major gives a translated extract of the journal in question, together with some other particulars relating to the same voyage, extracted from manuscript documents at the Hague. It must be from those particulars relating to the voyage of Willem de Vlamingh that Major translated his inscription.

(*Footnote. Early Voyages to Terra Australis. Introduction page cviii.)

According to that narrative it appears evident that Dirck Hartog's plate was not treated with the same consideration which prompted the French captain to replace what he considered to be a relic dating from the year 1616; for the extract, after giving the inscription, with slight variations from the one given in Major's Introduction, the variance being in the orthography of the names, runs thus:

"This old plate, brought to us by Willem de Vlamingh, we have now handed over to the commander, in order that he might bring it to Your Nobilities, and that you may marvel how it remained there through such a number of years unaffected by air, rain, or sun. They erected on the same spot another pole, with a flat tin plate, as a memorial, and wrote on it as to be read in the journals."

The second inscription, relating to Vlamingh's arrival and departure, which was found added to the first on the plate described by Peron, corresponds with the one published by Major, and is no doubt the one referred to above as a memorial *to be read in the journals.*

We have therefore to look to Vlamingh's account for the authenticity of the claim. We must take his word for it that he really did carry away a plate placed on that island in 1616 by Dirck Hartog.

But we come now to the most mysterious part of the whole transaction. In Vlamingh's journal we find the following entries:

"On the 1st of February (1697), early in the morning, our little boat went to the coast to fish. Our chief pilot, with De Vlamingh's boat, again went into the gulf, and our skipper went on shore *to fix up a commemorative tablet*..." The commemorative tablet was fixed up on the 1st of February. We pass over the doings of the 2nd, which do not refer to the subject, and we arrive at the 3rd. "On the 3rd Vlamingh's chief pilot returned on board; he reported that he had explored eighteen leagues, and that it was an island. *He brought with him a tin plate*, which in the lapse of time had fallen from a post to which it had been attached, and on which was cut the name of the captain, Dirck Hartog, as well as the names of the first and second merchants, and of the chief pilot of the vessel, *De Eendragt*, which arrived here in the year 1616, on the 25th October, and left for Bantam on the 27th of the same month."

Of course several plates may have been fixed up *in localities distant from each other*. It is not probable that two would be placed in the same locality. Then, how could the first commemorative tablet, fixed up two days before, contain the information said to have been found on another tablet two days later? Besides, there is something suggestive in Vlamingh's voyage to the coast of New Holland so soon after Dampier's visit and the publication of various voyages relating to Australia.* Were the Dutch afraid that the English would claim New Holland as having been discovered by them?

(*Footnote. An Account of Several Late Voyages and Discoveries to the South and North, towards the Straits of Magellan, South Seas, the Vast Tracts of Land beyond Hollandia Nova, etc. By Sir John Narborough, etc.; was published in 1694, the year before Vlamingh's expedition was first mooted.)

The avowed object of Vlamingh's expedition was to search for the *Ridderschap Van Hollandt*, lost between the Cape of Good Hope and Batavia in 1685. This searching for a ship and survivors, lost eleven years before, looks very much like an excuse for the furtherance of some other object; one other object of the expedition being apparently the fixing up of claims of discovery. The authenticity of one of these claims--the one founded on Dirck Hartog's discovery in 1616--was, according to the Dutch account, only obtained a couple of days after the erection of one of their memorials.

The authenticity however of Dirck Hartog's discovery would be perhaps better established from a manuscript chart by Eessel Gerrits, of Amsterdam, 1627, if it were to be found. According to Flinders* it is referred to by Dalrymple in his collection concerning Papua, note page 6. Major also mentions this reference in Dalrymple's work, but quoting Flinders, we believe. We have neither seen Dalrymple's collection concerning Papua nor Eessel Gerrit's manuscript chart, or even a copy of it.

(*Footnote. Flinders, Introduction page xlix.)

Vlamingh's replica of Dirck Hartog's or Hatich's plate must be lying perdu in some corner of the French *Institut*. It must have been deposited there by Freycinet. The other day in the Sydney Free Library we had occasion to go once more into this matter more thoroughly, as that institution now possesses Freycinet's magnificent work, Vlamingh's narrative in Dutch, and Rienzi's compilations. Referring to the plate, and to the chances of its being lost for ever if he did not take it away, Freycinet says, very clearly*:

(*Footnote. Freycinet volume 1 page 449. Voyage autour du monde, etc.)

Je la destinais en consequence au cabinet de l'Academie Royale des inscriptions et belles-lettres de l'Institut de France, et *j'ai eu l'honneur d'en faire la remise ainsi que le constate le proces-verbal de cete illustre societe, du 23 Mars 1821.*

But the plate we should like to see when found, if it is ever to be found, indeed if it ever existed, is the one said to have been taken away by Vlamingh and entrusted to their Nobilities the Gentlemen Seventeen of Batavia.

What Major said in 1859 with reference to a considerable number of Dutch voyages still remains true with regard to Dirck Hartog's. A document "immediately" describing it has not yet been found.

CHAPTER 43. A.D. 1617 TO 1623.

OTHER DUTCH DISCOVERIES ON THE WESTERN COAST OF AUSTRALIA AND SOUTH COAST OF NEW GUINEA. ABRAHAM GOOS' GLOBE OF 1621. THE DISCOVERY OF THE LAND OF THE LEEUWIN. THE VOYAGE OF THE PERA AND ARNHEM TO THE GULF OF CARPENTARIA.

According to the *Instructions* the next voyage in chronological order "was undertaken with a yacht in the year 1617, by order of the *Fiscael d' Edel*, with little success, of which adventures and discoveries, through the loss of their journals and remarks, nothing certain is to be found."

If we make use of the above scanty information and apply it to the examination of old Dutch charts we shall find that a discovery mentioning the name *Edel* was made on the western coast of the southern continent, somewhere between 31 and 33 degrees of south latitude, i.e. between Wedge and Rottenest Island of modern charts. That discovery is recorded on the oldest Dutch chart we have come across, a map of the assigned date of 1630, by the legend, *I. de Edels Landt det. 1619*. The date 1619, as will be noticed, does not agree with the one given in the Instructions, but there may be a *lapsus* somewhere, or bad reading may account for the date of either the chart or the Instructions.

The next visit to the west coast was made in the year 1618, but no corroborative evidence of any discovery made that year can be found on old Dutch charts.

The Dutch recital mentions next a voyage to the west coast made in 1619. The only discovery made on the west coast of the Great South Land in 1619 is, according to old Dutch charts, the discovery already referred to, made "by order of the Fiscael d' Edel." The Instructions mention also another discovery made that year but on the south coast of New Guinea. The statement runs thus: "A ship named *'t wapen van Amsterdam* (the Arms of Amsterdam) destined to Banda, drove past that place and touched at the south coast of Nova Guinea, where some of the crew were murdered by the savage inhabitants, wherefore they acquired no certain knowledge of the country."

ABRAHAM GOOS' GLOBE, 1621.

We must now interrupt the course of Dutch recital of voyages of discovery in order to consider a Dutch globe which was published at Amsterdam in 1621, and is therefore in its proper chronological order here.

The globe we refer to is Abraham Goos', published by Joh. Jannssonius. We might expect to find marked on a globe of that period some of the Dutch discoveries described in the Instructions. Dirck Hartog's discovery, made in the year 1616, should at least be recorded. Such however is not the case, although a Latin legend on the globe in question indicates that *all the latest discoveries made have been set down. Hac jterata delineatjone Globi hydrographica, et geographica, non tantum ea quae a majoribus, sed et omnia jam noviter detecta, singulariquz studio collecta, benevolis inspectoribus liberali manu offeruntur, valete et frujmini.* ANNO 1621.

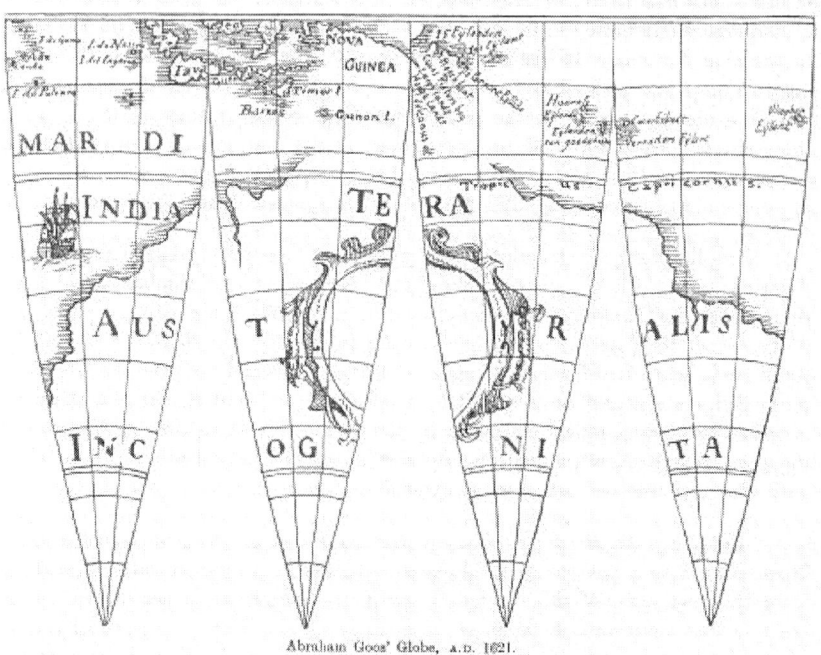

Abraham Goos' Globe, A.D. 1621.

Abraham Goos' globe shows a southern continent, occupying the position of Australia, called TERA AUSTRALIS INCOGNITA, without the slightest intimation of any Dutch discovery whatsoever; it is in fact nothing else but the Terra Australis that is represented there, discovered and charted before the arrival of the Dutch in Australasian regions. Nova Guinea nevertheless, detached from the Terra Australis Incognita, bears the Dutch nomenclature that obtained after Schouten and Lemaire's expedition of 1616.

Continuing now the Dutch recital we arrive at the discovery made in the year 1622. The Dutch lay claim to the discovery in that year of *'t Landt van de Leeuwin*, and would have us believe, according to the inscriptions on their charts, that that part of the south-west coast of Australia, so clearly marked on Jean Roze's chart of Portuguese origin dating as far back as 1542, was discovered by one of their captains in the ship *Leeuwin*. It was a re-discovery no doubt, and is only suggested in the Instructions; but as we have said an inscription on all old Dutch charts clearly records a discovery made in the year 1622. One strange feature of the oldest of these charts--which we shall consider further on--is that it still preserved among comparatively modern Dutch inscriptions the older half Portuguese and half Spanish appellation for Australia, i.e. TERRA DEL ZUR, Great Land of the South.

According to the Instructions the next voyage "was undertaken in the month of January 1623, with the yachts *Pera* and *Arnhem*, out of Amboina, under the command of Jan Carstens, with orders to make a nearer friendship with the inhabitants of the islands Key, Arou, and Tenimber, and better to discover Nova Guinea and the south lands, when an alliance was made with the said islands and the south coast of Nova Guinees nearer discovered. The skipper, with eight of the crew of the yacht *Arnhem*, was treacherously murdered by the inhabitants; and, after a discovery of the great islands Arnhem and the Speriet [by an untimely separation], this yacht with very little success came back to Amboina.

"But the yacht *Pera*, persisting in the voyage, sailed along the south coast of Nova Guinea to a flat cove on this coast, situated in 10 degrees south latitude, and ran along the west coast of this land to Cape Keer-Weer, from thence discovered the coast farther southward so far as 17 degrees south to Staten River (from this place what more of the land could be discerned seemed to stretch westward), and from thence returned to Amboina. In this discovery were found everywhere shallow water and barren coast, islands altogether thinly peopled by divers cruel, poor, and brutal nations, and of very little use to the company. The journal of this voyage is not now to be found; but the discovered countries may be seen in the maps which were made of them."

In the above description the passage "and after a discovery of the great islands Arnhem and Speriet," deserves notice. The conclusion one naturally comes to in reading that passage is that one of those islands was named after the yacht *Arnhem*; as to Speriet no reason is given for giving that name to the other island said to have been discovered. Speriet is written differently on Dutch charts, and in the translation of the Instructions published by Alex. Dalrymple it is given as Spult and Speult. Speriet is the orthography used in Swart's black letter copy from the original manuscript document once in the possession of the Van Keulen's of Amsterdam. It does not appear to be a *lapsus* because it is repeated in the 14th paragraph of the Instructions, where mention is made of the Sperietrivier.

We have contended elsewhere that the word Speult and Spult, to be found on Dutch charts in the locality of Torres Straits, were words corrupted from the Spanish words Spiritu Santo, written Spu St., in its abbreviated form.

The Dutch contend that Spult, or Speult, is the name of a Dutch official who resided at the Spice Islands for some time.

There certainly was a governor of that name who rendered himself notorious in the Spice Islands by destroying all the clove trees the produce of which the Dutch could not monopolise; but we do not see that the fact of there being a governor named Speult proves that it was his name that was first applied to the discovery made in the Gulf of Carpentaria. If however Governor Speult sent out the expedition that gave rise to his name being applied to the localities where it is to be found (which remains to be proved), how is it that his name is spelt Speriet in the most authentic printed Dutch document that we possess? Tasman's original manuscript chart, now in the possession of Prince Roland Bonaparte, might throw some light on the subject. The copy we possess of that document does not; for in it those words are not recorded, although the nomenclature in the Gulf of Carpentaria is in other respects the most extensive we know of in print.

As to the other word, Arnhem, there is apparently greater likelihood that Arnhem River and Arnhem Land were named after the second yacht of the expedition than there is with regard to Speult River and Island being named after the Dutch governor of Amboina. One fact however renders caution necessary and militates against a rash conclusion on the subject, and that is that an island in older charts than the Dutch ones occupies the site of the island called Arnhem Island and bears the name Arnim. We refer to the Henry II mappamundi of 1546, in which the Arouw Islands are set down in that locality under the name Arnim.

CHAPTER 44. A.D. 1624 TO 1629.

AN ENGLISH PETITION TO KING JAMES THE FIRST FOR THE RIGHT TO COLONIZE THE TERRA AUSTRALIS. DISCOVERY OF THE SOUTH COAST OF AUSTRALIA, 1627. THE VIANEN ON THE NORTH-WEST COAST IN 1628. THE WRECK OF THE BATAVIA IN 1629.

A close rivalry existed at this time between the Dutch and the English with regard to the trade in the Spice Islands. In 1621 a treaty between these two nations was signed. It prevented war for a time, but did not put an end to the disputes or animosities of the rival English and Dutch companies which culminated in the well-known massacre of the English at Amboina in 1622. The English notwithstanding continued to send out ships to the Australasian regions, and in 1624 a petition for the "privilege of erecting colonies" in Terra Australis was presented to King James the First by Sir William Courteen. We reprint here from E.A. Petherick's publication The Torch this interesting document, concerning which Mr. Petherick remarks*: "Sir James Lancaster, who had made voyages to the East Indies, frequently proposed to have a ship sent through the Strait of Magellan to the Solomon Islands, but without result. James the First was not favourable to colonies.

(*Footnote. The Torch, March 1888 page 89.)

"In the last year of his reign however an eminent London merchant-- probably the most enterprising English merchant of his time--Sir William Courteen, desiring to extend his trade to the *Terra Australis*, petitioned the king for the privilege of erecting colonies therein. Sir William, who was joint owner of more than twenty ships of burden, employing four or five thousand seamen, already carried on an extensive trade on his own account to Portugal, Spain, Guinea, and the

West Indies. The following is a copy of his petition, now printed for the first time:

"To the King's most Excellent Matie. The humble peticon of Sr William Courten, knt, Most humbly showeth unto Your Matie.:

That all the lands in ye South parts of ye world called Terra Australis, incognita, extending Eastwards and Westwards from ye Straights of Le Maire, together with all ye adjacente Islands, etc., are yet undiscovered, or, being discovered, are not yet traded unto by any of your Maties subjects. And your petitioner being very willing, att his owne charges, which wil be very greate, to endeavour ye discovery thereof and settle collonies and a plantation there which he hopeth will tend to ye glory of God, ye reducing of Infidells to Christianity, ye honour of your Matie, ye inlargemt of your Mat's Territories and Dominions, ye increase of your Maties' customes & revenue, & ye Navigation and imployment of your Maties' subjects.

"Your petr therefore humbly desireth yr Matie to bee pleased to grante to him, his heires and assignes, all ye said lands, islands, and Territories, with power to discover ye same, to erecte Colonies & a plantation there, and Courts of Justice, officers and Ministers for ye setling and governinge of ye said Colonies and plantations and those which are or shall inhabit or be there, and power to administer justice and to execute Marshall law by land and sea, and for your petr and those whom hee shall imploy to defend themselves and offend such others as shall oppugne or hinder the said discovery or plantation of your petr's shippes in going or returning; and with such other grantes and landes and privileges as in cases of discovery or setlinge of Colonies or plantations is usuall or shall be fitt. And to directe your Matie's Attorney generall to prepare a grante accordingly fitt for your Matie's Royal Signature. And your petr (as in duty bound) shall ever pray for your Matie's long and happie raigne."

Mr. Petherick adds the following: "Having lent large sums of money to the King, Sir William Courteen had some claim upon His Majesty's consideration. But it does not appear that '*All ye said islands and territories*' were granted to him. He appears to have been satisfied with a bad title to the island of Barbadoes, where he sent (1626) fifty settlers, who built a fort (1627), and remained there till it was taken from them (1628). He then sent eighty men to the island and re-took it in the name of the

Earl of Pembroke. Sir William died in 1666. His son's claim to the title was not deemed a good one, and was disallowed in 1660."

DISCOVERY OF THE SOUTH COAST OF AUSTRALIA, 1627.

A portion of the south coast of Australia is shown for the first time on old Dutch charts, where it appears under the name of *'t Landt van P[ieter] Nuyts*. The Dutch inscription further indicates that the discovery was made in the *Gulde Zeepaert* (the Golden Sea-horse), and the date varies according to the chart consulted. In the Mar di India chart it is 26 January 1627. In Pieter Goos' chart it is 26 January 1625. In Tasman's chart, published in Amsterdam in 1859, the legend reads as follows:

't Landt van p. Nuys opgedean met gulden Zeepert van middelburch. Ano. 1627 den 26 Februaris.

The passage in the Instructions refers to this discovery in the following terms:

"...but in the interim, in the year 1627, the south coast of the great south land was accidentally discovered by the ship *'t Gulde Zeepaert* (comende uit 't Patria) for the space of 250 miles." The date 1625, on P. Goos' chart, must be wrong, for the announcement of the arrival of the *Golden Seahorse* at Batavia on the 10th of April 1627 is to be found, says P.A. Leupe,* in the daily register of that town amongst the entries made from January to September 1627. We gather also from that author that the skipper's name was *Franchois Thysz*, and that *Pieter Nuyts* of the Counsel of Seventeen was on board, with a despatch for the Counsel of India: Aan boord van dit schip bevond zich PIETER NUYTS, door de Vergadering van Zeventienen aanges teld tot Raad Extraordinair van *Indie*.

(*Footnote. De Reizen der Nederlanders naar het Zuitland of Nieuw-Holland in de 17de en 18de eeuw, door P.A. Leupe. In the Verhandelingen volume 27 page 149 Anno 1867.)

The names of the islands on the south coast of Australia, I. St. Peter (or Pieter), and I. St. Francoys, appear to have been given in commemoration of the Christian names of the skipper, Franchois Thysz, and Peter Nuyts.

THE VIANEN ON THE NORTH-WEST COAST IN 1628.

"And again, accidentally," says the Instructions, "in the year following, 1628, on the north side, in the latitude of 21 degrees south, by the ship *Vianen*, homeward bound from India; when they coasted about 50 miles without gaining any particular knowledge of this great country, only observing a foul and barren shore, green fields, and very wild, black, barbarous inhabitants."

The involuntary visit of the *Vianen* to the north-west coast of Australia is recorded on Dutch charts, with slight variation, by the following inscription: G.F. de Witts Landt ontdeckt 1628. It appears that the commander's name was *Gerrit Fredericsz De Witt*,* which accounts for the initials and name found on Dutch charts. The skipper was Cornelis Schouten--De Schipper was Cornel is Sthouten, daar hij op den 13 Januarij 1628 het cognossement van de lading teekent.

(*Footnote. See Verhandelingen etc. vol 27 page 151.)

In the second part of the Introduction to the Voyages of the Dutch East India Company, volume 1 page 51, a short account is given of the wreck of the *Vianen*, which, it is stated, had sailed from Batavia in January 1628, in the hopes of passing the Straits of Bali in the good season, but not having succeeded she was driven out of her course to the shores of the Austral lands of the unknown Magellanica. There it was found necessary to jettison a quantity of precious merchandise, and at last the ship was set afloat again, not without great risk.

THE WRECK OF THE BATAVIA, IN 1629.

In 1629, in the month of June, the *Batavia*, commanded by Captain Francis Pelsart, on his passage from Holland to Java, was separated in a storm from the fleet with which he was sailing and driven on the reef known as Houtman's Abrolhos (western coast of Australia). The coast was found to be very rocky and full of shoals. They resolved however to run the risk of landing, as the ship was breaking up. They therefore exerted themselves to get bread and other provisions on deck, but did not take the same care of the water. On the first day, which was the 5th of June, they landed one hundred and eighty persons, twenty barrels of bread, and some small casks of water. Subsequently several parties were landed on various islands, where they expected to find water; but no water could be found. The captain, with a few of the crew, resolved to go in a small boat in search of water. They explored the coast of the mainland for several days without success. The wind was blowing from the south-east, and they discovered that the current was carrying them north, whereupon the captain resolved to steer for Java. Having arrived there safely he sought for help, and returned to the Abrolhos in the *Sardam* to save the remainder of his shipwrecked passengers and crew.

During his absence a shameful conspiracy had been set on foot, and he was obliged to execute some of the ringleaders and maroon others on the mainland before his return to Java with the remnant of his charge.

For further particulars of this event we refer our readers to R.H. Major's Early Voyages to Australia, where a full account of The Voyage and Shipwreck of Captain Francis Pelsart, in the *Batavia*, on the coast of New Holland, and his succeeding Adventures, will be found.

Shortly after the wreck of the Batavia another Dutch ship was near coming to grief in the same locality. She belonged to Admiral *Jacques Specx's* fleet that set sail a little more than a month after the fleet of eleven vessels to which the *Batavia* belonged.

On the 19th of August 1629, says Rechteren,* one of the passengers, we ran close to the South Land, or Land of Concord (Eendraght Landt), where we found bottom in 40 fathoms, and we ran north.

(*Footnote. Voiages de la Compagnie. Tom. ix. page 131.)

It was on this coast, continues Rechteren, that the ship *Batavia* was lost, etc. La nuit du 17 (sic. for 19) nous fumes proche de la Terre du Sud, ou de la Terre de Concorde, ou nous trouvames fond sur 40 brasses & nous courumes la bande du Nord. C'etoit sur cette cote que le vaisseau *Batavia* s'etoit perdu. J'ai parle moi meme, etant a Batavia au Pasteur qui y etoit, de qui la femme & les enfants furent egorgez par nos propres gens, a la reserve d'une fille que ces scelerats violerent; ce qui n'est qu'un echantillon des barbaries qu'ils commirent. Ce malheur arriva en cette maniere. Le *Batavia* etant echoue, les gens se sauverent dans des Isles ou il n'y avoit point d'eau douce. Le Maitre ayant offert d'aller avec la chaloupe en chercher au Continent, prit la route de Batavia, & laissa tout son equipage dans ces Isles. La mesintelligence se mit entre eux: ils se separerent en diverses troupes. Ce qu'il y eut d'honnetes gens se joignirent ensemble, & les autres commirent toutes les mechancetez qu'il leur fut possible de commettre, & dont ils se purent aviser. Le Commis et ses adherans, apres avoir fait beaucoup de mal, se rendirent a Batavia, ou ils furent supliciez, sur les plaintes & les temoignages du reste de ceux qu'ils avoient outragez, qui s'y etoient aussi rendus.

CHAPTER 45. A.D. 1630 TO 1640.

A PRE-TASMANIAN MAP OF AUSTRALIA. DISCOVERIES IN THE GULF OF CARPENTARIA. HOEIUS' MAP, CIRCA 1640.

e acquired some time ago an engraved hand-coloured, curious old Dutch map of the Indian Ocean, in which a large portion of the Australian continent as said to be known to the Dutch prior to Tasman's first and second voyages is delineated. It belongs to a folio printed in black letter, apparently one of Blaeu's early atlases.

The pagination of the verso, which describes the Mar d'India, Oder Das Ost-Indische Meer, is 69 & 70. The paper bears no watermark and is gilt on all the edges. The size of the map is 1 foot 10 inches by 1 foot 6 inches. The title is Mar di India. This map bears no date, but various discoveries marked on the Australian continent enable one to fix the date approximately. For instance Peter Nuyt's discovery of the south coast of the Southern Land is recorded for the year 1627. De Witt's discovery is also marked, which brings the date of the map to the year 1628. The discoveries made in the year 1636, when "the coast of Arnhem, or Van Diemen's Land, in 11 degrees south latitude," and "the unknown island of Timor Laut," were discovered, are not charted.

The inference is that it dates from between 1629 and 1636. In 1631 Blaeu and Hortensius were sent by the Dutch to Florence to study under Galileo, who was at the time applying his discoveries in astronomy to practical purposes in navigation and geography. The probabilities are therefore in favour of the supposition that this map, if compiled by Blaeu, was designed before his departure for Florence with Hortensius. We are aware that maps of the same regions published in Blaeu's atlases were drawn at a much later period; they are however most of them totally different to this one, inasmuch as they show Tasman's discoveries made in the years 1642 and 1644.

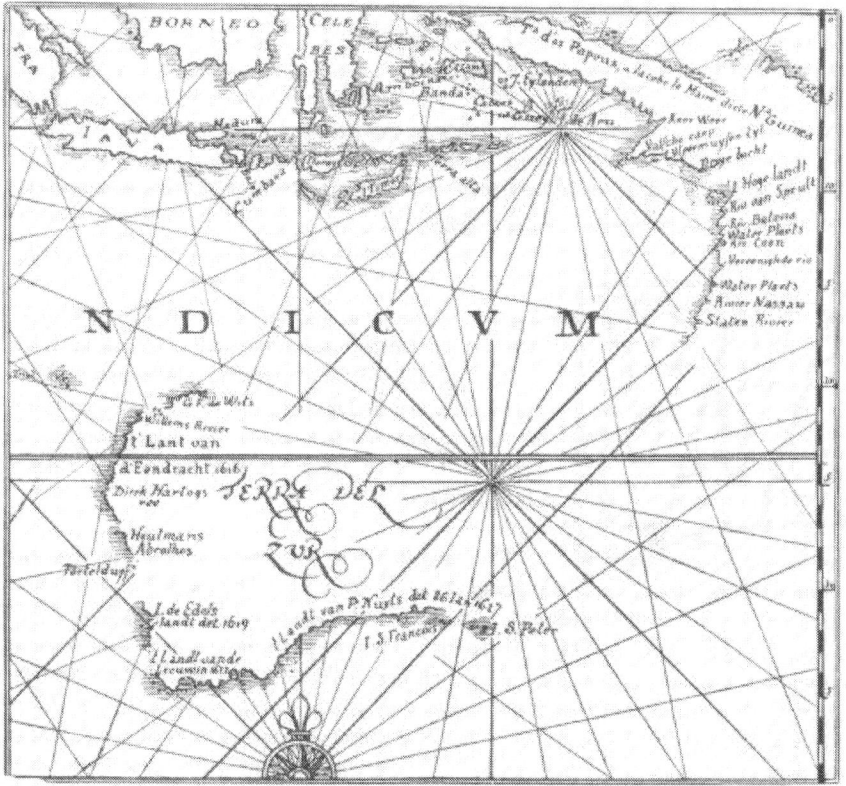

MAR DI INDIA MAP.

The name given to Australia is the most important feature of this map. It bears the half Portuguese and half Spanish name of TERRA DEL ZUR--the Land of the South. Originally this name must have been given either by the Portuguese or the Spanish. It is not at all likely that the Dutch would give such a name to Australia suggesting a discovery made by their rivals; and the only other way of explaining its presence is to consider it as the result of Portuguese or Spanish naming and as a remnant of an earlier and more extensive nomenclature.

DISCOVERIES IN THE GULF OF CARPENTARIA, 1636.

The next Dutch discoveries were made in the Gulf of Carpentaria, when the bottom of the gulf was visited and Arnhem Land discovered.

This was an expedition sent out from Banda in the year 1636, with Gerrit Thomasz Pool in command of the yachts *Amsterdam* and *Wesel*. They set sail in the month of April to discover the *East* and *South lands*; "when they first discovered the coast of Nova Guinea in 3 1/2 degrees south latitude, and coasted about 60 miles to the eastward to 5 degrees south, when the Commodore Pool, with three of the crew (by the barbarous inhabitants), was murdered, at the same place where the skipper of the yacht *Arnhem* was killed in the year 1623.

"Notwithstanding which the voyage was assiduously continued under the supercargo, Pieter Pietersz, and the islands Keij and Arouw visited. By very strong easterly winds they could not reach the west coast of Nova Guinea, but, shaping their course very near south, descried the coast of Arnhem, or Van Diemen's Land, in 11 degrees south latitude, and sailed along the coast for 30 miles without seeing any people, but many signs of smoke; when, turning towards the north, they visited the unknown islands of Timorland,* and the known islands of Tenimber, Kauwer, etc., but without ever being able to converse with the inhabitants, who were a very timid people; when, after three months' cruising, they returned in July to Banda, without (in this voyage) having done or discovered anything of consequence; which may be seen by the journals and maps."

(*Footnote. A corruption of Timor Laut.)

In reading Major's translation of the Instructions, and especially his Introduction (see Early Voyages to Australia page xcii.), it would appear that three yachts were sent instead of two, for, referring to Pool's expedition, he says: "Gerrit Tomaz Pool, or Poel, was sent in April of this year (1636) from Banda, with the yachts *Klyn, Amsterdam,* and *Wezel*."

In Tindall and Swart's account (see Verhandelingen en Berigten volume 4 page 73) the names of two yachts only are given, the *Amsterdam* and *Wesel*. We are inclined to believe that *Klyn* in Major's translation is derived from *klein* or *kleen*, which in Dutch means little, small, and that it qualified the word Amsterdam in the original text. We have come across two other original references to the above voyage. The first is in Valentyn's Beschryvinge van Banda. In that account, given also by Major, the *Amsterdam* and the *Weasel* are the only "two shallops" mentioned.

The second reference is to be found in the Voiages de la Campagnie, volume 7 page 377. It occurs in a passage where mention is made of the massacre of "Pierre Pauvelz" and two soldiers, who had come from Kei, beyond Banda, in a junk.

HOEIUS' MAP, *Circa* 1640.

We have already remarked that none of the early discoveries which the Dutch claim to have made on the shores of the Great South land were marked on a map published at Amsterdam in the year 1621. It appears strange that those early discoveries, and later ones, extending over a period of 30 years, from 1606 to 1636, should not be recorded on the map, the Australasian portion of which we reproduce here. Especially as this map, published for the first time in 1600, was republished at Amsterdam circa 1640, recording discoveries that had been made in other parts of the world since the year 1600.

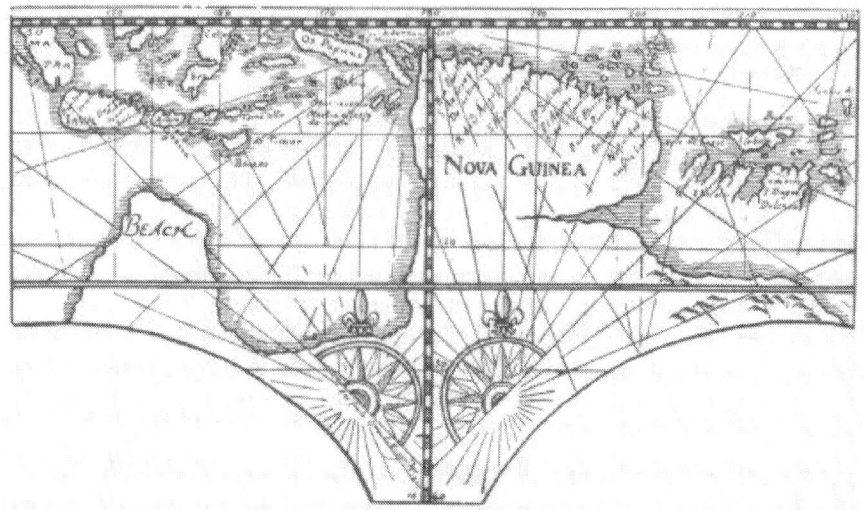

HOEIUS' MAP.

Franciscus Hoeius, apparently the engraver, and Hugo Allardt, the publisher, appear to be not only ignorant of Dutch discovery on Australian shores, but ignore also that part of Schouten and Lemaire's voyage and discoveries made along the north coast of New Guinea in 1616, although the *Fretum le Maire* between *Staten landt* and *Tierra del Fuego*, which belongs to the nomenclature of the same voyage, is set down. Instead of the Dutch nomenclature that obtained after Schouten and Lemaire's voyage the earlier nomenclature of Inigo Ortiz de Retez, Juan Gaetan, and Gaspar Rico, will be noticed on the north coast of New Guinea, and to the east of New Guinea Mendana's Solomon Islands.

What is probably a rough indication of some portion of the north-west coast of Australia receives on this map the name of BEACH, a fictitious name, to which we have already referred. There appears to be an indication of the Gulf of Carpentaria, and the separation between New Guinea and York Peninsula is also indicated, although not very apparently, owing to the scales of latitude which, in the original, form the margin of the map.

In joining, as we have done, the eastern margin with the western, NOVA GUINEA does not show the separation from Australia that one is led to expect to see from the indication on the side of the Gulf of Carpentaria. The eastern coast of Australia is very roughly indicated, but is not connected in the south with the Antarctic continent.

CHAPTER 46. A.D. 1642 TO 1658.

TASMAN'S FIRST VOYAGE ROUND ABOUT AUSTRALIA.
TASMAN'S SECOND VOYAGE ALONG THE NORTHERN AND NORTH-WESTERN COASTS OF AUSTRALIA.
WRECK OF THE GOLDEN DRAGON.

In the month of August of the year 1642 Anthonie Van Diemen, the Governor-General of the Dutch East Indies and the council of the East India Company, availing themselves of the noted ability of Abel Jansz Tasman, ordered a more extensive exploration of the South Land, t' Zuytland, than had hitherto been attempted. Their intention was principally to find out the extent of the Great South Continent, and ascertain whether a passage to the south of it led into the South Sea.

Two ships were equipped for the voyage, the *Heemskerk* and the *Zeehaen*. Besides Tasman, as commander of the expedition, there went, as pilot major, Fransz Jacobsz *alias* Vissher, and the skippers Yde Tjerksen and Gerrit Jansz. They set sail for Mauritius. In October they left Mauritius, and, steering south, reached the latitude of 54 degrees; they then steered east by north, with the intention of gradually gaining north until the Solomon Islands should be reached.

In this course they made the south coast of a land which they believed formed part of the Great South Land.

They named it Anthonie Van Diemen's Land. Having examined the southern shores of this land they continued their course in a north-easterly direction, and discovered another important land, which they called New Zealand. Then, steering north, they visited several islands of the Pacific, and returned to Java by the north of New Guinea. In the course of this extensive voyage of circumnavigation Australia was not touched upon.

TASMAN'S SECOND VOYAGE.

Tasman's second voyage was undertaken in the beginning of the year 1644. Its main object was to ascertain whether New Guinea and new Van Diemen's Land (Tasmania) were connected with the South Land (Australia) or not. Three ships were equipped for the expedition, the *Limmen*, the *Zeemeuw*, and the *Brack*. They sailed into the Gulf of Carpentaria with the intention of reaching new Van Diemen's Land; but, failing to find the strait through which Torres had passed in 1606 and which now bears his name, they steered along the northern and north-western coasts of Australia and returned to Java. The track which Tasman followed in his two voyages will be found traced in Captain T. Bowrey's map, which we give here (Illustration 7).

Captain Bowrey's map bears no date, but was probably made in 1687, says Major, from whose work (Early Voyages to Australia) we take it. Since Major published that map Tasman's original chart has been found, and Tasman's route is traced on it in a similar manner, showing that our copy is correct.

No new discoveries of any importance were made, strictly speaking, in Tasman's second voyage; nevertheless after 1644, when the first maps in which his track is laid down made their appearance, the outline of this continent assumed for the first time a relatively true position and a more accurate delineation of form. Whether, between the time of Tasman's return (which, according to the Instructions, was fixed for July 1644), and the publication of the first map, new expeditions were made it would be difficult to say. None are spoken of, and Dutch discoveries may be said to have ended with Tasman's second voyage and the death of A. Van Diemen, which happened on the 19th of April 1645.

About this time the Dutch, in addition to calling Australia *'t Groot Zuidlandt*, the Great South Land, which was only the translation of the previous name, Terra Australis and Terra del Zur, began calling it Nova Hollandia and Nieuw Holland, a name transferred by them to the southern continent from the icy regions they had explored in the Arctic Seas when attempting to reach India and the Spice Islands by a north-east passage.

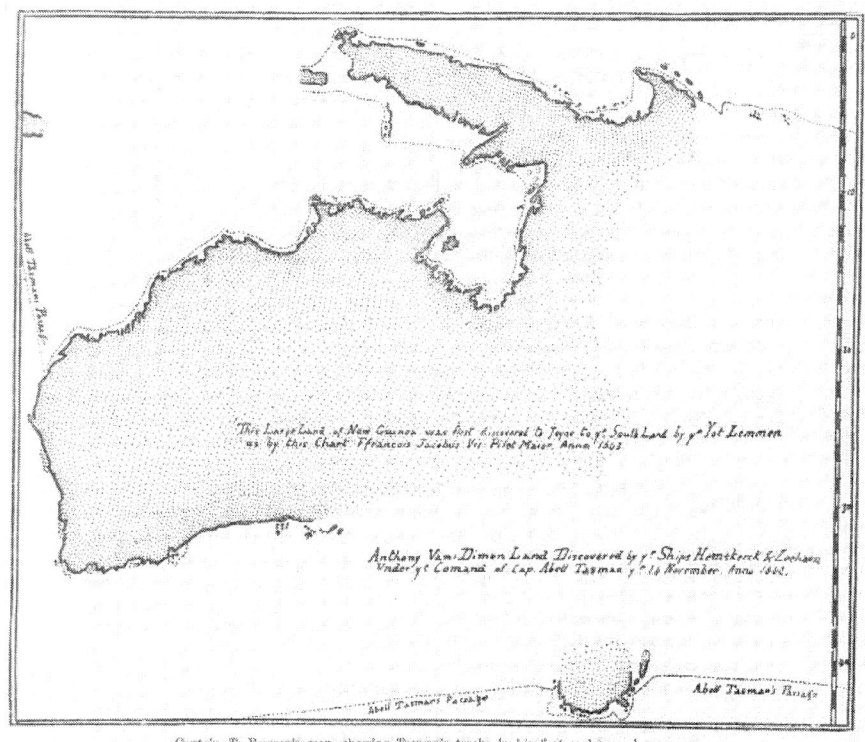

Captain T. Bowrey's map, showing Tasman's tracks in his first and second voyages. Date circa 1687.

The maritime power of the Dutch nation was now reaching its climax. Eight years after Tasman's last voyage, in 1652, Holland was the most powerful maritime state in Europe. Her preponderance however was soon to give way to that of England. In 1653 Van Tromp's fleet was beaten by Blake's. Another and more decisive battle, in which Monk had the command and in which Van Tromp was killed, dealt a death blow to the supremacy of the Netherlands. After this the Dutch seem to have lost all interest in connection with Australian discovery, and the occasions on which they sighted this continent seem to have been mostly when their ships were driven out of their course by storms or contrary winds and currents.

In 1656 the ship *Vergulde Draeck** (Golden Dragon) was wrecked on the same coast as Pelsart in 1629, but a little further south. She had sailed on the 4th of October from Holland, on her way to the East Indies, with a rich cargo, including 78,600 guilders in cash, in eight boxes; she was wrecked very suddenly on the 28th of April, at night, on a reef stretching out to sea about one mile and a half, latitude 30 2/3 degrees.

(*Footnote. In the Voyages of Gautier Shouten, published at Amsterdam in 1708 duod. volume 1 page 41 et seq., there is a curious account of the wreck of the *Vergulde Draeck*. P.P. King, in his narrative of a survey of the inter-tropical and western coasts of Australia, gives this account in French, page xviii. volume 1.

Of one hundred and ninety-three souls only seventy-five, amongst whom were the skipper, Pieter Aberts, and the under-steersman, reached the shore alive. The news was brought to Batavia on the 7th of June by one of the ship's boats, with the above-mentioned steersman and six sailors. The General and Council resolved to get ready without delay the *Witte Valck* (White Falcon). She was ordered to join company with the yacht *Goede Hoop* (Good Hope), then cruising in the Straits of Sunda, and to proceed with her towards the coast of the South Land. Apart from the rescue work they were sent to perform they were ordered to explore the coast with particular attention near the part where the ship had been wrecked, and to lay it down on a map.

These two vessels returned without having succeeded in their object, the *White Falcon* on the 14th of September, and the yacht *Good Hope* a month afterwards, having been forced by a severe storm to part company on the 18th of July, on their way south. According to the captain's journals lying at Batavia they had reached the coast just in the winter time, during which season the sea is so boisterous there that an approach to the coast is a matter of extreme danger.

Thus, as these documents inform us, they were compelled, after experiencing great dangers and exhausting every effort, to put off from the coast and return to Batavia, leaving behind them eleven men of the yacht *Good Hope*--three having wandered too far into the bush eight others were sent in search of them, but not one of the number returned. As the boat in which they had rowed to land was found dashed to pieces on the shore the whole number most probably came to an untimely end. According to the reports which were made some men or some signs of the wreck of the *Golden Dragon* had been noticed, although the *Good Hope*, which had been at the place when the ship was supposed to have been wrecked, gave a different statement.

Subsequently the commander at the Cape of Good Hope, according to instructions sent to him, gave orders in the year 1657 to the fly-boat *Vinck*, bound thence to Batavia, to touch *en passant* at the same place where the above-mentioned disaster had occurred, that search might be made for the unfortunate men. But his vessel, also having arrived at the unfavourable season, found no means of landing either with fly-boat or boat so as to make a proper search. Having sighted land in 29 degrees 7 minutes south latitude, on the 8th of June 1657, they continued to coast along it until the 12th, when they stood out towards Batavia, where they arrived on the 27th.

Although the rescue of these men seemed hopeless the General and Council resolved to despatch, for a third time, two galliots, the *Waeckende Boey* and *Emeloort*, the former with a crew of forty, the latter with twenty-five men, provisioned for six months. They set sail from Batavia on the 1st of January 1658. They had at last taken due consideration of the necessity of approaching these inhospitable shores in the proper season of the year. On the 19th of April they returned to Batavia, having each of them separately, after parting company by the way, sailed backwards and forwards again and again, and landed parties at several points along the coast. They had also continually fired signal guns night and day, without however discovering either any Dutchman or the wreck of the vessel. The only things seen were some few planks and blocks, with a piece of a mast, a taffrail, fragments of barrels, and other objects scattered here and there along the coast and supposed to be remnants of the wreck. The crew of the *Emeloort* also saw, at different points, five black men of extremely tall stature, without however daring to land there. Thus this expedition also failed in its object. On their return they left the cliff Tortelduyf on the starboard side. On the 14th of April they made for the west point of Java, and there fell in again with the *Waeckende Boey*, which had lost its boat and schuyt and fourteen men, and had got some timber from the *Golden Dragon*, at 31 degrees 15 minutes south latitude, without having perceived anything else. The *Waeckende Boey* had on March 31 passed at five miles' distance from Dirck Hartog's Reede. The following is a description of the west coast of Australia by Captain Volkersen of the *Waeckende Boey*:

"The south land has on its coasts downs covered with grass and sand so deep that in walking one's foot is buried ankle deep, and leaves great traces behind it. At about a league from the shore there runs a reef of rock, on which here and there the sea is seen to break with great force. In some places there is a depth of from one, one and a half, to two fathoms, so that a boat can pass, after which the depth becomes greater up to the shore; but it is everywhere a dangerous coral bottom, on which it is difficult to find holding for an anchor. There is only one spot, about nine leagues to the north of the island, and where these rocks are joined by a reef that shelter is afforded for a boat, and there one can effect a landing, but the ground is everywhere rocky. Further from the coast there is a raised ground, tolerably level, but of dry and barren aspect, except near the island, where there is some foliage. In nearly 32 degrees south latitude there is a large island* nearly three leagues from the continent, with some rather high mountains, covered with wood and thickets which render it difficult to pass across.

(*Footnote. Named afterwards Rottnest (Rat's Nest) Island.)

It is dangerous to land there on account of the reefs of rock along the coast; and moreover one sees many rocks between the continent and this island, and also a smaller island somewhat to the south. This large island, to which I have not chosen to give a name myself, thinking it right to leave the choice of name to the Governor-General, may be seen from the sea at seven or eight leagues distance on a clear day. I presume that both fresh water and wood will be found there in abundance, though not without considerable trouble."*

(*Footnote. Translated from a Dutch manuscript in the Royal Archives at the Hague. See Major's Early Voyages to Australia page 89.)

CHAPTER 47. A.D. 1660 TO 1669.

P. GOOS' MAP OF HOLLANDIA NOVA, CIRCA 1660 TO 1669.

The map of Hollandia Nova by P. Goos, which we reproduce here (Illustration 34), is a reduced copy of an engraved map published at Amsterdam between the years 1660 and 1669. It bears no date, but belongs to one of the numerous atlases published in Holland during the above-mentioned period.

In it Tasman's discoveries are duly recorded, and the name *Hollandia Nova*, written across the Australian continent, is followed by the legend *detecta 1644*, which is the date of Tasman's second voyage. This map differs slightly from the engraved copy of Tasman's original manuscript chart published in 1859 by G. Hulst Van Keulen, of Amsterdam: Owing no doubt to its smaller size, the nomenclature is less complete. The delineation of the discovered portions of coastline are similar. Unlike Goos' map the map published by G. Hulst Van Keulen shows a connection, albeit fictitious, of the south coast of Australia with the west coast of Tasmania, and the east coast of Tasmania is connected with a fictitious east coast of Australia running north beyond New Guinea, then connecting with New Ireland and New Britain, those islands being linked in the same erroneous way with New Guinea and Australia.

The strange consequence of this combination is that New Guinea is deprived of its name. Australia is called the COMPAGNIS NIEV NEDERLANDT, and the following legend is placed immediately under that title: *Int osten het groote landt van nouo guinea met het erste bekende Zuijt lant weesende een landt end altesaemen aen malkanderen vast als by deese gestippelde passagie by d'Jachten Limmen. Zeehmeeuw end het quel d' bracq-kan worden. Ano 1644.*

In P. Goos' map New Guinea bears the legend, *le Maire dicta Nova Guinea*, and the name for Australia is HOLLANDIA NOVA; *detecta 1644.*

The other comparative nomenclature of these maps, as far as Australia and Tasmania are concerned, is as follows :—

NORTHERN COASTS.

TASMAN'S MAP.	P. GOOS' MAP.	TASMAN'S MAP.	P. GOOS' MAP.
....	t' Hooge landt	survers revier	....
Waeter plaets	R. Van Spult	Laegh lant	....
Staeten revier	R. Batavia	cabo van diemens	C. Van Diemen
Prince revier	Water plaets	demmers revier	....
Revier met bosch	....	Wittes revier	....
Revier carpantier	....	revier croock	....
Vliege bay	....	Van alphen's revier	R. Van Alphen
revier coen	R. Coen	abeltasman revier	Abel Tasmans Riv.
Visschrs revier	....	waeter plaes	....
cap Keerweer	....	cabo van dorlms	C. Vander Lim.
laegh lant	....	cabo demarie	C. Maire.
Vereenigde revier	Vereenichde R.	limmens bocht	Limmens bocht
en water plaets	Water plaets	Laegh lant	....
revier nassaou	R. Nassau	arrnhems lant	Arnhems Landt
rivier pera	Staten R.	crocodils Eylant	Cocodrils Eyl.
revier arnhem	....	moijlick boch	....
Staten revier tot	....	Vuijlle hoeck	Vuyle hoeck
Hier toe hebbe dersonig	....	Laegh Lant	....
en de Keergewogt	....	Maria lant	....
Van diemen's revier	Van Diemens R.	Van Diemen's bay	Baya van Diemen
van der lins revier	....	Witte Waeter	....
revier caron	R. caron.	alhier laeghe bergen	....
revier maet skuykre	R. Maetsuycker	Van Diemens lant	Van Diemen's Landt

WESTERN COASTS.

G. F. de Witte-lant ondeck A^{no} 1628	G. F. de Wits Landt ontdeckt A° 1628	i. de. Edels lant bijseijlt A^{no} 1619	I. de Edels Landt ontdeckt A° 1619
Willems revier	Willems Riv.		Duyning Land baren met Lage Rurgte Gelyk Verdronke Boomen en Bosschagie*
't Lande van de Eendrachtondeck A^{no} 1616	t'Landt de Eendracht ontdeckt A° 1616		
dirck Hartogs Ree	Dirck Hartogs Ree		
Houtmans Albrogos	Houtmans Abrolhos	't Lant van de Leuwin	t' Landt van de Leeuwin
Tortel duijf	Tortelduyf	A^{no} 1622 Angedean	ontdeckt A° 1622

SOUTH COAST.

t' Landt van p. Nuys opgedean met gulden Zeepert van middelburch A^{no} 1627 den 26 Februaris	't Landt van P. Nuyts opgedaen met t' Gulde Zeepaert van Middelburch den 26 January, 1625	....	.... St. Pieter I. St. Fransoys

* A legend which evidently belongs to a period posterior to Tasman's second voyage. It is, no doubt, extracted from some notes on a chart by Captain Volkersen of the *Waeckende Boey*, who was in those parts in 1658.

The following is the nomenclature of Tasmania:—

Anthonio van diemens landt	Anthoni van Diemens Landt	Schouten Eylant	Schouten E
		maria Eylant	Marias Eyl.
dit is beseylt ende on-			Zuyd Caep
deckt met de schepen		Tasman Eylant	Tasman's E
Hemskerck ende			Storm Bay
Zeehaen onder com-		borel Eylant	Boereels Ey
mando van de E. abel		verthont als en	Pedra bran
tasman, in de yare A^no		plompen toren	
1642, de 24 novambre		maet suyckers Eylant	Wits Eyl.
		Suwers Eylant	Maet Suyck
Vanderlins Eylant	Vander lins Eyl.	Witte Eylant	Sweers Eyla

New Zealand, which is not charted in our copy of P. Goos' map, is name LANDT" in Tasman's map; then follows a legend relating to its discovery, thus *beseylt ende ondeckt met schepen hemskerck ende Zeehaen onder het comma E. abel Tasman. In de yare A^no 1642 de 13 desembre."*

The few names inscribed along the sea coast are the following:—

't dry Koningen Eylant   *abel tasman Reede*
cabo maria van diemens   *Steilhogh*
cabo pieter borels   *clyppen hoeck*
Zeehaen boecht

It will be noticed that P. Goos' map represents the western shores of Cape York Peninsula as a separate land from Australia and New Guinea, tinted in yellow, and bearing the name CARPENTARIA.

Peter Goos' Map of Hollandia Nova, Circa 1660 TO 1669.

The discoveries supposed to have been made during the government of Speult in the Spice Islands, and bearing his name on some charts, are not recorded in Tasman's chart, neither do we notice the Portuguese or Spanish inscription *Pedra branca* which occurs in P. Goos' map, and is written also *Piedra blanca* in other maps.

It is difficult to explain the presence of these words on maps supposed to be copies of Tasman's original chart. Other words, evidently of Portuguese or Spanish origin, appear also even on Tasman's chart in combination with his nomenclature. These names suggest an earlier discovery and the possession by the Dutch of maps relating to those discoveries.

Explorers and navigators who make discoveries give, as a rule, the reasons for naming the various places they discover. Tasman's journal makes no exception to this rule, and, while he mentions Pedra branca as resembling another *Pedra Branca* on the coast of *China*, he does not say that he named those rocks off the south coast of Tasmania.

CHAPTER 48. A.D. 1688 TO 1700.

THE DAWN OF THE ENGLISH PERIOD. W. DAMPIER'S FIRST VOYAGE TO NEW HOLLAND. W. DE VLAMINGH'S VOYAGE. W. DAMPIER'S SECOND VOYAGE.

The dawn of the English period of dominion in Australasia was heralded by the arrival of W. Dampier thirty years after the last recorded Dutch voyage, and precisely one hundred years before the arrival of our first English Governor.*

(*Footnote. Phillip sighted land on the 3rd of January 1788; Dampier on the 4th of January 1688.)

Dampier's first visit was to the north-western coast, which was approached from Timor. His narrative runs thus: "The 4th day of January 1688 we fell in with the land of New Holland, in the latitude of 16 degrees 50 minutes, having, as I said before, made our course due south from the shoal* that we past by the 31st day of December. We ran in close by it, and, finding no convenient anchorage, because it lies open to the north-west, we ran along shore to the eastward, steering north-east by east, for so the land lies. We steered thus about twelve leagues, and then came to a point of land from whence the land trends east and southerly for ten or twelve leagues; but how afterwards I know not. About three leagues to the eastward of this point there is a pretty deep bay, with abundance of islands in it, and a very good place to anchor in or to hale ashore. About a league to the eastward of that point we anchored, January the 5th 1688, two miles from the shore, in twenty-nine fathoms good hard sand and clean ground.

(*Footnote. Great Sahul Shoal.)

W. Dampier.

"New Holland is a very large tract of land. It is not yet determined whether it is an island or a main continent, but I am certain that it joins neither to Asia, Africa, nor America. This part of it that we saw is all low, even land, with sandy banks against the sea, only the points are rocky, and so are some of the islands in this bay.

"The land is of a dry sandy soil, destitute of water except you make wells, yet producing divers sorts of trees; but the woods are not thick, nor the trees very big. Most of the trees that we saw are dragon trees, as we supposed, and these too are the largest trees of anywhere. They are about the bigness of our large apple-trees, and about the same height, and the rind is blackish and somewhat rough. The leaves are of a dark colour; the gum distils out of the knots or cracks that are on the bodies of the trees. We compared it with some gum-dragon, or dragon's blood, that was aboard, and it was of the same colour and taste. The other sorts of trees were not known by any of us. There was pretty long grass growing under the trees, but it was very thin. We saw no trees that bore fruit or berries. When we had been here about a week, we hal'd our ship into a small sandy cove, at a spring-tide, as far as she would float; and at low water she was left dry, and the sand dry without us near half a mile, for the sea riseth and falleth here about five fathoms. The flood runs north by east, and the ebb south by west. All the neaptides we lay wholly aground, for the sea did not come near us by about a hundred yards. We had therefore time enough to clean our ship's bottom, which we did very well. Most of our men lay ashore in a tent, where our sails were mending; and our strikers brought home turtle and manatee every day, which was our constant food.

"While we lay here I did endeavour to persuade our men to go to some English factory, but was threatened to be turned ashore and left here for it.

"This made me desist, and patiently wait for some more convenient place and opportunity to leave them than here, which I did hope I should accomplish in a short time, because they did intend, when they went from hence, to bear down towards Cape Cormorin.

"In their way thither they designed to visit also the island Cocos, which lieth in latitude 12 degrees 12 minutes north, by our drafts, hoping there to find of that fruit, the island having its name from thence."

From Dampier's description it seems easy enough to determine the part of the coast visited by him, for although he gives no longitude this is indicated by his statement concerning the shoal that he fell in with to the south of Timor. Dampier, it must be remembered, was only a common sailor on this trip, and the captain of the *Cygnet*, the ship he was in, had no intentions of discovery. Their visit at New Holland was to see what that country "would afford" them. They did not give any names to the places where they stayed, nor did they know whether they had made any discoveries or not. The nomenclature that commemorates their visit was given in 1821 by P.P. King, who had no difficulty in fixing the locality described by Dampier, for, alluding to Dampier's description, he says*: "From this description, I have little hesitation in settling Cape Leveque to be the point he passed round. In commemoration therefore of his visit the name of Buccaneer's Archipelago was given to the cluster of isles that fronts Cygnet Bay, which was so called after the name of the ship in which he sailed. The point within Cape Leveque was named Point Swan* after the captain of the ship, and to a remarkable lump in the centre of the archipelago the name of Dampier's monument was assigned."

("Footnote. Narrative of a Survey of the Intertropical and Western Coasts of Australia, performed between the years 1818 and 1822, by Captain Phillip P. King, R.N. London 1827 volume ii. page 38 line 20.)

(*Footnote. At the time of the visit of the Cygnet to Australia Captain Reade was in command. Captain Swan and thirty-six of his men had abandoned the Cygnet at Mindanao, being heartily weary of buccaneering.)

W. DE VLAMINGH'S VOYAGE.

Wilhem de Vlamingh's voyage is the next in chronological order. The avowed object of Vlamingh's visit to the South Land was to search for the *Ridderschap Van Hollandt*, lost between the Cape of Good Hope and Batavia in 1685. The little fleet of three vessels composing the expedition set sail from Holland on May 3 1696. It was composed as follows: The frigate *De Geelvink*, Commodore Wilhem de Vlamingh; the hooker *De Nyptang*, Captain Gerrit Colaert; the galiot *Weseltje*, Captain Cornelis de Vlamingh, son of the Commodore.

The few extracts that we shall give are taken from *The Journal of a Voyage made to the unexplored South Land, by order of the Dutch East India Company, in the years 1696 and 1697. Printed at Amsterdam in 1701.*

"On the morning of the 29th December 1696 at half-past two o'clock we discovered the South Land...They cast anchor in from fourteen to fifteen fathoms. At nearly half a league from the island, on the south side, they had good holding ground.

"There are very few birds there and no animals except a kind of rat as big as a common cat, whose dung is found in abundance over all the island."*

(*Footnote. The island mentioned above is the one seen thirty-eight years before by Captain Samuel Volkersen, and which he did not name, "thinking it right to leave the choice of name to the Governor-General." It received a name after Vlamingh's sojourn there (Rottnest), which was suggested no doubt by Vlamingh's description.)

On the 4th (January) de Vlamingh's boat made sail for the mainland. On its return a council was held with the view of making an expedition on shore on the morrow.

"At sunrise on the morning of the 5th the resolution which had been taken was put into execution, and I, in company with the skipper, pushed off to the mainland with the boats of the three South land navigators. We mustered, what with soldiers and sailors, and two of the blacks that we had taken with us at the Cape, eighty-six strong, well armed and equipped. We proceeded eastwards; and after an hour's march we came to a hut of a worse description than those of the Hottentots. Further on was a large basin of brackish water, which we afterwards found was a river, on the bank of which were several footsteps of men, and several small pools in which was fresh water, or but slightly brackish. In spite of our repeated searches however we found no men.

"Towards evening we determined to pass the night on shore, and pitched our camp in the wood, in the place where we found a fire which had been lighted by the inhabitants, but whom nevertheless we did not see. We fed the fire by throwing on wood, and each quarter of an hour four of our people kept watch.

"On the morning of the 6th at sunrise we divided ourselves into three companies, each taking a different route, to try if we could not by this means find some men. After three or four hours we rejoined each other near the river without discovering anything beyond some huts and footsteps. Upon which we betook ourselves to rest. Meanwhile they brought me the nut of a certain fruit tree, resembling in form the drioens, having the taste of our large Dutch beans, and those which were younger were like a walnut. I ate five or six of them, and drank of the water from the small pools; but after an interval of about three hours I and five others who had eaten of these fruits began to vomit so violently that we were as dead men; so that it was with the greatest difficulty that I and the crew regained the shore, and thence in company with the skipper were put on board the galiot, leaving the rest on shore.

"On the 7th the whole of the crew returned on board with the boats, bringing with them two young black swans. The mouth of the said river lies in 31 degrees 46 minutes, and at eleven, nine, and seven gunshots from the mainland are five and a half fathoms of water on good bottom. Between the river and Rottenest Island, which is at nearly five leagues distance, Captain de Vlamingh had the misfortune to break his cable."

On the 10th and 11th they renewed their exploration of the river where they had found the black swans (since called the Swan River), ascending it six or seven leagues (some thought it was ten).

They then continued their course along the coast in a northerly direction, landing at various places, finding footsteps of men, dogs, and cassowary (emus). On the 23rd and 24th they passed through the channel now known as the Geelvinck Channel, landing now and again. On the 25th and 26th they were on shore searching for water, which they discovered near a little hut. They were now in the latitude of Hutt Lagoon and Port Gregory of modern charts. On the 28th they put to sea again. On the 30th they cast anchor in "an extensive gulf, which probably must have been that named *Dirk Hartog's Reede.*" On the 31st two boats entered the gulf to explore it, and two others to go fishing, which brought back in the evening a good quantity. The same evening the chief pilot reported that they had been in the gulf but had seen nothing further to show whether the part to the north of the gulf were an island or not. They saw there a number of turtles.

The narrative then runs thus: "On the 1st of February, early in the morning, our little boat went to the coast to fish. Our chief pilot, with de Vlamingh's boat, again went into the gulf, *and our skipper went on shore to fix up a commemorative tablet.**

(*Footnote. We have italicised the above passage, which should be compared with another further on, equally italicised by us, both being worthy of some consideration. See also above, Chapter 42.)

"On the 2nd we took three great sharks, one of which had nearly (sic) thirteen little ones, of the size of a large pike. The two captains (for de Vlamingh had also gone on shore) returned on board late in the evening, having been a good six or seven leagues up the country. Our captain brought with him a large bird's head, and related that he had seen two nests, made of boughs, which were full three fathoms in circumference.

"On the 3rd Vlamingh's chief pilot returned on board. He reported that he had explored eighteen leagues, and that it was an island. *He brought with him a tin plate*, which, in the lapse of time, had fallen from a post to which it had been attached, and on which was cut the name of the captain, Dirk Hartog, as well as the names of the first and second merchants, and of the chief pilot of the vessel *De Eendraght*, which arrived here in the year 1616, on the 25th of October, and left for Bantam on the 27th of the same month."

From the above we observe two items of importance: first, that they went on shore on the 1st of February to fix up a commemorative tablet; and secondly, that Dirk Hartog's tin plate was brought on board by de Vlamingh's chief pilot on the 3rd. These two occurrences, as related by a member of de Vlamingh's expedition, are difficult to reconcile unless we admit that two commemorative tablets were erected at Dirck Hartog's Island, which does not appear probable and is not recorded in the narrative.*

(*Footnote. See above, Chapter 42.)

Dirck Hartog's plate was taken away by Vlamingh and another one erected in its place commemorating Hartog's visit in 1616 and Vlamingh's in 1697, "as to be read in the journals," says the narrative.

To conclude the description of this voyage: They now shaped their course in a northerly direction. Whether they passed between Dirck Hartog's Island and the mainland is not very clear. Having reached North West Cape they report having sailed up that bogus river known on old Dutch charts as Willems' River. They then steered their course for Batavia.

W. DAMPIER'S SECOND VOYAGE, IN THE YEAR 1699.

The next voyage to Australia was directed to the same shores by W. Dampier, now captain of the *Roebuck* and on a voyage of discovery.

(*Footnote. The initial letter shows Dampier's Rosemary: Conyza Nova Hollandia angustis Rorismarini foliis.)

At a time when Englishmen barely credited the existence of a continent south of the East Indies it is noteworthy that amongst Dampier's patrons was Edward Harley, Earl of Oxford, one of the principal Lords of the Admiralty, and possessor of that valuable document, the Dauphin chart. He, at least, believed in the existence of a southern continent.

Dampier fell in with the coast of Australia to the north of the Abrolhos, "an appellative name for shoals" as he calls it, and "strove to run in near the shore to seek for a harbour to refresh us after our tedious voyage; having made one continued stretch from Brazil hither of about 114 degrees; designing from hence also to begin the discovery I had a mind to make on New Holland and New Guinea. The land was low and appeared even"..."with some red and some white cliffs; these last in latitude 26 degrees 10 minutes south, where you will find fifty-four fathoms within four miles of the shore...

"When I saw there was no harbour here, nor good anchoring, I stood off to sea again, in the evening of the second of August...I made sail and stood to the north; and at eleven o'clock the next day, August 5th, we saw land again at about six leagues distance. This noon we were in latitude 25 degrees 30 minutes.

"The 6th of August, in the morning, we saw an opening in the land, and we ran into it...The mouth of this sound, which I called Shark's Bay, lies in about twenty-five degrees south latitude.

"Twas the 7th of August when we came into Shark's Bay, in which we anchored at three several places, and stay'd at the first of them* till the 11th. During which time we searched about, as I said, for fresh water, digging wells, but to no purpose.

(*Footnote. On the south-west side of the bay, vide map (Illustration 17.)

"On the 11th about noon I steered farther in, with an easy sail, because we had but shallow water...Then we saw the land right ahead that in the plan makes the east of the bay. We could not come near it with the ship, having but shoal water; finding by the shallowness of the water that there was no going out to sea to the east of the two islands* that face the bay, nor between them, I returned to the west entrance. going out by the same way I came in at, only on the east instead of the west side of the small shoal to be seen in the place; in which channel we had ten, twelve, and thirteen fathoms of water, still deepening upon us till we were out at sea.

(*Footnote. Dorre and Bernier Islands.)

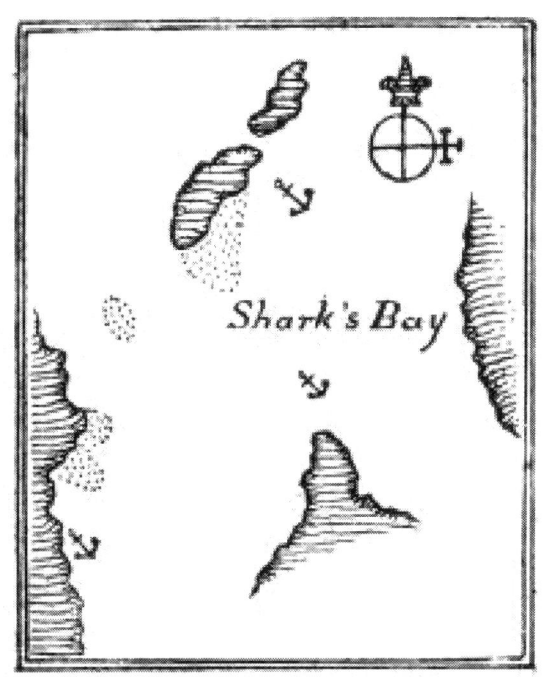

Dampier's Map of Shark's Bay.

"It was August the 14th when I sailed out of this bay or sound...designing to coast along to the north-east till I might commodiously put in at some other part of New Holland...The 20th we were in latitude 19 degrees 37 minutes, and kept close on a wind to get sight of the land again, but could not get to see it...The 21st we did not make the land till noon...There were three or four rocky islands about a league from us...and we saw many other islands...as far as we could see either way from our top-mast head; and all within them to the south there was nothing but islands of a pretty height, that may be seen eight or nine leagues off. By what we saw of them they must have been a range of islands of about twenty leagues in length, stretching from east-north-east to west-south-west, and for aught I know as far as to those of Shark's Bay, and to a considerable breadth also (for we could see nine or ten leagues in among them) towards the continent or mainland of New Holland, if there be any such thing hereabouts, and by the great tides I met with awhile afterwards more to the north-east, I had a strong suspicion that here might be a kind of archipelago of islands, and a passage possibly to the south of New Holland and New

Guinea into the great south sea eastward, which I had thoughts also of attempting on my return from New Guinea (had circumstances permitted), and told my officers so; but I could not attempt it at this time because we wanted water, and could not depend upon finding it there.

"This place is in the latitude of 20 degrees 21 minutes, but in the draught that I had of this coast, which was Tasman's, it was laid down in 19 degrees 50 minutes, and the shore is laid down as all along joining in one body or continent, with some openings appearing like rivers, and not like islands, as really they are...There grew here two or three sorts of shrubs, one just like rosemary,* and therefore I called this Rosemary Island."

(*Footnote. See (Illustration 18) where Dampier's design of the Australian rosemary is given.)

Dampier was then amongst the islands which afterwards received the name of *Archipel de Dampier* on the occasion of the visit to them made on the 29th of March 1803 by the commander of the French ship le Casuarina.*

(*Footnote. See Peron volume 2 page 234.)

He was greatly in need of fresh water and a better place to ride in; he consulted with his officers; "they all agreed to go from hence."

"Accordingly, August the 23rd at five in the morning we ran out...On the 25th of August we still coasted along the shore that we might the better see any opening...The 30th day, being in latitude 18 degrees 21 minutes, we made the land again...The 31st of August, betimes in the morning, I went ashore with ten or eleven men to search for water. We went armed with muskets and cutlasses for defence, expecting to see people there (they had seen 'smoaks' near the shore), and carried also shovels and pickaxes to dig wells." They had an encounter at this place with the natives, of which Dampier says: "These New Hollanders were probably the same sort of people as those I met with on this coast in my voyage round the world,* for the place I then touched at was not above forty or fifty leagues to the north-east of this...Upon returning to my men I saw they had dug eight or nine feet deep, yet found no water. So I return'd aboard that evening, and the next day, being September 1st, I sent my boatswain ashore to dig deeper, and sent the sain with him to catch fish."

(*Footnote. See volume 1. page 464 etc. Dampier's Voyage Round the World.)

The passage to the South Sea still haunted Dampier's mind. Such a passage was not indicated on the Dutch charts, which were those that Dampier used, but he may have had also a draught of the Dauphin chart, on which a passage is indicated. It will be borne in mind that Ed. Harley, the Earl of Oxford and one of the principal Lords of the Admiralty, had been instrumental in sending Dampier out on this expedition of discovery, and that Harley was the possessor of the Dauphin chart, which has also been called the Harleyan chart by some cartographers.

The "passage to the South Sea" was suggested to Dampier by the tides at the place where he was, for he says: "By the height and strength and course of them hereabouts it should seem that, if there be such a passage or straight going through eastward to the great South Sea, as I said one might suspect, one would expect to find the mouth of it somewhere between this place and Rosemary Island, which was the part of New Holland I came last from."

After all their trouble, the only water they could get was brackish.

"And thus, having ranged about a considerable time upon this coast without finding any good fresh water, or any convenient place to clean the ship, as I had hoped for, and it being moreover the height of the dry season, and my men growing scorbutick for want of refreshments, so that I had little encouragement to search further, I resolved to leave this coast, and accordingly in the beginning of September set sail towards Timor." From Timor, where Dampier made a lengthy stay, a straight course was made for New Guinea, which was sighted on January 1 1700.

CHAPTER 49. A.D. 1700 TO 1717.

VOYAGE OF THE NOVA HOLLANDIA, THE WAJER, AND VOSSENBOSCH TO MELVILLE ISLAND AND THE COBURG PENINSULA, IN 1705. DAMPIER AND WELBE.

Five years and twenty-three days after we left W. Dampier in sight of New Guinea three Dutch vessels left Batavia--the fluyt *Vossenbosch*, the sloop the *Wajer*, and the *phantiallang* or patsjalling *Nova Hollandia*. These three vessels were commanded by Martin Van Delft. The journals appear to have been lost, as usual, but a report has been preserved which was addressed to the Governor-General and Council. The three Dutch ships remained some considerable time at Timor, then in April 1705 proceeded to the north-west corner of Van Diemen's Land. This north-west corner of Van Diemen's Land is what is now known as Cape Van Diemen, Melville Island, Northern Territory. They were instructed to survey with care a large bay that, owing to the flow of water and other signs, was believed to run right through to the South of New Holland. They only visited however "a very small portion of that great bay, which it was recommended to them to sail over and explore as much as possible." The great bay in question is Van Diemen's Gulf, which retained on old Dutch charts the term *Baya*, given to it no doubt by the Portuguese, who must have been there before.*

(*Footnote. In 1818, when P.P. King was on a surveying expedition to the locality, and determined the insularity of Melville Island, the natives "repeatedly asked for axes by imitating the action of chopping," and invited the white men to land, one in particular, a native woman, frequently repeated the words "Ven aca, Ven aca," come here, come here, "accompanied with an invitation to land." P.P. King volume I. pages 111 and 113.)

Having reached *Cape Van Calmoerie*, Croker Island, the expedition returned home. A map of the surveys made during that expedition was published at Amsterdam in 1868 in Jacob Swart's *Verhandelingen en Berigten*. The above expedition is the last one recorded in which discoveries were made before the arrival of our illustrious Cook.

DAMPIER AND WELBE.

The publication of Dampier's voyages, in which *New Holland* is described as the *barrenest spot upon the globe*, seems to have damped the ardour for Australian exploration, for the several schemes of colonisation that were projected about this time met with no encouragement. The great Australian Continent was a drug in the market. None would have it. One of these schemes is worth recording because it appears to have been suggested by Dampier, who, after his return to England, viewing the profession of the sea with the old yearnings of the buccaneer, started on a privateering expedition to despoil the Spaniards.

On this occasion Dampier commanded the *St. George*, and a certain John Welbe, author of the scheme we refer to, accompanied him, it appears, for he mentions having done so in his petition. Welbe does not mention however that most of his information came from Dampier; in fact he pretends to ignore that others had visited the regions in which he proposes to settle colonies. Burney (volume iv. page 517) gives the following account of John Welbe's proposal, which is to be found among the Sloane Manuscripts in the British Museum:

"In 1713 John Welbe, a person who had been in the South Sea with Captain Dampier, offered a plan to the British Ministry for a voyage to make a full discovery of Terra Australis. Welbe was an ingenious but distressed projector, and, it appearing that his proposals were made principally with a view to his own relief, they obtained little attention. They were referred to the Admiralty, and afterwards to the South Sea Company, a committee of which company examined and 'found the matter out of their bounds.'"

The heads of Welbe's scheme were, to give them in his own words, as follows:

"For a good fourth-rate ship of the navy to be equipped for the voyage, to carry 180 men, having only her upper tier of guns mounted, leaving the rest ashore for the convenience of storing additional provisions, and for the ease of the ship; the cooking copper to be hung like a still so that, when water is wanted, we can distil salt water and make fresh. Also a brigantine tender to be provided. To go round Cape Horne to the island Juan Fernandez, thence to the Solomon Islands, discovered 150 years ago by the Spaniards. But the Court of Spain did not think fit to settle them by reason they had not entirely settled the main land of Peru. On arriving, to search and discover what that country abounds in, and to trepan some of the inhabitants on board and bring them to England, who, when they have learned our language, will be proper interpreters."

Welbe proposes afterwards to sail to New Guinea, which he believed to form part of Terra Australis, and there to make the like examination. He renewed his proposals several times. His plan and application have been preserved in the Sloane collection of manuscripts, and his last application is dated in the latter part of the year 1716, from Wood-street Compter, where he was then confined for debt. He complains in it that he presented three petitions to the king, besides petitioning the Treasury and the Admiralty Board, without receiving any definite answer.*

(*Footnote. History of New South Wales, from the Records. By G.B. Barton page 569.)

It will be noticed that Dampier's experience was made use of, and that the absence of fresh water on the coasts of Australia was to be provided against. In the above proposal Welbe acknowledges that he had been in the South Sea with Dampier, and also that the Spaniards had discovered the Solomon Islands; but in a later proposal made in 1716, just after Dampier's death, he boastfully states that "from the coast of Peru West to the East Indies is upwards of 2,500 leagues, which to the south of the line is *undiscovered to any European, Captain Welbe excepted.*"

Only one copy of the original of this second proposal, which we give here, is known to exist, and that is in the Bibliotheque Nationale, Paris. Mr. G.B. Barton remarks, "That in the light of present knowledge, this document is of great interest, especially in connection with the reference to the gold and silver mines, and the name of New Wales."

CAPTAIN JOHN WELBE'S PROPOSALS for Establishing a Company, by the name of the London Adventurers, for carrying on a Trade to (and settling Colonies in) TERRA AUSTRALIS, and Working and Improving the Gold and Silver Mines which there abound.

"Whereas 'tis well known that there is no nation that do Trade from the South Seas to the East Indies but the Spaniards, whose India trade is from Acapulco (on the coast of Mexico, in the South Seas), to the Philippine Islands in the East Indies, which ships in going keep always to the North-East Trade Wind; and in coming back they run to 40 or 45 Degrees North, to meet with a Westerly Wind, to run them to the Eastward, for which Reason those Southern parts are not yet fully discovered, nor any part of them settled by any European whatsoever, they lying out of the way of all Trading Ships.

"If we look back and trace the Course of those European Ships Voyages that have sailed round the Globe it may easily be seen how far they were from making any Discoveries in those Southern Parts, the Course of their Voyages not giving them any Opportunity for so doing.

"Magellanus, the Discoverer of the Streights called after his Name, the first that sailed West from the South Seas to the East Indies, sailed along the Coasts of Peru and Mexico till he came to California, and thence took his Departure for India, keeping in the North-East Trade Wind.

"Sir Francis Drake, said to be the first Commander that sailed round the Globe (Magellanus being kill'd by the Indians of Mindanos Island) kept the Coast of Peru and Mexico on board, and sailed West for India in the North-East Trade Wind.

"Sir Thomas Cavendish the same.

"Captain Swann, one of the Buccaneers of America, with whom Captain Dampier sailed the first time round the Globe, kept in the North-East Trade Wind from California to India, and was killed at Mindanos, as Magellanus was.

"Captain Rogers, in the *Duke and Duchess*, with the *Acapulco* ship, kept likewise in the North-East Trade Wind.

"It is here to be observed that from the Coast of Peru West to the East Indies is upwards of 2,500 Leagues, which to the Southward of the Line is undiscovered to any European (Captain Welbe excepted), who, in the course of his Voyage round the World with Captain Dampier, in the years 1703, 1704, 1705, and 1706, having many extraordinary Opportunities of satisfying and informing himself what Discoveries had been made, by Order of the Viceroys of Peru, for 150 Years past, Was thereby well assured that the Islands named (by the said Captain Welbe) St. George's Islands and New Wales, and some other Islands thereabouts, which abound with Mines of Gold and Silver, belong to no European Prince or State, and are therefore free for the first Discoverer to take Possession of, which Mines the Undertaker doubts not to prove, will enrich the British Nation upwards of 50,000,000 sterling if taken Possession of and Colonies settled, which is not half what the Kingdom of Peru has produced to the Spaniards since their first Settlement there under Francisco Pizaro, the first Viceroy.

"It is therefore proposed that a Joint Stock, not exceeding 2,500,000, be raised to fit out Ships and settle Colonies forthwith, that the Improvements and Advantages of such Valuable Discoveries may not be lost. And in order thereto the said Captain Welbe is now ready to grant Permits to such Persons who are willing to be Proprietors and Adventurers in this said Undertaking. On Grant of which Permits the Proprietors are to pay in 1 shilling on every Share, namely 10 shillings for every 1000 pounds, to enable the Undertaker to apply for and obtain a Patent, and defray other charges; and no more is to be paid in until at a General Meeting of and by the Proprietors Directors and Treasurers be chosen; and then no more on each Share than what the Directors at such Meeting shall agree on and find necessary for carrying on effectually so valuable and advantageous a Trade.

"N.B. The proposer has no Sinister Ends nor Self-Interest In View, and expects no Pay nor any Reward but such Part of the neat Produce of Profits as the Directors shall think fit and agree to allow him."*

(*Footnote. From E.A. Petherick's valuable publication, *The Torch*. Number 3 page 91.)

CHAPTER 50. A.D. 1717 TO 1770.

JOHN PURRY'S PROPOSITIONS. ROGGEWEEN'S EXPEDITION. THE LOSS OF THE ZEEWYCK. CONCLUSION.

A year after Welbe's proposal, in 1717, Jean Pierre Purry, a Swiss born at Neuchatel, addressed a memoir to the Governor-General of the Dutch East India Company, proposing the settling of a colony in the *Land* of NIGHTS (Nuyts Land).

Neither this memorial nor another which accompanied it were well received, and a friend of Purry's told him privately that he had better get out of the way, for that some things had been observed in both memorials which ought not to be made public. P. Purry took the hint and went to France. "It was supposed by some," says Major (Early Voyages to Australia, page cxvi.) "that the voyage of Roggeween to the South Seas in 1721 was a result of this application (Purry's), but it is distinctly stated by Valentyn that it was an entirely distinct expedition. In 1699 Roggeween's father had submitted to the West India Company a detailed memoir on the discovery of the Southern Land; but the contentions between Holland and Spain prevented the departure of the fleet destined for the expedition, and it was forgotten. Roggeween however, who had received his father's dying injunctions to prosecute this enterprise, succeeded at length in gaining the countenance of the directors, and was himself appointed commander of the three ships which were fitted out by the company for the expedition. According to Valentyn the principal object of this voyage was the search for certain "islands of gold," supposed to lie in 56 degrees south latitude; but the professed purpose was distinctly avowed by Roggeween to be directed to the South Lands. Although the expedition resulted in some useful discoveries it did not touch the shores of New Holland."

The survivors of the wreck of the *Zeewyk* were apparently the last Europeans to catch sight of Australian shores before the arrival of the English on the eastern coast. Relics from this vessel, which was lost in 1727, are constantly turning up on the guano islands known under the name of Houtman's Abrolhos. Messrs. Broadhurst, Macneil, and Company have been exporting guano from the Abrolhos the last eight years, the total output in 1893 amounting to some 3,500 tons, and the trade is still a very profitable and prosperous one. In shifting the guano relics from shipwrecked vessels are uncovered, and no doubt when the lower stratas are reached older relics of the Portuguese period will be found.

We give here a short account of the wreck of the *Zeewyk* because it is interesting, and in this document we have an example of the marvellous sagacity of the Hollanders for Netherlandising expressions that otherwise would not be Dutch to anyone. The original Venetian expression, *Apri-l'occhio*, used by mariners as a warning to have a good look out, literally to keep their eyes open, and which became Portuguese under the modified form of *Abrolhos*, is in the following document corrupted to Ambrollossen*:

(*Footnote. Our extract is from Major who is responsible for the orthography of Ambrollossen.)

"To His Excellency and the Noble Councillors of the Netherlandish India:

"We take the liberty of informing you that, in sailing from the Cape of Good Hope to Batavia with the company's late ship *Zeewyck*, we were wrecked on a reef on the ninth of June 1727 at seven o'clock in the evening, in the first watch.

"The reef against which the vessel struck is surrounded by a very high and heavy surf, and runs in the shape of a half-moon. On the inner side lie many small islands, called Frederick Houtman's Ambrollossen (Abrolhos), which we gained on the eighteenth of June, and upon which we remained from that day until we had fetched from the wreck everything that seemed to us necessary for the preservation of our life-- spars, ropes, timber, and provisions. As soon as we had got these materials on shore our carpenter at once set to work with his men, by order of the officers, and by the help of the common people, to build a vessel, so that we might save our lives, if it pleased God. We called it the *Slopie*, that is the little sloop, made up from the wreck of the *Zeewyck*. When it was ready for sea we made sail with a south wind and fair weather on the twenty-sixth of March, having with us the money chests of the company as well as provisions for the voyage. We continued to enjoy favourable weather throughout the voyage, and so arrived by God's blessing, on the twenty-first of April 1728, in the Straits of Sunda, eighty-two souls, of whom we herewith subjoin a list for the information of your nobility and council.

"We beg to wish you and the council, from the bottom of our heart, every prosperity and happiness, and present respectfully our humble services. Yours, etc.,

(S.) JAN. STEYNS.

JAN. NOBBENS."

England was now coming to the front. In 1762 Admiral Cornish and General Draper reduced the Philippines, and after the siege of Manila Dalrymple became the possessor of the document which revealed Torres' passage through the straits that bear his name.

After the peace of Paris England became the greatest maritime and colonial power in the world.

We have reached the period of great expeditions, sent out no longer for piratical purposes but in the interests of science and commerce-- Bougainville's, Byron's, Wallis', Carteret's, Crozet's, Kerguelen's, and Cook's.

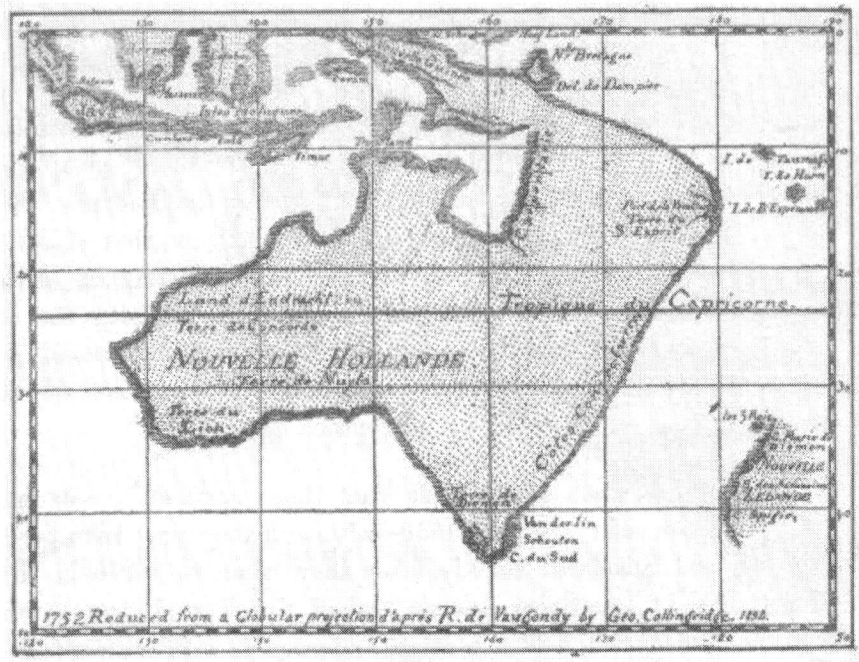

R. de Vaugondy's Map of New Holland, A.D. 1752.

R. De Vaugondy's Map of New Holland, A.D. 1752.

The map which closes the series of maps of Australia, which we have given in this work, shows the idea that the world possessed of the configuration of this continent prior to the arrival of Lieutenant Cook. It is by Robert de Vaugondy, the geographer to the King of France. Corrected and published in 1752 it is a fair specimen of the maps of New Holland of that date. It will be noticed in it that the early discoveries of Mendana, de Quiros, and Torres are set down as forming part of the Australian continent. Torres Straits are indicated, although with some hesitation. Such is not the case in many maps of the same period, the Australian continent being decidedly joined to New Guinea, whereas in another map by the same cartographer, published in 1756, New Guinea is quite separate from New Holland. Indeed the ignorance of the geography of New Holland was such that we find English maps assuming the very same outline as this one even after the world-famed voyage of Lieutenant Cook. We have one now before us in which the inscription New South Wales, discovered 1770, takes the place of the French *Cotes conjecturees*, without the slightest alteration in the outline of this eastern coast, which runs north to the

New Hebrides, with the legend *Espiritu Sancto*, and, as the Straits of Torres are blocked, Lieutenant Cook was supposed by the cartographer to have reached Batavia by the north of New Guinea.

CONCLUSION.

In conclusion we feel inclined to say with Alexander Dalrymple that "there is nothing new under the sun," and that Australia must have been known from the remotest antiquity.

As far as its cartography is concerned the first appearance of something less problematical than the *Terra Australis* of the ancients is the outline of the Western coasts of that *Terra Australis* on the British Museum mappamundi of 1498.

Then comes a long period of uncertainty, and the Portuguese and Spaniards find their way to these seas. No mention however of any positive discovery of Australian shores is made by them, and the Lusitano-French maps of the Dieppese School of Hydrography are the only documents which prove conclusively that Australia had been discovered, since those documents bear witness to the charting of at least the western and eastern coasts of this great South Land. Concerning the southern coasts the cartography of the period does not furnish any absolute proof of discovery, and with reference to the northern coasts some hitherto impenetrable mystery envelops the history of their discovery by Europeans.

It would perhaps be rash to conclude that those northern coasts had been charted at the period we refer to--1511 to 1550--although they must have been known to the Portuguese and Spaniards shortly after they came to settle in the Spice Islands. The natives of the Spice Islands and of the East Indian Archipelago, having from time immemorial held a constant intercourse with traders from China, the Philippines, New Guinea and islands in close proximity to Australia, must have known all the countries that those traders were acquainted with. The Chinese and Malays were acquainted with the northern coasts of Australia, where they came to fish for trepang. Whatever facts concerning the Great Southern Continent those traders became acquainted with must have soon been known to the Portuguese and Spaniards, always on the look out for fresh information and the discovery of new territory.

With regard to the northern coasts of Australia we wish to draw particular attention to the following facts:

1. That on certain early charts New Guinea is shown as an island.*

(*Footnote. See Illustration 32, the F. Monachus Mappamundi of 1526/1527.

2. That on other charts of the same period* (actually only 3 or 4 years later in point of date) that part of the Australian Continent which is nearest to New Guinea--Cape York--is shown as it should be, i.e. unconnected with New Guinea.

(*Footnote. Dauphin and other charts, 1530 to 1550. See Chapter 30 et sequit.)

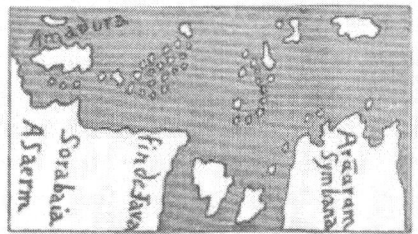
Portion of Dauphin Chart.

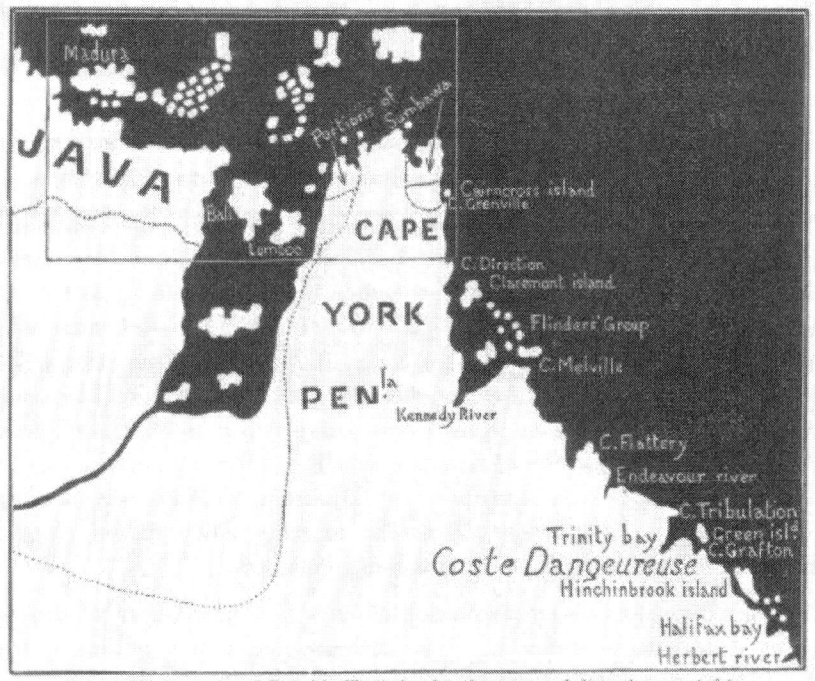
Adaptation of portion of Dauphin Chart showing the process of distortion resorted to.

Portion of Dauphin Chart.

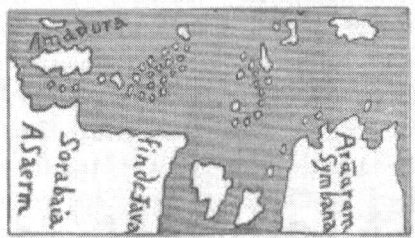

Portion of Dauphin Chart.

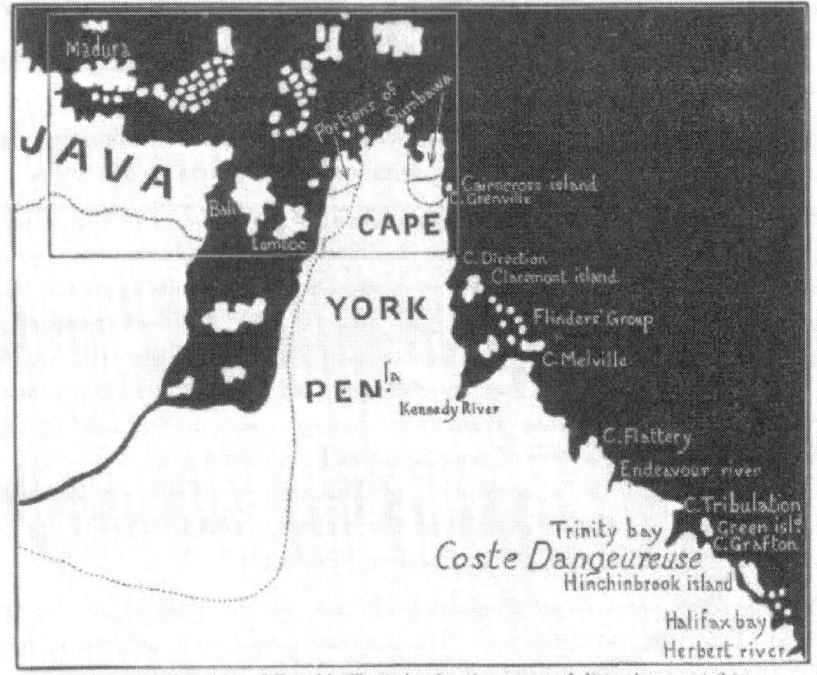

Adaptation of portion of Dauphin Chart showing the process of distortion resorted to.

Now, although in the former charts no Australian Continent is represented, and in the latter only a portion of New Guinea bearing the name of Papuas, yet the fact remains that an open sea is shown between New Guinea and Australia in the two classes of maps referred to. This points to the fact that the straits now known as Torres Straits were known at an early date.

Nevertheless there remains some strange mystery, as we have said, in connection with this matter which has not yet been solved. The mystery, if cleared up some day, will be found to relate to the peculiar distortion to which the charts of the Desceliers type have been subjected to. We have seen that the Portuguese and Spaniards must have known of an open sea between Timor and Sumbawa, yet on all the charts of the Desceliers type, which, it must be remembered, are charts of Portuguese origin, Sumbawa forms part of Australia, since it is shown as attached to and forming one with York Peninsula. Timor* is so situated (off the coast of Queensland) that Sebastian del Cano, with the remnant of Magalhaens' expedition, could not have left that island to reach the Cape of Good Hope on a south-westerly course without coming into immediate contact with Australia.

(*Footnote. See map, Illustration 38.)

Java, Bali, Lomboc and Sumbawa form the northern coasts of Australia on the Desceliers maps. Bali and Lomboc, being represented as detached islands, are either in the Gulf of Carpentaria or in their correct and respective positions with regard to Java and Sumbawa.*

(*Footnote. See note above.)

The two preceding woodcuts (Illustrations 2 and 65) will illustrate the process of distortion that has been adopted in the compilation of the Lusitano-French charts of Australia.

The small woodcut is a facsimile outline of a portion of the Dauphin Chart, showing part of Java, Madura, Bali, Lomboc, and Sumbawa through which protrudes Cape York Peninsula. A few names have been left by us for purposes of identification, they are: Amadura (Madura Island, north-east coast of Java), Asaerm (Gresic, also on the north-east coast of Java), Sorabaia (the well-known modern Surabaya), fin de Java (end of Java, a much repeated indication found on numerous old charts), Araaram (Kamara? a native village in Sumbawa, probably a bad reading or an elliptical form of Aramaram in F. Rodriguez' Portolano 1511/1512, see above; or it may be a corruption of Masaram or Massaram, another name for Bramble Bay, an island situated at the extreme north end of Cape York). Symbana (the name of the island, the modern Sumbawa).

The larger woodcut is an adaptation of ours for the purpose of showing the process of distortion we refer to. The exterior (coastline) outline is from the Dauphin Chart, as will be noticed by comparing it with the smaller woodcut. In it will be seen a dotted outline showing a portion of the rectified line of the south coast of Java, eastern and portion of more south-eastern coast of the Gulf of Carpentaria.

This woodcut illustrates at a glance how the seaway was blocked between Java and Australia, although a river communication, that of the *Rio Grande*, was left. *Coste Dangereuse* belongs to the nomenclature of the Dauphin Chart; the other names belong of course to the modern nomenclature of Queensland. The cape which forms the apex of York Peninsula, i.e. Cape York, divides Sumbawa in two, and the islands of Bali and Lomboc may be considered as either belonging to the hydrography of the Gulf of Carpentaria or to the eastern prolongation of islands from Java to Sumbawa.

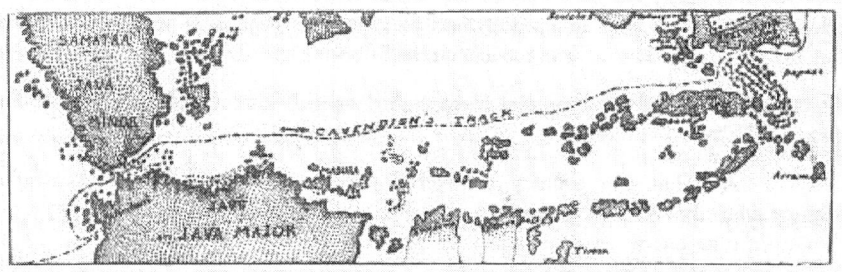

Cavendish's track, as it would appear on the Dauphin Chart.

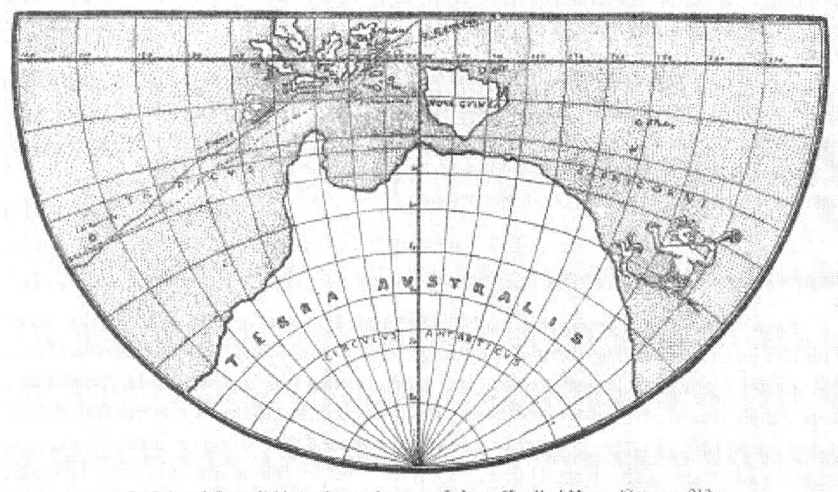

Drake's and Cavendish's tracks, as shown on Jodocus Hondius' Map. (See page 212.)

Cavendish's track as it would appear on the Dauphin Chart.

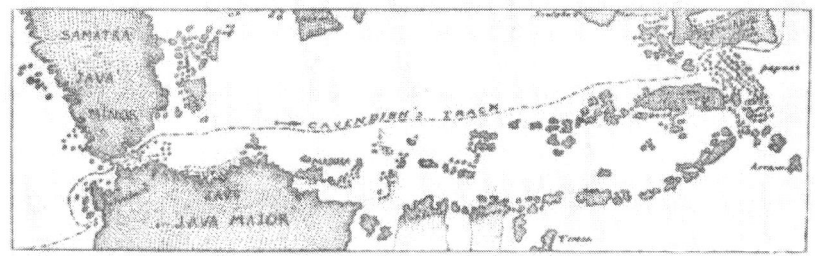

Cavendish's track, as it would appear on the Dauphin Chart.

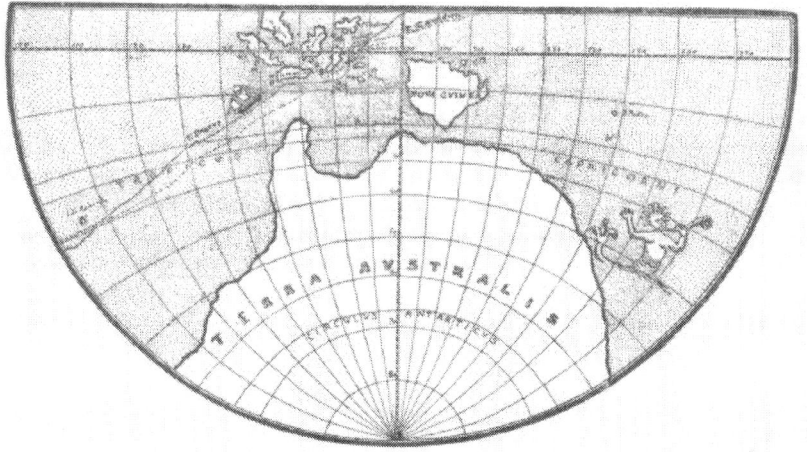

Drake's and Cavendish's tracks, as shown on Jodocus Hondius' Map.

Drake's and Cavendish's tracks, as shown on Jodocus Hondius' Map.

APPENDIX.

DE GONNEVILLE DISCOVERS AN AUSTRAL LAND IN THE YEAR 1503/1504.

A few French writers* on Australasian maritime discovery have attempted to set up a claim in favour of a discovery of Australia by one of their countrymen.

(*Footnote. D'Avezac is the principal French geographer who has written about de Gonneville's Voyage, and the result of his investigation was that de Gonneville landed in South America.)

It is said by them that the Sieur de Gonneville discovered Australia in the year 1503. This claim having been endorsed by certain English writers it is necessary to point out here that such a claim is untenable on the following grounds:

1. That the country discovered does not correspond with Australia geographically.

2. That the country discovered does not correspond with Australia ethnographically; and

3. That the term *Terre Australle*, Austral Land, would apply at the time to any land south of the equator--Madagascar or South America for instance.

Mr. E. Marin La Meslee, who was the first and last to deal exhaustively with this claim as far as Australia is concerned, fails to convince one that J.B. Paulmier de Gonneville actually landed in Australia.

We need not enter into all the details of Mr. La Meslee's lengthy dissertation, in which he tries to explain such difficulties as those which refer to a people carrying bows and arrows, and wearing "mantles either of skins or of woven mats, and some of them made of feathers, with a kind of apron just above the haunches, which the men wear down to the knee, and the women to the calf of the leg."

The first part of de Gonneville's narrative, relating to the place where he landed, may be summarized as follows:

Soon after the Portuguese had discovered the way to the East Indies some French merchants, having formed the design of following the steps of Vasco da Gama, and invited by a prospect of sharing the gains of the Portuguese trade, fitted out a ship, which was entrusted to de Gonneville. He left Honfleur in the month of June of the year 1503 in the good ship L'Espoir, rounded the Cape of Good Hope, and, being on his way to the East Indies, was driven out of his course into calm latitudes by a furious storm, which left him uncertain in what part of the world he was. Being in want of water, and his ship having suffered much by storm, the sight of some birds from the south induced him to hold his course that way, when he soon discovered a large country to which he gave the name of Austral India and Terre Australle, naming the inhabitants Australians.

Now it must be remembered that, prior to the discovery of Madagascar in 1505, the route followed by the Portuguese, once the Cape of Good Hope rounded, was along the African coast to Sofala, leaving Madagascar to their right.

There are no degrees of longitude or latitude mentioned in de Gonneville's narrative, and we have only his statement that he was on the "true course to the East Indies" when (in about October) he met with adverse winds.

We must suppose therefore that he was somewhere between the coast of Zanzibar and the Seychelles Islands, and that by going south he landed on the coast of Madagascar.

The periodicity of the monsoons in this part of the Indian Ocean would explain de Gonneville's statement with regard to the "tempestuous weather and calm latitudes," and give colour to the following theory, which we venture for the consideration of our readers:

De Gonneville, on his way to India, passed through the Mozambique Channel, and arrived towards October within a few degrees of the equator with a fair south-easterly monsoon.

At this time of the year however in these latitudes the wind changes and blows from the north-east. De Gonneville therefore must have been driven out of his course by a head wind into calm latitudes; then, falling in with the north-easterly monsoon, between 3 to 10 degrees south of the line, he was carried to the coast of Madagascar.

GOMEZ DE SEQUEIRA'S VOYAGE IN THE YEAR 1525. AN ALLEGED DISCOVERY OF AUSTRALIA.

There is an account of a voyage by Gomez de Sequeira that is worth while considering, because it is quite possible that Sequeira's discovery of some islands near Australia led to its discovery as suggested by Mr Barbie du Bocage.

The celebrated French geographer of that name, commenting on the Desceliers Lusitano-Spanish charts,* was led to believe that the Portuguese had discovered Australia between the years 1512 and 1542, but that they kept the matter secret because the Spanish at the time claimed all territories lying under the meridian of the Spice Islands. Of this discovery Barbie du Bocage says*:

(*Footnote. In the *Magazin Encyclopedique 12ieme annee*, tome iv. 1807, and also Major, Early Voyages to Australia, page xxxv.)

(*Footnote. Major's translation.)

"There is however no mention made of it in the voyages of the time, which would sufficiently prove that the Portuguese had suppressed, or at least concealed, the account of it. But I propose to endeavour to supply this defect from the narrative of two of their historians.

"Castanheda, a Portuguese author, who had been in India, tells us that in the beginning of July 1525 the Portuguese of Ternate, one of the Moluccas, dispatched a vessel to the Island of Celebes to traffic there; that this vessel on its return was driven by violent winds and currents into an open sea between the Straits of Magellan and the Moluccas; that the Portuguese found themselves thrown more than three hundred leagues out of their route, and were several times nearly lost. One night their rudder was carried away, and they beat about till the morning, when they discovered an island thirty leagues in circumference, on which they landed, with thanks to God for affording them this asylum. The islanders gave them an excellent reception; they were of a tawny colour, but well made and good looking, both men and women. The men had long black beards. The Portuguese remained four months in this island, not only for the purpose of refitting but because the winds were contrary for the return to the Moluccas. At length they departed and reached Ternate on the 20th January 1526.

"Such is the narrative of Castanheda. The Jesuit Maffei, who has given us a history of India, has supplied us with less details, but his account is not less valuable inasmuch as he gives us the name of the captain who commanded the ship. He says: Some Portuguese of the Moluccas, having gone to the islands of Celebes to seek for gold, but not having been able to land, were driven by a fearful tempest upon an island which is distant therefrom three hundred leagues, when they went ashore. The inhabitants, who were simple people, received them very well, and soon became familiar with them. They comprehended their signs, and even understood a little of the language spoken at the Moluccas. All the inhabitants were well-looking, both male and female; they were cheerful, and the men wore beards and long hair. The existence of this island was previously unknown, but, in consideration of the account given of it by the captain, whose name was Gomez de Sequeira, *and of the map which he drew of this island, his name was given to it.*

(*Footnote. We have italicised this passage referring to a map that was made because we have found the name on a map which we give further on. George Collingridge.)

"From the details supplied to us by these two authors it is evident that the island on which Gomez de Sequeira was thrown was to the eastward of the Moluccas, because, in returning, the Portuguese had to sail westward. Now three hundred Portuguese leagues, starting from the Moluccas or the Island of Celebes, lead us to within a trifle of Endeavour Straits; we may therefore conclude that it was upon one of the rocks in this strait that Gomez de Sequeira lost his rudder, and that the island on which he landed was one of the westernmost of those which lie along its western extremity. The Portuguese did not advance far into this strait, for it is plain that they met with no obstacle in returning to the Moluccas. I think therefore that the island on which Gomez de Sequeira landed was one of those which were called Prince of Wales Islands by Captain Cook, and which are inhabited, because this navigator states that he saw smoke there. What confirms me in this opinion is the agreement of our two authors in stating that the men of Gomez de Sequeira's Island had long and black hair and beards. We still find this characteristic distinguishing the natives of New Holland from those of New Guinea, whose hair and beards are crisped. This island therefore was nearer to New Holland than to New Guinea, which is in fact the case with the Prince of Wales Islands." And Mr. Barbie du Bocage adds: "The Portuguese having discovered in 1525 an island so near as this to New Holland, we must believe that the discovery of that continent followed very soon after that of this island. It was at that time that the controversies between the Courts of Portugal and Spain were at their highest; the Portuguese therefore needed to be cautious respecting their new discoveries; they were obliged to conceal them carefully. It will not therefore be surprising that no mention was made in their works of the discovery of New Holland."

Major does not agree with Barbie du Bocage, and points out that he appears to have neglected to consult de Barros, the most distinguished of all early Portuguese historians. It is certainly strange that Barbie du Bocage does not mention that author; but, had he availed himself of the minute description of the voyage in question, to which de Barros devotes the 5th chapter of the 10th book of his 3rd *Decada*, he would not have been any wiser than Major, who may be said to be equally at variance with any of the three authors' descriptions quoted, as Barbie du Bocage is. For Major, in refuting Barbie du Bocage's opinion, lays stress on the passage in de Barros, where it is said that they were driven *into an open sea*, with not a single island in sight, *but constantly towards the east*. Yet, notwithstanding this passage, Major is inclined to believe that the island to which Gomez de Sequeira had drifted is Tobi or Lord North's Island, which lies to the north of New Guinea in a latitude which precludes the possibility of the voyage having been accomplished in a direction *constantly towards the east*, since the island in question lies to the north-east of Celebes and Ternate, and only at *sixty leagues* instead of *three hundred*, which is the estimated distance to which they had drifted. Furthermore Tobi Island cannot be said to lie "between the Straits of Magellan and the Moluccas." Yet Barbie du Bocage's suggested route is not *in an open sea*, and the Prince of Wales' Islands lie at considerably more than three hundred leagues from the Moluccas.

Thus a careful examination of Barbie du Bocage's and Major's theories shows them to be both faulty. We were hesitating between the conflicting evidence of these two authorities when we came across an additional bit of information afforded by those "*eyes of history*" not sufficiently consulted, called maps.

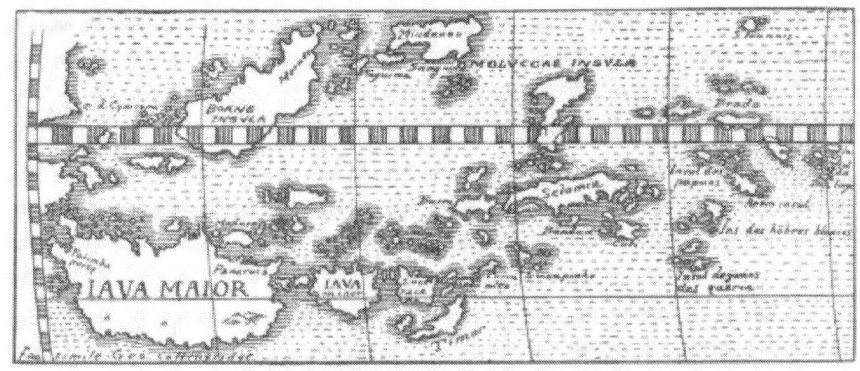

Portion of Gastaldi's Map, showing Gomez de Sequeira's Islands.

The evidence of the particular map we refer to--Gastaldi's remarkable map of the world, published in Venice by Tramezini in 1554--is decidedly in favour of Barbie du Bocage's ideas. The portion of Gastaldi's map which we reproduce here shows a group of islands named *Insul de gomes des queria*, Islands of Gomez de Sequeira. They lie in about 8 degrees of south latitude and in the longitude of the Northern Territory of Australia; the only Australian continent represented on the original map being the *Terra incognita* of the *Circulus Antarcticus*. New Guinea and Celebes are left out also, and therefore, in order to arrive at some kind of identification of Gomez de Sequeira's Islands, we must consider them in relation to the other landmarks which this map affords. These are: Timor, which is well charted to the south-east of Java (IAVA MAIOR) and Sumbawa (IAVA MINOR). Booro (*Burro*), Ceram (*Selamia*) and Banda (Bandan) which are equally well charted. Islands relating to New Guinean discoveries, such as: *Insul de Don Iorge* (Islands of Don Jorge de Menezes), *Insul das Papuas* (Islands of the Papuas), which are recognisable. *Apem insul?* seems to correspond with either Adi Island or the Arru Islands. *Ins des hobres blancos* (Islands of the White Men) correspond, as far as locality is concerned, to the Arru Islands. It would appear then that Gomez de Sequeira's Islands, which are the south-easternmost of those represented, must correspond with the Timor Laut group.

These islands however are not sufficiently far from the Spice Islands to answer exactly, and if we look further east we must look a little south to find any other island or islands which would correspond with the distance given. The Australian islands known as Wessel Islands are the nearest to the distance specified, and they would be reached in the latter part of the voyage through an open sea--the Sea of Arafura. These difficulties however are not the only ones which require elucidation with reference to Gomez de Sequeira's discovery.

Galvano reports a discovery made by Gomez de Sequeira, albeit under different circumstances, but the same year. Therefore the question arises, did Gomez de Sequeira make two voyages that year, or is the voyage reported by Galvano the same as the one which, according to Barbie du Bocage, led to the discovery of Australia?

With reference to the voyage in which Gomez de Sequeira was driven three hundred leagues out of his course Castanheda tells us that it was undertaken in the beginning of July, and that they returned to the Moluccas in the year 1526. The voyage referred to by Galvano may therefore have been accomplished during the first five months of the year 1525. It was directed to the north of New Guinea for purposes of discovery when some islands in 9 or 10 degrees latitude were discovered and named Islands of Gomez de Sequeira, but Alvaro de Saavedra two years afterwards in 1527 came across the same islands, it appears, naming them the *Islas de los Reyes* (Galvano, page 174).

Galvano mentions that Gomez de Sequeira went afterwards on an Indian voyage. A voyage to the Celebes would be called an Indian voyage, and this appears to settle the question. Gomez no doubt made the two voyages that year--the one to the north of New Guinea being made during the first five months of the year.

The following is Galvano's account which we take from the Hakluyt Society's edition, page 168:

"In this yeere 1525 Don George de Meneses, captaine of Maluco, and with him Don Garcia Henriquez, sent a foyst to discouer land towards the north, wherein went as captaine one Diego de Rocha, and Gomes de Sequeira for pilot, who afterwards went as pilot on an Indian voyage. In 9 or 10 degrees they found certaine islands standing close together, they passed among them, and they called them the Islands of Gomes de Sequeira, he being the first pilot that discouered them. And they came backe againe to the fort by the Island of Batochina do moro."

MANOEL GODINHO DE EREDIA'S ALLEGED DISCOVERY OF AUSTRALIA IN THE YEAR 1601.

In the year 1861 the learned and indefatigable Major read a paper on the discovery of Australia by the Portuguese. He had come to the conclusion that this continent was discovered by the Portuguese Godinho de Eredia in the year 1601.

Some years after however, having come across fresh data, he altered his views and wrote again as follows:

"In the year 1861 I laid before the Society of Antiquaries, and thereby made known to the world for the first time, the apparently important fact that the great continental island of Australia had been discovered in the year 1601 by a Portuguese navigator named Manoel Godinho de Eredia. Up to that time the earliest *authenticated* discovery of any part of the great southern land was that made a little to the west and south of Cape York by the commander of the Dutch yacht the *Duyfhen*, or Dove, about the month of March 1606. Thus the supposed fact which I announced in 1861 gave a date to the first authenticated discovery of Australia earlier by five years than that which had been previously accepted in history, and transferred the honour of that discovery from Holland to Portugal. The document on which this assumption was based was a manuscript mappemonde in the British Museum, in which, on the north-west corner of a country which could be shown beyond all question to be Australia, stood a legend in Portuguese to the following effect: Nuca Antara was discovered in the year 1601 by Manoel Godinho de Eredia, by command of the Viceroy Ayres de Saldanha. This mappemonde had the great disadvantage of being only a copy, possibly made even in the present century, from one the geography of which proved it to be some two centuries older. Still the mere fact of its being a copy laid it open to a variety of possible objections, which fortunately I was able to forestall by arguments that I believed to be unanswerable, but which need not be repeated here. I need now merely say that I had the good fortune at the time to find an apparently happy confirmation of what was stated in the map in a little printed work which described the discoverer as a learned cosmographer and skilful captain, who had received a special commission from the Viceroy at Goa to make explorations for gold-mines, and at the same time to verify the descriptions of the southern islands. The Viceroy thus mentioned was the immediate predecessor of Ayres de Saldanha, under whose viceroyalty the map declares the discovery to have been made.

"The map, as I afterwards discovered from a letter addressed to Navarette by the Vicomte de Santarem in 1835, was a copy by a foreign hand from one in a manuscript Atlas made in the seventeenth century by one Teixeira. The name Nuca Antare is shown in Sir Stamford Raffles' Java to apply also to the land of Madura, north-east of Java, but as that island was distinctly laid down in this very mappemonde, it seemed clear that no mistake was involved on that account; and that the country delineated was really Australia was proved by a second legend in Portuguese below the first to this effect: 'Land discovered by the Dutch, which they called Endracht or Concord.' Eendraghtsland, as we all know, was the name given to a large tract on the west coast of Australia, discovered by the Dutch ship the Eendraght in 1616. The reader then will see that in 1861 I had before me in a map (the original of which was made two centuries and a quarter ago) a distinct and unequivocal declaration of the actual discovery of a country which the map itself showed to be Australia, by a man whose contemporary history described as a distinguished cosmographer, and at a time which corresponded with the periods of office of the two viceroys mentioned respectively in the printed document quoted, and in the map. The viceroyalty of Francisco de Gama, from whom Eredia first received his commission to make similar explorations, extended from 1597 to 1600, and the asserted discovery was made in 1601 under the viceroyalty of Ayres de Saldanha, the immediate successor of Da Gama. I am not ashamed that I accepted the declaration as sound. It was so accepted by all who had the above evidence before them, and became recognised as an historical fact. Being so recognised, it carried back, as I have said, the first discovery of Australia by *any known ship or navigator* from 1606 to 1601, and transferred the honour of such discovery from the Dutch to the Portuguese. One thing of course remained to be desired, namely: that the original report of the discovery might some day be found. That day at length arrived. In the year 1871 M. Ruelens, the librarian of the Royal Burgundian Library at Brussels, discovered among the manuscripts there the original report of Eredia to Philip III of all his doings in the South Seas, and his excellency the Chevalier d' Antas was good enough to have a transcript made for me of all that portion which related to my subject. I no sooner looked into this more ample statement than I detected the work of an impostor, and as, in the preparation of my work on Early Voyages to Terra Australis, my memory had become charged with all the details of the subject, I was able to trace not only the documents which, as he was not a discoverer in reality, supplied him with the materials for being a discoverer on paper, but also blunders in those documents of which I was cognizant, but he had not been, and which, as he had been himself deceived, clearly betrayed the utter falsity of his statements. Believing, for reasons which I shall presently explain, that there were wealthy countries in the south which had never been explored, Eredia procured for himself the appointment of official Discoverer in those regions, an ambiguous and misleading title which implies by anticipation the credit due only to success. The delusion which the ambiguity of that title rendered possible became a reality, for we have seen that on the map which came before me in 1861 the declaration was distinct and absolute, 'Nuca Antara was discovered in the year 1601 by Manoel Godinho de Eredia,' whereas the pretended discoveries described in the report are not professed to have been made by Eredia in *propria persona*.

"Before giving the translation of the words of Eredia's report I will merely premise that the reputed country in the south, about which he treats, has received from him the name of India Meridional, a designation which I will retain in preference to Southern India, for the sake of avoiding confusion with the country to which the latter name more properly belongs. I shall presently explain how this country received its existence on maps, became a subject of ambitious thought to Manoel Godinho de Eredia, and finally became identified with the genuine Australia, of which he really had no knowledge whatever."

"The India Meridionale [or Southern India]," says Eredia, "is that continent which extends from the Promontory of Beach, the province of gold, in 16 degrees of south latitude, to the tropic of Capricorn and Antarctic circle, with many large provinces, such as Maletur, Locach, and others as yet unknown in that sea, in which lies the island called Java Minor, so celebrated by the ancients and so unknown by the moderns, with other adjacent islands, such as Petan, Necuran, Agania; and nearly all these produce a great quantity of gold, cloves, mace, nutmegs, sandalwood, and spices not known or seen in Europe, as is testified by Ptolemy and Vartomannus in their writings, and by Marco Polo from eye-witness, for he lived a long time in Java Minor." [Here follows a learned dissertation on Marco Polo and Java Minor which need not be quoted until he approaches the part which concerns our subject]. "The annals of Java Major," he says, "make mention of the India Meridional and of its commerce and of the ancient navigation from Java Major to Java Minor, where was the greatest emporium in the world for gold and spices. This commerce was subsequently stopped by wars for the space of 331 years until the year 1600, when by chance a boat from Luca Antara, in the India Meridional, driven by weather and currents, arrived in the harbour of Balambuan in Java Major, where the king of the province, who was present at the time with some Portuguese, gave them a good reception and entertainment. These strangers of Luca Antara, although in form and features like the Javanese of Bantam, differed from them in language, and showed themselves to be Javanese of another race. This novelty caused so much pleasure to the Javanese and satraps of Balambuan, and especially to Chiaymasiuro, King of Damuth, that the latter, being a prince, resolved for curiosity's sake to venture on the discovery of Luca Antara. Embarking with some companions in a calaluz or rowing-boat provided with necessaries, he left the port of Balambuan for the south, and after twelve days' voyage arrived at the said harbour of Luca Antara, a peninsula or island of 600 leagues in circumference, where he was well and hospitably received by the Xabandar of the country; and, while Chiaymasiuro was enjoying the freshness of the country, he took note of its wealth, for he observed in it much gold, cloves, mace, nutmegs, sandalwood, both white and coloured, with other spices and aromatics of which he took samples. With the south monsoon he returned safely to the harbour of Balambuan, where he was received by the king in presence of the Portuguese and particularly of Pedro de Carvalhaes, overseer at Malacca, who will bear witness to his arrival and to his voyage from Luca Antara to Balambuan in the year 1601. According to the roteiro or log of Chiaymasiuro's voyage Luca Antara must be the general name of that peninsula in which are the harbours of the kingdoms of Beach and Maletur, because between the sixteen degrees of latitude of Beach and the nine degrees of Balambuan is a space of eight degrees, which amount to the 140 Spanish leagues of Chiaymasiuro's twelve days' voyage from Balambuan to Luca Antara. This shows that Luca Antara cannot be the Java Minor of Marco Polo, because it is in a higher latitude of the tropic of Capricorn, namely in 23 degrees 30 minutes. And for this enterprise was Manoel Godinho de Eredia at the same time despatched in the said year 1601 and provided with the habit of the Order of Christ and the title of Adelantado of the India Meridional, to pass to the southward in order to carry out the southern discoveries and to take possession of these lands for the Crown of Portugal. But this did not take place because, being in Malacca ready to make the voyage of the India Meridional, there supervened the wars of that fortress with the Malays and Dutch, which prevented the discoveries, as the people were wanted for the defence of Malacca, the Governor of which was Andrea Furtado de Mendoca."

Major adds: "This is Eredia's report, and it is followed by a statement to the same effect written by Chiaymasiuro, King of Damuth, to the King of Pam, but embodying the following additional facts: The king of the country presented Chiaymasiuro with handfuls of gold coin, such as that of Venice. The natives wore their hair long, down to the shoulders, and had the head bound with a fillet of wrought gold. They wore kreeses adorned with precious stones, and with curved blades like the kreeses of Bali. Their common pastime was cock-fighting. This letter of Chiaymasiuro's is followed by a like statement, agreeing in all particulars with the two preceding, indicted by the Portuguese, Pedro de Carvalhaes, who declares that he received it from the lips of Chiaymasiuro and his companions whom he met in Surabaya. This document contains one statement in addition to the foregoing, namely: that Luca Antara contained many populous cities and towns. At the close of the document Carvalhaes swears on the Holy Gospels to the truth of his statement, and signs it with his name. Accompanying the extract which I received from Brussels were two maps, also by Eredia, the one of Luca Antara and its surroundings, the other a map of the world in which Luca Antara is placed on the north-west of that part of the great southern land, which, if it represented a truth, COULD only tally with what we know to be Australia. Now it does not require much knowledge of geography to see that the Luca Antara of Eredia thus described would in no way agree with what we know of Australia. Here therefore I might stop; but, when I reflect how many thousands have been led by my means erroneously to connect the name of Eredia with the first authenticated discovery of Australia, I think it likely that some may look to me for the completion of the story.

"Not being Australia, then, what was Luca or Nuca Antara? Finding that in Sunda Nusa is the ordinary, and in Java the ceremonial, word for island, while to the eastward and northward not Nusa, but Pulo and other equivalents are used for that word, and, remembering that Luca Antara was an alternative name for the Island of Madura, which lies close to the east coast of Java itself, I reverted to the description of Luca Antara given by the native prince Chiaymasiuro and by P. Cavalhaes, and found that it tallied with Madura to a nicety. The men of Luca Antara who were driven by stress of weather into the port of Balambuan are described as in figure, face, and complexion like the Javanese of Bantam, but differing somewhat in their language, insomuch as they showed themselves to be Javanese of another species or race. Crawford, in his History of the Indian Archipelago, t. 2, page 69, says that the language of the two islands are scarcely more like than any other two languages of the western portion of the Archipelago. The long hair down to the shoulders, the fillet of cloth of gold round the head, the kreese adorned with precious stones and with the blade curved, the cock-fighting, the gold and spices and sandalwood, all bear their abundant testimony to the fitness of the application of the description to the Island of Madura. The island itself was described as six hundred leagues in circuit, and containing well-peopled cities and towns, which is all in accordance with the real description of Madura, nor can we find any other island presenting such elements of identity. Here then we come to the first stage of the great falsehood. The Javanese prince reports himself to have made a voyage of twelve days to the *south* from Balambuan to reach an island whose name and description in every particular belong to an island lying *north* of Balambuan. The distance from Balambuan to the coast assumed to be reached by the southward course, namely Australia, would be about six hundred miles; that by the northern course to Madura would be barely ninety, and the time occupied in accomplishing the voyage with oars, namely twelve days, would apply much more reasonably to the former distance than the latter. The question then naturally arises, how came Eredia, having elected the Island of Madura, under its little known Malay name of Luca Antara, as the source from which to draw the materials for circumstantial description in his report to Philip III to apply that description to a locality which corresponds, as our map shows, with a country which, had he been speaking truth, *could* be no other than Australia? A fact of which he was utterly ignorant, but which had come to my knowledge in the elaboration of my Early Voyages to Terra Australis for the Hakluyt Society in 1859, laid bare to me the whole machinery of this impostor's process of deception, and showed how, in attempting to deceive the king, he himself was deceived by the blunders of others who had gone before him. The facts are as follow: In the seventh chapter of the third book of Marco Polo's travels we read these words:

"'When you leave Java and sail for 700 miles on a course between south and south-west you arrive at two islands, a greater and a less. The one is called Sondur and the other Condur. As there is nothing about them worth mentioning let us go on five hundred miles beyond Sondur, and then we find another country which is called Locach. In this country the brazil which we make use of grows in great plenty, and they also have gold in incredible quantity. They have elephants likewise and much game. In this kingdom too are gathered all the porcelain shells which are used for small change in all those regions.'

"Now although all the manuscripts and texts of Marco Polo read as above 'when you leave Java,' Marsden has shown that the point of departure should really be Champa, a name in old times applied by Western Asiatics to a kingdom which embraced the whole coast between Tongking and Cambodia, including all that is now called Cochin China. Colonel Yule has shown that the country meant by Locach was Lo-Kok, or the Kingdom of Lo, which previous to the middle of the fourteenth century formed the lower part of what is now Siam. Sondur and Condur are the Pulo Condore Islands. The introduction of the word Java into the text instead of Champa was a digression, the retention of which inevitably led geographers to place Locach in the Southern Ocean. So much for blunder number one, of which Eredia knew nothing; we now come to blunder number two, of which he was equally unconscious. In the Basle edition of Marco Polo in 1532, the printer unluckily altered the L into a B, and the first c into an e, so that the word Locach became Boeach.*

(*Footnote. See above, Chapter 20 with reference to Locach and Beach.)

"This was afterwards shortened into Beach, and the blunder was repeated in books and on maps with so much confidence that we find it even occurring on a semi-globe which adorns the monument of the learned Sir Henry Savile in Merton College Chapel, Oxford; and strangely enough it is the only geographical name thereon inscribed. As however some editions of Marco Polo retained the word Locach and others Beach both names came to be copied on to maps, and, the point of departure being Java, the mapmakers, following the course indicated in Marco Polo, laid these countries down as forming part of the great southern land which was supposed to occupy the entire south part of the globe. This was the India Meridionalis of Eredia's dreams and ambition. It will have been observed that Luca Antara was said to be also reached by Chiaymasiuro after a voyage of twelve days *south* from Java, and accordingly it is domiciled by Eredia on this same southern land with Locach and Beach, a thought evidently suggested by Marco Polo's text.*

(*Footnote. It must be understood that, long before Eredia's time, Mercator, in his map bearing date 1569, had already set down the countries of Beach and Locach. See above, Illustration 5. George Collingridge.)

"But it will also have been noticed that in this Locach, mis-spelt Beach, there was gold in considerable quantity. And the result was that Beach was specially described on many of the maps of that time as provincia aurifera, and Eredia at the commencement of his report speaks of it as 'the province of gold.' Let us now trace the effect which this produces on Eredia's geography. In the first place he lays down *both* Locach and Beach, showing in common with the other geographers his ignorance of the misprint. To these he adds Luca Antara with an elaborate and complex outline, even with the rocks and shoals minutely laid down, which I fear he never derived from the surveying skill of his friend Chiaymasiuro, but in the same manner as the Portuguese named the Cape Verde Islands from the promontory off which they lay; so also off the coast of Beach Eredia lays down an island to which he gives the name of Luca Veach. In Spain and Portugal the B and V are interchangeable. 'The island,' says Eredia, 'is called Luca Veach, because among the natives of Ende, Sabbo, and Java Luca signifies an island, and Veach of gold. The printer's devil in Basle* in 1532 little dreamed that he was inventing a Javanese word, nor does Crawford, the great Malay authority, corroborate that he did so. So far is it otherwise that, in a list of all the words representing gold throughout the Archipelago, not one in the slightest degree approaches to either Beach or Veach. Nevertheless the next chapter in Eredia's report consists of a certification from our friend Pedro de Carvalhaes, captain of the fortress of Ende, in which he swears on the Holy Gospels that it is all true, and affixes his signature thereto under date of Malacca, 4th of October 1601; the same date as his other certificate.

(*Footnote. See Chapter 34 footnote.)

"In one of the chapters of Eredia's report, entitled Of Discovery by Chance, he tells us that a vessel from Malacca was carried to the south by the Bali currents between Java and Bima, and discovered the Islands of Luca Tambini* peopled only by women, like Amazons, who with bows and arrows prevented anyone from landing. 'These women,' he says, 'must have their husbands from another separate island.'

(*Footnote. According to E. Modigliani (the Italian author of L'Isola delle Donne, viaggio ad Engano) the island to the south-west of Sumatra, which the Portuguese Diego Pacheco called *Engano* (the Deceitful) in 1520, appears to have been known previously under the name of the Island of Women by the inhabitants of Sumatra. Early Italian authors who gathered their information from the Arabs place the Male and Female islands in the Indian Ocean, near Socotra Island. Rottenest Island, near Perth, Western Australia, was called *Meisjes Eylandt* (Island of Girls) on old Dutch charts, and *Isle des Filles* on French charts. See Vaugondy's map 1756. The origin of *Isle des Filles* is to be traced to Martin Behaim's Globe, A.D. 1492. George Collingridge.)

"Everyone has heard of the fable of the Male and Female Islands. It has existed from time immemorial, and was repeated by Marco Polo, but I doubt if the noble Venetian would have sworn on the Holy Gospels, as of his own knowledge in the character of a local and official authority, that a vessel from Malacca went there. This however Pedro de Carvalhaes did in his last mentioned certification, and I am glad that he tells us that after having discovered the island of women (Pulo Tambini) they then came in sight of Luca Veach. The one statement deserved to be made in the same breath with the other. I need not weary the reader with any further details from the utterances of these vile accomplices. Suffice it that there are plenty more falsehoods in them, built up on the basis of the low country maps, the conjectural or imaginary portions of which are dressed up by Eredia as solid realities, confirmed by all the circumstance of detail. That Eredia received a commission from the Viceroy Ayres de Saldanha to make discoveries of supposed islands in the south is pretty certain. The Alvara, or patent, signed 5th of April 1601, accompanies the report. It constitutes him Governor-in-Chief of any such islands falling within the limits of the Crown of Portugal, promises him the Order of Christ, and engages that, in the event of his death being ascertained, provision should be made for the honourable marriage of his daughter, to whom the extreme recompense and honours would be accorded as the services of her father might merit. He was to receive also the twentieth part of the profit of his discoveries, or what his majesty was in the habit of giving to discoverers of mines in his own kingdoms. It is very clear that he occupied a responsible position, and that much might be expected from him. Carvalhaes in both his certificates uses the words, 'The discoverer, Manoel Godinho de Eredia, asked me for this information for the good of his voyage and for the accomplishment of the service of the king.' It was evidently requisite that he should be a discoverer on paper, since fate had not made him a discoverer at sea. In the map of the world which accompanies his report, and which is itself a reduction from a map by Ortelius, he writes on the southern land, India Meridional descoberta anno 1601. The mapmaker who followed him, and from whose handiwork was made the copy which I brought forward in 1861, had a constructive mind. On a country which bore a legend which proved it to be Australia he with unflinching positiveness grouped into one distinct declaration the reputed discovery, the date, the name of Eredia, and the name of the Viceroy. 'Nuca Antara was discovered in 1601 by Manoel Godinho de Eredia, by order of the Viceroy Ayres de Saldanha.' I repeat that I am not ashamed that with the amount of evidence that then lay before me I believed him; but I am very happy in the thought that, so soon as the field of evidence was enlarged, it was I, who alone had been responsible for its promulgation, that had the good fortune at once to detect the imposture."*

(*Footnote. From Major's Prince Henry the Navigator 1877.)

Some years after the publication of Major's altered views in connection with Godinho de Eredia's alleged discoveries Mr. Leon Yanssen published in French a translation of Godinho de Eredia's original manuscript.* Mr. Ch. Ruelens wrote a preface to that work, in which he seeks to defend Godinho's character against Major's perhaps somewhat hasty remarks. At all events he shows that the title *descobridor* (discoverer) was a term often given in advance to a person that received a commission to make discoveries.

(*Footnote. Malacca L'Inde Meridionale et le Cathay. Manuscript originale autographe de Godinho de Eredia, appartenant a la Bibliotheque Royale de Bruxelles reproduit en facsimile et traduit par M. Leon Yanssen, membre de la Societe de Geographie de Bruxelles. Avec une preface de M. Ch. Ruelens, conservateur a la Bibliotheque Royale, membre du Comite de la Societe de Geographie de Bruxelles 1882.)

Mr. Delmar Morgan, in his paper on the Early Discovery of Australia, read at the Geographical Congress at Berne and printed in 1891, says (page 7 note 1), speaking of Godinho de Eredia:

"This explorer and his discoveries have been discussed by M. Ruelens, Dr. Hamy (*Bulletins de la Soc. de Geographie*, vime serie tome 15), and by Mr. Major (*Archaeologia* volume xliv.), all of whom leave the matter in some doubt. The general inference to be derived from a study of their writings is that Godinho's claims to rank as a discoverer rest wholly on his surveys in Malacca, not on any presumed discovery by him of Australia."

A LETTER FROM R.H. MAJOR WITH REFERENCE TO THE WORD QUABESEGMESCE ON THE WEST COAST OF AUSTRALIA.

Corona d' Italia, Via Palestro 4. Florence, March 28 1890.

DEAR SIR,

Your very kind letter and accompanying number of the Centennial Magazine, sent to my address in London, have just reached me here, and I beg you to accept my best thanks for them.

I have read your article with great interest, and, seeing that great obscurity surrounds the actual explorations on which the early sixteenth century French maps of Australia are founded, minutely critical observations on individual expressions occurring on them are of great interest, and, in the endeavour to progress from the unknown into the known, one is never sure what fresh stepping-stone may not be gained sight of by means of any the slightest glimmer of new light. Another interesting problem lies before you, if you care to follow it out, in tracing the value of the word on the west coast, QUABESEGMESCE. At present my own mind is fully occupied with another subject; but in the event of your happily lighting on any fresh tracks it would always be a great pleasure to me if you would do me the favour to let me hear of them.

Faithfully yours,

R.H. MAJOR.

George Collingridge, Esq.

Since the receipt of the above letter we have followed out R.H. Major's suggestion, and have been fortunate enough to trace the meaning and origin, to a certain extent, of the word *Quabesegmesce*, or *Quabe se quiesce* as it should read. It will be noticed on the Dauphin chart, and refers, we have not the slightest doubt, to *Calmia* on Martin Behaim's globe. (See Chapter 16.)

THE END.

GEOGRAPHICAL INDEX.

See also the special nomenclature of the Lusitano-French and Dutch Charts, given above.

Abaie a Besse:
a name on J. Roze's chart Number 1.

Abaie bressille (Brazil Bay):
a name on J. Roze's chart Number 1.

Abaie de:
a name on J. Roze's chart Number 1.

Abbey of All Saints:
an extraordinary mistake.

Abrolhos group:
on the western coast of Australia.
Dampier fell in with the coast of Australia to the north of the.

Abyssinia:
Suakem in.

Acacan:
an island near Inuagana, reached by Magellan.

Acapulco:
an expedition sent out from by Cortez.
De Quiros landed by his mutinied crew at.
Trade from.

Accad:
Zenith of the Heaven over.

Acheen Head:
referred to by Couto.

Achen:
Captain Lancaster went to.

Aden:
Gulf of, on Turin mappamundi.

Envoys go via.
Covilham embarked at.

Adenara:
mentioned.

Africa limited to the northern hemisphere in Copenhagen mappamundi.

Africa:
belongs to the Great World according to the School of Pergamos.
Asia and Europe surrounded by the sea.
Canary Islands on the west coast of.
Terra incognita connected with, in Ptolemy's map.
On an early mappamundi.
Southern coasts of, bent round on maps so as to almost join the Malay Peninsula.
Stretches beyond the equator in third type of map.
The coasts of, visited.
The southern extremity of, called Cavo di Diab.
Voyages along the west coast continued.
Western coast of.
Mentioned.
The eastern parts of, supposed to be under the sway of Prester John.
Sofala on the eastern coast of.
Southern extremity of, rounded.
Coast of China connected with the eastern extremity of.
A coastline in the latitude of the southern parts of.
With reference to Columbus' arguments.
A work on the Discoveries of the Portuguese in.
Position of Zanzibar with reference to, explained.
The protuberant part of the south-east coast of.
Dauxety Island some distance from.
New Holland does not join.

Afrike:
mentioned.

Agama (Angaman):
in Ruysch's mappamundi.

Agania:
in Eradia's description.

Aidoema Island (south coast of New Guinea, Dutch Territory):
named Isla del Capan luis Vaes de Torres, discovered by Torres.

Aimoey Bay:
in China, mentioned.

Ainioro Island (south coast of New Guinea):
named by Torres isla de la madera, or wooded island.

Aiolie:
mentioned by Homer.

Albans, St.:
the knight of (see Mandeville).

Albert Nyanza:
on Turin mappamundi.

Al Camar:
another name for Madagascar.
Corrupted on charts.

Alcacer Quibir:
the battle of, a death-blow to Portugal.

Alcobaza:
a map found in the study of.

Alexandria:
centre of eastern and western commerce of the world.
Erathosthenes, the chief librarian of.
Meridian of.
Envoys go via.

Algarves:
and of Mauritania, Dom Joao II, named King of Portugal of the.

Algoa Bay:
an island in, reached by Dias.

Allas:
Strait of, mentioned.

Almaine:
Dom Pedro goes to.

Alter Orbis:
referred to by Santarem.

Amadura:
island (same as Madura), north-east coast of Java.

Amberno River:
in Papua, discovered by Inigo Ortiz de Retez and Gaspar Rico, and named the St. Augustin River.

Amboina (same as Amboyna):
written Amboino in Galvano's account.
Serrano escaped to.
Mentioned by Torres.
A voyage to Australia from.
Jan Carstens' expedition returned to.
The yacht Pera returned to.
Massacre of the English at.

Amboyna (same as Amboina):
Paul Van Soldt met the Duyfken at the fort of.

Ambrollossen:
a corruption of Abrolhos.

America:
International Exhibition held in, to commemorate the 400th anniversary of her discovery.
Revealed to the world.
Sighted by John and Sebastian Cabot.
Early intercourse with.
"Did the Phoenicians discover."
Discovery of, due to Italians.
Novel objects brought from.
Regions between Bay of Bengal and, omitted on Cosa's map.
The Arabs and Rodriguez's map with reference to.
A strait to the south of, in Schoner's gores.
Mendana returned to, in 1569.
South of, occurs Brasilie Regio.
New Holland does not join.

American Continent:
with reference to Strabo's ideas.

Amsterdam:
Cornelius Houtman addressed the merchants of.
The merchants of, sent the two brothers Houtman to Lisbon.
Commelyn's work published at.
A Dutch map published at, in 1640, without any discoveries that the Dutch claim to have
  made on the shores of the Great South Land, recorded.
Vlamingh's voyage printed at, in 1701.

Anamba Islands:
referred to.

Andalusia:
slaves sold there.
Inhabitants of.

Andaman Islands:
described under the name of Angaman by Marco Polo.

Anda ne barcha:
a legend on the Dauphin chart.
Altered to Autane bamcha on P. Desceliers' chart.

Angaman:
of Marco Polo.

Angania:
on Fra Mauro's map.

Angiana:
is Marco Polo's Angaman on the Apianus mappamundi.

Angra das Voltas:
named by Bartholomew Dias.
A negress left at.

Angra do Salto:
two negroes restored to.

Angra dos Ilheos:
named by Bartholomew Dias.
Negroes left at.

Angra dos Vaqueiros:
named by Dias.

Angra Pequena (Angra dos Ilheos).

Anguana:
on Behaim's globe.
Occupies the site of New Zealand.

Anjane:
in Galvano's description.

Annoban (Annobon):
an island more than eighty leagues from the mainland.

Antarctic Continent:
the fictitious, left out on S. Cabot's mappamundi.

Antarctic Pole:
the crown of the, should have been discovered by De Quiros.

Antarctic Regions:
with reference to position of Hades and Tartaros.

Antichthone:
referred to by Santarem.

Antichthonos:
of Strabo.

Antic Ocean:
the Chaldean and Greek circumfluent ocean.

Antilia:
Diogo de Teive in search of.
A pretended discovery of.
Near the middle of the Atlantic.
Ten spaces from, to Cipango.
Of marvellous wealth.

Antipodes:
on Turin mappamundi.

Antwerp:
Themara's work published at.

Ap quieta:
with reference to Quabe se quiesce.

Arabia deserta:
mentioned.

Arabia felix:
mentioned.

Arabian Sea:
with reference to Conti's location of Malepur.

Aramaram:
a name in Francisco Rodriguez's portolano.

Archaic Ocean:
bursting of the.
Fra Mauro's pseudo-equatorial line ran parallel with the.

Archipelago:
East Indian, the sumpit (blow pipe) of the, mentioned by Odoric.

Achipel de Dampier:
Dampier amongst the islands that received the name of.

Arctic Pole:
the dry star of the.

Arenes:
occupies the site of the Abrolhos on the western coast of Australia. Not a corruption of Arenas (Sand), but rather of Abrolhos.

Argira:
island, on 11th century mappamundi.

Arguin:

Bay of, first reached by Lorenzo Dias.

Arnheim:
Cape, a group of islands occupying the position of.

Arnhem:
or Van Diemen's Land, the discovery of, not recorded on the Mar d'India map.
Discovered by Pieter Pietersz after the murder of Pool.
The Great Island of, discovered.
Named probably after the yacht Arnhem.
An island on older charts than the Dutch ones occupies the site of the island called,
  and bears the name Arnim.

Arnhem River:
named after the second yacht of Jan Carstens' expedition.

Arnim (see also Arnhem) island:
on Henri II mappamundi of 1546.

Arou:
Jan Carstens ordered to visit.

Aroum Islands:
the Duyfken sailed by the.

Arouw Islands:
named Arnim on the Henri II mappamundi (1546).

Arques:
near Dieppe.

Arrecifes:
an island discovered and named during Mendana's expedition.

Arus:
passed by Abreu.

Asaerm (same as Gresic).

Asia:
belongs to the Great World according to the school of Pergamos.

Europe and Africa surrounded by the sea.
In connection with Fra Mauro's Malay Archipelago.
Gold and silver, etc. brought from.
Early commerce to ports in.
Atlantic Ocean, stretching to the shores of.
In Galvano's description.
In an early mappamundi.
Stretches beyond the equator in third type of map.
When Affonso V should send an expedition to east coast of.
A picture of.
The larger part of, supposed to be ruled by Prester John.
The regions of, assumed more correct dimensions.
The term Brazil may have applied to some continental land south of.
And America joined by Schoner.
On the eastern part of.
Gataio fails to join, at Catigara.
New Holland does not join.

Asiatic Archipelago:
the Spaniards did not know when to sail from the, to reach New Spain.

Assyria:
mentioned.

Asturias:
inhabitants of.

Atlas:
in the south.

Atlantes:
of Plato.

Atlantic Ocean:
the, mentioned by Strabo.
As considered by Strabo.
The mystery of.
mentioned.
Antilla Island, near the middle of.
Unauthorised voyages in.

Au fane bacha:
a corruption of Anda ne barcha.

Aujaue Island of:
passed by Abreu, is named Anjano in the Portuguese text of Galvano.
Corresponds with Lomboc.
Dr. Hamy suggests Rindjani as the origin of.

Aureus Chersonesus (Malay Peninsula).

Austral-Asia:
early commerce to ports in.

Australasia:
opening of the sea-way to.
The regions of, assume more correct dimensions.
Portion of Barthema's travels which refer to.
The voyage of the Vittoria had a marked influence on the geography of.
Journal and proceedings of the Royal Geographical Society of, referred to.
The Dutch of the first expedition to.
The dawn of the English period of dominion in.

Australasian regions:
the effect of Marco Polo's writings on the cartography of.
Described from hearsay by Marco Polo.
Interpolations in Odoric's narrative of the.
Information concerning the, obtainable only from Italians.
To recognise them in Fra Mauro's Map.
Invaded.
The Land of Spice.
Bartholomew Columbus' continent in the.
On Behaim's globe.
Made the centre of the eastern and western configurations.
Left bare.
The term Brasil may have applied to.
The first cartographical appearance of the term Brasil in the.
A strait between the, and an Antarctic continent in Schoner's globe.
Totally different configuration for the, identical in Schoner's globe of 1515 and 1520.

Austral continent:
Schoner the first to give a more decided form and different name to the.
Supposed by A. Corsali and others to extend from the regions of New Guinea to the Land of Sanctae Crucis.
Believed to have been discovered by Francisco de Hoces.

Australia:
possibility of an International Exhibition being held in, to commemorate the 400th anniversary of her discovery.
Discovery of.
Dauphin chart of.
Or southern world according to the school of Pergamos.
And the ancients.
Northern portion of, obliterated.
Early voyages to, quoted.
A portion of, might be intended to be represented in Ptolemy's map.
Islands set down to the north of, in Ptolemy's map.
And Java considered as one by Marco Polo.
Java Major does not refer to, on fantastic maps.
Odoric of Pordenone reached nearer to, than Marco Polo.
Discovered.
Ignorant remarks concerning.
Themara on.
The western coasts of, may have been marked on an Arabian portolano.
Fantastic representation of.
Java Minor set down to the south-east of.
Its eastern coasts with reference to Neucuram and Pentam.
Its western and north-western coasts made to serve for the coast of a bogus Sumatra.
Its westerly coasts known.
A passage which applies to.
Bogus Malay Peninsula in latitude and longitude of.
Terra Australis may apply to.
The east coast of.
Some island off the west coast of.
Coachs in Behaim's globe is between New Guinea and.
The term Brazil applied to.
And New Guinea supposed to be connected.
De Gonneville said to have landed on the western coast of.
Barthema visits regions in proximity to.
A country south of Java must be.
A remarkable reference to.
Distorted charts of.
Between Madagascar and.
Bears the name of Loac Provincia in the Hunt-Lenox globe.
A curious continental land that has been taken for.
The western coastline of.

Seylan insulae pars of Ruysch's mappamundi corresponds with the western parts of.
Western coasts of, in Frankfort gores.
South of, occurs Laco int Montaras.
Western coast on Apianus' mappamundi.
Named Gataio or China.
Islands discovered not far from the western coasts of.
The most important document in connection with the early discovery of.
The strongest evidence of discovery as yet brought to light is shown in the drafting of
  the Dauphin and similar charts of.
The discovery of, due to the Portuguese and Spanish.
Western coasts of, charted by the Portuguese.
Eastern coasts charted by the Spaniards.
Occupies the site of the continent set down on Portuguese and Spanish maps.
Connected with Java and an imaginary continent around the South Pole.
placed in its true position.
Supposed to be connected with the Tierra del Fuego.
Called Jave-la-Grande.
Islands on the western coast of, represented in G. Mercator's map.
Bears no name on Jean Roze's chart Number 1.
Called The Londe, or Land of Java, in chart Number 2.
Supposed to be inhabited by tigers and lions.
The earliest account of the natives of.
Remarkable features of the western coast of.
Previous representation of, disregarded.
Drake and Cavendish stood as good a chance as the Dutch of coming in contact with.
The eastern and western coasts of, roughly delineated in Wytfliet's map.
Major speaking of the indications of, in Mercator's and Ortelius' maps.
Strait between New Guinea and, known to the Spaniards.
Port Denison, one of the best ports on the eastern coast of.
Captain Saris' notes with reference to the first Dutch voyage to.
Dutch discovery in.
The early history of.
Tasman passed round the east side of.
A doubt cast on the discovery of the south-west coast of.
A cruise among the islands and gulfs of.
In the voyage of the Duyfken, nothing said about.
Did the Duyfken reach.
Various voyages published relating to.
Discovery of a portion of the south coast of.
The involuntary visit of the Vianen to the north-west coast of.

The name given to, in the Mar d' India map.
Called Terra del Zur in the Mar d'India map.
A rough indication of the north-west of, with the name Beach.
Called the Compagnis Niev Nederlandt in the copy of Tasman's original manuscript chart.
Nomenclature of, and Tasmania, in P. Goos' and Tasman's maps.
Dampier's second voyage to.
When the Cygnet reached, Captain Read was in command.
Absence of fresh water on the coasts of.
A map of.
Discovered.
Islands in close proximity to.
The country discovered by Gonneville does not correspond with.
Islands near, discovered by Gomez de Sequeira.
Discovered by Gomez de Sequeira.
The discovery of, by the Portuguese.
The Chinese and Malays acquainted with the northern coasts of.
Northern coasts of.
An open sea between, and New Guinea.
The seaway blocked between Java and.
A French claim of discovery in.

Australian Continent:
with reference to Psittacorum regio.
Omitted for want of space.
The term Beach used by Mercator on the.
Altered to New Holland.
Sumbawa indicated as forming part of the.
Disappearance of the.
Left out on the F. Monachus mappamundi.
Only a small portion of the, given on Jean Roze's chart.
Peculiar shape of the.
The outline of the.
No, represented on Sebastian Cabot's mappamundi.
Called Iava-la-Grande on P. Desceliers' mappamundi.
G. Mercator's map based on a vague knowledge of the existence of the.
New Guinea separated from the, by a narrow strait on G. Mercator's map.
Joined to the Antarctic Lands in the map which appeared with Frobisher's voyages.
A colony to be settled on the.
De Quiros determined to discover and settle the.
A document which proves a discovery of the, before the arrival of the Dutch.
The great, a drug in the market.

Not represented.

Austral-India:
two islands in.
A name given by De Gonneville.

Australis Terra (see also Terra Australis):
an important passage with reference to the, in Wytfliet's work.

Austral regions:
called Terra Australis.

Austral world:
according to the school of Pergamos.

Austria:
for the sake of the name of, says De Quiros.

Austrialia (see also La Austrialia):
a matter for discussion.
The term used unmistakably.

Aynan (Hainan):
in Galvano's description.

Azores:
the, with reference to its volcanoes.
Adventurers from.
Marked on maps.
Joao, first discoverer of.
Bamboo stalks driven to the shores of.
The, an expedition to start from.
The hot-bed of transatlantic expeditions.
In connection with the line of demarcation.

Babylon:
Berosus, priestly historian of.

Baccalearum:
a region in the north.

Bachan :

and Ternate, the southern hemisphere to be explored between the Baia de San Felipe y Santiago and.
Torres continued his voyage to.

Bachian (same as Bachan):
reached by Torres.
The King of.
Or Labova, the Dutch had Fort Barneveldt at.

Bada (Banda):
near Muthil, reached by Magellan's expedition.
Mistaken for Badjane or Batchian.

Badajos:
a commission appointed to meet at.
Referred to.

Badam (for Bada, i.e. Banda):
on alleged Schoner globe.

Bagdad:
visited by Odoric.

Baia (same as Baia de San Felipe y Santiago):
Torres prevented by stress of weather from making the circuit of the land of the.

Baia de San Felipe y Santiago (same as Baia):
the southern hemisphere to be explored between Peru and the.
Discovered by De Quiros.

Baibara Island (south coast of New Guinea):
and another island in its neighbourhood are called isla de don diego barrantes and islas
  de mayorga in De Prado's map.

Bajador (Bogador):
Joao the first to double Cape.

Balabero:
channel of.

Balambuam:

on the south-east coast of Java.

Balambuan:
mentioned in Eredia's description.

Bali:
in Galvano's description.
Straits of, mentioned by De Barros.
One of Nicolo de' Conti's Javas.
South coast of, little known.
On the confines of the world.
Charted in Fra Mauro's map.
Passed by Abreu.
Bears names difficult to reconcile with.
Difficult navigation in the Straits of.
Charted as a distinct island.
Charted by Francisco Rodriguez.
Is called Ballaram in F. Rodriguez's chart.
Reached by the Dutch of the first expedition to Australasia.
The Dutch set sail from.
The Vianen hoped to pass the Straits of.
Forms part of Australia.

Banca:
in Galvano's description.

Banda:
Sea of, with reference to volcanoes.
Sea, Ptolemy's islands of the.
Gunong Api in the Sea of.
Islands in the Sea of, included in Gilolo.
Islands of, in Galvano's description.
Island, one of the Spice Islands.
On the confines of the world.
Nutmegs from.
Three ships sent to.
A nautical phrase which refers to.
An island of snakes not far from the island of.
Abreu's expedition leaves.
Mentioned by Torres.
The Duyfken returns to.
The Flemings Pinnasse returned to.
An expedition sent out from, in command of Gerrit Thomasz Pool.

Pieter Pietersz after the death of Pool and discoveries made returned to.

Bandan (Banda):
Described by Nicolo de' Conti.
Described by Barthema.

Bantam:
Peter Both arrived at.
Captain Lancaster went to.
A Dutch yacht despatched from.
The Dutch trade at.
Captain Saris at.
The Little Sun arrived at.
In Java.
The Eendraght left for.
Mentioned in connection with Dirck Hartog's visit to Australia.

Barateue (Bouton ?):
An island reached by Drake.
Departing from, Drake sails for Java Major:

Barbadoes:
Island of, Sir W. Courteen got a bad title to the:

Barusae:
In Ptolemy's map:

Basilisk Island:
Named by Moresby, previously named the Tierra de San Buenaventura by the Spaniards:

Basles:
A Pomponius Mela, printed at.

Batavia:
Van Diemen governor of.
Old archives turned over at.
Captain Cook's visit to.
The Ridderschap van Hollandt lost between the Cape of Good Hope and.
Vlamingh steered for.
Three Dutch vessels leave.
The Golden Seahorse arrives at.
The Vianen sailed from.

The Waeckende Boey and the Emeloort set sail from.

Batochina:
reached by Cavendish's expedition.
Some confusion about the name.

Baxos de la Candelaria:
named by Mendana.

Baya:
a Portuguese term given to Van Diemen's Gulf.

Bay of St. Peter of Arlanza (south coast of New Guinea):
a name given by Torres to the bay named Triton Bay by the Dutch.

Bay of St. Philip and St. James (see also Baia):
De Quiros appointed officers in the.

Beach:
a corruption of Locach.
A name on the north-west coast of Australia in Hoeius' map.

Bead Island (coast of New Guinea):
De Prado's isla de la palma.

Bengal, Bay of:
with reference to location of Malepur.
Same as Sinus Gangeticus.

Benghalla:
reached by Barthema and his friend.

Berlin:
a work mentioning Behaim's globe published at.

Bernier Island:
an island facing Shark's Bay.

Bintan (Bintang):
in Galvano's description.

Bintang:
near Singapore.

Same as Pentan.
Marco Polo's Pentam.

Blanchard Island:
called isla de san facundo in Spanish chart.

Blue Mountains:
early colonists stopped by the.

Blue Nile:
on Turin mappamundi.

Bordeaux:
a mappamundi coming from the Geographical Society of.

Borneo:
left out in Fra Mauri's mappamundi.
Left out in Ptolemy's map.
Volcanoes of.
Southern or eastern, visited by Odoric.
Barthema proceeds to Java by way of.
Camphor from.
Claimed by the Spaniards.
Not named Java by Marco Polo.

Borneos (Borneo):
in Galvano's description.

Bramble Cay:
an island off the extreme north end of Cape York.

Brasielie Regio (same as Brasilie regio):
a Schonerean term.

Brasilae regio:
Schoner's.

Brasilia regio:
on a globe.

Brasilie regio (or Brasielie Regio):
referred to.
On an Antarctic continent.

South of America.

Brazil:
Island of, Lloyd searched for it.
Ships equipped to go in search of.
The country of, discovered by Cabral.
Not original term.
The first cartographical appearance of the term in the Australian regions.
the term, on an Arabian map.
The term, applied to Australia (?)
The alleged proximity of, to Malacca.
In Schoner's map is called Sacte Crucis.
Terra de Brazil situated eighty degrees away to the west of the real.
Dampier came from.

Bresil (Brazil):
with reference to Rodriguez' map.
The coast of, near Australia.
Or Verzino.

Bristol:
the people of, equipped ships.
John and Sebastian Cabot left, and returned to.

Broad Sound:
in the latitude reached by Torres.
Bears the name of Baia Perdita (Lost Bay) in the Dauphin chart.
Torres reached a point somewhere between New Caledonia and.

Bruges:
a canon of, concocted Mandeville's wonderful travels.

Bruxelles:
a work mentioning Behaim's globe printed at.

Buccaneer's Archipelago:
a name given in commemoration of W. Dampier's visit.

Buena Vista:
discovered and named during Mendana's expedition.

Burney:
appears for Borneo on Oronce Fine's map.

440

Burro, Island of:
Antonio de Abreu went to.
Sebastian del Cano at.

Cabo Fresco:
the limit of Torres' exploration in Milne Bay.

Cabo Godanige:
appears for the first time on the alleged Schoner globe.

Cabo Tormentoso:
the name first given to the Cape of Good Hope.

Cadiz:
vessels returned to.
Inuagana, 158 degrees west of.

Cainam Sabadibe insule tres:
an erroneous appellation for New Guinea on G. Mercator's map.

Cairo:
envoys go via.
Covilham meets messengers at.

Calicut:
mentioned as being discovered.
Trade with.
Covilham went to.
Vasco da Gama made his way to.
Barthema met the Portuguese at.
Gloomy class of.
Money circulated as in.
Referred to.
Indian fleet at.
The Portuguese navigations to.
Cloth of.

California:
Geographical Society of.

Callao, in Peru:
Mendana sailed from.

Mendana's second expedition set sail from.
De Quiros and Torres sailed from.

Callenzuaz:
perhaps a variation of Ptolemy's Caladadrua.

Callezuan:
on Schonerean gores.
Written Callensuan.

Calmia:
becomes quiesce.
On M. Behaim's globe.

Camabam:
an island near New Guinea on Sebastian Cabot's map.

Camaeocada:
corrupted from Camar diva, Island of the Moon.

Camar diva, or Al Camar, Island of the Moon (Madagascar; see also Al Camar).

Cambala (Sumbawa):
passed by Abreu.

Cambalu:
mentioned by Conti.

Cambodia:
with reference to a route indicated by Marco Polo.
Called Lochac.
Produces gold, etc.
And Cochin-China made to serve for the Malay Peninsula in Oronce Fine's map.

Cananor (or Cannanore):
Covilham embarked for.
Barthema reached.

Canary Islands:
Ptolemy's map commences at the.
Joao first discoverer of the.

Candin, or Candyn:
may be same as Odoric's Dondin and Dondyn.
On Schonerean gores.

Candur:
meant for Kondur.

Canduz, for Kondur.

Candyn (see Candin):
on Behaim's globe.
Outside the Australasian sphere.
On Ruysch's mappamundi.

Canton:
visited by Odoric.

Cape bima, modern Bima:
north-east coast of Sumbawa.

Cape de Bona Sperace (Cape of Good Hope):
in Linschoten's description.

Cape Diab (same as Cavo di Diab):
an inscription on, mentioned.

Cape Inscription:
a well determined point.

Cape King William, New Guinea.

Cape Kollf:
with reference to Torres' route.

Cape of Bona Speranca:
called the forefront of Afrike, and marked on an early map.

Cape of Good Hope:
distorted on maps.
Rounded.
Anticipated.
First land beyond.

Named by Joao.
The discovery of, alluded to.
An inscription near.
regions south of the equator revealed by the Portuguese navigations to the.
Schoner's Brasilae regio near the.
Mentioned.
Barthema returns to Europe by the.
Magellan's expedition arrived at.
North-west extremity of New Guinea.
The commander at the, gave orders to the fly-boat Vinck bound for Batavia to touch en passant
   at the west coast of the South Land.
The Ridderschap Van Hollandt lost between the, and Batavia.

Cape Santa Cruz:
named by Magellan.

Cape Van Calmorie (Croker Island):
reached by Martin Van Delft.

Cape Van Diemen:
in Van Diemen's Land.

Cape Verde:
Prince Henry discovered that beyond, the coast trended eastwards.
And the land of the blacks first reached by Diniz Dias.
Islands, with reference to volcanoes.
Discovered by accident.
With reference to line of demarcation.

Cape York:
placed under Sumbawa.
The site of, occupied by an island bearing the name Ye de Tnbanos.
With reference to the course of the Duyfken.
Unconnected with New Guinea.
Divides Sumbawa in two.

Cape York Peninsula:
from Cairncross Island to Cape Grenville.
Torres near the Islands of.

Capogat:
Indian fleet at.

Capraria, islands:
mentioned.

Capricorn, tropic of:
Coasts of Australia set down at the.
Confounded with the equator.
Cuts Pentam in two.
Java Minor placed to the north of the.
The word Calmia near the.
Egtis-Silla to the south of the.
Malacca, near the.
A Malay peninsula extending to.
Southern parts of Ruysch's Sumatra crossed by the.
Lac regnum situated near the.
Islands discovered under the.
Countries known to the Portuguese beyond the.
The Portuguese made no difficulty about sailing twelve degrees south of the.
Magellan had almost reached again the, when he came in sight of two islands.
The eastern coast of Australia at the.
Islands placed on the, in Schoner's 1515 map are represented on the equator in his 1533 map.

Capture, Bay of the (Angra do Salto).

Carpentaria, Gulf of:
with reference to Anda ne barcha.
The Duyfken sailed into the.
Roughly indicated on Wytfliet's map.
With reference to the voyage of the Duyfken.
The nomenclature of the, most extensive in the copy of Tasman's original chart.
Represented as separate from Australia and New Guinea on P. Goos' map.

Castilla (Castille):
with reference to a letter by Toscanelli.
Inhabitants of.

Castille, and Leon.

Cataio (same as Cathay):
in Conti's description.

Cathay:
visited by Odoric of Pordenone.
Yule's work on, quoted.
Khan of, mentioned.
Yule's, referred to.
Mango near.
The residence of the Grand Khan.
Maximilian's advice to go in search of.
Quinsay in.
Distorted.
A continental.

Catherine, Cape St.:
passed.

Catigara:
in Ptolemy's map.
Distance from the Fortunate Islands to.
The Spaniards sailed to the Cape of.
The Spaniards did not find.

Catoira:
the manuscript of, gives a more complete account of Mendana's expedition than Gallego's journal does.

Cauo alto (south coast of New Guinea):
a cape named by Torres.

Cauo de Cocos (south coast of New Guinea):
a cape named by Torres.

Cauo del entredos (south coast of New Guinea, Dutch Territory):
a name given by Torres.

Cauo de S. Antonio de Padua (south coast of New Guinea):
a name given by Torres.

Cauo de S. lucas (south coast of New Guinea, Dutch Territory):
a name given by Torres.

Cauo hondo (south coast of New Guinea, Dutch Territory):
a name given by Torres.

Cauo llano (south coast of New Guinea):
a cape named by Torres.

Cavo di Diab:
name for southern extremity of Africa.

Cayln:
name given to a bogus Sumatra set down to the south of the Malay Peninsula.

Caylur:
from regnum Cayln.

Caypassia, flats of:
spoken of by Galvano.

Celebes:
Drake sailed to an island south of.
A vessel despatched to the Island of.

Ceram:
taken for Ceylon.
Included in Gilolo.

Ceylon, and Taprobana:
And Sumatra described as Taprobana.
Placed in longitude and latitude of Sumatra.
Sumatra placed where Ceylon stands.
Enlarged to correspond with Sumatra.
Islands south of the equator taken for.
In Ptolemy's map.
On 11th century mappamundi.
Visited by Odoric.
Described as Sillan by Marco Polo and Odoric.
Written Saylam.
The Indian Peninsula with regard to.
May be regnum Cayln.
Suggested as another name for Taprobana.
Called Ceilam in Ruysch's mappamundi.

Chaldea:
the author of.

Challis Head:

the Cabo Fresco of Torres.

Champa (same as Chiampa):
visited by Odoric.
As a point of departure.

Cheribon, in Java.

Chiampa:
the word Java used instead of, causes great mistakes.

Chicago:
International Exhibition held in, to commemorate the 400th anniversary of the discovery of America.

China:
the Arabs extend their trade to.
Limit of Ptolemy's map.
In Galvano's description.
Trade of, in the hands of the Arabs.
Seaway to, laid open by Prince Henry the Navigator.
Or Zaiton.
Columbus endeavoured to reach.
Coast of.
Or Cathay.
Shores of, distorted.
Connected with Fra Mauro's Sumatra.
Sarnau, a place in.
Precious commodities from.
Sea, in Ptolemy's map.
Misplaced.
People of.
Andrade and Perestello went to.
Represented in the Australasian regions.
Coast of, claimed by the Spaniards.

China Straits:
Discovered and named by Moresby.
The southern portion of, set down as a port on De Prado's chart.

Chinese Sea:
Represented as a gulf in Ptolemy's map.
Islands of, omitted.

Chucopia (Tucopia):
An island named.

Ciambo, same as Ciamba.

Ciampo porto:
On Behaim's globe.

Cincapura (Singapore):
In Galvano's description.

Cipango, Island of:
Ten spaces distant from Antilla Island.
Not Japan, but Java.
East of Mangi and Cathay.

Circobena:
Corresponds with Cirtena.
An island near Madagascar on Apianus' mappamundi.

Cloues, Island of (Spice Islands):
The first Portuguese that went to.

Coachs:
a corruption of Marco Polo's Lochac.

Cochin:
mentioned as being discovered.
Viceroy in.
Barthema factor for the Portuguese at.

Cochin China:
Marco Polo sojourned on the coast of.
With reference to Chiampa.

Cochin-terra (Cochin China):
Andrea Corsali writes from.

Cocos, Island of:
the buccaneers of the Cygnet intended to make for the.

Cohol (a misprint for Bohol):

an island reached by the survivors of Magellan's expedition.

Coilum, the modern Quilon.

Coilu regnu:
in Schonerean gores of date 1515.

Cologne:
Maximilian's letter printed at.

Comarim, Cape of (Comorin):
described by Galvano.

Comarin, Cape:
mentioned.

Condore, Pulo, Islands:
mentioned with reference to a route indicated by Marco Polo.

Condur:
not mentioned on maps before Nicolo de' Conti's return.
In Fra Mauro's map.

Congo:
King of, received Portuguese hostages.
River, same as Zaire and Rio do Padrao.

Constantinople:
visited by Odoric.

Copenhagen:
an early mappamundi from the library of.

Cormorin Cape:
the buccaneers of the Cygnet intended to make for, after leaving New Holland.

Coromandel Coast:
called Malabar by Nicolo de' Conti.
Called Provincia di Ma'bar or Mobar.
Several towns on the, visited by Conti.

Coruna:

an expedition to the Spice Islands sails from.

Coste Dangereuse:
on the coast of Queensland.

Coste Dangerose (Dangerous Coast):
a legend on J. Roze's chart, at the spot where Cook was nearly wrecked on the coast of Queensland.

Cranganor:
visited by Odoric.

Crete:
on Turin mappamundi.
An island near the Straits of Magalhaens.

Crisa, island:
on Turin mappamundi.

Crise:
island on 11th century mappamundi meant for Malay Peninsula.

Croker Island:
reached by Martin Van Delft.

Cul de sac de l'Orangerie:
the name given by Bougainville to the country at the back of Orangerie Bay.

Cumberland, Islands:
in the latitude reached by Torres and so well charted on the Dauphin map.

C: Vatraar, or ratraar:
probably a bad reading for Aramaram in F. Rodriguez's portolano.

Cygnet Bay:
a name given in commemoration of W. Dampier's visit.

Cyprus:
on Turin mappamundi.

Dampier's Monument:
a name given to commemorate Dampier's visit to New Holland.

Dampier's Archipelago:
a sea chart must have existed showing the western coasts of Australia from Cape Leeuwin to.
A portion of the north-west coast of Australia left out from, to King Sound.

Darien, Gulf of:
Balboa in command at the.
Isthmus of.

Dauxety, Island:
a name for Madagascar.
At some distance from Africa.
The origin of.
Corruption of Laurentij.

Dead Sea:
towards the south (Australasian regions) in Odoric's narrative. See also Anda ne barcha.

Debana, Point:
at the northern entrance to Mullen's Harbour, New Guinea, called Cauo llano by Torres.

Dembea, Lake, or Tzana:
on Turin mappamundi.

Deptford:
Drake's old ship, long an object of veneration to the seamen of.

Dias Point:
or Pedestal Point.

Didymus, Island (New Guinea):
the Spanish isla de manglares.

Dieppe:
mariners of.
Jean Roze, a Frenchman, native of.

Diey, St.:
in Lorraine, the cosmographiae introductio first printed there.

Dimo baz, or Margabim (Mauritius).

Dina aroby, or Arobi (Rodriguez).
On Schonerean gores.

Dinamora:
on Schonerean gores.

Dina Morare, or Moraze (Bourbon).

Dina norca, corrupted from Diva Moraze.

Dina robin, corrupted from Diva Arobi.

Dino baz:
on Schonerean gores.

Dirck Hartog's Island:
with reference to Dirk Hartog's plate.
In connection with Vlamingh's course.

Dirck Hartog's Reede:
visited by Vlamingh.
Passed by the Waeckende Boey.

Diva Arobi:
corrupted to Dina Aroby.

Diva Margabim:
corrupted to Dimo baz.

Diva Moraze:
corrupted to Dina Morare.

Dondin, and Nicoverra Islands:
in Odoric's narrative (see Dondyn).

Dondyn (or Dondin):
in Odoric's narrative may refer to Candin or Candyn.

Dorre Island:
an island facing Shark's Bay.

Dufaure, or Mugula Island (native):

named by Torres isla de Santa Clara.

East, The:
the Dutch had premeditated their designs in the.
The Dutch seek to establish themselves in.

East and South Lands:
Thomasz Pool sent out from Banda to discover the.

Eastern Islands:
removed from their actual position in Ptolemy's map.

Eastern Ocean:
reached by the West.

East Indian Archipelago:
on the Sebastian Cabot mappamundi.
The Dutch gaining ground in.

East Indian Islands:
reached by the Phoenicians.

East Indies:
an early map showing navigation to the.
Houtman promises to reveal the route to the.
Captain Lancaster settled the first English factory in the.
Captain Saris' observations in the.
A yacht called the Duyfken accompanied Steven Van der Hagen's expedition to the.
Englishmen barely credited the existence of a continent south of the.
Trade from the South Sea to the.
De Gonneville on his way to the.

Eendraghtsland:
a name given to a large tract on the west coast of Australia.

Egtis-Silla:
the origin of Hame de Sylla.

Egydienplatz:
in Nuremberg.

Egypt:

Covilham returns to.
Mentioned.

El puerto de la vera cruz (port of the true Cross):
named on the 3rd of May.

El sonbrero (sombrero) (south coast of New Guinea, Dutch Territory):
a name given by Torres.

Elvas:
a commission appointed to meet at.

Ende:
an island named.

Endeavour Straits:
Gomez de Sequeira lost his rudder on some rocks in the.

Engano:
the Dutch of the first expedition to Australasia reach the vicinity of.
The island of women.

England:
Galvano's work published in.
Dom Pedro goes to.
Owes discovery of America to Italians.
John Rotz went to.
The daring sea-rovers of.
Holland and, combined to defeat the Spanish Armada.
Dampier after his return to.
Coming to the front.

Equator:
a fourth part of the world beyond the, on Turin mappamundi.

Erzerum:
visited by Odoric.

Espiritu Sancto:
on the eastern coast of Australia.

Espiritu Santo:
the land of the, named by De Quiros.

Discovered by De Quiros.
De Quiros' crew mutinied at the bay of the island.

Estramadura:
inhabitants of.

Estrecho de S. Roque:
the channel between Mugula Island and the mainland of New Guinea (Orangerie Bay), a name
  that ought to be maintained.

Ethiopia:
mentioned.
People of the coast of, conquered.
Cinnamon the product of.

Eunauro or Euna (south-west coast of New Guinea):
named Villada by Torres.

Euphrates:
mentioned.
Circular boats of the.

Europa:
in an early mappamundi.

Europe:
belongs to the Great World according to the school of Pergamos.
The coastline of.
Columbus thought he could reach the Land of Spice direct from, by sea.
With reference to North America.
Asia and Africa surrounded by the sea.
In Galvano's description.
Represented on an early mappamundi.
Barthema on his way to, met the Portuguese at Calicut.
The Victoria returned to.
How did the news of the discovery made by Francisco de Hoces reach (?)

Europia (Europe).

Falkland Islands:
discovered by the Spaniards.

False Cape, to Cape Kollf:
with reference to Torres' route.

Fayal:
Diogo de Teive goes to the south-west of, in search of the Antilia.
Behaim's wife lived at.

Ferrara, Duke of:
with reference to Toscanelli and Columbus.
Hercules d'Este was.

Fin de Iaoa:
is corrupted in later charts to Fideoia.

Fin de Jaua:
end of Java.

Firenze (Florence):
Pope Eugenio IV there.

Flesh Bay:
near Gauritz River.
Dias at.

Florence:
a letter by Fernam Martins dated from.
Toscanelli's letter dated from.
The Duke of Ferrara requested his ambassador to institute researches at.

Flores:
deformed.
Islands between Java and, set down on Sebastian Cabot's mappamundi.
Placed latitudinally.

Florida:
a region in the north.

Fort St. George:
Mailapur near.

Fortunate Islands:
Joao first discoverer of the.
Distance from the, to Catigara.

France:
vessels equipped in the ports of.
Dom Pedro goes to.
Owes discovery of America to Italians.
Pierre D'Ailly, called the Eagle of the Doctors of.
Maximilian fought against.
Munzmeister wrote about his travels in.
Lyons in.
A globe found in.
Jean Roze's atlas first dedicated to the King of.
The Dieppese school of hydrography the first in.
The daring sea-rovers of.

Frankfort, gores:
mentioned.
Described.

Frederick Henry Island:
with reference to Torres' route.
Keer-Weer in the latitude of.

Fremose C: de:
in the position of Cape St. George (Jervis Bay).

Fretum le Maire:
between Staten landt and Tierra del Fuego, marked on Hoeius' map.

Galav, or Guliam:
passed by Abreu.

Galera:
discovered and named during Mendana's expedition.

Galicia:
inhabitants of.

Gange (River Ganges):
with reference to St. Thomas.

Ganges:
passed by the Phoenicians.
With reference to the location of Malepur.

Gascony:
St. Sever, monastery in.

Gataio:
a continental land in the southern hemisphere.
Meant for Cataio.

Gatigara:
30 leagues from Java the Less.

Gauritz River:
Near Flesh Bay.

Geelvink Bay:
isla de los Crespos at the entrance to.

Geelvinck Channel:
Vlamingh's fleet passed through the.

Genoa:
Bartholomew Columbus' native country.

George St. da Mina:
Dias puts in at.

Germany:
Marco Polo's work published in.
Monetarius from.
Maximilian became Emperor of.
Munzmeister wrote about his travels in.
Was Ruysch's map made in.

G.F. de Witt's Landt:
ondeckt 1628, an inscription on the north-west coast of Australia, where the Vianen was stranded.

Giava:
visited by Barthema.
Barthema remained fourteen days in.

Giava mazor:Fra Mauro's.

Giava minore, & maggiore:
in Nicolo de' Conti's text.
Cannot be Marco Polo's Java Minor.

Giave:
the Javas in Nicolo de' Conti's text.

Gibeth:
an island reached by Magellan's expedition.

Gibith:
stands for Gibeth.

Gibraltar, Straits of:
like the straits mentioned in Schoner's pamphlet.

Gilolo:
referred to.
Gelolo vel Siloli in Oronce Fine's map.
An island near, espied by Cavendish's expedition.
Once called Batochina.

Gilona:
reached by Magellan's expedition.

Globe, the:
circumnavigated.

Goa:
Covilham went to.

Gobubu:
a native village at the back of Baibara Island (south-west coast of New Guinea), in a bay
  called by the Spaniards Cala de Helvires.

Golden Chersonesus:
on Turin mappamundi.
Mentioned.
Spices brought from the, by the Portuguese.
Called Malacca.

Golphe de la Louisiade:

a name given by Bougainville to Orangerie Bay, New Guinea.

Gomez de Sequeira's Islands:
correspond with the Timor Laut group.
Another group to the north of New Guinea.

Good Gardens Islands:
discovered by Saavedra.

Gouffre (Gulf):
occupies on the Dauphin chart the position of Corner Inlet and Wilson's Promontory.

Grafton Cape:
the Australian continent cut off at, in Jean Roze's chart of Australia.

Great Australian Continent:
De Quiros set sail again in search of the.

Great Bay of St. Lawrence, and Port of Monterey the (New Guinea):
the modern Orangerie Bay.

Great Bay of St. Philip and St. James, the:
discovered by De Quiros.

Great Fish River:
the same as the Rio do Infante.

Great Java:
a description of the.

Great Sahul Shoal:
passed by W. Dampier.

Great Southern Continent:
with reference to a Malay skipper.
Facts concerning the.

Great South Land:
appears in a new form.
The earliest English references to the colonization of the.
A discovery made on the west coast of the.

Great World:
according to the school of Pergamos.

Greece:
the Argo only sailed from.

Greenland:
the great island of.

Greenwich:
our zero corresponds with 120 degrees east of.

Gresic:
on the north-east coast of Java.

Guadalcanal, or Guadalcanar:
believed to be New Guinea.
Discovered and named during Mendana's expedition.

Guadalupe:
discovered and named during Mendana's expedition.

Guadiana:
the council convened on the shores of the.

Guinea:
coast depicted as far as.
A sea route by way of.
Lord of.
Supplies left off the coast of.
People of the sea of, conquered.

Gulf of Carpentaria (see also Carpentarie):
islands of the.
The rectified line of the south-eastern coast of the.
Arnhem Land discovered in the.
Appears to be indicated on Hoeius' map.
The three ships of Tasman's second expedition sailed into the, with the intention of
  reaching New Van Diemen's Land (Tasmania).

Guli Guli:
a haven where Abreu came to anchor.

Gumape (see Gumnape), modern Gunong Api:
on Jean Roze's chart.

Gumnape (meant for Gunong Api).

Gunong Api:
a small island off the north-east coast of Sumbawa.

Hades:
situation of, according to the Greeks.

Hague:
the State archives at the.
Manuscript documents at.

Haynes Mt. (New Guinea):
mentioned.

Hame de Sylla:
derived from Egtis-Silla.

Hayter Island:
marked as a peninsula on Spanish charts.

Head Island (New Guinea):
not reached by Torres.

Heath Island (New Guinea):
mentioned.

Hesperides:
now called Cape Verde Islands.

Hispaniola:
Sir John Hawkins crossed the Atlantic to.

Hogaleas:
in Galvano's description.

Holland:
the second, third and fourth expedition of the Dutch left, in 1598, according to Constantin.

The third expedition of the Dutch sailed from, by way of Magalhaens' straits.
Sebaldt de Weerdt's ship, the only one of seven that returned to.
Incertitude about the departure of ships from.
England and, combined to defeat the Spanish Armada.
Important documents in, relating to Australia.
A yacht named the Duyfken accompanied the first Dutch expedition from, to Java.
The Vergulde Draeck sailed from.
Vlamingh's fleet set sail from.

Hollandia Nova:
P. Goos' map of.
Tasman's discoveries are recorded in P. Goos' map of.

Holy Land:
Dom Pedro goes to.

Honfleur:
de Gonneville sailed from.

Hong Kong:
limit of Ptolemy's map.

Hormuz:
visited by Odoric, where he embarks for Tana.
Reached by Barthema.

Horne, Cape:
Captain Welbe's proposal to go round.

Houtman's Abrolhos:
Captain Francis Pelsart wrecked on.
Pelsart returned to, in the Sardam.
Relics found on.

Huon, Gulf of, New Guinea:
mentioned.

Hutt lagoon:
near Port Gregory, locality visited by Vlamingh.

Iaoas, or Iauos:
a generic term for islands.

Iaua, the noble island of:
passed by Abreu.
The course of Magalhaens' fleet set down to the south of, on the alleged Schoner globe.

Iava maior:
on Ruysch's mappamundi.

Iava Minor:
on Ruysch's mappamundi.

Iavva Maior:
on Schonerean gores.

Iberia:
mentioned by Strabo.

Iceland:
with reference to its volcanoes.

I. de Edels Landt:
discovered in 1619.

Ilha de fonti (probably Penedo das Fontes).

Illa da:
On Jean Roze's chart, Number 1.

Ille de llame:
On Jean Roze's chart, Number 1.

Imsa:
Of modern charts, named by Torres la enbaidora.

Indes:
With reference to J. Codine's memoire.

Indes Occidentalles (West Indies):
With reference to early French voyages.

India:
Ships sent to, in early days.

St. Thomas goes to.
Mentioned by Strabo.
Columbus maintained he had reached.
Of Marco Polo.
Of the ancients.
Galvano speaks of.
Trade of, in the hands of the Arabs.
On 11th century mappamundi.
Seaway to, laid open.
Things of, to be learnt by the subjects of the King of Portugal.
Christians in.
In the 15th century, published by the Hakluyt Society.
Portuguese in search of.
Learned scholars from.
Covilham directs his course towards.
Passages to, anticipated.
Columbus believed he had reached.
The possibility of reaching, by sea westwardly entertained.
Barthema retraced his steps to.
Mentioned in connection with Barthema.
Magalhaens served seven years in.
The Portuguese arrived at the shores of.
The Dutch tried to collect all the documents that might guide them on the way to.
English settlement made in.
Trade to.

India interiore, or inferiore (?)

India meridional:
A country in the south described by Godinho de Eredia.

Indian Archipelago:
South coast of the islands of the, were little known.
Gunong Api belongs to the.

Indian Ocean:
Alteration made by the Arabs in the, of Ptolemy.
Ptolemy's fantastic islands of the.
Traffic carried on in the.
Of Ptolemy.
The, an enclosed sea in Ptolemy's map.
On Turin mappamundi.

Covilham, the first of his countrymen to sail in the.
Vasco da Gama's fleet the first European fleet to enter the.
The coastline of the.
The Arabian navigations confined to the.
Called Seylan Oceanus on Ruysch's mappamundi.
Islands of the, visited by Malays and charted by Arabs.
A chart of the.
An engraved hand-coloured curious old Dutch map of the, in the author's possession.
The periodicity of the monsoons in the.

Indian Peninsula:
Suppressed on Ptolemy's chart.
The large size of Ceylon prevented the proper charting of the.
The, duplicated.
The true.
Brought down in Fra Mauro's map.
Travancore on the.
Ceilam to the east of the.

Indian Sea:
in an Arabian mappamundi.

Indie Orientali (East Indies):
mentioned.

Indies:
History of the, by Las Casas, mentioned.
Themara's work on the.
Mentioned.
Augmentation of the.

Infernal regions:
position of the.

Insulae Fortunatae (Canary Islands).

Insulae Infortunatae:
on Magalhaens' track, placed near Rarotonga.

Insul de gomes des queria (Islands of Gomez de Sequeira).

Insulindia:

Synoptic table of the first voyages of the Dutch to.

Inuagana:
an island north of the equator reached by Magellan.
In 11 degrees north and 158 degrees west of Cadiz.

Inuana (the Inuagana of Maximilian's letter):
an island on the alleged Schoner globe.

Ioach:
answers to Loach.

Irlanda (Ireland):
with reference to an interpolation.

Isabel Island:
placed in its true latitude.

Isla berde (south-west coast of New Guinea):
an island named by Torres.

Isla de Jesus:
named by Mendana.

Isla de la Madera (south-west coast of New Guinea):
an island named by Torres.

Isla de las altas Palmas (south-west coast of New Guinea):
an island named by Torres.

Isla de la Savana (south-west coast of New Guinea):
an island named by Torres.

Isla del Oro:
name given to New Guinea by Saavedra.
In Herrera's description.

Isla de los Crespos:
visited and named by Grijalva's expedition.

Isla de Nogales (south-west coast of New Guinea):
an island named by Torres.

Isla de Ranedo (south-west coast of New Guinea):
an island named by Torres.

Isla de san bernardo (south-west coast of New Guinea):
an island named by Torres.

Isla llana (south-west coast of New Guinea):
an island named by Torres.

Island of St. Francoys (south coast of Australia):
a name given in commemoration of the Christian name of the skipper Thysz who
  commanded the Golden Seahorse.

Island of St. Peter (south coast of Australia):
a name given in commemoration of the Christian name of Nuyts.

Island of the Moon:
a name given to Madagascar by the Moors.
The, to be inquired for.
Al Camar in Arabic.

Islas bartolome (south-west coast of New Guinea):
an island named by Torres.
Toulon Island of modern charts.

Islas de los Reyes:
named by Alvaro de Saavedra.

Islas de Sta leocadia (south coast of New Guinea, Dutch Territory):
a name given by Torres.

Islas de Timoteo (Port Glasgow, New Guinea):
islands named by Torres.

Islas Rocos, Roc Islands:
on S. Cabot's mappamundi.

Isle Mege, or Nege:
on J. Roze's chart, Number 1.

Isola Atreguada:
placed in its true latitude.

Italy:
Odoric returned to, in 1330.
Dom Pedro goes home by.
A fact that redounds to the honour of.
Nicolo de' Conti returned to, in the year 1444.
Ramusio could not find a copy of Nicolo de' Conti's travels in.
Copies of Nicolo de' Conti's travels obtained in, in 1457 to 1459.
Dom Pedro brought a map from.
Skilled cartographers of.
The first impulse which led to the re-discovery of the New World came from.

Jaavaa:
a name set down on a detached section of Sumatra.

Japan:
in connection with Fra Mauro's Malay Archipelago.
With reference to its volcanoes.
With reference to Columbus' route.
The early cartography of, by George Collingridge.
Not Cipango.
Precious commodities from.

Japara, in Java.

Jaua (Java):
in Galvano's description.
On P. Desceliers' mappamundi.

Jaua Maior, or Great Java:
described.
On G. Mercator's mappamundi.
Applies to Java on S. Cabot's mappamundi.

Jaua Minor:
applies to the islands from Java to Flores in the S. Cabot mappamundi.
In Drake's and Cavendish's narratives, applies probably to some islands east of Java.

Java:
its volcanoes referred to.
Reached at an early time.
In Ptolemy's map

470

Called Zaba in Ptolemy's map.
In Galvano's description.
May be marked on Turin mappamundi.
Mentioned.
Australia and, considered as one by Marco Polo.
South coast of, unknown.
Sumatra called Java Minor by Marco Polo.
Used instead of Chiampa causes great mistakes.
Termed Java Major on fantastic map.
Visited by Odoric.
Described by Odoric.
Islands in vicinity of, mentioned by Odoric.
Islands mentioned by Odoric set down near, on Behaimean maps and globes.
Sumbawa and, must be Nicolo de' Conti's two Javas.
South coast of, little known.
The equator, with reference to, in Fra Mauro's map.
On the confines of the world.
Charted on Fra Mauro's map.
Is Cipango.
Referred to.
Described from hearsay.
Barthema and his party agree to visit.
A country south of, referred to in Barthema's narrative.
Description by a Malay skipper of people to the south of.
Barthema and party must have landed in some out-of-the-way part of.
Set down as a distinct and separate island.
Charted by F. Rodriguez.
An inscription on Rodriguez's map of.
Deformed.
Called Simbabau in Reinel's chart.
Supplied the first model of special deformation.
Assumes a longitudinal instead of a latitudinal position.
Described as a very large island by Marco Polo.
The largest island in Reinel's chart is.
Claimed by the Spaniards as being within their territory.
Open sea to the south of, in Diego Ribeiro's mappamundi.
Bali and, with reference to the legend Anda ne barcha.
With reference to the blocking of the seaway to the south of.
The south coast of, connected with Australia.
The Portuguese and Spanish knew of an open sea to the south of.
Australia and, believed to be one and the same continent even after the return of Sebastian del Cano.
Called Little Java contrary to all precedent.

Called Lytil Jaua.
Islands between, and Flores set down on S. Cabot's map.
Bears the name of Iava petite on P. Desceliers' map.
And Australia one and the same island.
Bears a double name on P. Desceliers' mappamundi.
Resembles a hog.
The Dutch firmly established in.
The Dutch of the first expedition to Australasia sailed along the north coast of,
With Bali, Lomboc and Sumbawa forms the northern coast of Australia in the charts of the Desceliers type.
The seaway blocked between Australia and.

Java Major:
occurs frequently in Marco Polo and Nicolo de' Conti.
In Marco Polo's description applies to Java and Australia.
Described by Marco Polo as the largest island in the world.
Not mentioned on maps before Nicolo de' Conti's return.
Represented on Fra Mauro's mappamundi.
Australian continent called.
Does not refer to Australia on map of fantastic type.
A name given to Java on fantastic maps.
Supposed to be of great size.
On Behaim's globe.
A description of.
The terms Java Major and Java Minor first made use of by Marco Polo.
Drake arrives at.
Drake sails from, to the Cape of Good Hope.
Cavendish came to anchor under the south-west parts of.

Java Menor:
mentioned.

Java Minor:
occurs frequently in Marco Polo and Nicolo de' Conti.
Applies to Sumatra in Marco Polo.
Not mentioned on maps before Nicolo de' Conti's return.
Represented on Fra Mauro's map.
Misplaced.
Of Marco Polo cannot be Nicolo de' Conti's Giava Minore.
Corresponds with Sumbawa in Nicolo de' Conti's text.
With reference to Pentam and other islands.
On Behaim's globe.

On Ruysch's mappamundi.
On the Schonerean gores.
corresponds with Sumbawa in Schoner's Weimar globe.
Refers to Sumatra on G. Mercator's map.
Cavendish passes through the Straits of, and Java Major.
In Eredia's description.

Javas:
Nicolo de' Conti stops nine months in the.

Java the Less:
thirty leagues from.

Jave-la-Grande:
placed under Java.
Australia called.
Blocked out.

Jave-la-Petite:
suggested.

Jenkins' Bay (New Guinea):
named by Moresby.
The Baya de San Millan of early Spanish maps.

Jentana:
in Galvano's description of Ptolemy's Geography.

Jerusalem:
Envoys returned from.
Seen by Barthema.

Jones' River (New Guinea):
mentioned.

Jordan:
one of the rivers that flowed into the Bay of St. Philip and St. James (New Hebrides).

Juan Fernandez:
Captain Welbe's proposal to reach the island of.

Juan Gallego, the port of, in New Spain.

Kashan:
visited by Odoric.

Kauwer, Island:
visited by Pieter Pietersz.

Keer-Weer (Turnagain):
the point in the Gulf of Carpentaria reached by the Duyfken.
A point or cape on the coast of New Guinea.
On the coast of New Guinea, the extreme point visited by the Duyfken according to Ch. Ruelens.
Set down in 14 degrees 15 minutes south latitude on a copy of the original manuscript chart of
   Tasman in the author's possession.
The Pera ran along the west coast to Cape.

Keij (same as Key) and Arouw Islands:
visited by Pieter Pietersz after the murder of Pool.

Key Islands:
the Duyfken sailed by the.
Jan Carstens ordered to visit the.

Kilauea, Mount:
a volcanic peak in the Sandwich group.

Kimmerie:
a northern country described by Homer.

King Sound:
Jean Roze's chart of Australia cut off at.

Kirke:
an island mentioned by Homer.

Koi Koi (south-west coast of New Guinea):
named by Torres isla de Villabonillos.

Kondur:
in Marco Polo's description.

Kulam:

visited by Odoric.

La Austrialia, del Espiritu Santo:
the name given by De Quiros to the land discovered in the New Hebrides group,

Labadii (same as Sabadibae):
in Ptolemy's map.
Another name for Java.
Confounded with New Guinea by Mercator.
And Sabadibae are corrupted forms of Jawa, Dwipa or Jaoa diva of Sanscrit or Arabic origin.

Lack:
on Behaim's globe, a remnant of the word Malacca.

Laco int Montaras:
appears to be a repetition of Lac regnum.

Lac regnum:
on Frankfort gores.
Near the tropic of Capricorn.
On Apianus' mappamundi.

Ladrones:
Alonso de Salazar steered for the.
Placed to the south of the equator.
Mentioned by Torres.

La enfaidora (embaidora):
south coast of New Guinea, an island named by Torres.
Imsa of modern charts.

La enpanada (south coast of New Guinea, Dutch Territory):
a name given by Torres.

La fuente de Argales (south coast of New Guinea, Dutch Territory):
a name given by Torres.

Lago and Lago regno:
mention of.

Lago regno:

the evolution of Fra Mauro's.
Does not resemble Calmia.
Is Loac Provincia of the Hunt-Lenox globe derived from (?)

La guardia (south coast of New Guinea):
an island named by Torres.

Laistrugonas:
a western country in Homer.

Lampong, territory, or district of Palembang in Sumatra.

Land of Brazil:
of the Copia not the land in South America.

Land of Java:
New Holland called the.

Land of Nights (Nuyts Land):
Jean Pierre Purry's proposal to settle.

Land of Spice:
with reference to Toscanelli and Columbus.
Columbus proposed to the King of Portugal to reach the.
A better result obtained than reaching the.

Land of St. Bonaventure, the (New Guinea).

Land of the Papuas:
the Bay of St. Peter of Arlanza discovered by Torres in the.

Land of the South (Terra del Zur):
the name given to Australia in the Mar d'India map.

Landt van de Leeuwin:
the Dutch claim the discovery of the.

Landt van Pieter Nuyts, the:
an inscription in Dutch charts on the south coast of Australia.

Laon, the, globe:
mentioned.

La Peninsula (south coast of New Guinea, Dutch Territory):
a name given by Torres.

La piedra fuerte (south coast of New Guinea, Dutch Territory):
a name given to an island by Torres.

Laponia:
mentioned.

Las encubridores (south coast of New Guinea):
islands named by Torres.
Two rocky islets at the entrance to Millport Harbour.

Las entretexidas (south coast of New Guinea, Dutch Territory):
a name given by Torres.

Las Roccos insule:
on the western coast of Australia.
On S. Cabot's mappamundi.

Las tres hermanos (south coast of New Guinea, Dutch Territory):
a name given by Torres to three small islands.

Las Virgines:
some islands named by De Quiros.

Laurence, Island of St.:
information about the, procured by Covilham.

Laut chidol, or South Sea.

Lazaro (same as Lazarus), Archipelago of St., the:
Magalhaens killed in.

Lazarus (same as Lazaro), Archipelago of St., the:
discovered by Magalhaens.
It invited the eager enterprise of the Spaniards.

Leeuwin, Cape (Lioness):
the Londe of Java terminates at, in J. Roze's chart, Number 2.
The discovery of, suggested.
Lions or lionesses represented near (see map).

The coast of Australia prolonged from, to the South Pole in the Dauphin chart.
A doubt cast on the discovery of.
North-west cape to, visited by Dutch ships.
A sea chart must have existed showing the western coasts of Australia from the vicinity of
  Dampier's Archipelago to.

Leon:
Inhabitants of.

Leppe (Aleppo):
De Prado mentions that he will go by.

Lequeos:
in Galvano's description.

Leveque Cape:
the point that Dampier passed round.

Levant Sea:
mentioned.

Libia (Africa):
Europia, and Asia surrounded by the sea.

Lima:
De Quiros sailed from.
Distance measured from.

Lisboa (Lisbon):
mentioned.

Lisbon:
a copy of Nicolo de' Conti's travels found by Ramusio in.
Marco Polo's work translated and published in.
Italian agents at.
Distance from Quinsay to.
Fernam Martins, a canon in.
Envoys leave.
Lumiar near.
Dias proceeds to.
Behaim not successful in.

A vessel returned to.
Marco Polo's and Nicolo de' Conti's voyages published in.
Rodriguez's atlas preserved at.
The courts of.
Linschoten lived for two years in.

Loach provin:
for Lochac in Schonerean gores.

Loac Provincia:
in Hunt-Lenox globe.
Seilan to the east of.

Locach (same as Lochac):
Corrupted to Coachs.
Is Loac on the Hunt-Lenox globe derived from (?)
Lo-kok or the kingdom of Lo.
In Eredia's description.

Lochac, or Locach:
in Marco Polo's description.
Part of Cambodia.
Produces gold, etc.
Marco Polo's, referred to.
As a point of departure.

Loech:
the capital of Cambodia was named.

Lo-Kok, or the kingdom of Lo:
the lower part of what is now Siam.

Lo Loach ac:
for Lochac in Ruysch's mappamundi.

Lomblen:
mentioned.

Lomboc:
one of Nicolo de' Conti's Javas.
South coast of, little known.
On the confines of the world.
Charted on Fra Mauro's mappamundi.

Named Autane.
Aintama or Amjama in the Henry II map of 1546, and au tane in Jean Roze's map of 1542.
A nautical phrase which refers to.
Difficult navigation between Bali and.
Charted as a distinct island.
Charted by F. Rodriguez.
Is called Lomboquo in F. Rodriguez's chart.
Forms part of Australia.

Londe of Java (or Lande of Java):
in J. Roze's chart terminates at Cape Leeuwin.

London:
mentioned.
The Royal Geographical Society of.
Yule's Cathay published in.
Bartholomew Columbus made a map of the world in.

Loo Choo:
gold from.

Lopez, Cape:
mentioned.

Lopo Gonzalvez, Cape, now Cape Lopez.

Louvain:
an English edition of Wytfliet's work was published at, in 1597.

Luca Antara (see also Nuca Antara):
an alternative name for Madura.

Lucach, and Beach:
derived from Loac Provincia.
On G. Mercator's map.

Lucapinho:
Serrano wrecked on the flats of.

Lucones (Luzon):
in Galvano's description.

Lumiar, near Lisbon.

Lusuparam, Islands of:
Abreu went to the.

Lyons:
a mappamundi published at.

Lytil Java (Little Java):
on Jean Roze's chart.
Java is called.

Ma'bar:
is indicated by Regnum Var on Apianus' mappamundi.

Machian:
the Dutch had three forts at.

Madagascar:
and Marco Polo's bird.
Named Island of the Moon.
Called Al Camar.
Charted by the Arabs.
On Behaim's globe.
An island which may be intended for.
Discovered in 1506.
Marco Polo's.
Three nameless islands between, and Loac Provincia.
Called Camaeocada on Ruysch's mappamundi.
Called San Lourenco by the Portuguese.
The Dutch of the first expedition to Australasia made a long stay at.
De Gonneville carried to the coast of.

Madagastar:
for Madagascar on Apianus' mappamundi.

Madeira:
Joao, first discoverer of.
A caravel sailed from.

Madras:
Meliapur near.

Madrid, Ateneo de:
referred to.

Madura, Island of:
passed by Abreu.
On F. Rodriguez's chart.
Sometimes called Java Minor.
An island near Java.
Called also Nuca Antara.

Magelan, Streight of:
called The Dragon's taile.

Magellanica:
a name for Australia in the account of the wreck of the Vianen.

Magna Margarita:
a name given to New Guinea in Don Diego de Prado's letters to the King of Spain.
Named by Torres.

Mahabar:
in Nicolo de' Conti's description.

Mailapoor:
visited by Odoric (See also Meliapur).

Mailapur:
same as Meliapur.

Mailapuram:
means Peacock Town.

Maine, State of.

Maiorca & Minorca:
mentioned by Galvano.

Majorca:
Mestre Jayme came from.

Malabar:
Galvano speaks of.

Visited by Odoric.
Referred to by Nicolo de' Conti.
On the coast of Malabar.
Written Melibaria in Hakluyt Society's edition of Nicolo de' Conti's travels.
Cananor on the, coast.

Malacca:
in connection with Fra Mauro's Malay Archipelago.
The Arabs extend their trade to.
Galvano speaks of.
Marco Polo near Straits of.
Straits of, shown in Fra Mauro's mappamundi.
Straits of, obliterated.
An island near.
Brazil near.
A strait near.
Sequeira anchored at, in 1509.
Abreu's expedition returns to.
Magalhaens in the vicinity of the Spice Islands when 600 leagues from.
And the Great Gulf, in Spanish territory.
The blocking of the Straits of.
Fortress in the Straits of, useless.
Godinho de Eredia's surveys in.

Malacha (Malacca):
Barthema, arrived at.

Malaiur:
a kingdom spoken of by Marco Polo.
Identified as the Malay Peninsula.

Malay Archipelago, Islands of:
in Fra Mauro's mappamundi.

Malay Peninsula:
Sumatra removed from the, in Ptolemy's map.
In 11th century mappamundi.
With reference to the Cape of Good Hope.
Or Aureus Chersonesus.
Bogus.
Omitted on Cosa's map.
Position of the, on Cantino map.
Double.

Duplicated.
Identified with Malaiur.
Part of it claimed by the Spaniards as being within their territory.
The line of demarcation made to pass through the.

Male and Female Islands:
near Socotra.

Malepur (same as Mailapoor, Meliapur and Maliapor):
reference made to.
Where the body of St. Thomas is buried.
On the Coromandel coast.
Mentioned.

Maletur:
on G. Mercator's map, it should occur under Beach.
Belongs to Asia in Marco Polo's writings.
In Eredia's description.

Mallaqua:
on the Schonerean Frankfort gores.
Near the Cape of Good Hope.
Set down on Schonerean gores where Lack occurs on Behaim's globe.

Mallua:
passed by Abreu.

Malo, St.:
mariners of.

Malua (Ombai, modern):
Sebastian del Cano passed by.

Malucas (same as Moluccas):
Torres near the.
The Moors gave Torres news of the events at the.

Maluco (Moluccas):
three ships sent to.
Kings of, sent for the shipwrecked Portuguese.
Galvano's account of the return from.
People of, call the New Guineans Papuas.

Manga das Areas:
passed by Bartholomew Dias.

Mangi (same as Mango):
referred to by Conti.
Distorted.

Mango, province of.

Manila:
bombarded and plundered by the English.
The remainder of Mendana's expedition taken to.
Torres continued his voyage to.
The Royal Audience of, failed to give despatches to Torres for the completion of his voyage.
The crew of De Quiros's ship designed to go to.
Succour from.
Torres' letter addressed from.
After the siege of, Dalrymple became the possessor of the document which revealed Torres' passage.

Maniole:
in Ptolemy's map.

Maranon, or river of the Amazons:
Measuring from the.

Mar del Sur:
sighted by Balboa.

Mar d' India:
a description of, mentioned.
Title of a map.

Mare (Maru):
one of the Moluccas reached by Magellan's expedition.

Mare Lant (for Laut):
Chidol, South Sea.

Mare Rubrum:
on Turin mappamundi.

Maroabyn:
corrupted from Diva Margabym.

Mar Oriental:
in Fra Mauro's mappamundi.

Marquesas:
discovered by Mendana.

Martoban:
with reference to location of Malepur.

Massana:
some of Magellan's men driven by a storm to.

Massaram, or Masaram:
another name for Bramble Cay, north extremity of Cape York.

Matalota:
placed in its true latitude.

Matanza:
an island named by De Quiros.

Mathien (Mutjan):
one of the Moluccas reached by Magellan's expedition.
A small island.

Maulua:
in Galvano's description.

Mauritania:
mentioned.

Mauritius:
Tasman first set sail for.
Tasman left, in October.

Mauthan:
the nearest island to Subuth.
Magellan ordered 40 of his men to pass over to.
The king of, led 3000 of his people into the field.
Magellan attacked the islanders of.

Meccah:
mentioned.

Mediterranean:
on Turin mappamundi.

Melbourne Review:
an article by Petherick contributed to the.

Meliapur, or Maliapor:
St. Thomas' tomb outside.

Melibaria:
the name for Malabar in the Hakluyt Society's edition of Nicolo de' Conti's travels.

Melville Island:
known formerly as part of Van Diemen's Land.
Insularity of, determined by P.P. King.

Menuthias:
the modern Zanzibar in Ptolemy's map.

Mexico:
an alleged Phoenician mariner's compass found at.
Mentioned.
Mendana returned to.
Acu-pulco on the coast of.

Milapur (Conti's Malepur).

Millport Harbour (south-west coast of New Guinea):
called by Torres Puerto de Valdetuexar.

Milne Bay:
represented on De Prado's chart.
Not thoroughly explored by Torres.

Mindanao, Isle of:
mentioned.
Captain Swan, of the Cygnet, left that vessel at.

Mindanaos (Mindanao):
in Galvano's description.

Minor:
an island answering to either Sumbawa or Timor.

Mirapolis, same as Mailapur.

Mirapor:
in Catalan map (same as Meliapur).

Moluccas (or Molucca Islands):
the seaway to the, laid open.
Mentioned.
Cloves from.
Galvano the conqueror and apostle of the.
First depicted.
Or Spice Islands.
The Spaniards pretended that the, were in the hemisphere allotted to them.
In Portuguese territory.
Those who returned from the, maintained they were in Spanish territory.
The distance between the, and the line of demarcation examined.
Spaniards not permitted to trade with the.
The Portuguese could not show discoveries under the meridian of the.
A letter concerning the.
Magellan ordered to sail for Terra Firma and seek for a passage to the.
In the extreme east.
Magellan's expedition sails to the.
The Spaniards examined the position of the.
After the return of the remnant of Magalhaens' expedition the longitude of the,
   remained as unsettled as ever.
The King of Spain renounced his claim to the.
Bernardo de La Torres' fleet reached the.
Torres observed the variations near the.
Events of a stirring nature at the.
A vessel sent from the.
Portuguese of the, in search of gold.

Moluques:
referred to.

Monoch, or Maluch (Molucca).

Moro or Maro:
may be intended for Maio, a small island at the entrance to Salee Gulf, Sumbawa.

Morocco:
mathematicians obtained from.

Mortir:
the Dutch of Fort Nassau at.

Moscovia, the Grand Duke of.

Mountain of the East:
Columns at the, on which the Chaldean Heaven rested.
Position of the.

Mountain of the South:
position of the.

Mount Sinai:
Tor at the foot of.

Mozambique Channel:
followed by De Gonneville.
The Portuguese navigations through.

Muar d'Amboina:
mentioned.

Mugula (or Dufaure) Island:
the channel between the mainland of New Guinea and, is called estrecho de S. Roque
   in De Prado's chart of Torres' expedition.

Mullens' Harbour (New Guinea):
unknown to Moresby, named by Torres the baya de N.S. de la Assumpcion-- The Bay of
   Our Lady of the Assumption.

Murano, the cathedral convent of San Miguel of.

Murcia:

inhabitants of.

Mushkah Bay:
on Turin mappamundi.

Muthil (Moter):
one of the Moluccas reached by Magellan's expedition.

Mutyr:
an island reached by Drake.

Myos-Hormos:
ships sailed from, in early days.

Naples:
envoys go via.

Necuram:
on Schonerean gores.
In Eredia's description.

Neuchatel:
Jean Pierre Purry born at.

Neucuram:
on Fra Mauro's map.
On Behaim's globe.
Belongs to Marco Polo's nomenclature.
The eastern coastlines of, with reference to the east coast of Australia.

Nevca (Neucuram):
in Ruysch's mappamundi.

New Britain:
the passage between New Guinea and, made according to the pilot Gaetan.

New Caledonia:
Torres reached a point somewhere between, and Broad Sound.

New Guadalcanal (same as Guadalcanal and Guadalcanar):
discovered by Mendana.
Near New Guinea.
Torres thought he had reached.

New Guinea:
a portion of, may be represented on Ptolemy's map.
A strait between Terra Australis and.
Coachs in Behaim's globe is between Australia and.
Andrea Corsali describes land in the vicinity of.
Supposed to be connected with Australia.
Terra de Brazil in the longitude and latitude of.
Some islands near, reached by Magalhaens.
Named Papua by Don Jorge de Menezes.
Further discovery of.
Equal in size to Sumatra on the Franciscus Monachus mappamundi.
Periplus of, shown.
Portion of, named Gilolo.
Islands on the north coast of, visited.
Named by the Spaniards during Villalobos' expedition.
Formal possession of, taken in the name of the King of Spain.
Called Nueva Guinea on account of the "frisled hair" of the inhabitants.
The Spaniards of de Retez' expedition knew not that Saavedra had made a prior discovery of.
The Spaniards intended to make use of Torres' discoveries in.
Several Spaniards left in.
A discovery made by the Dutch on the south coast of.
Schouten and Lemaire's voyage and discoveries made along the north coast of, alluded to.
Separation between York Peninsula and, indicated on Hoeius' map.
A portion of, represented on the S, Cabot mappamundi.
Forms an important feature in G. Mercator's map.
Insularity of, doubted.
The insular character of, doubtful on Peter Plancius' map.
A legend on, showing the date assigned to the map referred to.
Le Maire made to appear to be the discoverer of.
Strait between Australia and, known to the Spaniards.
A chart of, published by Dalrymple.
Belongs to the Southern Hemisphere.
The insularity of, known to the Spaniards.
Torres sailed along.
The beginning of.
Peopled with Indians.
Torres observed the variation in all the land of.
Tasman sailed along the northern shores of.
To be explored.
The course of the Duyfken from.

Supposed to be connected with Cape York Peninsula.
Van der Hagen's Little Dove is the yacht that was sent to.
Dutch killed at.
Dampier's intentions of discovery on.
Dampier believes in the existence of a passage to the south of.
Dampier sailed for.
Dampier in sight of.
Welbe proposes to sail to.
Joined to the Australian Continent.
Traders from.
Shown as an island.
A portion of, bearing the name Paplas.
An open sea between, and Australia.

New Hebrides:
Torres steered in a south-west direction from the.
The reason for representing the, as connected with the Great Southern Land.
Included in the eastern coast of Australia.

New Holland:
traces of Behaim's nomenclature to be found on maps of.
More to the east than the Moluccas.
Referred to.
With reference to Vlaming's voyage to the coast of.
Were the Dutch afraid that the English would claim?
Dampier fell in with the land of.
Dampier's description of.
The buccaneers of the Cygnet wanted to know what, "would afford."
Dampier's intentions of discovery on.
A passage to the south of.
A large bay supposed to run right through.
Described by Dampier as the "barrenest spot upon the globe."
Not reached by Roggeween.
A map of referred to.
New Guinea separate from.
The ignorance of the geography of.
The discovery of, kept secret.

New Jerusalem:
the town in De Quiros' new colony to be called the.

New South Wales:
discovered in the year 1770.

New Spain:
mentioned.
Joam de Resaga reached.
Villalobos set sail from the Port of Juan Gallego in.
Bernard de La Torre and Gaspar Rico fail to reach.
The Spaniards had not acquired the necessary knowledge to reach.

New Wales:
with reference to John Welbe's scheme of colonisation.
Named by Captain J. Welbe.

New World:
mentioned.
Disclosed.
Clandestine expeditions to.
A few years after the discovery of.
The first impulse which led to the rediscovery of the, came from Italy.

New York:
the latitude of, would have been reached by Columbus.
Mentioned.

New Zealand:
Behaim's Anguana occupies the site of.
With reference to Patalis regio.
Not charted in our copy of P. Goos' map.
Called Staete Landt in Tasman's map.
Discovered by Tasman.

Nicobar, Islands:
described under the name of Neucuram by Marco Polo.

Nicoveran (same as Nicoverra, Neucuram, and Nicobar):
Described by Marco Polo.

Nicoverra and Dondin, Islands of:
in Odoric's narrative.

Nineveh:
sculptures of, representing circular boats.

Nombre de Jesus:

placed in its true latitude.

North America:
the discovery of, a work by Harrisse, quoted.
With reference to Europe.
Villalobos on his way from, to the Philippines discovered many islands.

Northern Territory (Australia):
Melville Island in the, known formerly as part of Van Diemen's Land.

Northern World:
according to the school of Pergamos.

North Pacific Ocean:
as considered by Strabo.
Islands discovered in.

North Pole:
with reference to position of Hades and Tartaros.
northern limit of Antic Ocean.
Of the ancients.

North West Cape (Australia):
reached by Vlamingh.
From Cape Leeuwin to, visited by Dutch ships.

Noua Ginnea, and Noua Ginny (New Guinea):
according to Purchas.
The Flemings Pinnasse which went on discovery to, returned to Banda.

Nova Guinea (New Guinea):
with Schouten and Lemaire's nomenclature.
The Duyfken discovered the south and west coasts of.
A discovery made on the south coast of.
Jan Carstens ordered to "better discover."
The yacht Pera sailed along the south coast of.

Nuca Antara:
discovered by Godinho de Eredia.

Nueva Guinea (New Guinea):
named.

Nuremberg:
Behaim's country.
Behaim's globe removed to the School of Arts of.
The archives of the Behaim family at.
Ghillany published a work at.
Doppelmayr published a work at.
Monetarius from.

Nurmberg (Nuremberg):
with reference to Marco Polo.

Ocean:
the old river.

Oceanic Sea:
discovery in.

Oceanus Indicus Meridional:
on British Museum map.

Okeanos:
the earth-surrounding river of the Greeks.

Omaun:
traded to, by Arabs.

Ophinsa, Island of:
now Formentera, numerous snakes in.

Orangerie Bay (New Guinea):
called by the Spaniards the Great Bay of St. Lawrence.
Discovered on the 10th of August 1606.

Orange River:
and Cape Votas.

Oriental Sea:
in Fra Mauro's map.

Ormuz:
De Prado mentions that he will travel via.

Oronoco:

reached by Vincent Yanez Pinson before Cabral discovered Brazil.

Os Papuas, north-west coast of New Guinea:
Extensive discoveries made in, by Inigo Ortiz de Retez and Gaspar Rico.

Ostrich Point:
a remnant of the nomenclature belonging to Grijalva's expedition to the Spice Islands and New Guinea.

Ovo Islands:
mentioned.

Pacific Ocean:
its real size realised.
Not known.
Entered.
Proposition to explore a portion of the southern hemisphere lying in the.

Padan, Bay of, south-west coast of Bali:
Drake in the.

Palembang, district of:
long believed to be an island.
Named Ilha de Jaavaa on an early map.

Palimbam (Palembang), Islands of:
Abreu went to the.

Panama:
De Quiros died at.

Pandarani:
visited by Odoric.
Indian fleet at.

Pannani:
Indian fleet at.

Panten:
in Odoric's description.

Papagalli terra:
the Land of Parrots.

Paples Island (New Guinea):
the isla de Sanbenito, of Torres.

Papoia:
occurs on F. Rodriguez's portolano of Spice Islands.

Papua:
islands misnamed between, and Sumatra.
Don Jorge de Menezes carried by currents to the north of.
A further survey of.
Inigo Ortiz de Retez and Gaspar Rico make extensive discoveries on the north coast of.
Torres in the Gulf of.
Dalrymple's Collection concerning Papua mentioned.

Papuas:
name given to New Guinea people by the inhabitants of the Spice Islands.

Papuasia:
Saavedra sailed along the north coasts of.

Paris:
a wooden globe found in.
A mappamundi of the 11th century in.
National Library of, mentioned.
Poggio's treatise edited by the Abbe Oliva at.
After the peace of.
Codine's Memoire published at.
A work on Behaim's globe published at.
Dirck Hartog's plate in the Museum of the Institute of.

Paseos de Borne:
on J. Rotz's chart.

Patalie regio:
a name given to Terra Australis.

Patalis regio:
answers to New Zealand.
Suggested origin of name.
Its origin.

Peacock Town (Mailapuram?).

Pedestal Point, or Dias Point.

Pedir, in Sumatra.

Pedra branca, or Piedra blanca:
names unaccounted for.
Which occurs on P. Goos' map is not recorded on Tasman's chart.
Difficulty of explaining the presence of such Portuguese and Spanish words on Dutch charts.

Pegu:
mentioned.
Precious commodities from.
A fort on the coast of.
Given as Pego on P. Desceliers' chart.

Penedo das fontes:
Santa Cruz named, by some.

Peninsula:
Mathematicians obtained from the.

Pentam:
an island spoken of by Marco Polo.
Belongs to Marco Polo's nomenclature.
Identified with Bintang.
The eastern coast of, with reference to eastern coast of Australia.

Pentan (same as Pentam):
not mentioned on maps before Nicolo de' Conti's return.
Represented on Fra Mauro's map.
Misplaced.
On Schonerean gores.

Pergamos:
school of, mentioned.

Persepolis:
visited by Odoric.

Persia:

mentioned.

Persian Gulf:
on Turin mappamundi.
Omaun on.
Visited by Odoric.

Peru:
Governed by Lopez Garcia de Castro.
De Quiros set sail from the coast of.
The part of the southern hemisphere between, and Bachan and Ternate to be explored.
Mendana sailed from, for the last time.
De Quiros despatched to the Viceroy of.
The mainland of, not entirely settled.

Petan:
and Jaua Minor appear to occupy the Gulf of Carpentaria on G. Mercator's map.
Has been identified with Bintang.
In Eredia's description.

Pevtan, meant for Pentan:
in Ruysch's mappamundi.

Philippine Islands:
trade to.
Traders from.

Philippines, the:
left out in Fra Mauro's map.
Called first Archipelago of St. Lazaro.
The remnant of Loaysa's fleet sailed for.
Named after Philip II of Spain.
The settling of.
Bernardo de La Torre compelled to return to.
The remnant of Mendana's disastrous expedition repaired to.
Reduced by Admiral Cornish and General Draper.
Mentioned by Torres.

Phrygia:
Midas, King of, in conversation with Silenus.

Piccinacoli, the land of:
in Andrea Corsali's description.
Is the name given to New Guinea in G. Mercator's map.

Pider:
in Sumatra.

Piedra Blanca, or Pedra branca:
unaccounted for.
A probable Spanish survey to the south of Tasmania.

Point Swan:
named after the captain of Dampier's ship.

Polar Continent:
resembles what we know of those regions.

Pontos:
in Homer.

Porne (Borneo):
reached by Magellan's expedition.

Port Denison:
mentioned.

Port Gregory:
locality visited by Vlamingh.

Porto de Borneo:
on J. Rotz's chart.

Porto Santo:
discovered by accident.
A piece of wood and thick canes driven to.

Portugal:
John III, King of.
Sebastian, King of.
Dom Pedro returns to.
Dom Manoel, King of, obtained a copy of Nicolo de' Conti's voyages, and had it
  translated into Portuguese.

Affonso V of, sent documents to Italy.
Fra Mauro's map sent to.
The bold seafaring men of.
A copy of a map by Toscanelli sent to.
An appeal to the King of.
Islands near the coast of, marked on maps.
Peace between Spain and.
Death of Affonso V of.
Natives of the Congo River taken to.
Covilham determines to convey information to.
Negroes and negresses well affected towards.
When Dias reached.
At war with Spain.
Columbus had made propositions to the King of.
Wolf Holzschuer lived in.
Letter sent to Joao of.
Munzmeister wrote about his travels in.
Barthema goes to.
Terminates the quarrel over the Moluccas.
Other nations on the eve of contending with.
The decline of the power of Spain and.
Vessels equipped in the ports of.
A copy of a map sent to the King of.
Barthema's return to.
Disputing with Spain for the possession of the Moluccas.
Never recovered from the blow at Alcacer Quibir.
Linschoten and Houtman had been in the service of.

Potutis regio:
on Behaim's globe.

Presillg Landt:
the name for Land of Brazil in the Copia.

Prince of Wales Islands:
Gomez de Sequeira landed on one of the.
Nearer New Holland than New Guinea.

Promontory of Beach:
in Eredia's description.

Provincia di Ma'bar, or Mobar:
on the Coromandel coast.

Provincia di Malabar:
on the coast of Malabar.

Provincia Seilan:
on Lenox globe.

Psitacorum terra:
on a globe.
With reference to Bresil.

Psittacorum regio (Australian continent).

Pudipeten:
in Nicolo de' Conti's description

Puerto de Monte Rey:
a port near Mugula Island, south-west coast of New Guinea, named by Torres after
   the Count of Monterey, Viceroy of Peru.

Puerto de San Francisco:
The port where Torres first sighted land in New Guinea.

Puerto de S. Juan del Prado (south coast of New Guinea, Dutch Territory):
A name given by Torres.

Pulo Condor, Islands:
Called Sandio and Candur on Schonerean gores.

Pulo Tambini, the island of women.

Punta de fontiduena (south coast of New Guinea, Dutch Territory):
A name given by Torres.

Punta de la aguja (New Hebrides).

Puta (for Punta) di Melata, Point of Malacca.

Quabesegmesce:
A bad reading for Quabe se quiesce.
A letter from R.H. Major to George Collingridge with reference to the word.

Quabe se quiesce:
Corresponds with Calmia.

Quarequa, Sierra de:
Mar del Sur sighted from the heights of the.

Queen Charlotte's Islands:
A name given by Carteret to a group of islands discovered by Mendana.

Queensland:
The coast of, from Curtis Island to Great Sandy Island.
At the spot where Cook was nearly wrecked in the Endeavour occurs the name Coste
 dangerose in J. Roze's chart of Australia.
The coast of, erroneously supposed to have been discovered.
A true picture of the inhabitants of, 250 years ago.
Annual report on British New Guinea published in.
Timor situated off the coast of.

Quilon, or Coilum.

Quinsay:
distance from Lisbon to.

Ramos, or Mailata:
discovered and named during Mendana's expedition.

Red Sea:
on Turin mappamundi.
Tor on the.

Regio Petalis:
referred to.

Regnum Cayln:
on British Museum map.
Became a bogus Sumatra.
Separated from Regnum Lac.
Becomes Caylur.

Regnum lac:
on British Museum map.
Became a bogus Malay Peninsula.

Separated from Regnum Cayln.
Does not resemble Calmia.

Regnum Var:
indicates Ma'bar on Apianus' mappamundi.

Repulse Bay:
in the latitude mentioned by Torres.

Rhodes:
envoys go via.

Rindjani:
suggested by Dr. Hamy as the origin of Anjano.

Rio de brazil:
on the Cantino map.

Rio de la batalla:
a name on De Prado's chart of the Bay of St. Philip and St. James (New Hebrides).

Rio de San Antonio (New Hebrides).

Rio de S. Pedro (New Hebrides).

Rio do Infante:
named after Joao Infante.
Reached.

Rio do Padrao:
named by Diogo Cam.

Rio Grande:
a fictitious river between Australia and Java.

Rocky Pass (New Guinea):
between Hayter and Basilisk Islands, called the boca de la batalla in De Prado's chart.

Rome:
Matrons of.
Dom Pedro goes to.

A map in the Pope's library at.
Varthema's Itinerary first published at.
Barthema arrives in.
Ruysch's map of.
The Theatines established at.

Rosalaguin:
in Galvano's description.

Rosalanguin:
passed by Abreu.

Rosemary Island:
an island named by Dampier.

Rottenest Island:
on the west coast of Australia.
Captain Vlamingh broke his cable near.
Called the Island of Girls.

Rottnest Island (same as Rottenest):
named.

Rouen:
with reference to De Gonneville.
De Constantin's work published at.

Sabadibae:
in Ptolemy's map.

Saban, Straits of:
passed.

Sacte Crucis:
the name used in Schoner's map for the country called afterwards Brazil.

Sadales:
an island on Magalhaens' track, set down between Java and the Cape of Good Hope.
It recalls the Sandalos silve of the Frankfort Schonerean gores.

Sagres:
Prince Henry's school of navigation and astronomy at.

Salites, Islands:
passed by Abreu.

Salitres:
in Galvano's description.

Salsette:
visited by Odoric.

Samarcand:
Barthema started for.

Samaria (New Guinea):
Sir William Macgregor sent a despatch from.

Samatra (Sumatra):
Galvano speaks of.

Sambaba:
the name for Sumbawa on Wytfliet's map.

Sambana (Sumbawa):
in Galvano's description.

San bernardo:
an island in pieces.

San Bras:
named by Dias.

San Christobal:
Discovered by Mendana.
Mendana sent out to, to found a colony.

Sandai:
described by Nicolo de' Conti.
May be one of the Spice Islands.
Identified with Sunda in Fra Mauro's mappamundi.
Written Sondai.

Sandalos silve:
a name on Madagascar in the Schonerean gores.

San dimas:
an island discovered and named during Mendana's expedition.

Sandio, meant for Sondur.

Sandwich:
group, with reference to volcanoes.
Charted on Fra Mauro's map.
With reference to Marco Polo.
Discovered by the Spaniards.
Named by Cook, discovered by Villalobos.

San Felipe y Santiago (same as Baia de, etc.):
a bay named by De Quiros.

San Francisco:
Geographical Society of, mentioned.

San German:
an island discovered and named during Mendana's expedition.

Sanghir:
volcanic disturbances in.

San Jorge:
discovered and named during Mendana's expedition.

San Lourenco:
the name given by the Portuguese to Madagascar.

San Lucar:
Magellan sailed from.
Sebastian del Cano returned to.

San Marcos:
discovered and named during Mendana's expedition.

San Nicolas:
an island discovered and named during Mendana's expedition.

San Pablo:
a monastery at Seville.

Santa Cruz:
named by Dias.
A river beyond.
Dias' emotion when leaving.
Islands, named by Mendana.
De Quiros set sail for.
Discovered by Mendana.
De Quiros decided to go to.
De Quiros kept in the latitude of.
Information given concerning the Island of.
No necessity to go to the Island of.

Santa Maria, an island of the name of.

San Thome (see also Thomas, St.):
on the Coromandel coast.
The projected town of, placed (cartographically) on the Tenasserim coast by mistake.
Placed in the Sinus Magnus.

Santiago (New Hebrides):
One of the Cape Verde Islands, the Spaniards landed at.
An island discovered and named during Mendana's expedition.

San Urban:
an island discovered and named during Mendana's expedition.

San Valerio:
an island named by De Quiros.

Saragossa:
secret treaty signed at.
Vessels sent when the King was at.

Sarnau:
a place in China.

Satiroru:
in Ptolemy's map.

Sava:
answers to Java in Juan Vespuccius' map.

Saylam, i.e. Ceylon:
mentioned.

Scelebes:
left out in Fra Mauro's map.
Volcanoes of.

Sciamuthera:
another name for Sumatra.

Scolera (same as Socotra), Island:
on 11th century mappamundi.

Scotland:
the coastline of Europe from.

Scoyra, Island:
on Frankfort gores, meant for Socotra.

Scythia:
the Appollonians of.

Sea of Arafura:
an open sea.

Sea of Okhotsk:
with reference to North Pole of the ancients.

Sea of Orient:
a chart of the.

Segarga:
a volcano named by Mendana.

Segovia:
treaty of.

Seilan:
corresponds with Behaim's Seylan Insula.

Seilan Insulae Pars:
in Ruysch's mappamundi.

Seillan:
Cayln in earlier charts.

Seillan insulae pars:
name given to a bogus Sumatra.

Selamia (Ceram):
in Gastaldi's map.

Selani:
an island reached by Magellan.

Serra Parda:
mentioned.

Seven Cities, the Island of:
granted.
Ships equipped to search for.

Sever, St.:
monastery of.

Seville:
San Pablo, a monastery at.
Only port of equipment.
Two vessels sailed unlawfully from.
Spaniards returned to.
Treaty of.

Seychelles Islands:
on De Gonneville's route to the East Indies.

Seyla:
on Schonerean gores.

Seyla:
on Apianus' mappamundi.

Seylan insulae:
on Behaim's globe.

Seylan insule pars:

on Ruysch's mappamundi.

Shark's Bay:
a name given by Dampier.

Shiraz:
visited by Odoric.
Barthema arrived at.
Barthema returned to.

Siam:
precious commodities from.

Siamotra (Sumatra):
name given by Conti.
Name used by Fra Mauro.
The island, distorted on Behaim's globe.

Sian (Siam):
in Galvano's description.

Siberia:
mentioned.

Sidayu:
in Java.

Sierra Leone:
reached by Drake.

Sillan (Ceylon):
in Odoric's and Marco Polo's nomenclature.

Siloli:
larger than Porne (Borneo).

Simancas:
Torres' original manuscript letter relating his expedition with De Quiros is in the archives of.
Don Diego de Prado's original maps in the archives of.
Diligent research made at, for De Prado's map of New Guinea.

Simbabau:

a name applied erroneously to Java in Reinel's chart.

Sinbana (the modern Sumbawa):
in F. Rodriguez's portolano.
Applies to Sumbawa in the S. Cabot mappamundi.

Simbana (the modern Sumbawa):
on Jean Roze's chart.

Sindae:
in Ptolemy's map.

Sindoba:
duplicated, stands for Sumbawa.

Singapore:
island of Bintang near.

Sinus Gangeticus:
an important gulf of Ptolemy's map.

Sinus Magnus, same as Chinese Sea:
Brought down below the equator.
In Ptolemy's map.

Sinus Persicus:
in Ptolemy's map.

Sismondi:
a name for Sumatra.

Siuill (Seville):
in Galvano's account.

Socotra, Island:
written Scolera and Scoyra.

Sodur, meant for Sondur.

Sofala:
to be inquired for.
Covilham goes to.
On the route followed by the Portuguese.

Soffala (Sofala):
in Fra Mauro's map.

Solo:
an island reached by Magellan's expedition.

Solomon Islands:
for point of departure.
Discovered by Mendana.
The earliest map of the.
Confounded with New Britain and New Ireland in De Bry's map.
Stand too far south in Wytfliet's map.
Captain Welbe's proposal to steer for the.
Discovered by the Spaniards.

Solor:
in Galvano's description.
Passed by Abreu.
Mentioned.

Soltania:
visited by Odoric.

Sondai:
written Sandai in Ramusio.

Sondur:
in Marco Polo's description.
In Fra Mauro's map.
On Apianus' mappamundi.

Sorabaia (same as Surabaya).

South America:
according to the school of Pergamos.
Columbus on the north coast of.
Mentioned.
With reference to the term Brazil.
Joam de Resaga ran along the coast of.

South Atlantic Ocean:
a passage from the.

Southern Continent:
alluded to.

Southern Hemisphere:
early notions concerning the.

Southern Land:
a detailed memoir on the discovery of.

Southern Sea:
studded with islands in map of third type.

Southern World:
according to the school of Pergamos.

South Georgia, or South Sandwich Islands:
discovered by Francisco de Hoces.

South Land:
or Land of Concord (Eendraght Land) in Rechteren's account.
The Witte Valck and Goede Hoop ordered to proceed to the.
Willem de Vlaming's voyage to the, and its object.
Journal of a voyage to the unexplored.
Discovered in the year 1696.
Navigators.
The charting of the eastern and western coasts of the Great.

South Pacific Ocean:
a passage from the South Atlantic to the.
Studded with Marco Polo's islands.
Discoveries in the, referred to.

South Pole:
enveloped by Austral regions called Terra Australis.
The unknown continent relegated towards the.
An imaginary continent around the, connected with Australia.
De Quiros took possession as far as the.

South Sea:
afterwards to be called the Pacific Ocean.
The Dutch sailed with the intention of reaching the.
A passage into the, sought for.

Divided from the Western Sea.
Captain Welbe had been in the.
Company.
Trade from the, to the East Indies.

Spain, or Iberia:
Owes the discovery of America to Italians.
When C. Columbus started from.
Skilled cartographers of.
Peace between, and Portugal.
At war with Portugal.
Columbus went to.
With reference to Columbus' argument.
Munzmeister wrote about his travels in.
Vessels equipped in the ports of.
With reference to lawful enterprises.
Magellan makes his way to the Court of.
Formal possession taken of New Guinea in the name of the King of.
Disputing with Portugal for the possession of the Moluccas.
Maps used in.
King of, renounced his claim to the Moluccas.
Other nations on the eve of contending with Portugal and.
Power of Portugal and, on the decline.
The throne of Portugal an appanage of.
Wytfliet's map dedicated to the King of.

Speriet:
The Great Island, discovered.
No reason given for the name.
Written differently on Dutch charts.
Is the orthography used in Swart's black letter copy from the original manuscript document.

Sperietrivier:
in the 14th paragraph of Tasman's instructions.

Speult:
another form of Speriet and Spult.
A word found on Dutch charts near Torres Straits.
The Dutch contend that, or Spult, is the name of a Dutch official.

Spice Islands:
in Ptolemy's map.

Near Nicolo de' Conti's Javas.
Banda is one of the.
Described from hearsay.
The race to the, began.
Columbus believed he had reached the.
Voyages in search of.
Said not to have been visited by Barthema.
Australians with a practical knowledge of the.
Magellan sailed in search of the.
Nomenclature of the, derived from Maximilianus' letter.
A route to the, sought for.
The Portuguese appear to have reached the, before the conquest of Malacca.
With reference to white people.
Papoia and the, charted by F. Rodriguez.
Attempts made to reach the, by the west.
Or Moluccas.
The remnant of Loaysa's expedition make for the.
Saavedra's ship unable to reach America, returned to the.
In Spanish territory.
A close rivalry between the Dutch and the English with regard to the trade to the.
The Portuguese and Spaniards at the.
The Spaniards claimed all discoveries under the meridian of.

Spult:
given for Speriet in the translation of Tasman's Instructions published by Alex Dalrymple.
May be a corruption of the Spanish Spiritu Santo written Spu St.

Sta Isabella (island):
named by Mendana.
A brigantine built at.

Sta Polonia:
an island named by De Quiros.

Staten River:
the yacht Pera ran along the west coast as far as 17 degrees south to.

St. Christoval:
a port in 11 degrees south named by Mendana.

St. George's Islands:

named by Captain Welbe.

St. Julian's Bay:
Magellan arrived at.
Magellan sailed out of.

Stockholm:
a map by La Salle in the Royal Library of.

Stormy Cape (Cabo Tormentoso).

Straits of Sunda (see also Sunda):
the survivors of the Zeewych arrive in the.

Strasburg:
a work on Behaim's globe published at.

Suakem:
Payva directs his course towards.

Subuth:
a very large island reached by Magellan.

Suez, Isthmus of:
on Turin mappamundi.

Sumatra:
and Ceylon described as Taprobana.
Ceylon placed in same latitude and longitude as.
Placed where Ceylon stands.
Known to be cut in two by the equator.
Its earliest name was Tamravarna.
A portion of, should show in Southern Hemisphere on Ptolemy's map.
Removed to Northern Hemisphere on Ptolemy's map.
On Turin mappamundi.
On 11th century mappamundi.
Described by Marco Polo under the name of Java Minor.
Visited by Odoric.
Duplicated.
Missing, receives the name of Cayln.
The west coasts and probably north-west coast of bogus, were the west and north-west coasts of Australia.
Described as Anticamente detta Taprobana in Nicolo de' Conti's text.

On the confines of the world.
Charted nearly as well as Java, on Fra Mauro's map.
Believed to be formed of several islands.
Mentioned.
Bears the name first given to it by Conti.
No mistaking it.
Written Sciamuthera.
A bogus.
How did our western coasts get confounded with the western coasts of?
Fra Mauro's placed in the Southern Hemisphere.
Cut in two by the Tropic of Capricorn instead of the equator.
With reference to the western shores of Australia.
Barthema and party sailed from.
Assumes a greater likeness to the real Sumatra in Ruysch's mappamundi.
Gold from.
Southern parts of, split up into islands in Fra Mauro's mappamundi.
Islands between and Papua misnamed.
Claimed by the Spaniards as being within their territory.
Disconnected in Juan Vespuccius' map.
The Dutch of the first expedition to Australasia reached the south-west coast of.

Sumbawa (the island of):
with reference to its volcanoes.
Reached at an early time.
Called Zibala in Ptolemy's map.
Java and, must be Nicolo de' Conti's two Javas.
South coast of, little known.
On the confines of the world.
Charted as a distinct and separate island.
Charted by F. Rodriguez.
Represented as two islands in F. Rodriguez's portolano.
Deformed.
Called Frroresta erroneously in Reinel's chart.
Charted as Sindoba.
Placed over Cape York.
Called Jaua Minor.
To the east of Bali and Lomboc.
Undistinguishable because forming the apex of York Peninsula.
The nomenclature of the island of.
An open sea between, and Timor.
Forms part of Australia on charts of the Desceliers type.

Sunda (see also Straits of Sunda):
in Galvano's description.
Sandai identified with.
Written Sondai.
The blocking of the straits of.
Fortresses in the straits of useless.
Meant for Java in Camoens' poem.
Described.
The yacht Goede Hoop cruising in the straits of.

Swan River:
black swans found in the, by W. de Vlamingh.

Sydney:
Captain Carpenter in.
Free Public Library of, mentioned.
Museum of, mentioned.

Sydrapetta River:
Mailapur near.

Symbana:
the modern Sumbawa.

Synti bvgd:
in the Australasian regions.

Synus Gangeticus:
limit of Cosa's mappamundi.

Syria:
mentioned.

Tabriz:
visited by Odoric.

Tagulanda:
an island reached by Drake.

Tamravarna:
corrupted to Taprobana.

Tana:

in Salsette, visited by Odoric.

Taomaco (same as Taumaco):
mentioned.
An island like that of.
Islands named by the Indians of.

Tappaprone I Indie (Taprobana):
on 11th century mappamundi.

Taprobana, and Ceylon:
Ceylon and Sumatra described as.
A Greek corruption of Tamravarna.
Name given to Ceylon in Ptolemy's map.
Same as Sumatra in Nicolo de' Conti's description.
Alias Zoilon is the name given to Sumatra in Ruysch's mappamundi.
Ceylon suggested as another name for.

Taprobane:
mentioned.
Now called Zamatara.
No island to be identified with.

Tarante (Ternate):
one of the five Spice Islands according to Maximilian's account.
A small island.

Tarasa River (New Guinea):
Mentioned.
The delta of the, well charted in de Prado's map.

Tartaros:
Situation of, according to the Greeks.
The Earth Genii of.

Taraze (for Tarante, i.e. Ternate):
On alleged Schoner globe.

Tasmania:
Java Minor occupies the site of.
For goal.
Named after Tasman.
More generally known as Van Diemen's Land

Discovered by Tasman.
Nomenclature of, and Australia on P. Goos' and Tasman's maps of Australia.

Tassaso:
A Dutch fort at Machian.

Taumaco (island):
Indications of a great southern continent given by the Indians of.
De Quiros put in at the island of.
The chief of, informs De Quiros of a Terra Firma in the south.
Torres disembarked in, and went on board the Almirante.

Tenasserim Coast:
The projected town of San Thome erroneously placed (cartographically) on the.

Tenimber:
Jan Carstens ordered to visit.
Visited by Pieter Pietersz.

Ternate:
Galvano governor of.
With reference to Gumnape.
Serrano wrote from, to his friends and to Magalhaens.
Juan de Esquivel the Maestro de Campo of.
Torres departed for.
Drake decides to go to.
The King of, possesses seventy islands besides, according to Drake.
Torres asked to subdue one of the islands of.
The nations of, in rebellion.
The Dutch had Fort Melaia and Tacomma at.
The Portuguese of.

Terra Australis Incognita:
the name for Australia on Abraham Goos' globe.

Terra Alta:
of the Ribeiro maps marked on Mercator's map.

Terra Australis:
discovery of the.
On fantastic maps.
A strait between New Guinea and.

Called Patalie Regio.
In Oronce Fine's map.
Schoner's Brasielie Regio and Regio Patalis found on Oronce Fine's map of.
Described in Frobisher's voyages.
The only name which is not fictitious on Wytfliet's map of Australia.
An important passage with reference to the.
Separated from New Guinea.
With reference to the course of the Duyfken.
A petition to "erect colonies in," was presented to King James the First.
Captain Welbe offered a plan for the full discovery of.
New Guinea supposed to form part of.
Captain Welbe's proposals for establishing a company for carrying on a trade to.
Of the ancients.

Terra Australis Incognita:
first appearance of, on a map.

Terra de Brazil:
in the longitude and latitude of New Guinea.

Terra del Fuego (see also Tierra del Fuego):
with reference to Terra Australis.

Terra della Vera Cruz (or Brazil).

Terra del Verzino:
a continental land near or connected with New Guinea.

Terra del Zur (Great Land of the South):
a name for Australia.
Thus called in the Mar d' India map.

Terra de Piccinacoli (the Land of Piccinacoli):
Apparently New Guinea.
Described by Andrea Corsali.
Believed to be connected with Brazil or Terra del Verzino.

Terra de Santa Cruz:
for Serra Sanctae Crucis, a name given previously to Brazil.
With reference to its western shores.
Near the Spice Islands.

Terra dos Papous:
a legend on New Guinea.

Terra en negade:
on J. Roze's chart, Number 1, a corruption of terra anegada (submerged land).

Terra firma:
Magellan ordered to sail for the, and search for a strait.
To be found in the south.
Or continent (Australian) to be discovered by Mendana from San Christoval.

Terra Incognita:
of Ptolemy.
The absence of the, a provisory measure.
Some think Java belongs to the.

Terra Rubra:
Bartholomew Columbus of.

Terre Australle:
on an imaginary continental part of Australia prolonged towards the South Pole.
Corresponds with any land south of the equator.
A name given by De Gonneville.

Terrestrial Paradise:
near Gatigara.

Texel:
the first Dutch fleet to Australasia sailed from the.
The first Dutch fleet returned to.

Texoxtica (Mexico):
discovered.

Thalamassin (see also Thalamasyn):
a land of that name described by Odoric.

Thalamasyn (same as Thalamassin):
or Panten, in Odoric's description.

Thalassa:

in Homer.

Thedori (Tidore):
one of the Moluccas reached by Magellan's expedition.
King of, submitted to the Spanish Imperial Government.

Thome, S.:
on British Museum map.

Tidore, Island of:
two of Magalhaens' vessels arrived at.
Inigo Ortiz de Retez and Gaspar Rico sail from.

Tierra del Fuego (see also Terra del Fuego):
believed to be connected with an Austral continent.
Set down as an island on the Carta da navigar.

Tigris:
mentioned.
Circular boats of the.

Timor:
an island intended for, in Schoner's globe.
Sandalwood from.
Not represented on Reinel's chart.
Sebastian del Cano went to.
The Portuguese could not believe that the island of, was situated to the east of the
  peninsula set down on the Dauphin and similar charts.
Out of place.
Sebastian del Cano passed through an open sea from, to Spain.
Larger on P. Desceliers' map.
Dampier approached Australia from.
Dampier fell in with a shoal to the south of.
Dampier set sail for.
Martin Van Delft's fleet remained some time at.
The Portuguese and Spaniards must have known of an open sea between, and Sumbawa.
Situated off the coast of Queensland.
In Gastaldi's map.

Timor Laut:
a group of islands mentioned.

The discovery of, not recorded on the Mar d' India map

Timona-ilha:
probably Timor.

T' Landt Van d'Eendracht:
said to have been discovered in the year 1616.

Tobi, or Lord North's Island:
to the north of New Guinea.
Not on the route to the straits of Magellan.

Toledo:
the Courts of.

Tona:
the remnant of some prototypic name.

Tor:
on the Red Sea.

Tormapatan:
Indian fleet at.

Torres Straits:
with reference to the course of the Duyfken.
Indicated.
Blocked.
Known at an early date.

Tortelduyf, cliff:
passed by the crew of the Emeloort.

Toulon, Island (or Mairu, native):
the Islas Bartolome of Torres.

Travancore:
where Quilon is situated.

Trebizond:
visited by Odoric.

Treguada:

an island discovered and named during Mendana's expedition.

Tres Marias:
an island discovered and named during Mendana's expedition.

Tuban, in Java.

Tucopia (same as Chucopia):
to the north-east of the New Hebrides.

Tunis:
a map of that name.
Referred to.
The meridian of.

Tzana, Lake:
on Turin mappamundi.

Underworld:
of Homer.

Unfortunate Islands:
reached by Magellan.

Valladolid:
the remnant of Magalhaens' expedition went up to.
Maximilian's letter written at.

Valsche Kaep (False Cape), New Guinea:
Keer-Weer to the north of.

Van Diemen's Gulf:
visited by Martin Van Delft.

Van Diemen's Land:
with reference to Markham's communication.
A name for Tasmania.
Martin Van Delft's fleet proceeded to.
The north-west corner of, now known as Cape Van Diemen.

Varre regio:
on Schonerean gores.

Varr var regnum:
in the British Museum map.

Venetia (Venice):
Ramusio could not find a copy of Nicolo de' Conti's travels in.

Venezuela:
a small island off the coast of.

Venice:
Ptolemy's geography published in.
Marco Polo returns to.
Reached overland by Odoric.
Dom Pedro goes to, brings back a map and a copy of Marco Polo's travels.
A fine map made in.
Draughts of maps sent to.
De Prado mentions that he will travel by.

Vermont, the State of:
mentioned.

Versailles:
a work of Prince Roland Bonaparte published at.

Versija:
probably Waigiu, where Don Jorge de Menezes landed.

Verzino (the same as Brazil):
the size of.
The Italian for Brazil-wood.

Victoria Nyanza:
on Turin mappamundi.

Vienna:
a map published at.

Vintara:
in Galvano's description.

Vitara:
passed by Abreu.
Sebastian del Cano passed by.

Voltas, Cape (same as Angra das Voltas).

Waigiu:
Menezes arrived at.

War ein Konigreich:
a legend on Behaim globe.

Washington:
the Hunt-Lenox globe taken to.
A lecture published at.

Wedge Island:
on the west coast of Australia.

Weimar:
mappamundi referred to.

Wessel Islands:
might be Gomez de Sequeira's Islands.

Western Australia:
the Portuguese could only claim, according to Diego Ribeiro's map.

Western Sea:
divided from the South Sea by a narrow neck of land.

West Indies:
reached by Columbus.
Reached by Dieppe and St. Malo mariners.

West Island (New Guinea):
is called in De Prado's chart the isla de San Antonio.

White Nile:
on Turin mappamundi.

Willems' River:
Vlamingh reports having sailed up.

Xengibar (Zanzibar):
on Fra Mauro's map.

Ya de los hobres blancos:
on S. Cabot mappamundi.

Yciagina (?):
a name not to be found in Maximilian's letter.

Yezd:
visited by Odoric.

York, Cape, of Australia:
connected with the southern shores of Sumbawa near Bali and Lomboc.
Bramble Cay, an island situated off the extreme north end of.

York Peninsula:
a legend between, and the east end of Java.
Sumbawa forming the apex of.
forts and castles represented on.
Connected with Sumbawa on charts of the Desceliers type.

Ysles de Magna:
on the Dauphin chart, a probable corruption of the Anguana of Behaim's globe.

Zaba (a form of Java).

Zaire:
the native name for Rio do Padrao.

Zaitam (same as Zaiton):
the extremity of the empire of the Great Khan.

Zaiton (China):
sudden transition from, to Giava in Nicolo de' Conti's text as given in Ramusio.
The port of, famous.

Zamatara, or Taprobane.

Zanzibar:
Menuthias in Ptolemy's map.
On Behaim's globe.
On Apianus mappamundi.

Inhabited by giants.
On De Gonneville's route to the East Indies.

Zaragoza:
treaty of, mentioned.

Zeilan, Island of:
described by Galvano.
In Barthema's description.

Zelon:
an island reached by Drake.

Zewarra:
an island reached by Drake.

INDEX TO NAMES.

See also the special nomenclature of Navigators given above.

Abel Yansz Tasman (see also Tasman):
the manuscript map of, mentioned.

Aberts, Pieter:
one of the survivors of the Vergulde Draeck, wrecked on the west coast of Australia.

Abraham Goos:
his globe published by Joh. Jannssonius.
Shows a southern continent occupying the position of Australia without any Dutch
  discoveries recorded thereon.

Abraham of Beja, Rabbi:
a messenger from King Joao.

Abreu, Antonio de (see also D' Abreu and Antonio de Breu):
reached the Spice Islands.

Pathways traversed by.

Adam, and Eve:
represented on Turin mappamundi.
On 11th century mappamundi.

Aelian:
a fragment of the works of Theopompus preserved by.

Aelianus:
translated by Fleming.

Affonso V, of Portugal:
sent some documents to Italy.
Seconded Prince Henry.
Spared no expense.
Fra Mauro made a copy of maps while elaborating the one for King.
Followed the example set by Prince Henry.

Affonso de Payva:
sent to search for the country of Prester John.

Agnesina, Madonna:
mentioned.

Albert-le-Grand:
pre-eminent in his time.

Alberuni:
his India quoted.

Albuquerque:
refers to a lost map.
Some letters of his, recently found.
The text of a letter by.
Went unto Mossambique.
Lost no time in sending out an expedition to the Spice Islands.

Alexander-the-Great:
with reference to Marco Polo.
Quoted by Maximilian.

Alexander VI, Pope:

his line of demarcation.
Line of demarcation of, did not extend much beyond the east coast of Timor.

Alfonso:
King Joao's second son.

Alfragano:
no notice to be taken of.

Alfred, King:
builds boats.

Allan Cunningham:
at the Bay of Rest, W. Australia.

Al-Mamoun:
with reference to Ptolemy's geography.

Almeyda, Don Francisco de, the Portuguese Viceroy.

Alonso de Salazar:
appointed to the command of Loaysa's expedition.
Died on his way to the Philippines.

Alonso Medel, one of Columbus' officers.

Alonso Corzo, Captain, one of the officers of De Quiros' expedition.

Alvarado, Fernando de:
went out with Grijalva.
Returned to New Spain, it is supposed.

Alvaro da Torre:
translated Monetarius' letter to Joao II.

Alvaro de Mendana (see also Mendana and Alvaro Mendana de Meyra):
mentioned.

Alvaro de Mesquita:
in command of one of Magellan's ships.
Put in irons.

Alvaro de Saavedra, Cortez's kinsman:

sent to the Spice Islands from New Spain.
On his way back to America discovered the north coast of New Guinea.

Alvaro Mendana de Meyra (see also Alvaro de Mendana and Mendana):
first discovered New Guadalcanal.

Alvaro Telez:
ran out of his course and reached Sumatra.
Was he driven on the western coast of Australia.

Alvrin (see also Dalvim), John, Lopez:
with reference to Java.

Amherst, Tyssen Amherst W.:
possesses the original manuscript of Catoira giving the account of Mendana's expedition.

Ana, or Zi-Ana:
the spirit of the Heaven of the Chaldeans.

Andrade:
went to China.

Andrea Bianco:
called by Fra Mauro to help in making a map.

Andrea Corsali:
With other Italians gave information concerning the Australasian regions.
With reference to the term Brazil.
With reference to Terra de Piccinacoli.
Never saw New Guinea.
Writing from Cochin China, describes the Terra de Piccinacoli.

Andrea Furtado de Mendoca, Governor of Malacca.

Anghierra:
his decadas quoted.

Anne of Cleves:
went to England.

Anson, Admiral:
a Spanish map found by.

Antonio de Arostegui, King of Spain's secretary:
letter of Don Diego de Prado to.

Antonio de Breu (see also Abreu and D'Abreu):
went to the Spice Islands.
Took his course towards the north.
Returned to Malacca.

Antonio de Lisboa:
sent out to search for Prester John.

Antonio Gallo:
referred to.

Apianus:
his mappamundi referred to.

Aratus:
speaks of a southern continent.

Argensola:
with reference to D'Abreu's expedition.
With reference to Magalhaens.

Arias:
his memorial referred to by Dalrymple.

Aristotle:
speaks of two segments of the globe.
His ideas revived.
Quoted.

Ayres de Saldanha:
Godinho de Eredia discovered Nuca Antara by command of the Viceroy.
The successor of Da Gama.

Bacon:
pre-eminent in his time.
Derived his ideas concerning the existence of transatlantic lands from Aristotle.
With reference to Bartholomew Columbus.

Badger, George Percy:
refers to Barthema.

Banks, Sir Joseph:
presented the Dauphin chart to the British Museum.
Knew of the existence of Torres' Straits.
A document with information relating to Australia fell into the hands of.
Tasman's Instructions supposed to have been found in Batavia by.

Barbie du Bocage:
on Gomez de Sequeira's discovery of some islands near Australia.

Barentz:
Linschoten accompanies him in his attempt to reach India by the Polar Seas.

Barreto (same as Garreto), Da Isabel de, Mendana's wife.

Barros, de (same as de Barros):
mentioned.
Quoted.

Barthema, Ludovico (same as Varthema):
visited Java.
supposed not to have visited the Spice Islands.
His narrative little known.
The Australasian portion of his narrative.
At the time of his travels the Chinese used to visit the Spice Islands.
His guides.
Addressed by the Christians.
Leaves Calicut.
Escorted to the Viceroy.
His account of the appearance of the Indian fleet.
Factor to the Portuguese of Cochin.
Descriptions on P. Desceliers' Map of Australia taken from the writings of Marco Polo and.

Bartholomew Columbus, C. Columbus' younger brother:
Made a map in London.
His presence in London.
A copy of the lost map of.
May be the author of a prototypic map.

Bartolome Colin:

Set sail.

Bartolomeo de Lasso, the cosmographer:
Sent 25 charts to Plancius.

Barton, G.B.:
With reference to Torres' Straits.
Referring to the account and map of Terra Australis published with Frobisher's voyages.
With reference to J. Welbe's scheme of colonisation.

Behaim, M.:
His globe the earliest extant.
Islands mentioned by Marco Polo and Odoric set down on his globe.
Accompanies Diogo Cam to the Congo River.
A parallel between, and Dalrymple.
Copied Fra Mauro's mappamundi.
A more primitive mappamundi than his.
May be the author of a prototypic map.
His globe has Seylan insulae.
Baron Frederic Carl Von, senior familiae.
The archives of the family of.
Furnished the geographical data and legends for his globe.
The geographical notions of his globe.
To go and search for Cathay.
Mentions Doctor Ieronimus.
Degrees of longitude and latitude first revived on the globe of.
An indication that his globe was copied from Toscanelli's map.
Features of a western coast of Australia to be found in the globe of.
Marco Polo's writings compared with the interpretation given to them on the globe of.
Malaiur does not appear on the globe of.
Position of Java Minor on the globe of.
Islands of the Australasian regions on the globe of.
Locach altered to Coachs on the globe of.
The prototype of his globe was no doubt of Arabian origin.
His globe mentioned.
His Africa.
His Java Major is nameless on the Hunt-Lenox globe.
His Seylan Insula rendered by Seilan on the Hunt-Lenox globe.
His Seylan Insula rendered Seylan Insule pars on Ruysch's mappamundi.
First model of deformation to be found on his globe.
Toscanelli or, corrected the direction of Fra Mauro's pseudo-equatorial line.

Belga, G.N.:
a mappamundi published by him at Lyons.

Benedetto Bordone (see also Bordone):
a mappamundi of, mentioned.

Bennet & Van Wyk, M.M.:
their map shows Keer-Weer on the coast of New Guinea, and not on the Australian coast.

Bernardino, Monsignor:
Barthema's travels dedicated to.

Berosus:
corrupted EA-han to Oannes.

Binot Paulmier de Gonneville (same as de Gonneville):
an affidavit subscribed by.

Bisagudo, Simao Afonso:
commanded a ship in D'Abreu's expedition.

Blaeu:
his atlases mentioned.
Sent to Florence by the Dutch.
Some maps of, show Tasman's discoveries.

Bolamboam (see also Balambuam), the Rajah of:
in Java at the time of Cavendish's visit.

Bonaparte, Prince Roland:
on Linschoten's and Houtman's knowledge of the route to India.
Quoted.
Tasman's chart of Australia the property of.
With reference to Dutch discovery in Australia.

Bordone (see also Benedetto Bordone):
Sebastian Cabot's mappamundi drawn on the projection of.

Bougainville:
visited and named Orangerie Bay, the Golphe de la Louisiade (New Guinea).
His description of Orangerie Bay corresponds with the Spanish description.

Quoted.
His expedition mentioned.

Boulengier:
his gores referred to.

Bowrey, Captain:
his map shows the track followed by Tasman in his first and second voyage.

Branca, King Joao's first son.

Breusing:
mentions Behaim's globe.

Broadhurst, Macneil and company:
with reference to Houtman's Abrolhos.

Burleigh, Lord:
a manuscript endorsed by.

Burney:
first printed the Relation of Luis Vaes de Torres, translated by Alexander Dalrymple.
His account of John Welbe's proposal.

Byron:
his expedition mentioned.

Cabot, John and Sebastian:
sighted America.

Cabots, the, Venetians.

Cabral:
his discovery of Brazil.
Did the Arabs know about his discovery?

Calvert, A.F.:
Author of The Discovery of Australia, with reference to a mistake of ours.

Camers:
published Apianus' mappamundi.

Camoens:
quoted.

Cantino, Hercules d'Este's ambassador.

Carpenter, Captain, of the Costa Rica packet:
with reference to the Straits of Bali.

Carteret:
re-named islands discovered by Mendana.
His expedition mentioned.

Carvalhaes, Pedro de:
mentioned in Eredia's report.

Castanheda:
with reference to D'Abreu's expedition.
A Portuguese author.
With reference to Gomez de Sequeira's voyage.

Castro Da Mariana de, Lope de Vega's wife.

Cavendish, Sir Thomas:
the gale he experienced.
Sailed through the straits to the north-west of Australia.
The Australasian portion of his narrative.
A passage with reference to the track of.
An English pilot who had been round the world with.
Sailed in the track of Drake.

Cazazionor (same as Cogiazanor), the Persian merchant who travelled with Barthema.

Charles V, of Spain:
Magellan in his service.
Spain governed by Cardinal Ximenes in the absence of.
With reference to the dispute concerning the Moluccas.
Continued to allow his subjects to trade with the Spice Islands.
Voyage made under his auspices.

Chesney, Colonel:
on the shape of the circular boats of the Tigris and Euphrates.

Chiaymasiuro, King of Damuth:
in Eredia's description.

Christ:
200 years before.

Christofero di Arco, a clerk of Seville.

Codine, J.:
his Memoire referred to.
His conclusions with reference to the Arabian Islands.

Coen, Jan Pietersz, Governor-General of the Dutch East Indies.

Cogiazanor (or Cazazionor):
objected to Barthema leaving him.

Collingridge, George:
with reference to the Early Cartography of Japan.
With reference to Point Cloates, Western Australia, and the bird called Ruck or Rock by Marco Polo.
A letter from R.H. Major to.

Colonna:
Fabricio, mentioned.
Ascanio, mentioned.

Columbus, C.:
discovers America.
Endeavours to put Strabo's ideas into practice.
The course his ship might have taken.
Maintained that he had reached India.
Spain owes the discovery of America to.
Mentioned.
Mentioned by Harrisse.
Endeavours to reach China and Japan.
The map which he took with him.
A map in which the islands discovered afterwards by, were set down.
An article called, by Professor Ruge.
May have received a letter and map from Toscanelli.
Directed his course to the Land of Spice.
Wrote a letter to Toscanelli.

Wanted particulars from Toscanelli concerning the route to the Land of Spice.
In search of Cipango.
Only received Martins' letter years after it was sent.
Copy of Toscanelli's letter to.
With reference to the Duke of Ferrara.
A parallel between him and Cook.
America practically re-discovered by.
Had made a proposition to the King of Portugal.
Went to Spain.
His expedition.
America unknown to him.
Made a globe.
His younger brother Bartholomew, an efficient cartographer, demonstrated to him that
  a continent would be reached.
His arguments, the same as those used by Munzmeister.
His glowing accounts.
His 10%
Two of his officers elope with two armed vessels.
Rivarolla, his friend and banker.
His ideas not generally accepted.

Commelyn:
his Begin ende Voortganh referred to.

Constantin:
quoted.
A passage in, which shows that the Spaniards wished to avail themselves of Torres' discoveries in New Guinea.

Conti, Nicolo de' (see also Nicolo de Conti):
referring to the location of Malepur.
His narrative could not be found by Ramusio.
Mentioned.
Quoted.
His nomenclature.

Cook, Captain:
did he discover the east coast of Australia?
A parallel between him and Columbus.
Australia practically re-discovered by.

The Sandwich and Falkland Islands known and charted by the Spaniards a long time before.
At the spot where he was nearly wrecked in the Endeavour occurs the name coste dangerose
  in Jean Roze's chart of Australia.
Named the Sandwich Islands discovered previously by Villalobos.
Knew of the existence of Torres Straits.
At Batavia.
Lieutenant James, his arrival and re-survey of the eastern coast of Australia alluded to.
The last recorded expedition previous to the arrival of.
His expedition mentioned.
A map before his arrival.
Supposed to have reached Batavia by the north of New Guinea.
Named the Prince of Wales' Islands in Endeavour Straits.

Coote, C.H., of the British Museum:
With reference to the Hunt-Lenox globe.
His opinion on Ruysch's mappamundi.
With reference to Maximilianus.
On a legend in Java.

Coquebert, Montbret:
with reference to Jean Valard's maps.

Cordier:
his Bibliotheca Sinica referred to.

Cornelis Schouten:
the name of the skipper of the Vianen.

Cornelius Claez, of Amsterdam:
procured charts.

Cornelius Houtman (see also Houtman):
inquired into the state of the East Indies.
Put into prison.
Addressed the merchants of Amsterdam.
Supercargo.

Cornish, Admiral:
reduced the Philippines,

Correa, and de Goes:
with reference to D'Abreu's expedition.

Corsali (same as Andrea Corsali):
his remarks cast a doubt on the insularity of New Guinea.

Cortez:
received an account of a voyage by Joam de Resega.
Sent Alvaro de Saavedra in search of Loaysa's expedition.

Corzo Felipe:
commanded the San Felipe in Mendana's second expedition.

Cosmo de Medicis:
at Naples.

Courteen, Sir William:
presented a petition for the "privilege of erecting colonies" in Terra Australis to King James the First.
Carried on an extensive trade to Portugal, Spain, Guinea and the West Indies.
Had some claim on the King's consideration.
Died in 1666.

Couto (see also Diego do Couto):
gives an account of Don Jorge de Menezes' voyage.

Covilham, Pedro de:
directed his course towards India.
Embarked at Aden.
Had heard of cloves and cinnamon, etc.
His letters taken to King Joao.

Cowley:
his fine lines on Drake's ship.

Crates (200 B.C.):
mentions an earth globe.
With reference to Geminus.
His terrestrial globe described by Strabo.
Mentioned.

Crawford:
quoted.

Creuszner, Fricz:
with reference to the Editio Princeps of Marco Polo.

Cristobel Guerra:
alluded to.

Crozet:
his expedition mentioned.

D'Abreu:
back in the year 1512.
A possible copy of his chart of the East Indian Archipelago.

Dalrymple, Alexander:
a parallel between him and M. Behaim.
Quoted with reference to Mendana's first voyage.
His letter to Hawkesworth concerning Torres' Straits.
Torres' track marked on his map determined the course of the Endeavour.
His map showing Torres' track and Straits compiled from facts.
A copy of a memorial communicated to.
Published a chart of New Guinea showing Torres' Straits.
Published a document that fell into the hands of Sir Joseph Banks.
His faulty translation of the Instructions.
Refers to a manuscript chart by Eessel Gerrits, of Amsterdam.
Became the possessor of the document which revealed Torres' passage.
Said "there is nothing new under the sun."

Dalvim (see also Alvrin):
was captain of one of the vessels ordered by Albuquerque to remain at Malacca.

Dampier, W.:
strange rocks seen by, on the western coasts of Australia.
Vlamingh's voyage made after the visit of.
The arrival of, in Australasia.
Sighted New Holland (Australia) on the 4th of January 1688.
His landfall in New Holland easily determined.
Only a common sailor when on his first visit to New Holland.
Captain of the Roebuck.
Edward Harley, one of the patrons of.
Fell in with the coast of Australia to the north of the Abrolhos.
Had Tasman's chart of west coast of New Holland.

Amongst the islands that received the name of Archipel de Dampier.
His description of the New Hollanders.
The passage to the South Sea haunted his mind.
Set sail for Timor.
In sight of New Guinea.
His voyages published.
A scheme of colonisation suggested by.
In command of the St. George.
His experience to be made use of.
His death.
Sailed with Swann.

Dante:
pre-eminent in his time.
His verses on the Southern Cross.

D'Avezac:
wrote about De Gonneville's voyage.

De Barros:
with reference to Odoric and the Straits of Bali.
With reference to D'Abreu's expedition.

De Brosses:
with reference to the insularity of New Guinea.

De Bry:
his map of the Solomon Islands.

De Constantin (same as Constantin):
his translation of Commelyn's work referred to.

De Goes, and Correa:
say that Simao Afonso Bisagudo commanded the third ship in D'Abreu's expedition.

De Gonneville (same as Binot Paulmier de Gonneville):
his claim not substantiated.
A French claim of discovery in favour of.

Delmar Morgan:
on the La Salle map.
Quoted.

Endorses a statement made by Petheric.
Did not refer to Ramusio's text.
On Juan Gaetan's narrative.
On Godinho de Eredia.

De Murr:
reproduced legends on Behaim's globe.

Desceliers (see also Pierre Desceliers):
with reference to ap quieta and quabe se quiesce.
Lomboc called Autane on his map of 1550.
Dauphin chart drawn by.
With reference to Anda ne barcha.
A priest of Arques.
Charts of the, type, referred to.

De Witt, G.F. (see also Gerrit Fredericsz):
his discovery marked on the Mar d' India map.

De Wit, F.:
his map does not show Keer-Weer on the coast of Australia.

Dias Bartholomew:
left supplies on the coast of Guinea.
Put in at St. George da Mina.
His successful voyage.
Sailed under the Portuguese flag.

Dias Diniz:
the first to reach the land of the blacks.

Dias Joao:
the first to double Cape Bogador.

Dias Lorenzo:
the first to reach the Bay of Arguin.

Dias Pedro, Bartholomew's brother.

Diaz Bartholomew:
mentioned.
Practically discovered the Cape.
Erected a pillar.

Named Angra das Voltas.
Named Angra dos Vaqueiros.
At Flesh Bay.
Reached an island in Algoa Bay.
Anxious to proceed.
Compelled to return.

Diaz de Solis, Juan:
sailed from San Lucar.

Dicearchus:
his cartographic views.

Diego do Couto:
with reference to the blocking of the seaway south of Java.
His description of Java.

Diego Pacheco:
named Engano Island.

Diego Ribeiro:
his mappamundi.
The Australian continent left out in his mappamundi.

Diogo Cam:
sets up a padrao.
Ascended the Congo River.
Took negroes back.
Accompanied by Martin Behaim.
His padrao passed.
Captured two negroes.
Dias discovered more than.

Diogo de Teive:
where did he direct his ship?

Diogo Lopez de Sequeira:
commissioned to discover Malacca.

Dirck-Hartighs (same as Dirck Hartog):
a name on a plate found by the French expedition commanded by Baudin.
The replica of the plate recording the discovery of, must be in Paris.
A document "immediately" describing the voyage of, has not yet been found.

His discovery ought to be recorded on Abraham Goos' globe.

Dirck-Hartog:
Many inexactitudes in connection with the plate of.
The authenticity of his discovery.
The French did not find the original plate of.
A plate containing a copy of the inscription of.

Dirk Hartog:
a name cut on a tin plate taken away by Vlamingh.

Dom Henry:
imitated.

Dom Manoel (same as Emanuel), King of Portugal:
obtained a copy of Nicolo de' Conti's voyages.
Refused to recognise Magalhaens' services.

Dom Pedro:
returned to Portugal.
Devotes himself to scientific studies.
The map he brought back from Venice probably the same as the one seen by Tavarez.
Brought back from Venice a manuscript of Marco Polo's travels.
With reference to the islands of the western seas.

Dona Isabel Garreto (same as Barreto), Mendana's wife:
taken to Manila.

Don Antonio, of Portugal:
the Portuguese ask Cavendish for news of.

Don Diego Barrante y Maldonad, an officer of De Quiros' expedition.

Don Diego de Prado y Touar:
made Depositario-General in the Bay of St. Philip and St. James.
Before his maps were found Dr. Hamy had pointed out the discoveries made by the Spaniards.
Two letters of, to the King of Spain.
Speaks of a map, which has not yet been found.
His first letter to Antonio de Arostegui.
His second letter.
Repeats in his second letter what he said in the first.

Sends to the King of Spain the discovery of the Magna Margarita (New Guinea).
Blames Don Juan de Silva, the Governor of Manila.
Blames De Quiros for not discovering the southern continent.
His antagonism to De Quiros.
Does not blame De Quiros for leaving Torres.

Don Jorge de Menezes:
discovered, it is said, New Guinea.

Don Juan de Silva, Governor of the Spice Islands:
took from the Dutch the Fort of Sabongo in Gilolo.
Governor of Manila.

Don Pedro de Acunha:
mentioned.

Don Peter (same a Dom Pedro).

Don Sebastian, of Portugal:
defeated and killed at the battle of Alcacer Quibir.

Doppelmayr:
gives a reduced copy of the configurations of Behaim's globe in his work.

Drake, Sir Francis:
The first commander who sailed round the globe.
The rise of the naval fame of England begins with.
Sailed through the straits to the north-west of Australia.
Reaches the Molucca Islands.
Resolved to go to Ternate.
On the south-west coast of Bali.

Draper, General:
bombarded and plundered Manila.
Reduced the Philippines.

Dumont D'Urville:
mentioned.

Ea, the Chaldean Fish-God:
The Exalted Fish.
Legend concerning his arrival from the East.

-Han (Ea, the fish).

Edel d':
a voyage undertaken by order of the Fiscael.
A discovery mentioning the name of.

Eessel Gerrits:
a manuscript chart by.

El Istahkri:
the Arabian geographer.

Elizabeth (Queen of England):
the spirit of commercial enterprise awakened under Mary developed under.
Mere piratical expeditions undertaken during the reign of.

Emanuel, Don, the First, King of Portugal:
heard of a manuscript account of Nicolo de' Conti's travels.

Erathosthenes:
the Indian Ocean an open sea in the geography of.
Chief Librarian at Alexandria.
His cartographic views.

Eredia, Manoel Godinho de:
his claim somewhat similar to that of De Gonneville.

Eucharius Cervicornus:
Maximilian's letter printed at the house of.

Eugene IV, Pope:
ordered Nicolo de' Conti to narrate his travels to his secretary.
An envoy from the Grand Khan visited Pope.

Eve, and Adam:
represented on Turin mappamundi.
On 11th century mappamundi.

Faria y Souza:
on Magalhaens.

Favenc, E.:
his History of Australian Exploration mentioned.

Speaking of Dirck Hartog's plate

Federico, Signor, Duke of Urbino:
mentioned.

Ferdinand, and Isabella:
Columbus' arguments to convince.
Charter three vessels.

Fernam d' Ulmo:
an island granted to him.

Fernam Martins:
a map by Toscanelli addressed to him.
His letter.

Fernam Tellez:
what island did Alfonso V concede to?

Fernando, Don, the King of Portugal's son:
showed a map to F. Tavarez.

Fernando Calaco, a scrivener from Lumiar.

Fernando Columbus:
a map said to have belonged to him.
Said to have translated a letter of Toscanelli.

Figueroa:
quoted by Dalrymple.

Finaeus (same as Oronce Fine):
with reference to his map.

Fleming, Abraham:
his Thirde Booke of Aelianus.

Flinders:
with reference to Behaim's nomenclature.
On the course of the Duyfken.
Came across native huts on the coast of western Australia similar to those depicted on P. Desceliers'
  chart of Australia.

Makes use of information furnished by Dalrymple, and endeavours to trace the course of the Duyfken.
Speaks of a manuscript chart by Eessel Gerrits of Amsterdam.

Fogaza, Joao commander.

Fra Mauro (see Mauro).

Francesco de Rivarolle:
owner of vessels and Columbus' banker.

Franchois Thysz:
the name of the skipper that discovered the land of Peter Nuyts (south coast of Australia).

Francisco de Hoces:
driven to 55 south latitude.
Believed he had discovered an Austral continent.

Francisco Pizaro, the first Viceroy of Peru.

Francisco Rodriguez:
made use of a map, now lost.
His portolanos referred to.

Francisco Themara:
his book referred to.

Franciscus Monachus (or Monacus):
his De Orbi Situ mentioned.

Francis I, of France:
the Dauphin chart executed in the time of.

Fransz Jacobsz, alias Vissher:
accompanied Tasman as pilot major.

Fray Juan de Merlo:
sent to the King of Spain by Torres.

Fray Juan de Silva:
several memorials to the King of Spain by.

Freville, M. de:
published Dalrymple's letter to Hawkesworth.

Freycinet, de, M. L.:
took Dirck Hartog's plate home with him and placed it in the Museum of the Institute, Paris
His work, Voyage Autour du Monde mentioned.

Frobisher:
his voyages referred to.
His attempt to reach India by the Polar Seas.

Gaetan, Juan (see also Juan Gaetan):
his description of New Guinea natives erroneously taken for a description of Queensland natives.

Galileo:
Blaeu and Hortensius, sent to Florence to study under.

Gallego, Hernan:
with Mendana's expedition.
His journal referred to.

Galvano:
describes early traffic in the Indian Ocean.
Quoted.
On Ptolemy's geography.
On a Venetian map taken to Portugal by Dom Pedro.
With reference to Alvaro Telez.
His description of the first expedition to the Spice Islands.
His Anjano a bad reading for Anda ne, with reference to Anda ne barcha (no boats go here).
A digression in.
His description of D'Abreu's expedition corresponds with Reinel's charts.
His reference to the discovery of certain islands.
Informs us that only one vessel of Loaysa's fleet reached the Moluccas.
On Saavedra's expedition.
On Villalobos' expedition.
Reports a discovery made by Gomez de Sequeira.

Garcia Jofre de Loaysa (see also Loaysa):
entrusted with an expedition to the Spice Islands.

Gaspar Corte Real:
mentioned.

Gaspar de Cruz:
says that Loech is the capital of Cambodia.

Gaspar Rico, pilot:
with Bernardo de La Torre.
With Inigo Ortiz de Retez.
His nomenclature on a Dutch chart.

Gastaldi:
his remarkable map published by Tramezini.

Gautier Schouten, or Shouten:
in the Voyages of, published at Amsterdam, there is a curious account of the wreck of the Vergulde Draeck.

Geminus:
speaks of a southern continent.

Gerard, Abbot, afterwards Cardinal Maffei.

Gerard Van Beuningen, supercargo in the first Dutch fleet to Australasia.

Gerrit Colaert, captain of the hooker De Nyptang.

Gerrit Fredericsz De Witt (see also De Witt, G.F.):
the name of the commander of the Vianen, wrecked on the north-west coast of Australia in the year 1628.

Gerrit Jansz:
one of the skippers in Tasman's expedition.

Gerrit Thomasz Poole:
sent out from Banda.
In command of the yachts Amsterdam and Wesel, discovered the coast of Nova Guinea in 3 1/2 degrees south latitude.
Murdered.

Ghillany:
his reproductions of legends on Behaim's globe.
Quoted.

Gilles Mibais (same as Miebais):
Major leaves out words after.

Gilles Miebais:
a name on Dirck Hartog's plate.

Giovanni da Empoli:
with other Italians gave information concerning the Australasian regions.
Terra Sanctae Crucis known to him.

Giuliani de Medici:
Andrea Corsali's letter addressed to.

Gladstone:
on the boat-shaped form of the earth.
With reference to position of the Infernal regions.
With reference to Phoenician reports.
Fails to notice that Homer reversed the Chaldean position of the terrestrial globe.

Godinho de Eredia:
the valuable manuscript of, mentioned.
Discovered Australia according to Major.

Gomara:
quoted.

Gomez de Sequeira:
his voyage.
Did he make two voyages the same year?

Goncalo d'Oliveira, pilot in D'Abreu's expedition.

Gonzales de Leza, the pilot of De Quiros' expedition.
Gives an account of the ceremony of taking possession.
Uses the word Austral.

Gonzalo Velho Cabral:
sent by Prince Henry.

Grand Khan (or Great Khan), of Cathay:
mentioned.

In Marco Polo's description.
The Empire of the.
Discovery in his province.
The King of Kings.

Gregoire, l'Abbe:
a manuscript executed under his guidance.

Gregory X, Pope:
Marco Polo travelled in his time.

Grijalva, Hernando de:
and Fernando de Alvarado, sent out from Acapulco on an expedition of discovery.
Murdered by his revolted crew.

Groland, Nicholas:
with reference to Behaim's globe.

Guidobaldo:
mentioned.

Guillaume Yanss, Captain:
commanded the Duyfken.

Guillemard, F.H.H.:
his Life of Ferdinand Magellan quoted.

Guppy, Dr.:
his book, the Solomon Islands, referred to.

Hakluyt, Richard:
publishes Galvano's work.
Society's edition of Galvano, quoted.
Of Yule's work.
Of Nicolo de' Conti's travels.
With reference to Bartholomew Columbus.
Society's edition of Barthema quoted.
A sentence translated wrong in Barthema of.
Notes in Barthema are of great interest.

Hamelin, Captain:
Major quoting Peron refers to.

Hamy, Dr. E.T.:
quoted.
Believes Barthema never visited the Spice Islands.
Suggests Rindjani as the origin of Anjano.
With reference to the islands reached by Magalhaens in 1511.
Describes the geographical work of the Reinels.
Refers to the special deformation of Java, Sumbawa, Flores.
Assigns the date of 1517 to Reinel's chart.
With reference to Jean Roze and his maps.
Found Mendana's original narrative.
His views on the discoveries made by the Spaniards in New Guinea.
The author wrote to him.
A member of the French Institute.
On Dirck Hartog's plate.

Harley, Edward, Earl of Oxford:
Owned the Dauphin chart.
Instrumental in sending Dampier out to Australia.
One of Dampier's patrons.

Haro, Christopher:
carried on a trade with Eastern countries.

Harper's Monthly Magazine:
mentioned.

Harrisse, Henry:
on the Paris wooden globe.
His remarks with reference to Christopher Columbus.
Mentioned.
On Toscanelli's letter.
His indefatigable researches.
On Bartholomew Columbus' map.
On Behaim's globe.
Referring to Finaeus' map.
Referring to Western expeditions.
Assigns the date circa 1511 to the Hunt-Lenox globe.
On Ruysch's mappamundi.
His remarks with reference to the alleged Schoner globe of 1523.
On the Franciscus Monachus mappamundi.
On the Harleyan or Dauphin chart.
On the Desceliers-Lusitano French maps.

Hawkins, Sir John:
acquired celebrity.
Lost his fleet.

Henry, Prince, the Navigator:
Major's biography of, referred to.
Much helped by an old map.
Never weary of his purpose.
In the year 1428 he and his brother became possessed of a manuscript of Marco Polo and of a map of the world.
A note in.
King Affonso V followed his example.
His object accomplished.
Major's work on, quoted.
Where did he send Gonzalo Velho Cabral?
His motto.
His ruling desire.
Joao preferred to carry out the designs of.

Henry VIII, of England:
John Rotz dedicates his book of hydrography to him.
Mentioned in connection with J. Roze's chart of the Londe of Jaua (Australia).

Henry II:
his map of 1546 referred to.

Henry VI, of England:
Bartholomew Columbus made a map of the world for.

Hercules d'Este:
Cantino, the ambassador of.

Herodotus:
quoted.
Quoted by Rawlinson with reference to circular boats of the Tigris and Euphrates.

Herrera:
with reference to Bartholomew Columbus.
With reference to New Guinea.
His maps.

Quoted.
An account of his corroborated.

Hieronimo da San Stephano:
with other Italians gave information concerning the Australasian regions.

Hilgard, Dr.:
saw the Hunt-Lenox globe.

Hipparchus:
his cartographic views.

Hoeius, Franciscus:
apparently the engraver of the map published by Hugo Allardt.

Holzschuer, George:
with reference to Behaim's globe.
Constructed, painted and inscribed Behaim's globe.

Homer:
a verse of, quoted.
The Indian Ocean represented as an open sea in the days of.
Quoted by Gladstone.
His Phoinikes the same people as the later Phoenicians.
His River Okeanos.
Reversed the Chaldean position of the terrestrial globe.
Sets his Heaven upon columns.
Places his north above.
Places his Heaven in the south or south-west.
His views corroborated by Strabo.
Position of Mountain of the South or South-West.

Hondius, Henricus:
a map by, in Linschoten's work, referred to in Nordenskiold's atlas.

Hondius, Jodocus:
his map shows tracks of Drake and Cavendish.

Hortensius:
and Blaeu sent to Florence by the Dutch to study under Galileo.

Houtman, or Hootman:
and Linschoten, the pioneers of Holland in the East.

Only the commercial chief of the first Dutch expedition to Australasia.

Huerter, Job de:
Behaim's wife daughter of.

Hugo Allardt:
published a map at Amsterdam.
Ignorant of Dutch discoveries on Australian shores.

Hulst, G. Van Keulen:
published Tindal and Swart's Verhandelingen.
Published a copy of Tasman's original manuscript map.

Humboldt:
mentions Behaim's globe.

Hunt, Jonathan:
R.M. Hunt's father.

Hunt, R.M.:
the architect of the Lenox Library.
Presented the Hunt-Lenox globe to the Library.

Hyde Clarke:
on the legend of the Atlantes of Plato.

Ieronimus, Doctor, same as Munzmeister.

Im, or Mermer, the Wind-God of the Chaldeans.

Infante Joao:
accompanies Bartholomew Dias.
First to land.

Infant Henry:
a captain in the employ of referred to.

Inigo Ortiz de Retez (see also Retez):
mentioned.
His nomenclature of New Guinea marked on a Dutch map.

Iniquez de Carquicano, Martin:
died poisoned.

Isabella, and Ferdinand:
Don John II makes an arrangement with.

Isabella, Queen:
her subjects alone granted licenses.

Isidore, of Seville:
a legend on Terra Australis by him.
Spoken of by Santarem.
Referred to.

Iwan III:
celebrated for his great territorial accessions.

Jacob Mahu:
seven ships under the command of.

Jacques Specx, Admiral:
a ship of his fleet nearly wrecked on Houtman's Abrolhos.

James the First:
a petition by Sir William Courteen presented to.
Not favourable to colonies.

Jan Carstens:
sailed from Amboina.

Jansen:
published in French a work on Behaim's globe.

Janstins:
a name on Dirck Hartog's plate.

Jason:
the Argonauts who sailed to Colchis with.

Jean Dignumsz, of the first Dutch fleet to Australasia.

Jean Jacobz Schellinger, of the first Dutch fleet to Australasia.

Jean Jansz Molenaar, of the first Dutch fleet to Australasia.

Jesus Christ:
St. Thomas gives up his life for.

Joam de Resaga:
ran along the coast of Peru and reached New Spain.

Joam Fernandez, of Terceira:
with reference to letters patent granted.

Joao de Coimbra:
went to Calicut.

Joao Gomez d'Abreu:
discovered and named Madagascar.

Joao, King:
Don Henry his fifth son.

Joao II:
granted an island to Fernam d'Ulmo.
The Perfect, son and successor of Affonso V.
Stone pillars erected in his reign.
Greatly gratified.
King of Portugal and the Algarves.
Determines to reach the country of Prester John.
Sends messengers to Cairo.
Covilham's letter to him.
Sent two vessels to the south.
A report to.
Dias' discovery of the Cape, the last great discovery in the reign of.
Did not listen to Columbus' proposition.
Dissatisfied with the Pope's bull.
With reference to Behaim's globe.
A letter from Monetarius sent to.
Maximilian was the cousin of.
Date of Maximilian's letter to.
Arguments used by Munzmeister to convince.

Johan Muller, the artist:
reproduced Behaim's globe for the French Government.

Johanna Macedo:
Behaim's wife.

Johannes Bohemus:
referred to.

Johann Schoner:
professor of Mathematics at Nuremberg.

Joh, Jannssonius:
published Abraham Goos' globe.

John Davis:
caused a chair to be made out of the timbers of Drake's ship.

Johnston, Thomas, Crawford:
a paper of his entitled Did the Phoenicians discover America? referred to.

John III, King of Portugal:
ordered the remains of St. Thomas to be sought for.
Begged Charles V to have the question of the position of the Moluccas examined.

Jomard:
his collection of maps.
Facsimiled Behaim's globe.
Malaiur does not appear on Behaim's globe copied by.

Joseph, of Lamego:
a messenger of King Joao.

Juan Bernardo de Fuentiduena:
an officer of De Quiros' and Torres' expedition.

Juan de Esquivel:
the Maestro de Campo who governed the islands of Ternate.
Put the affairs of the island in good order.

Juan de Iturbide:
blames De Quiros for parting company with Torres.
Blames De Quiros for not following instructions, which were "to go as far as 40 degrees south latitude."

Juan de la Cosa:
his mappamundi.

Juan Diaz de Solis:
sailed with the intention of reaching the Spice Islands by the west.

Juan Gaetan:
reports that the Portuguese purposely distorted their charts.
One of Villalobos' pilots wrote an account of Inigo Ortiz de Retez' expedition.
His account published by Ramusio.
His nomenclature on a Dutch chart.

Juan Vespuccius:
his mappamundi, a pre-Magellanic one.
His southern continent.

King, P.P.:
with reference to Behaim's nomenclature.
Fixed the locality described by W. Dampier, and gave the nomenclature that commemorates his visit.
His Narrative of a Survey, etc., mentioned.
Determined the insularity of Melville Island.

Kerguelen:
his expedition mentioned.

Kohl, J.G.:
mentions Behaim's globe.
With reference to a map found by Admiral Anson.

Kunstmann:
published Munzmeister's account of his travels in Germany.

Lafrere:
his copperprint of G. Mercator's mappamundi published in Rome.

Lancaster, Captain:
sailed from London, the founder of the first English settlement in the East Indies.
Frequently proposed to send a ship to the Solomon Islands.

Lansdowne:
manuscript, referred to.

La Salle:
map, published by La Salle.

Las Casas:
with reference to circuit of the globe.
A chart in his possession.
A translation of a letter by Toscanelli inserted in his Historia.
Quoted.
Verses preserved by.

Lawrence, St.:
Madagascar discovered on the feast of.

Lavanha:
mentioned in connection with Menezes' discoveries.

Lelewel:
mentions Behaim's globe.

Le Maire, or Lemaire:
made to appear to be the discoverer of New Guinea.

Lemos, Gaspar de:
brought some parrots to Europe from Brazil.

Lenormant, F.:
author of Chaldea.
His description of the boat-shaped form of the earth.

Lenox, James:
of New York.
A globe named after him.

Leon Janssen:
translated Godinho de Eredia's Malacca.

Leonora, of Portugal:
Maximilian was the son of.

Leupe, P.A.:
on the arrival of the Golden Sea-Horse at Batavia.

Leyva, Alonzo de:

commanded the Santa Catalina in Mendana's expedition.

Linschoten:
his Discours of Voyages, etc., referred to.
Refers to Cavendish's voyage.
And Houtman, the pioneers of Holland in Australasia.
Lived for two years in Lisbon.
Resided for thirteen years in India.
His book appears to be a translation from the Portuguese.
Accompanies Barentz.
Twenty-five charts relating to India, China and Africa procured by the Dutch before his return from India.
Added fresh information on his return.
His book contains a passage similar to one in Wytfliet's work.
Quoted.
His information not up to date.
His map of Java.
The London edition of his work.
A map by Peter Plancius, with indications of Australia, in the English edition of his work.
A map said to be from the work of, in Nordenskiold's atlas.

Lloyd, Thomas:
in search of the Island of Brazil.

Loaysa (see also Garcia Jofre de):
on his way to the Spice Islands.
Very sick.
Death of.
Only one vessel of his fleet reached the Moluccas.
An account of his proceedings reached Cortez.

Lodovico Barthema (same as Ludovico Barthema):
his Itinerary.

Lopez Garcia de Castro, Governor of Peru.

Lorenzo, Don:
met at Cannanore by Barthema.

Ludovico:
Toscanelli's nephew.

Ludovico Barthema:
with other Italians gave information concerning the Australasian regions.
The account of his travels.

Ludovico di Varthema (same as Barthema).

Luys Botim:
pilot in D'Abreu's expedition.

Magregor, Sir William:
sketch map of part of British New Guinea, referred to by.
Explored the Tarasa River (New Guinea).

Maffei:
on Gomez de Sequeira's voyage.

Magalhaens (see also Magellan):
and Serrano, in the Moluccas.
Sailed with a special and secret mission for Albuquerque.
Back in Lisbon in 1512.
His letters to Serrano.
Death of.
Returned to Europe after seven years' service in India.
His services not recognised.
His great achievement first made known.
His squadron.
His course marked in the alleged Schoner globe.
Survivors of his expedition went on a second expedition.
The second voyage through the Straits of, tedious and dismal.
After the return of his expedition the question of longitude still remained unsettled.

Magellan (see also Magalhaens):
his voyage referred to.
Reach the regions of the Spice Islands.
Pathways traversed by.
The Straits of, referred to.
Life of, quoted.
In Sequeira's expedition to Malacca.
Made his way to the Court of Spain.
Suggested the idea that the Moluccas fell within Spanish territory.
Well received by Cardinal Ximenes.
A plan proposed by, and Haro.

Perceiving that the voyage would be a long one.
Irritated about the conversations of his men.
Executed the ringleader.
Sailed out of St. Julian's Bay.
Determined to sail along the channel.
Gave orders to turn away from the great continent.
Converts the Chief of Subuth.

Magellanus:
the discoverer of the Streights.

Major, R.H.:
on traditions relating to the existence of an island of immense extent beyond the known world.
with reference to the earliest opinions concerning a knowledge of an Australian continent.
With reference to "When you leave Java."
On Prince Henry the navigator.
A remark by, redounding to the honour of Italy.
Refers to a translation of Marco Polo's work made in Lisbon.
Edited the first English translation of Nicolo de' Conti's travels.
Inscription on Fra Mauro's map not noticed by.
Says navigators left the coast with impunity.
Quoted.
On Joao II.
On Prester John.
With reference to Spanish ideas concerning Australia.
Identifies Malaiur with Malay Peninsula.
A communication of G.P. Badger to.
Arias' memorial in extenso in the Early Voyages to Australia by.
His answer to Badger with reference to a country south of Java.
Named the Dauphin chart.
Came to the conclusion that the French claim of Australian discovery was untenable.
With reference to Beach.
On Peter Plancius' map with indications of Australia.
On Dutch discovery.
Used Dalrymple's faulty translation.
Quotes Saris.
On Dirck Hartog's plate.
Gives some particulars relating to Vlamingh's voyage.
Appears to mention three yachts in Pool's expedition.

Malte-Brun:
mentions John Rotz's book of hydrography.
An erroneous opinion of.

Mandevilla, Johan de:
mentioned on Martin Behaim's globe.

Mandeville, (same as Mandevilla):
his influence on the cartography of the Australian regions.

Manilius:
a quotation of his referring to the southern continent.
The date at which he wrote.

Mann, John:
with reference to the navigation of the Bali Straits.

Manoel, Dom (same as Don Emanuel):
had a manuscript of Nicolo de' Conti's travels translated into Portuguese.
Wolf Holzschuer rendered services to.
Sent three vessels.

Marco Polo:
erroneous interpretations of his writings.
no geographical progress made by Europeans before his time.
Returns to Venice.
Compelled to wait near the Straits of Malacca.
Geographical terms used by.
Considered Java and Australia as one.
News of his voyages.
An important description of his.
With Marsden's rectification.
Five types of maps appeared after his and Nicolo de' Conti's return.
Maps which appeared after his, but before Nicolo de' Conti's return
Says Lochac produces gold, etc.
Islands named after his descriptions.
With reference to Java Major.
A fantastic type of map bearing his nomenclature.
The influence of his writings.
And Odoric of Pordenone.
Did not reach so near Australia as Odoric of Pordenone.
Probable interpolations.
Describes Nicoveran.

His nomenclature on Behaim's globe.
A copy of his travels taken to Portugal in the year 1428.
With other Italians gave information concerning the Australasian regions.
Nicolo de' Conti, his emulator.
His voyages to be read in connection with Nicolo de' Conti's.
Went to the East in the time of Gregory X.
Nicolo de' Conti found the lands described by.
Referred to in connection with Nicolo de' Conti.
A manuscript of, given to Dom Pedro in 1428.
His works translated and published in Portugal.
His Java Minor cannot be Nicolo de' Conti's Giava Minore.
Mentioned.
Manuscript copies of, difficult to obtain.
His eastern seaboard.
His Mangi and Cathay distorted.
Our zero the point of departure of the descriptions of.
Speaks of Lochac.
Speaks of Malaiur.
By Marsden.
His Angaman.
Quoted.
Described Java from hearsay.
His Madagascar.
His islands stud the South Pacific Ocean in Ruysch's mappamundi.
Descriptions on P. Desceliers' map, taken from the writings of.
his islands on the Schonerean gores.
The Javas of his descriptions.
His islands on the Apianus mappamundi.
Described Java from hearsay as being the largest island in the world.
His writings form the basis of G. Mercator's map.

Marino Sanuto:
a map by, mentioned, which appeared before the return of Nicolo de' Conti.

Marin La Meslee, E.:
on De Gonneville's discovery.

Markham, C.R.:
a communication of G.P. Badger to, and answer.

Marsden:
has shown that Java should read Chiampa.
Ditto, that Lochac is some part of Cambodia.

His Sumatra.
Identifies Malaiur with Malay Peninsula.
His Marco Polo.

Martin Alonzo Pinzon:
with reference to a map.

Martin of Bohemia (same as M. Behaim).

Martin Van Delft:
in command of three Dutch vessels.

Maximilian, Emperor:
his advice to go in search of Cathay.
Date of his letter to Joao II.

Maximilianus, Transylvanus:
referred to.
Peter Martyr sent to him the men who had returned from Magalhaens' expedition.
Sent his Latin exercise to Cologne.
His letter.
The alleged Schoner globe considered as a result of the publication of his letter.
With reference to the vastness of the Pacific Ocean.
No place for his nomenclature on the alleged Schoner globe.

Mauro, Fra (see also Fra Mauro):
with reference to the difficulties that early cartographers had to contend with.
His regions of darkness
The equatorial regions on his map.
His map referred to.
His India.
The circumfluent ocean of the ancients still retained in his mappamundi.
Nicolo de' Conti's Sandai identified with Sunda in his map.
His monument of geography compiled between the years 1457 and 1459.
A commission given to him to construct a map.
Paid the draughtsman Andrea Bianco.
Death of.
His bird called Rukh.
His map a ground plan for Toscanelli.
A departure made from his map.
Prototypic map.

The construction of his map.
His map borrowed from.
The evolution of his lago regno.
With reference to the western shores of Australia.
The period at which his errors were found out.
Had no room on his mappamundi.
His Sumatra placed in the southern hemisphere.
Behaim's Java Major a distorted representation of Fra Mauro's Siamotra.
His mappamundi with reference to Calmia.
Is Loac Provincia derived from his Lago regnum (?).
His legends referring to parrots.
His pseudo-equatorial line corrected.
His Giava Mazor appears to have been set down from actual knowledge of its coastlines.

Meda, Don Francisco dal (same as Almeyda).

Medici, Duke of:
Andrea Corsali writes from Cochin-China to him.

Mela:
spoken of by Santarem.

Mendana (see also Alvaro de Mendana):
his expedition of 1567 described.
The original manuscript in which his voyage is narrated was found by Dr. E.T. Hamy.
Sent out to San Christoval to found a colony.
The fleet of, composed of four vessels.
His galleon was named the San Jeronimo.
In search of the Solomon Islands.
Named the Santa Cruz Islands.
Death of.
Began the work of exploration continued by De Quiros.
Discovered the Solomon Islands.
His Solomon Islands marked on a Dutch chart.
The early discoveries of.

Mercator, Gerard:
with reference to a fantastic type of map.
Used the term Beach on the Australian continent.
His mappamundi.
In certain respects failed to improve the geography of his time.

Made use of Ptolemy's and Marco Polo's nomenclature.
Indications of Australia on the map of, referred to by Major.

Menezes, Don Jorge De:
was carried by currents to the North Coast of Papua.

Mestre Jayme:
no work of his to be seen.

Mermer, or Im, the Wind-God of the Chaldeans.

Midas, King of Phrygia:
in conversation with Silenus concerning an island of immense extent beyond the known world.
His familiarity with Silenus.

Middleton:
his expedition mentioned.

Modigliani, the author of Isola delle Donne, the Island of Women.

Monetarius, Hieronymus (Munzer or Munzmeister).

Monterey, Count of, Viceroy of Peru:
De Quiros' expedition sent out under the auspices of.
De Quiros followed the instructions given by.
Desired De Quiros to discover the southern continent.

Montesclavos, Marquis of:
with reference to De Quiros' character.

Moresby, J.:
his visit and re-survey in New Guinea.
His book referred to.

Mortier, Pierre:
an atlas published by, at Amsterdam.

Munchhausen:
his adventures compiled by Raspe.

Munzmeister:
derived his ideas from Aristotle.

His suggestion.
His arguments used to convince Joao.

Napoleon I:
documents appropriated by, now returned.

Narborough, Sir John:
his Account of Several Late Voyages, etc. alluded to.

Navarette:
quoted.
A letter addressed to, by the Vicomte de Santarem.

Navis:
on Australia and the Ancients.

Naya, Signor, of Venice:
made a photograph of Fra Mauro's map.

Nicholson, E.B.:
with reference to Mandeville.

Nicolas Coelho:
went to Calicut.

Nicolas Struyk:
his Inleidning tot de Algemeen Geographie, mentioned.

Nicolas Witsen:
his Noord en Oost Tartarye, mentioned.

Nicolo de' Conti:
erroneous interpretation of his writings.
No progress made by European geographers before his time.
His India.
Mentions Java Major and Java Minor, not the same islands as Marco Polo's.
Maps which appeared before his return from the East.
His information used in Fra Mauro's map.
With other Italians gave information concerning the Australasian regions.
The emulator of Marco Polo.
Don Emanuel of Portugal ordered his manuscript to be translated into Portuguese.
Went to India in the time of Eugene IV.

Referred to in connection with Marco Polo.
His voyages translated by Valentino Fernandez.
Referring to Malepur.
Original Latin description of his travels.
Missing passages in his descriptions in Ramusio's text.
Stays nine months in the Javas.
Describes Sumatra as Anticamente detta Taprobana.
His descriptions traceable on Fra Mauro's map.
Describes the Spice Islands from hearsay.
First to name Sumatra.
Dr. Ruge with reference to.
Quoted.
The influence of his writings on the cartography of the Eastern regions.
With reference to parrots.
With reference to papagalli terra.
His description of the Nestorian Christians.

Nobbens, Jan:
one of the survivors of the Zeewyck.

Nockhoda Tingall:
arrived at Bantam from Banda.

Nordenskiold:
his collection of maps, referred to.
A map said to be from Linschoten's work in his atlas.

Nutzel, Gabriel:
with reference to Behaim's globe.

Nuyts, Pieter:
was on board the Golden Seahorse when Franchois Thysz, the skipper, made a discovery on the south coast of Australia.
Of the Counsel of Seventeen.
His discovery marked on the Mar d' India map.

Oannes, the Greek Fish-God:
The name corrupted from Ea-han.

Odoardo Barbosa:
his book tampered with.

Odoric, of Pordenone (Odoric de Pordenone):

no geographical progress made by Europeans before his time.
His influence on the cartography of the Australasian regions.
His descriptions plagiarised.
One of the most renowned travellers in his days.
Visited Java and other islands of the Eastern Archipelago.
Manuscripts of his travels.
His course of peregrinations.
His account of the regions south of the equator.
Eats of a paste (sago).
With other Italians gave information concerning the Australasian regions.
Describes Candin under the name of Dondin.

Oliva, Abbe:
edited Conti's travels.

Oronce Fine:
celebrated French astronomer and mathematician.
His information borrowed from Lusitano-Spanish charts.

Ortega Pedro:
with Mendana's expedition.

Ortelius:
with reference to a fantastic type of map.
The Australasian regions on his map similar to those of G. Mercator's map.
Indication of Australia on maps of, referred to.

Owen Stanley:
mentioned.

Paolo da Gama:
went to Calicut.

Paul (same as Paolo Toscanelli):
copy of a letter by him to Columbus.

Paul Van Caerden:
proclaimed Governor of all the Spice Islands.

Paul Van Soldt:
the author of the journal that deals with Etienne Van der Hagen's second voyage.
Met the Little Dove (Duyfken), which had returned from New Guinea.

His narrative shows that the Little Dove and the Little Sun were together at the Spice Islands.

Payva, Affonso de:
directs his course towards Suakem.
His death.

Pedro Bernal Cermeno:
commanded the Tres Reyes, the launch of De Quiros' expedition.

Pedro Correa:
Columbus' brother-in-law.

Pedro de Covilham:
sent to search for the country of Prester John.

Pedro de Montarryo:
sent out to search for the country of Prester John.

Pedro Nunez:
went to Calicut.

Pelsart, F., Captain:
describes some ant-hills on the western coast of Australia.
The Batavia commanded by.
Driven on Houtman's Abrolhos.
Resolved to steer for Java.
A full account of the shipwreck of, given in R.H. Major's Early Voyages to Australia.
The Vergulde Draeck wrecked on the same coast as.

Pero de Alemquer:
went to Calicut.

Pero Escobar:
went to Calicut.

Peron:
describes some ant-hills on the western coast of Australia.
The French account of the finding of Dirck Hartog's plate given in the work of.
Was on board the Naturaliste when Dirck Hartog's plate was found.
Referred to.

Peter Both:
his fleet of eight ships arrived at Bantam.

Peter de Alyaco (Pierre D'Ailly):
quoted.

Peter Dirckz Keyser:
commanded the first Dutch fleet to Australasia.
Died in the Straits of Sunda.

Peter Martyr, of Anghierra:
his observations concerning the dispute between the Portuguese and Spaniards.

Peter Plancius:
procured charts for Cornelius Claez.
Indications of Australia on a map by.

Petherick, E.A.:
on Patalie Regio.
A statement of his corrected.
An article contributed to the Melbourne Review by.
Did not refer to Ramusio's text.
His publication The Torch referred to.
On Sir W. Courteen's petition.
Quoted.

Petrarch:
quoted on Sebastian Cabot's mappamundi.

Phillip:
the first Governor of New South Wales.
sighted Australia on the 3rd of January 1788.

Pierre d'Abano:
pre-eminent in his time.

Pierre d'Ailly:
his India.
Derived his ideas from Aristotle.
Quoted.

Pierre Desceliers (see also Desceliers):
a priest of Arques, and celebrated cosmographer and cartographer.

Pierre Pauvelz, the same as Gerrit Thomasz Pool.

Pieter Dockes (see also Pieter Ecorres):
a name on Dirck Hartog's plate according to Major Doore, according to Rienzi, quoting Freycinet.

Pieter Ecoores:
a name on Dirck Hartog's plate according to Peron's account.

Pieter Goos:
his chart with reference to the discovery of 't Landt Van Pieter Nuyts.
A wrong date on the chart of.

Pieter Pietersz:
of Gerrit Thomasz Pool's expedition, continued the voyage of discovery and lighted on Arnhem or Van Dieman's Land.
Visited Timor Laut.

Pigafetta:
describes the guanaco.
His description suggested the wooden houses depicted on the P. Desceliers' chart of Australia.

Pingre:
Captain Cook wished to follow his authority.

Pinkerton:
quoted.

Pinzon, Vicente, Yanez:
sailed from San Lucar.
Sailed as far as the Oronoco.

Pires:
in China.

Plato:
the Atlantis of.

Pliny:

quoted by Galvano.
Articles of commerce mentioned by.
His geography referred to.
Quoted by Maximilianus.

Poggio Fiorentino, Messer, secretary to Pope Eugene IV:
His treatise De Varietate, etc., referred to.

Poggio Bracciolini:
writes Sumatra Sciamuthera.
Referred to.

Polo Marco (same as Marco Polo):
mentioned.

Pomponius Mela:
a work of that name printed at Basles.

Prester John:
supposed to rule over vast tracts of country.
Information wanted concerning.

Ptolemy:
errors attributed to him.
His fantastic islands.
Placed Java and Sumbawa in the northern hemisphere.
Develops the views of early cartographers.
His map of the world referred to.
His ideas revived.
Period at which he compiled his works.
Islands set down by guess on his map.
Galvano's views of his geography.
No other charts but those of, at the time the projected San-Thome was placed (cartographically) on Tenasserim coast.
Two important gulfs on his map.
Duplication of Malay Peninsula suggested in his map.
Sumatra and Ceylon confounded in his map.
The first edition of his atlas.
The British Museum map compared with his map.
His fictitious coastline.
His geography.
His map served to form a prototype.
Theoretical arguments based on the geography of.

Our zero placed at the extreme end of the world of.
Western shores of Fra Mauro's Sumatra and the coasts of China connected as in the map of.

Purchas:
with reference to Gaspar de Cruz.
With reference to Bartholomew Columbus.
Gives a passage from Saris.
A passage of his quoted.

Purry, Jean Pierre:
his memoire referred to.
Went to France.

Quaritch, Bernard:
with reference to Sir John Mandeville's travels.

Quiros, Pedro Fernandez de:
Mendana's captain and chief pilot.
The leader of another expedition.
Two important items in connection with the expedition of.
Only continuing the work of Mendana.
Took Mendana's wife and the remainder of the fleet to Manila.
Petitioned at Valladolid for another expedition.
Sailed on an expedition to colonize the island of Santa Cruz and follow out the intentions of Mendana.
Put in at Taumaco.
Abandoned the project of going to Santa Cruz.
Left the Almiranta.
Sailed for Mexico.
Died at Panama.
His ship or galleon was named the San Pedro y San Pablo.
Torres' condition different to his.
The expedition of, closes the period of Spanish activity.
Appointed officers.
Discovered Espiritu Santo in the New Hebrides group.
Makes use of the word Australia in his diary.
An alteration made in the manuscript of, changing Austrialia to Australia.
The memorial of, sent to Philip III.
Two letters of Don Diego de Prado respecting the expedition of.
Called liar by de Prado.
Only discovered rocks and small islands.
Blamed by de Prado for not discovering the southern continent.

Would have discovered New Zealand and perhaps Australia had he obeyed instructions.
The early discoveries of.

Rafael Perestello:
and Andrade, went to China.

Raffles, Sir Thomas Stamford:
his History of Java quoted.

Ragozin, Zenaide A.:
referred to.
Position of the Mountain of the East according to.

Ramusio:
his account of Nicolo de' Conti.
Could not find a single copy of Nicolo de' Conti's narrative in Venice and many other Italian towns.
Obliged to have recourse to a Portuguese translation of Nicolo de' Conti's travels.
His work called Navigationi et viaggi.
Mentions Valentino Fernandez.
His opinion of Valentino Fernandez' translation of Nicolo de' Conti's voyages.
His text of Nicolo de' Conti's travels contained a passage that led to the distortion of maps.
The Latin edition of Nicolo de' Conti's that he could not find was found afterwards.
Referred to.
Missing passages in, with reference to Nicolo de' Conti's text.
Says D. Manoel obtained in 1500 a copy of Nicolo de' Conti's travels.
Mentioned,
Sciamuthera is written Sumatra in his translation.
Quoted.
His account of Barthema's travels.
On Portuguese secrecy.
His account of Inigo Ortiz de Retez' expedition written by the pilot Gaetan.
The portion of Juan Gaetan's account relating to New Guinea as given in.

Raspe:
compiled the adventures of Munchhausen.

Rawdon Brown:

mentioned.

Rawlinson:
a note of, on Herodotus, referred to.

Reade, Captain:
in command of the Cygnet when Dampier first landed in Australia.

Rechteren:
a passenger by Admiral Jacques Specx's fleet, gives an account of the wreck of the Batavia on Houtman's Abrolhos.

Reinel, Pedro:
mentioned.
His map shows the geographical evolution.
Misnamed nearly all the islands on his chart of the East Indian Archipelago.
Bali and Lomboc are not distorted on his chart.

Rene Van Hel:
supercargo on the first Dutch fleet to Australasia.

Retez, Inigo Ortiz de (see also Inigo Ortiz de Retez):
in command of the San Juan with Gaspar Rico as pilot.

Ricardo Beltram y Rozpide:
referred to.

Rienzi, author of Oceanie:
mentioned.
With reference to Dirck Hartog's plate.

Robert de Vaugondy:
a map of Australia by.

Rodrigo de Bastidas:
referred to.

Rodriguez Francisco (see also Francisco Rodriguez):
set out with Abreu.
made an adaptation from a map, now lost.
Pilot in D'Abreu's expedition.
His charts well known.
His charts served as models.

His surveys are independent of Pedro Reinel's surveys.
His chart of part of Java, Bali, Lomboc, Sumbawa, etc., bears additional nomenclature.

Rogers, Captain:
in the Duke and the Duchess.

Roggeween:
his voyage to the South Seas.

Rotz, John (same as Jean Roze):
a book of hydrography of his dedicated to King Henry VIII.

Roze, Jean (same as Rotz, John):
his map referred to.
Two maps of his described.
His chart Number 2 described.
The Land of the Leeuwin of Dutch charts shown on the chart of.

Ruelens, Charles:
Maintains that the Duyfken (Little Dove) never reached the shores of Carpentaria.
Makes Flinders responsible for the confusion with regard to the voyage of the Duyfken.
Other documents have turned up since the conclusion arrived at by.
The librarian of the Royal Burgundian Library at Brussels.
Wrote a preface to Yanssen's work.

Ruge, Dr., Author of Columbus:
With reference to Nicolo de' Conti.

Ruy Lorenzo, de Tavora:
ex-Viceroy of India.

Ruysch:
his mappamundi has Seilan Insulae Pars.
His mappamundi mentioned.
Various opinions as to the origin of his mappamundi.
His mappamundi unique in many respects.

Saavedra:
sailed along the coast of New Guinea.
The survivors of his expedition return from the Moluccas.

Saltzburg, Cardinal of:
Maximilian's letter addressed to the.

Samis:
Cazazionor's niece.

Santarem:
on early maps.
Refers to the alter orbis and antichthone.
Referred to.
Rodriguez's portolanos reproduced in outline in his collection.
Ignored that Rodriguez was already at Malacca in 1511.

Saris, Captain:
of Middleton's expedition, at the Moluccas.
His notes with reference to the first Dutch voyage to Australia.
A passage from.
His Christian name was John.
Supposed to have mistaken the word Duyfken for another similar.

Schefer:
with reference to Barthema.

Schoner:
used the term Brazil in connection with the Australasian regions.
Timor in his 1533 globe.
A passage marked on his globe of 1515.
With reference to Magellan's Strait.
His Luculentissima quoted.
The information in Schoner's Luculentissima not given at first hand.
His gores of 1515 show two straits.
His globe of 1515.
Is the first to give a different name to the Austral Continent.
His alleged globe.
Credited with having laid down the precise routes of Magellan's fleets.
The 1523 globe not his.
His maps and globes used by Oronce Fine.
His Weimar globe mentioned.
His lost globe.

Schouten:
and Lemaire, their expedition alluded to.

Their expedition ignored in Hoeius' map.

Sebaldt de Weerdt:
in command of a ship to Australasia.

Sebastian, King of Portugal:
mentioned.

Sebastian Cabot:
his mappamundi is an engraved one.

Sebastian del Cano:
returned to Europe with the Victoria.
One of the commissioners at Badajos and Elvas.
Pilot major of a second expedition to the Spice Islands.
His vessel wrecked.
Death of.
Passed through an open sea to the south of Java.
With the remnant of Magalhaens' expedition.

Selenus (same as Silenus):
his familiarity with Midas sonne of a nymphe, tells Midas of "certaine ilandes."

Seneca:
quoted

Serrano, Francis:
went to the Spice Islands with Abreu.
His ship burnt at Guliguli.
In the Moluccas.
Nine years in the Moluccas.
His letters to Magalhaens.
Death of.
Magalhaens wrote to, in the Moluccas.

Serrano, John:
chosen as new admiral after the death of Magellan.
Invited to a banquet.
Left on shore.

Shakespeare:
alludes to a chart.

Silenus (same as Selenus):
in conversation with Midas describes an island of immense extent beyond the known world.
Referred to.

Simon de Cordes:
in command of a ship to Australasia.

Simon Lambertsz Mau:
of the first Dutch fleet to Australasia.

Sinclair, Captain:
said to have discovered Port Denison.

Solinus:
his Polyhistor published by Camers.

Solomon, King:
his pilots brought gold and silver, etc., from Asia.
The gold and treasures of his temple reported to have been derived from the Solomon Islands.

Speult, a Dutch Governor of the Spice Islands:
destroyed all the clove trees which the Dutch could not use.
Was his name given to the island or river discovered in the Gulf of Carpentaria?
The discoveries supposed to have been made during his government in the Spice Islands are
  not recorded on Tasman's chart.

Stevens, Henry:
his Johann Schoner mentioned.
His narrative of the Hunt-Lenox globe.
Assigns the date 1506/1507 to the Hunt-Lenox globe.
The gores of the alleged Schoner globe formerly in his possession.

Steyns, Jan:
one of the survivors of the Zeewyck.

St. Luke, the Evangelist:
feast of, on the 18th of October.

St. Peter, of Arlanza (Alcantara):
feast of, on the 19th of October.

St. Philip and St. James:
feast of, 1st of May.

Strabo:
describes Crates' earth globe.
Speaks of a Southern Continent.
Develops the views of earlier cartographers.
Quoted by Galvano.
Articles of commerce mentioned by.
His geography referred to.
His ideas concerning the Atlantic Ocean.
With reference to Crates.

Swan (same as Swann), Captain:
abandoned the Cygnet at Mindanao.

Swann (same as Swan):
one of the buccaneers of America.

Swart, Jacob:
his Verhandelingen en Berigten mentioned.
His black letter copy from the original manuscript document (Tasman's Instructions)
  once in the possession of the Van Keulens of Amsterdam.

Tasman, Abel Yansz:
his claims of discovery.
New Holland drawn almost like in the charts of, of the 17th century.
His first expedition on the eve of being sent out.
His original manuscript chart of Australia offered to the author--Proposed to the
  New South Wales Government--Acquired by Prince Roland Bonaparte.
A copy of the Instructions to Commodore, published by Dalrymple.
The account of the voyage of the Duyfken given in the Instructions for the second voyage of.
Voyages made before the time of.
The passage in the Instructions to, referring to the voyage of the Duyfken, confirmed.
His original chart might throw some light on the discovery of an island and river said to

have been named after Speult.
His chart referred to.
Australia set down on a chart as said to be known to the Dutch prior to the first and second voyages of.
Some of Blaeu's maps show the discoveries of.
Discoveries of, recorded on P. Goos' map of Hollandia Nova.
Words, evidently of Portuguese and Spanish origin, appear on his chart of Australia.
Two ships equipped for his voyage of discovery.
Steered for the Solomon Islands.
Reached land which he called Anthonie Van Diemen's Land.
Discovered New Zealand.
Visited islands of the Pacific.
Returned to Java by the north of New Guinea.
Did not touch upon Australia in his first voyage.
His second voyage.
The object of the second voyage was to ascertain whether New Guinea and New Van Diemen's
 Land (Tasmania) were connected with the South Land (Australia).
Failed to find Torres Straits.
Sailed along the north coast of Australia, and returned to Java.
His original map found.
Made no new discoveries in his second voyage.
Dutch discoveries in Australia end with the second voyage of.
Dampier had a copy of his chart of west coast of New Holland.

Tavarez, Francisco de Souza (same as Francis de Sosa Tauares):
saw a map showing all the navigation to the East Indies.

Teixeira:
attributes the discovery of some islands near New Guinea to Magalhaens.
A manuscript atlas by.

Thales:
drew the equator across the globe.

Themara, F.:
referred to.

Theopompus:
a fragment of the works of, referring to a southern island beyond the known world.

Thevenot, Melchisedech:
his Relations de divers voyages curieux, mentioned.

Thevet:
with reference to the giants of Zanzibar.

Thomas, St., or San Thome:
a town called after him.
Preached the Gospel to the Parthians and Persians, and went to India.
His shrine visited by Odoric.
His body buried at Malepur.

Thommaso San (same as Thomas):
referred to.

Tiberius:
in connection with Manilius.

Tiele:
with reference to Barthema.

Tindal, Jhr. G.A.:
and Jacob Swart, their Verhandelingen en Berigten mentioned.
Dutch accounts given by.
Mentions two yachts in Pool's expedition.

Tolomeo (Ptolemy), Claudio Alexandrino:
his geography published at Venice.

Tomai:
the chief of Taumaco.

Torre, Bernardo de La:
commander of the San Juan with Gaspar Rico as pilot, made an unsuccessful attempt to reach New Spain.
Discovered many islands.

Torre, Hernando, della:
the fifth commander of Loaysa's expedition.

Torres, Francisco de:
returned to Spain in command of de Solis' expedition.

Torres, Luis Vaes de:
the periplus of New Guinea known before he passed through the straits that bear his name.
His track marked on a map by Dalrymple.
His name marked on a map by Dalrymple.
De Quiros' Admiral.
Left in the bay.
His ship named the San Pedro.
Reached 21 degrees south latitude.
May have been in search of the Lost Bay of the Dauphin and similar charts.
Did the Dutch learn about the voyage of?
His expedition closes the period of Spanish activity.
The track of, pointed out by Dr. E.T. Hamy.
Discovered the Bay of St. Lawrence and Port of Monterey (Orangerie Bay, New Guinea)
  on the 10th of August 1606.
Left Orangerie Bay towards the end of August of the year 1606.
Put in at Triton Bay, which he named the Bay of St. Peter of Arlanza.
Port of St. Luke and Port of St. John del Prado discovered on the 18th of October 1606.
Took formal possession of New Guinea, which he called the Magna Margarita, on the feast of St.
  Marguerite, one week after his arrival at the east end of New Guinea.
The map of the discovery made by.
His discoveries remarkably well charted by De Prado.
His passage revealed.
The early discoveries of.

Toscanelli:
his India.
Landing places referred to by.
Derived his ideas from Aristotle.
The first to map certain islands.
Gained information from Nicolo de' Conti.
Lived to be a hundred years old.
With reference to Columbus.
With reference to the size of the globe.
His letter sent to Columbus.
The Latin text of his letter.
Sends a map and a copy of a letter to Columbus.
Geographical descriptions borrowed from.
Columbus' discovery, as viewed by the Duke of Ferrara.
Used Fra Mauro's mappamundi as a model.

C. Columbus sent a globe to.
Made use of degrees of longitude and latitude.
May be the author of a prototypic map.
His arguments the same as those used by Munzmeister.
Argued that the sea was smaller than the earth.
A particularity about his description not generally noticed.
The date of his map.
With reference to the western shores of Australia.
Wished to fill in the open spaces on his map.
An innovator.
The prototype of his map was no doubt of Arabian origin.
Corrected Fra Mauro's pseudo-equatorial line.

Touar (Tovar):
one of Don Diego de Prado's names.

Tramezini:
a map published by.

Trevigiano, Stephano:
went to Portugal with Fra Mauro's map.

Tristan de Acuna:
went unto Mossambique.

Unrug, Pateh, a Prince of Java:
defeated by Fernam Peres, at Malacca.

Valard, Jean, of Dieppe:
referred to.

Valentim, Fernandez, is no doubt same as Valentino Fernandez.

Valentino, Fernandez:
translated Nicolo de' Conti's manuscript from Latin into Portuguese.
In his proem refers to Marco Polo.

Valentyn:
His Oud en Nieuu Oost Indien mentioned.
His Beschryvinge Van Banda mentioned.
With reference to Roggeween's expedition.

Van der Hagen:

the Duyfken (Little Dove) of his expedition is the one that sailed into the Gulf of Carpentaria.
His expedition of three vessels.
The Duyfken accompanied the expedition of.
His second voyage.

Van Diemen, Antonio, or Anthonie:
signed the Instructions given to Tasman.
Governor-General of the Dutch East Indies.
Ordered a more extensive exploration of the South Land.

Van Keulens, the, of Amsterdam:
referred to.

Varthema (same as Barthema and Ludovico Barthema):
mentioned.

Vasco da Gama:
a map of the Cape of Good Hope before that cape was rounded by, referred to.
Mentioned.
Serrano said he had discovered a richer and larger world than.
The French followed the steps of.

Vasco Nunez, de Balboa:
sighted the South Sea.

Vega, Lope de:
commanded the Santa Isabel in Mendana's second expedition.

Verazzano:
France owes the discovery of America to.

Verschoor, John Williamson:
directed the Dutch trade at Bantam.

Villalobos, Ruiz Lopez de:
his expedition gave rise to a further survey of Papua and to its being named Nueva Guinea (New Guinea).
Juan Gaetan, one of his pilots.
Mentioned.

Visscher, Frans Jacobsz:

the chief pilot and second in command of Tasman's second expedition.

Vittoria, Lady, Marchioness Dal Guasto:
mentioned.

Vlamingh:
took away Dirck Hartog's plate.
Major did not get his text of the inscription on Dirck Hartog's plate from the account of.
The narrative of, does not contain the inscription on Dirck Hartog's plate.
An inscription on Dirck Hartog's plate relating to the arrival and departure of.
Entries in the journal of.
His chief pilot brought back a plate with him.
Something suggestive in the voyage of.
The avowed object of the voyage of.
His replica of Dirck Hartog's plate must be in Paris.

Vlamingh, Cornelis de:
son of the commodore and captain of the galiot Weseltje.

Vogado, Joao:
a captainship given to him.

Volkersen, Samuel:
captain of the Waeckende Boey, his description of the west coast of the South Land (Australia).
Discovered, but did not name Rottnest Island (Western Australia).

Volkhamer, P.:
with reference to Behaim's globe.

Wallis:
his expedition mentioned.

Walsingham:
a project in the handwriting of, to trade beyond the equinoctial.

Welbe, John:
Author of a scheme of colonisation.
Got information from Dampier.
Acknowledges that he had been in the South Sea with.
Islands named by.
Ready to grant permits.

Wieser, Dr.:
believes that the Frankfort globe of 1515 (Schonerean gores) is the work of Schoner.
His derivation of Patalie.

Wilhem de Vlamingh (same as Vlamingh):
with reference to Dirck Hartog's plate.
His voyage to the South Land.
Commodore of the fleet.
His boat made sail for the mainland.
His description of Rottenest Island.
Broke his cable near Rottenest Island.
On shore.
The chief pilot of, went on shore and brought back a tin plate.
A plate left on Dirck Hartog's island to commemorate the visit of.

Winter, Jones:
his translation of The Travels of Ludovico di Varthema quoted.

Woodford, C.M.:
his book, A Naturalist among the Head Hunters, referred to.

Woods, Reverend F.T.:
quotes Saris.
His friend should have left out the paragraph referring to the "little sunne."

Wytfliet:
his map places the Solomon Islands too far south.
The straits between Nova Guinea and Terra Australis (Torres Straits) placed correctly in the map of.
His nomenclature for Australia the same as G. Mercator's.
His map dedicated to the King of Spain.

Ximenes, Cardinal:
governed Spain in the absence of Charles V.

Yanssen, Leon:
published in French a translation of Godinho de Eredia's original manuscript.

Yde Tjerksen:
and Gerrit Janz, the skippers that went with Tasman.

Yule, Sir Henry:
with reference to Mandeville.
With reference to real difficulties in Odoric's narrative.
His work Cathay and the way thither quoted.
His work referred to.

Zenaide, A. Ragozin:
mentioned.

Zi, the Spirit.

Zi-Ana, the Spirit of Heaven.

THE END

Made in the USA
San Bernardino, CA
06 May 2020